'This manuscript covers both the pandemic from a Marxist angle and also explores some related issues in Marxist theory. As such, it is on the whole a good effort that demonstrates a grasp of many of the core issues, both in theory and in social reality. The topic is an important and compelling one that is in need of discussion, including for a global audience.'

Kevin Anderson, *Distinguished Professor of Sociology, University of California, USA.*

'This manuscript deals with a critical issue that could hardly be more timely – the impact of the COVID-19 pandemic on India, and its overall social, political, and ideological consequences. The author has marshalled a considerable amount of data, reports, and information on India's response to the pandemic, which will fill an important gap in the growing body of literature concerning the pandemic's global impact. It also has the virtue of not limiting itself to an empirical analysis, drawing from a wide range of theoretical works in arguing that the pandemic highlights the need for an alternative to both neoliberal and statist models of development. The work has the potential to be an important addition to Routledge's catalog of works on critical social theory.'

Peter Hudis, *Distinguished Professor, Humanities and Philosophy, Oakton College, USA.*

Pandemic Fissures

This book analyses India's response to COVID-19, using an intersectional framework that highlights the roles of the central government, regional governments, and community organisations, both formal and informal. The volume brings forward the immense potential embedded within collective communitarian formations by exploring themes such as disaster capitalism, municipal socialism, civic capitalism, apocalypse or disaster communism, and Marxist humanism in relation to the management strategies exhibited by the Indian government towards the COVID-19 pandemic. It underscores the necessity for imagining a scenario where egalitarian and socially just policies replace the dominance of capitalism.

Part of the *Academics, Politics and Society in the Post-COVID World* series, the book will be an essential read for scholars and researchers of sociology, political studies, cultural studies, social anthropology, South Asia studies, pandemic studies, and postcolonial studies.

Suddhabrata Deb Roy is a PhD Candidate at the University of Otago, New Zealand.

Academics, Politics and Society in the Post-COVID World

Series Editors:
Lewis Gordon
Professor, University of Connecticut, USA
Rozena Maart
Professor, University of KwaZulu Natal, South Africa
Epifania Amoo-Adare
Independent Researcher, UK and Ghana
Sayan Dey
Postdoctoral Fellow, University of Witwatersrand, South Africa

This book series focuses on various forms of academic, social and political transformations that are taking place/are expected to take place in a post-COVID World. The biomedical crisis of COVID-19 has opened up a floodgate for all kinds of crisis like communal violence, racial discrimination, geographical hierarchies, socio-political hegemonies, and academic exclusivities. These crises are also catalyzing massive geo-political shifts in various epistemological and ontological frameworks of knowledge production across the globe. These shifts in turn are bound to influence patterns of thinking and doing in a post-COVID era, including shifts affecting pedagogical frameworks, curricular structures, institutional infrastructures, evaluation patterns, international policies, political ethics, communal relations, gender existence, racial connotations, mental health and physical wellbeing. With respect to academic shifts, many elite academic institutions have transferred their courses online, while other institutions are forced to shut down, due to the lack of sufficient technological infrastructure. With respect to politics, countries are experiencing several shifts in terms of social, cultural, economic and political policy-making that are bound to bring major changes in internal as well as international relations. With respect to society, the global pandemic has aggravated already existing racial, communal and cultural differences. At the same time, there are consistent efforts towards new forms of solidarities, reconciliations and humanity. All these are transformations that will continue to take place in a post-COVID era. Keeping these shifting scenarios at the forefront, this book series critically analyzes the various forms of transformation taking place in academic, social and political systems across the globe, during this post-COVID era.

Green Academia
Towards Eco-Friendly Education Systems
Sayan Dey

Pandemic Fissures
COVID-19, Dehumanisation, and the Obsolescence of Freedom in India
Suddhabrata Deb Roy

For more information about this series, please visit: www.routledge.com

Pandemic Fissures
COVID-19, Dehumanisation, and the Obsolescence of Freedom in India

Suddhabrata Deb Roy

LONDON AND NEW YORK

Designed cover image: Gettyimages/ajijchan

First published 2025
by Routledge
4 Park Square, Milton Park, Abingdon, Oxon OX14 4RN

and by Routledge
605 Third Avenue, New York, NY 10158

Routledge is an imprint of the Taylor & Francis Group, an informa business

© 2025 Suddhabrata Deb Roy

The right of Suddhabrata Deb Roy to be identified as author of this work has been asserted in accordance with sections 77 and 78 of the Copyright, Designs and Patents Act 1988.

All rights reserved. No part of this book may be reprinted or reproduced or utilised in any form or by any electronic, mechanical, or other means, now known or hereafter invented, including photocopying and recording, or in any information storage or retrieval system, without permission in writing from the publishers.

Trademark notice: Product or corporate names may be trademarks or registered trademarks, and are used only for identification and explanation without intent to infringe.

British Library Cataloguing-in-Publication Data
A catalogue record for this book is available from the British Library

ISBN: 978-1-032-26070-9 (hbk)
ISBN: 978-1-032-82567-0 (pbk)
ISBN: 978-1-003-50516-7 (ebk)

DOI: 10.4324/9781003505167

Typeset in Sabon
by Apex CoVantage, LLC

To my parents for all the love, support, and kindness!

Contents

	Acknowledgements	*x*
	List of Abbreviations	*xi*
	Introduction	1
1	India and the Unequal Pandemic	27
2	The Monstrosity of Disasters under Capitalism	67
3	Pandemics of Capitalism and Everyday Disasters	115
4	Benefits and Pitfalls of Local Governance during Apocalyptic Times	161
5	Radical Possibilities of the Apocalyptic Times	206
6	Morbidities of Disaster Civility	258
	Conclusion	311
	Index	*345*

Acknowledgements

A book can never be complemented without the support of numerous individuals who stand by an author. Likewise, this book too could not have been completed if I had not received the support of certain very important people in my life, who need to be thanked for the completion, and publication, of this book.

My parents for supporting me. Without them, I would have been nothing. Thank you.

Marcelle Dawson for being a pillar of support throughout my academic journey. Without her support, this journey would have been impossible. Marcelle has been the kindest and most supportive supervisor that anybody can think of. Thank you, Marcelle.

Annabel Cooper, Simon Barber, Steve Jackson, and Erik Olssen for their continued support towards me.

Vellikad Janardhan and Purendra Prasad for being the people who had introduced me to Marxist theory per se.

Kevin Anderson, Peter Hudis, Sandra Rein, and Heather Brown for their support, criticisms, and appreciations.

Sayan Dey, for always being there, as both a series editor and a wonderful friend and mentor.

My sincere thanks to the series editors, Lewis Gordon, Rozena Maart, and Epifania Amoo-Adare for accepting the manuscript.

Debasreeta for standing beside me, both in life and during the writing and editing of the book.

Amitabh, Saurav, Himangshu, Rituraj, Utpal, and Ratul for supporting all my endeavours for more than a decade and for always being there.

Paul, Brandon, Angus, Jonas, Kieran, Grace, Suraj, Manuel, Lotte, Nelson, Arun, Mrinmoy, Sepoy, Ayush, Lokendra, Arif, Bankim, and Joe for their support and the many interesting (and heart-wrenching) discussions regarding COVID-19.

Thanks to the University of Hyderabad and the University of Otago for being my *almae matres*.

My sincere thanks to the anonymous peer reviewers of the manuscript, whose comments have greatly contributed to the improvement of the book.

Last of all, thanks to all my colleagues, students, and friends – discussions with whom have seriously contributed to the book.

Abbreviations

AAP	Aam Aadmi Party
AIMED	Association of Indian Medical Device Industry
AITC	All India Trinamool Congress
AKCDA	All Kerala Chemists and Druggist Association
AMTZ	Andhra Pradesh MedTech Zone
API	Active Pharmaceutical Ingredient
ASHA	Accredited Social Health Activist
BJP	Bharatiya Janata Party
BRS	Bharat Rashtra Samithi
CHC	Community Health Centre
CII	Confederation of Indian Industry
CSO	Civil Society Organization
CSR	Corporate Social Responsibility
DC	District Collectorate
DMO	District Medical Office
FAO	Food and Agriculture Organization
FYE	Fiscal Year-End
GDP	Gross Domestic Product
HIMS	Health Information Management System
HPEC	High Powered Expert Committee
ICDS	Integrated Child Development Services
ICT	Information and Communication Technology
IIPH	Indian Institute of Public Health
INC	Indian National Congress
IPR	Intellectual Property Right
LMIC	Low- and Middle-Income Country
MAI	Multiplex Association of India
MNC	Multinational Corporation
MWSN	Migrant Workers Solidarity Network
NCW	National Commission for Women
NGO	Non-governmental Organization
NRHM	National Rural Health Mission
NFHS	National Family Health Survey
NHP	National Health Policy

NPPA	National Pharmaceutical Pricing Authority
NSSO	National Sample Survey Office
OECD	Organisation for Economic Co-operation and Development
OOP	Out-of-Pocket
PDS	Public Distribution System
PHC	Primary Health Centre
PMO	Prime Minister's Office
PPE	Personal Protection Equipment
PPP	Public-Private Partnership
PRIA	Participatory Research in Asia
SBM	Swachh Bharat Mission
SCAI	Shopping Centres Association of India
SII	Serum Institute of India
SHG	Self-help Group
SWAN	Stranded Workers Action Network
TB	Tuberculosis
TERI	The Energy and Resources Institute
TRIPS	Trade-Related Aspects of Intellectual Property Rights
UFO	Unidentified Flying Object
ULB	Urban Local Body
UNICEF	United Nations Children's Fund
UNESCO	United Nations Educational, Scientific and Cultural Organization
WCD	Women and Child Development
WHO	World Health Organization
WPI	Wholesale Price Index
WTO	World Trade Organization

Introduction

Viruses have lived among human beings for centuries. The plagues which have come upon the human society in the past are a proof of that. Plagues and pandemics are nothing fundamentally new to human society, and human society has not experienced a pandemic for the first time with COVID-19. There have been pandemics and pandemics with a far more devastating impact than COVID-19 in the past. The Black Death of 1346 that went on a rampage through Europe is often considered to be one of the worst disasters in recorded history, despite the fact that it occurred when Europe was doing considerably well, both economically and socially.[1] The impact of a viral outbreak, however, is not only contingent upon the material conditions but also on the psychological state of the people. The fear of death plays an important role in the way in which *disasters by themselves* influence the formulation of the policies around them. As Frank Ryan states in a recent book:

> Viruses frighten us. They elicit a primal fear of the unknown. They are capable of crashing through our natural barriers and defences, turning healthy cells into microscopic factories to produce exponential numbers of daughter viruses. These swarm through the bloodstream, drawing the attention of the immune system . . . every infection becomes a pitched battle that will determine the outcome for us, the host.
> (Ryan, 2019, 'Introduction')

However, the way in which COVID-19 has affected the human society has been unique, something that both the governments across the globe and the citizens under them have experienced for the first time. COVID-19, if one follows Naomi Klein (2007), constitutes a unique 'shock' which has become an important weapon at the hands of capital to further dominate the world. The COVID-19 pandemic has exposed that the world as we know it under capitalism has been wrecked by the rising inequality, which has become a fundamental characteristic of all the major democracies in the world.

The pioneering Marxist Sociologist from India, Akshay Ramanlal Desai had written – way back in 1975 – that 'The Fundamental issue of the twentieth century is the battle against poverty, against disease, against illiteracy, against the economic misery and the ruthless exploitation of the majority of population by a handful of capitalist owners in every capitalist country' (Desai, 1975, p. 104). After more than four decades, which also includes the turn of the century, Desai's proposition is as true as it was in 1975. The COVID-19 pandemic has been disastrous for the entire globe, killing as many as 6.9 million people globally as of 31st of December 2023.[2] In the context of India, COVID-19 has caused a massacre. As of the first week of September 2022, as per the World Health Organization (2022a), there have been 44,432,862 confirmed cases of COVID-19, which have resulted in 528,030 deaths. The vaccination numbers remain at 2,20,67,79,081 till 31st of December 2023.[3]

India found itself at its wits end during the pandemic. It tested little during the initial days of the pandemic with one of the lowest testing rates in the world, as a report by Biswas (2020) shows for the BBC. This data becomes further relevant because like most of the Global South, India's healthcare structure too is heavily privatised with a significant gap between medical accessibility and requirement. The COVID-19 pandemic has inflicted innumerable pains upon the *body politic*. The surveillance capitalistic model and the lockdowns initiated as responses to COVID-19 by various governments have been the causes of numerous economic and social issues, the full effects of which remain to be seen. Neoliberal models of governance have failed to provide the people with the institutional and social support that they need to overcome the crisis. Because of the growing apocalyptic nature of COVID-19 even after two and a half years of its genesis, it has again mainstreamed some of the ideas surrounding disasters and apocalyptic dystopias. However, as Slavoj Žižek writes:

> Hegel wrote that the only thing we can learn from history is that we learn nothing from history, so I doubt the epidemic will make us any wiser. The only thing that is clear is that the virus will shatter the very foundations of our lives, causing not only an immense amount of suffering but also economic havoc conceivably worse than the Great Recession.
>
> (Žižek, 2020a, p. 3)

Vaccines emerged as a ray of hope against the virus. Vaccines usually take years to come up and be functional, as Gilbert and Green (2021) rightly state in their book on the AstraZeneca vaccine. The complexities involved in the process of its development have been noted in accounts by their creators. However, if one goes through the accounts that have been released regarding the development of the Pfizer-BioNTech or the Oxford-AstraZeneca vaccine, the dynamics of the interrelationship between the market and science becomes extremely clear.

Natural disasters caused by climatic conditions and viruses have been an important part of human history. The rapid progress of science and technology had made some believe that viruses do not have the capacity to influence and disrupt human lives – an assumption which has been shattered by COVID-19. The history of pandemics and epidemics is an old one. During the Influenza pandemic of 1918–19, it became commonly accepted by the general masses that diseases and viruses can prove to be more harmful to the human society than wars (Kupperberg, 2008). The first virus to reach the shores of India after 1947 was the Asian flu (influenza) virus – named because its origins lay in East Asia – and within a month the country was witnessing over a million cases of a flu which went on to kill around 1.1 million–2 million lives before a vaccine was invented (Lundquist-Arora, 2022). Daniel Defoe's (1908/2010) *A Journal of the Plague Year* talks about how diseases such as plagues were thought of as being divine interferences in the lives of human beings from God. Epidemics and pandemics have been part of human history for centuries. It dates way back to 1346, when the Black Death went on to wipe out around 60% of Europe's total population (Slavicek, 2008). However, the Spanish flu of 1918 was one of the first pandemics, which gained recognition globally as a mass killer of human beings and resulted in approximate 50 million deaths worldwide. The Asian flu, another disease caused by an influenza virus originated from Eastern Asia in 1947 which caused a death of around 2 million people (Lundquist-Arora, 2022).

The severe acute respiratory syndrome (SARS) epidemic, appearing in 2002, infected around 8,000 people spanning across 26 countries, as per the World Health Organization (WHO). The virus SARS-CoV, identified in 2003, was also one of the precursors of the novel coronavirus that was unleashed upon human beings in 2019. A few years later, Swine flu caused by the H1N1 subtype of the influenza virus, first identified in 2009, had caused around 151,700–575,500 deaths globally, while the Middle East respiratory syndrome (MERS) epidemic killed around 659 people across 22 countries since its first detection in 2012 in the Arabian Peninsula (Koley & Dhole, 2021). Swine flu was the most recent pandemic that had left a mark on the globe, caused by the influenza subtype H1N1 (Mahapatra, 2021). Ebola, another virus, emerged in Western Africa in 2013, spreading across Guinea, Liberia, Nigeria, Sierra Leone, and Senegal (Wallace et al., 2016). The emergence of Ebola and its subsequent spread exhibited that social and political factors play a crucial role in the context of whether an outbreak or an epidemic becomes a pandemic, potentially resulting in the loss of many lives.

Zoonotic viruses such as the Nipah virus have been around there for centuries but have only recently begun to cause epidemics and outbreaks in the human society – as per human recorded history at least. The bat-borne zoonotic virus was discovered in 1994 when several livestock and people in Australia and later in Malaysia were observed to develop severe respiratory illness (Amaya & Broder, 2020). The virus subsequently has been making a mark in countries such as Bangladesh and Philippines, with the former suffering from annual seasonal outbreaks and the latter suffering an outbreak in 2014 with a fatality rate of 82% (Aditi & Shariff, 2019). The Zika virus, a mosquito-borne virus, was first discovered in monkeys in the forests of Zika in Uganda in 1957, with a large outbreak being witnessed for the first time in many years in Brazil in March 2015, which has subsequently spread to around eighty-six countries and territories (Koley & Dhole, 2021). Similar to Ebola, Zika too has no vaccine till date. The avian flu or bird flu, another disease caused by the zoonotic virus H5N1 and with no mainstream vaccine till date, was first identified in South Korea in 1997, when the virus made a jump from a waterfowl onto a human body (Davis, 2005) and has a mortality rate of around 60% (Poovorawan et al., 2013). The state of Kerala still suffers from annual outbreaks of the bird flu with the recent outbreak occurring as recently as in December 2021 (Shaji, 2021).

Among these different epidemics and pandemics, SARS, MERS, and COVID-19 are caused by coronaviruses – at least among the ones that science knows of. Mahapatra (2021) has identified, however, some of the reasons behind COVID-19 being a pandemic which has ushered in newer dimensions with regards to the ways in which human society engages with pandemics. The first being that COVID-19 can spread through human carriers who are infected but have yet not exhibited any signs of being sick, making it more difficult to identify and engage with patients. At the same time, it spreads very quickly – one person can infect more than two people within a very short period of time. Third, COVID-19 is lethal, though its mortality rate is lower than that of SARS. COVID-19 is lethal because it tends to have long-term effects on those it infects, especially elderly people and those with existing medical conditions. In other words, as Mahapatra argues:

> [A] disease can be much more lethal than COVID-19 but be limited in the manner in which it spreads and how fast it spreads. A disease can be much more contagious than COVID-19 and spread faster but be very mild and not cause major sickness or death in a substantial portion of the population.
> (Mahapatra, 2021, p. 134)

Koley and Dhole (2021) note that COVID-19 is far more infectious than any other virus that has infected the lives of human beings. And, with the low levels of testing that had characterised the Indian response to the pandemic (Biswas, 2020), it was almost a foregone conclusion that COVID-19 was going to become the catastrophe that the human society has been fearing, albeit mostly on religious terms, for a very long term.

One would have ideally assumed that with the extent to which science and technology have developed in the last century, the world would have gradually moved beyond these tendencies avoiding them to the best of its capabilities. However, as capitalist development has exhibited, the world has gradually moved towards the possible realisation of apocalyptic tendencies at *an increased pace*. A key reason for which is that capitalism today increasingly relies on globalised structures of supply to maintain its hegemony on the world (Lin, 2022) evading any kind of considerations focused on the environment and climate. India, as such, is placed at a critical juncture. Recently, India surpassed the United Kingdom in terms of its economy and emerged as the fifth-largest economy in the world on the 3rd of September 2022 (The Hindu, 2022). However, the critical question which stands relevant in this context is the human cost of this economic upsurge, especially when more than 90% of the workforce remains employed in informal modes of employment (Sengupta et al., 2007). A recent report by Abhishek et al. (2021) has highlighted the ways in which the vaccine delivery system in India has been characterised by a massive inequality, which has disproportionately affected these informal workers. The Oxfam report by them stated that women, Muslims, Adivasis, and Dalits, have faced discrimination over the delivery of vaccines with even healthcare workers actively taking part in the discriminatory practice. Because of the way in which the pandemic has been managed, it has instilled fear amidst the citizens, causing mental trauma for a lot of them (Singh, 2021, June 7).

Vaccines had become critical for India to come out of the crisis caused by COVID-19 because unlike some other countries in the world – proportionately akin to India in geographical size and population numbers – India was *gasping for its breath during the second wave* as Unninathan (2021) had put it in a recent issue of *India Today*. With a highly compromised media structure, whose sanctity and truthfulness have been brought under question in recent times, the crisis caused by COVID-19 has received a coverage which has combined the pandemic with the broader social ideology at play under the contemporary neo-fascist regime where terms such as *Corona jihad* and *Muslim Virus* have been rendered mainstream (Daniyal, 2022). At the same time, because of the slow policymaking that has characterised India's response to the crisis, caused an acute shortage of essential equipment such as masks, medical goggles, and gloves. This shortage was made scarcer by the complete marginalisation of domestic manufacturers (S & Nandan, 2020). When COVID-19 became the *killer* that one knows it as, specifically during the second wave in India, certain changes occurred in the general fabric of the society as well.

The most visible one became the manifestations of the ways in which certain businesses decided to make a profit out of the disaster by using the psychological and material vulnerabilities that people face during emergencies such as COVID-19 (Klein, 2007; Davis, 1998). For example, the fear that people harbour towards any viral infection has been used by right-wing forces to rapidly generate anti-vaccination drives (Shepherd, 2020). Another example can be cited of the oximeter – a device which became critical during the pandemic, especially during the second wave – continues to remain in high demand with brick-and-mortar stores failing to cater to the surge in demand. It has gone through a price increase of nearly 150% since the second wave of the pandemic – from around INR 800 to around INR 2000, with many e-commerce platforms selling them for INR 1900–3500 (The Hindu, 2021).

Big Tech and Big Pharma being the two most obvious examples in this regard. Wallace (2016) has laid bare the crucial interjections that Big Pharma makes in the creation of the conditions under which diseases such as COVID-19 can emerge in the society.

COVID-19 has provided a unique opportunity for Big Pharma and Big Tech to make immense profits and potentially target those who stand opposed to their domination in the society. The pandemic constitutes a perfect moment for the disaster capitalists to inflict their overarching domination over the society because the pandemic has provided them with a unique opportunity to push through the desired policies which can increase social inequality since people *are too busy surviving through their everyday lives* (Solis, 2020). It is also in situations such as these that people tend to put too much uncritical trust upon those in power (Klein, 2017) – such as the state, capitalists, and the philanthropists.

Capitalists engaged in the production and maintenance of Big Tech have gained immensely during the pandemic, with many of the technological companies generating substantial profits. There has also been an increased surveillance networking in the society which has allowed states to keep a more vigilant eye on its citizens, such as the usage of Google and Facebook to target environmental activists in India (Klein, 2021). With COVID-19, disaster capitalism has been unleashed with its full potential in India largely stemming from India's increasing integration with the global economy (Harshvardhan, 2020). He goes on to say that in the name of fighting against the virus, the central government has repeatedly violated human, environmental, and labour rights along with the continued suppression of dissenting voices. Naomi Klein (2020) has argued, quite effectively, that once the pandemic is over, the kind of vision which has been rendered mainstream by the pandemic will be difficult to get rid of. As Naomi Klein writes:

> It's a future in which our homes are never again exclusively personal spaces, but are also, via high-speed digital connectivity, our schools, our doctor's offices, our gyms, and, if determined by the state, our jails. . . . This is a future in which, for the privileged, almost everything is home delivered, either virtually via streaming and cloud technology, or physically via driverless vehicle or drone, then screen 'shared' on a mediated platform.
>
> (Klein, 2020, Paras 8–9)

That disaster capitalists could make a mark in countries such as India, which have historically been defined by traditional communitarian values, also shows that the sense of a community is on the decline under capitalist neoliberal economies. With globalisation of capital, communicable diseases had also become globalised as Sainath (2020a) argues, which has posed an incremental amount of risk to the marginalised populace with a constantly rising privatised healthcare infrastructure designed to reduce accessibility.

The shortage of medical drugs and oxygen had completely baffled the society and the state during the second wave in 2021 when the number of confirmed cases had reached 1.99 crore (Firstpost, 2021). In May 2021, the Supreme Court, reacting to the crisis, had asked the government to consider fixing a ceiling price for essential COVID-19-related drugs under the Drugs (Price Control) Order, 2013, which allows the government to intervene in the retail pricing of certain drugs during situations of distress (Business Today, 2021). However, the government claimed that there was no shortage of oxygen and drugs and issued a strict warning against hoarding, as Firstpost (2021) reported. The hoarding of oxygen and medicines had, during the second wave, created a shortage of the essential drugs and equipment which the common people needed to counter the viral infection (The Indian Express, 2020b). This aptly becomes an example of Mbembe's (2019) fundamental observation of a necro-political framework wherein the social solidarity concerning human beings has, under capitalism, degraded immensely leading the world down a path where the problems of the other person do not invoke compassion but rather a sense of self-preservation and a feeling of respite that one is not affected by the same. The section of the society which suffered the most from the pandemic and its associated response from the government were the migrant workers, often left stranded across different parts of the country. The crisis faced by the migrant workers in India has led one to question the biopolitics involved within the larger domain of crisis management by the state and the market. The state, if it wished to do so, could have avoided the mass perpetuation of hunger and crisis in the society, but instead it went ahead with the numerous reforms it had been seeking to bring in with the intention of creating docile and compliant human lives. The worst affected of which were the migrant workers (Raja, 2020), most adequately represented by the crisis faced by the migrant workers due to the crumbling healthcare infrastructure in the country.

Noted journalist, P. Sainath (2020b) wrote that the migrant exodus, which occurred during the first lockdown, was an indicator of the kind of inequality that has been institutionalised in the society since the neoliberal economic reforms of 1991. This agrarian crisis has ravaged the nation and has had a devastating impact on rural India, leaving millions of people without any option but to return to substandard levels of living in urban areas performing cheap labour for the new middle class and the elites. Numerous reports have elaborated upon the plight that migrant workers have faced during the pandemic. The Stranded Workers Action Network (SWAN) (2021) stated:

> For the poor, the last few months have been [characterised by] a crisis of livelihood and hunger that has been compounded by the ubiquitous healthcare crisis that has paralysed the country. Images of hungry and tired migrant workers making long journeys home were at the forefront of the public discourses in 2020.
>
> (SWAN, 2021, p. 6)

The crisis caused by the COVID-19 pandemic had revealed the degenerated state of collective conscience of the nation in terms of how the nation views the most precarious of all the workers in the country – the migrant informal labour force. Deka writes:

> Many of these workers are 'circular migrants' – who come to the cities seeking work in the non-agricultural season – and would have returned to their native places after the monsoon . . . their invisibility is the reason why the urban poor and migrant workers in the informal sector fall below the radar of central and state government officials.
> (Deka, 2020, p. 17)

Migrant workers usually cannot avail the different benefits that governments and municipalities plan for the residents because of not being permanent residents of the place. This is being done in a context where the approximate number of rural to urban migrants is around 120 million, contributing around 10% of the economic output of the nation (Tripathi, 2020). Reports by the SWAN (2020) and the Migrant Workers Solidarity Network (MWSN) (2020) prove that migrant workers have not only been left homeless and penniless but also had been at the risk of losing their basic dignity as human beings during the first lockdown. The migrant workers' crisis exhibited the limitations that India possesses even in the contemporary times as far as the operational functionality of its democracy among the informal and vulnerable sections of the working class. Shoaib Daniyal wrote, 'That India saw a bruising episode of mass death and economic collapse with almost no political expression might be a significant example of India's current moment of democratic malfunction' (2022, Para 20).

Responses to disasters such as pandemics requires an elaborate plan which needs to focus on public expenditure – at least in certain sectors which are considered to be essential for survival – or an alternative method of providing the people with the basic necessities of life – food, clothing, shelter, healthcare, and education being the most important ones of them. Neoliberal reforms in the healthcare and education sector have ensured that the public education and healthcare sector is in shambles. The accessibility to these services in India is contingent upon the ways in which the state has allowed the market forces to intervene directly into the everyday lives of the people. At the same time, the introduction of the market forces in general has been encouraged in such a way that it does not temper with the heretical notions of oppression which have existed in the Indian society. Evidence of this can be seen in the way in which sanitation – a job that became the most important one during the pandemic – is still performed mostly by the lower castes with the state actively enforcing the same (Counterview, 2019).

The workers under the contemporary neoliberal capitalism in India have been suffering from a string of newer models of oppression which have emerged during the pandemic – some caused by the state and central governments themselves, the bodies which are supposed to protect them – with those in the lowest strata as per the hierarchical division of labour suffering the most such as the pyre workers (Narayani, 2021) and care workers, including those who are not directly involved in the medical profession (Deol, 2022). In countries such as India, where the per capita expenditure is low, the care workers face the highest and the most brutal brunt of the budget restrictions imposed on the healthcare by neoliberal policies (Nelson, 2020). The COVID-19 pandemic has exposed the mutual relationship that exists between global capital and the precariat workers in the Global South as 'Capital relies on these workers to produce commodities destined for global circulation, while the workers are highly dependent on their wage work, which renders them particularly exploitable and disposable' (Zanoni & Mir, 2022, p. 371). This nexus, in turn, affects the kind of healthcare that vulnerable workers and others from the marginalised sections can have access to. This also has an adverse impact on the kind of workers who provide the requisite healthcare services to these people. COVID-19 did not make many positive alterations to these conditions, instead, it amplified that. Mishra and Santosh (2021) bring forward the fears that many of the frontline workers, who are not as such medical workers per se, have had to face during the pandemic with increased workloads, compromised protection mechanisms, and the like, in addition to the constant devaluation – both economically and socially – of the kind of work that they do.

Blakeley (2020) argues that the arrival of the recession, which was about to hit the world in the near future – as argued by numerous economists – has been accelerated by COVID-19. The COVID-19 pandemic, as Žižek (2020a, 2020b) has argued, has brought forward issues surrounding the global vision of the human society that states and governments possess with important questions regarding how human societies are segregated on the basis of newer aspects, such as the split between those who are masked and who do not want to wear one. There have been issues around the ethics of forced vaccination and the implications it has for the working people (King, 2021), which had not been the major issues they are today. Lupton (2022) argues that the COVID-19 pandemic has shown that biopolitical modes of control are still as relevant as they were years ago, and that citizens across the globe are still affected by them. India has been the one of the most affected countries by the pandemic with around 4.7 million deaths as of May 2022 as per the data provided by the WHO (Daniyal, 2022). The havoc caused by COVID-19 has not been constructed out of thin air. Decades of neoliberal and capitalist exploitation of the natural world has degraded the subtle balance that exists between human society and the broader environment in general. Large-scale capitalist agriculture produces pathogens that promote disastrous and unhealthy food habits across the globe (Nelson, 2020). This in turn creates the conditions under which pandemics such as COVID-19 can become the global catastrophe that it has turned out to be. The dynamic nature of capitalism has enabled the spread of COVID-19 globally. The manner in which capitalism has become a part of the everyday lives of human beings has brought about a major change in the ways in which human beings have begun to imagine lives altogether, creating alienation and estrangement on a mass scale.

The current book talks mainly about four different perspectives and the ways in which they can be used to analyse the effects of the pandemic, as well as the response that different governments showed towards the pandemic. These are disaster capitalism, municipal socialism, civic capitalism, and apocalypse or disaster communism. The six chapters of the book engage with these tendencies, as well as with Gandhian and Nehruvian ideas, to provide an analytical and critical discussion surrounding the state of affairs in India. The focus on local governance has caused a massive stir among the Indian governmental apparatus, which has historically relied on the assumption that a strong state is necessary for the effective functioning of a society.

The issues associated with local governance are also intricately associated with those of large-scale urbanisation, which has often been of an unplanned nature in India, causing an unnecessary pressure on the healthcare infrastructure of the country (Mishra et al., 2021). And healthcare crisis inevitably affects the social fabric of the society because health affects everybody ontologically at a highly intimate level of being. Under neoliberalism, the powers accorded to bodies such as the WHO, which could have been more effective in battling such crises, are severely curtailed because of the way in which their finances are structured, which allows increasing private wealth to be pushed into the organisations reducing their autonomy (Sengupta, 2000/2020b). This aggravates the chances of outbreaks and epidemics transforming into pandemics, which then have a direct impact on the social fabric of the society with self-preservation taking over the psyche of collectivity and co-operation even in societies where traditional values are held in high esteem, such as India.

One of the major challenges that India faced in the wake of the COVID-19 pandemic is to reinvent its own social fabric. The pandemic has given rise to a diverse range of tendencies within the society – from disaster capitalism to a newfound admiration for municipal socialism. Admiration for a new kind of socio-administrative system is nothing new for India. India has had trysts with both Gandhian socialism and Nehruvian socialism, but it is essential to realise that both these tendencies have tried to reduce the individual to a mere object of study. It is essential, at the critical juncture, to go back to these tendencies and evaluate them in light of the new challenges that COVID-19 has thrown up. Different pandemics have brought forward newer challenges for the human society to deal with. These challenges are contingent upon the ways in which developmental practices and the process of socio-economic and cultural restructuring have progressed in the society. Such a nuanced analytical framework becomes essential in engaging with the broader dimensions of the society. The book is based on the premise that during times of crisis, it becomes essential to engage with ideas that are otherwise considered to be marginalised voices because the voices from the margins often invoke reflective ideas which are not usually considered to be relevant under *normal* times.

Numerous philosophers have begun to become relevant with the coming of apocalyptic probabilities such as climate change, and especially with the pandemic, and the increasing influence of the state within the lives of common citizens. Thomas Hobbes, can be taken as one such example, who has gained in relevance over the last few years, especially after the publication of Joel Wainwright and Geoff Mann's (2018) *Climate Leviathan*, where they have put forward an argument in favourable advocacy for asserting the continued political relevance of Hobbes's concept of the *Leviathan* and how the concept can be used to construct a socialist vision in times of rapidly emerging apocalyptic tendencies which characterise the twenty-first century. However, the task which remains is to relate the philosophical tendencies to actually existing events as, 'Our life and times impart an urgency to the task of working out a new relationship of philosophy to actuality. Thought and deed cannot forever stand far apart' (Dunayevskaya, 1958, p. 16). The relation between theory and praxis is critical to the ushering in of a theoretical framework which goes beyond the normalised theories of the yesteryears. The perpetual condition of crisis that infests human society today is a multipronged one as Shantz (2016) argues – which has been made further complicated after COVID-19 emerged – in which the state plays an active role through the many resources it has at its disposal, both materially and psychologically. Societies are characterised by internal contradictions, which become critical within any conceptualisation of socialism. There are aspects related to caste, class, gender, and race which become critical during conditions of disasters, as the book will go on to exhibit. The state through its ushering in of control and disciplinarian force attempts to either render obsolete or aggravate these internal contradictions as it deems fit. The crucial importance of internal contradictions in the society has to be realised, in light of tendencies such as apocalypse communism – most famously propagated by Juan Posadas of the Latin American Bureau of the Fourth International – who went against the dominant tide of left-wing thinkers and politics which advocated the complete disarmament of nuclear weapons (Gittlitz, 2020). While most left-wing tendencies – which include both Stalinism and orthodox Trotskyism – often make a fetish out of the particular struggles while delving into the universal struggles of the working class insufficiently, Juan Posadas committed the reverse. Posadas (1968) argued that it was the universal struggle which mattered the most, often at the expense of the local or national ones. While people like Posadas, might look to be irrelevant under contemporary modes of social organisations, it is indispensable to engage with them because the twin assaults of the Coronavirus and capitalist policies have created a situation where the *end of the world* does not seem to be a mere object of speculation. The COVID-19 pandemic provides a unique opportunity to rethink many of the socio-economic and cultural policies which one has taken for granted in the twenty-first century. The COVID-19 pandemic provides the world with an opportunity to re-analyse the contemporary public policies, as well as the effects that these policies have had on the creation of increasing inequality (Garicano, 2021).

12 *Introduction*

One of the major debates which has emerged during the pandemic is the relevance of the welfare state. The welfare state, or rather the conceptualisation of the welfare state under capitalism, has found itself to be the centre of attention during COVID-19. With increasing demands focused on the public takeover of the key industries, and the emerging debate about the moral responsibility of the state, ideas such as municipal socialism have been, since the pandemic, gaining increasing grounds in major democracies where the government management of essential services has become a major electoral issue. Shabi (2021) reports that ideas such as council housing and collectivism focused on community wealth-building projects and people-driven policies have become issues which concern the populace in any social context during the COVID-19 crisis. Models such as Preston Model, under the leadership of politicians such as Matt Brown, have brought in newer dimensions to the age-old argument advocating for economic reforms to bolster local production and well-being through collectivism and localism (Dennett, 2021). Such models have often become the answers that many on the centre-left – which has often found itself searching for alternatives (Rentoul, 2020) – had been searching for decades in opposition to the *Big Capital, its leaders, and its ideas*. Such models as Dennett and Shabi note have provided a common-sensical and concrete answer to critical questions surrounding public welfare, employment, and local economic growth, which have become more enticing to citizens, especially with the COVID-19 pandemic-induced disruption in their everyday lives. Paul Dennett writes, in the context of Salford that:

> [We] have challenged the assumption that nothing is achievable in local government without national political change. . . . National contexts do have a huge impact on our fortunes locally, it's true – but with will and determination, there is still much which can be done in our cities, towns, communities, and neighbourhoods, to make life better for working people.
> (Dennett, 2021, Section 'Changing the Future')

The plea for a truly welfare state becomes critical in contexts, when a report in May 2020 stated that around 130 migrants had lost their lives in road accidents while returning back to their homes during the first lockdown (The Indian Express, 2020a). The issue surrounding other kinds of scarcities such as the food scarcity during the first lockdown brought up certain critical questions regarding the responsibility which rests with the state and the society in general – the centre of which again lay in India's mega urban cities (Bhakti, 2020). As A. R. Desai would have argued:

> Judged by all the indices, the welfare state does not satisfy any of the claims attributed to it. In fact, the functioning of the welfare states does not reveal that these states will be able to satisfy any of the claims

attributed to them. On the contrary, welfare states are developing those tendencies and processes which are quite the opposite of their avowed intentions. [They] are not able to provide minimum securities to the citizens. They are strengthening the hold of monopoly capital [because they] have not been able to create the social forces which would control the power of monopoly capital.

(Desai, 1975, p. 71)

The debates surrounding the welfare state have found a new lease of life because of the COVID-19 pandemic. These debates have provided a new lease of life to the centuries' old demand of public provisioning of essential services which has often resulted in governments, especially local administrative bodies themselves, engaging with the establishment of companies such as the Glasgow Water Company which was established in 1805 when the council and magistrates of Glasgow invested in a company to secure water for the residents leading to political debates surrounding the relationship between state (The Water Enterprise of Some of our Large Towns V. Glasgow, 1899; Kellett, 1978).

It is imperative to note that existent methods of social analysis of pandemics, or for that matter, any kind of disaster might not help much in the context of COVID-19 because the challenges that came up with COVID-19 have been largely unprecedented ones. In this context, it also becomes essential to talk in terms of newer theoretical endeavours and frameworks, which not only reform the demerits associated with old frameworks but also provide pathways towards a more affirmative future for the marginalised sections of the society. To achieve this, one needs to ground oneself in the idea that the contradiction between capital and labour is fundamental to a capitalist society, something which emerged to be a critical difference between Marx and the other Utopian socialists. Marx devised his theories based on the idea that the contradictory relationship between capital and labour is the central contradiction under capitalism, which made him successful in analysing capitalism as a social relationship, rather than simply a moral or an ethical one (Dunayevskaya, 1956, 1965).

Critiquing capitalism today cannot only mean critiquing it from a materialistic standpoint, but also needs to engage with the philosophical point of view. The lack of philosophical understanding of the onslaught of capitalism and the methods in which resistance can be effected can gain immensely if the point of production can be problematised. The pandemic has revealed the relevance of human solidarity and the relationship that human solidarity shares with the theoretical and the practical basis of an organisational structure which can struggle against the unequal social structure under conditions where neoliberal economic policies have fused with neo-fascism, especially in countries such as India. This have in turn given an opportunity for the far-right to be backed by the forces of corporate capital thus becoming more deeply rooted in the economic and cultural life of a society (Patnaik, 2021), which have had a drastic effect on different sectors of the economy. Hupkau and Petrongolo (2021) argue:

> Covid-19 is hitting most economies as hard as the deepest recessions, but given the exceptional nature of this crisis, the distribution of jobs and workers affected is potentially different from previous recessions. The Great Recession, as well as other previous downturns, tended to affect male-dominated industries more severely such as construction and manufacturing. In contrast, the social distancing and lock-down associated with the Covid-19 crisis has hit service sectors with frequent interactions between consumers and providers, sectors whose activities, sectors whose activities involve social contact, such as retail, restaurants and hospitality have been shut down, with temporary and permanent job losses concentrated among low-skill service workers.
> (Hupkau and Petrongolo, 2021, p. 2)

Nagpal and Uppal (2020) brought forward the issues surrounding numerous sectors – from the salaried workers to those who earn from *hand-to-mouth* on a daily basis. They have, unsurprisingly, argued that workers employed in transportation sectors – such as auto-rickshaw drivers and gig workers in the Ola or Uber application-based services found it hard to pay even their monthly rent. Although the gig workers, retail workers, and other freelance workers suffered because of their lowered incomes, the situation faced by others such as sanitation workers and domestic workers was worse.

The pandemic has revealed that certain sectors which are otherwise not considered to be key ones, are, in fact, important ones in the context of a health crisis. Issues surrounding the state of sanitation in the country, where the Swachh Bharat Mission has been functioning, have found themselves to be at the centre of attention. Sanitation in India is intimately connected with other issues such as proper sewerage mechanisms and access to water – aspects which do not receive the kind of attention that they deserve (Kanwar, 2019b). This becomes critical in places such as Dharavi, the largest slum in Asia located in Mumbai, where a humongous population lives in cramped spaces working to earn the money required for their sustenance – a major portion of whom are migrant workers in the informal sector which contributes a major portion of the economic output of India (Yardley, 2011). The condition of sanitation in India under the neoliberal economic framework demands an emphasis on the dialectical relationship between philosophy and organisation as Dunayevskaya (1953) had put it. It cannot be denied that the primary agency of social change are the organisations which engage with the problems at the grassroots, the effectiveness of which has been demonstrated by numerous social movements. These movements have continued to be relevant even amidst the pandemic, especially during the pandemic.

The complexities associated with the spread of COVID-19 have made grassroots action critical in countries such as India, where vaccine inequity has been institutionalised by the state itself. With widespread usage of digital frameworks and a constantly diminishing supply chain of vaccines, the vaccine delivery mechanisms in India had been characterised by inequality before it had even begun. Buckshee (2021) argues that the overt dependence on technology during critical public health emergencies has been fatal to many without the necessary social and economic capital to make use of the technology:

> People with disabilities, the economically disadvantaged and daily wage earners have been particularly impacted. [A 27-year-old domestic worker from Mumbai] said she finally got her first doseafter a month of trying – at a local temple that organized a free vaccine drive.
> (Buckshee, 2021, 'Cruelly out of Reach')

Public health measures initiated during times such as COVID-19 must ensure that they are framed, as Buckshee correctly argues, to include the widest section of the people, something which already unequal avenues such as the accessibility to technology in India can never provide if they are taken to be the foundation of a supposedly equality-driven healthcare program. The report by Barman (2021) proves that during the pandemic, the marginalised sections of the society, especially those coming from the poorest sections of the working class, were unable to access the relief benefits that the government had been offering because the plans were not streamlined enough to reach the most vulnerable workers such as the informal migrant workers, who were often relatively deprived of some critical relief packages, including midday meals under the *Atma Nirbhar* relief package – the financial benefits promised by the *Pradhan Mantri Garib Kalyan Yojana* (PMGKY), and so on. Reading Sainath (2020a), however, would make one argue that the debate about the delivery of the packages should be related to the fact that most of these packages under the Public Distribution System (PDS) that the government had initiated during the lockdown were allocated from sums that had already existed for other schemes for marginalised workers. Sainath says, 'What's also surfacing is demonisation of migrant workers, domestic maids, slum-dwellers, and other poor by housing societies convinced that they are *the* problem. The truth: the carriers of COVID-19, as also of SARS earlier, are the flying classes: us' (2020a, Para 11).

Initially, there were reports of COVID-19 being very similar to SARS, with many claiming that the impact that both of them have on the human society will be similar (Petrosillo et al., 2020). COVID-19, however, is different from SARS because of the fact that it has a lower fatality rate than SARS, but it is much more infectious (Koley & Dhole, 2021). However, the way in which COVID-19 has spread in the society has been very different than that of SARS because of the ways in which globalisation of trade and services has been managed and rendered mainstream under global capitalism. It is worthwhile to note here that SARS still does not have an effective vaccine. The race for the vaccine reminded one of the *space-race* between the United States of America (USA) and the Union of Soviet Socialist Republics (USSR) that had characterised much of the twentieth century, which was – like COVID-19 – a global affair intertwined with broader questions surrounding foreign policy, world peace, and nationalist policymaking (Mukherjee, 1988). India's vaccination drive had begun on the 16th of January 2021, and on the 1st of May 2021, every citizen had become eligible to receive a vaccine. However, the vaccination drive in India was infused with political propaganda, with unreal claims – such as the ability to vaccinate the entire population by 2021 – and the organisation of large-scale events to celebrate important milestones while vaccine shortages and issues surrounding accessibility remain abound (Ramachandran, 2021; Ramakrishnan & Salam, 2021). The Indian healthcare system is a mix of the public sector working in conjunction with the private sector, something that came into public focus during the pandemic due to the massive fund crisis and the disjunction between the private and public providers, which crippled the healthcare infrastructure of the country in terms of planning, equipment rationing, testing facilities, and human resource management (Baru, 2020). Salve (2020) reports that even major urban metropolitan areas such as Mumbai and Delhi had to face significant workload issues because of the dilapidated state of primary healthcare funding, which often remains in a state of crisis, despite more funds being allocated to secondary and tertiary care facilities.

Fuelled by a combination of these factors, the vaccine delivery mechanism in India has failed to ensure the smooth administration of the vaccines in India. Sridhar (2021b) has written in details about the ways in which the vaccine has been used for the generation of profits by those tasked with the responsibility to manufacture it, even though bodies such as the Serum Institute of India (SII) had initially stated that they would not try to make profits out of the vaccine because most of the research was initiated by non-corporate bodies. The shortage of vaccines and the unpreparedness of the government had ensured that black marketing and hoarding could go on unabated in most cities (Sridhar, 2021a). At the same time, as Sridhar (2021a) notes, the government of India's fetish with the development of an indigenous vaccine gave Bharat Biotech International Limited (BBIL) virtually a free-ride through the system bypassing critical, ethical, and scientific procedures producing unrealistic claims and market-driven revenue mechanisms through the institutionalised usage of Intellectual Property Rights (IPRs). It is critical to realise that vaccine delivery mechanisms in the context of India have to be devised extremely carefully because there is an existent inequality – even though it has been decreasing – in the way in which vaccines are delivered in India (Bettampadi et al., 2020).

Commentaries on the pandemic from Wallace (2016), Honigsbaum (2020), and Quammen (2012) have all agreed that human civilisation, as it stands today, will be vulnerable to future pandemics. Honigsbaum (2020) lays out that when bureaucracy and criminalisation of informal modes of communication takes precedence over localised forms of governance and tries to stifle out democratic voices from the bottom, the chances of any local yet critical news – such as that of the 70-year-old patient zero who fell ill in Wuhan on the 1st of December 2019 – finds itself difficult to be reported in the wider media. He noted that since the 1992 report from the Institute of Medicine on emerging infections, it was clear to most that 'globalization, coupled with climate change and the increasing demand for animal protein, had made the word "intrinsically more vulnerable" to infectious diseases, both known and unknown, than in the past' (Honigsbaum, 2020, p. 268). SARS was the first disease which made the world realise how interconnected it was to these processes, COVID-19 only exhibited how bad it has become over the last few years. The impact of COVID-19 was further accentuated in India because of the political crisis, which followed the first emergence of the disease. As Harsh Mander writes:

> India had a window of over a month and a half between its first reported infection and the nationwide lockdown. The first case of Coronavirus was detected in Kerala on 30 January 2020. . . . Even as late as 18 March, there were only 161 confirmed cases. . . . There is [however] little evidence that the Indian government used these precious weeks of low infection to strengthen its capacities for testing, tracing and cure; or to educate its people about precautions they could take or prepare them for restrictions on movement and large gatherings that would become necessary.
>
> (Mander, 2021, p. 148)

These factors ensured that the government remained focused on maintaining the political stability of the nation, while retaining the power in the hands of those already empowered. Reduced public expenditure on a variety of different schemes has left the marginalised sections of the population completely helpless in the face of a global pandemic like COVID-19. Citizens of most countries in the world do not have the capacity to respond to disasters like COVID-19. The lack of a social and economic capacity to respond to health emergencies can be seen in the ways in which even advanced industrial nations such as the United States of America (USA) and the United Kingdom (UK) responded to COVID-19 – which has caused a stir in the global media. Globally, COVID-19 has caused an indelible impact, not only on the physical health of people but has also been having a massive impact on the mental health of the people with loss of sleep, weird dreams, and the like becoming normalised elements of everyday life during the pandemic (Koley & Dhole, 2021), especially during the lockdowns.

There is a widespread argument coming from psychologists and sociologists alike that times and crises are always a dual-edged sword, one that might bring out the best or the worst from the human society. The COVID-19 pandemic, in that regard, has been an ambiguous one, as the book will go on

18 *Introduction*

to show. The lessons that humanity has learnt – and continues to learn – from the COVID-19 will be critical because, as Quammen (2020) argues, pandemics *will be* recurrent to human civilisation unless human civilisation begins making changes to the basic ways in which life is sustained on the planet, which includes transforming the human-non-human relationship to that of respect and empathy and devising stronger barriers against the viruses by the employment of robust medical systems in place which remain independent of the effects of political opportunism characterising most democracies. Honigsbaum (2020) argues, on the other hand, that the fact that COVID-19 could become a global catastrophe even with all the stringent mechanisms in place is a reminder that human society, as of now, still remains vulnerable to forces of nature such as pandemics. Quammen (2020) quite rightly states, 'We must remember, when the dust settles, that COVID-19 was not a novel event or a misfortune that befell us. It was – it is – part of a pattern of choices that we humans are making' (p. 526).

Naomi Klein (2007) had argued that capital uses shocks to push forward its own agendas for the further accumulation of profits. The COVID-19 pandemic, in this regard, has been used for passing through decisions that can have massive implications on the marginalised population of the country. These include the replacement of the labour laws by the labour codes, the farm laws which could have potentially opened up Indian agriculture to further corporate control, major changes in the educational infrastructure in the country, and the like (MWSN, 2020). The construction of a public health emergency as a war-like situation grants the governments with certain executive powers, which can be used by the state to maintain secrecy around the developments of the spread of the disease and control the people in the name of national security (Rutzen & Dutta, 2020). The constant glorification of the *war on Corona* has allowed the central government to invoke wartime measures which often result in the suspension of basic human rights and further marginalisation of the already exploited, as was the case with migrant informal workers (MWSN, 2020; Rutzen & Dutta, 2020). The accessibility to healthcare has become further complicated in the Global South because of the increasing privatisation of the healthcare services, which has characterised the healthcare infrastructure in most of these low- and middle-income countries (Sengupta, 2013/2020a).

With the COVID-19 pandemic, the world has witnessed the havoc which can be wrecked when health services are not accessible to everybody, especially those who come from the vulnerable sections. Sengupta et al. (2017/2020) had noted long ago that the incessant privatisation of healthcare and the constant promotion of the non-governmental organisations (NGOs) and the not-for-profit sector has resulted in major corporates operating through trusts and charities in the sector taking up the space occupied by the erstwhile public provisioning of health services. The world, however, has not learnt much from COVID-19. As the world continues to battle with COVID-19, another viral infection Monkey Pox has emerged, the treatments to which also remain unavailable in most of the poorer nations in the globe (Nolen, 2022). Italy, the country which was once labelled by the *New York Times* as being the 'grim epicenter' of the COVID-19 pandemic in Europe with deaths rising to 800 per day (Povoledo, 2022), has elected one of the most right-wing governments in its recent history (Albanese, 2022). In India, as well, the popularity of Narendra Modi and the Bharatiya Janata Party (BJP) remained relatively stable in July 2021, despite the sharp drop in April–May 2021 caused by the mismanagement of the pandemic as noted by various scholars, journalists, and activists. This phenomenon has been attributed to public negligence rather than the government's management of the pandemic (Menon, 2021; Miglani & Ghoshal, 2021). As Menon writes, in cases where criticisms were being made, it was due to the campaigns that the PM had attended in Bengal during the pandemic, and not the management of the pandemic itself. David Broder (2022) in a recent article notes about the kind of pattern which has been emerging in global politics with the gradual move towards the right-wing bloc in recent times, which emphasises the global right-ward shift in politics based on the constant othering of immigrants and minorities.

Arundhati Roy (2021) notes that the mismanagement which had characterised India's COVID-19 response was a *crime against humanity* itself because of the hasty decisions that the government had made by locking down the country – of the size of India – in four hours, and the government's complete reliance on corporate houses to manufacture the vaccines who will 'roll out two of the most expensive vaccines in the world, to the poorest people in the world' (p. 15). At the same time, the official death toll which had been published in 2021 by the government – a mere 220,000 – has come to be criticised as being an undercounted one by major experts (Ellis-Petersen & Alam, 2021; Rao, 2021), much like how the government had suppressed the Malaria death counts in 2016 – reporting 561 deaths in 2016, while the experts predicted it to be around 200,000 (Rao & Namana, 2016). Ellis-Petersen and Alam (2021) note that the allegations of such manipulation of data were particularly stark in the state of Uttar Pradesh according to data collected by *The Observer*, a state ruled by the BJP, and which plays an important role in its national electoral dynamics.

Capitalist urbanisation processes and the incessant greed of accumulation are what propelled the pandemic to the levels that it is in the contemporary times, as Nail (2022) elaborates. There have numerous claims that the economic downturn brought about by COVID-19 can cause the fall of the existent socio-economic order *as one knows it*. There has been a consistent effort to label the difficulties faced by people as being triggered by the virus, while in reality they are largely the faults of the structural logic of capitalism itself (Waitzkin, 2020), which has propelled states such as India to move towards further pro-business policies during the pandemic taking advantage of the situation which deters protests and social movements (Kumar, 2021). The passing of the labour codes highlights the apathy that the state shows towards the migrant workers, especially those in the informal sector, who will be particularly affected by the reduction in the security and accountability ensuring frameworks guaranteed by the labour laws (Varma et al., 2020). Arun Kumar (2021) writes that the pro-business attitude of the government had already been exposed when lockdowns were lifted when the number of cases decreased, rather than following the more scientific and logical method of lifting them when new cases decreased.

The reaction that the local governments exhibited towards the pandemic reflected the kind of financial distress that they have been going through along with the functional overlaps, ambiguity with regards to duties and finances, and the potential wastage of resources as Kaur and Gupta (2020) have highlighted. Local bodies, it must be emphasised, are expected to be the first ones to react to the crisis. It is important to realise in this context that capitalism does not abhor the idea of lesser human beings or human deaths en masse, because it has already created the grounds for a massive *Robotization* of the production process and the economy itself (Marder, 2020). COVID-19 has resulted in massive bailouts being issued to major capitalists to lift them out of the crisis caused by the pandemic – which had been allowed by capitalist processes to become the *pandemic that it became* (Nail, 2022). Multiple layers of contradictions have been exposed by the pandemic, from the disparities existing in internet accessibility for education (Kumar & Kumar, 2020) to the inability of a significant section of the population to practice social distancing because of their conditions of living (Sur & Mitra, 2020). All of these have pointed out the fact that issues such as sustainable housing and urban policies cannot be formulated without taking into cognisance the *urban* needs of the marginalised even when the worst phase of the pandemic is over, as Das (2020) and Kanwar (2019a) have argued.

With the pandemic, the stark reality of life under capitalism has been exposed. A state of social crisis has an indelible effect on the individual human being, both physically and psychologically affecting both the modes of one's being and thoughts. The cycle of crisis that capitalism produces is provided with certain solutions by capitalism itself. However, the major issue with those solutions always have been that they have either been based structurally on already existing inequalities or have led to further conditions of crises. It is only through a crisis that capitalism is able to ascertain the renegade elements contributing to the crisis, get rid of the same, and proceed towards a new mode of profit accumulation. 'It is in the course of crises that the instabilities of capitalism are confronted, reshaped and re-engineered to create a new version of what capitalism is about. Much gets torn down and laid waste to make way for the new' (Harvey, 2014, p. ix).

Under such circumstances, hope, or rather militant optimism – a mode of thinking which falls in between naive optimism and abject pessimism – along the lines of Ernst Bloch can be a powerful weapon at the hands of the marginalised (Menozzi, 2020). At the same time, it is essential to take into cognisance that under capitalism, there has been, as Fromm (1976) had argued, a constant change in the ways in which people define themselves. Contemporary capitalism derives significant benefits from the manner in which people define themselves through the commodities they own, and health under the modern capitalist mode of production is a commodity, *one which can be owned*. At the same time, the way in which, in spite of the mismanagement, the popularity of the statist paradigm under right-wing neoliberal governments continues to grow brings up the question of the very conception of freedom that people have developed within themselves through years of capitalist and neoliberal exploitation.

Notes

1 During those days, 'Better nutrition, combined with a long period of peace and the absence of any major disease epidemics, [had] caused the continent's population to triple between 1000 and 1250, from approximately 25 million to 75 million. As the population swelled, new cities and towns sprang up, and trade flourished within Europe as well as with Asia and North Africa' (Slavicek, 2008, p. 13).
2 The latest data is retrieved December 31, 2023, from www.worldometers.info/coronavirus/
3 Latest numbers are retrieved December 31, 2023, from www.mygov.in/covid-19/

References

Abhishek, S., Taneja, A., Vyas, A., & Jadhav, N. (2021). *Securing rights of patients in India: Lessons from rapid surveys on people's experiences of patient's rights charter and the Covid-19 vaccination drive*. Oxfam India.
Aditi, A., & Shariff, M. (2019). Nipah virus infection: A review. *Epidemiology and Infection, 147*(e95), 1–6.
Albanese, C. (2022, September 26). Meloni wins big in Italian election to turn page on Draghi era. *Bloomberg*. www.bloomberg.com/news/articles/2022-09-25/meloni-s-right-wing-bloc-set-for-clear-majority-in-italian-elections
Amaya, M., & Broder, C. C. (2020). Vaccines to emerging viruses: Nipah and Hendra. *Annual Review of Virology, 7*(1), 447–473.
Barman, A. (2021). *Atmanirbhar Bharat meets digital India: An evaluation of COVID-19 relief for migrants*. Migrant Workers Solidarity Network & The Centre for Internet and Society.
Baru, R. V. (2020, April 3). Making the private sector care for public health. *The Hindu*. www.thehindu.com/opinion/lead/making-the-private-sector-care-for-public-health/article31241291/
Bettampadi, D., Lepkowski, J. M., Sen, A., Power, L. E., & Boulton, M. L. (2020). Vaccination inequality in India, 2002–2013. *American Journal of Preventive Medicine, 60*(1), 565–576.
Bhakti, G. (2020, April 25). A cruel lockdown: Lessons from relief work in Mumbai. *The Wire*. www.thewire.in/article/rights/coronavirus-lockdown-mumbai-relief-work
Biswas, S. (2020, March 20). Coronavirus: Why is India testing so little? *BBC*. www.bbc.com/news/world-asia-india-51922204
Blakeley, G. (2020). *The Corona crash: How the pandemic will change capitalism*. Verso.
Broder, D. (2022, July 22). The future is Italy, and it's bleak. *The New York Times*. https://nyti.ms/3RMqK6l
Buckshee, D. (2021, July 21). Dispatches from India: Vaccine inequity and the pandemic rages on. *Yale School of Public Health*. www.ysph.yale.edu/news-article/dispatches-from-india-vaccine-inequity-and-the-pandemic-rages-on/

Business Today. (2021, May 2). COVID-19: SC asks centre to consider fixing ceiling price for drugs. *Business Today*. www.businesstoday.in/latest/economy-politics/story/covid-19-sc-asks-centre-to-consider-fixing-ceiling-proce-for-drugs-used-for-treatment

Counterview. (2019). Gujarat govt "reserves" sanitation workers' job only for Dalits: Activists Protest. *Counterview*. www.counterview.net/2019/01/gujarat-govt-sanitation-workers-job.html

Daniyal, S. (2022, May 9). The Indian fix: How did a democracy like India rack up the highest Covid death count in the world? *Scroll*. www.scroll.in/article/1023500/the-india-fix-how-did-a-democracy-like-india-rack-up-the-highest-covid-death-count-in-the-world

Das, P. K. (2020, April 22). Sustainable housing can't slip under the radar once the Covid-19 crisis subsides. *The Wire*. www.thewire.in/article.urban/mumbai-housing-social-distancing

Davis, M. (1998). *Ecology of fear: Los Angeles and the imagination of disaster*. Metropolitan Books.

Davis, M. (2005). *The monster at our door: The global threat of avian flu*. The New Press.

Defoe, D. (2010). *A journal of the plague year*. Everyman. (Original work published 1908)

Deka, K. (2020, June 8). The migrant mess. *India Today*.

Dennett, P. (2021, January 19). Sensible socialism: The Salford model. *Tribune*. www.tribunemag.co-uk/2021/01/sensible-socialism-the-salford-model

Deol, T. (2022, April 21). Anganwadi, ASHA work massively disrupted during COVID-19 pandemic: Survey. *Down to Earth*. www.downtoearth.org.in/news/governance/anganwadi-asha-work-massively-disrupted-during-covid-19-pandemic-survey-82500

Desai, A. R. (1975). The myth of the welfare state. In *State and society in India: Essays in dissent*. Popular Prakashan.

Dunayevskaya, R. (1953). Letter on Hegel's science of logic (May 12, 1953). In P. Hudis & K. B. Anderson (Eds.), *The power of negativity: Selected writings on the dialectics in Hegel and Marx*. Lexington Books.

Dunayevskaya, R. (1956). Marx and the Utopian socialists. In *The Raya Dunayevskaya collection – Marxist-humanism: A half century of its world development*. Wayne State University Archives of Labor and Urban Affairs.

Dunayevskaya, R. (1958). *Marxism and freedom . . . from 1776 until today*. Bookman Associates.

Dunayevskaya, R. (1965). Marx's humanism today. In E. Fromm (Ed.), *Socialist humanism*. Doubleday.

Ellis-Petersen, H., & Alam, M. S. (2021, May 1). 'We're burning pyres all day': India accused of undercounting deaths. *The Guardian*. www.theguardian.com/world/2021/01/were-burning-pyres-all-day-india-accused-of-undercounting-deaths

Firstpost. (2021, May 3). COVID-19 news: Centre claims no shortage of oxygen, warns against hoarding cylinders; India's tally at 1.99 crore. *Firstpost*. www.firstpost.com/india/centre-claims-no-shortage-of-oxygen-warns-against-black-marketing-indias-tally-news-two-crore-mark

Fromm, E. (2011). *To have or to be?* Continuum. (Original work published 1976)

Garicano, L. (2021). Introduction. In L. Garicano (Ed.), *Capitalism after Covid: Conversations with 21 economists*. CEPR Press.

Gilbert, S., & Green, C. (2021). *Vaxxers: The inside story of the Oxford AstraZeneca vaccine and the race against the virus*. Hodder and Stoughton.

Gittlitz, A. M. (2020). *I want to believe: Posadism, UFOs and apocalypse communism*. Pluto Press.

Harshvardhan. (2020, August 22). COVID-19 and disaster capitalism in India. *Jamhoor*. www.jamhoor.org/read/covid-19-and-disaster-capitalism-in-india/

Harvey, D. (2014). *Seventeen contradictions and the end of capitalism*. Oxford University Press.

The Hindu. (2021, April 28). As positive cases rise, oximeter prices jump by nearly 2.5 times. *The Hindu*. www.thehindu.com/news/telengana/as-positive-cases-rise-oximeter-prices-jump-by-nearly-25-times/

The Hindu. (2022, September 3). India overtakes U.K. to become fifth-largest economy in the world. *The Hindu*. www.thehindu.com/news/national/india-overtakes-uk-to-become-fifth-largest-economy-in-the-world/

Honigsbaum, M. (2020). *The pandemic century: A history of global contagion from the Spanish flu to Covid-19*. Penguin.

Hupkau, C., & Petrongolo, B. (2021). *Work, care and gender during the Covid-19 crisis*. Centre for Economic Performance, London School of Economics and Political Science.

The Indian Express. (2020a, April 26). Hoarding of oxygen and medicines creates panic shortage: Experts. *The Indian Express*. www.indianexpress.com/article/india/hoarding-of-oxyfen-medicines-creates-panic-shortage-experts-7289367/

The Indian Express. (2020b, May 18). Coronavirus lockdown: So far, over 130 Migrants killed in Accidents en route to their home states. *The Indian Express*. www.indianexpress.com/article/india/coronavirus-lockdown-count-of-migrants-killed-in-accidents-enroute-their-home-states-6412475/

Kanwar, S. (2019a, May 16). Without an overhaul, smart cities won't fulfill urban needs. *The Wire*. www.thewire.in/article/urban/smart-cities-mission-reality

Kanwar, S. (2019b, May 17). Four years on, how Swachh is Bharat? *The Wire*. www.thewire.in/article/urban/swachh-bharat-mission-urban-sanitation

Kaur, P., & Gupta, S. (2020, December 24). Examining urban local governance in India through the case of Bengaluru. *PRS Legislative Research*. www.prsindia.org/theprsblog/examining-urban-local-governance-in-india-through-the-case-of-bengaluru

Kellett, J. R. (1978). Municipal socialism, enterprise and trading in the Victorian city. *Urban History Yearbook*, 5, 36–45.

King, L. (2021, November 11). 'Vulnerable' care worker not taking Covid jab over health fears to lose 'job she loves'. *Mirror*. www.mirror.co.uk/news/vulnerable-care-worker-not-taking-25429739

Klein, N. (2007). *The shock doctrine: The rise of disaster capitalism*. Penguin.

Klein, N. (2017). *No is not enough: Resisting Trump's shock politics and winning the world we need*. Haymarket Books.

Klein, N. (2020, May 13). How big tech plans to profit from the pandemic. *The Guardian*. www.theguardian.com/news/2020/may/13/how-big-tech-plans-to-profit-from-the-pandemic

Klein, N. (2021, March 4). How big tech helps india target climate activists. *The Guardian*. www.theguardian.com/news/2021/mar/04/how-big-tech-helps-india-target-climate-activists

Koley, T. K., & Dhole, M. (2021). *The COVID-19 pandemic: The deadly coronavirus outbreak*. Routledge.

Kumar, A. (2021, March 26). What changed and what didn't in one year of a pandemic and lockdown. *The Wire*. www.thewire.in/article/economy/what-changed-what-didnt-one-year-covid-pandemic-lockdown-india

Kumar, A., & Kumar, M. (2020, June 17). Data of disparity shows why its critical that digital learning is inclusive. *The News Minute*. www.thenewsminute.com/article/data-disparity-shows-why-its-critical-digital-learing-inclusive

Kupperberg, P. (2008). *The influenza pandemic of 1918–1919*. Chelsea House Publishers.

Lin, W. (2022). Automated infrastructure: COVID-19 and the shifting geographies of supply chain capitalism. *Progress in Human Geography*, 46(2), 463–483.

Lundquist-Arora, S. (2022). *The Asian flu pandemic of 1957*. Reference Point Press.

Lupton, D. (2022). *COVID societies: Theorizing the Coronavirus crisis*. Routledge.

Mahapatra, A. (2021). *COVID-19: Separating fact from fiction*. Penguin.

Mander, H. (2021). *Locking down the poor: The pandemic and India's moral centre*. Speaking Tiger.

Marder, M. (2020, August 17). Only a virus can save us? *Thesis Eleven: Living and Thinking Crisis*. www.thesiseleven.com/2020/08/17/only-a-virus-can-save-us/

Mbembe, A. (2019). *Necro-politics*. Duke University Press.

Menon, A. (2021, July 13). Can PM Modi's popularity withstand a third covid wave? Here's what surveys say. *The Quint*. www.thequint.com/news/politics/pm-narendra-modi-popularity-survey-covid-third-wave-opinion-poll

Menozzi, F. (2020, July 20). Militant optimism: A state of mind that can help us find hope in dark times. *The Conversation*. www.theconversation.com/militant-optimism-a-state-of-mind-that-can-help-us-find-hope-in-dark-times

Miglani, S., & Ghoshal, D. (2021, May 18). PM Modi's rating falls to new low as India reels from COVID-19. *Reuters*. www.reuters.com/world/india/pm-modis-rating-falls-india-reels-covid-19-second-wave-2021-05-18/

Migrant Workers Solidarity Network. (2020). *Citizens and the sovereign: Stories from the largest human exodus in contemporary Indian history*. MWSN.

Mishra, A., & Santosh, S. (2021). *Aren't we frontline warriors? Experiences of grassroots health workers during Covid-19*. Azim Premji University.

Mishra, A., Seshadri, S. R., Pradyumna, A., Pinto, E. P., Bhattacharya, A., Saligram, P., & Benny, G. (2021). *Health care equity in urban India*. Azim Premji University.

Mukherjee, S. (1988). *Socialism and the nuclear space age*. Sterling Publishers Private Limited.

Nagpal, J., & Uppal, T. (2020). *Caught in Corona conflict: An approach to the working population*. National Book Trust.

Nail, T. (2022). What is Covid capitalism? *Distinktion: Journal of Social Theory* [Online]. https://doi.org/10.1080/1600910X.2022.2075905

Narayani, A. (2021). Labourers are the backbone of a capitalist economy: India can't leave them unattended in Covid. *The Print*. www.theprint.in/opinion/labourers-are-backbone-of-a-capitalist-economy-india-cant-leave-them-unattended-in-covid

Nelson, A. (2020). COVID-19: Capitalist and postcapitalist perspectives. *Human Geography*, 13(3), 305–309.

Nolen, S. (2022, September 12). Monkeypox shots, treatments and tests are unavailable in much of the world. *The New York Times*. https://nyti.ms/3qtUx1

Patnaik, P. (2021, July 19). Why neoliberalism needs neofascists. *Boston Review*. www.bostonreview.net/articles/why-neoliberalism-needs-neofascists/

Petrosillo, N., Viceconte, G., Ergonul, O., Ippolito, G., & Petersen, E. (2020). COVID-19, SARS and MERS: Are they closely related? *Clinical Microbiology and Infection*, 26(6), 729–734.

Poovorawan, Y., Pyngporn, S., Prachayangprecha, S., & Makkoch, J. (2013). Global alert to avian influenza virus infection: From H5N1 to H7N9. *Pathogens and Global Health*, 107(5), 217–223.

Posadas, J. (1968). Flying saucers, the process of matter and energy, science and socialism. In *Socialism and human relationships with nature and the cosmos*. Scientific, Cultural and Political Editions.

Povoledo, E. (2022, May 31). Italy, once the pandemic's grim epicenter, lifts requirements for visitors. *The New York Times*. www.nytimes.com/live/2022/025/31/world/covid-19-mandates-vaccines-cases

Quammen, D. (2020). *Spillover: Animal infections and the next human pandemic*. Vintage. (Original work published 2012)

Raja, I. (2020). India's migrant crisis: The sovereign injunction that was not. *Thesis Eleven: Living and Thinking Crisis*. www.thesiseleven.com/2020/08/18/indias-migrant-crisis-the-sovereign-injunction-that-was-not/

Ramachandran, R. (2021, November 19). Grand cover-up: The Narendra Modi government's celebration of one billion Covid doses. *Frontline*.

Ramakrishnan, V., & Salam, Z. U. (2021, November 19). India's Covid vaccination drive infused with doses of propaganda. *Frontline*.

Rao, A. (2021, May 6). India is hiding its Covid crisis – and the whole world will suffer for it. *The Guardian*. www.theguardian.com

Rao, A., & Namana, V. (2016, January 11). Revealed: The malaria crisis India doesn't want to acknowledge. *Aljazeera*. www.america.aljazeera.com/articles/2021/1/11/malaria-crisis-india-doesnt-want-to-acknowledge

Rentoul, J. (2020, February 4). Labour's war on capitalism was futile without a real alternative. *Independent*. www.independent.co.uk/independentpremium/long-reads/capitalism-socialism-corbyn-mcdonnell-labour-leadership

Roy, A. (2021). It's a crime against humanity. *The Guardian Weekly*, 204(20), 10–16.

Rutzen, D., & Dutta, N. (2020, March 12). Pandemics and human rights. *Just Security*. www.justsecurity.org/69141/pandemics-and-human-rights

Ryan, F. (2019). *Virusphere: From common colds to Ebola epidemics: Why we need the viruses that plague us*. William Collins.

S. S., & Nandan, R. (2020, March 30). Shortage of masks, gloves worsened by slow policymaking. *Mint*. www.livemint.com/news/india/coronavirus-shortage-of-maks-gloves-worsened-by-slow-policymaking-11585510974016.html

Sainath, P. (2020a, June 8). The migrant and the moral economy of the elite. *India Today*.

Sainath, P. (2020b, March 27). In India, neither tokenism nor panic can help counter this unique crisis. *The Wire*. www.thewire.in/article/government/india-coronavirus-migrants-agricuture

Salve, P. (2020, July 10). COVID-19: Low primary health spending, staff shortages overburden Mumbai, Delhi's staff systems. *IndiaSpend*. www.indiaspend.com/covid-19-low-primary-health-staff-shortages-overburden-mumbai-delhis-health-systems/

Sengupta, A. (2020a). Universal Health Coverage: Beyond Rhetoric. In P. Purkayastha, I. Mukhopadhyay, & R. Chintan (Eds.), *Political Journeys in Health: Essays by and For Amit Sengupta*. Leftword. (Original work published 2013)

Sengupta, A. (2020b). Global governance of health: A minefield of contradictions and sectional interests. In P. Purkayastha, I. Mukhopadhyay, & R. Chintan (Eds.), *Political journeys in health: Essays by and for Amit Sengupta*. Leftword. (Original work published 2000)

Sengupta, A., Kannan, K. P., Srivastava, R. S., Malhotra, V. K., Papola, T. S., & Yugandhar, B. N. (2007). *Report on conditions of work and promotion of livelihoods in the unorganised sector*. National Commission for Enterprises in the Unorganised Sector.

Sengupta, A., Mukhopadhyay, I., Weerasinghe, M., & Karki, A. (2020). The rise of private medicine in South Asia. In P. Purkayastha, I. Mukhopadhyay, & R. Chintan (Eds.), *Political journeys in health: Essays by and for Amit Sengupta*. Leftword. (Original work published 2017)

Shabi, R. (2021, May 15). Municipal socialism is winning – what a shame the labour leadership isn't shouting about these success stories. *Independent*. www.independent.co.uk/voices/labour-socialism-localism-collectivism-b184815

Shaji, K. A. (2021, December 20). Bird flue scare in Kerala: What's pushing sudden rise in cases again? *Down to Earth*. www.downtoearth.org.in/news/wildlife-biodiversity/bird-flu-scare-in-kerala-what-s-pushing-sudden-rise-in-cases-again-80751

Shantz, J. (2016). *Crisis states: Governance, resistance and precarious capitalism*. Punctum Books.

Shepherd, T. (2020, June 7). 'It's psychologically easier': How anti-vaxxers capitalised on coronavirus fears to spread misinformation. *The Guardian.* www.theguardian.com/society/2020/jun/06/its-psychologically-easier-how-anti-vaxxers-capitalised-on-coronavirus-fears-to-spread-misinformation

Singh, S. (2021, June 7). The age of fear. *India Today.*

Slavicek, L. C. (2008). *The black death.* Chelsea House Publishers.

Solis, M. (2020, March 13). Coronavirus is the perfect disaster for 'disaster capitalism'. *VICE.* www.vice.com/en/article/5dmqyk/naomi-klein-interview-on-coronavirus-and-disaster-capitalism-shock-doctrine

Sridhar, V. (2021a, May 21). The Fiasco that is India's Covid-19 vaccine policy. *Frontline.*

Sridhar, V. (2021b, June 18). Covid-19: Vaccine follies. *Frontline.*

Stranded Workers Action Network (SWAN). (2020). *21 days and counting: Covid-19 Lockdown, migrant workers, and the inadequacy of welfare measures in India.* SWAN.

Stranded Workers Action Network (SWAN). (2021). *No country for workers: The Covid-19 second wave, local lockdowns and migrant worker distress in India.* SWAN.

Sur, P., & Mitra, E. (2020, March 30). Social distancing is a privilege of the middle class: For India's slum dwellers, it will be impossible. *CNN.* www.cnn.com/2020/03/30/india/india-coronavirus-social-distancing-intl-hnk

Tripathi, B. (2020, May 3). Migrants build cities but face exclusion during crisis: Here's how this can change. *IndiaSpend.* www.indiaspend.com/migrants-build-cities-but-face-exclusion-heres-how-this-can-change/

Unninathan, S. (2021, May 10). Gasping for breath. *India Today.*

Varma, D., Bharadkar, K., & Mehrotra, R. (2020, September 27). India's new labour codes fail migrant workers whose vulnerability was highlighted by lockdown crisis. *Scroll.* www.scroll.in/article/974137/indias-new-labour-codes-fail-migrant-workers-whose-vulnerability-was-highlighted-by-lockdown-crisis

Wainwright, J., & Mann, G. (2018). *Climate Leviathan.* Verso.

Waitzkin, H. (2020). COVID-19 as cause versus trigger for the collapse of capitalism. *International Journal of Health, 51*(2), 203–205.

Wallace, R. (2016). *Big farms make big flu.* Monthly Review Press.

Wallace, R. G., Gilbert, M., Wallace, R., Pittiglio, C., Mattioli, R., & Kock, R. (2016). Did Ebola emerge in West Africa by a policy-driven phase change in agroecology? In R. G. Wallace & R. Wallace (Eds.), *Neoliberal Ebola: Modeling disease emergence from finance to forest and farm.* Springer.

The water enterprise of some of our large towns V. Glasgow. (1899). *The British Medical Journal, 1*(1987), 219–221.

World Health Organization. (2022a, September 7). *India situation.* www.covid19.who.int/region/searo/country/in

Yardley, J. (2011, December 28). In one slum, misery, work, politics and hope. *The New York Times.* www.nytimes.com/2011/12/29/world/asia/in-indian-slum-misery-work-politics-and-hope

Zanoni, P., & Mir, R. (2022). COVID-19: Interrogating the capitalist organization of the Economy and the society through the pandemic. *Organization, 29*(3), 369–378.

Žižek, S. (2020a). *Pandemic!: COVID-19 shakes the world.* OR Books.

Žižek, S. (2020b). *Pandemic! 2: Chronicles of a time lost.* OR Books.

1 India and the Unequal Pandemic

Introduction

The sociologist Ulrich Beck had argued back in the early 1990s that the contemporary society was, in fact, a risk society, where risks are unevenly distributed across the social, economic, and cultural spectrum (Beck, 1992). The idea that societies are unequally distributed as far as risks are concerned becomes extremely threatening in contemporary times because of the widespread existence of potential apocalyptic processes and events such as climate change, nuclear warfare, and pandemics (Murdoch, 2020). Some of these processes might even put the COVID-19 pandemic to shame in the coming decades. COVID-19 has endangered the very sense of security that citizens of most modern democracies possess (Horton, 2020). Various governments have reacted to this crisis in different ways, contingent upon the ways in which they are structured. When major crises come upon on any society, then 'Nations' people and governments regularly seek to reinforce national identity by recounting history in a way so as to foster national pride. Such recounting of history constitutes "national myths"' (Diamond, 2019, p. 433). Similar tendencies can be seen in the context of India with regular calls being made in India by the authorities that COVID-19 was not a risk any more as far as India was concerned, with India being the *Vishwaguru*[1] in terms of the management of the pandemic; however, the validity of that claim did not last for long when the country descended into the chaos of the second wave in May 2021 (Sood, 2021, May 4). However, as time went on, the claim has been dismantled and the precarious nature of the healthcare and social infrastructure of India has been established for the world to see. Arundhati Roy rightly claimed that the way in which the pandemic had been managed in India, especially during the second wave, was a crime against humanity itself (Roy, 2021, May 7).

COVID-19 according to the WHO had claimed around 14.9 million lives, either directly or indirectly between January 2020 and December 2021 and India accounted for one-third of those deaths (Ramachandra, 2022, June 3). India has also been accused of meddling with the number of deaths due to COVID-19 when it denied the feasibility of the methodology adopted by the

WHO, even though many claimed that the deaths that India has reported are only a fraction of the actual numbers (Rao, 2021, May 6; Ramachandran, 2022, June 3). The central government and some other state governments have continued to push forward claims surrounding its supposedly exemplary management of the pandemic, disregarding material realities. These claims have tried to camouflage the fact that between the 7th of May 2021 and the 10th of June 2021, the total number of deaths in India was around 1.29 lakhs – higher than the 79,000 between the 8th of February to the 6th of May 2021, the time when the first wave of COVID-19 was raging through India (Rajalakhsmi, 2021). That a country can debate over *how many people have died* highlighted the complete disregard for human lives that characterises governmental decision-making processes and the popular discourse that it generates.

COVID-19 has brought in so many changes in the way in which human beings live and sustain others in the world that even when the pandemic is over, it would be very difficult, even for capitalism, to go back to its old self (Lal, 2020). It can be said with a reasonable amount of certainty that small scale shopkeepers, gig workers, domestic workers, sanitation workers, and large sections of informal workers will find it very difficult to return their earnings to pre-pandemic levels – not only in India but across the globe (Turner et al., 2021; Chen et al., 2022). Though some monetary benefits and assistance was made available to them, they found it very difficult to apply for them because of the ways in which the policing mechanisms and local governance often works in India, which is highly bureaucratic and as such remains outside the accessibility of the poor and the marginalised (Banerji, 2020, September 1).[2] Among all the sectors of public services, where such tendencies are prevalent, the one which affects people the most during a pandemic is healthcare.

The possession of a fair and equitable health service remains a testimony to the shared commitment and solidarity of people in the society. Richard Horton (2020) argues that when there is a public support for the constant development of a public health system, it also means that people are willing to go through some material constraints in the form of taxes if they can get adequate protection from diseases and other health-related issues from the government. The human society is an interdependent one, and reciprocity of responsibilities is crucial to its sustenance, especially when COVID-19 has adversely affected most of the economies across the globe, especially the urban spaces, and more so because the effects of the same have not been uniform. Growing urbanisation has further accentuated these differences because of its role in economic development focused on the availability of cheap labour, structural violence, and exclusion. The urban space in India is disproportionately tilted in favour of the elites and the urban middle class (Desai & Pillai, 1990). The process of urbanisation in India has been fraught with tendencies of crisis, ranging from the existence of large-scale slums to the most abject forms of caste and class segregation, even within the urban spaces.

When diseases like COVID-19 emerge, they alter the society at a fundamental level affecting the basic ways in which human life is lived and thought of (Shah, 2010; Honigsbaum, 2020). Such diseases also have broader social and political effects, which continue to have impacts on human lives long after they are technically over. Each epidemic or pandemic affects the human society in different ways – the effects of some are visible, like smallpox, while the effects of some others, such as AIDS, are more personal in nature often invisible to the naked eye. The COVID-19 pandemic caught the entire world by surprise, leaving almost every major country – democracy or otherwise – in the world almost completely unprepared to handle the impending crisis (Egan, 2020).

Newer viruses can crop up anywhere in the world and, in most cases, their impact on human life is very limited. But when such viruses become life-threatening in nature in the form of diseases, immediate responses towards the situation become extremely critical because human society often remains unprepared for viral outbreaks of such magnitude (Sternfeld, 2020). A Healthcare emergency such as COVID-19 requires both pharmaceutical and non-pharmaceutical responses. Pharmaceutical responses towards the pandemic emerge in the form of drugs and vaccines, while non-pharmaceutical responses such as sanitation practices and usage of face masks also remain critically important. However, under global capitalism both these aspects become mere commodities for profit, affecting the already marginalised through the proliferation of structural violence and material inequalities (Shah, 2010; Mukul, 2022).[3] Taking cognisance of these issues, the current chapter is divided into three subsections. The first section discusses the socio-political dynamics associated with COVID-19 in India, while the second section speaks about the impact of neoliberalism. The third and final section extends the discussion of neoliberalism with a particular focus on the pharmaceutical industry.

The Socio-Political Causality of the COVID-19 *Mega*-Pandemic

The first reports of COVID-19 emerged from China on 30th of December 2019 (Mackenzie, 2020). It took root in and around the Huanan Seafood Wholesale Market in Wuhan – a city in China where around 11 million people live – which 'sold the meat of a huge range of wild animals, including wolf cubs, crocodiles, and snakes' (Honigsbaum, 2020, p. 262). There are two critical factors that have emerged as being extremely important as far as the spread of the COVID-19 pandemic is concerned, and both of these factors are found in abundance in urban India. These are wet markets and slums. Wet markets have emerged as major contributors of epidemics and pandemics (Wallace, 2016). Like China, India too has a significant number of wet markets[4], some of which pose significant threats of future viral outbreaks (Goyal, 2020). Wet markets constitute an important part of the informal trading ecosystem in India and hence are difficult to completely let go unless the state brings in reforms catering to the marginal, small, and family businesses which feature in and run these markets – often based on caste, creed, or the sense of a community. The second factor found critical to the spread of the pandemic are slums. A slum, in general:

> may be described as a chaotically occupied, unsystematically developed, and generally neglected area which is overpopulated by persons and overcrowded with ill-repaired and neglected structures. The area has insufficient communications, indifferent sanitary arrangements, and inadequate amenities necessary for the maintenance of physical and social health, the minimum needs and comforts of human beings and the community' which gets amplified because most of the residents in these areas do not possess the income or social capital, which is necessary to ensure a certain standard of living suitable to maintain a healthy life.
> (Ramachandran, 1970/1990, pp. 136–137)

Slums in urban areas usually result from a sustained housing crisis (Pillai, 1970/1990) which has become almost endemic to structures of contemporary capitalist urbanisation. The residents of slums form a major section of what has come to be known as the 'Urban Poor' in India, who have proliferated in numbers because of the unplanned urbanisation that has characterised Indian cities after the neoliberal economic reforms creating newer forms of marginalisation and urban poverty based on class, caste, gender, the kind of work they do, and the kind of living spaces that they possess (Bose & Saxena, 2016). These people get highly affected in the case of events such as pandemics because they often do not have the right to access citizenship in the regions in which they live, and as such cannot enjoy the socio-cultural benefits that a community or a society might provide during times of disaster. Their situation becomes particularly volatile during pandemics or other forms of public health crisis, which undermine the regular socio-medical order of the day, changing the social perceptions regarding individual safety and security in the world (Honigsbaum, 2020). Slums and other forms of informal settlement are a result of a combination of unplanned urbanisation and population explosion (United Nations, 2003). The United Nations stated that as of 2001, around 924 million people had been living in slums, which had increased significantly since the 1990s. It projected that by 2030, the global number of slum dwellers will increase to approximately 2 million if no action was taken. The pioneering Marxist Sociologist, A. R. Desai had brought out the abysmal conditions of slums in India back in 1991 itself, when he had stated:

> The path of development pursued by the ruling classes has generated a distorted economic development resulting in a concentration of assets in few hands on one side, and pauperisation of the majority on the

other, driving them to the tensions of unemployment or underemployment, lumpen activities, begging, garbage collection, etc., thus creating diverse situations with respect to shelter, essential commodities, and services.

(Desai, 1991, p. 175)

Such a mode of economic development also has had its impact on the healthcare services. Health emergencies exert a humongous pressure upon the local bodies – because it is often the local bodies who are the 'first responders' to the crisis – and they are often not equipped well enough to engage with the same. The municipal corporation of Wuhan was the first administrative body in the world, which had to react to COVID-19 and as such it reacted with the only option it thought was responsible and plausible – a lockdown (Mackenzie, 2020). Following the confirmation of COVID-19 and its potential to become a pandemic, the WHO issued an advisory for countries to take precautions against the virus. However, the advisory largely analysed COVID-19 as any other coronavirus, which have been living among humans for centuries now (Mukul, 2022).

In India, the first case of COVID-19 was detected in the southern state of Kerala on the 27th of January 2020, when a student who had returned from China tested positive (Srivastava & Priyadarshini, 2020, January 30). After the report was confirmed, Kerala implemented emergency protocols, setting up a 24-hour control room, and isolation rooms, and engaging the District Medical Office (DMO) and District Collectorate (DC) (Perappadan, 2020, January 30). India's first step towards stopping the pandemic came in the form of establishing mechanisms for basic health check-ups at airports from the 17th of January 2020. The WHO subsequently declared COVID-19 as a pandemic on the 11th of March 2020. The central government, following WHO's declaration, went ahead to declare a nationwide lockdown on the 24th of March 2020 when the number of cases in India reached 500 (Bajpai & Wadhwa, 2020). The government also implemented a *National Containment Plan* focusing on 'early detection, primary care for mild infection cases, tertiary care for severe infection cases, and emphasised health education through media and facilitate reduction of person-to-person transmission' along with the setting-up of quarantine centres, surveillance procedures, and the like (Bajpai & Wadhwa, 2020, p. 14).

An analysis of the initial few COVID-19 patients in India found that their mean age was close to 40.3 years and most of them were males (Gupta et al., 2020). However, as time passed, the virus refused to be constrained by such factors. However, states soon came to realise that mere travel restrictions and other such mandates would not serve the purpose, rather they should move towards more stringent measures such as lockdowns and partial curfews. Globally, the basic guidelines for lockdowns were clearly established – *stay at home if one is unwell*. However, the 'potentially infected' people who could not afford to stay at home, subsequently carried the virus to their workplaces and then to the society in general (Egan, 2020). The same was the case in India as well.

India imposed its first lockdown in March 2020, which was then extended thrice and finally concluded in May 2020. After around 10 months, the second wave of COVID-19 in India began in March 2021, which brought global attention to the prevailing scenario in India. The number of deaths between April and June 2021 were almost 240,000 as per a report by the United Nations (The Economic Times, 2022, January 13). The lockdown that was imposed in India was one of the strictest lockdowns in the world because of the number of personnel involved and the scale of the population affected by it (Hale et al., 2020). However, when it was imposed in India for the first time, the news that caught the attention of most was not the lockdown itself, but the terrible human tragedies that followed its hasty implementation in India, especially its effects on the marginalised section of the populace – who were affected more by the response to the pandemic than the pandemic itself.

Disasters are *events*[5] which cause massive historical and social impacts that continue to affect human societies for decades to follow. COVID-19 disrupted the natural course of humanity in a fashion in which the society could find little time to respond to the crisis. However, responses to all kinds of disasters – be they natural or man-made – harbour within themselves the fetish of outsourcing under neoliberal capitalism.[6] Wars, conflicts, and disasters are natural elements of a capitalist world order. However, as against the mainstream world view, where even scientists such as Albert Einstein (1931/2012c, 1934/2012b, 1934/2012a) argued against wars and conflicts, the Argentinian Trotskyist thinker Juan Posadas found hope in such apocalyptic events because he visualised them as a vehicle of social transformation. The primary drive behind Posadas's claims were his beliefs surrounding the existence of a superior group of beings – a hyper vanguard – who could come and rescue the human beings from the misery that capitalism exerts on the human society (Posadas, 1968, 1978). The idea was similar to how many people believe in religious sermons and godmen. During COVID-19, such mode of devotion shown by the general people towards supposedly higher beings fuelled by their religious and community beliefs played a key role in countries like India, Indonesia, South Africa, and the like. In India, religion enabled the segregation of the society during the pandemic creating newer versions of offenders and victims (Mander, 2021; Sibanda et al., 2022).

Such events of exclusion and segregation allowed crony capitalist governments to distract the public discourse from getting exposed to the perils of capitalism. Many governments across the world used such events to camouflage the economic issues that the capitalist mode of production faced during the pandemic. Vinay Lal (2020) writes that, perhaps, the COVID-19 pandemic might be the only significant hurdle that *viral capitalism* has faced over the past few decades. However, while it is true to a certain extent, considering that the pandemic has resulted in a significant loss of money and the very credibility of capital being able to regulate the society as harmoniously as it claims, it is also true that capital itself has worked through the crisis through the many avenues which exist under most neoliberal governments – *vaccines being one of them*. The ways in which the vaccine has been administered among the people of most major democracies in the world, as well as the methods by which vaccines have been denied to some, have resulted in a disproportionate vaccine accessibility as far as the marginalised population is concerned.

Vaccines, first proved scientifically by Dr Edward Jenner in Gloucestershire, are basically, the introduction of a small dose of the disease into the body of the patient (Kupperberg, 2008). The science of effective vaccines during the pandemic has been appropriated by the forces of global capital, causing widespread profit accumulation. Under contemporary capitalism, there is a peculiar enmeshment of innovative science and profit accumulation, one which has made life-saving innovations an integral part of the circuit of global capital. Divya Trivedi writes – on the situation of vaccination in north India – in late 2021 that, the vaccination:

> drive has not been [even] across north India. The Narendra Modi government's obsession with mega events and projecting India as an achiever in the vaccine race has reportedly resulted in a haphazard vaccination policy that has led to a record number of doses being administered on particular days', creating a political spectacle.
> (Trivedi, 2021, November 19, pp. 20–21)

The fetish with mega-events and spectacles is a result of the ways in which political communication has been implemented in contemporary India. Political communication and the usage of the media have played a key role in India's Pandemic Response strategy. The growth of mass communication in India has been adequately used by the BJP to offset the rational arguments coming from the scientific community (Gandhi-Mody, 2022). Modes of communication do not become mainstream overnight but rather are related to the wider socio-economic changes in the society (Vilanilam, 2003). Under neoliberalism, commercial interests have tended to dominate over factors such as neutrality, dignity, and social justice in the media houses (Pradhan, 2019). The change in the role and prowess of the media was bolstered by the fact that the contemporary media houses, unlike their colonial counterparts, have both mass appeal and mass circulation (Vilanilam, 2003). In the contemporary times, the mainstream press possesses both. Television channels such as *Aaj Tak* and *Zee News* which have been often accused of being pro-establishment which also enjoy a humongous viewership.[7] With such a drastic growth of private TV Channels and newspapers, it has been extremely easy for the political milieu to become a part of the everyday life of the people that it seeks to influence.[8] The domination of the media, especially the corporate owned media houses, has transformed the manner in which public health policies had been propagated during COVID-19 in India, transforming health advisory into marketable commodities which have gone on to create commodities out of disasters.

Barring a few, most of the mainstream media houses have actively attempted to camouflage the flaws of the healthcare structures in place, which has been characterised by massive outsourcing and privatisation. However, it would be a mistake to argue that outsourcing only happens in such drastic conditions. Conversations with healthcare workers who worked during the pandemic has led the current author to argue that the problems with outsourcing healthcare delivery in India during crises such as the one caused by the COVID-19 pandemic are something which are caused by long waves of neoliberal reforms in the healthcare sector. The healthcare sector, referred to here, encompasses both the personnel engaged in the sector and the pharmaceutical companies. The corporate takeover of the Indian healthcare sector has been one of the prime hallmarks of the neoliberal growth trajectory of the country since 1991 that has concentrated on the complete demolition of the public sector in India, which is essential to fulfil the responsibilities that the government has towards the citizens of a nation (Prasad, 2018; Ghosh, 2019–2020).[9] The India Exclusion Report 2016 concluded that after 25 years of the economic liberalisation of India, the inequality between the extremely rich and poor have only increased, the effects of which are starkly noticed in the labour market. The way in which COVID-19 has 'shocked' the global labour market has made one realise that the power of the market is not infallible, with the pandemic affecting the employers and the employed at the same time (Hupkau et al., 2020). The uncertainty regarding the lockdown has made matters worse by heightening financial, educational, and professional fears.

COVID-19 has impacted the society not only at a macro level but also at a micro level altering an individual's communitarian, personal, and familial lives. Once somebody in the family gets infected with coronavirus, there is a widespread fear of discrimination in the society, and even within the family (Harsheeta & Arora, 2020). There is an increasing risk of social isolation which goes beyond the mandated 'social distancing' and penetrates right into the very self of the individual who has been infected. The issues concerning stigmatisation of individuals[10] has caused grave concerns for majority of the population. A government sponsored report notes in this regard:

> One of the major concerns during such time is of stigmatisation belonging to certain region/ethnicity/country which is associated with the origin of the virus. . . . There are reports from across the globe, particularly in India where this fear has led individuals to hide and conceal their travel history, the experience of symptoms and association/interaction with an affected person. This, in turn, makes them less likely to get timely medical help and treatment.
>
> (Harsheeta & Arora, 2020, p. 26)

While on one hand, one is noticing newer forms of social segregation reinforcing conservative beliefs emerging in India, as Dutt (2022) and Kapri (2021) report, on the other hand, one is also witnessing a constant rise of the idea that it is okay to profit during the pandemic by increasing prices and hoarding essential supplies. Such tendencies among people in a society such as India, which has historically been known to possess strong communitarian values, are indeed worrisome for humanity as a whole. Whenever a disease becomes a pandemic, its effects are not only felt at the level of healthcare but also in other spheres of one's social and individual life.[11] Honigsbaum (2020) notes that different epidemics in human history have had different effects on different sections of the population and as such their long-term effects are difficult to be put into a homogenised perspective. The first aspect of a pandemic that one needs to take cognisance of is that diseases – and more so, infectious diseases – are rarely factors which affect only the infected individual. They are, more often than not, socially constructed. There are various factors related to the social customs of the particular social context in which one resides which might have an impact on the probability of someone contracting a disease such as smoking, irregular diet, and the like (Heraud, 1979). The contemporary world is a world where human beings are potentially more at risk of getting infected with infectious diseases such as COVID-19 because of the kind of lifestyles that are becoming mainstream today, which often endorse practices considered to be harmful to long-term immunity. For example, the kind of diet that has become mainstream today consists of a significant amount of junk and fast food (Ashton & Toland, 2021). However, junk and fast food did not emerge out of a vacuum but were rather structurally ingrained within the population, first in the United States (Schlosser, 2001), and then globally. COVID-19-induced disaster capitalism, likewise, has not arrived all of a sudden but is rather a result of the long-drawn processes of the constant degradation of human life under capitalism.

There have been some accounts from writers and commentators which have exhibited the impact that COVID-19 has had on the human society. Gokhale et al.'s (2022) book narrates the ordeals that an upwardly mobile family had to face during the pandemic in India. The book mainly focused on the condition of healthcare that the upper middle class and the elite in India can access, along with the mental impact that the pandemic has had on that section of the population. Mukherjee's (2020) book, on the other hand, focuses on the way in which the common people have faced the pandemic. Mukherjee's work focuses on issues faced by people on an everyday basis, such as gender discrimination, class exploitation, and the like. One of the major characteristics of India as a nation that becomes evident in all of these works is the public provisioning of essential commodities services, something which the early leaders of Independent India, including Jawaharlal Nehru, had emphasised. The way in which economic development has proceeded in India speaks volumes about the ways in which certain key sectors were emphasised by the early planners.[12] The reduction of mortality rates, especially for infants and women, was a particular focus of the Tenth and Eleventh Five-Year plans, which ran from 1997 to 2002 and 2007 to 2012. The Eleventh Plan could effectively relate healthcare improvement to other factors such as water and malnutrition (Dharia, 2011). The brief note about the progress of India's planned development is an important one in this context because the trajectory and contours of neoliberal development in India has constituted the conditions under which the impact of the pandemic could reach such spiralling heights in the country. Neoliberalism in India has led to a constant demonisation of the public sector. Scholars such as Das (2000, 2012) and Jalan (2005, 2019) have written about the problems that the public sector apparently posed for the rapid economic development of the nation through the institutionalisation of the bureaucracy, which they mostly ascribe to be one of the basic effects of Nehruvian socialism on the Indian society. These accounts often neglect the fact that public employees are often at the worst receiving end of adverse events on a mass scale, both natural and man-made.[13]

Neoliberal India and the Pandemic

Neoliberalism's coming of age in India has been praised by many, such as Jalan (2021) for its continued undermining of the public sector and the state because to them, centralised planning in India since 1947 had given rise to corruption as a socially acceptable aspect of the Indian socio-economic and political fabric of the nation. However, such simplistic causal analysis fails to take into cognisance that the buyer-seller relationship that neoliberalism promotes, does not attack corruption structurally, but instead, makes it starker in the society as it gains a socio-political legitimacy because it is primarily focused on the question of access that an individual within a position of power possesses – the numbers of which proliferate under neoliberalism in relation to those who do not, as access is made more difficult for the marginalised sections by the constant introduction of austerity policies (Visvanathan, 2018). Pande (2020) has argued that neoliberalism has in fact caused a resurgence of the idea of India as a superpower because of 'its sustained democracy, its embrace of technology – especially informational technology – and its open, plural and diverse society' (p. xi). However, unlike Jalan and Das, Pande takes a much more pragmatic approach towards neoliberalism in India and has also pointed out the immense challenges that India faces in terms of health and employment. The continuous defaming of public services is an important aspect of neoliberal capitalism, with advocates of privatisation arguing that under private regulation, all kinds of service delivery would improve qualitatively, with better funds and revenue systems available to them. The opposers of privatisation, on the other hand, bring forward the inherently unequal nature of privatised services which include low wages, unaffordable costs, lay-offs, practising poor health and safety standards, and the like (McDonald & Ruiters, 2005).

Within the healthcare sector, as Reddy (2019) writes, privatisation has had a drastic effect. The government expenditure on the healthcare sector has been abysmally low for many years now, accounting for just 1.4% of the gross domestic product (GDP) for 2019–20 and 1.8% for 2020–21. During the pandemic, the country faced the perils created by the rampant privatisation of the healthcare sector, which had left the primary and secondary healthcare infrastructure in a state of financial crisis. Even in 2022, when the benefits of the primary health centre (PHC) system have been fairly established due to the pandemic, the budgetary allocation for PHC has been insufficient, as Srinath Reddy informs. The expenditure on health, however, has increased marginally to 2.1% of the GDP, with the allocation for Covid vaccines being only Rs 5,000 crore (USD 6 billion) (Reddy, 2022, February 2). The SII had discounted only the first 100 million doses to the Government of India and capped them at Rs 200 (USD 2.5 app.) per dose, before SII was granted the market license (Das, 2021, January 4). However, just before the central government announced booster doses for everyone above 18 years of age in April 2022, both Covishield and Covaxin prices were slashed to Rs 225 (USD 3 app.) per dose (Vora et al., 2022, April 9). Market licenses have now been granted to both Covishield and Covaxin manufacturers, which makes it almost certain that at some point, the users can purchase them from the retail market *legally*. In January 2022, Covaxin was being sold for Rs 1,200 per shot while Covishield for Rs 780 (USD 9.5 app.) per shot in private centres, which had also been charging around Rs 150 (USD 2 app.) for service charges. Until recently, covid vaccines could only be distributed by the government, but with the market licenses, they can now be distributed by virtually anyone with a trade license (Sharma, 2022, January 27).

Neoliberalism has caused a fundamental alteration in the process in which governments react to issues, including issues of accessibility during the COVID-19 pandemic. Market licenses are frequently evoked as the solution to all forms of accessibility issues within the society. The general capitalistic argument runs along the lines that once market licences are provided for any commodity, the citizens are provided with innumerable options regarding the place from which they desire to obtain the commodity. However, under conditions where the general accessibility to medicines and drugs remain extremely low, making any essential commodity available to the market *in general* also comes with the risk of black marketing and hoarding. Both of these became major issues faced by the common masses in India during the second wave. Hoarding and black marketing of drugs required for treating COVID-19, including oxygen cylinders and other medical equipment, became a common event across the country during the second wave affecting vulnerable individuals and communities with a major shortage of medical oxygen for usage by the general populace, especially during the second wave of the pandemic. The central government, however, claimed that India had no shortage of medical oxygen, even when the cases in India had reached a massive tally of 1.99 crores (USD 19.9 million) (Firstpost, 2021, May 3). Hoarding of essential goods and commodities in India is criminalised in accordance with The Prevention of Black Marketing and Maintenance of Supplies of Essential Commodities Act, 1980, which was enacted to prevent the hoarding of commodities deemed essential for the maintenance of a healthy life. This act also enables the legal and administrative personnel to make preventive arrests as well. Additionally, India has a host of other major laws related to the continuous supply of essential commodities in the country, including the Essential Commodity Act, 1955, the Drugs and Cosmetics Act, 1940, and the Epidemic Diseases Act, 1897. Each of these laws were formulated in such a way as to prevent the exploitation of poor people during crises such as COVID-19. Smith et al. write:

> Pricing policies have as their object to establish the right Price for the product. The 'right price' may be determined by cost influences, the nature of the market, the nature of the competition, and a variety of other factors, The pharmaceutical industry has been criticised for: having the same Price for the same products, having different Prices for the same product; having different Prices for different customers for the same product; and for having too high Prices.
>
> (Smith et al., 2021, p. 41)

The pricing of essential drugs and their control during a public health crisis is not only a pharmaceutical issue but rather a social issue. Prices are also inevitably related to profits, and have been under governmental scrutiny for a long time (Smith et al., 2021). The increase in the prices of medicines required for the treatment of COVID-19 is not a case which is particular to India only but is rather a global issue. Between February and July 2020, the prices of as many as ten critical drugs required for the effective treatment of COVID-19 have risen in over eighty countries, with diazepam increasing by 16% and azithromycin by 6.5% being the drugs with the highest in prices in terms of percentages (Ando, 2020, July 8). This is a critical data in the context of India because around 70% of the expenditure on health by Indians goes towards the procurement of medicines (Chintan, 2022, April 5). The left-wing news website, Newsclick reports:

> If we compare the trend of price rise (inflation) for Medicines (Allopathic) with the general price rise, we see that during the pandemic, the price rise for medicines was higher than the general price rise throughout 2021. The price rise of medicines began in August 2020 and crossed the general price rise in September 2020 [, staying] higher [than the average] throughout the peak pandemic period. . . . Only in September 2021, it reduced a little to hit the same level as the general inflation in December 2021.
>
> (Chintan, 2022, April 5, Paras 8–9)

The physical and psychological impact of a disaster like COVID-19 often carries with itself certain opportunities for the egalitarian forces to emphasise the importance of public accountability. Public accountability is something that has often been reported to have been missing from the public services (Sastri & Bandyopadhyay, 2021). However, neoliberal market structures cannot be said to generate much public accountability because they rely on a cheap and highly exploitable workforce. Most market structures under neoliberalism depend on cheap migrant labour in India's urban spaces, who are often denied socio-economic rights as workers and human beings and cannot even seek accountability from those who employ them because of the absence of formal contracts (Jayaram & Jain, 2020). During the first lockdown, which was announced without any significant notice period by the central government, a huge proportion of the migrant workers living in the urban centres of India had to leave the cities and return back home. Pithode's (2022) account of the management of the COVID-19 pandemic speaks favourably of the ways in which the municipalities reacted to the COVID-19 pandemic, with adequate help and support being provided to the migrant workers. However, the accounts that people such as Tarun Kapri and Barkha Dutt have recounted in their books, paint a different picture. Kapri (2021) speaks about how the travelling migrant workers were discriminated against by the local residents in some places, something which he referred to as a new form of untouchability. Similarly, Barkha Dutt (2022) provides insights into the manner in which the migrant workers were being discriminated against by local people while travelling back home. The urban local bodies (ULBs) have tremendous ability to mitigate these kinds of issues. However, most ULBs failed to perform these duties.

The ULBs, out of compulsion, instead of advocating for greater control and resources had to resort to further exploiting the marginalised workers. They used people working in various schemes, such as the Anganwadi and Accredited Social Health Activist (ASHA) workers, to take care of COVID-19 patients, especially those put in isolation, and conduct surveys (Pithode, 2022). COVID-19 not only caused problems in the lives of the low-paid migrant workers but also caused major problems in the lives of the care workers engaged in these semi-formal low paid 'social voluntary' labour under the directives of the government. The pandemic drastically increased their already existing workload, with a lot of them being forced to do work which does not fall within their official responsibilities. There are scores of reports from across the country where these workers have worked tirelessly for the safety of the citizens during the pandemic. There were some care workers in Delhi, who were quite vocal about the ways in which their services have been disproportionately used during the COVID-19 pandemic and not adequately remunerated by the state. However, they did bring out the important role that ULBs have in the overall process of ensuring public health, especially the safety of the primary health workers, which has been severely impacted by the pandemic. Many of the primary caregiving workers were not given the protective equipment that they required to battle the disease (Mishra & Santosh, 2021).

The lack of protective medical equipment for the workers came into effect when the medical device industry in India was making huge profits and gains – both financially and socially India has been a leading producer of personal protection equipment (PPE) kits and the second-largest producer of medical textiles, making it one of the leading players in the world market in these sectors during the pandemic (J. Sharma, 2022). It can be safely assumed that industries such as the medical device industry in India have actually benefited from the pandemic. The sale of devices such as Oximeters have gone up manifold during the pandemic and the lockdowns (Agarwal, 2020, August 2; The Hindu, 2021, April 27). And, because of the poor regulatory framework surrounding the Minimum Retail Pricing (MRP) in India, there has been a surge in prices of these devices which has allowed the costs of such devices to increase from Rs 900 or so before the pandemic to around Rs 2000–3000, despite the MRP being marked at INR 3,500–4,000 (USD 42–48 approx) (Bhadala, 2021, May 20). The larger issue is that there have been certain untested brands as well, which have found their way into the market without the necessary certifications taking advantage of the dire conditions (Yadav, 2020, July 13; Agarwal, 2020, August 2). It is worthwhile to mention here that oximeters do not come under the Essential Commodities Act, and as such there is no way that bodies such as the National Pharmaceutical Pricing Authority (NPPA) could have controlled their prices during the pandemic.

The condition of the healthcare infrastructure is such that the out-of-pocket (OOP) for medical-related costs constitutes around 70% of all the healthcare expenditure in India. India ranks 154th out of 195 countries in terms of quality and accessibility to healthcare services according to a study done by Lancet and fails to satisfy the global standards on many counts.[14] The abysmal conditions of healthcare infrastructure ensured that the impact of the pandemic in India would be faced unequally across the society – the worst affected of which were the informal migrant workers. They were at the receiving end of the worst aspects of both COVID-19, and the response that the government showed towards the virus. Many informal migrant workers had to walk back to their homes – often hundreds of kilometres away – because they were not provided with any means of transport or money by the government. The government issued a circular on the 29th of March 2020 stating that:

> [All] employers would have to pay wages, without deductions, to workers during the duration of the lockdown. The 29th of March circular and appeals from the PMO, however, did not suffice to ensure wage payments to workers, who largely remained unpaid throughout the lockdown.
>
> (Jayaram & Jain, 2020, p. 261)

Such cases of non-payment are not surprising because only around 48% of the workers in India earn regular salaries, of which only about 27% have written contracts with a fewer percentage having access to benefits such as provident funds, sick pay, and insurance. Their conditions worsened further when the government began to focus more on the remedial aspects of the pandemic rather than the preventive ones (Bhalotia et al., 2020; Dhingra & Kondirolli, 2021). The effects of the pandemic were felt acutely by the marginalised populace, particularly due to the highly privatised healthcare system in place in India today, mostly serving those who can afford them. Health policies at a national level in India have been sporadic in nature, coming in at large gaps. The first health policy of India was introduced in 1983, while the second one was brought forward in 2002. The third and the latest one was introduced in 2017. Because of such abnormal delays in the timings of these policies, they remained largely discrete with a lack of continuity between them. Most of the healthcare policies and analysis rests upon the report prepared by the Bhore Committee in 1946,[15] which focused on the universalisation of healthcare in India (Aiyar, 2020). However, the state of affairs in India has not been able to realise the recommendations of the Bhore Committee in practice, and as such healthcare has remained an elitist sector accessible only to the few in the country (Rao, 2017). The ways in which a person spends on healthcare is contingent upon the ways in which other associated sectors function in an economy. The COVID-19 pandemic spread in India at a time when a large proportion of Indian citizens have continued to be gripped by lifestyle diseases such as heart conditions, diabetes, and obesity, all of which contribute to the deteriorating condition of the health in the country. The lifestyles that most of the people follow under contemporary capitalism create the conditions for certain ailments to become general issues affecting almost everyone in the society (Ramin, 2017; Egan, 2020). There are certain parts of the diets that one follows in general as well as the structuring of one's everyday life that makes it impervious that people from certain regions, especially urban areas, will get more affected by COVID-19 than others.

The speed with which COVID-19 made its way through India is a proof of the rapid pace at which infectious diseases can make their progress, given the kind of developmental trajectory that India has produced over the past decades or so. When any crises such as the pandemic strikes human society, the worst affected are always the lowest-paid workers, who often have nothing to hold on to. Hupkau et al. (2020) have argued that in the United Kingdom, the young and lowest-paid workers, who are often contractual workers, have suffered a considerable decline in their earnings and future employment prospects. This has also been seen in the context of India, where a significant proportion of workers have lost their jobs during the lockdown.[16] Lockdowns have been a major setback for the forces of capital during the pandemic, and the corporates have lost no time in protesting against lockdowns, despite the common sensical *fact* that well-coordinated lockdowns are often the only options that can help resist the onslaught of COVID-19. However, to arrive at a complete picture of the lockdown, a dialectical view is required, one that does not focus only on one aspect of the lockdown, but rather looks at the totality surrounding the lockdowns. It is true that lockdowns are often necessary to stop the spread of the disease, but at the same time, almost all forms of lockdowns – localised, national, or global – also have certain pitfalls, which enable certain other social evils to express themselves in the society, such as caste and gender-based violence.[17]

When movement is restricted by law, it sometimes becomes even more necessary to move (Mukul, 2022). COVID-19 has brought forth numerous aspects of Indian public life that had been hitherto unexplored by mainstream media and policy analysts. One such issue was the way in which the state managed the crisis faced by the migrant workers in India's urban centres. With the lockdown imposed upon the country by the central government, many migrant workers were forced to walk or cycle for thousands of kilometres back to their homes, some even losing their lives in the process.[18] Migration is not the central topic of the current book, but since the migrant workers are an important part of the book, it is customary to provide some background on the scale of migration in India. Under global capitalism, migration has become central to the process of capitalist accumulation and exploitation and is having an indelible impact on the society (Arnold, 2012). It has become one of the tools by which capitalism ensures a certain biopolitical control over the people (Tazzioli, 2020). In India, migration is often juxtaposed with failed developmental projects, or with failed policies of the state during times of crises. Writing about the exceptionality of the Indian scenario, historian Chinmay Tumbe writes:

> What makes the Indian case unique is the sheer persistence and magnitude of [the phenomenon of migration], one that has lasted for well over a century now. It is also a phenomenon that affects regions covering at least 20 per cent of the Indian population, currently comprising over 200 million people. I call it the 'Great Indian Migration Wave', and it ranks among the largest and longest migration streams for work in documented history. It led to the rise of cities like Kolkata and Mumbai in India and Yangon and Dubai abroad.
>
> (Tumbe, 2018, pp. 39–40)

Factors such as this have contributed to the nature in which the Indian society and the state has reacted to the COVID-19 crisis. There are certain important facets of the way in which India reacted to the pandemic. One of the main strategies remained the way the bureaucracy has been unleashed on the marginalised sections of the populace. This is where NGOs become critical. NGOs and community organisations can be extremely helpful in spreading public health awareness within communities which are populated by marginalised people who often exhibit a certain distrust surrounding governmental instructions (Digital Medic, 2021, March 29) – such tendencies got manifested in the widespread vaccine hesitancy exhibited by many (Trivedi, 2021). The NITI Aayog CEO, Amitabh Kant-led Empowered Committee actively sought help from NGOs in combating vaccine hesitancy. NGOs played a critical role in the way India responded to the pandemic as has been noted by many authors, journalists, and think tanks (Marwaha, 2021, February 27; Anand, 2021, October 5; Digital Medic, 2021, March 29). The NITI Aayog reached out to as many as 90,000 or more NGOs along with other civil society organisations (CSOs) for help during the first lockdown (Marwaha, 2021, March 1). As Digital Medic (2021, March 29) noted, community organisations possessed certain unique characteristics which are difficult for existing public bodies to internalise, including their intimate – and often lived – understanding of community needs, their ability to adapt to changing circumstances, their ability to spread public awareness about pandemics and epidemics by using the access they have in local communities, and their ability to customise the education and information required during a pandemic.[19] The state sought to use the NGOs, community organisations, and other CSOs for a variety of reasons, which ranged from their involvement in the community to their large volunteering base within the society (Marwaha, 2021, March 1). The NGOs were instrumental forces in bringing in imported medical devices to India during the pandemic (Anand, 2021, October 5). They devised plans such as Mission *Sanjeevani*[20] that provided large quantities of hospital equipment and supplies, while actively being engaged in training and providing critical medical equipment to 60,000 ASHAs (Anand, 2021, October 5), who were instrumental forces behind the government's pandemic response plan.

The Pandemic, Neoliberal Logic and Its Implications

The COVID-19 pandemic in India exhibited the abysmal conditions of the various local bodies in the 739 districts in the country (Mathew, 2020; Raj, 2020, July 2). It is always beneficial to counter healthcare emergencies such as COVID-19 at the local level because it helps the society have a better chance to contain the infection.[21] Municipalities are other forms of ULBs play a crucial role in busting certain myths that inevitably crop up during a health emergency such as the COVID-19 pandemic. For example, Krishnan (2022) narrates a brief note about the history of TB to illustrate this point. She writes, 'Consumption [, a historical name for a mysterious illness] is a remarkably enduring disease. Once it arrives, it stays. It ravages cities and plunders populations. . . . Today, we know the disease as tuberculosis' (Krishnan, 2022, pp. 22–23). The public's viewing of:

> TB – as mysterious, romantic malady – changed once slum clearances, municipal sewage systems, and safe and sterile drinking water were provided to urban centres in the US and Europe. Access to modern

medicine became a reality, and tuberculosis was never again considered the captain of the men of death.

(Krishnan, 2022, p. 75)

Things, however, are not so simple, when the very access to medicine – which played such a crucial role in busting the myths surrounding TB – itself is disproportionately balanced under contemporary capitalism.

Poor finances and widespread corruption in the healthcare sector contribute to its dilapidated state. This has been a major setback in keeping the healthcare structure in India skin to a low-income country despite India becoming a middle-income country (Rao, 2017; Reddy, 2019). The categorisation of any service or commodity as a public good implies within itself the basic idea that those commodities or services would be made universally available and accessible to all, something which has been missing in India since 1991 (Mander, 2016). The COVID-19 pandemic has exhibited that quite blatantly, with even quarantining facilities being segregated on the basis of class, where the elite could enjoy a host of different facilities, and 'the gravest consequence of this class bias on the pandemic was by portraying the worst victims of this pandemic as the criminals and most dangerous, rather than victims and their confinement in subhuman quarantine facilities' (Mander, 2020, p. 27).

Proponents of free market capitalism were quick to argue that the vaccines exhibited that Big Pharma had a tremendous power to innovate during adverse circumstances – and with negligible state funding – which often makes it common sense and imperative for humanity to bow down to free-market capitalism (Paqué, 2020). Capitalism promotes free trade by arguing that it benefits economic well-being and enhances the efficiency of the different sectors (Hart-Landsberg, 2013). During pandemics, a quick response saves countless lives, however, it is important to note that a quick response does not always mean a sound response. Free market capitalism believes that the incentives that the market has to offer for innovation is far more than any state. COVID-19, in a way, has reinforced this belief with widespread disaster capitalism becoming the order of the day during the pandemic. Capitalism today almost makes it imperative for societies to adjust, affecting the health and safety of the communities and individuals, often by considering the short-term economic gain that those policies might bring forward (Smedley, 2019). Such adjustments often put the marginalised populace under extreme levels of risk that mere structural rearrangements at a city level cannot address (Singh, 2018; Smedley, 2019).

The pandemic exposed the vulnerabilities faced by certain communities during such apocalyptic times. The class nature of accessibility to essential services such as clean water, healthcare, education, and the like has ensured that even during times such as a pandemic, there is a very prominent gap between how issues get covered in the media. Singh (2018) argues that the urban middle class in India is increasingly dependent on private providers for most of the services that it considers essential for survival. And, since it is the middle class that controls the discourse in the society, the only issues that get media coverage in India are often the issues that concern the middle class. This can be seen from the way in which most mainstream media covers, in general, the rise of digitalisation in the society. These media houses and outlets often fail to take into cognisance that they are reporting in a country where internet penetration is only about 43% as of 2020 (KANTAR and IAMAI, 2020). Exclusion from the digital ecosystem can be due to the shortage of skill, as well as because of the unavailability of physical access to digital means of communication (Kularski & Moller, 2012). And, since in this day and age, and especially during the pandemic, digital access has become the key to access other services, it is of utmost necessity that digital access be established as a public good, one that can be used and accessed by everyone in the society (Manzar et al., 2016). One's access to digital services also get impacted by the ascribed social status that one possesses. In India, the deep-seated social exclusionary mechanisms in place infiltrate the accessibility that one possesses, which in turn affects their social positioning giving rise to a teleological relationship between these two factors where one reinforces the other and vice versa. The government, as per the report presented by Kamath and Kumar (2017, November 24), did not take into account the inaccessibility with regards to the use of technological artefacts like smartphones caused by factors other than the accessibility to the internet. At the same time, there is also a miniscule number of people who have gone on to become social influencers on social media who do not come from the upper caste (Mandal, 2020). A combination of these factors results in Dalits and people from other backward castes finding it extremely difficult to be a part of the *smart* ecosystem.[22]

Schemes such as the Swachh Bharat Mission (SBM) only scratch the surface when it comes to the needs of sanitation in India by focusing more on the construction of toilets rather than their actual everyday usage (Unni & Panwar, 2019, April 5). Housing, sanitation, and community healthcare have become extremely critical in situations such as the one that COVID-19 has constructed globally, where there has been an *enforced* increase in the volumes of home production – both of commodities and services. The way in which home production is carried out depends on the way in which the various members of a householding unit are placed occupationally (Hupkau & Petrongolo, 2021). Under free market capitalism, certain aspects of activities such as childcare and housekeeping had come within the market, but with COVID-19, a significant proportion of these activities again came within the fold of the household activities, especially for the women (Hupkau & Petrongolo, 2021).

The pandemic has forced many additional responsibilities on the households as well. One of the major ones is education. Eyles et al. (2020) argue that the availability of online platforms for continuing education has helped significantly in some cases. The possibility of parental instruction substituting formal education can be a successful one provided that parents are able to 'adjust educational expenditure and instruction time in response to the number of educational inputs received elsewhere' proportionately' (Todd & Wolpin, 2003; Eyles et al., 2020, p. 4). However, the students from poorer households are at higher risk of getting their education impacted by loss of school days because of their inability to invest in high-end private tutoring (Cooper et al., 1996; Major et al., 2021). Fiorini and Keane's (2014) argument which has been echoed by Eyles et al. (2020) in the context of the Global North, that the amount of time that children spend with their parents on educational issues enhances their cognitive skills, does not hold much ground, especially when considering the marginalised population in India. This is because the requisite parental effort that is necessary for adequate cognitive development (Houtenville & Conway, 2008) is difficult to be provided by the marginalised populace.

In spite of the fact that there were differences between how different countries and their economies reacted to the Covid crisis, losses in educational continuity and healthcare inaccessibility were common aspects of almost all the major democracies, including India. Egan (2020) narrates how South Korea and America, even though both reported their first cases on 21st of January 2021, responded to the issue were grossly different – while South Korea moved towards testing and contact tracing, the American state was largely dismissive. Similarly, the reactions from countries such as Australia and New Zealand, though effective, were also recipients of a certain amount of criticism from social commentators, like Shraya (2022), for the methods in which they tended to isolate sections of population from the globe. This had a negative impact on the mental health of population. Travel restrictions had become one of the major hurdles that many people – including those from the extremely marginalised sections – had to face throughout the duration when lockdowns had become the order of the day (Mukul, 2022). The effects on the mobility of human beings during the pandemic made many realise the importance of the right to mobility on their experience of the space around them. This right to mobility also affects the accessibility to the various services during a pandemic, or any kind of emergency for that matter. The corporatisation of any healthcare sector can be broadly defined as:

> [The] provision of health care services through market relationships to those able to pay; investment in, and production of those services, and of inputs to them, for cash income or profit, including private contracting and supply to publicly financed health care; and health care finance derived from individual payments and private insurance.
> (Mackintosh & Koivusalo, 2005, p. 3)

The constant neoliberal reforms in the healthcare sector have made human beings more vulnerable to disasters by following Perrow's (2007) arguments, increasing the target-concentration, and enabling the continuous impoverishment of regulation in the private sector while at the same time increasing the concentration of economic power and resources (both lethal and non-lethal) at the hands of a tiny minority. Disaster capitalism has permeated every aspect of the society during COVID-19, working through the complete disruption of the public sector in developing economies. The outsourcing of public services and the over-reliance on NGOs to perform the responsibility of the state is one of the basic indicators of disaster capitalism. The implications of this becomes particularly critical in sectors such as education in India, which is a highly unequal terrain. There are widespread disparities surrounding accessibility and infrastructural developments in the sector, which make it one of the most important markers of profiteering under neoliberalism by monopoly capital in India.

The disparities surrounding education extend right from the pre-primary schooling level to the university level. School education, especially in India, is massively underfunded, and as such government schools are in abysmal condition. Education in such schools and food security for the children – considering that a huge proportion of children in government public schools come from families with meagre incomes – are seen as interlinked aspects in the Indian context, and as such:

> In most States no fees are charged for schooling and there is a midday meal programme which is to attract children to school and provide nourishment at the primary stage. Many states have made education free for girls, some even up to the professional stage.
> (Ramachandran & Ramkumar, 2005, p. xix)

The emphasis placed on schemes such as midday meals point towards two important issues that are highly relevant in the context in which the current book is laid out. The first being the workers involved in the process. The second being the issue of food security in India. Both of these aspects have been drastically affected during the COVID-19 pandemic in India.

In the context of this chapter, the focus will be on healthcare. Priya (2018) argues that even though the Indian state had taken up the responsibility of providing healthcare to its citizens, this also caused numerous issues surrounding the biopolitics of healthcare to crop up. The use of the community in public health has always been a contested and controversial issue in the public domain. Numerous definitions have been put forward in that aspect, focusing heavily on the element of commonality within a social group, without taking into consideration the diversity that might be pre-existent within the social group in terms of social identities based on class, caste, and gender along with other social and personal values and interests. Hence, even though the Indian pharmaceutical industry has been one of the best among the low- and middle-income countries (LMICs) since the 1980s (Sengupta, 2018), the Indian pharma industry:

> represent[s] only one element of the Health Care system, and their appropriate use is based on many factors. Proper diagnosis, prescribing, manufacture, distribution, and patient use all combine to determine the extent to which patients benefit from pharmaceutical therapy.

> Essentially, pharmaceutical marketing must strive to inform a technically sophisticated audience about dramatically changing product and service mixes in a climate of constant governmental Regulation, Public scrutiny, and industry competition.
>
> (Smith et al., 2021, p. 25)

Pharmaceutical companies, as Sismondo (2018) puts forward, 'sustain large networks to gather, create, control, and disseminate information. They provide the pathways that carry this information, and the energy that makes it move. Through bottlenecks and around curves, knowledge is created, given shape by the channel it navigates' (p. 8). The companies that benefit the most out of healthcare disasters are the pharmaceutical conglomerates. The sales of paracetamol and other such drugs increased dramatically during the pandemic, and especially during the lockdown (Ali, 2022, January 22). However, even with such huge sales, the prices of paracetamol are set to increase from 2022 (Nihalani, 2022, April 11). The management of the pandemic by the neoliberal state has left the medical-based knowledge that pharmaceutical companies possess unchecked and unconstrained even during the times of despair so as to enable them to create profits out of their ability to direct that knowledge where it is most profitable. Sismondo (2018) argues that 'In a knowledge-based economy, knowledge itself becomes an object of investment, trading, and deployment' (p. 9). Nothing more symbolises this than the ways in which innovations have been used in the healthcare sector, which have exhibited that such innovative technologies can be used for profit during emergency situations.

In the case of the pharmaceutical monopolies, this continuous impoverishment of the public sector coupled with a certain secrecy around the government mandates regarding rules and regulations surrounding COVID-19 has created a vacuum in which they can operate at a more exploitative pace. For example, it had become a common practice for passengers, mostly ordinary middle-class people, to take a paracetamol on flights during the landing process so as to escape the arduous, yet necessary, process of checks at the airports (The Times of India, 2020, March 21; Thakur, 2020, May 25; Arakal, 2020, May 28). The point here is not the mere activity of the individuals popping those pills, but rather the fear of the government procedures that are often structured in a manner so as to intimidate people. Liberal social analysts such as Das (2000, 2012) have discussed at length the way in which the common citizens feel uncomfortable with the growth of the bureaucracy in the society. However, the solution that they propose usually remains entrapped within a framework which speaks about the potential of the market to solve the issues rather than any form of egalitarian solution.

Conclusion

The extreme levels of risk that the marginalised people face is a result of the ways in which capitalist development has undermined the natural balance in the world. The fragile relationship that many societies share with nature has pushed human civilisation to the brink of the current apocalyptic scenario (Honigsbaum, 2020; Quammen, 2020). The intensity of human interference into the natural order varies proportionally to the amount of alienation from nature that human beings have developed over time (Williams, 1978).[23] The relation between capitalism and nature is infested with contradictions. Capitalism thrives on nature, which provides it with its geographical advantage of resources, but capitalism in return, almost always, undermines nature to productivity. Human beings do not constitute their modes of living (Marx, 1844/1975) in isolation but rather constitute the same through their interaction with nature and various other social beings and institutions. Much of these tendencies have particularly affected the community lives of people – something that often serves as the only barrier between marginalised individuals and death due to a viral infection during times of a neoliberal healthcare crisis.

The community life of individuals has been massively affected by the growth of neoliberal tendencies in the society which have prioritised productivity over human dignity. These tendencies have come to affect the marginalised populace more starkly than others. This becomes even more evident if one begins to analyse the social reality that people from different sections of the population went through during the pandemic. The effects of the lockdown, as faced by the informal workforce of this country, was very different than that experienced by the middle-class workforce in the country. Barkha Dutt (2022) writes:

> [A]cross India, through 2020 and 2021 – the virus was anything but the great equaliser. It exacerbated existing inequalities and birthed new ones. In an already stratified society, it created a new social order. The assumption that the calamity was inherently egalitarian – that the pandemic had somehow created a level playing field on which death and illness were the great levellers, flattening out the ground for India's wealthiest and poorest – was grossly incorrect.
>
> (Dutt, 2022, 'The Village with Yellow Water')

Neoliberalism has also created jobs which are specifically designed for people from lower end of the socio-economic spectrum, who suffer the most from these kinds of policy changes, especially during a pandemic. Even the Organisation for Economic Co-operation and Development (OECD) (March 17, 2022) has agreed that in spite of possessing economic prowess of a much higher quality than the Global South, it cannot deny that migrants, ethnic and racial minorities, and especially the young people in vulnerable jobs are most likely to lose their lives during the pandemic. Dhingra and Kondirolli (2021) have stated that in Mumbai, where around 40% of the urban workers in their research stated that they had struggled to obtain work or payments even after 10 months of the first lockdown, young and low-income urban workers remained at the greatest risk. Young workers, of 18–25 years of age, were already much more vulnerable because they were likely to be employed either informally receiving lesser pay or have no work at all (Bhalotia et al., 2020). With the complete disruption of routine lives, along with a very strategic disinvestment from the public sector, this section of the population is expected to be the most adversely affected, not only when the pandemic rages on but also when the pandemic subsides in its intensity. Social Capital, which these vulnerable sections often lack, is critical to making informed choices regarding one's own health and well-being during a pandemic (Samantha, 2020, March 30). With the increasing amount of digitalisation of the basic services, these sections have found themselves at the risk of being further marginalised. As a gravedigger recounted:

> Sometimes, it feels like democracy is a privilege only the rich can afford. People like me, and jobs like mine are taken for granted. Our work is often termed 'disposable' or 'replaceable' with very little consideration given to those who are actually doing it.
>
> (Shameem, 2022, p. 12)

These are the people who got affected by the higher price of medicines and drugs, which characterised the failures of the pandemic response in India. There was an increase in the prices of drugs hitherto under price control by the government such as ibuprofen, ranitidine, and carbamazepine by the NPPA, which are essential drugs for treatment of any disease associated with rising temperatures – a move that benefitted companies such as Torrent Pharmaceuticals, Cadila Pharmaceuticals, Zydus Cadila, and J. B. Chemicals (Das, 2021, July 3). The increase in drug prices has continued even after the pandemic. In April 2022, again, there has been a 10.8% hike in the prices of essential drugs such as paracetamol and metformin attributed mainly to the rise in the Wholesale Price Index (WPI) (Chintan, 2022, April 5). There was a tendential increase in the price of the raw materials required for manufacturing the medicines for treatment of COVID-19 during the first wave. From the month of May 2021, the All Kerala Chemists and Druggist Association (AKCDA) asserted that during the months of April and May 2021, the prices of most of the raw materials necessary for the treatment of COVID-19, including Ivermectin, Methylprednisolone, Meropenem, Paracetamol, Azithromycin, and Doxycycline, increased by approximately 40–200% (Mohan, 2021, May 13). The reasons for the same are not entirely local in nature. According to the same report which quotes the AKCDA, the price hike was also partially due to the ban on imports from China. Before 1991, the import of active pharmaceutical ingredients (APIs) from China – the largest API manufacturer by volume in the world – used to be around only 0.3%, which has increased drastically under neoliberal globalisation (Dadhich, 2020, April 22). The other importers had also increased their prices in response to the increased demand for these raw materials. The ways in which COVID-19 has impacted the transport of raw materials has greatly affected the production of medicines in India, especially those related to the treatment and prevention of COVID-19.[24] Coupled with a dilapidating funding into public healthcare, such shortages and price-rises have wreaked havoc on the marginalised populace.

Since the 2017–18 financial year, the central government's expenditure on healthcare has been declining with an increasing reliance on state governments for approximately 72% of the total requisite expenditure (Jain, 2017, August 2). The state governments have repeatedly accused the central governments of denying funds to them (Singh, 2021, April 20). Some have even gone on to breach protocols of high-security meetings to make their voice heard to the general public and the central government (Business Today, 2021, April 23). The government, however, has been instrumental in providing an absolute monopoly to private facilities like the SII by granting them huge funds (Das & Seth, 2021, April 20; The News Minute, 2021, April 20) rather than investing in the publicly funded vaccine manufacturing units (Basu, 2021, April 18). Under a healthcare system, which is massively tilted in favour of the rich and which receives an approximately 1.2% of the total GDP of the country (Raj, 2021, February 1), it is not surprising to find state governments gasping for amenities during a crisis as grave as that of COVID-19, many of which do not exist at all. In the nineteenth century, municipalities were the bodies which mainly controlled the healthcare provisioning as private capital did not find the sector profitable enough to invest in leaving health to be managed by the local authorities. This also ensured, in certain ways, the complete absence of the local authority's interference in commercial activities per se (Leopold & McDonald, 2012, p. 1844).

The classical assumption was that the competition over health services would involve the politicians and medical officials and would not necessarily interfere with commercial practices (Leopold & McDonald, 2012). Under neoliberalism, however, this assumption has been proved to be a false one. The privatised healthcare sector in India, which has blossomed at the expense of the public sector (Sengupta & Nundy, 2005, p. 1158) now occupies a staggering 72% of the total infrastructure of the country according to research conducted by the Institut Montaigne (Jaffrelot & Jumle, 2020, November 3). The total impoverishment of the public sector, both financially and technologically, has created a highly unbalanced structure with almost no public or community accountability, whereby competent healthcare has become accessible only to the urban middle and upper classes (Dehury et al., 2019).

Healthcare is not a personal entity in the urban space, but rather a culmination of the ways in which different forms of essential services have been provisioned in the particular space. In the *India Exclusion Report 2016*, Nambiar et al. (2016) and Anand et al. (2016) have noted that the health of the urban poor is further degraded due to factors such as water provisioning and sanitation, which continue to work in a structurally violent fashion in most urban areas in India. Bisen (2019) has noted in his work about the degrading state of sanitation for a majority of the population which is a result of the way in which structural inequalities have been bolstered by the constant and unplanned urbanisation strategies that have been taken up in India. He argues that if the situation of urban sanitation is to be improved, then the local bodies need a complete revamp if the problem of sanitation is to be solved in the context of India. Additionally, the impact that traditional structural inequalities such as caste and gender have had on the overall picture of sanitation in India has also had an adverse effect on the way in which different people experience sanitation in different types of urban spaces in India (Harriss-White, 2019).

Neoliberal reforms in India have argued in favour of a *lack of government* but more of governance (Mathur, 2008). Interestingly, that was also the election campaign rally cry of the BJP in 2014 (Price, 2015). Governance, as per the World Bank and the one that neoliberal governments usually follow, effectively refers to the network of relationships formed between state, market, and the civil society where the will of the government – democratic or dictatorial – is only contingent to the will of the other actors, with the state merely acting as an actor in the process on equal terms with others (Mathur, 2008). However, under neoliberal capitalism, the market very soon comes to dominate over the state because the state – by itself – simply becomes redundant with increasing influence of the market over every aspect of the citizens' lives. In other words, the government elected by the people becomes akin to the description of the corrupt managing agencies, as put forward by Goswami (2016), whose single drive remains to profit at the expense of the shareholders. In the context of the citizens and the state, the state assumes the role of the agency, while the citizens become the unfortunate shareholders of the neoliberal state. Thinkers who align with the neoliberal growth trajectory such as Bimal Jalan and Gurcharan Das – both of whom have been extensively engaged with in the current book – have argued that except for certain critical factors in some very specific contexts, the state should withdraw from providing services and instead focus on other issues, such as legislative ones. However, the COVID-19 pandemic has proved that public sector services – if not the state-form in itself – are crucial to the sustenance of human life as it exists, especially during emergencies where it has become difficult for the people to access other services. As Jayati Ghosh writes:

> [Public] employment should not be seen as a fiscal cost, which has become the approach of the government in recent times. Instead, it is not only crucial for a just, healthy, equitable and peaceful society, but can also play a hugely important role in economic revival.
> (Ghosh, 2019–2020, p. 258)

COVID-19 has resulted in a massive loss of the idea of selfhood among many people, and the effects of the pandemic will be felt for years to come. Vinay Lal argues, '*If, in our capitalist economy, homo sapiens is fundamentally homo economicus, what might be the implications of living in a time, and for a protracted period of time, when as human beings we ceased to be primarily economic agents?*' (Lal, 2020, 'Viral Capitalism', emphasis self). It is essential here to realise that the implications of this kind of changes are felt variably across the globe. COVID-19 has exhibited that a close relationship does exist between the state and the forces of global capital by establishing that both private firms run by global capital and the state are essential for the effective functioning of each other (Zanoni & Mir, 2022). Capitalist globalisation and the concurrent upsurge of nationalist politics has ensured that the internationalist oppressive models of capitalism remain intact with a global shift from agrarian modes of production and welfarism, while keeping intact the context and geography-specific modes of exploitation and oppression. Globalisation, as Waterman (2001), argues spreads the ills of capitalism throughout the world sharpening 'the combinations, unevenness, ambiguities and contradictions of high modernity' (p. 210). In the Global South, there is an ingrained precarity within a certain section of the working populace who even find it difficult to express themselves as workers and as such remain outside of the traditional wage struggles (Munck, 2013), and the migrant workers' crisis that India faced is a testimony to that. Migrant workers in India are some of the worst paid informal workers in the world. Most of them, as Jha and Pankaj note, are:

> [Labour] migrants . . . engaged in manual labour in formal sectors, such as street vendors, construction workers, service providers, and rickshaw pullers, but due to the lockdown, they became unemployed, which resulted in shortage of food and other essentials required to survive in the city [leaving them with no choice but to leave the city and move towards their homes].
>
> (Jha & Pankaj, 2020, p. 56)

The migrant workers' crisis must be analysed both as a local and as a universal one. While on the one hand, they had to struggle against the complete absence of apathy from the *universal* state, they also had to battle against the localised forms of exploitation that the citizens exhibited towards them. Many of the people from the lower ends of the economic spectrum – many of who also exploited the migrant workers on their way home – also showed a good amount of vaccine hesitancy globally, which only added to the crisis. Instead of ridiculing them, one of the most beneficial policy responses would have been that 'If you *are* going to seek integrative medicine, you have to integrate it. It's a resource to help treat the root causes and side effects of illness, but it should be used in conjunction with the rest of your healthcare' (Goldberg, 2019, p. 55).

Disasters such as COVID-19 present social scientists with a unique framework through which it becomes possible to analyse the relationship that social sciences share with technological advancement. A dialectical approach towards science and technology leads one to question the hegemonical descriptions of technological development that the ruling class proposes. Mosley's (2020) account of the pandemic and the virus points one to the complete uncertainty that reigned during 2020, and the trust that citizens were supposed to show towards the government and the global pharmaceutical conglomerates designing the vaccines. Erich Fromm's humanist psychoanalysis of the human mind under capitalism points one towards the manner in which under contemporary capitalism, human beings are structured in such a way that they completely lose the sense of their own self and feelings. The constant promotion of capitalism's desire to integrate the individual within the *world outside* often results in the complete obliteration of the true sense of feeling itself, which can result in the support many show for authoritarian figures in the political realm (Fromm, 1942/2001).

Dunayevskaya's (1987/2002a) philosophical vantage point on dialectics as a philosophy of revolutionary social change is based on the Hegelian concepts of 'Abstract Negativity' and 'Concrete Universality' emphasising that both materialism and idealism are co-existent in Marx. This can be of immense importance here because it has the potential to provide pathways towards a more detailed comprehension of the social conditions existing in the underdeveloped or developing nations (Dunayevskaya, 1979). Such a mode of analysis allows one to take the focus back on the human being as it does not succumb to either crude materialism or to romantic idealism. Revolutionary theories of the past have to be referred to, not imitated, in the contemporary struggles. Dunayevskaya's arguments surrounding the dialectical Lenin can be taken up as a case-in-point which was in contradiction to others' 'concept of capitalist growth in a straight line, or via a quantitative ratio, Lenin's own work holds on tightly to the dialectical principle, "transformation into opposite"' (Dunayevskaya, 1967, quoted from Anderson, 2020, pp. 69–70).

Societies do not progress in straight lines (Dunayevskaya, 1979, 1983/2002b) and cannot be streamlined to fit into particular models, but rather have to be analysed subjectively. They have to be analysed as part of the overall mode of production in the society, which need to be analysed as actual revolutionary revolutions. This would enable Marxist theory to come to terms with the fact that some societies can 'choose a different path' (Dunayevskaya, 2002c, p. 259). It is in this light that one needs to take note of the workers in the Global South who, as such, do not form part of the mainstream workers' struggle and remain entrapped within a non-capital per se but equally capitalistic mode of exploitation whose conditions of life have been analysed by Žižek (2017) in details. That requires an analysis of not only the means of production but also the relations of production. The chronic rise of unemployment in the factories, industries, and various market-based industries has put the entire human society on the shopping racks for capitalism to choose from. The COVID-19 pandemic demands a critical analysis of not only the response that states such as India exhibited but also the ingrained causality behind the responses and the kind of reactions – both physical and psychological – that they garnered within the society. This is because the non-capitalist classes today are entrapped within a system where policies – framed by the holistic combination of neoliberalism and statism – and the response that the non-capitalist classes and sections show towards those policies are all part of *one big whole*, the controls of which are firmly placed at the hands of Capital.

Notes

1. *Vishwaguru* means 'the one who teaches the entire world'.
2. As of June 2022, only 40% of the street vendors could repay the loans under PM SVANidhi scheme, that the government had provided them with during COVID-19 (N. Sharma, 2022, July 8). Most of these vendors and informal workers need direct assistance from the state along the lines of direct transfer of money and the assurance of safe and hygienic vending spots along with bringing more of them within the scheme of governmental plans and benefits (Majithia, 2020).
3. Shah's (2010) book on Malaria points one towards the innumerable vulnerabilities that a pharmacological response to a health emergency has to go through, which often results in violent effects, especially on vulnerable populations. Similarly, the quest for non-pharmacological responses to pandemics often results in structural violence against a large section of the populace, such as the one that was inflicted on India's migrant workers during the first lockdown in India (Mukul, 2022).
4. Given the nature of such markets, it is often difficult to put a number on such wet markets in India in a city, let alone the country as a whole, and as such no concrete and reliable data is available for the same.
5. The definition of 'event' in this context comes from Hannah Arendt, who defines 'events' to be 'occurrences that interrupt routine processes and routine procedures; only in a world in which nothing of importance ever happens could the futurologists' dream, come true. Predictions of the future are never anything but projections of present automatic processes and procedures, that is, of occurrences that are likely to come to pass if men do not act and if nothing unexpected happens; every action, for better or worse, and every accident necessarily destroys the whole patterns in whose frame the prediction moves and where it finds its evidence' (Arendt, 1969, p. 7).
6. During the Afghanistan War, the United States saw private outsourced security as the only means through which it could protect its assets in Afghanistan. Similar issues also abound elsewhere, where security agencies had been hiring thousands of people in different parts of the world with little experience in the strategic nuances of the region (Lowenstein, 2015).
7. The viewership of such Hindi channels remains at an upwards of 350,000 on an average every day. For example, see retrieved December 3, 2023, from https://bestmediainfo.com/2023/12/aaj-tak-india-today-tv-dominate-live-concurrent-viewership-on-counting-day#:~:text=a%20huge%20margin.-,On%20December%203%2C%202023%2C%20Aaj%20Tak%20recorded%20an%20average%20concurrent,145k%20between%20the%20same%20period
8. The rapid rise of private media houses in the country has been most aptly spoken about by journalist Rajdeep Sardesai who recounts: 'In 1989 – the first election I covered as a journalist – only Doordarshan was on air. In 2004, there were half a dozen major "national channels" and about a dozen regional channels. By 2014, the information and broadcasting ministry list suggested that there were almost 400 24/7 news and current affairs channels beaming out of India, a crazy number, way more than any other country in the world' (Sardesai, 2015, p. 220).

9 In lieu of employment provisioning, the government has initiated numerous plans such as the *Swachh Bharat* (Clean India) campaign which instead of advocating for further public expenditure, focuses on the civility that citizens possess to get things done and 'In a bid to create a spirit of civic responsibility, government . . . advertisements even invoked Hindu gods to encourage citizens to achieve a Clean India' (Waghmore & Gorringe, 2019, p. 2).

10 During the lockdown, there have been reports of both communal violence and caste-based violence in India (Veeraraghav, 2020; Salam, 2021).

11 Vidya Krishnan's (2022) analysis of Tuberculosis (TB) points one towards how TB affected the fashion sense of citizens, especially bringing forward shoes for women, shorter skirts, and the like. For men, the change was largely related to the obliteration of the moustache and beards due to the germ theory's rise in public acceptance since the 1900s, and beards being ascribed as 'a dust trap' (Krishnan, 2022, p. 61).

12 The first two Five-Year Plans focused on the irrigation, energy, agriculture, community development, transport, communication, industry (especially heavy industry), social services, land rehabilitation, and the like. During the Third Five-Year Plan (1961–1966), the State Electricity Boards and the State Secondary Education Boards were established to ensure the public provisioning of electricity and education. The drive towards nationalisation was emphasised heavily during the prime ministership of Indira Gandhi, which resulted in the nationalisation of as many as nineteen banks in India during the Fourth Five Year Plan (1969–74). The Five-Year plans, which subsequently came into being until the Planning Commission itself was dissolved to establish the NITI Aayog, focused on issues such as poverty alleviation, provisioning of guaranteed employment, and inclusive growth during the Fifth Plan (1974–79), construction of highways during the Sixth Plan (1980–85), improved manufacturing productivity during the Seventh Plan (1985–89), etc (Dharia, 2011). From 1990 to 1992, there were only annual plans. In 1991, India faced a massive economic crisis in its Foreign Exchange (FOREX) Reserves, which prompted the ushering in of the neoliberal reforms.

13 For example, Singh (2009), in his book on the public sector postal system in India narrates that during the Bombay and Surat riots of 1928, the post offices delivered post while being under police protection but even then 'in February 1929 . . . 17 post offices including the G.P.O were badly affected and 17 post offices had to be closed down for a number of days' (p. 97) while many in the postal department – public employees – delivered exceptional courage in saving letters and money orders from being burnt and looted.

14 The norm set by the WHO is that any country should ideally possess 1 doctor for every 1,000 people, whereas in India the ratio is almost 1:1,456. Similarly, India has around 1.7 nurses per 1,000 people whereas the WHO standards set it to be 1 nurse for every 500 people. The number of beds for every 1,000 people in India is reportedly as low as 0.53, while the global average stands at 2.9 as per data from the OECD in 2017 (DebGupta, 2021).

15 The Bhore Committee was set up by the Government of India in 1943 under Joseph William Bhore. It was also known as the Health Survey and Development Committee. For more details, one can refer to Duggal, R. (1991). Bhore Committee (1946) and its relevance today. *The Indian Journal of Paediatrics*, 58, 395–406. Retrieved December 1, 2023, from https://doi.org/10.1007/BF02750917

16 For the first time in over 40 years, India registered a negative growth rate. At the same time, the unemployment rate in India has been on the rise since January 2020. As per the data provided by the Centre for Monitoring Indian Economy, the rate of unemployment in India reached its peaked in May 2020 at 24%

which includes 26% in urban India and 23% in rural India. The rate came down to 7% by November 2020 (UNESCO, 2021). An UNESCO report which cites this data states, 'Close to 122 million Indians had lost their jobs in April alone. Of these, 91.3 million were small traders and labourers. A significant number of salaried workers (17.8 million) and self-employed people (18.2 million) also lost work' (2021, p. 12). These are the conditions under which COVID-19 made its way into the Indian society.

17 Cases of domestic violence almost increased by 100% during the pandemic, especially during lockdowns as recorded by the National Commission for Women (NCW) (Mander, 2021). The NCW data has been reproduced in Chapter 6.

18 The horrors faced by migrant workers is nothing new in the history of independent India. Even during the Bhopal gas disaster in 1984 – arguably the most famous man-made disaster in post-independent India – migrant workers have always remained the worst sufferers (Lapierre & Moro, 2001).

19 Despite the government's reliance on them, larger and trusted NGOs such as ActionAid, Save the Children, Oxfam India, American India Foundation, SaveLIFE Foundation, Caritas, and World Vision have emphasised the role of the PHCs and CHCs in combating the pandemic (Anand, 2021, October 5).

20 Refers to a mythical plant from the Hindu epic Ramayana that supposedly cures deathly ailments and injuries.

21 Vidya Krishnan (2022), in her recent book, brings forward the various efforts that certain municipal bodies in the United States undertook to halt the spread of TB. These measures included a strict ban on spitting, which made the municipalities realise that ingrained habits are difficult to control and prevent through mere advertisement campaigns, 'So, cities stationed police officers on eery public conveyance and within every public building, and to mitigate gaps in enforcement, civilians were encouraged, even expected to stand up to spitters' (2022, p. 55). However, even some of the police officers, as she adds, remained unconvinced with the anti-spitting campaign, and saw no harm in it.

22 The housing situation of Dalits in India is extremely worrisome indicating massive inequalities in terms of sanitation, healthcare accessibility, and mortality rates (Ahmad, 2015). During the lockdown, the Dalit community found themselves to be facing the worst aspects of the lockdown, which included heightened social exclusionary measures and a process of rendering invisible their plight (Anand, 2020, October 5) through a rhetoric of universalism.

23 The pandemic is an important reminder to human beings that nature cannot be seen as alienated from human existence and vice versa. Right from the inception of primitive communism, nature and non-human beings have occupied an important position in the development of human society. The numerous relationships between nature and human society have never been static in nature, but rather have always been a highly dynamic one composed of a complex web of dynamic events. It has made one realise that even though non-human beings have been used for furthering human productivity since centuries, given the chance, these beings can easily reclaim *humanised* spaces. Ashton and Toland (2021) have argued that one of the major *takeaways* of the pandemic was the re-emergence of the social ethos towards animal welfare and empathy for other non-human beings. Empathy for animals has been found to be one of the most critical aspects of the human society's relationship to pandemics.

24 This is a consequence of the ways in which India's foreign policy has been shaped in recent years, which are increasingly moving away from previous positions of non-alignment and using the increased pharmaceutical manufacturing prowess during the COVID-19 pandemic to offset China's strategic advantages in the South Asian region as per Jaishankar (2020).

References

Agarwal, S. (2020, August 2). Oximeter sales soar but there is no guarantee of accurate reading and 'no govt regulations'. *The Print*. Retrieved December 1, 2023, from www.theprint.in/heath/oximeters-sales-soar-but-there-is-no-guarantee-of-accurate-reading-and-no-govt-regulations/472281/

Ahmad, S. (2015). Housing poverty and inequality in urban India. In A. Heshmati, E. Maasoumi, & G. Wan (Eds.), *Poverty reduction policies and practices in developing Asia*. Springer.

Aiyar, S. (2020). *The gated republic: India's public policy failures and private solutions*. Harper Collins Publishers India.

Ali, S. (2020, January 22). Dolo breaks sales record; sells over 350 crore pills during COVID-19 pandemic. *Business Today*. Retrieved December 1, 2023, from www.businesstoday.in/industry/pharma/story/dolo-breaks-sales-record-sells-over-350-crore-pills-during-covid-19-pandemic-319974-2022-01-22

Anand, G., Wankhede, K., Raman, R. V., Deb, A., & MJ, V. (2016). Tracing exclusions in urban water supply and sanitation. In *India exclusion report 2015*. Centre for Equity Press and Yoda Press.

Anand, P. (2021, October 5). How NGOs have silently helped Indians combat the Covid-19 pandemic. *The News Minute*. Retrieved December 1, 2023, from www.thenewsminute.com/article/how-ngos-have-silently-helped-indians-combat-the-covid-19-pandemic-156115

Anderson, K. B. (2020). *Dialectics of revolution*. Daraja Press.

Ando, G. (2020, July 8). Prices of essential Covid-19 Medicines have increased 4% globally since February. *Pharmaceutical Technology*. Retrieved December 1, 2023, from www.pharmaceutical-technology.com/pricing-and-market-access/prices-essential-covid19-medicines-increased-4-percent-globally.htm/

Arakal, R. A. (2020, May 28). Karnataka: Passengers pop pills to evade thermal screening, government says trick won't work. *The Indian Express*. Retrieved December 1, 2023, from www.indianexpress.com/article/cities/bangalore/airport-flights-paracetamol-thermal-screening-6431453/

Arendt, H. (1969). *On violence*. Harcourt Brace Jovanovich Publishers.

Arnold, G. (2012). *Migration: Changing the world*. Pluto Press.

Ashton, J., & Toland, S. (2021). *The new normal: A roadmap to resilience in the pandemic era*. William Morrow.

Bajpai, N., & Wadhwa, M. (2020). *Covid-19 in India: Issues, challenges and lessons*. ICT Working Paper # 34. Center for Sustainable Development.

Banerji, A. (2020, September 21). Indian street vendors 'shattered' as Coronavirus wrecks trade. *Reuters*. Retrieved December 1, 2023, from www.reuters.com/artcile/healthcoronavirus-india-workers-idUSL8N2GB44R

Basu, S. (2021, April 18). State-owned vaccine manufactures sit idle as India scours for jabs: Report. *The National Herald*. Retrieved December 1, 2023, from www.nationalheraldindia.com/india/state-owned-vaccine-manufacturers-sit-idle-as-india-scours-for-jabs-report

Beck, U. (1992). *Risk society: Towards a new modernity*. Sage.

Bhadala, T. (2021, May 20). Oximeter for Covid-19: Sellers using loopholes in India's MRP regime to overcharge. *Down to Earth*. Retrieved December 1, 2023, from https://downtoearth.org.in/health/oximeter-for-covid-19-sellers-using-loopholes-in-indias-mrp-regime-to-overcharge-77018

Bhalotia, S., Dhingra, S., & Kondirolli, F. (2020). *City of dreams no more: The impact of Covid-19 on urban workers in India*. Covid-19 Analysis Series. Centre for Economic Performance, London School of Economics and Political Science.

Bisen, A. (2019). *Wasted: The messy story of sanitation in India, a manifesto for change*. Pan Macmillan.

Bose, R., & Saxena, N. C. (2016). Strife in a metro: Affirming rights to admission in the city of Delhi. In *India exclusion report 2016*. Centre for Equity Studies.
Business Today. (2021, April 23). BJP slams Delhi CM for breaking protocol; CM Kejriwal's office 'regrets' televised appeal. *Business Today*. Retrieved December 1, 2023, from www.businesstoday.in/current/economy-politics/bjp-slams-delhi-cm-for-breaking-protocol-cm-kejriwal-office-regrets-televised-appeal/story/437401.html
Chen, M. A., Grapsa, E., Ismail, G., Rogan, M., Valdivia, M., Alfers, L., Harvey, J., Ogando, A. C., Reed, S. O., & Roever, S. (2022). COVID-19 and informal work: Evidence from 11 cities. *International Labour Review*, 161(1), 29–58.
Chintan, R. (2022, April 5). Increase in drug prices will hit people hard – need for reorienting drug pricing and production policy. *Newsclick*. Retrieved December 1, 2023, from www.newsclick/in/Increase-Drug-Prices-Will-Hit-People-Hard-Need-Re-orienting-Drug-Pricing-Production-Policy
Cooper, H., Nye, B., Charlton, K., Lindsay, J., & Greathouse, S. (1996). The effects of Summer vacation on achievement test scores: A narrative and meta-analytic review. *Review of Educational Research*, 66(3), 227–268.
Dadhich, A. (2020, April 22). The Covid-19 pandemic and the Indian pharmaceutical industry. *European Pharmaceutical Review*. Retrieved December 1, 2023, from www.europeanpharmaceuticalreview.com/article/117413/the-covid-19-pandemic-and-the-indian-pharmaceutical-industry/
Das, G. (2000). *India unbound: From independence to the global information age*. Penguin.
Das, G. (2012). *The elephant paradigm: India wrestles with change*. Penguin.
Das, S. (2021, January 4). Covishield to cost Rs 200/dose for first 100 MN doses to govt: Serum CEO. *Business Standard*. Retrieved December 1, 2023, from www.business-standard.com/article/current-affairs/covishield-to-cost-rs-200-does-for-first-100-mn-doses-to-govt-serum-ceo-121010300906_1.html
Das, S., & Seth, D. (2021, April 20). Serum, Bharat Biotech to get suppliers' credit for 300 MN Covid-19 doses. *Business Standard*. Retrieved December 1, 2023, from www.business-standard.com/article/current-affairs/serum-bharat-biotech-to-get-suppliers-credit-for-300-mn-covid-19-doses-121042000059_1.html
DebGupta, A. (2021). Dynamics of the public healthcare model. In K. Sarkar (Ed.), *The sickness of health: Journey of India's healthcare from colonial era to Corona*. BEE Books.
Dehury, R. K., Samal, J., Coutinho, S., & Dehury, P. (2019). How does the largely unregulated private health sector impact the Indian mass? *Journal of Health Management*, 21(3), 383–393.
Desai, A. R. (1991). Housing: Chaos? – Blame the victims! In A. R. Desai (Ed.), *Expanding governmental lawlessness and organised struggles: Violation of democratic rights of minorities, women, slum dwellers, press and some other violations*. Popular Prakashan.
Desai, A. R., & Pillai, S. D. (1990). Portrait of a Bombay slum. In A. R. Desai & S. D. Pillai (Eds.), *Slums and urbanization*. Popular Prakashan.
Dharia, M. (2011). *India's glorious freedom struggle and the post-independence era*. National Book Trust.
Dhingra, S., & Kondirolli, F. (2021). *City of dreams no more, a year on: Worklessness and active labour market policies in urban India*. Covid-19 Analysis Series. Centre for Economic Performance, London School of Economics and Political Science.
Diamond, J. (2019). *Upheaval: How nations cope with crisis and change*. Allen Lane.
Digital Medic. (2021, March 29). *The role of NGOs in Covid-19 community-based education*. Retrieved December 1, 2023, from www.digitalmedic.stanford.edu/general/the-role-of-ngos-in-covid-19-community-based-education/
Dunayevskaya, R. (1967). *State-capitalism and Marx's humanism or philosophy and revolution*. News and Letters.

Dunayevskaya, R. (1979). Marx and Engels' studies contrasted: Relationship of philosophy and revolution to women's liberation. In *The Raya Dunayevskaya collection – Marxist-humanism: A half century of its world development*. Wayne State University Archives of Labor and Urban Affairs.

Dunayevskaya, R. (2002a). Marxist-humanism: The summation that is a new beginning, subjectively and objectively. In P. Hudis & K. B. Anderson (Eds.), *The power of negativity: Selected writings on the dialectic in Hegel and Marx by Raya Dunayevskaya*. Lexington Books. (Original work published 1983)

Dunayevskaya, R. (2002b). Presentation on the dialectics of organisation and philosophy. In P. Hudis & K. B. Anderson (Eds.), *The power of negativity: Selected writings on the dialectics in Hegel and Marx*. Lexington Books. (Original work published 1987)

Dunayevskaya, R. (2002c). Marxist-humanism: The summation that is a new beginning, subjectively and objectively. In P. Hudis & K. B. Anderson (Eds.), *The power of negativity*. Lexington Books.

Dutt, B. (2022). *To hell and back: Humans of Covid*. Juggernaut.

The Economic Times. (2022, January 13). Deadly Delta Wave stole 240,000 lives in India between April-June, 'similar episodes' could take place in near term: UN report. *The Economic Times*. Retrieved December 1, 2023, from www.economictimes.indiatimes.com/news/india/deadly/-delta-wave-stole-240000-lives-in-india-between-april-june-similar-episodes-could-take-place-in-near-term-un-report/articleshpw/88883714.cms

Egan, T. (2020). Introduction. In J. Sternfeld (Ed.), *Unprepared: America in the time of Coronavirus*. Bloomsbury.

Einstein, A. (2012a). The question of disarmament. In J. Green (Ed.), *Albert Einstein: Selected writings*. Leftword. (Original work published 1934)

Einstein, A. (2012b). America and the disarmament conference of 1932. In J. Green (Ed.), *Albert Einstein: Selected writings*. Leftword. (Original work published 1934)

Einstein, A. (2012c). The world as I see it. In J. Green (Ed.), *Albert Einstein: Selected writings*. Leftword. (Original work published 1931)

Eyles, A., Gibbons, S., & Montebruno, P. (2020). *Covid-19 school shutdowns: What will they do to our children's education?* Centre for Economic Performance, London School for Economics and Political Science.

Fiorini, M., & Keane, M. (2014). How the allocation of children's time affects cognitive and noncognitive development. *Journal of Labour Economics*, 32(4), 787–836.

Firstpost. (2021, May 3). Centre claims no shortage of oxygen, warns against hoarding cylinders; India's tally at 1.99 crore. *Firstpost*. Retrieved December 1, 2023, from www.firstpost.com/centre-cliams-no-shortage-of-oxygen-warns-against-black-marketing-indias-tally-news-two-crore-mark-9588991.html

Fromm, E. (1942/2001). *The fear of freedom*. Routledge.

Gandhi-Mody, P. (2022). *A nation to protect: Leading India through the Covid crisis*. Rupa Publications.

Ghosh, J. (2019–2020). Public employment for public purpose. In *India exclusion report*. Three Essays Collective and Centre for Equity Studies.

Gokhale, M., Bavadekar, R., & Chaudhuri, S. (2022). *Cheating Covid: A family's journey to hell and back*. Vitasta Publishing House.

Goldberg, S. (2019). *How to be a patient: The essential guide to navigating the world of modern medicine*. Harper Wave.

Goswami, O. (2016). *Goras and Desis: Managing agencies and making of corporate India*. Portfolio.

Goyal, P. (2020). Wet markets and food laws in India: What is needed to ensure safety and hygiene? *Economic and Political Weekly*, 55(31). www.epw.in/engage/article/wet-markets-and-food-laws-india-what-needed-ensure-safety-hygiene

Gupta, N., Agrawal, S., Ish, P., Mishra, S., Gaind, S., Usha, G., Singh, B., Sen, M. K., & Safdargunj Hospital COVID 19 Working Group. (2020). Clinical and epidemiological profile of the initial COVID-19 patients at a tertiary care centre in India. *Monaldi Archives for Chest Disease*, 90(1). https://doi.org/10.4081/monaldi.2020.1294

Hale, T., Webster, S., Petherick, A., & Phillips, T. K. (2020). *COVID-19 government response tracker*. Oxford University Press.

Harriss-White, B. (2019). Small town waste and its lifeworld. In *India exclusion report, 2018–19*. Three Essays Collective and Centre for Equity Studies.

Harsheeta, & Arora, M. (2020). *Alienation and resistance: Understanding Corona affected families*. National Book Trust.

Hart-Landsberg, M. (2013). *Capitalist globalization: Consequences, resistance and alternatives*. Monthly Review Press.

Heraud, B. (1979). *Sociology in the professions*. Open Books.

The Hindu. (2021, April 27). Demand for pulse oximeters up. *The Hindu*. Retrieved December 1, 2023, from www.thenhindu.com/news/national/kerala/demand-for-pulse-oximeters-up/article34418510.ece

Hindustan Times. (2021, November 27). Which states and UTs are among India's poorest? List here. *Hindustan Times*. Retrieved December 1, 2023, from www.hindustantimes.com/india-news/which-states-and-uts-are-among-india-s-poorest-list-here-101639365634094

Honigsbaum, M. (2020). *The pandemic century: A history of global contagion from the spanish flu to Covid-19*. Penguin.

Horton, R. (2020). *The Covid-19 catastrophe: What's gone wrong and how to stop it happening again*. Polity.

Houtenville, A., & Conway, K. (2008). Parental effort, school resources, and student achievement. *The Journal of Human Resources*, 43(2), 437–453.

Hupkau, C., Isphording, I., Machin, S., & Ruiz-Valenzuela, J. (2020). *Labour market shocks during the Covid-19 pandemic: Inequalities and child outcomes*. Centre for Economic Performance, London School for Economics and Political Science.

Hupkau, C., & Petrongolo, B. (2021). *Work, care and gender during the Covid-19 crisis*. Centre for Economic Performance, London School of Economics and Political Science.

Jaffrelot, C., & Jumle, V. (2020, November 3). Private healthcare in India: Boons and banes. *Institut Montaigne*. Retrieved December 1, 2023, from www.institutmontaigne.org/en/blog/private-healthcare-india-boons-and-banes

Jain, M. (2017, August 2). Private sector profits in healthcare soar as Indian government investment stagnates. *Scroll*. Retrieved December 1, 2023, from www.scroll.in/pulse/845539/private-sectors-profits-in-healthcare-soar-as-indian-government-investment-stagnates

Jaishankar, S. (2020). *The India way: Strategies for an uncertain world*. Harper Collins Publishers India.

Jalan, B. (2005). *The future of India: Politics, economics and governance*. Penguin Viking.

Jalan, B. (2019). *Resurgent India: Politics, economics and governance*. Harper Collins Publishers India.

Jalan, B. (2021). *India after liberalisation: An overview*. Harper Collins.

Jayaram, N., & Jain, P. (2020). Protection of wages of seasonal, circular migrant labour in India. In *India exclusion report, 2019–20*. Three Essays Collective and Centre for Equity Studies.

Jha, M. K., & Pankaj, A. K. (2020). Insecurity and fear travel as labour travels in the time of pandemic. In R. Samaddar (Ed.), *Borders of an epidemic: Covid-19 and migrant workers*. Calcutta Research Group.

Kamath, A., & Kumar, V. (2017, November 24). In India, accessible phones lead to inaccessible opportunities. *The Wire*. Retrieved December 1, 2023, from www.thewire.in/article/caste/india-accessible-phones-lead-to-inaccessible-opportunities/

KANTAR and IAMAI. (2020). *Internet adoption in India: ICUBE 2020*. IAMAI and KANTAR.

Kapri, V. (2021). *1232 KM: The long journey back home*. Harper Collins Publishers India.

Krishnan, V. (2022). *Phantom plague: How tuberculosis shaped history*. Penguin Random House.

Kularski, C., & Moller, S. (2012). The digital divide as a continuation of traditional systems of inequality. *Sociology, 51*.

Kupperberg, P. (2008). *The influenza pandemic of 1918–1919*. Chelsea House Publishers.

Lal, V. (2020). *The fury of Covid-19: The politics, histories, and unrequited love of the Coronavirus*. Pan Macmillan.

Lapierre, D., & Moro, J. (2001). *Five past midnight in Bhopal*. Grand Central Publishing.

Leopold, E., & McDonald, D. A. (2012). Municipal socialism then and now: Some lessons for the global South. *Third World Quarterly, 33*(10), 1837–1853.

Lowenstein, A. (2015). *Disaster capitalism: Making a killing out of a catastrophe*. Verso.

Mackenzie, D. (2020). *COVID-19: The pandemic that never should have happened and how to stop the next one*. Hachette Books.

Mackintosh, M., & Koivusalo, M. (Eds.). (2005). *Commercialisation of health care: Global and local dynamics and policy responses*. Palgrave Macmillan.

Majithia, A. S. (2020). *Impact of COVID-19 on street vendors in India: Status and steps for advocacy*. Women in Informal Employment: Globalizing and Organizing. Retrieved December 1, 2023, from www.wiego.org/impact-covid-19-street-vendors-india-status-and-steps-advocacy

Major, L. E., Eyles, A., & Machin, S. (2021). *Learning loss since lockdown: Variation across the home nations*. Centre for Economic Performance, London School for Economics and Political Science.

Mandal, D. (2020, July 19). India's oppressed groups had high hopes from Internet: But upper castes got in there too. *The Print*. Retrieved December 1, 2023, from www.theprint.in/opinion/indias-oppressed-groups-had-high-hopes-from-internet-but-upper-castes-got-in-there-too/463431/

Mander, H. (2016). Public goods, exclusion, and 25 years of economic reforms: A blotted balance sheet. In *India exclusion report 2016*. Centre for Equity Studies.

Mander, H. (2020). In the shadow of Covid-19. In *India exclusion report, 2019–20*. Three Essays Collective and Centre for Equity Studies.

Mander, H. (2021). *Locking down the poor: The pandemic and India's moral centre*. Speaking Tiger.

Manzar, O., Kumar, R., Mukherjee, E., & Aggarwal, R. (2016). Exclusion from digital infrastructure and access. In *India exclusion report 2016*. Centre for Equity Studies and Yoda Press.

Marwaha, P. (2021, February 27). Celebrating the role of Indian NGOs in combating the Covid-19 pandemic. *Down to Earth*. Retrieved December 1, 2023, from www.downtoearth.org.in/blog/governance/celebrating-the-role-of-indian-ngos-in-combating-the-covid-19-pandemic-75597

Marwaha, P. (2021, March 1). The role of NGOs in combating Covid-19 pandemic. *The Hans India*. Retrieved December 1, 2023, from www.thehansindia.com/hans/opinion/news-analysis/the-role-of-ngos-in-combating-covid-19-pandemic-674577

Marx, K. (1844/1975). Economic and philosophical manuscripts of 1844. In *Marx Engels collected works: Volume 3*. Lawrence and Wishart.

Mathew, C. K. (2020). *The historical evolution of the district officer: From early days to 1947*. Azim Premji University Press.

Mathur, K. (2008). *From government to governance: A brief survey of the Indian experience*. National Book Trust.

McDonald, D. A., & Ruiters, G. (2005). Introduction: From public to private (to public again?). In D. A. McDonald & G. Ruiters (Eds.), *The age of commodity: Water privatisation in South Africa*. Earthscan.

Mishra, A., & Santosh, S. (2021). *Aren't we frontline warriors? Experiences of grassroots health workers during Covid-19*. Azim Premji University.

Mohan, S. (2021, May 13). Price hike of raw materials for Covid drugs adds to Kerala's woes. *The New Indian Express*. Retrieved December 1, 2023, from https://newindianexpress.com/states/kerala/2021/may/13/price-hike-of-raw-materials-for-covid-drugs-adds-to-keralas-woes-2301869.html

Mosley, M. (2020). *COVID-19: What you need to know about the coronavirus and the race for the vaccine*. ATRIA Books.

Mukherjee, U. (2020). *Essential items and other tales from a land in lockdown*. Bloomsbury India.

Mukul, J. (2022). *The great shutdown: A story of two Indian Summers*. Harper Collins.

Munck, R. (2013). The precariat: A view from the South. *Third World Quarterly, 34*(5), 747–762.

Murdoch, D. (2020). The next once-in-a-century pandemic is coming sooner than you think, but Covid-19 can help us get ready. In M. Glassey (Ed.), *2020: The year that changed us*. Thames and Hudson.

Nambiar, D., Ganesan, P., Rao, A., Motwani, G., Alkazi, R., Murugan, G., Sundararaman, T., & Sinha, D. (2016). 'Who cares?' Urban health care and exclusion. In *India exclusion report 2015*. Centre for Equity Press and Yoda Press.

The News Minute. (2021, April 20). Govt to boost vaccine production: SII to get Rs 3000 cr, Bharat biotech Rs 1500 crore. *The News Minute*. Retrieved December 1, 2023, from www.thenewsminute.com/article/govt-boost-vaccine-production-sii-get-rs-3000-cr-bharat-biotech-rs-1500-crore-147490

Nihalani, J. (2022, April 11). From paracetamol to stroke medicine: Check how much medicine prices increased this year. *The Hindu*. Retrieved December 1, 2023, from www.thehindu.com/data-from-paracetamol-to-stroke-medicine-check-how-much-medicine-prices-increased-this-year/article65311448.ece

OECD. (2022, March 17). *The unequal impact of COVID-19: A spotlight on frontline workers, migrants and racial/ethnic minorities*. Retrieved December 1, 2023, from www.oecd.org/coronavirus/policy-responses/the-unequal-impact-of-covid-19-a-spotlight-on-frontline-workers-migrants-and-racial-ethnic-minorities/

Pande, A. (2020). *Making India great: The promise of a reluctant global power*. Harper Collins Publishers India.

Paqué, K.-H. (2020, December 17). Covid-19 vaccine: Why we should bow to capitalism right now. *Friedrich Naumann Foundation for Freedom*. Retrieved December 1, 2023, from www.freiheit.org/turkey/covid-19-vaccine-why-we-should-bow-capitalism-right-now

Perappadan, B. S. (2020, January 30). India first Coronavirus Infection confirmed in Kerala. *The Hindu*. Retrieved December 1, 2023, from www.thehindu.com/news/national/indias-first-coronavirus-case-confirmed-in-kerala/

Perrow, C. (2007). *The next catastrophe: Reducing our vulnerabilities to natural, industrial and terrorist disasters*. Princeton University Press.

Pillai, S. D. (1990). Slums and squatters. In A. R. Desai & S. D. Pillai (Eds.), *Slums and urbanization*. Popular Prakashan. (Original work published 1970)

Pithode, T. (2022). *The battle against Covid: Diary of a bureaucrat*. Bloomsbury.

Posadas, J. (1968). Flying saucers, the process of matter and energy, science and socialism. In *Socialism and human relationships with nature and the cosmos*. Scientific, Cultural and Political Editions.

Posadas, J. (1978). The crisis of capitalism, war and socialism. In *War, peace, and the function of the socialist countries*. Scientific, Cultural and Political Editions.

Pradhan, B. (2019). *S. Ramesh Chandra Agarwal: The man who created the Dainik Bhaskar group*. Amaryllis.
Prasad, P. (2018). Health care reforms: Do they ensure social protection for the labouring poor? In P. Prasad & A. Jesani (Eds.), *Equity and access: Health care studies in India*. Oxford University Press.
Price, L. (2015). *The Modi effect: Inside Narendra Modi's campaign to transform India*. Hodder and Stoughton.
Priya, R. (2018). State, community, and primary health care: Empowering or disempowering discourses. In P. Prasad & A. Jesani (Eds.), *Equity and access: Health care studies in India*. Oxford University Press.
Quammen, D. (2020). *Spillover: Animal infections and the next human pandemic*. Vintage. (Original work published 2012)
Raj, A. (2021, February 1). Budget 2021: 'Increase healthcare expenditure from 1.2% to 2.5% of GDP'. *Business Today*. Retrieved December 1, 2023, from www.businesstoday.in/union-budget-2021/expectations/increase-healthcare-expenditure-from-12-to-25-of-gdp/story/429780.html
Raj, C. A., & K., M. (2020, July 2). As Covid-19 Puts India's largest cities under strain, municipalities must rethink finance strategies. *Scroll*. Retrieved December 1, 2023, from www.scroll.in/article/966210/as-covid-19-puts-indias-largest-cities-under-strain-municipalities-must-rethink-finance-strategies
Rajalakhsmi, T. K. (2021, July 2). Perils of vacuous claims. *Frontline*, 20–23.
Ramachandran, P. (1990). The slum: A note on facts and solutions. In A. R. Desai & S. D. Pillai (Eds.), *Slums and urbanization*. Popular Prakashan. (Original work published 1970)
Ramachandran, P., & Ramkumar, V. (2005). *Education in India*. National Book Trust.
Ramachandran, R. (2022, June 3). Controversial count. *Frontline*, 46–49.
Ramin, C. J. (2017). *Crooked: Outwitting the back pain industry and getting on the road to recovery*. Harper.
Rao, A. (2021, May 6). India is hiding its Covid crisis – and the whole world will suffer for it. *The Guardian*. Retrieved December 1, 2023, from www.theguardian.com/commentisfree/2021/may/06/india-covid-crisis-narendra-modi-government-hiding
Rao, K. S. (2017). *Do we care? India's health system*. Oxford University Press.
Reddy, K. S. (2019). *Make health in India: Reaching a billion plus*. Orient Blackswan.
Reddy, K. S. (2022, February 2). Budget lacks push for primary healthcare: K Srinath Reddy, President, public health foundation of India. *Financial Express*. Retrieved December 1, 2023, from www.financialexpress.com/budget/budget-lacks-push-for-primary-healthcare/2423447/
Roy, A. (2021, May 7). "It's a crime against humanity": Is India's Covid catastrophe of Modi's making. *The Guardian Weekly*, 204(20).
Salam, Z. U. (2021, July 2). The virus of hate. *Frontline*.
Samantha, T. (2020, March 30). A beginner's guide to the importance of social capital during a pandemic. *The Wire*. Retrieved December 1, 2023, from www.thewire.in/article/government/physical-distnacing-social-capital-coronavirus-pandemic-public-confidence
Sardesai, R. (2015). *2014: The election that changed India*. Penguin.
Sastri, S., & Bandyopadhyay, A. (2021). *The ventilator project: How the IIT Kanpur consortium built a world-class product during India's Covid-19 lockdown*. Macmillan.
Schlosser, E. (2001). *Fast food nation: The dark side of the all-American meal*. Houghton Mifflin Company.
Sengupta, A. (2018). Globalisation, intellectual property rights, and pharmaceuticals. In P. Prasad & A. Jesani (Eds.), *Equity and access: Health care studies in India*. Oxford University Press.

Sengupta, A., & Nundy, S. (2005). The private health sector in India. *BMJ, 331*(7526), 1157–1158.
Shah, S. (2010). *The fever: How malaria has ruled humankind for 500,000 years*. Penguin.
Shameem, M. (2022). Digging deeper wounds. In D. Aggarwal & S. Sundaram (Eds.), *A world on hold: A living record of the global pandemic*. Om Books International.
Sharma, J. (2022). *Made in lockdown: India's MedTech growth powered by AMTZ*. Rupa.
Sharma, N. (2022, July 8). Only 40% street vendors repay working capital loan given during Covid-19. *The Economic Times*. Retrieved December 1, 2023, from www.economictimes.com/industry/finance/only-40-street-vendors-repay-working-capital-loan-given-during-covid-19/articleshow/92733078.cms
Sharma, N. C. (2022, January 27). What is full market authorisation and why did Covishield, Covaxin get it? *Business Today*. Retrieved December 1, 2023, from www.businesstoday.in/coronavirus/story/what-is-full-market-authorisation-and-why-did-covishield-covaxin-get-it-320553-2022-01-27
Shraya, V. (2022). *Next time there's a pandemic*. University of Alberta Press.
Sibanda, F., Muyambo, T., & Chitando, E. (2022). Religion and public health in the shadow of COVID-19 PAndemic in Southern Africa. In F. Sibanda, T. Muyambo, & E. Chitando (Eds.), *Religion and the COVID-19 pandemic in Southern Africa*. Routledge.
Singh, A. K. (2009). *India post: A journey through ages* (S. Das, Trans.). National Book Trust.
Singh, S. (2018). *The great smog of India*. Penguin.
Singh, S. S. (2021, April 20). Centre evading responsibility on vaccines: Mamata Banerjee in letter to PM Modi. *The Hindu*. Retrieved December 1, 2023, from www.thehindu.com/news/national/other-states/mamata-banerjee-accuses-pm-modi-of-allowing-open-market-sale-of-vaccines-after-depleting-stocks-through-gifts-abroad/article34367373.ece
Sismondo, S. (2018). *Ghost-managed medicine: Big pharma's invisible hands*. Mattering Press.
Smedley, T. (2019). *Clearing the air: The beginning and end of air pollution*. Bloomsbury.
Smith, M. C., Kolassa, E. M., & Pray, W. S. (2021). *Government, big pharma, and the people: A century of dis-ease*. Routledge.
Sood, R. (2021, May 4). Collapse of the 'vishwaguru' in 60 days. *The Print*. Retrieved December 1, 2023, from www.theprint.in/opinion/opinion/collapse-of-the-vishwaguru-in-60-days/
Srivastava, V., & Priyadarshini, S. (2020, January 30). India reports first case of novel Coronavirus. *Nature*. Retrieved December 1, 2023, from www.nature.com/articles/nindia.2020.15
Sternfeld, J. (2020). Author's note. In J. Sternfeld (Ed.), *Unprepared: America in the time of Coronavirus*. Bloomsbury.
Tazzioli, M. (2020). *The making of migration: The biopolitics of mobility at Europe's borders*. Sage.
Thakur, A. (2020, May 25). No, the Paracetamol trick won't work with airport staff anymore. *Deccan Chronicle*. Retrieved December 1, 2023, from www.deccanchronicle.com/nation/current-affairs/250520/no-the-paracetamol-trick-wont-work-with-airport-staff-anymore.html
The Times of India. (2020, March 21). Covid-19: 'Many took meds to dodge isolation'. *The Times of India*. Retrieved December 1, 2023, from www.timesofindia.com/india/covid-19-many-took-meds-to-dodge-isolation/articleshow/74740303.cms
Todd, P., & Wolpin, K. (2003). On the specification and estimation of the production function for cognitive achievement. *Economic Journal, 113*(485), 3–33.
Trivedi, D. (2021, November 19). Uneven drive. *Frontline*, 20.

Tumbe, C. (2018). *India moving: A history of migration*. Penguin Random House India.

Turner, S., Langill, J. C., & Nguyen, B. N. (2021). The utterly unforeseen livelihood shock: COVID-19 and street vendor coping mechanisms in Hanoi, Chiang Mai, and Luang Prabang. *Singapore Journal of Tropical Geography*, *42*. https://doi.org/10.111/sjtg.12396

UNESCO. (2021). *India case study: Situation analysis on the effects of the responses to COVID-19 on the education sector in Asia*. UNESCO.

United Nations. (2003). *The challenge of slums: Global report on human settlements 2003*. Earthscan.

Unni, A., & Panwar, T. (2019, April 5). What the last five years of urban policies reveal about our cities. *The Wire*. Retrieved December 1, 2023, from www.thewire.in/article/urban/urban-planning-india-elections

Veeraraghav, S. (2020). *No lockdown on caste atrocities: Stories of caste crimes during the Covid-19 pandemic*. Zubaan.

Vilanilam, J. V. (2003). *Growth and development of mass communication in India*. National Book Trust.

Visvanathan, S. (2018). Socio-logic of corruption. In S. Nundy, K. Desiraju, & S. Nagral (Eds.), *Healers or predators: Healthcare corruption in India*. Oxford University Press.

Vora, R. V., Sridhar, N., & Law, A. (2022, April 9). Bharat biotech, serum institute slash vaccine prices to Rs 225 per dose. *Business Line*. Retrieved December 1, 2023, from www.thehindubusinessline.com/companies-bharat-biotech-serum-institute-slash-vaccine-prices-to-rs-225-per-dose/article65306318.ece

Waghmore, S., & Gorringe, H. (2019). Towards civility? Citizenship, publicness and the politics of inclusive democracy in India. *South Asia: Journal of South Asian Studies*, *42*, 301–309. https://doi.org/10.1080/00856401.2019.1573714

Wallace, R. (2016). *Big farms make big flu*. Monthly Review Press.

Waterman, P. (2001). *Globalisation, social movements and the new internationalisms*. Continuum.

Williams, R. (1978). Problems of materialism. *New Left Review*, *1*(109).

Yadav, S. (2020, July 13). Pulse oximeter sales surge, but imports hurt market share: Indian firms. *The Indian Express*. Retrieved December 1, 2023, from www.indianexpress.com/article/india/coronavirus-pulse-oximeter-sales-surge-but-imports-hurt-market-share-indian-firms-6502809/

Zanoni, P., & Mir, R. (2022). COVID-19: Interrogating the capitalist organization of the economy and the society through the pandemic. *Organization*, *29*(3), 369–378.

Žižek, S. (2017). *The courage of hopelessness: Chronicles of a year of acting dangerously*. Allen Lane.

2 The Monstrosity of Disasters under Capitalism

Introduction

Apocalyptic disasters are extremely common under capitalist modes of production that value profits over and above human lives and nature, especially in countries such as India that are plagued by widespread semi-feudal exploitation along with mainstream capitalist oppression. Marginalised individuals face the risk of becoming victims of disasters every day in urban India. The genesis of these highly marginalised workers in the urban areas, however, lies in rural India, where the people have been facing *disasters on repeat* for many years now. The development of neoliberalism in India has contributed to the construction of a high-risk society that has created a society, where marginalised people are always at the risk of being severely affected by disasters. Rural India, over the course of the last few decades, has also been at the centre of the economic disaster that neoliberal capitalism has produced, creating growing poverty, distress migration, and health issues (Sainath, 1996; Hardikar, 2013, 2021; Iyer, 2021). Rural India suffers from many malaises, one among which is the lack of drinkable and irrigatable water, which also has an impact on the widespread migration that one has seen in the urban areas. As Iyer writes:

> Every year, thousands of farmer families fleeing water scarcity and near-total loss of crops in Marathwada[1] also arrive in the big cities. Even the squalor and disease of Mumbai's slums hold some promise for them. Migration cleaves families, as children are often left behind with relatives. Families that stay back in the villages walk miles for water in the summer and duel the lack of livelihood and the depletion of resources including livestock . . . [along with half of the rural families having] outstanding loans from banks and usurious private lenders.
>
> (Iyer, 2021, p. 9)

These migrant workers constitute an important part of the Indian economy creating discretionary wealth for the elites. This is also the section of the working class that had been forced to walk for thousands of kilometres back to their homes when the nation went into a complete lockdown in March 2020 (Dasgupta, 2022). The crisis faced by migrants in India forced the United Nations Children's Fund (UNICEF) to release a statement talking about the necessity of the public health responses to reach the most vulnerable sections of the populace. An early report in Reuters stated:

> Nearly 200 migrant workers died in road accidents in India returning to their village homes during the world's longest coronavirus lockdown. . . . More than 1,400 road accidents killed 750 people, including 198 migrant workers, between March 25 and May 31, according to the SaveLIFE Foundation.
> (Banerji, 2020, June 2, Paras 1–3)

Contemporary migrant workers are a result of the economic liberalisation in India, which has pushed, as many as 9 million farmers out of the agriculture sector – from 2001 until 2011 – creating widespread migration resulting in 35–40 million seasonal labouring migrants in urban India (Prasad, 2018). Migrant workers often perform essential tasks required for sustaining the society that are often more risk-laden than other jobs, and because of the precarious nature of their jobs, they have been affected the most by the social vulnerabilities that the lockdown has exposed (York, 2022, April 19). The emergence of lockdowns – often at shocking speeds – is an important part of the disaster capitalism framework as lockdowns are crucial to resisting the potential collapse of the healthcare infrastructure of a neoliberal economic system, which is characterised by rampant privatisation (Alexiou, 2021), thus saving the privatised healthcare infrastructure from a complete collapse.

Rural distress, which produces such widespread migration, has inevitably had an impact on the urban social fabric, especially during the pandemic. Sainath (1996) quite correctly argues that when rural India is in distress, then the entire fabric of the nation is affected. The rural distress in India, as both Hardikar (2021) and Iyer (2021) have described in detail, has contributed significantly to the overall economic downturn that the nation has been facing.[2] Because of the distressing economic conditions under which COVID-19 has been unleashed upon the Indian society, it has highlighted the 'killer phase of capitalism' in the Indian society, caused by the complete devaluation of bodies (Sagot, 2022, p. 86). The 'killer phase of capitalism' significantly reduces the possibilities of a dignified human life and diminishes the chances of survival for the marginalised populace during disasters, converting them into victims and:

> The victim of a disaster is . . . unavoidably marked. As a victim of a disaster, is [one] part of its continuum? Is such an ill-fated individual also a sign, a fallen star in whose situation the suffering of others has been placed, as in the case of the scapegoat, or is that person, by coming

upon the scene, a divine warning? Much of this turns on whether the victim emerges as a survivor.

(Gordon & Gordon, 2007, p. 26)

The chances that a victim will emerge as a survivor are often slimmed down by the kind of neoliberal healthcare infrastructure that has come to dominate most of the major democracies in the world. For example, in the context of the United States, 'the 2008 recession had been a bloodbath for local health departments, trimming their workforces by a quarter and closing a dozen major public-health laboratories' (Davis, 2020, p. 32), which has contributed immensely to the apocalyptic situation that the United States found itself in during the COVID-19 pandemic. There was a similar situation in India as well. Years of neoliberal reforms have transformed the Indian healthcare infrastructure into a profit-driven one, putting an intense amount of pressure on the public sector by dividing the healthcare services into various segments engaging with diverse aspects of healthcare and thereby initiating the emergence of a profit-driven market mechanisms in the sector (Fouskas & Gokay, 2020; Steinberger, 2020).

The contemporary Indian healthcare infrastructure, as of 2021, is such that there is a shortfall of 3.5 million hospital beds in the public hospitals, and when combined with the private sector, this shortfall improves marginally only to a lack of around 2.4 million beds. While the global average hospital beds for 1,000 people stands at 3.2, in India, it stands at 0.5 and 1.4 in public and private hospitals, respectively (Housing Research, 2021). There are also serious urban-rural divides operating in this context – around 69% of the total beds in India are placed in urban areas, which houses most of the private healthcare infrastructure of the country. The NITI Aayog's (2021) official report itself confirms that the best-performing hospitals at a district level across the country are all situated in urban areas.[3] This disproportionate distribution proves that the impact of the developmental policies taken by the Indian state post-1991 has not produced the all-encompassing development that was promised.

When a state allows private corporations to enter the healthcare ecosystem of a society, then it basically leaves one of the most crucial aspects of human sustenance at the mercy of private benefits and competition. Neoliberal public intellectuals and thinkers such as Das (2000) argue that not opening up an industry or a sector to the private sector is tantamount to discouraging entrepreneurship and competition in the nation. However, competition is the soul and substance of the capitalist mode of production (Marx, 1867/1976). The healthcare sector is one of the most respected sectors in India, and it is also the fourth-largest employer in the country (Thomas et al., 2022). Because the healthcare sector is so important financially, it is almost inevitable that factors such as competition and corruption will emerge within the sector.

When competition is left unchecked, it is inevitable that many sellers will try to sell a similar commodity for higher profits. This will create the grounds for the emergence of newer forms of monopolies using various factors such as economic desires, social needs, and the state of crisis. Marx had noted, 'It is essential that the immovable monopoly turn into the mobile and restless monopoly, into competition; and the idle enjoyment of the products of other people's blood and sweat turn into a bustling commerce in the same commodity' (Marx, 1844, p. 267). Marx had noted:

> The same commodity is offered by various sellers. With goods of the same quality, the one who sells most cheaply is certain of driving the others out of the field and securing the greatest sale for himself. Thus, the sellers mutually contend among themselves for sales, for the market. Each of them desires to sell, to sell as much as possible and, if possible, to sell alone, to the exclusion of the other sellers. Hence, one sells cheaper than another. Consequently, *competition* takes place *among the sellers*, which *depress* the price of the commodities offered by them.
> (Marx, 1849/1977, p. 205)

During the outbreak of COVID-19, the fear of death played a crucial role in bringing forward the worst aspects of the competitive social psychology that capitalism tries to preserve in the society. Contrary to popular beliefs that portray disasters as levelling events, they are actually highly unequal events, where even the fear of death is disproportionately distributed across the socio-economic and cultural spectrum. Taking cue from this, the current chapter is divided into four subsections. The first section engages with the conditions of public health and its role during a disaster. The second section speaks about the disruptions of public services that had been caused by COVID-19, while the third section discusses about the politics of mortality rates and the processes through which human beings are turned into quantitative figures under capitalism. The fourth and final section discusses the dynamics of Big Pharma and privatised healthcare and their role during the COVID-19 pandemic.

Public Health and Disasters

The Public healthcare infrastructure in India is divided into three segments: primary healthcare, secondary healthcare, and tertiary healthcare, all of which remain underfunded for the time being and require drastic improvements – something that has remained constant throughout the pandemic (Sharma, 2020, August 17; Reddy, 2021, October 28). Such a magnitude of underfunding in a crucial sector owes itself to the relatively undemocratic and economistic nature of the Indian ruling class, which has prioritised economic development over and above actual human and community development (Dréze & Sen, 2013). The neoliberal economic reforms characterised by a rapid growth of private and corporate healthcare providers have contributed to the bourgeoning inequality in India, with most structural changes effected within the Indian healthcare infrastructure remaining oblivious and insensitive to the growing inequality and the continuous impoverishment of the primary and secondary healthcare systems in the country (Prasad, 2018). These processes have led to a rapid rise in the OOP expenditure for a huge section of the population, especially those coming from marginalised sections. The health financing profile prepared by the WHO shows that in 2017, the world average for OOP expenditure was 18.2%, but in India, it contributed to around 67% of the total expenditure on health (Housing Research, 2021). Such massive OOP expenditures create the grounds under which inequitable distribution of healthcare services are made to thrive and are normalised within mainstream media and political discourse. Because of these very reasons, India found itself in a massively disadvantageous position at the outbreak of the second wave of the COVID-19 pandemic.

The Indian government, however, took no cognisance of such issues. After the first wave of the pandemic subsided in the later part of 2020, the Indian government prematurely declared at the World Economic Forum's Davos Dialogue in January 2021 that under its governance, the country had been successful in battling and had actually already emerged victorious against the COVID-19 pandemic (The Quint, 2021, April 23). Since April 2021, however, India began witnessing a massive surge in the number of cases of COVID-19 and found itself wanting in terms of vaccine availability, its manufacturing capabilities (Sriram, 2021, April 15; The Hindu, 2021, April 29), hospital beds (James, 2021, April 20), and essential medical supplies, especially medical oxygen (Moole, 2021, April 23; Ghoshal, 2021, April 24). It must also be taken into consideration that the vaccine and oxygen crises occurred despite the fact that, as of 2021, around 60% of the world's total vaccines come from India (Dhillon, 2021, April 16), and the country produces around 7,000 tonnes of industrial oxygen per day, which can be easily diverted towards medical needs (Krishnan, 2021, May 5). Repeated warnings by esteemed and highly respected professionals of a potential second wave (Jha, 2021, May 11) were continuously neglected, and the requisite planning was sacrificed for political gains in the then impending state elections (Sherwell, 2021, April 25). Based on a combination of these factors, the massive neoliberal healthcare ecosystem, which had been put in place by the private bodies, found itself wanting during the pandemic (Ratcliffe, 2021, April 23).

When such public health disasters occur, it is the marginalised community which gets affected the most. Differences in socio-economic status affect their accessibility to healthcare – which ideally should be a fundamental right (Bambra et al., 2021). These differences occur along the lines of class, caste, occupation, gender, race, and the like, that affect other aspects such as housing and sanitation, which in turn, have a direct impact on the kind of health that an individual and a community enjoys. Everything that becomes relevant in a context such as an apocalyptic event caused by climate change or a healthcare emergency such as that caused by the COVID-19 pandemic is related to each other, such that 'health systems [themselves] cause stress on the environment through their consumption of large quantities of energy, water and materials' (Soni & Pant, 2022, 'The Impact of Health Systems on Climate Change'). Factors such as climate and health are intimately related to the other essential aspects of human sustenance in the world. And, when these aspects get altered, apocalyptic tendencies grow within the society. Good health and well-being are two of the most fundamental aspects of human sustenance, to which material issues such as the availability of food and psychological factors such as the perception of risk are intrinsically related (Fabiansson & Fabiansson, 2016).

The situation in India demands special attention due to the way in which corporate capitalism has developed in India. Corporate capitalism usually emphasises the ways in which people can adapt to the healthcare crises without making many adjustments to their own profit-seeking healthcare models, which often constitute the very causality behind the healthcare crisis. Responses such as the one initiated by the central government in India which, quite literally, locked up the entire country within a matter of hours, left thousands of people, especially the migrant workers entrapped in various cities, in great distress (Mukul, 2022). This created the ideal ground for disaster capitalism to penetrate into the society through the usage of the avenues which are constructed by such 'shocks' – a term made popular by Naomi Klein's (2007) classic study of the disaster capitalism complex that talks about how global corporations benefit from disasters such as climatic events, wars, and the like. Disaster capitalism thrives because the contemporary society in most democracies under the capitalist mode of production are highly unequal societies that tend to exploit vulnerable people. And the ways in which states respond to disasters are part of the methodological arsenal of the process of the imposition of neoliberalism in society (Klein, 2017, July 6). This is aptly reflected in India if one takes the expenditure on the public healthcare system in India has not been adequate. In India:

> [The] public expenditure on healthcare has been in doldrums until recent years. Its share from total GDP, which was 1.0 percent in 2015 has reached 1.6 percent in 2019, showing a mere increase of 0.6 percent in the last four years, leading to no significant improvement in outcomes such as the number of beds, mortality rates or life expectancy.
> (Housing Research, 2021, p. 6)

Even with the OOP expenditure, the total expenditure on healthcare was only 3.5% in 2018, significantly lower than other countries such as the UK, US, and France (Housing Research, 2021). The limited resources available to public healthcare systems in almost all the major democracies in the world have resulted in a situation where 'new infections and deaths quickly rose exponentially as the virus rapidly spread to other countries, especially to advanced countries in the West, better connected by passenger air travel'

(Chowdhury & Sundaram, 2020, p. 517), from which the virus could then multiply exponentially in the Global South.

The rampant rise of COVID-19 was met with the idea of *flattening the curve*, which was based on the idea that if the curve, the ebbs of which point towards the rise of cases, can be flattened, then the healthcare infrastructures of the countries will be able to cope better with the pandemic and the rising number of cases (Chowdhury & Sundaram, 2020). In such a scenario, lockdowns emerged as the only viable solution – one that would not only save the profit-driven healthcare infrastructure to survive in a post-pandemic situation by saving it from the crisis but also reiterate the control that states have on the people. Mike Davis (2020) notes that instead of focusing on the 'flattening of the curve' – a phrase made famous during the pandemic – the better option would have been to create the conditions under which such a disaster should not have been allowed to occur in the first place.

Responses to most natural and man-made disasters under neoliberal regimes usually involve fragments of the privatised utopia that most corporations instil within the state and the society that they set out to control. Privatisation usually begins with the idea that privatised services would be cheaper and more competitive than the ones in the public sector (McDonald & Ruiters, 2005). However, experience proves that this is rarely the case, as private services usually are more unequal by design than their public counterparts. During the second wave of the pandemic in India, the lack of public resources had been felt acutely, especially in the urban spaces where the lockdown had been followed much more strictly than in the rural areas, which contributed to the severity of the disaster caused by COVID-19.

Disasters, especially under capitalism are not new, and will continue to occur as history progresses. In a highly dystopic sense, capitalism enjoys the prospect of disasters because with every disaster – be it economic, political, or ecological – capitalism is provided with newer opportunities for profit maximisation. Kelman (2020) argues that one cannot merely categorise disasters into those few moments of human tragedies, but that 'The disaster is these long-term processes, over years and centuries, not the short-term events, over seconds (earthquakes), minutes/hours (tsunamis), and days (hurricanes). The process of unrolling disaster is based on the long-term choices of people' (Kelman, 2020, p. 14). They have been an integral part of the development of capitalist profit accumulation procedures because of their effects within the realm of labour markets, patterns of conquest, and consumption practices (Scheidel, 2018, pp. 297, 315, 329).

Disasters like epidemics and pandemics have also been known to have an impact on the very structure of communities and states (McNeill, 1976). Under capitalism, disasters end up in revealing the material and psychological aspects of human tragedies rather than concealing them, which is the norm under routine circumstances (Diaz-Quiňones, 2019). This is extremely worrying because COVID-19 is not the first pandemic that the human society has faced, and nor will it be the last. In contemporary human life, disasters and risks have become the order of the day affecting human lives economically, socially, culturally, and politically. As Matthewman argues:

> Disasters are on the rise, increasing in magnitude, frequency and cost; We are also seeing new forms of disaster emerging in which 'the impossible' happens. These arise from growing interconnectivity and complexity in our world, which link back to questions of political economy and globalisation; Definitions of disasters have remained static in these most rapidly challenging times of all; disaster studies is threatened with intellectual marginality at the very moment of its greatest need; Even in wealthy countries we do not really know the true casualty figures from disasters, which has obvious policy implications, The spectacular events that disaster researchers focus on may not be the ones which take the greatest toll, A sociology of disasters which omits the most devastating types of damage is barely worthy of the name
> (Matthewman, 2015, pp. 8–9)

When disasters take place, there are certain events that occur at a rapid pace in the society – both at the individual level and at the social level. One of the instances that Klein (2007) narrates in *The Shock Doctrine* is related to the transactions between the Federal Emergency Management Agency (FEMA) and the State of Louisiana in the United States of America during the hurricane *Katrina*. When the state requested funds as a means to develop a contingency plan for a hurricane inflicted catastrophe, the funds were denied. However, in the same year, the FEMA was found to have awarded 500,000 USD to the *Innovative Emergency Management* to come up with a disaster management plan (Klein, 2007, p. 409). In case of COVID-19 in India, the trajectory is similar. India as Krishnan (2022) argues would always be at risk of being affected more by deadly epidemics and pandemics because of the ways in which urban infrastructure has been structured in India. This has resulted in extremely congested living conditions with little attention being given to aspects of public health. Ankur Bisen (2019) has also written about how unplanned urbanisation has resulted in poor sanitation systems in urban India – something which has become extremely important during the pandemic. It can be said with reasonable certainty that it is often the marginalised sections that suffers from the worst effects of such unplanned urbanisation, be it the racial minorities in the West or the marginalised sections in India based on caste, religion, and class. The ways in which the urban space is segregated have a very concrete effect on the health of people belonging to marginalised groups and contribute to their deteriorating health (Wallace & Wallace, 2021).[4]

In situations caused by pandemics, the healthcare infrastructure in any country is put under tremendous pressure by the way in which the disease spreads in the society. The conditions created by the pandemic rendered certain jobs as being essential for the continued functioning of the society, which included healthcare, pharmacies, food services, and the like (Schaffer, 2021). Even within these jobs, there are issues surrounding the social identity of these workers, which makes their lives extremely difficult. An overwhelming percentage of sanitation workers in India, who are mostly contractual, belong to the Scheduled Castes (SC) and Scheduled Tribes (ST) and face conditions of extreme poverty, as they are the most poorly paid workers in the country (Bisen, 2019). The kind of jobs that they have to do usually place them in direct contact with sites that are far more likely to hold the virus than other workers. During the pandemic and especially during the lockdown, sanitation workers found themselves to be increasingly vulnerable to the virus when they had to work in close contact with patients and high-risk sites, while continuously facing rebukes (Ravichandran, 2020, March 30) and having to work without protective gear despites orders from the Supreme Court (Kumbhare, 2020, May 7). These workers, in spite of the service that they have provided during the pandemic, are not recognised as frontline workers and remain bereft of the recognition and the possibilities of remuneration (Kumbhare, 2020, May 7).

Some suggested that the private bodies are more equipped to deal with the pandemic than the government bodies (Hampden-Turner & Trompenaars, 2021). However, as the pandemic has shown over the months, private bodies have found themselves to be inadequately equipped to deal with the pandemic. But, as Nail (2022) has shown, the pandemic is not merely a by-product of capitalist processes but also a window for capital to cause further exploitation. Especially in the urban areas of developing nations, this gets further accentuated because most of them remain characterised by unequal access to certain resources considered to be essential for responding to a disaster (Pelling, 2003). During any major crises under contemporary capitalism, there are certain common events that occur across the globe, such as massive price hikes of essential commodities with a certain relaxation of government oversight. These events happen almost automatically during disasters (Matthew & Upreti, 2018).

Price changes provide one of the most vital avenues to analyse the impact of a disaster such as COVID-19 because they alter wages and influence the power of consumption, thus affecting the economy of any society, often for years to come (Davies, 2021). These effects, in turn, also impact the social mobility prevalent in any society. Effective policies framed with an intention of preventing adverse shocks to economic conditions and essential service provisioning are needed, including the framing of policies such as job guarantees, wealth taxation, educational infrastructural development, and the like (Major & Machin, 2020). Different kinds of disasters evoke different kinds of responses from the common populace and the governments under which the disasters occur. It is almost impossible to establish direct relationships between various disasters, but there are certain similarities between all kinds of disasters that emerge from natural sources, including pandemics, earthquakes, floods, and the like. However, there are three crucial phases of managing a disaster: the first being the crucial phase when the impending disaster becomes imminent and the possibility of its occurrence turns from being a probability to a certainty, the second being the period of action when the effects of the disaster are instantly felt, and the third and final one being the management of the situation once the disaster has passed (Srivastava, 1983).

During the first phase, the responsibility is to maintain public awareness and make the public aware, the second phase starts with forecasting the approximate time in which the disaster might happen, while the third phase engages with reliefs, rehabilitation, and precautionary measures. Srivastava's (1983) categorisation was based on the state's response to earthquakes, but within liberal democracies under neoliberalism, the approach towards the management of any disaster has some similar characteristics. For example, price rise during disasters has almost become normalised in most societies. These activities create a situation where prices fluctuate rapidly in accordance with the profitability associated with certain commodities. And price changes are vital to understanding the economic impact of COVID-19, especially for the marginalised population in the Global South who remain entrapped within the disaster capitalism complex.

A major aspect of the disaster capitalism complex is the privatisation and outsourcing of essential services amidst the horrors that disasters cause (Klein, 2007)[5] along with a complete marginalisation of the problems that marginalised people face during and after disasters. In India the situation was no different, with reports coming in that the outsourced staff who were hired in massive numbers during COVID-19 were facing uncertainty about their future (Times of India, 2022, March 29). Conversations with the sanitation and care workers, mostly women, of certain hospitals in Delhi also revealed about the dire conditions that many of them are facing with widespread speculations about their employment contract. Many of them, it must be mentioned, were employed through contractors and middlemen, who had charged them money for providing them with the jobs. One of them recounted to the author, *'We were hired during the pandemic. We did more work than even the doctors and nurses who are permanent employees, but at the end, they have treated us as disposable entities'*.[6] The informalisation of such workers is a common feature of neoliberalism in India. When health emergencies take place due to a potentially deadly virus, a large section of the populace finds themselves at the risk of being 'exterminated' by the disease because the kind of labour they do does not pay them well enough to afford the best healthcare available. During such emergencies, disaster capitalism benefits because:

> Humans are so averse to the thought and threat of death that most religions dangle the carrot of an afterlife before our trembling gaze. One can go to heaven with the Christians and Islamics or get recycled in reincarnation with Buddhists, Hindus, and Jains. Jews have been

contaminated with their long sojourn in Christian societies and have folk tradition of a hereafter.
(Wallace & Wallace, 2018, p. 53)

The Disruption of Public Services

Public services are the backbone of the Indian democracy. They not only bring fiscal profits but also make the state accountable to the general public. The public sector in India, which was integrated into the Indian democracy since 1947, has suffered from constant attacks on its autonomy and operations since 1991. However, despite the widespread attacks, the public sector continues to be a major service provider to the majority of the population – something which got manifested during COVID-19. When disasters strike the society, the public services maintained by the public sector are often the ones that are closed down immediately because of the human and financial cost required to maintain them, which the State can rarely furnish or has the political will to furnish. No sector exhibits this better than the education sector in India. According to a United Nations Educational, Scientific and Cultural Organization (UNESCO) report on the impact of COVID-19 in India, the public sector schools suffered the most during the lockdown. The report mentions:

> A status report on schools during COVID-19 indicated that children studying in government schools were hit particularly hard, with more than 80 per cent of government school students in Odisha, Bihar, Jharkhand, Chhattisgarh, and Uttar Pradesh not receiving any educational materials during the lockdown.
> (UNESCO, 2021, p. 11)

It cannot be taken out of consideration that the above-mentioned states are also some of the poorest in India. Bihar, for example, also has the lowest number of hospital beds in the country (Housing Research, 2021). According to the NITI Aayog's Multidimensional Poverty Index (MPI), which takes into account health, education, and the standard of living and incorporates factors such as nutrition, mortality, schooling, sanitation, and the like into context, Bihar, Jharkhand, and Uttar Pradesh fare the worst with 51.91%, 42.16%, and 37.79% of their populace being poor, respectively (Hindustan Times, 2021, November 27). When government schools suffer, the food security in these states as well as the nation as a whole also suffers, as does the level of sanitation that many children from poor social backgrounds can practise. More than 27 crore students in the impoverished state of Chhattisgarh had been affected by the enforced closure of the schools due to the pandemic (Drolia, 2020, September 17). This has massively affected the food security of the children in the government schools, many of whom receive regular meals only in the schools.

Food security in India has always been an important issue of debates and discussions within polity. Food security depends to a large extent on the purchasing capacity of the household and the ways in which the distribution system is managed (Modgal, 2012). Jawaharlal Nehru's (1949/2015) resolution to problems of food security was based on the formation of an administrative authority, effective co-operation between national and provincial governments, statistical alertness, and an emphasis on the public's co-operation on matters of food security. Nehru's intellectual abilities as a politician and a social observer made him introspect about the ways in which wars, partition, and other major global events, such as wars and famines, had been having a disastrous effect on India's prospects of achieving food sovereignty. Nehru wrote:

> It is clear also that while we must and will import foodstuffs from outside to fill the gap in India, we cannot rely indefinitely on outside sources. This import of large quantities of food from outside is having a disastrous effect on our economy. It is not absolutely necessary for a country to be self-sufficient in food. But any large gap is a dangerous thing.
>
> (Nehru, 1949/2015, p. 150)

Under neoliberal economic reforms, corporates entered Indian agriculture contributing to the realisation of Nehru's fears. Despite the fact that the introduction of neoliberalism has resulted in a reduction of the role of middlemen in the agrarian sector, but at the expense of the autonomy of the agrarian working class (Modgal, 2012), the effects of neoliberal reforms on Indian agriculture have been horrific as far as food security is concerned. There has been a tendential fall in the percentages of food and cash crop cultivation in India. According to the Food and Agriculture Organization (FAO, 2022), 70% of all rural households in India are still dependent on agriculture for survival. The FAO states that out of these 70% rural households, around 82% of the people engaged in agriculture are small or marginal farmers. The Indian Council for Agricultural Research (ICAR) has stated that the total food grain production in the country is at a record 291.95 million tonnes in the 2019–21 cycle and will increase to 345 million tonnes by 2030. However, one has to analyse this data relatively. As of 2011, the share of agriculture in the GDP was about 15%, which is a tremendous drop from the 34% in 1983–84. The share of services has increased from 40% to 57% with the share of industry remaining constant at 20% (High Powered Expert Committee [HPEC] for Estimating the Investment Requirements for Urban Infrastructure Services, 2011). The Department of Economic Analysis and Research of NABARD claims that there has been a decline of 2.7% in the total agrarian production in India with declines in the allied sectors of poultry, fisheries, and livestock by 19.5%, 13.6%, and 8.5%, respectively. The farm gate prices of these important allied sectors within the agrarian economy, such as poultry, horticulture, dairy, and fisheries have also declined by 17.8%, 7.6%, 56%, and 4.8%, respectively. The HPEC Report of 2011 stated that one of the major reasons for the shifts in the percentages of population increase between urban and rural India is because of the migration of erstwhile agrarian workforce – which they classified as being a low-productivity sector – towards more productive sectors such as industry and services:

> India's growth has stabilized with its economy's diversification and transition towards services. The service sector makes up an outsized part of the economy, and knowledge sectors such as information technology have grown dramatically. By 1980, the share of agriculture in GDP fell to 36 per cent and, by 2013, it was only 14 per cent. By contrast, the share of service sector workers rose from 18 per cent to 24 percent.
> (Pande, 2020, p. 53)

In 2021, estimates suggest that the agrarian sector contributes 20.2% of the GDP, the only sector to have shown a positive growth despite decreases in all the other sectors, including the overall GDP (Shagun, 2021, January 29). The noted agrarian scholar and journalist, P. Sainath (2011, September 25) analyses this rapid growth of the urban population in India and argues:

> At 833.1 million, India's rural population is today 90.6 million higher than it was a decade ago. But the urban population is 91 million higher than it was in 2001. The Census cites three possible causes for the urban population to have risen by more than the rural: 'migration', 'natural increase' and 'inclusion of new areas as "urban"'. But all three factors applied in earlier decades too, when additions to the rural population far outstripped those to the urban. . . . In 2011, urban India's increase was greater than that of rural India's by nearly half a million, a huge change.
> (Sainath, 2011, Paras 2–3)

The previous instance when the urban population had grown more in numbers than the rural population was in 1921, following the 1918 Spanish flu pandemic.[7] A significant cause behind such changing population patterns is the constant migration that characterises the Indian agrarian workforce. The agrarian sector in India results in the employment of around 64% of the rural population in the country (Srivastava et al., 2017), and thus when the agrarian productivity goes down, it is safe to assume that rural productivity goes down. In a country like India, which sits at 101st position out of 116 countries on the Global Hunger Index Data 2021 (Global Hunger Index, 2021), the reduction in agrarian production, especially in food crop production, is disastrous.

Food scarcity has a drastic effect on women and children. According to the fifth round of the National Family Health Survey (NFHS-5), the number of undernourished people in India stands at 189.2 million, most of whom are women and children (Gupta, 2022, July 24). States such as Maharashtra, Bihar, and Gujarat have more than half of the over 33 lakh (3.3 million) malnourished children as per the data compiled by the Women and Child Development (WCD) Ministry (The Hindu, 2021, November 7). There has been a 91% increase in the number of severely acute malnourished children between November 2020 and October 2021, the period when the pandemic was on its peak in India (The Hindu, 2021, November 7). It goes beyond saying that these children would have been at more risk of contracting the virus because of their reduced immunity due to lower nutrition. Coupled with a lack of education, malnourishment and undernourishment played a key role in letting the pandemic wreak havoc in India.

Education also plays a critical role in the resistance shown by any society towards a pandemic. Education helps individuals in making informed decisions, which have become extremely important during the pandemic (Lahariya et al., 2020). In countries like India, where the literacy rates are still low in comparison to other western countries, schemes such as Integrated Child Development Services (ICDS) and Mid-Day meals, in this regard, perform dual functions. They provide children with food as well as a reason to come to school in the first place. COVID-19 disrupted that. Food and education were critical areas in which disaster capitalism has made a mark in India. Public provisioning of food would have solved matters had the PDS been functioning properly in the country. The PDS in India was formulated in 1939 to ration food during the World War (Swaminathan, 2000). However, as Swaminathan (2000) argues, that the PDS system in India has had a significant urban bias entrenched within it when it comes to the ratio of urban to rural consumption and price differentials, resulting in the system benefitting the urban populace over the rural ones. Swaminathan reproduces data from 1994 which puts forward that, on a national scale, PDS reaches only about 2% of the population. On the contrary, in Kerala, even in 1994, the reach of PDS was about 87% of the population (Swaminathan, 2000). Thus, it was only natural that almost all the people residing in Kerala could rely heavily on the PDS structure in place when COVID-19 came up in 2020 (Martin, 2020, May 23). The PDS was undermined and completely overwhelmed during COVID-19 in most of the Indian states. There were also variations in the way in which the PDS operated during the two waves. While during the first wave, the government provided food to additional households who did not have access to ration cards, this was not renewed during 2021 when only the ones with ration cards and identity cards issued by their respective states were provided with state-sponsored food (Chen et al., 2022).

Instead of the PDS, during the lockdown, the delivery of medical supplies and essential groceries was taken over by the private corporations. The failure of government mechanisms sparked groups such as Cognizant into action, which went on to deliver as many as 13,000 grocery kits and 5,000 meal packages to people, in addition to making philanthropic alliances with municipal bodies, sponsoring scholarships, and donating technological devices. Rajesh Nambiar states in *The Indian Express*:

> The Maharashtra Government has been our support partner since the beginning of the pandemic. Our partnership has enabled to serve the critical needs of our customers while protecting vulnerable communities. As a company with a strong social purpose, we are proud to support with Covid care beds in addition to the several community care program that our Foundation and Cognizant outreach volunteers are running on the ground.
> (The Indian Express, 2021, June 19, Para 5)

Neoliberal privatisation was thus something that India's pandemic response emphasised. Capitalists and the state have always been in synchronisation with each other. It becomes extremely easy for individuals possessing capital to make inroads into the political community (Bondre, 2014). Under neoliberalism, the state suffers from a decreasing social and financial influence over the society and the citizens, and private entities often become the de facto leaders of the society. In these situations, the private corporations treat the state as merely an appendage, while they attempt to posit themselves as being the more efficient managers of a crisis-ridden situation.

The Politics of Life Expectancy

Countless lives of common people, healthcare workers, and vulnerable sections of the population have been lost because of COVID-19. Epidemiologists use factors such as life expectancies and mortality rates to make inferences with regards to public health. Many individuals from disadvantaged communities are always at the risk of being further marginalised during a health emergency. As Wallace and Wallace state, epidemiologists:

> ultimately measure well-being of populations. Populations with low life expectancies and high age-adjusted mortality rates generally experience adverse social, economic, political and environmental influences that result in accelerated aging, high rates of violent deaths (murders and suicides), and high rates of fatal disease such as TB and AIDS and of chronic conditions (cancer, coronary heart disease, stroke, Alzheimer's disease, etc.).
> (Wallace & Wallace, 2018, p. 53)

When a disaster such as COVID-19 occurs, it is always the vulnerable community which suffers the most. Sonia Shah (2010) narrates how the migrant construction workers in Mumbai are more prone to getting infected by malaria than others. While it is true that the average life expectancy has rose to 68.8 in 2017 from a very low 32 in 1947 (Pande, 2020), accounts such as those from Singh (2018) make one believe that the conditions for the marginalised populace will be worse than this considering that they are more prone to be in high-risk situations. The ways in which the health emergency has endangered the lives of millions for reasons *other than health* have exhibited that any model of management engaging with a healthcare emergency in the society involves not only doctors curing the patients and pharmaceutical industrialists manufacturing medicines or vaccines but also a host of other sectors of workers and employees. There are sectors such as sanitation which become extremely essential during a health emergency. Disasters also exhibit the stark contrasts which exist in the everyday lives of the general masses in comparison with those in power. The lived experience of the marginalised populace during a disaster narrates the reality of capitalism in a way that under normal circumstances would not have been able to evoke similar emotions and reflections.[8]

One of the major sectors that the migrant workers engage within the urban spaces is sanitation. Sanitation work and its caste-based employment constitute one of the major aspects of caste-based segregation of people in urban areas (Mahalingam, 2007; Mahalingam et al., 2019). The pandemic has initiated a caste-based reassertion of the existing social relations in the society, which often bases itself on the construction of essentialist notions surrounding the identity-based inequality that Dalits face in India (Mahalingam, 2007). Vinod Kapri (2021) and Barkha Dutt (2022) have narrated how newer forms of untouchability had emerged in India during the lockdown because of the fears that people had harboured within themselves regarding the virus. These were often irrational and unscientific in nature. The possession of such flawed knowledge often made common people practice certain heinous discriminatory acts against the migrants. This raises certain larger issues as well surrounding the information that people from socially disadvantaged communities possess regarding their own health, which is often flawed. This creates further avenues for them to be more vulnerable to contracting the disease during a pandemic (Lahariya et al., 2020). Many of these migrant workers, who had to walk back home when the lockdown was announced, were engaged in jobs considered derogatory by most of the urban middle class.

Sanitation was one such job, which, although essential, has historically been relegated to the lower castes in the Indian society (Shruti & Majumdar, 2021, January 29). According to Shruti I. (2021), the total number of sanitation workers in India is around 1.2 million, most of whom come either from the Dalit community or from de-notified tribes. Urban municipal governments, such as the BMC, have tended to institutionalise the relationship between caste and labour by bringing in significant numbers of Dalit workers to perform sanitation work in urban areas to maintain urban sanitation. As Shruti I. writes:

> The large majority of sanitation workers are also migrant worker from another state. In our field sites in Karnataka, most workers were from

Andhra Pradesh or Telangana but had settled in Karnataka for two or more generation, in Mumbai many sanitation worker households are from Gujarat, Haryana or Karnataka but have been in Mumbai for more than 70 years.

(I, 2021, pp. 167–168)

Migrant workers live under some of the worst conditions unimaginable to the human society, with extremely bad conditions of sanitation and public health (Nazeer, 2014, February 1). During the pandemic, they found themselves to be further excluded from the society with newer forms of exclusionary measures being enacted. One such incident even involved the spraying of disinfectants on them (MWSN, 2020). Acts such as those were not only a result of the fear of the pandemic but rather indicated the combined reaction that the fear of death and institutionalisation attributed inequality by birth produce within the society in general. A paper from 'Participatory Research in Aisa' (PRIA) states:

> The occupation of sanitation work is intrinsically integrated with caste in India. This link earmarks sanitation as the sole concern of just one caste – the Dalits, and among them *Valmikis*.[9] An even wider gap of injustice appears on disaggregating the Valmiki community by gender. Women sanitation workers (specifically lower caste women) in a country in which patriarchy still thrives, live and work under the double burden of labour
>
> (PRIA, 2019, p. 5)

The issues that Dalits face are intimately related to other issues such as sanitation and family welfare. Jobs such as sanitation in India are primarily a caste-based occupation. Even though the Supreme Court had passed a judgement banning manual scavenging in India, there has not been a law penalising those who violate the terms of the judgement.[10] The system of caste-based employment has been particularly harsh towards Dalit women, who have suffered tremendously throughout the pandemic.

Being a sanitation worker in India is a difficult one and is ridden with stigmas and social corruption to the extent that even their deaths often do not get the attention that they deserve even though their death rates are pretty high in comparison to other sectors (I, 2021). India's issues with serious public health concerns such as sanitation encompass the methods in which sanitation responsibilities are often portrayed to be the sole domain of one particular caste. Manual Scavenging has been one of the most persistent evils that characterise modern India. The SBM focused more on construction of toilets rather than emphasising on the overall improvement of the state of sanitation in the country, which has left the communities engaged in jobs such as manual scavenging completely included from the aegis of the plan (Rajagopalan, 2019, October 2). According to Wilson and Singh (2016), there have been disproportionate allocations to schemes, which has left the 1.3 million mostly Dalit women employed in manual scavenging in complete disarray:

> Why does the country allocate a budget of INR 16,248 Crore for the Swachh Bharat Abhiyan while it has only INR 5 Crore to spare for rehabilitation of manual scavengers, as per the Union Budget for the fiscal year 2017–18? Why is India unable to invest in finding a technology to clean sewer septic tanks without endangering human life? These are serious questions that the Indian democracy must answer.
> (Wilson & Singh, 2016, p. 298)

These people from the marginalised communities have been stigmatised not only because of their caste but also because of the kind of work they do, which in turn is reinforced by their caste in the first place. With very little political mobilisation around the vulnerability and non-dignified nature of the profession, manual scavenging has become almost a perennial characteristic of India, something that even neoliberalism could not erase (Singh, 2012). The sanitation workers in India have faced a time of immense crises during the pandemic, and especially during the lockdown. And, considering that the sanitation workforce in India is largely composed of Dalits, the discrimination and stigmatisation of these workers also causes a double exploitation of the individual workers – one that attacks both their social and economic well-being (Thorat & Thorat, 2022, February 11). These are the vulnerabilities that characterise modern India.

The dire situations that Dalits and Muslims face under neoliberal capitalism in India, even when they form around 16% and 14% of the population, respectively, have accentuated during the pandemic. Guru (2013) argues that the institution of caste in India has made it difficult for Dalits to become integrated into the society as equals given the tremendous pressures they face to respect the upper castes and the socially enforced demonstration of that reverence. According to Vyas et al. (2022), Dalits, Adivasis (Tribals), and Muslims in India are much more likely to die early. Adivasis, Dalits, and Muslims live for 4 years, 3years, and 1 year less, respectively, than those from the upper caste Hindu communities. Their analysis is based on the data collected from above 20 million people from nine Indian states, which total to around half of India's total population. The same situation persists for Dalit, Adivasi, and Muslim women as well. Women in India cannot be a universal category because there are vast differences between how they are treated in different micro social contexts, in accordance with their caste and class (Rege, 2020). The life expectancy of Adivasi, Dalit, and Muslim women is 62.8 years, 63.3 years, and 65.7 years, respectively, while the upper caste women live for around 66.5 years on an average. When pandemics become a reality, they play a great role in revealing such man-made policy-driven disasters (Wallace & Wallace, 2016).

Mortality rates in India are contingent upon the various social attributes and ascriptions that an individual possesses. Dalits are always more at risk of facing high mortality rates than caste Hindus, which have remained the same over two decades after neoliberalisation (Gupta & Sudharsanan, 2022). After the 1991 economic reforms, which had resulted in the creation of a new middle class in India, especially in the urban areas, the situation of Dalits did not undergo any significant change in terms of micro or macro factors (Vidyarthee, 2014). Dalit and Muslim workers have found themselves to be increasingly vulnerable during the pandemic, not only because of the institutionalised structural inequalities but also because the response to the pandemic did not pay adequate attention to their contemporary social and occupational marginalisation. As a Muslim gravedigger informs:

> Covid-19 changed the demands my job made of me. I felt like a participant in a psychological experiment – only, my consent wasn't mine. It was being forced out of me because of the simple reason that no one else was willing to do the job. . . . There was nothing in the rulebook mandating I had to touch a body affected by Covid-19 . . . we were repeatedly encouraged to maintain our distance and direct people from afar. The World Health Organisation (WHO) guidelines clearly stated that [frontline workers] should wear appropriate personal protection equipment (PPE). . . . We were barely provided with any of that.
> (Shameem, 2022, p. 13)

This testament from the worker accurately sums up the situation that Schaffer (2021) describes through the theory of necro ethics, where even though certain services are deemed to be essential under certain circumstances, the workers performing them are not. Workers from essential services, especially if the service has to engage with diseased people, tend to be mostly from the marginalised communities globally. Most of the workers who have had the liberty to work from home during the pandemic are those who have had a higher social status because of their caste, class, or gender. Dalits, arguably, are the worst sufferers in this. Marginalised communities like Dalits are the individuals who have the highest chances of contracting viral diseases, and they are also the ones who are mostly rendered voiceless through years of social oppression and stigmatisation (Nanda, 2021; Parsons, 2021).

The kinds of professions that Dalits engage in, such as sanitation work, manual scavenging, and rag picking, were considered essential activities during a pandemic, but unlike doctors and nurses, they continued to face stigmatisation and suffer from the further institutionalisation of their outcast existence within the society due to aggravation of the already existing socio-economic, structural, cultural, and historical inequalities (Agarwal, 2020, April 6). With the coming of large-scale privatisation of healthcare, the tendency to devalue Dalit lives has increased further. Under neoliberal regimes, the state's own public healthcare infrastructure remains in a dilapidated state.

This is especially 'shocking' considering that, as of 2016, there existed around 426 medical colleges in India with an approximate number of 60,000 students in them (Madhiwalla, 2018). This has been made possible, as Madhiwalla (2018) explains following Amin et al. (2010), by the manner in which private hospitals and medical colleges have caused brain-drain from publicly funded hospitals and medical facilities to the private ones, leaving the public sector with limited options to choose from during times of crisis. The constant privatisation of medical education has led to a state of complete inaccessibility of primary healthcare for a majority of the population, as '[f]rom the 1960s, the trends in the development of academic specialisation have led to specialist dominated and privatised healthcare system without adequate attention to the development of primary care as an important discipline in the Indian setting' (Zachariah, 2018, p. 105). One of the most important components of a healthcare system produced and sustained through such processes is pharmaceuticals.

Big Pharma, Privatised Healthcare, and the Pandemic

The idea of 'good health' has been used by corporates to enhance profit maximisation. During the times of disaster, this becomes easier for them because disasters bring out some of the worst fears within the human mind. This is what drives corporate interests to use these fears for their own benefits. And, because healthcare is such a large avenue for profit maximisation, it is no surprise that even smaller set-ups have been able to bring out innovative solutions during the pandemic within extremely short durations. Numerous examples can be taken in this regard. The start-up, Nocca Robotics, assisted by the IIT Kanpur Ventilator Consortium, successfully built the Noccarc V310 in a record-breaking time. The mentoring team formed around the start-up consisted not only of technological and scientific experts but also Padmaja Ruparel, the president of the *Indian Angel Network* (IAN). The account provided by Sastri and Bandyopadhyay (2021) is detailed and is extremely well-researched in terms of how the market and socio-political scenario influence innovation mechanisms in India.

The initial price set for the ventilator was at Rs 50,000. Another case in point is the Andhra Pradesh MedTech Zone (AMTZ) as has been documented by Jitendra Sharma (2022). Established in 2018, AMTZ according to Sharma has been a crucial factor in India's response to the global pandemic. Sharma states, 'Every crisis is an opportunity for nation building. When the world went into lockdown due to the unprecedented, global COVID crisis, the same proved true for newly visualised AMTZ, Asia's first exclusive medical devices technology and manufacturing zone' (2022, p. 1). However, medical devices have come under some very serious criticisms, which have argued that medical devices and implant technologies – the uses of which have significantly increased in the past decade – have greatly affected the pricing of healthcare services: '*Healthcare is expensive because technological breakthroughs are costly; patients who have health insurance can afford pricey solutions, and hospitals are happy to provide therapies that boost their bottom line*' (Schneider, 2021, p. 327, emphasis self).

When a particular aspect of an overall market structure suffers from an increase in prices or rates, one can see a corresponding increase in other areas as well. These increases are most visible in the domain of devices and drugs that promise to offer instant data, remedies, or solutions. Such tendencies are prevalent even within the domain of mental health, where because of the domination of managed care and short-term therapeutical remedies within the healthcare sector, the sector has moved towards privileging instant solutions rather than preparing the ground for a complete prevention of all health emergencies (Gnaulati, 2018). Such issues point towards the existence of widespread discrepancies and corruption within the sector as well. Considering that a such a tremendous amount of money is brought in within the healthcare sector, it is only natural that profit seeking exercises will creep in within the profession (Yoho, 2021). Healthcare corruption must be seen in the context of the control that medical practitioners hold over the society and individuals in general. Doctors and others associated with the practice of medicine in the society have an indelible control over the society that has shaped the profession itself, especially in fields such as surgery (Schneider, 2021). Brian Heraud notes that '[o]f all the professions, that of medicine is probably the most prestigious and powerful. Medicine is often seen as the archetype of the professions because of its special relation to matters of life and death, its basis in science, its control of and influence over related occupations' (1979, p. 62).

The Indian pharmaceutical industry, known for its generic medicines and low-cost vaccines, ranks third globally in terms of production by volume growing at a rate of 9.77% annually (Department of Pharmaceuticals, 2022). The rapid rise of the pharmaceutical sector in India had come through the way in which the patent laws had been established in India. The 1970 Patent Act prohibited the establishment of product patents, especially within the sectors of food, medicine, and other drugs. Because of these relaxations, the Indian pharmaceutical industry could make huge inroads into the genetic medicine industry (Chaudhuri, 2002). After the explosion of capitalist globalisation across the globe, the international pharmaceutical firms have been trying to use India as a combination of two critical aspects essential for manufacturing at a large scale, that is as a base for supply of raw materials and cheap labour, along with exploiting the large market that India provides by employing the rigid patent rights that have been rendered mainstream (Abrol et al., 2011). Under the neoliberal capitalism, multinationals are re-entering the Indian market at a much higher level, thereby placing the local manufacturers at a highly precarious position. This will undoubtedly result in a reduction of the cost-advantage that India previously enjoyed, and also contribute to the increase in drug-prices, which are again related to the cost of imports, which will inevitably increase with the multinational corporations' (MNCs) presence in the market (Loitongbam, 2016).

The Indian pharmaceutical sector has progressed steadily since the early 1990s and is one of the most financially viable sectors in the country, fulfilling around 50% of the global vaccine demand, apart from catering to 40% of the generic demand in the United States and 25% of the total medicine requirement in the United Kingdom (Festa et al., 2022). Like anywhere else in the world, the pharmaceutical companies in India not only create medicines and construct the basis of a health-based capitalism but also construct other forms of capital – cultural, social, and symbolic – which they manage by active interference in various healthcare related sectors, including medical education. Neha Madhiwalla writes:

> Medical educationists are preoccupied with updating curricula to keep abreast with latest developments in hi-tech medicine and 'cutting edge' fields, such as genetics, while there has been virtually no movement to revitalise disciplines such as preventive and social medicine. Students are socialised into a professional culture that privileges employment in the highly capital-intensive, technology focused, and corporatized medical industry, rather than comprehensive primary health care or public health.
>
> (Madhiwalla, 2018, p. 96)

Sismondo (2018) refers to this domination as Big Pharma's 'Ghost Management' under capitalism. The medical and pharmaceutical companies, before and during the pandemic, have constantly engaged actively with the patenting mechanisms put in place by the capitalist system. Naomi Klein argues:

> The patenting of drugs and vaccines to treat public health emergencies remains a controversial subject. The U.S. has been epidemic-free for several decades, but when the polio outbreak was at its peak in the mid-fifties, the ethics of disease profiteering were hotly debated. . . . When Jonas Salk . . . developed the first polio vaccine in 1952, he did not patent the lifesaving treatment.
>
> (Klein, 2007, p. 290)

However, the world has 'evolved' since the 1950s. The contemporary world stands at a juncture where the regime of patenting has been globalised, with most of the major democracies in the country agreeing to its norms. Amit Sengupta argues:

> [I]t is now possible to convey ideas from one mind to another without ever making them physical, ideas themselves are sought to be given ownership, and not merely their expression. And since it is likewise now possible to create useful tools that never take physical form, there is a move towards patenting abstractions, sequences of virtual events, and mathematical formulae – the most unreal terrain imaginable
>
> (Sengupta, 2000, p. 3)

Sengupta sees the patenting regime as an inevitable part of the knowledge economy, which characterises the post-industrial society as Bell (1973/1999) would have put it, where the sustenance of the global economy depends not on physical goods but rather on an abundance of ideas and thoughts that can be used for extracting profits. The healthcare sector has been particularly affected by this, especially in developing nations in the Global South. The trade in pharmaceuticals, which roughly accounts to around 55% of all health-related trade (Sengupta, 2018), is one of the most important aspects of the global healthcare industry. TRIPS or the agreement related to Trade-Related Intellectual Property Rights was devised to protect the IPRs of businesses. Anurag Agarwal argues:

> With geographical boundaries losing relevance in the field of information sharing, handling intellectual property issues in a holistic manner for the world is the need of the hour. Efforts in the field of intellectual property to harmonise the law and other practices have been undertaken for more than a century, however, there has been a tremendous momentum in the last decade and a half.
>
> (Agarwal, 2010, pp. 1–2)

The way in which IPRs operate globally makes it impossible for poor people residing in rural areas in developing nations to be able to afford medicines and drugs. There are various additional social, structural, and infrastructural inequalities that contribute to the constant degradation of rural health, especially in conditions created by the COVID-19 pandemic. In rural areas, not only are the people suffering because of the deplorable conditions of PHCs under neoliberalism but also because they cannot even avail the basic services available at those PHCs due to the restrictions on their mobility imposed by the lockdown (NT, 2021, May 18). The works that traditionally fell under the purview of governments, such as the provisioning of food, employment, and providing other basic amenities during a health crisis had been performed by CSOs such as *Swabhiman Society*, GIVEIndia, and the like.

The relevance of NGOs in any society only arises if the government has already failed to perform some of its primary responsibilities (Padel & Das, 2010). Within the healthcare sector, NGOs play an important role in India. NGOs are so critical to the healthcare infrastructure in the country that the Indian prime minister had to directly make an appeal to use NGOs and other civic volunteers during the pandemic (Sharma, 2021, May 1). Even though NGOs have been finding it difficult to maintain their status quo in the country, especially financially, with all the relief packages which they had released due to COVID-19, they are still a force to reckon with (Bhusan, 2022, June 6), especially in sectors such as mental health, which are traditionally not priority areas of intervention within the Indian healthcare sector (Dasson, 2021, October 10). During the pandemic, bodies such as the *Rapid Community Response to COVID-19*, which was composed of twenty NGOs engaged in grassroots healthcare campaigns, and *GIVE India*, a tech-based retail fundraising platform aimed at collecting Rs 500 crore could be formed much more quickly by the private sector than the public sector (Kudva & Vyavaharkar, 2020, April 24). NGOs could generate a humongous amount of money and human resource within a very short time for causes such as supporting the migrant workers, daily wage earners, and minority communities, notably through programs such as the Action COVID-19 Team, which was worth Rs 100 crore funded by India's start-up community (Kudva & Vyavaharkar, 2020, April 24).

The immense amount of money that the private sector can generate *at a moment's notice* makes one realise the power that the private and non-profit sectors hold in the contemporary society. In India, the growth of the private sector in healthcare has come at the expense of the publicly funded healthcare infrastructure in the country. As of 2018, the private healthcare sector contributes more than 60% of the healthcare services in the country, operating a total of 43,487 hospitals out of the total 69,265 hospitals in India (DebGupta, 2021). Additionally, there are other issues such as medical insurance and financial aid which are only available to a select percentage of the population (Sarkar, 2021; Festa et al., 2022), which makes the healthcare infrastructure in India a highly unequal terrain catering mostly to the relatively affluent sections of the population.

The general middle-class bubble about the benefits of the private healthcare system had also been done away with those being overburdened by the number of cases related to COVID-19, something for which they were not prepared at all. The shortage of vaccines had become so acute that the central government had to immediately authorise the private import of many vaccines, bypassing the traditional laws of the country (Thacker, 2021, May 6). This has catastrophic implications for a country where the OOP expenditure on healthcare is one of the highest globally, with high rates of poverty and low rates of insurance cover (Ladusingh & Pandey, 2013, pp. 58, 70). The world, on an average, spends around 10% of its GDP on healthcare, including both public and private expenditure, within which China spends around 5.5% of its GDP on healthcare and the US spending around 17%. India spends only 5.5% of its GDP on health, as per data in 2017 which includes 1.4% by the government and the rest 3.3% by private players (Jain, 2017, August 2). As of 2021, the percentage of GDP that is spent on healthcare remains at an abysmal low of approximately 1.3 (DebGupta, 2021). This creates the conditions for disasters such as COVID-19 to become profit maximisation avenues for private hospitals. As Purendra Prasad writes:

> Poor government spending on health, resulting in inefficient and inadequate services is one of the reasons why people seek private health providers in high OOP expenses. The National Accounts and Statistics data indicates that private expenditure on health care is about Rs 2,750 billion, of which 98 per cent is OOP spending. In addition, the

public expenditure on health care is about Rs 600 billion. Together this adds up to a health expenditure amounting to 5.7 per cent of GDP of which expenses account for 78 per cent.

(Prasad, 2018, p. 53)

Even with the New Health Policy (NHP) of 2017, the situation is not set to be improved drastically. The NHP 2017 states that the government will try to improve the healthcare expenditure to 2.5% of the GDP by 2025 (Reddy, 2019). The biggest challenge in front of the NHP 2017 is the articulation of the role of the private sector in the healthcare infrastructure of the country. The NHP declares that it will strive to integrate the private sector with the public sector with a focus on the creation of Public Health Management Cadres in every state by engaging with the already employed ASHAs in those areas (Reddy, 2019). However, the plan remains seemingly robust only in appearance because it still does not address the basic question of the poor working conditions of the workers with whom it aims to bring in all these major changes. Big Pharma in situations such as these plays a critical role in favour of the state because it brings in a sector-specific attitude where profit is maximised at the cost of human lives and workers (Wallace, 2016). Countering Big Pharma in times such as the one presented by COVID-19 makes it imperative to theorise about the domination that commodities hold over the human society, both on a social and individual level.

Under capitalism, commodities are not just an usable entities but are infused with exchange value that creates the value-form – something that it draws from the very nature of labour under capitalism (Dunayevskaya, 1958). Because the commodity inherits the inherent contradictions within the nature of labour under capitalism, the commodity, '*in embryo contains all the contradictions of capitalism*' (Dunayevskaya, 1958, p. 85, emphasis self). Disaster capitalism benefits from the commodity fetishism that is rendered mainstream under the capitalist mode of production in the society. Commodity fetishism is an intrinsic characteristic of capitalism and, as such, dominates the social relationships that arise under capitalism, at the core of which lies:

> [The] commodity form, and the value-relation of the products of labour within which it appears, have absolutely no connection with the physical nature of the commodity and the material relations arising out of this . . . (the commodity) is nothing but the definite social relation between men themselves which assumes here, for them, the fantastic form of a relation between things.
>
> (Marx, 1976, p. 165)

The severity of COVID-19 in India has been bolstered by the way in which the economic policies of the country have been shaped up, especially after the 1991 economic reforms, which have focused more on the production of commodities and consumers, rather than on the production of human capital or making life better for the marginalised sections, which contribute the most to the human capital that India possesses. Neoliberalism has laid the groundwork for disaster capitalism and apocalyptic cultures to take shape in contemporary society. Many technology-based companies have made huge profits throughout the pandemic.[11]

Naomi Klein (2020, May 13) has argued that the growth of technology during COVID-19 has rendered mainstream the surveillance that global capital has always desired to implement. At the same time, it has also attempted to fast track a version of the future where privacy, public spaces, and public services become non-existent and in case they do, they do so while remaining under strict protocols that discourage all forms of labour or civil rights. Disaster capitalism has numerous facets, which has continued to affect the world during COVID-19 because a pandemic affects the human society in many different ways. Sagot argues:

> The crisis [generated by Covid-19] is transforming our ways of envisioning the world and how we live. . . . This is why this is not a health crisis, as some have called it. The COVID-19 pandemic has the potential to become a *civilizational crisis* that could disrupt social relations, the organization of production, the role of states, the path of neoliberal globalization and even the place of humans in history and nature.
>
> (Sagot, 2022, p. 86)

This becomes further complicated for India because it has been going through a massive geopolitical and geographical change over the last decade, resulting in worsening foreign relations, a declining GDP, and a rapidly urbanising population. Global profits which are being produced on an everyday basis have been increasingly concentrated at the hands of a tiny minority. With the era of welfare capitalism long past, monopolistic capitalism has been an active participant in the further marginalisation of labour in the contemporary world.

Conclusion

Risks associated with potentially apocalyptic disasters such as nuclear warfare has increased rapidly over the past few years. However, public health emergencies, in recent times, have posed a much graver threat at an immediate level than nuclear wars to civilisations including the advanced, industrial nations such as the United States and the United Kingdom. Health emergencies constituted by pandemics and epidemics often create situations where there is a disjoint between the knowledge of the treatment and the actualisation of the treatment (Kupperberg, 2008). This disjoint is the space where disaster capitalism finds an ideal ground to creep in. The impact of disaster capitalism on human society gets accentuated by the fact that among governments of major democracies across the world, there is an increasing dominance of corporates (Klein, 2017). This makes disasters often seem favourable to governments, because they allow such governments to take certain decisions that would have been contested under normal circumstances (Matthew & Upreti, 2018). From medicines and vaccines, throughout the onslaught of the pandemic, one has been able to notice the deep connections which exist between the desire for secrecy and the tendency to fetishise large-scale shocks as drivers of the global capitalist economy.

Disasters always create 'aftershocks', and under the neoliberal management of the society and the state, the propensity of the aftershocks becoming fatal drastically increases. This becomes critical under contemporary neoliberal capitalism where even medical education is mostly focused on issues that are beneficial to the development of the culture of capitalism. Bonilla and LeBrón argue:

> The concept of aftershocks is mostly used in the context of earthquakes to describe the jolts after the initial quake. Aftershocks can continue for days, weeks, months, and even years after the 'main shock'. The bigger the earthquake, the more numerous and long-lasting the aftershocks will be. Although aftershocks are often similar, their effects can compound the damage of the initial shock. . . . Although aftershocks can be often smaller, their effects can compound the damage of the initial shock and create new urgencies that complicate recovery efforts.
> (Bonilla & LeBrón, 2019, 'Introduction')

The analysis of aftershocks is critical to making one realise that disasters are not singular events but rather events in continuity. Likewise, Eva Kelman argues:

> Disasters are not natural. We – humanity and society – create them and we can choose to prevent them. . . . Stating that natural disasters do not exist because humans cause disasters seems insanely provocative. We witness nature ravaging our lives all the time: from a city underwater after a hurricane to rows of smouldering houses after a wildfire to the dust rising from the ruins after an earthquake.
> (Kelman, 2020, p. vii)

Mapping disaster capitalism and its effects on the Indian society is tantamount to analysing the effects of disasters on factors crucial to development, and sustenance, of India as a state of its people. There are certain sectors that demand special attention in this context – food, health, housing and education. COVID-19 put all of these aspects at risk for a majority of the population, especially due to the ways in which the lockdown was managed by the governments, both at the central level and across majority of states. All the aspects mentioned above had adversely affected by the governmental lockdown protocols.

Disaster capitalism encompasses aspects of contemporary society such as debt, privatisation, food sovereignty and security, as well as energy sovereignty (Klein, 2018). Talking about disaster capitalism inevitably leads one to talk about some of the critical aspects that get inevitably engaged with disasters such as food provisioning, health delivery and security. Disaster capitalism thrives under conditions where ordinary citizens are made to believe that corporatisation and privatisation are the only roads towards a better and healthy life. COVID-19 has again brought into focus the critical debate between the patient as a human being and the patient as a consumer. The manner in which the perceptions about good health have developed and altered through the centuries have tended to construct a social situation where certain ailments have been integrated into the very lifestyle of contemporary human beings. Ramin (2017) has engaged in detail about how life in modern societies is designed in such a manner as to enable the massification of ailments such as backpain, which increase profusely because of the modern social structure's emphasis on *getting things done while* sitting, as well as the rising prevalence of desk-jobs among the urban populace. This also provides the neoliberal healthcare sector with an opportunity to exploit the ailment for profit.

The continuous erosion of the role of the family doctor has resulted in a situation where there has been a general de-personalisation of the healthcare services that one receives (Goldberg, 2019). The devaluation of the family doctor has also resulted in the complete marginalisation of the importance of any form of humanistic and subjective treatment of individuals (Zachariah, 2018). It creates a homogenous structure, which is critical to accelerating profit accumulation (Klein, 2002). The way in which neoliberalism affects the healthcare industry are diverse. Under liberalised healthcare, as Goldberg (2019) argues, even the clothes that the patient wears have an effect on the kind of treatment that the patient received. In the case of India, the effects can be felt in the way in which India acceded to global laws regarding strong intellectual property rights (Sengupta, 2018), or in the way in which the primary healthcare system in the country has been structured so as to completely dismantle any role that the family doctor might have had in the country's healthcare system (Zachariah, 2018). This basically renders the patient completely invisible and produces, in place of the patient, a consumer who is now much more attracted towards the labels that the medicines carry rather than the actual composition of the medicines (Tomes, 2016).

The culture around brands and labels is an important aspect of disaster capitalism. Naomi Klein (1999) has written about the adverse impacts that brands and other such labelling procedures have on the society as a whole, creating constrained spaces with little public freedom and giving rise to monopolistic tendencies. It is critical to realise that the world that one inhabits today is a world which is populated by the power of brands (Deb Roy, 2022), and as such brand-culture plays a crucial role in disaster capitalism, especially when it is referred in the context of healthcare. Brands such as the

AMTZ rely on their productivity to leverage large scale subsidies from the government or gain a relatively affirmative public opinion, which in turn helps them to accumulate further profit by converting healthcare into a lifestyle commodity. The AMTZ manufactured around a million RT-PCR kits daily which has contributed to the rapid increase in India's domestic production of the kits. However, like Sastri and Bandyopadhyay (2021) have discussed in their book on Nocca Robotics, Sharma (2022) focuses more on the industrial aspects of the innovation and how it could be used for enhancing production and profits – which they frequently associate with the common good – rather than discussing the common good that these innovations can generate. The same goes for Big Pharma monopolies such as Pfizer and AstraZeneca. They have benefited tremendously from the commodification of health under capitalism, and especially under neoliberalism. Stuart Law argues:

> The idea of patients coming to believe, to a greater or lesser extent, that good health is an option is now fairly well-established. This conviction that health really is a commodity like any other, to be bought and sold, is one that rests easily with the vision of the future the pharma companies themselves hold. This is a vision that tends to marginalise the human aspect of doctoring – and promote the technical, over which pharma has greater control. The intuitive powers of the doctor, honed over years of clinical practice, naturally wane as the art of healing gives way to the certainty of science. . . . Drugs offer such certainty.
> (Law, 2006, p. 23)

The certainty that drugs, and vaccines to a certain extent, provide makes the corporates manufacturing them locate themselves in a more advantageous position than other industries during times of healthcare crises. The way in which healthcare innovations are marketed by capital makes it easy for powerful industrial bodies to advocate for bypassing the established regulatory frameworks in place, as was done in the case of Nocca Robotics by a member of the Confederation of Indian Industries (CII) (Sastri & Bandyopadhyay, 2021).

Naomi Klein (2007) argues that contemporary capitalism operates through shocks, which has been developed into a full-fledged strategy. Under the framework of free market capitalism, the accumulation of capital depended upon the power of the shock to advance 'corporate goals: using moments of collective trauma to engage in radical social and economic engineering' (Klein, 2007, p. 8). Klein further argues, 'Central to a shock doctrine strategy is speed – pushing a flurry of radical changes through so quickly it's virtually impossible to keep up. So, for instance, while most of the meagre media attention [focuses on] . . . privatisation plans, an equally significant attack on regulations and independent oversight' pertaining to fiscal planning and regulations go unnoticed (Klein, 2018, 'Shock-After-Shock-After-Shock Doctrine'). As Matthewman (2015, p. 99) argues, under neoliberalism the state has been continuously supressed to give way to neoliberal corporations emphasising the normality of the ever expanding 'market'. At times like the present, when the state has actually been functioning *in absentia* in most of the major democracies around the world, the management of the crisis, especially in a situation where medical oxygen, the key to saving people affected by COVID-19, is produced by both government and private manufacturers (Khan, 2021, May 8).

The rampant corruption in the procurement and distribution of these supplies has led to disaster capitalists reaping profits by illegally hoarding and selling oxygen in the black economy (The Hindu, 2021, May 9) in a pandemic ravaged country. These kinds of events, it must be emphasised, do not occur in isolation, but are rather the result of the long years of capitalist deregulation of private enterprises under neoliberal regimes. Disaster capitalism is tied up with states attempting to rally widespread public sentiment against the public services that are required for a smooth administration of the economy and the society for a majority of the people. Klein (2007) highlights the procedural nuances of how capitalism and the state work in coalition to make this happen. During events such as earthquakes, floods, and pandemics, it becomes extremely easy for the state to rally public support for private replacement of public services. Walter Scheidel writes:

> Large social structures may unravel with different degrees of intensity and severity. At one end of the spectrum, we find processes that are primarily related to the exercise of political power, conventionally known as state failure. From a contemporary perspective, states are considered to be failing if they are unable to supply public goods to their members: corruption, lack of security, breakdown of public services and infrastructure, and loss of legitimacy serve as markers of state failure.
>
> (Scheidel, 2018, p. 257)

However, with disaster capitalism becoming mainstream, such markers of state failure have become obsolete. The private sector uses disasters to push its own agendas surrounding the complete demolition of the public sector, creating grounds for corporates to make entries into sectors deemed essential for the survival of the citizens and thus placed under the regulatory powers of the state (In These Times, 2020, April 16). These acts of rapid privatisation often result in increased inequality in terms of accessibility. Naomi Klein argues:

> In times of crisis, seemingly impossible ideas suddenly become possible. But whose ideas? Sensible, fair ones, designed to keep as many people as possible safe, secure and healthy? Or predatory ideas, designed to further enrich the already unimaginably wealthy while leaving the most vulnerable further exposed? The world economy is seizing up in the face of cascading shocks.
>
> (Klein, 2020, March 19, Para 2)

With the onset of the COVID-19 pandemic, the worst aspects of Naomi Klein's theoretical framework of disaster capitalism have come true. Not only have large conglomerates profited from the disaster that COVID-19 brought forward, but they have also initiated many large-scale social processes that are set to effect human society for decades to come.[12] Disaster capitalism combined with the neoliberal exploitation of the society makes human beings more compliant to the norms set by capitalism by propagating that the society as it exists is the only alternative. In other words, the TINA, that is *there is no alternative*, syndrome becomes a mainstream political force in the society. This inherently exploitative nature of contemporary capitalism has transformed it into a social system that not only controls but also disciplines individuals. Capitalism, today, ruptures the basic idea of being human. It turns human beings into commodities and commodities into 'spiritual beings'. In such circumstances, struggling against merely the economic aspect of capital is not sufficient, and it is necessary to struggle against the core of capitalism – the dehumanisation of human life and the commodity form. In situations like these, it is necessary to combine egalitarian philosophical ideas of revolution with actual revolutionary praxis, one of the primary elements of which is the articulation of the domination of dead labour over actually existing living labour, which converts human beings to parts of a capitalistic social machine. This can only be done when philosophical schools who believe in social justice get liberated from various forms of disciplinary sectarianism (Dunayevskaya, 1965).

It becomes extremely crucial in times like the present when it can be said that the pandemic has exposed the vulnerabilities of capital with economic downturns occurring, if only for a brief time, in major stock markets across the world. Negative growth rates became prevalent during a significant amount of time in 2021, when the pandemic was at its peak (Alexiou, 2021). The lure of capitalism, which drives advocates of freer markets and global circuits of capital, has found itself to be at odds with the material reality when it has become clear that it is global capitalism which, in the first place, created the conditions under which COVID-19 could achieve such monstrous heights. Zanoni and Mir argue, 'The stark contrast between death and misery on the one hand and grotesque levels of profit for big capital on the other hand have contributed to denaturalizing capitalism as the most desirable way to organize societies across the globe for all' (2022, p. 370). Social change in circumstances becomes not only possible, but also probable, provided that those responsible can struggle for the same.

Marx (1976) had argued that when the overaccumulation of capital rises, it creates massive conditions of relative impoverishment for the workers, thus constructing the social basis for change in the socio-economic and cultural organisation of the society. The COVID-19 pandemic demonstrates this in the most brutal sense possible. The society, as it stands today, has been transformed into a set of individuals who exists to follow orders and protocols, believing – often quite uncritically – that the decisions made by the state are for the benefit of *all* the citizens (Alexiou, 2021). Disaster capitalism ignores the plight that common people face during crises. Disaster capitalism, as it exists today during the pandemic, is a result of the ways in which the state and market have combined with each other – reinforcing each other into the lives of common people, especially those coming from the marginalised sections of the populace – to promote a society where the possession of private property serves as the driving force. Juan Posadas argued:

> With the rise of private property, people developed the fear of shortage, and this fear created egoism. The lack of food in sufficient quantity and for everybody provokes the sentiments of egoism, possession, and envy. It is not true that these sentiments are innate. The church says that they are, but the upholding of this falsehood is not even in its interests, for how come God created such a being? You see the stamp of private property on every church notion, like the devil and hell.
> (Posadas, 1978, p. 2)

The solution that Posadas posed is the creation of a *Revolutionary State*, which acts as an agent of transition between capitalist state and the workers' state by challenging capitalism by radically altering property structures, operational modes, and attempts to formulate relations of production that are free from the desires of profit accumulation (Posadas, 1969/2014). The subsequent chapters will delve deeper into this concept. Some people have argued that the solution to disaster capitalism is the gradual supersession of all sorts of private bodies by the state such as Dean and Heron (2020) who argue:

> Few are persuaded by the denial of the political nature of climate change [one of the major precursors to disaster capitalist tendencies]. Persistent mobilisation by the grassroots activists has placed climate clearly on the political agenda . . . voters recognize climate change as a matter of politics: it's an issue that simultaneously divides and necessitates a political response. Moreover, as is clear to nearly everyone, the scale of the catastrophe requires a state response.
> (Dean & Heron, 2020, Para 21)

The state has become an important aspect of the resistance that progressive forces are conceptualising to confront tendencies such as disaster capitalism, which, as Yee (2018) argues, has almost become a policy response in some states. Yee argues, 'the aftermath of disasters provides an enticing opportunity for states, corporations, and multilateral institutions – the disaster capitalism complex – in exploiting the reconstructing process to push for a free-market agenda to the detriment of the people' (2018, p. 161). While the roles that corporations and multilateral institutions have been playing have been debated quite vociferously during the pandemic, the state-form has escaped that kind of attention because to most people, it seemed essential as a regulating body. However, not many critically analysed the long-lasting effects that the domination of the state-form might have on the society at large once the pandemic is behind the society. Most such responses lose sight of the fact that in many states such as China, Iran, and North Korea, there has been no difference made between an authoritarian and highly privatised disaster capitalist complex and the State.

The state has occupied a central stage in most of the responses that societies have shown towards the pandemic, both in the Global North and in the Global South. However, when certain states in the Global South have become successful in controlling the spread of the disease, such as China, North Korea, Cuba, or Vietnam, the success has also raised certain questions with regards to how these states are structured and the methods through which they employ strategical surveillance and state control during health emergencies such as COVID-19. The success of the aforementioned states has brought forward the power that states command, or can command, over the economy and the society during times of distress. China's response to the pandemic has been one which has been characterised by a combination of strict lockdowns, mobilisations in support of governmental mandates, health provisioning by the state along with a suppression of information for the citizens as well as the globe, while maintaining a shroud of normalcy (Shih, 2021). Similar is the case with Vietnam which has managed the pandemic well, but the response has initiated widespread debates about the secretive methods that the state had employed (Troung, 2020). Cuba, similar to China, has used its local bodies to suppress the pandemic (Burke, 2021). The common thread binding all of these responses by different states governed by state capitalist regimes is the way in which they used their existing surveillance methods in conjunction with the services they have built over the past few decades. A. R. Desai, speaking in the context of such developmental activities had argued:

> The experience of these countries had proved that even the elementary bourgeois-democratic tasks . . . , which were resolved by the bourgeoisie in advanced capitalist countries through the democratic revolution can be resolved in colonial and semi-colonial countries only through Socialist Revolution.
>
> (Desai, 1974, p. 45)

Social development cannot be made to fit into straight lines, as most dialectical Marxists argue. The mainstream global media, which quite rightly focuses on the ability of strongarming the local bodies and the citizens that these states possess, fails to take note of the exemplary development that these small states have made in the domain of state provisioning of essential services. Lal (2021) brings out the inequalities within the media discourse itself which characterise the contemporary world, which glorifies the reaction that countries such as New Zealand showed – there is nothing wrong in it as

New Zealand did exemplary work in restricting the spread of the pandemic – but completely downplays the response that similar small nation states such as Cuba showed. This is similar to the ways in which historians and social commentators conveniently, even some on the left, have marginalised certain historical disasters and the effects that they have had on the populace of the affected regions, especially if they are from the Global South (Davis, 2002). This is, again, not to argue that one needs to avoid being critical towards these states, but rather the point is to bring them into the discussion – appreciate the benefits and condemn the pitfalls. One of the major causalities behind such actions might be the structural basis of the state, which operates in the Global North and in the Global South. For several states of the Global North, surveillance has been an everyday affair for decades albeit with a greater degree of subtlety incorporated in the process. States such as China and Vietnam do not operate on the basis of any such subtlety as accounts by Fang (2020) and Yang (2022) exhibit. However, it cannot be denied that these states did significantly better than many others on the Global North.

Hobbes's (1651/1996) Leviathan has again become relevant in the wake of the increasing statist interventions which are becoming mainstream during the current pandemic. Climate change and the rapidly degrading environment had already converted Hobbes' Leviathan into a relevant idea in the twenty-first century, but COVID-19 makes it look *almost* imminent. Multiple thinkers and commentators have argued that the pandemic presents society with a critical juncture where the *mighty state* is uncritically accepted as an authority in almost every matter which concerns the citizens. Hobbes' Leviathan was proposed as a remedy to the *state of war* which exists in the society because of the way in which human beings behave when they are left by themselves. Leviathan, as a concept, has been widely debated among social scientists of all hues. Some argue that the Leviathan is merely a concept referring to the state of absolutism with a purpose of protecting the citizens from the chaos that characterises society in general, while others see it as nothing better than a social order based on bourgeois property relations (Mann & Wainwright, 2018). To Hobbes, human beings are almost always at odds with each other over their own self-interests, which makes them behave in a manner that constitutes a society where planning becomes absolutely essential. The task of making a constitution is designated to a central figure by the will of the citizens themselves, *the Leviathan* (Oliver, 2020).

During the pandemic, right-wing populism has been one of the major factors that has influenced the global order of things. Figures such as Narendra Modi and Donald Trump have continued to enjoy widespread popularity, despite their apparent failures in handling the public health crisis caused by the pandemic. In spite of the failure, both of them have continued to follow the exact same political, social, and economic trajectory that they had been following before the pandemic. These leaders have worked upon the destructive nature of human society when left to themselves, which is the core of Hobbes' Leviathan (Botting, 2021), and have brought forward their own version of populist authoritarianism, one which actively reinforces the submission of one's freedom to authority as Fromm (1942/2001) had argued to be natural state of affairs under capitalist restructuring of the human psyche *en masse*. The Leviathan does not see much hope in parliamentary democracy but rather in monarchy (Oliver, 2020) and, in the context of the contemporary situation, in populist authoritarianism. One also needs to consider that contemporary authoritarianism does not need to be overtly exploitative in nature, but it can be performed under the guise of democracy because democracy itself has become an institution which has been under the constant threat of being overpowered, and in certain contexts completely overpowered, by the market-state. It is in this context that even steps such as surveillance have been rendered mainstream because they carry within themselves, in the wake of the otherwise oppressive nature of capitalist social structure, a factor being cared for by both the state and the market. The pandemic has exhibited the immense power that state surveillance has with regards to the implementation of resources to monitor the daily activities and movement of the citizens (Mahadevan et al., 2021). Mann and Wainwright (2018) have argued that more than the economic crisis, it is the crisis surrounding the climate, which has been promoting the kind of responses from the states.

The challenge that lies ahead for global thinkers and practitioners is to work on the response to the pandemic *in the long run*. This would require a much more innovative and universal policies being formed. For example, the rules and regulations framed in the Global North regarding the benefits of social distancing work only partially in countries such as India because in India, the major stakeholders, in such a milieu, are those who cannot afford to socially distance themselves. The migrant workers who live in tiny huts in slums cannot afford social distancing because that would mean the destruction of their livelihoods itself, given the kind of work that most of them are engaged, which frequently involve direct skin-to-skin contact such as care work and domestic work. The world, in this context, also needs to move away from the fetish of privatisation towards more innovative means of public provisioning of essential services.[13]

COVID-19 and the associated lockdowns have posed newer challenges to capitalism, in terms of the manner in which it frames the property relations in the society. One of the major issues that has surfaced during the pandemic is the issue of inequality, which is on the rise in India – the highest since the days of the British Empire according to the World Inequality Report 2022 (Chancel et al., 2022). Taxation has often been cited as a solution to India's inequality problem. Multiple social and economic thinkers in India have argued in favour of much more radical tax reforms to be brought into action, so that wealth can be redirected towards the essential service provisioning, thereby reducing the inequality in the society (Malhotra & Kundu, 2016; Patnaik, 2019–2020). Taxation reforms, though revolutionary, would still depend on the state to implement the associated benefits. This is again laden with the risk of giving rise to statism and state-capitalism. The question that looms large before humanity, as Mike Davis (2018) put it, especially when it is fairly evident that the society as one knows it is headed towards an inevitable collapse, is 'Who will build the ark?'. Davis's answer to the question is quite pessimistic – along the lines that it is the elites in the society who will build walls around themselves and their loved ones, both the living and the non-living ones, to protect themselves, leaving the rest of humanity to fend for themselves.

The solution to such a situation can be neither with the agency of the state nor with that of the market, as both the state and the market today act in conjunction with each other. The COVID-19 pandemic has made it evident that governments across the world, when working in conjunction with the forces of the market, can act as both destroyers and rebuilders of people's lives – a classical trait within disaster capitalist tendencies according to Naomi Klein (2005). Klein also argues that the primary motive behind such reconstruction is not reconstruction at all, but rather about reshaping the society through radical social and economic engineering for the benefit of the forces of the market. This is evident in the ways in which companies like Pfizer could make around US$ 3.5 billion in profits during the first 3 months of 2021, as Robbins and Goodman (2021) have reported – with sales constantly increasing since then (Robbins, 2021). The ways in which Pfizer and companies such as Moderna and AstraZeneca have experienced spiralling profits during the pandemic have exposed the fact that disaster capitalism is a permanent fixture of the global economic order.

Pfizer, AstraZeneca, and Moderna, along with the others in the global vaccine race, have been engaged in constant battles both among themselves and with states themselves regarding their patents, while a major section of the world's population has remained bereft of the vaccines (Stolberg & Robbins, 2021; Robbins & Gross, 2022). This has again made relevant the critical importance of the resistance that people and governments should show towards the patent regimes imposed by the corporates in the pharmaceutical sector. Without a timely intervention in these matters, even a partial waiver such as the one granted to India, would make little sense as global capitalism controls every aspect of the production process, from the knowledge to the furnace. It reserves the ability to constrain any aspect of the process, such as the supply of raw materials or technological know-how, which can in turn jeopardise the entire process itself (The Hindu, Editorial, 2022). Waivers in that situation would mean nothing better than empty promises. The constantly rising prices of medicines and vaccines coupled with the inability of the generic industry to respond to the crisis has exhibited the shortfalls of the generic supply chain in the world caused by resource concentration and competition for monopolistic control (Gustafsson, 2020).

Wars and pandemics have always been major disruptors of global and national economies.[14] However, the possibilities of that are severely restricted in the contemporary times because there has been a constant impoverishment of human society through years and decades of neoliberal reforms. Unlike the majority of previous pandemics, the COVID-19 pandemic did not create any scarcity in the labour force available to capitalism, but it has strengthened the segregations in the society by reinforcing the class, caste, and geopolitical lines of segregation in India (Sur, 2020; Wankhede, 2020) – by creating new kinds of inequality based on the ability of workers to work from home and by exploiting the technological advances in the field of digitalised service provisioning, creating an accessibility crisis. Hence, unlike the previous instances, capitalism did not suffer from a lack of labour supply, because it has, as Tronti (1962/2019) had put it, converted the entire society into a means of production. This has resulted in a situation where inaccessible essential services and a crumbling infrastructure has led to the death of around 14.9 million people (Daniyal, 2022). Contemporary society is a society where human beings have *turned on* each other, and as such are causing an indelible mark on the basic fabric of not only the human society but also the environment in general. Such a state of affairs makes it imperative for human societies to rethink, re-analyse, and rearticulate the radical possibility of a new social order, one that privileges human lives over profit accumulation.

Notes

1 A region in Maharashtra that comprises the districts of Aurangabad, Osmanabad, Jalna, Beed, Latur, Nanded, Hingoli, and Parbhani.
2 Prior to the emergence of COVID-19 as a global pandemic, the Indian economy had constantly slowed down, with GDP growth being registered at 4.1% for 2019–20 Financial Year, the lowest in over two decades (Mehrotra, 2021). The condition of the economy in India prior to COVID-19 was such that it had created a situation in which COVID-19 could have a much greater impact than in other societies. According to the First Advance Estimates of National Income during the 2020–21 Financial Year, there has been an 8.7% drop in the per-capita GDP of India – from Rs 1,08,620 in 2019–20 to Rs 99,155 in 2020–21 (Sengupta, 2021, January 7). This is in stark contrast to the continuous growth – from 4.4% during the 1970s–80s to 5.5% during the 1990s–2000s and then further to 7.1% during the 2000s–2010s (Pande, 2020) – which had characterised the Indian economy during the 1990s and 2000s.
3 According to the report, Delhi is the best performing State, while Uttarakhand is the worst.
4 Wallace and Wallace (2021) argue that in New York, the impact of COVID-19 varied in accordance with race and social class, and that, 'Like AIDS and tuberculosis (TB), COVID-19 hits marginalised communities and population sectors harder than wealthy, white ones. Black and Latinx people, the elderly, and the working class and poor suffer higher incidence of morbidity from the virus, as well as more severe illness' (p. vi).
5 The roots of outsourcing amidst disasters dates back to the 1980s and 1990s, when the privatisation agenda '. . . had successfully sold off or outsourced the large, publicly owned companies in several sectors, from water and electricity to highway management and garbage collection . . . . By the late nineties, a powerful move was afoot to break the taboos protecting "the core" from privatisation. It was, in many ways, merely a logical extension of the status quo' (Klein, 2007, p. 288).
6 Original statement was in Hindi. Translation provided by the author.

7 It is worthwhile to mention here that data about the Spanish flu and its impact on the human civilisation reveals that the Spanish flu had been more severe in its impact than COVID-19, at least until mid-2022, killing around – according to epidemiological estimates – 50 million people globally (Barry, 2005). COVID-19 is, yet, nowhere near that.
8 For example, the migrant workers' crisis in India has been there for decades now, accentuating with each passing year especially after the neoliberal economic reforms, but it is only with the onset of the pandemic that internal migration in India became a global issue both for policy analysts and social thinkers despite it being widely known that the kind of work that migrant workers engage with in the urban spaces is highly discriminatory in nature.
9 A sub-caste among the Dalits that mainly engages in sanitation work.
10 According to the *International Dalit Solidarity* Network, the number of dry latrines that are cleaned by human beings in India amounts to a staggering figure of 794,390, along with which around 4,97,236 toilets remain unattended until a human being, or an animal comes in to clean it (Parvati, 2020, August 31).
11 Companies such as Zoom, Amazon, and Google Meet have made tremendous progress in their social usefulness during the pandemic. During the third quarter of 2020, 'Zoom' reported that there had been a fivefold increase in its client-base during the pandemic, along with Amazon, which said that there was a 37% increase compared with the same quarter in the 2019–20 Financial Year, when the pandemic was at its peak globally (Lalé & Osotimehin, 2021).
12 For example, Matthew and Upreti (2018) write, in their analysis of disaster capitalism in Nepal, 'It is sad to think that through years of crisis, profiteering and corruption continuously countered acts of great courage and selflessness. . . . One of the main causes of disaster capitalism [observable is] the poor coordination of key stakeholders at the time of the crisis' (p. 181).
13 Dharavi, the largest slum in Asia, stands as an example of this. In spite of the warnings from the health authorities that it would be virtually impossible to stop a virus spreading through areas which are as congested with cramped housing and extremely dilapidated condition of sanitation as Dharavi, the authorities used existing equipment such as traffic cameras, heat maps, and advanced technologies such as drones to track and identify patients (Srivastava, 2020). The '4T' strategy consisting of tracing, tracking, testing, and treating made the Dharavi model gain widespread acclaim from public policy practitioners (Golechcha, 2020).
14 The combined effects of the World War and the Spanish flu brought down the then established order in Europe (Jordan, 2020). During the Spanish flu of 1918, India lost around 18 million people, which initiated a scheme of different events such as the protests against the Rowlatt Act and the Jallianwala Bagh massacre in colonial India – similar challenges lie ahead for the Indian government. as well as the failures that have come along with the upsurge of the pandemic (Parikh et al., 2020).

References

Abrol, D., Prajapati, P., & Singh, N. (2011). Globalization of the Indian pharmaceutical industry: Implications for innovation. *International Journal of Institutions and Economics*, 3(2), 327–365.

Agarwal, A. (2020, April 6). The Murky underbelly of sanitation during the pandemic. *The Wire*. Retrieved December 2, 2023, from www.thewire.in/article/rights/lockdown-delhi-ragpickers-sanitation-workers

Agarwal, A. K. (2010). *Business and intellectual property: Protect your idea*. Penguin.

Alexiou, C. (2021). Covid-19, capitalism and political elites: The real threat to humanity. *Human Geography*, 14(2), 284–287.

Amin, Z., Burdick, W. P., Supe, A., & Singh, T. (2010). Relevance of the Flexner report to contemporary medical education in South Asia. *Academic Medicine*, 85(2), 333–339.
Bambra, C., Lynch, J., & Smith, K. E. (2021). *The unequal pandemic: Covid-19 and health inequalities*. Policy Press.
Banerji, A. (2020, June 2). Nearly 200 migrant workers killed on India's roads during Coronavirus lockdown. *Reuters*. Retrieved December 2, 2023, from www.reuters.com/article/us-health-coronavirus-india-migrants-idUSKBN2392LG
Barry, J. M. (2005). *The great influenza: The epic story of the deadliest plague in history*. Penguin.
Bell, D. (1973/1999). *The coming of post-industrial society*. Basic Books.
Bhusan, R. (2022, June 6). COVID-19 relief hits cash-strapped NGOs hard, finds survey. *Money Control*. Retrieved December 2, 2023, from www.moneycontrol.com/trends/news/trends/health-trends/covid-19-relief-hits-cash-strapped-ngos-finds-survey-8649271.html
Bisen, A. (2019). *Wasted: The messy story of sanitation in India, a manifesto for change*. Pan Macmillan.
Bondre, S. (2014). *Dhandha: How Gujaratis do business* (S. Walimbe, Trans.). Penguin Portfolio.
Bonilla, Y., & LeBrón, M. (2019). Introduction: Aftershocks of disaster. In Y. Bonilla & M. LeBrón (Eds.), *Aftershocks of disaster: Puerto Rico before and after the storm*. Haymarket Books.
Botting, E. H. (2021). A novel (Coronavirus) reading of Hobbes' Leviathan. *History of European Ideas*, 47(1), 33–37.
Burke, N. J. (2021). Care in the time of Covid-19: Surveillance, creativity and socialism in Cuba. In L. Manderson, N. J. Burke, & A. Wahlberg (Eds.), *Viral loads: Anthropologies of urgency in the time of Covid-19*. UCL Press.
Chancel, L., Piketty, T., Saez, E., & Zucman, G. (2022). *World inequality report 2022*. World Inequality Lab.
Chaudhuri, S. (2002). TRIPS agreement and amendment of patent act in India. *Economic and Political Weekly*, 37(30), 3354–3360.
Chen, M. A., Grapsa, E., Ismail, G., Rogan, M., Valdivia, M., Alfers, L., Harvey, J., Ogando, A. C., Reed, S. O., & Roever, S. (2022). COVID-19 and informal work: Evidence from 11 cities. *International Labour Review*, 161(1), 29–58.
Chowdhury, A., & Sundaram, J. K. (2020). "Flattening the curve" through Covid-19 contagion containment. In C. M. Flood, V. MacDonnell, J. Philpott, S. Thériault, & S. Venkatapuram (Eds.), *Vulnerable: The law, policy and ethics and COVID-19*. University of Ottawa Press.
Daniyal, S. (2022, May 9). The Indian fix: How did a democracy like India rack up the highest Covid death count in the world? *Scroll*. Retrieved December 2, 2023, from www.scroll.in/article/1023500/the-india-fix-how-did-a-democracy-like-india-rack-up-the-highest-covid-death-count-in-the-world
Das, G. (2000). *India unbound: From independence to the global information age*. Penguin.
Dasgupta, B. (2022). Corona Pandemic, sudden visibility of migrant workers, and the Indian economy. In R. Bandyopadhyay, P. Bannerjee, & R. Samaddar (Eds.), *India's migrant workers and the pandemic*. Routledge.
Dasson, B. (2021, October 10). Mind the gap: How NGOs have been supporting the fractured Indian mental health infrastructure. *News18*. Retrieved December 2, 2023, from www.news18.com/news/india/mid-the-gap-how-ngos-have-been-supporting-the-fractured-indian-mental-health-infrastructure-4306307.html
Davies, R. (2021). *Prices and inflation in a pandemic: A micro data approach*. CEP Covid-19 Analysis Series. Centre for Economic Performance, London School of Economics and Political Science.

Davis, M. (2002). *Late Victorian holocausts: El Niño famines and the making of the third world*. Verso.
Davis, M. (2018). *Old Gods, new enigmas: Marx's lost theory*. Verso.
Davis, M. (2020). *The monster enters: COVID-19, avian flu, and the plagues of capitalism*. OR Books.
Dean, J., & Heron, K. (2020, June). Revolution or ruin. *E-flux Journal*. Retrieved December 2, 2023, from www.e-flux.com/journal/110/335242/revolution-or-ruin/
DebGupta, A. (2021). Dynamics of the public healthcare model. In K. Sarkar (Ed.), *The sickness of health: Journey of India's healthcare from colonial era to Corona*. BEE Books.
Deb Roy, S. (2022). *Social media and capitalism: People, communities and commodities*. Daraja Press.
Democracy Now. (2020, March 19). "Coronavirus capitalism": Naomi Klein's case for transformative change amid Coronavirus pandemic. *Democracy Now*. Retrieved December 2, 2023, from www.democracynow.org/2020/3/19/naomi_klein_coronavirus_capitalism
Department of Pharmaceuticals. (2022). *Annual report 2021–22*. Ministry of Chemicals and Fertilisers, Department of Pharmaceuticals.
Desai, A. R. (1974). "Two-stages" theory of revolution in the third world: Need for its evaluation. In *A positive program for Indian revolution*. Popular Prakashan.
Dhillon, A. (2021, April 16). Why is India, the world's No. 1 vaccine maker, struggling to inoculate its own people against the coronavirus? *South China Morning Post*. Retrieved December 2, 2023, from www.scmp.com/week-asia/health-environment/article/3129886/why-india-worlds-no-1-vaccine-maker-struggling
Diaz-Quiñones, A. (2019). Foreword. In Y. Bonilla & M. LeBrón (Eds.), *Aftershocks of disaster: Puerto Rico before and after the storm*. Haymarket Books.
Dréze, J., & Sen, A. (2013). *An uncertain glory: India and its contradictions*. Penguin.
Drolia, R. (2020, September 17). Chhattisgarh tops survey, scores 95% in midday meal during Covid crisis. *The Times of India*. Retrieved December 1, 2023, from www.timesofindia.com/city/raipur/chhattisgarh-tops-survey-scores-95-in-midday-meal-during-covid-crisi/amp_articleshow/78159267.cms
Dunayevskaya, R. (1958). *Marxism and freedom . . . from 1776 until today*. Bookman Associates.
Dunayevskaya, R. (1965). Marx's humanism today. In E. Fromm (Ed.), *Socialist humanism*. Doubleday.
Dutt, B. (2022). *To hell and back: Humans of Covid*. Juggernaut.
Fabiansson, C., & Fabiansson, S. (2016). *Food and the risk society: The power of risk perception*. Routledge.
Fang, F. (2020). *Wuhan diary: Dispatches from a quarantined city*. Harper Collins.
Festa, G., Kolte, A., Garli, M. R., & Rossi, M. (2022). Envisioning the challenges of the pharmaceutical sector in the Indian health-care industry: A scenario analysis. *Journal of Business and Industrial Marketing*, 37(8). https://doi.org/10.1108/JBIM-07-2020-0365
Food and Agricultural Organization (FAO). (2022). *India at a glance*. Food and Agricultural Organization of the United Nations. www.fao.org/india/fao-in-india-/india-at-a-glance-/en
Fouskas, V., & Gokay, B. (2020). COVID-19 and the bankruptcy of neoliberalism in the context of global shift. *Open Democracy*. Retrieved December 2, 2023, from www.opendemocracy.net/en/can-europe-make-it/covid-19-and-bankruptcy-neoliberalism-context-global-shift
Fromm, E. (1942/2001). *The fear of freedom*. Routledge.
Ghoshal, D. (2021, April 24). Why India is facing an oxygen crisis as COVID cases mount. *Reuters*. Retrieved December 2, 2023, from www.reuters.com/world/india/why-india-is-facing-an-oxygen-crisi-as-covid-cases-mount-2021-01-23/

Global Hunger Index. (2021). *India, 2021*. www.fao.org/india/fao-in-india-/india-at-a-glance-/en

Gnaulati, E. (2018). *Saving talk therapy: How health insurers, big pharma and slanted science are ruining good mental health care*. Beacon Press.

Goldberg, S. (2019). *How to be a patient: The essential guide to navigating the world of modern medicine*. Harper Wave.

Golechcha, M. (2020). COVID-19 containment in Asia's largest urban slum Dharavi-Mumbai, India: Lessons for policymakers globally. *Journal of Urban Health*, 97, 796–801.

Gordon, J. A., & Gordon, L. R. (2007). Reading the signs: A philosophical look at disaster. In K. J. Saltman (Ed.), *Schooling and the politics of disaster*. Routledge.

Gupta, A., & Sudharsanan, N. (2022). Large and persistent life expectancy disputes between India's social groups. *Population and Development Review* [Online]. https://doi.org/10.1111/padr.12489

Gupta, N. (2022, July 24). Malnourishment in Indian women: The hidden crisis. *The Times of India*. https://timesofindia.indiatimes.com/blogs/voices/malnourishment-in-indian-women-the-hidden-crisis/

Guru, G. (2013). Limits of the organic intellectual: A Gramscian reading of Ambedkar. In C. Zene (Ed.), *The political philosophies of Antonio Gramsci and B. R. Ambedkar: Itineraries of Dalits and subalterns*. Routledge.

Gustafsson, L. (2020, May 7). COVID-19 highlights problems with our generic supply chain. *The Commonwealth Fund*. Retrieved December 2, 2023, from www.commonwealthfund.org/blog/2020/covid-19-highlights-problems-with-out-generic-supply-chain

Hampden-Turner, C., & Trompenaars, F. (2021). *Culture, crisis and COVID-19: The great reset*. Cambridge Scholars Publishing.

Hardikar, J. (2013). *A village awaits doomsday*. Penguin.

Hardikar, J. (2021). *Ramrao: The story of India's farm crisis*. Harper Collins Publishers India.

Heraud, B. (1979). *Sociology in the professions*. Open Books.

The High Powered Expert Committee (HPEC) for Estimating the Investment Requirements for Urban Infrastructure Services. (2011). *Report on Indian urban infrastructure and services*. ICIER.

The Hindu Editorial. (2022, March 19). Too little, too late: On Covid-19 vaccines and patent rights. *The Hindu*. Retrieved December 2, 2023, from www.thehindu.com/oppinion/editorial/too-little-too-late-the-hindu-editorial-on-covid-19-vaccines-and-patent-rights/article65237446

The Hindu. (2021, April 29). Shortage and wastage: On cutting vaccine wastage. *The Hindu*. Retrieved December 2, 2023, from www.thehindu.com/opinion/editorial/shortage-and-wastage-the-hindu-editorial-on-cutting-covid-19-vaccine-wastage/article34433580.ece

The Hindu. (2021, May 9). Crime branch to probe hoarding of oxygen concentrators at posh eateries in Delhi. *The Hindu*. Retrieved December 2, 2023, from www.thehindu.com/news/cities/Delhi/crime-branch-to-probe-hoarding-of-oxygen-concentrators-at-posh-eateries/article34517524.ece

Hobbes, T. (1996). *Leviathan: Revised student edition* (R. Tuck, Ed.). Cambridge University Press. (Original work published 1651)

Housing Research. (2021). *State of Indian healthcare: Indian cities through the lens of healthcare 2021*. Retrieved December 2, 2023, from www.housing.com/research-reports

I, S. (2021). Of sewage, struggle, and the state: Caste and contractorization in contemporary sanitation work. In *India exclusion report 2019–20*. Three Essays Collective and Centre for Equity Studies.

I, S., & Majumdar, M. (2021, January 29). How caste oppression is institutionalized in India's sanitation jobs. *Scroll*. Retrieved December 2, 2023, from www.scroll.in/article/984297/how-caste-oppression-is-institutionalised-in-indias-sanitation-jobs

Iyer, K. (2021). *Landscapes of loss: The story of an Indian drought*. Harper Collins Publishers India.

Jain, M. (2017, August 2). Private sector profits in healthcare soar as Indian government investment stagnates. *Scroll*. Retrieved December 2, 2023, from www.scroll.in/pulse/845539/private-sectors-profits-in-healthcare-soar-as-indian-government-investment-stagnates

James, N. (2021, April 20). Young doctors 'overwhelmed' as beds, oxygen shortage leaves patients gasping. *Business Line*. Retrieved December 2, 2023, from www.thehindubusinessline.com/news/amid-crippling-shortages-of-hospital-beds-and-oxygen-healthcare-workers-are-struggling-to-save-lives/article34365229.ece

Jha, P. (2021, May 11). Government didn't pay heed to warnings about second wave: Uttarakhand HC. *The Times of India*. Retrieved December 2, 2023, from https://timesofindia.indiatimes.com/city/dehradun/govt-didnt-pay-heed-to-warnings-about-second-wave-uttarakhand-hc/articleshow/82540392.cms

Jordan, B. (2020, April 6). Covid-19 versus Leviathan. *Citizen Network*. Retrieved December 2, 2023, from www.citizen-network.org/library/Covid-19-versus-leviathan.html

Kapri, V. (2021). *1232 KM: The long journey back home*. Harper Collins Publishers India.

Kelman, I. (2020). *Disaster by choice: How our actions turn natural hazards into catastrophes*. Oxford University Press.

Khan, S. A. (2021, May 8). Ramping up medical oxygen production, distribution can save lives. *The Indian Express*. Retrieved December 2, 2023, from https://indianexpress.com/article/opinion/columns/ramping-up-medical-oxygen-production-distribution-can-save-lives-7306360/

Klein, N. (1999). *No logo: No space, no choice, no jobs*. Vintage Canada.

Klein, N. (2002). *Fences and windows: Dispatches from the front lines of the globalization debate*. Vintage Canada.

Klein, N. (2005, April 14). The rise of disaster capitalism. *The Nation*. Retrieved December 2, 2023, from www.thenation.com/article/archive/rise-disaster-capitalism/

Klein, N. (2007). *The shock doctrine: The rise of disaster capitalism*. Penguin.

Klein, N. (2017). *No is not enough: Resisting Trump's shock politics and winning the world we need*. Haymarket Books.

Klein, N. (2018). *The battle for paradise*. Haymarket Books.

Klein, N. (2020, March 19). "Coronavirus Capitalism": Naomi Klein's case for transformative change amid coronavirus pandemic. *Democracy Now*. Retrieved December 7, 2023, from www.democracynow.org/2020/3/19/naomi_klein_coronavirus_capitalism

Klein, N. (2020, May 13). How big tech plans to profit from the pandemic. *The Guardian*. Retrieved December 2, 2023, from www.theguardian.com/news/2020/may/13/naomi-klein=how-big-tech-plans-to-profit-from-coronavirus-pandemic

Krishnan, M. (2021, May 5). COVID: Why is India facing an oxygen shortage? *DW*. Retrieved December 2, 2023, from www.dw.com/en/india-covid-oxygen-shortage/a-57425951

Krishnan, V. (2022). *Phantom plague: How tuberculosis shaped history*. Penguin Random House.

Kudva, R., & Vyavaharkar, R. (2020, April 24). How the non-profit sector is helping India respond to Covid-19. *Business Line*. Retrieved December 2, 2023, from www.thehindubusinessline.com/opinion/how-the-non-proift-sector-is-helping-india-respond-to-covid-covid-19/article31423401.ece

Kumbhare, S. (2020, May 07). Sanitation workers: At the bottom of the frontline against COVID-19? *The Wire*. Retrieved December 2, 2023, from www.thewire.in/article/urban/sanitation-workers-covid-19

Kupperberg, P. (2008). *The influenza pandemic of 1918–1919*. Chelsea House Publishers.

Ladusingh, L., & Pandey, A. (2013). Health expenditure and impoverishment in India. *Journal of Health Management, 15*(1), 57–74.

Lahariya, C., Kang, G., & Guleria, R. (2020). *Till we win: India's fight against the Covid-19 pandemic*. Penguin.

Lal, V. (2021). Socialized healthcare and medical internationalism: Cuba and the Coronavirus. In K. Mahadevan, S. Kumar, M. Bhoot, & R. Kharat (Eds.), *The Covid spectrum: Theoretical and experiential reflections from India and beyond*. Speaking Tiger.

Lalé, E., & Osotimehin, S. (2021). Technology and globalisation in the post-Covid economy. In J. L. Denis, C. Régis, D. M. Weinstock, & C. Champagne (Eds.), *Pandemic societies*. McGill-Queen's University Press.

Law, J. (2006). *Big pharma: Exposing the global healthcare agenda*. Carroll and Graf Publishers.

Loitongbam, B. S. (2016). *Globalization and innovation in the Indian pharmaceutical industry*. Munich Personal RePEc Archive, 75925. Retrieved December 2, 2023, from https://mpra.ub.uni-muenchen.de/75925/

Madhiwalla, N. (2018). Social roots of medical education. In P. Prasad & A. Jesani (Eds.), *Equity and access: Health care studies in India*. Oxford University Press.

Mahadevan, K., Kumar, S., Bhoot, M., & Kharat, R. (2021). Uncertain consociates, unsettling conditions: The predicament of Covid-19. In K. Mahadevan, S. Kumar, M. Bhoot, & R. Kharat (Eds.), *The Covid spectrum: Theoretical and experiential reflections from India and beyond*. Speaking Tiger.

Mahalingam, R. (2007). Essentialism, power and the representation of social categories: An integrated perspective. *Human Development, 50*(6), 300–319.

Mahalingam, R., Jagannathan, S., & Selvaraj, P. (2019). Decasticization, dignity, and 'dirty work' at the intersections of caste, memory, and disaster. *Business Ethics Quarterly, 29*(2), 213–239.

Major, L. E., & Machin, S. (2020). *Covid-19 and social mobility*. CEP Covid-19 Analysis Series. Centre for Economic Performance, London School of Economics and Political Science.

Malhotra, R., & Kundu, S. (2016). Towards a tax system for inclusive development. In *India exclusion report 2015*. Yoda Press and Centre for Equity Studies.

Mann, G., & Wainwright, H. (2018). *Climate Leviathan: Our new planetary future*. Verso.

Martin, K. A. (2020, May 23). Keralites relied heavily on PDS during lockdown, says study. *The Hindu*. www.thehindu.com/news/national/kerala/keralites-relied-heavily-on-pds-during-lockdown-says-study/article31660893.ece

Marx, K. (1975). Economic and philosophical manuscripts of 1844. In *Marx Engels collected works* (Vol. 3). Lawrence and Wishart. (Original work published 1844)

Marx, K. (1976). *Capital, Vol. 1: A critique of political economy*. Penguin. (Original work published 1867)

Marx, K. (1977). Wage, labour and capital. In *Marx Engels collected works* (Vol. 9). Lawrence and Wishart. (Original work published 1849)

Matthew, R., & Upreti, B. R. (2018). Disaster capitalism in Nepal. *Peace Review, 30*(2), 176–183.

Matthewman, S. (2015). *Disasters, risks and revelation: Making sense of our times*. Palgrave.

McDonald, D. A., & Ruiters, G. (2005). Introduction: From public to private (to public again?). In D. A. McDonald & G. Ruiters (Eds.), *The age of commodity: Water privatisation in South Africa*. Earthscan.

McNeill, W. (1976). *Plagues and peoples*. Anchor Books.

Mehrotra, S. (2021). An alternative fiscal package to mitigate India's covid economic crisis. *The Indian Economic Journal* [Online First], 10.1177/00194662211021366

Migrant Workers' Solidarity Network. (2020). *Citizens and the sovereign: Stories from the largest human exodus in contemporary Indian history*. MWSN.

Modgal, S. C. (2012). *Food security of India: An overview*. National Book Trust.

Moole, J. (2021, April 23). A nightmare on repeat – India is running out of oxygen again. *BBC*. Retrieved December 2, 2023, from www.bbc.com/news/uk-56841381

Mukul, J. (2022). *The great shutdown: A story of two Indian Summers*. Harper Collins Publishers India.

Nail, T. (2022). What is Covid capitalism? *Distinktion: Journal of Social Theory* [Online]. https://doi.org/10.1080/1600910X.2022.2075905

Nanda, S. (2021). Inequalities and Covid-19. In J. M. Ryan (Ed.), *COVID-19: Vol. I: Global pandemic, societal responses, ideological solutions*. Routledge.

Nazeer, M. (2014, February 1). Health and hygiene in times of migration. *The Hindu*. Retrieved December 2, 2023, from www.thehindu.com/news/national/kerala/health-and-hygiene-in-times-of-migration/article5642482.ece

Nehru, J. (1949/2015). From a letter dated February 3, 1949. In M. Khosla (ed.), *Letters for a nation: From Jawaharlal Nehru to his chief ministers, 1947–1963*. Penguin.

NITI Aayog. (2021). *Best practices in the performance of district hospitals*. Government of India.

NT, S. (2021, May 18). Unseen warriors of COVID: Sanitation workers in rural Haryana unable to access ration, primary health care. *Firstpost*. Retrieved December 2, 2023, from www.firstpost.com/india/unseen-warriors-of-covid-sanitation-workers-in-rural-haryana-unable-to-access-ration-primary-health-care-96132141.html

Oliver, C. (2020, April 30). Of Leviathan and lockdowns. *Politico*. Retrieved December 2, 2023, from www.www.politico.eu/article/thomas-hobbesof-philosophy-coronavirus-leviathan-and-lockdowns/

Padel, F., & Das, S. (2010). *Out of this earth: East India Adivasis and the aluminium cartel*. Orient Blackswan.

Pande, A. (2020). *Making India great: The promise of a reluctant global power*. Harper Collins Publishers India.

Parikh, S., Desai, M., & Parikh, R. (2020). *The Coronavirus: What you need to know about the global pandemic*. Penguin.

Parsons, R. (2021). Business as usual: Poverty, education, and economic life amidst the pandemic. In J. M. Ryan (Ed.), *COVID-19: Vol. I: Global pandemic, societal responses, ideological solutions*. Routledge.

Participatory Research in Asia. (2019). *Lived realities of women sanitation workers in India*. PRIA.

Parvati, P. (2020, August 31). Dalit woman sparks hope for manual scavengers during COVID-19 pandemic. *International Budget Partnership*. www.internationalbudget.org/2020/08/dalit-woman-sparks-hope-for-manual-scavengers-during-covid-19-pandemic/

Patnaik, P. (2019–2020). Taxing the super-rich to institute universal socio-economic rights. In *India exclusion report*. Three Essays Collective and Centre for Equity Studies.

Pelling, M. (2003). *The vulnerability of cities: Natural disasters and social resilience*. Earthscan.

Posadas, J. (1978). Childbearing in space, the confidence of humanity, and socialism. In *Socialism and human relationships with nature and the cosmos*. Scientific, Cultural and Political Editions.

Posadas, J. (1969/2014). *The revolutionary state, its transitory role and the construction of socialism*. Scientific, Cultural and Political Editions.

Prasad, P. (2018). Health care reforms: Do they ensure social protection for the labouring poor? In P. Prasad & A. Jesani (Eds.), *Equity and access: Health care studies in India*. Oxford University Press.

The Quint. (2021, April 23). In January, PM Modi had expressed India's victory over Covid-19. *The Quint*. Retrieved December 2, 2023, from www.thequint.com/news/india/in-january-pm-modi-had-expressed-indias-victory-over-covid-19

Rajagopalan, S. (2019, October 2). Swachh Bharat toilets without sanitation is why Dalits are at the receiving end. *The Print*. Retrieved December 2, 2023, from www.theprint.in/opinion/swachh-bharat-toilets-without-sanitation-is-why-dalits-are-at-the-receiving-end

Ramin, C. J. (2017). *Crooked: Outwitting the back pain industry and getting on the road to recovery*. Harper.

Ratcliffe, R. (2021, April 23). Delhi hospitals issue SOS alerts over oxygen supplies as India's Covid crisis mounts. *The Guardian*. Retrieved December 2, 2023, from www.theguardian.com/world/2021/apr/23/delhi-hospitals-run-out-of-oxygen-as-india-covid-crisis-mounts

Ravichandran, N. (2020, March 30). Sanitation workers holding the fort against COVID-19 have no protective equipment. *The Wire*. Retrieved December 2, 2023, from www.thewire.in/article/rights/sanitation-workers-covid-19-working-conditions

Reddy, K. S. (2019). *Make health in India: Reaching a billion plus*. Orient Blackswan.

Reddy, K. S. (2021, October 28). Strengthening healthcare: ABHIM can fix the weakness in India's health system. *The Hindu*. Retrieved December 2, 2023, from www.thehindu.com/opinion/op-ed/strengthening-healthcare/article37200628.ece/

Rege, S. (2020). Brahmanical nature of violence against women. In S. Arya & A. S. Rathore (Eds.), *Dalit feminist theory*. Routledge.

Robbins, R. (2021, November 2). Pfizer's Covid vaccine could break sales records again next year. *The New York Times*. Retrieved December 2, 2023, from www.nytimes.com/2021/11/02/business/pfizer-covid-vaccine-revenue-profits.html

Robbins, R., & Goodman, P. S. (2021, May 4). Pfizer reaps hundreds of millions in profits from Covid vaccine. *The New York Times*. Retrieved December 2, 2023, from www.nytimes.com/2021/05/04/business/pfizer-covid-vaccine-profits.html

Robbins, R., & Gross, J. (2022, April 26). Moderna sues Pfizer and BioNTech over Covid vaccine technology. *The New York Times*. Retrieved December 2, 2023, from https://nyti.ms/3Klno7O

Sagot, M. (2022). Necropolitics and biopower in the pandemic: Death, social control or well-being. In B. Bringel & G. Pleyers (Eds.), *Social movements and politics in a global pandemic*. Bristol University Press.

Sainath, P. (1996). *Everybody loves a good drought: Stories from India's poorest districts*. Penguin.

Sainath, P. (2011, September 25). Census findings point to decade of rural distress. *The Hindu*. www.thehindu.com/opinion/columns/sainath/article60501688.ece

Sarkar, K. (2021). *The sickness of health: Journey of India's healthcare from colonial era to Corona*. BEE Books.

Sastri, S., & Bandyopadhyay, A. (2021). *The ventilator project: How the IIT Kanpur consortium built a world-class product during India's Covid-19 lockdown*. Macmillan.

Schaffer, S. (2021). Necroethics in the time of COVID-19 and Black lives matter. In J. M. Ryan (Ed.), *COVID-19: Vol. I: Global pandemic, societal responses, ideological solutions*. Routledge.

Scheidel, W. (2018). *The great leveler: Violence and the history of inequality from the stone age to the twenty-first century*. Princeton University Press.

Schneider, D. (2021). *The invention of surgery: A history of modern medicine from the renaissance to the implant revolution*. Coronet.

Sengupta, A. (2000). Genesis of intellectual capital as property. *The Marxist*, 16(1).

Sengupta, A. (2018). Globalisation, intellectual property rights, and pharmaceuticals. In P. Prasad & A. Jesani (Eds.), *Equity and access: Health care studies in India*. Oxford University Press.

Sengupta, R. (2021, January 7). Drop of 8.7% in India's per-capita GDP in 2020–21: First advance estimates. *Down to Earth*. Retrieved December 2, 2023, from www.downtoearth.org.in/news/agriculture/drop-of-8.7-in-india-s-per-capita-gdp-in-2020-21-first-advance-estimates-74956

Shagun. (2021, January 29). Agri share in GDP hit 20% after 17 years: Economic survey. *Down to Earth*. Retrieved December 2, 2023, from https://www.downtoearth.org/news/agriculture/agri-share-in-gdp-hit-20-after-17-years-economic-survey-75271

Shah, S. (2010). *The fever: How malaria has ruled humankind for 500,000 years*. Penguin.

Shameem, M. (2022). Digging deeper wounds. In D. Aggarwal & S. Sundaram (Eds.), *A world on hold: A living record of the global pandemic*. Om Books International.

Sharma, H. (2021, May 1). PM wants NGOs, volunteers to help health sector. *The Indian Express*. www.indianexpress.com/article/pm-wants-ngos-volunteers-to-help-health-sector-7297401.html

Sharma, J. (2022). *Made in lockdown: India's medtech growth powered by AMTZ*. Rupa.

Sharma, N. C. (2020, August 17). How Covid-19 pandemic exposed India's chronic underinvestment in healthcare? *Mint*. Retrieved December 2, 2023, from www.livemint.com/news/india/how-covid-19-pandemic-exposed-india-s-chronic-underinvestment-in-healthcare/amp-11597670943972.html

Sherwell, P. (2021, April 25). Modi leads India out of lockdown…and into a Covid apocalypse. *The Australian*. Retrieved December 2, 2023, from www.theaustralian.com.au/world/the-times/modi-leads-india-out-of-lockdown-and-into-a-covid-apocalypse/news-story/

Shih, V. C. (2021). China's Leninist response to Covid-19: From information repression to total mobilization. In S. L. Greer, E. L. King, E. M. da Fonseca, & A. Peralta-Santos (Eds.), *Coronavirus politics: The comparative politics and policy of Covid-19*. University of Michigan Press.

Singh, B. (2012). *Unseen: The truth about India's manual scavengers*. Penguin.

Singh, S. (2018). *The great smog of India*. Penguin.

Sismondo, S. (2018). *Ghost-managed medicine: Big pharma's invisible hands*. Mattering Press.

Soni, P., & Pant, M. (2022). The role of health systems in the Indian and global context. In A. Thomas, K. S. Reddy, D. Alexander, & P. Prabhakaran (Eds.), *Climate change and the health sector*. Routledge.

Sriram, J. (2021, April 15). Breaking down the reasons behind India's vaccine shortage. *The Hindu*. Retrieved December 2, 2023, from www.thehindu.com/sci-tech/health/breaking-down-the-reasons-behind-indias-vaccine-shortage-the-hindu-in-focus-podcast/article34329784.ece

Srivastava, H. N. (1983). *Earthquakes: Forecasting and mitigation*. National Book Trust.

Srivastava, R. (2020, July 7). Don't forget us in Coronavirus battle, say businesses in India's Dharavi slum. *Reuters*. Retrieved December 2, 2023, from https:///www.reuters.com/article/us-heath-coronavirus-india-slum-trfn-idUSKBN248004

Srivastava, S. K., Chand, R., & Singh, J. (2017). Changing crop production cost in India: Input prices, substitution and technological effects. *Agricultural Economics Research Review*, 30, 171–182. https://doi.org/10.5958/0974-0279.2017.00032.5

Steinberger, J. (2020). Pandenomics: A story of life versus growth. *Open Democracy*. Retrieved December 2, 2023, from www.opendemocracy.net/en/oureconomy/pandmeonics-story-life-versus-growth

Stolberg, S. G., & Robbins, R. (2021, November 9). Moderna and U.S. at odds over vaccine patent rights. *The New York Times*. Retrieved December 2, 2023, from https://nyti.ms/3bZgzrn

Sur, P. (2020, April 16). Under India's caste system, Dalits are considered untouchable: The Coronavirus is intensifying that slur. *CNN*. Retrieved December 2, 2023, from www.edition.cnn.com/2020/04/15/asia/india-coronavirus-lower-castes-hnl-intl/index.html

Swaminathan, M. (2000). *Weakening welfare: The public distribution of food in India*. Leftword Books.

Thacker, T. (2021, May 6). India's drug regulator clears the way for import of Covid-19 vaccines into India. *The Economic Times*. Retrieved December 2, 2023, from https://economictimes.indiatimes.com/industry/healthcare/biotech/healthcare/indias-drug-regulator-has-cleared-the-way-for-import-of-covid-19-vaccines-into-india-/articleshow/82399814.cms?from=mdr

Thomas, A., Alexander, D., & Gyani, G. (2022). Health sector leadership to combat climate change. In A. Thomas, K. S. Reddy, D. Alexander, & P. Prabhakaran (Eds.), *Climate change and the health sector*. Routledge.

Thorat, A., & Thorat, S. (2022, February 11) Employment and the Dalit question. *Outlook*. Retrieved December 2, 2023, from www.outlookindia.com/magazine/story/india-news-employment-and-the-dalit-question/305415

The Indian Express. (2021, June 19). Maharashtra joins hands with Cognizant Foundation to set up 100-bed Covid care facility in Pune. www.indianexpress.com/article/cities/pune/state-govt-joins-hands-with-cognizant-foundation-to-dedicate-100-bed-covid-care-facility-in-pune-7364588/

The Times of India. (2022, March 29). Lucknow: Staff hired for Covid management face uncertainty. *The Times of India*. Retrieved December 2, 2023, from www.timesofindia.com/cities/lucknow/staff-hired-for-covid-mgmt-face-uncertainty/

Tomes, N. (2016). *Remaking the American patient: How Madison avenue and modern medicine turned patients into consumers*. The University of North Carolina Press.

Tronti, M. (1962/2019). Factory and society. In *Workers and capital*. Verso.

Troung, M. (2020, August 6). Vietnam's COVID-19 success is a double-edged sword for the communist party. *The Diplomat*. Retrieved December 2, 2023, from www.thediplomat.com/2020/08/vietnams-covid-19-success-is-a-double-edged-sword-for-the-communist-party/

UNESCO. (2021). *India case study: Situation analysis on the effects of and responses to COVID-19 on the education sector in Asia*. Retrieved February 2, 2022, from www.unicef.org/rosa/media/16511/file/India%20Case%20Study.pdf

Vidyarthee, K. B. (2014). Trajectories of Dalits' incorporation into the Indian neoliberal business economy. In C. Still (Ed.), *Dalits in neoliberal India: Mobility of marginalisation*. Routledge.

Vyas, S., Hathi, P., & Gupta, A. (2022). Social disadvantage, economic inequality, and life expectancy in nine Indian states. *PNAS*, *119*(10). https://doi.org/10.1073/pnas.2109226119

Wallace, D., & Wallace, R. (2018). *Right-to-work laws and the crumbling of American public health*. Springer.

Wallace, D., & Wallace, R. (2021). *Covid-19 in New York city: An ecology of race and class oppression*. Springer.

Wallace, R. (2016). *Big farms make big flu: Dispatches on infectious diseases, agribusiness, and the nature of science*. Monthly Review Press.

Wallace, R., & Wallace, R. G. (2016). The social amplification of pandemic and other disasters. In R. G. Wallace & R. Wallace (Eds.), *Neoliberal Ebola: Modeling disease emergence from finance to forest and farm*. Springer.

Wankhede, H. S. (2020, April 6). The Coronavirus pandemic has strengthened class segregation in India. *The Wire*. Retrieved December 2, 2023, from www.thewire.in/article/rights/the-coronavirus-pandemic-has-strengthenes-class-segregations

Wilson, B., & Singh, B. (2016). The long march to eliminate manual scavenging. In *India exclusion report, 2016*. Yoda Press and Three Essays Collective.

Yang, G. (2022). *The Wuhan lockdown*. Columbia University Press.

Yee, D. K. P. (2018). Violence and disaster capitalism in post-Haiyan Philippines. *Peace Review*, 30(2), 160–197.

Yoho, R. (2021). *Butchered by "healthcare": How doctors and corporations try to kill you for the money and how to survive anyway*. Inverness Press.

York, J. (2022, April 19). How Covid-19 has made life more dangerous for migrant workers. *Migrant Data Portal: The Bigger Picture*. Retrieved December 2, 2023, from www.migrationdataportal.org/blog/how-covid-19-has-made-life-more-dangerous-for-migrant-workers

Zachariah, A. (2018). Medical education and basic health care. In P. Prasad & A. Jesani (Eds.), *Equity and access: Health care studies in India*. Oxford University Press.

Zanoni, P., & Mir, R. (2022). COVID-19: Interrogating the capitalist organization of the economy and the society through the pandemic. *Organization*, 29(3), 369–378.

3 Pandemics of Capitalism and Everyday Disasters

Introduction

COVID-19 has left an indelible mark on humanity. Not only has it caused a massive economic downturn but it has also resulted in tremendous loss of human capital globally. It has forced the society to question some of the most mundane assumptions that the society has held dear to itself since time immemorial (Pikoli, 2020). The pandemic has questioned the capitalist organisation of the economy and the ways in which capital influences the reproduction of life on the planet (Zanoni & Mir, 2022). COVID-19 presented an antithesis to the global capitalist growth model, in the sense that it showed the massive problems that capitalist globalisation had caused by being one of the most important carriers of the virus globally through its global modes of communication and transport designed in a manner which maximises profits often at the expense of other social benefits (Tooze, 2021). The COVID-19 pandemic is a result of the progress of human civilisation over the past few decades, which has resulted in the continued increase of vulnerability among the already marginalised section of the populace. Women, Muslims, Dalits, people from other backward castes, and young people have been severely impacted by the pandemic. This is not only because of the sectors in which they work but also because of the kind of disproportionate responsibilities – such as care-giving in the case of women, sanitation work in the case of Dalits, and social responsibility of finding a paid work in the case of young people – that are often entrusted upon them by the dominant social order (Blundell & Machin, 2020; Bell et al., 2020a).

The fragility of capitalism, property, is often equated with liberty and life itself. COVID-19 has expressed the fragility of this entire structural system, which has not only endangered life but also property – by bringing in a financial apocalypse for many – and liberty – by enabling the state to take autocratic decisions without consultation with the people. Books such as Greger's (2020) talk about how the health of an individual depends upon the individual's own activities as well as the way the individual communicates with the society, and the processes through which the measures advertised would only serve temporal gains, because 'To avoid the disease completely

DOI: 10.4324/9781003505167-4

would mean a divorce from society' (p. 271). COVID-19 has provided the human society and the socio-economic systems that govern the society with the task of choosing between private wealth and public health (Gans, 2020b), of which it has mostly chosen the former renouncing the importance of the latter.

Parikh et al. (2020) and Greger (2020) bring forward how previous pandemics had some amount of positive impact on the population, either by enabling the employment of women, bringing down rents, or increasing the per capita income in the early twentieth century. COVID-19 did not provide any such optimistic possibilities, except that it allowed massive profiteering processes to emerge out of the despair of the vulnerable populace by bringing in methods which produced 'vaccine inequality', having a disastrous impact on – and caused by – the already existing health inequalities (Nichols, 2022) and vulnerabilities that capitalism has produced through decades of uneven development. All of this has been taking place while Big Pharma has been reaping in huge profits: making around 1,000 US$ every second as of November 2021 (Oxfam, 2021, November 16). The political unaccountability, which has often been a part of the far-right denial of the lethal nature of COVID-19, has allowed these profiteering tendencies to grow and develop. Such denials have completely overlooked the apprehension that a steady and resolute viral infection, even with a comparatively low mortality rate, can kill a lot more people than one which manifests itself more prominently with concrete symptoms and high mortality rates (Gans, 2020a).

The COVID-19 crisis has often been equated with the apocalyptic changes that climate change has brought to the human society. Prabhakaran (2022) has argued that climate change is the biggest public health challenge confronting the entire human civilisation in the twenty-first century. In the context of India, as she narrates, the possibilities are more apocalyptic because there is already an estimate that the GDP will contract by around 2.8% by 2050. With thousands of people dying in events such as floods and heatwaves, these projections seem more fatal. However, there are certain differences, which need to be emphasised in any narrative regarding apocalyptic tendencies and COVID-19. Climate Change has not yet attacked capitalism at an immediate level for capitalism to react to it; unlike COVID-19, which has attacked global capitalistic socio-economic and cultural order at an immediate level (Malm, 2020).

With the introduction of neoliberal reforms in India, the effects of global capitalism transformed itself into an everyday reality for millions of Indians. Even within the pharmaceutical industry, global capitalism's drive for profiteering has become the norm in India after 1991, with major multinational companies entering the Indian market. With the economic reforms of 1991, the market for medical goods increased manifold, especially the demand for medical devices. Sharma (2022) argues that even with such a drastic change in the pattern of consumption, referring to the increasing household costs which neoliberalism brought forward, the primary market for such devices remained medical practitioners and hospitals with imported products (as of 2020) occupying a market size of approximately $6 billion out of the estimated $8 billion. At the same time, the medical device market in India is estimated to be valued at $5.9 billion (INR 44,580.8 crores) during the 2020–21 Financial Year with around $2.6 billion (INR 19,471.2 crores) of exports. During that period, exports grew by 7%, while imports grew by 7.2%. The data from the Department of Pharmaceuticals (2022) validates this with around US$ 6240.55 million imports and US$ 2531.62 million exports during 2020–21 Financial Year.

The COVID-19 crisis caused a massive compounding of existing inequalities globally because global capitalism has for decades functioned through a tremendously unequal relationship between supply and demand. This has allowed capitalism to accumulate further profits (Tooze, 2021). 'Shocks' such as COVID-19 present certain unique challenges in terms of supply and demand for commodities, especially if they are essential in nature. COVID-19 saw newer commodities emerging in the society, many of which have subsequently gone on to become major drivers of certain economies. Commodities such as masks have become essentialised during the pandemic. The OECD (April 4, 2022) reported that it was trading three essential commodities, which had enabled the world to launch a struggle against COVID-19 – vaccines, face masks, and testing kits. According to the OECD, global trading helped different countries overcome their production lacunae, giving them time and space to respond to the pandemic. The OECD, however, was only partially correct. In reality, the rampant trading in commodities such as face masks has converted them into fetishised commodities – a product that is more than a healthcare and preventive equipment against the virus (Subramaniam, 2020, April 28). Face masks with time turned into a 'normal' commodity reflecting the commodity-form capable of reaping in exorbitant profits and thus conformed to other market dynamics.[1]

Commodities under capitalism are not only valued for their use value but also because they produce a certain value. They are not just an entity focused on utility, but are rather focused on the creation of a class conscious value-form drawn from the dual-nature of labour under capitalism (Dunayevskaya, 1958). The commodity inherits the inherent contradictions within the nature of labour under capitalism and becomes 'in embryo [as an entity containing] all the contradictions of capitalism' (Dunayevskaya, 1958, p. 85). The centrality of the commodity form which became evident even during the pandemic, is such that any quantitative or qualitative change in their production, distribution, and consumption mechanisms greatly affects actual human lives. Capitalist production focused on the creation of profits does not only produce commodities but rather it produces the human being itself 'as a *commodity*, the *human commodity*, [a human being] in the role of *commodity*' in such a way that the human being only exists in the capitalist society in a completely dehumanised form' (Marx, 1844/1975, p. 284). COVID-19 is merely an event in this entire process of everyday dehumanisation. Taking cue from this idea, this chapter begins with a discussion about Big Pharma and ends with a section on digital apartheid. The arguments in these two sections are then related to issues such as vaccine shortages in the third section. The penultimate section discusses the most visible aspect of India's pandemic response strategy – the migrant exodus that occurred during the first lockdown.

Big Pharma and the Apocalypse

The contemporary society is a society characterised by risks, with lower income countries and the marginalised populace positioned at the bottom of the risk-facing hierarchy. Low-income countries often suffer from multiple ailments. It is completely possible that the Global North might consider these ailments as being, apocalyptic in nature. For example, Osho and Sareen (2022) write about the ways in which electricity deficiency causes a crisis in the healthcare delivery sector in many countries of the Global South, most of which are either low or middle income ones. At the same time, there are multiple other factors, such as issues with cold storage and transportation, which have become important aspects of the continued assurance of a good health during the pandemic (Yadav, 2022). Because the delivery of healthcare services in India is highly fragile and insufficient, pharmaceuticals assume a tremendous importance in India. This is due to the fact that medicines and drugs often become the first line of defence for the poor and marginalised. And, when Big Pharma enters these spaces, it creates avenues through which all forms of local production of medicines are rendered vulnerable (Wallace, 2016). Big Pharma also creates the conditions under which profitable industries can develop afresh in societies that have been previously resistant to changes in their medical regime, such as India.

The Department of Pharmaceutical (2022) Report for 2020–21 labelled the medical device industry as one of the most critical industries which 'has the [highest] potential of growing . . . among all the sectors in the healthcare system' (p. 6). With people becoming conscious of their own health and becoming aware that they can do so on their own, there occurred a massive surge in the sale of medical devices in the country's urban spaces during the pandemic.[2] However, the government investment into the sector remains extremely low. Around four-fifths of the manufacturers of medical devices in India are small, micro, and medium enterprises, which require governmental support to compete against the multinational companies that dominate the Indian market, in terms of medical devices (Barnagarwala, 2022, July 19). With regard to pharmaceuticals, the situation is a lot more promising. India produces around $40 billion worth of pharmaceuticals, around half of which is exported to other countries (Sharma, 2022). At the same time, it is also important to mention here that a large proportion of this production is occupied by generic medicines, which has its own flaws.[3]

Generic medicines had an important role to play in India's pandemic response strategy, considering that India supplies generic medicines to more than 200 countries (Department of Pharmaceuticals, 2022). Although Eban's arguments surrounding the issues of Indian generic medicines are legitimate and deserve to be taken into cognisance, but the prime issue that she highlights is not with the drugs but rather with the market that these drugs are sent to. As Feldman and Frondorf (2017) argue generic medicines are crucial to global health, because they allow countries with poorer health infrastructure to either manufacture or buy medicines at lower costs than the ones available from multinationals engaged in Big Pharma. This becomes critical in countries such as India, where the expenditure on health is low, while at the same time, the health care sector has to ensure wide outreach, affordability, longevity of the care framework, and easy accessibility (Reddy, 2019). Many medicines which have a global market today have risen to the level of being necessities – essential services – for those who use them, especially if they have a rare disorder, and the users would not hesitate to pay high prices for them even if the demand and pricing is at a disjunction and does not follow any ethical protocols (Feldman & Frondorf, 2017). The case of Remdesivir – the first COVID-19 drug, and its black marketing and hoarding in certain parts of India, which has also led to numerous arrests in 2021 – proves that during disasters, black marketing and hoarding are major concerns for law and order authorities in India (The New Indian Express, 2021, April 26). There were also pleas for initiating the National Security Act (NSA) against those who hoard and black market essential drugs and medicines, which had resulted in drugs such as Remdesivir being sold for Rs 70,000 in certain parts of Delhi while its normal price is only Rs 899 (The Hindu, 2021, May 30).

The same can be said about vaccines. The hoarding of vaccine shots contributed to the growing scarcity of vaccines. The phenomenon of vaccine hoarding is related to the widespread vaccine inequality that characterised COVID-19. Hoarding of vaccines manufactured by Big Pharma, such as Pfizer-BioNTech and Moderna, by the wealthy countries has resulted in the inability of low and middle income countries in Asia, Latin America, and Africa to vaccinate their population (Jishnu, 2022, February 11). This becomes critical because since the onset of the pandemic in 2020, as of March 2022, 'fewer than 15% of people in low-income countries have had at least one does of a vaccine, whereas in some high-income countries, people are being offered fourth doses' (Nature Editorial, 2022, March 31, Para 4). The demand to waive off patents on the vaccines has been backed by researchers, academics, NGOs, and other critiques of the capitalisation of a disaster. The Nature Editorial of 31st of March 2022 also states some of the issues with the removal of the IPRs during the pandemic. For example, Big Pharma has the capacity to block the compulsory licensing procedures, which gives countries the right to override IPRs during a pandemic. The second being that the proposal that has been forwarded by the anti-IPR bloc led by India and South Africa does not claim any right on the non-procedural knowledge that might be critical to the manufacturing process. The Center for Disaster Philanthropy (CDP) and Candid in their report state:

> As of April 14, 2022, 21% of the people worldwide who have received at least one vaccination are from North America or Europe, and 25% are from high-income countries. The wealthiest 30 countries have just 10.9% of the world's population but have access to 14.4% of the vaccines.
> (CANDID and Center for Disaster Philanthropy, 2022, p. 27)

Most of the headquarters of Big Pharma are located in the powerful western nations, including Pfizer and AstraZeneca. Apart from their economic prowess, since these companies are located in the Global North, the countries of the Global North also find it relatively easy to transport and stock the vaccines.[4]

The richest countries of the world are holding an abnormal amount of the best vaccines, while the poorer nations are left to make-do with the remaining ones (Bhutto, 2021, March 17). Companies such as Moderna are exclusively selling their vaccines to richer countries, and its forecasted sales numbers for 2021 was around US$ 18 billion, making it profitable for the first time since its formation. Big Pharma was selling the vaccine at increased prices in the Global South, which exceeded the cap placed by the companies themselves on the cost of the vaccines.

The spread of the virus in the Global South, with only around 3% of the population vaccinated in low income countries as of November 2021, had already unsurprisingly paved the path for newer variants to emerge (Brown, 2021, November 26). Both Fatima Bhutto and Gordon Brown's pieces for *The Guardian* emphasised the point that the issue was not with vaccine production – around 2 billion doses were being produced monthly in 2021 – but rather with the deeply skewed distribution mechanisms around the vaccines, which favoured rich countries' intentions of stockpiling and the companies' desires of profit maximisation out of the disaster. It is true that Big Pharma developed the vaccine in record time, but that in no way gives them the leverage to deprive the poorer countries of effective vaccines. As of January 2022:

> Globally, 50.03% of people of people have been fully vaccinated, according to the WHO. In total, 9.36 billion doses have been administered globally, and 32.69 million are now administered each day, as of January 16. But those vaccines are unevenly rolled out, with only 9.5 percent of people in low-income countries having received at least one dose.
> (The Global Times, 2022, January 17, Para 10)

India was one of the countries facing acute vaccine shortage, especially during the second wave (Alluri, 2021, May 1). This was especially apparent considering that India produces around 60% of the vaccines globally catering to fulfilment of demands ranging from 40% to 90% of vaccine requirement for various diseases globally, as mandated by the WHO, including diphtheria, tetanus, and measles (Dadhich, 2020, April 22). India, as Dadhich (April 22, 2020) and Guerin et al. (2020) mention, supplies approximately 30% to 40% of the generic APIs required in the United States and about a quarter of that in the European States, despite the fact that India itself remains dependent on China for approximately 70% of its own medicine formulations. However, the point here is to realise that even with this rapid growth of manufacturing, the accessibility to standard medicines for the labouring poor, or the working class, has remained extremely low (Reddy, 2019). The excess expenditure on medicines and healthcare contributed to the impoverishment of 38% of the 55 million people in India who experienced poverty during 2011–12 (Selvaraj et al., 2019). The way in which the Indian pharmaceutical industry has been structured has benefited immensely from the Indian Patents Act of 1970, which provided some special provisions for the pharmaceutical sector in the sense that it 'did not provide for pharmaceutical product patents and thus supported the domestic industry's endeavour to introduce new medicines at a fraction of the global price, unencumbered by the patent protection' (Sengupta, 2018). This made the Indian pharmaceutical industry grow by leaps and bounds.[5]

The growth of the private and corporate pharmaceutical sector in India has occurred through a constant impoverishment of the public sector companies. The meteoric rise of private capital undermines the role of economic planning in India, something which had been instilled in as a national agenda after independence and the public sector has been a part of that process. The nationalist leaders of the Indian freedom struggle were correct in establishing the immense contribution that science, technology, and freedom from foreign aid played in the development of a nation (Chandra et al., 2016). However, they remained oblivious of the idea that all of these can with time be completely dominated by networks of capitalist profit accumulation. As India progressed towards the twenty-first century, these issues even cropped up within the local governments. The distinctive characteristic of local socialistic tendencies such as municipal socialism was its focus on the municipal mayor who would *have to* walk through one's local neighbourhood on an everyday basis. The mayor or councillor here was at the focal point of all the major activities around municipal socialism. However, in India, ward elections are frequently contested by individuals who are either from the dominant caste or wealthy enough to dominate the capitalist electoral process. In India, the ways in which the national developmental trajectory was articulated, even though progressive, remained within the parameters of bourgeois developmental ideologies adherent to capitalist processes (Chandra et al., 2016). When such processes take place, there are usually certain demerits that occur along with them. For example, when municipalities are elected democratically under a capitalist free-market democracy, it is inevitable that money and elitism would also play a part within the process of elections.

Digital Apartheid and the Crisis of Essential Equipment

Technology has become a central element of the response to the pandemic. Numerous technology-based companies have made significant gains during the pandemic. In sectors such as health and education, the usage of technology before the pandemic and lockdowns were insignificant, which has greatly altered with the pandemic. There has been a considerable growth of online teaching and digital courses, which have been offered once the pandemic has sunk in among the people (Lalé & Osotimehin, 2021). The persistent use of technology in various sectors, including healthcare, has rendered normal ideas such as telemedicine, that is prescribing medicines over audio or video calls (Ashton & Toland, 2021) and digitalised state surveillance (BBC, 2020, April 24). Many of these digital alterations are expected to become permanent fixtures in human lives and society, even after the pandemic has receded. The Central Government of India also took recourse to digital means for its vaccine delivery process and announced that vaccines could only be received after the users registered themselves through the website launched by the government specifically for the purpose – *CoWin*.

Such over-reliance on digital modes is particularly problematic in India, where internet penetration is only about 67% and 31%, respectively, in urban and rural areas as of 2021 (Business Standard, 2021, June 3). However, the government did not take cognisance of such issues and launched a host of different internet-based services, such as the tracking application called the Arogya Setu App, which has raised a considerable amount of concern among many. Such digital innovations contributed to the normalisation of state surveillance, especially with them being pitted as the prime weapon against the virus (Sampath & Ghosh, 2020, June 15). Jayati Ghosh, one of India's most reputed economists, has argued that the kind of disaster capitalism which has been unleashed on India is much more likely to be referred to as 'disaster authoritarianism' (Sampath & Ghosh, 2020, June 15, Para 3). Jayati Ghosh has related to the ways in which the government has used its powers to impose unplanned lockdowns and throw millions of people into disarray at a moments' notice. The pandemic response and its associated large scale use of the internet have initiated an important debate surrounding whether access to the internet should be considered an essential service. In the context of COVID-19, the internet is an essential commodity because the internet has become essential for the exercise of other related human rights, including the crucial right to access healthcare and education in India (Archer & Wildman, 2021).

The disaster caused by COVID-19 cannot be analysed merely through GDP figures and unemployment percentages, but rather should be analysed taking into cognisance the disruption that it had brought to the everyday lives of the people it had affected and continues to affect (Tooze, 2021). The psychological security of individuals is an essential part of their ability to experience the space and time. Berman (1983) mentions the experience of time and space, with respect to both the self and the others, to be a vital criterion of living through modernity itself. Routines enable the proper functioning of solitary activities, which become important elements to construct the consciousness of the individual. Consciousness forged out of a feeling of being safe allows them to navigate their ways through the everyday life created by and creating the urban space and temporalities around themselves. It is this consciousness that enables the individuals to live and work with others while protecting their ideas of their own selves within the urban space. COVID-19 disrupted that, and capitalist science and technology attempted to replace this individual consciousness with a technocratic and mechanical one. The increase in anxiety among the people during the pandemic caused them to live a life where the distinction between fear and anxiety often blurred with significant effects on their ideas of selfhood. Ontological security is related to this relationship between the self and the anxieties prevalent in social life (Kinnvall & Mitzen, 2020).[6] Ontological security engages with, in the words of Giddens, ' "being" or, in terms of phenomenology, "being-in-the-world". But it is an emotional, rather than a cognitive, phenomenon, and it is rooted in the unconscious' (Giddens, 1990, p. 92).

Ontological security is a measure of how individuals cope with change, both at the social and at the personal level. Communities and local bodies play a crucial role in that. Co-operation and communities have been important parts of the human society, especially with regard to the marginalised communities. However, the primary problem faced by the workers' movement in this regard has been to rescue the sense of community from the forces of alienation that run amok under capitalism. Michael Lebowitz (2020) in his recent work has realised a dialectical approach towards analysing the relation between capital and community by focusing on the relationship between the whole and the parts. Communities are classically understood as bodies where neighbourhoods manage the society and attempt to steer it in favour of the established norms in the society. Democratic communities, however, can be immensely beneficial in contexts such as COVID-19 because such communities operate with a highly decentralised model of governance where individual subjectivity has a better chance of getting heard. Communities can play an important role in ensuring care to the most vulnerable (Means & Smith, 1994). And municipalities are a crucial part of the community in contemporary times. The tendency known as 'municipal socialism' becomes relevant in this context.

Municipal socialism can be defined as a system through which the socialist politicians and activists tend to mould the municipality in accordance with their overall socialist views (Jowett, 1907). The pandemic has provided a unique opportunity to do that. Because of the ways in which COVID-19 has impacted communities and localities, it has become almost mandatory for the governments to include the municipalities within their pandemic response framework. Also, because COVID-19 has initiated the requirement of widespread technological innovations, the municipalities also have to engage with this process. Innovation is critical for the development of long-term sustainable developmental programmes, especially in countries that have lagged behind others in terms of technological usage (Stern & Valero, 2021). Innovation policies in such countries need to take cognisance of building adequate knowledge capital and generating demands for innovations directing resources towards solutions that protect both the health and the economy (Stern & Valero, 2021).

With the coming of COVID-19, there have been a string of new innovations which have come into being, with vaccines being developed almost at the pace of light, *relatively* (Yadav, 2022). But innovation has a very distinct class character in itself, with small firms being a lot less likely to innovate than the large ones (Stern et al., 2020). While most businesses innovated with digital technologies and capabilities, management practices and the quality of their products (Valero et al., 2021) that increased the chances of the business surviving the COVID-19 downturn, the workers remained neglected amidst the financial distress caused by the same.

The emphasis by the Indian government on the drive towards digitalisation is nothing new. However, it was inappropriate to engage in such a process during a pandemic, considering that a significant part of the urban informal workforce does not possess the requisite technical knowledge to use digital platforms. The introduction of the digital platform, was of course, a shock to many, especially those who did not have access to a fast internet, the elderly who are not proficient in using smartphones or internet, and the like. This gave rise to small disaster capitalists in the various localities and cities who charged exorbitant sums of money to register people on the website. According to a senior citizen in Delhi, the charges varied from Rs 20 to 100 for booking, while those for other complicated tasks such as updating phone number and altering details were often capped at Rs 50 to 75. Similar issues were faced by people in Bengaluru, Hyderabad, Guwahati, and the like. In Tier-III cities such as Silchar, the cost of a single vaccine booking service at informal computer centres ranged from Rs 50 to nearly Rs 200, depending upon the customer and the service provider. Conversations with domestic workers who do not have access to the internet revealed that they were often forced to beg other people for booking their slots. At the same time, for Indian citizens not living within India and still having to book slots for people back home or for themselves when they would be returning to India was made impossible because of the way in which the website was coded which made it impossible for anyone living outside India to log in, adversely impacting the accessibility of many elderly people whose wards and relatives lived outside India. Naomi Klein (2007) argues that methods such as these are part of the strategy of shock doctrine, which emphasises the opportunities created by the trauma of disasters: 'A state of shock, by definition, is a moment when there is a gap between fast-moving events and the information that exists to explain them' (p. 458). The way in which global Big Pharma took recourse to disaster capitalism during the pandemic is a testimony to Klein's theory.

Drugs and medicines save a lot of lives, and help many others to maintain a healthy lifestyle, but as Feldman and Frondorf (2017) argue, the basic question is 'why do we (and our insurers) pay so much for them? Why are such large price increases possible?' (p. 13). Smith et al. (2021) have also highlighted the ways in which the knowledge about medicine has fused with marketing strategies in the contemporary society. Contemporary pharmaceutical companies have been able to amass tremendous power over human life because the industry has been able to somehow manage, although ineffectively, the dual responsibilities of serving the social need for safe and sound health and the industry's own need for generating profits (Law, 2006). With rising inflation in the healthcare sector, especially among medical goods, the poor in India are likely to be exploited further, especially with the price increase of certain essential drugs under the WPI (Oriel & Ghosh, 2022, May 31).

The other important aspect of the pandemic in India is the issue of masks. As soon as the government put forward the public health directives regarding the pandemic, masks were rendered mainstream in most societies – which also points towards a biopolitical control that states possess over the people. While masks have been traditionally associated with hospitals, COVID-19 rendered them mainstream turning them into commodities. This is again a testimony to the analyses of Tomes (1998) and then later on of Krishnan (2022), that global pandemics affect the people through a myriad of ways which penetrate right up to the most trivial aspects of their everyday life. The procurement of masks, however, became nightmarish for most people across the globe.

According to officials of *Invest India*, India required around 38 million masks, as against the 9.1 million available from various companies, in March 2020 to control the spread. This was when the total number of cases in India was only 873 with 19 deaths till then (Kalra & Ghoshal, 2020, March 28). The shortage of masks for India's citizens, most acutely faced by the marginalised populace, had even resulted in the construction of an entirely informal economy around masks.[7] There were many official newspaper reports that talked about the rising costs of masks, especially the N95 masks, which were being sold for up to Rs 150 (The Economic Times, 2020, March 5). According to some reports, surgical masks, usually Rs 10, were being sold for Rs 40 (The Economic Times, 2020, March 19). There is no standardisation of prices because these are informal prices that fluctuate based on the whims and fancies of the retailer. The WHO (March 3, 2020) claimed that the costs of surgical masks had increased almost sixfold during the pandemic. This becomes extremely problematic because the total number of requisite medical masks at that stage were around 89 million. Additionally, the global requirement of examination gloves was around 76 million while goggles requirements were 1.6 million every month.

The marginalised populace suffers the most from a lack of masks, and they are also at the risk of losing their jobs when oxygen fell short during the second wave of the pandemic (Pandey, 2021, May 5). There were numerous cases where medical oxygen had fallen short in the hospitals and nursing homes (The Indian Express, 2021, April 26). The health workers, who have been at the forefront of this struggle against the disease, suffered the most due to such shortages. The frontline workers not only have suffered from physical discomfort but have also faced tremendous amounts of mental stigma and trauma during the pandemic (Arora & Sidhu 2020). Bureaucratic and administrative accounts by Pithode (2022), Dighavkar (2021), and Kakani and Debroy (2022), focused on Bhopal, Dharavi, and Mumbai, respectively, have all emphasised the crucial role that the health workers, especially the women from the ICDS and ASHA schemes along with the Anganwadi workers, have performed during the pandemic. However, while their accounts were largely optimistic in nature, Lahariya et al. (2020) have emphasised the excruciatingly difficult conditions of work that these women had to go through during the pandemic, often without the necessary protective equipment. Bismark et al. (2022) write, '*By the middle of 2021, over four million people around the world had died from COVID-19, including many tens of thousands of healthcare workers*' (p. 217, emphasis self).[8]

The original insurance scheme that the government released for frontline workers did not include the Anganwadi workers, their incorporation was only implemented in late 2021 (The Hindu, 2021, October 5). Anganwadi workers, along with other scheme workers, have been struggling against the pandemic with increased workloads, which include going from door-to-door spreading information and obtaining statistics regarding the well-being of the community, with extremely little or no added remuneration. The health workers, especially those from the ICDS schemes were often treated in an extremely precarious way by their supervisors. Some of them even confessed that they had been instructed to use their *dupatta* or *sari* because the PHC did not have adequate masks for these vulnerable workers. Similar reports were abounded in the country, which faced serious shortages of hospital beds, medical oxygen, and above all, PPE kits and masks (Aljazeera, 2021, May 5). While cries of mask shortages were heard far and wide, the industrialists with the Association of Indian Medical Device Industry (AIMED) declared that India had a production capacity of 31.2 million pieces of N95 masks and 59.4 million pieces of four-layer masks, out of which 1.05 million and 1.9 million pieces, respectively, were surplus pieces.

At the same time, it also declared that a surplus of 5.05 million pieces of reusable or washable masks were also being produced (The Economic Times, 2020, June 7). By May 2021, India was also producing around 450,000 pieces of PPE kits through around 1,100 manufacturers (Bhardwaj, 2021, May 10). Start-ups such as SWASA face masks received widespread publicity because of the prime minister's endorsements of their products during the inauguration of the Ram Mandir in Ayodhya. Globally, there had been a shortage of masks in 2020 and much of 2021, as many countries had banned the export of critical medical equipment. An OECD report of 2020 analysed that there was a global shortage of masks, especially the N95 and surgical masks (OECD, 2020, May 4, p. 10). Regardless of the questions that one might pose towards the OECD's credibility in putting forward these reports, one of the major points specified by the OECD report has indeed come true in light of the pandemic's progress through time and space:

> Meeting demands for face masks has become one of the main issues for governments fighting the pandemic. Masks may play an even greater role in the next phase of the crisis, when lockdowns are gradually lifted and economic activity resumes, while the virus remains a threat.
> (OECD, 2020, May 4, p. 3)

In India, the production capacity of PPE kits, of which masks are a vital part, had increased manifold during the pandemic. In May 2021, India had been producing more than 25–30 million N95 masks per month with around 241 manufacturers, from being an under-producer in 2020 at merely 2 million units per month (Bhardwaj, 2021, May 10). The OECD report noted that the relationship between import and export would be critical with the progress of the pandemic because that would directly affect the state of affairs in many countries, especially those with minimum manufacturing capacities. During the initial days of the pandemic, the Government of India had banned the export of medical equipment. However, the export of medical equipment from India was resumed in June 2020 because of the demands coming from the manufacturing industry, especially the AIMED (The Economic Times, 2020, June 7). Associations such as the AIMED are the ones which make corporate exploitation look human under capitalism. Such civic organisations mainly comprise middle class and urban elites who remain oblivious of the social reality that most of the marginalised people face. These associations often do not emphasise the blatant exploitation that the patent regime performs on the people, especially during crises such as pandemics. Martin et al., in their paper on innovation and sustainable recovery, divide newer technologies which are emerging during the pandemic into two categories:

> ... in 'the "Covid core" category [they] include technologies of the type that are relevant for directly limiting the health impact of Covid-19 (e.g., vaccines, medical equipment). "Covid supporting" refers to innovations which can help the economy to cope with the pandemic in terms of working practices, which more recent analysis have seen increased patenting activity. . . . While a wide range of innovations fall into this category, [they] focus here on innovations which relate to automating office processes'.
> (Martin et al., 2020, pp. 10–11)

The latter category also includes numerous automation methods surrounding time management, meeting procedures, and so on – most of which contribute to heightened productivity. For disaster capitalists, many of whom populate the governing bodies of associations such as the AIMED, the pandemic is a classic situation to advance their class and social interests.

These moves by major corporate firms conform to the idea that disasters are events whereby global capitalists become critically engaged in 'a crisis and then sell themselves as the only ones who can resolve it' (Lowenstein, 2015, 'Introduction'). Such a position is achieved through the use of massive instruments for resource exploitation and uncontrolled private powers that multifaceted agents of capitalism possess, which inevitably leads to privatisation and loosening of state or public control over services and resources (Klein, 2007, pp. 391–394, 2018, Ch. 'A Solar Oasis') along with an increase in surveillance and corporatisation of human rights organisations (Zuboff, 2019; Lowenstein, 2015). The COVID-19 pandemic has provided an immense window of opportunity for neoliberal capitalism to practice newer forms of accumulation on a global scale based on the exploitation of workers along with the monopolistic appropriation of vaccines, medical supplies, and IPRs (Cao, 2021, April 28).

Neoliberal capitalism, by slowly doing away with the public ownership of essential resources and services in its drive 'to create a "good business climate" and therefore to optimize conditions for capital accumulation no matter what the consequences for . . . social well-being' (Harvey, 2006/2019, 'Neo-liberalism'), constitutes the conditions whereby crises such as COVID-19, almost inevitably reach deathly extremities. Rob Wallace (2016) argues that global pharmaceutical companies would lose profits if international aid was provided generously to vaccine manufacturers in poor and developing countries, which basically makes the wealthiest supporters and members of the WHO feel uncomfortable. Similar is the case with India. The same goes for bodies such as the United Nations, which though essential in times of global distress, fall short in terms of their adherence to neoliberalism as an ideological prerogative. The role that NGOs have played during the pandemic and the lockdowns has been extremely beneficial to the marginalised population.[9] However, NGOs are a part of the global circuit of capital and as such constitute an important part of the overall neoliberal and corporatist framework. Hence, the role that NGOs and other CSOs have played during the pandemic should not be seen in complete disjunction with tendencies of disaster capitalist frameworks.

Vaccine Shortages and Corporate Rivalries

Humanity today has extremely limited time to respond to crisis, and as such, a certain amount of foresightedness and quick responses formed on the basis of that become necessary to avert an apocalyptic crisis (Morgan, 2013). In the context of the pandemic, vaccines turned out to contain most of these characteristics. Vaccines constituted an important part of the response towards the pandemic, globally. Most governments, after a certain point of time, shifted their focus from remedial measures to preventive ones – vaccinating people rather than treating those affected. One of the major reasons behind this was the capitalist infatuation with prediction. Capitalism does not like many surprises, and during a pandemic, surprises are all that one has. Uncertainty, as Blundell and Machin (2020) argue, causes problems with investments, something that is fundamental to private accumulation of profits under contemporary capitalism. Natural disasters, such as pandemics, are manifestations of the uncertainty that nature still possess and the capacity of those uncertainties to affect human life, even in this day and age of scientific progress (Jones, 2018).

COVID-19 has proved that capital can create avenues for profit even amidst chaos. Capitalism has always been reliant on chaos as one of the fundamental elements of contemporary modernity (Bauman, 2000). Dunayevskaya (1949) was able to relate the chaos exhibited within the lives of people under capitalism to the process of capitalist expropriation and accumulation. Planning and chaos has been a central element of the debate between capitalism and socialism, with the former been associated with socialist or state-capitalist tendencies while the latter with capitalist systems *per se*. The analysis, however, should stand somewhere in between this duality. Dunayevskaya noted:

> Yes, planning is essential to capitalism and has always characterized the factory production and production relationship for it is the wherewithal of extraction of the greatest amount of surplus value. No, planning is not essential, chaos is, because while within production there resides the tendency to go outside the limits of production, class relations and existing values impose a limit on it, which expresses itself in the anarchy of the market. At the same time capitalism can never really plan because its law of motion is impelled by reproduction according to socially necessary labour time set by the world market, and thus even if all conditions are met as to plan in factory, external planning as to market, and labour paid at value, the incessant revolutions in production of necessity mean the 'development of productive forces of labour at the expense of the already created productive forces'.
>
> (Dunayevskaya, 1949, p. 9217)

This gets accurately manifested in the case of India. India is one of the largest producers of vaccines in the world with the SII – the largest vaccine manufacturer in the world (Gilbert & Green, 2021) – also located in India (Yadav, 2022). But, when vaccines had become available and usable, India was one of the first countries to fall short of the requisite number of vaccines, despite possessing a significant amount of vaccine production mechanisms globally (Alluri, 2021, May 1). As a result, it had to bring forward liberalised pricing on April 19, 2021, which though made vaccines available to everyone, but also opened the gates for the private sector to enter the vaccine economy

(Yadav, 2022). This created ideal conditions for disaster capitalism to thrive. The planned management of the vaccine has been rightly praised by Yadav (2022), but he also advocates support for the central government's advocacy for free trade of vaccines within the country, which had resulted in a massive vaccine inequality especially for the poor. The chaos that resulted from the shortfall of vaccines was used by profiteers to profit. The SII, in any way, was making profit. Thus, both planned production and chaos enabled the accumulation of capital during the pandemic.

The vaccine-crisis happened despite India being often labelled as 'the pharmacy of the world' by global media – a country that had been donating COVID-19 drugs to more than 120 nations (Business Standard, 2020, June 21). The SII could play a crucial role in getting the vaccine to every corner of the world because of its large manufacturing prowess 'irrespective of a country's ability to pay' (Gilbert & Green, 2021, p. 145). Large sections of the global populace suffered because of the kind of untouchability that were exhibited by Big Pharma towards poorer countries, when companies such as Pfizer and AstraZeneca realised that it would be almost impossible for any government body to fund the kind of money-intensive research that was required to bring up a vaccine against the virus in such a short time (Gilbert & Green, 2021; Bourla, 2022). This is because almost all Big Pharma research is carried out by large profit-seeking corporates (Zuckerman, 2021). Patents are an integral part of the profit-making mechanisms. Countries with large profit-making pharmaceutical sectors, such as Switzerland and Britain, are trying to halt any Intellectual Property (IP) removal from the vaccines (Shalal & Farge, 2022, March 17). The EU proposal as of March 2022 has argued that the international patent rights on the vaccines might be removed for a period of 5 years following the dispute regarding patents between the EU and the bloc led by India and South Africa (Koshy, 2022, March 16). However, such temporary waivers might not even benefit the LMICs because some of the most widely used vaccines, such as the ones manufactured by Pfizer and Moderna, are not even manufactured in the LMICs. Without sharing the technical and manufacturing knowhow, it would be nothing but an ineffective deal.

Most of the countries today do not have the approvals in place to produce COVID-19 vaccines. The campaign to remove the IP rights on the vaccines was initiated by India and South Africa, who were then backed by more than 100 countries along with the WHO and the United Nations AIDS charity (UNAIDS) (Nature Editorial, 2021, May 27). Despite India's own controversial position regarding waiving its own IP and sharing the knowhow regarding the indigenously produced Covaxin by Bharat Biotech (BB) (Jishnu, 2022, February 11). In the case of India, manufacturers such as the SII and others had already been engaged with either licensing arrangements with *Big Pharma* or had been developing indigenous vaccines, such as Bharat Biotech, a Hyderabad-based laboratory and manufacturer. The proposed waiver would have allowed manufacturers in developing countries to not only develop the vaccines but also export them without explicit permission from the patent holders, who charge exorbitant amounts of money for the same. Koshy further writes that since exigencies can already grant emergency authorisation powers to governments to manufacture medicines and vaccines in case of emergencies, and that India had already exceeded the maximum limit on the export of vaccine doses – which was set at 10% – the patent waiver would not make much of a sense for India. The European industry groups have come out in opposition to the World Trade Organization (WTO) patent waiver on the COVID-19 vaccines, arguing that IPRs constitute the basic foundation of all kinds of scientific research and development (Silver, 2022, June 20). During the discussion for the waiver on IPR on the vaccines, the issues concerning future investments on life-saving drugs became a contested one with many arguing that since production was sufficient there was no requirement for the waiver (Lopez & Bultman, 2022, June 21). These arguments did not consider that even with the *oversupply* of vaccines, there are continents such as Africa with only 15% of the population vaccinated (WHO, 2022, March 17).

In June 2022, the WTO finally agreed upon the partial IPR waiver with regards to patents, industrial designs, and copyright, for the production of COVID-19 vaccines for a period of 5 years, even though it said nothing about waivers on diagnostics and therapeutics (Barnagarwala, 2022, June 17). The absence of waivers on the diagnostic techniques will eventually mean that testing kits' availability and their cost will continue to haunt the LMICs. This move by the WTO despite strong resistance from powerful pharmaceutical lobbies and other critics has been appreciated by many, albeit with a pinch of salt (Rushe & Inman, 2022, May 3). During the pandemic, Big Pharma has behaved in an obnoxious manner, vying for supremacy of the industry in a pandemic-ridden world. In the context of India, there were bitter disputes between the SII and Bharat Biotech over the prices and government fundings (Das, 2021, January 5). The abject domination that the SII has, and continues to, enjoyed in terms of vaccine delivery and production has left many, including Bharat Biotech, thinking about the state of the public sector in the country. The SII far outsmarts Bharat Biotech's (BB) indigenous production, which has the capacity to produce only about 150 million doses a year, while the:

> SII is the largest vaccine maker in the world. It produces roughly 70 million doses of Covishield every month, accounting for nearly 90 percent of the total vaccine that India produces and consumes. The rules of the game are clear. Of these 70 million doses, 50 percent goes to the central government and 50 to the state government, which then passes it on to its private hospitals. This is what SII calls 'commitment in advance'.
>
> (Bhusan, 2021, April 29, Paras 4–5)

However, both SII and BB had not been producing to their full capacity because they were not earning enough revenue from their vaccines despite the government granting around US$ 610 million in April 2021 to both of these makers (Ahmed, 2021, April 19).

Despite a widespread shortage of vaccines, the government did not enforce any license transfers to initiate the production of the vaccines to the capable public sector undertakings (Jishnu, 2022, February 11). In spite of the allegations against Big Pharma corporates such as Pfizer for being too insistent on the fact that they were ahead of their competition rather than actually reacting to the crisis caused by the Coronavirus, especially in low and middle income countries (Gandhi-Mody, 2022), governments across the world continued to toe the line set by these large conglomerates. Gandhi-Mody's book also talked about how Pfizer's data from its clinical trials did not consider the particular traits that the population from countries such as India could show in reacting to the vaccine. Albert Bourla, the CEO of Pfizer, also affirmed to the lack of racial and ethnic data within most data from clinical trials:

> Historically, several minority groups have been underrepresented in research, including people of colour and women. Black Americans account for roughly 13 percent of the US population but make up only 5 percent of clinical trial participants. Latinx people account for roughly 19 percent of the US population but make up only 1 percent of clinical trial participants.
>
> (Bourla, 2022, p. 53)

Such realisations, however, did not deter Pfizer and its other compatriots in Big Pharma from placing massive roadblocks in the way of the free and accessible public delivery of the vaccines. Historically, India had led other low- and middle-income countries (LMICs), such as South Africa, in resisting:

> [The] harmonised laws on IPRs at the Uruguay Round of negotiations that culminated in the formation of the World Trade Organization (WTO). Resistance was systematically broken down during the negotiations. India's capitulation to pressures by the developed countries – leading to its agreeing to include IPRs under the WTO – was also a consequence of the changing trajectory of domestic economic policies in India.
>
> (Sengupta, 2018, p. 4)

During the COVID-19 pandemic, India along with South Africa had also vehemently protested against the imposition of the *patent regime* on the vaccine (Ranald, 2022, February 23). The opposition that Big Pharma puts up to generic medicines is thus a part of its accumulation mechanisms (Wallace, 2016). Generic medicines often, as Sengupta (1986/2021) notes, constitute a large portion of the accessible pharmacological care that people in the LMICs possess. Capitalism however, and Big Pharma especially, tries to displace that by bringing in mechanisms such as monetary and other non-monetary benefits to doctors and practitioners, enticing them to prescribe branded medicines to patients. Almost all the major generic medicine manufacturers in the country, instead of standing up to Big Pharma, took the easy way out by becoming contracted manufacturers to Big Pharma, including Cipla, one of the most prominent Indian generic manufacturers (Jishnu, 2022, February 11). The competition between Big Pharma and the generic manufacturers is an old one, with Big Pharma often exerting its influence to delay the approval process for its generic competitors. In addition, Big Pharma often engages with their generic competitors through proposals surrounding profit sharing with certain agreements surrounding the mitigation of competition from the generic manufacturers (Feldman & Frondorf, 2017).

However, this does not offset the effects that the patent regime that Big Pharma promotes has on the countries which do not have sufficient wealth to pay for the health of their citizens, specifically the low- and middle-income countries. Law (2006) correctly argues that 'all countries are driven by political agendas that have always put far greater weight on the creation of wealth than health' (Law, 2006, p. 16). In most wealthy countries, the consumers often do not pay in full for the drugs they consume. This is often taken care of by their insurers, who often act as brokers legitimising the marketing strategies that pharmaceutical companies undertake (Sismondo, 2018). In countries such as India, especially now with the long-standing and deeply penetrative effects of the neoliberal reforms brought in in 1991, the pharma companies have been able to influence almost all the other major sectors engaged in some way to ensuring healthcare for the common people.

The Migrant Exodus

Migration in India is a truth that everyone has had to wake up to during COVID-19. Most major urban centres have depended on cheap migrant labour, mostly coming from the rural parts of Bihar, Jharkhand, Chhattisgarh, Uttar Pradesh, West Bengal, and Assam.[10] Because of the unplanned manner in which the lockdown was imposed, millions of migrant workers were left stranded in the urban areas with absolutely no work and no means to survive. Having no other option, they had to begin walking towards their homes. The imposition of a complete lockdown on the 24th of March 2020, within four hours of its declaration, created a state of mass panic among the citizens, especially among the migrant workers. The noted agrarian and informal economy scholar, P. Sainath in an interview, quite correctly, puts forward the class nature of the manner in which the society has treated the migrant workers. Sainath says that the urban India had suddenly come to care about migrant workers because it had lost access to all the cheap services that the migrant workers had previously been providing (MN, 2020).

Factors such as regionalism and nationalism play a key role in the policies that are devised during a pandemic. Whenever an apocalyptic situation arrives, it is usually *the other* who becomes responsible for it within the public discourse (Lal, 2020). The same was the case with COVID-19. The public opinion was influenced in such a way that for most of the population, globally, the virus was something that could be only carried to their communities by agents coming from outside. Within this kind of a public perception, the migrants, *of all kinds*, found themselves to be at the centre of attention, both in India and globally. Migrants in India were demonised by the general populace because of their perceived role as the carriers of the virus (Kapri, 2021). However, the kind of apathy that the migrants received was unheard of in recent Indian history. At the same time, it would be a fatal mistake to think that the hate that the migrants received was only because of the pandemic. There has always been a growing discontent against the migrant populace in the urban regions because the popular perception has been that they adversely impact the employment of locales. However, there has been no sound economic evidence which proves that (Banerjee & Duflo, 2019).

Sainath's statement about the complete apathy of the urban middle class towards the migrant workers under normal circumstances proves the existence of the inhumane treatment that is meted out to them in the cities. The most disparaging event from the migrant exodus was reported in May 2020, when a group of migrant workers from Umaria and Shahdol in Madhya Pradesh were walking home from Jalna where they used to work in the Maharashtra Industrial Development Corporation (MICD) were run over by a goods train in Maharashtra between Badnapur and Karmad,[11] which killed fourteen of them and left five of them seriously injured (Banerjee & Mahale, 2020, May 8; The Wire, 2020, May 8). As *The Hindu* (2021, March 27) reports, as of March 2021, the families of the migrants had still been awaiting death certificates. Sainath says:

> How many English Publications even bothered to give names of the workers crushed under the train? They just had to go faceless, and nameless. That is our attitude towards the poor. If it had been a plane crash, you would have helplines giving information.
>
> (MN, 2020, Para 2).

Scroll (March 29, 2020) reported in late March 2020 that in the first month of lockdown itself, twenty-two migrants had lost their lives. The economic shock that COVID-19 has brought forward has affected the young and the lowest-paid workers unimaginably harder with a significant impact on the deepening of the existing inequalities in the labour market (Adams-Prassl et al., 2020; Bell et al., 2020a, 2020b). It is common knowledge that when disasters like COVID-19 come up, the worst affected are the *poorest of the poor*. This becomes especially problematic in India where the percentage of informal labour in the workforce is exceptionally high – at about 93% (Sengupta, 2007) – with financial assistance from the government being available to less than 25% of the total workforce (Bhalotia et al., 2020). The issues pertaining to the migrant workers is nothing new in the context of India, but:

> The visibility of the exodus made it so powerful that even the most ignorant of the urban middle class began to identify internal migration as a massive phenomenon. As they moved in number from the host states to their homes, they became the vehicles for spreading the horror stories of lockdown, contagion, looming unemployment and hunger. Their sheer mobility on foot threatened society.
> (Bandyopadhyay et al., 2022, p. 3)

During disasters, certain revelations about the society one inhabits are forced to come out in the open. David Harvey (2014) argues that human beings often tend to avoid the knowledge of the workers who produce the commodities that one uses in their everyday lives. However, during disasters such as the COVID-19 pandemic and the migrant exodus that followed, the urban populace was forced to wake up to the harsh reality of the living conditions of the cheap labour that they employ on an everyday basis.

The closure of the means of transportation, especially the railways – often labelled as being the lifeline of the nation[12] – has had an important effect on the way in which the migrants constituted their own selves within the social fabric (Mukul, 2022). The percentage of traffic on Indian trains is often an adequate measure of the countries progress because it reflects the largest proportion of paid movement in the country (Rao, 1975). Railways play a critical role in bridging the gap between urban and rural India and as such also have a cultural effect on the society, as Chatterjee (2019) writes. The rural-urban divide today is not only constructed by physical distance but also is part of a larger framework of finance capital under neoliberal capitalism to promote inequality *consciously* because it is only under a highly unequal society that consumerism can be adequately implanted as an ideology. The domination of finance capital[13] along with neoliberal consumerism have played a key role in the construction of these highly precariat workers. Neoliberal capitalism has depended heavily on the domination that Finance Capital had constructed in the post-war global economy, where banks and industries were tied to each other in a much more intimate relationship than how they had been previously. Hilferding had stated back in 1915:

> The newest phase of high capitalist development creates from its processes still other conservative tendencies. The rapid development of world capitalism since the middle of the 1890s shortened periods of depression, and tempered unemployment. The developed capitalist countries . . . had no reserve workforce in the traditional sense, rather they needed a continual infusion of foreign workers in both agriculture and industry, especially in times of economic crisis.
> (Hilferding, 1915, p. 514)

In India as well, the situation was not radically different. The formation of almost all the major urban labour forces in the country have deep-rooted histories that intersect with patterns of migration and a dialectical relationship that exists between the urban and rural citizens of India. The manner in which the urban workforce maintains itself in India with regards to its numbers depends to a large extent on the condition of the rural areas. The conditions of farming and the loss of livelihoods in rural areas greatly affect the migration patterns in India, creating a kind of seasonal migration in many urban areas such as Mumbai (Morris, 1991).

The migrant workforce in India's urban centres have historically been oppressed by a wide range of factors. Veeraraghavan (2013) writes about the employment of workers in Chennai during the early years of the industrial development of the city, arguing that most of the employment was performed through informal channels where there was ample influence of contractors and middlemen. These contractors and middlemen often come from affluent social backgrounds, with significant social capital, to make their way through disasters such as the one brought forward by COVID-19 (Kapri, 2021), while the workers that they manage are forced to suffer through the worst effects of the pandemic. The manner in which the working class has been shaped in India has been tremendously impacted by migration, especially the migration of the rural populace to the urban centres. In the Introduction to the present book, the author has referred to the influential work of Chinmay Tumbe (2018) who has, in recent times, brought out the intricacies of migration in India. Migration is an important aspect of the community's construction in India. However, at the same time, migration has also caused some major issues in modern-day India. Civic relations are greatly altered when migrants entered the community. During conversations with a homemaker in Delhi, the author was informed of the kind of emotions that some of the urban populace harbour towards the migrant workers. The concerned person argued,

> It is good that these migrants left the city. They make the city dirty and occupy all the pavements you know. At least during the lockdown, the city will be cleaned off all the *people and garbage* that has accumulated on its roads.

These attempts at stigmatising the migrant workers remain abound in spite of the locales being aware of the immense contribution that these migrant workers make towards the efficient functioning of the city. Daniel Monti argues:

> A Community that is trying to keep its civic act together can't do that when people are more busily engaged in posturing and making noise than they are in tending to important civic chores. Men and women trying to muscle their way to the top may appear insatiable, while the

ones already at the top either are not inclined to make room for them
or to do much more than smile at all their striving.

(Monti, 2013, p. 69)

Monti's theory about civic capitalism points towards a theory that often appears to justify existing infrastructures and their control by the ruling elites, while putting the aegis upon the oppressed for maintaining civic order – despite it being widely known that the kind of life that groups such as migrant workers lead in India is one of the worst forms of human lives possible. Analysing the conversation that the author had with a migrant worker who returned home to Katigorah, Assam during the pandemic from Bengaluru, it is easy to realise that the migrant workers in urban areas have realised the utter neglect that the society possesses towards them. The worker narrated the horrific living conditions that he had been living in while employed as a security guard at an MNC in Hyderabad. The state could do nothing to make his life, or of the thousand others like him, better. It is not because the state does not want to engage with these workers, but more because it does not have the capacity to engage with them under neoliberal capitalism.

Neoliberalism renders the state completely powerless in light of the domination that the market possesses over individuals and society. And it is the market that has created the migrant workers in India's urban centres, and it is that which sustains them. A brief travel through the streets of Delhi or Kolkata or Mumbai, or for that matter, most of the urban settlements in India will reveal that migrant workers are some of the worst paid and least acknowledged parts of the urban workforce in the country. In cities such as Delhi and Bangalore, even after the worst phases of the pandemic are over, the remnants of the crises caused by the exodus, both material and psychological, are still playing key roles in the informal economy of the regions. During the crisis caused by the migrant exodus, the demands for public expenditure on infrastructure increased manifold, such as the demand for public transportation, food distribution systems, emergency healthcare systems, and the like.[14] Most of the political and civil society formations on the left have been openly voicing their concerns over the massive privatisation of essential services in India, albeit with little success. However, mere nationalisation would rarely solve the issues, because even with nationalisation, the capitalist law of value would continue to function. In plain and simple terms, nationalisation would mean that the role of the market would be taken over by the State, and under neoliberalism, those who control the market are also the ones who have come to control the State. Hence, in effect, it would mean merely a change of terminology. The issues concerning devising policies that work for everyone – the core idea behind the use of the word within civic capitalism (Hay & Payne, 2015) – would continue to function akin to neoliberal capitalism. However, neoliberal capitalism has successfully created a model where both these concepts – citizenship and democracy – are in peril. Under capitalism, citizenship is a means of exercising power, and under neoliberalism, it is a means of exercising not only power but also abject domination. Democracy, as well, under neoliberal capitalism is a merely a means for party bureaucracies to dominate the common people. With free market capitalism taking control, states have little choice but to allow the market to dominate. This frequently leads to an erosion of democratic values creating newer modes of exploitation and oppression for the marginalised populace.

Global economic forces today make a direct impact on the various sectors of the economy of any nation state (Leys, 2008) and as such tend to render invisible the oppression that is caused as an aftereffect of their policies in certain localised settings. This allows the inhumane nature of the global system percolate down to the lowest level of governance. Migrant workers are the most pertinent examples of this. During the first lockdown, the migrant workers were left completely helpless not only by the central government but also by the local modes of governance, including the ULBs (Kapri, 2021; Dutt, 2022). In circumstances like these, local bodies such as municipalities and the like could have been very helpful, but they failed to respond to the crisis sufficiently (Dutt, 2022). The apathy that the government has shown towards the migrant workers has resulted in a situation where the government itself has been found lacking in terms of data regarding the migrant workers' situation in India, both quantitatively and qualitatively (Dasgupta, 2022). According to a report, out of the 3,196 migrant construction workers that they interviewed during the early days of the lockdown, about 92% had already lost their jobs by April 2020 (Nath, 2020, September 14). Sainath's apprehension that the state cares little about the migrant workers and the fate they met during the pandemic proved to be correct, as the data about the number of migrant workers who had lost their lives while *potentially* walking back to their homes was only revealed after a year of the first lockdown in June 2021. The walk-back home had claimed the lives of more than 8,000 migrant workers, according to the Railway Board's statement in response to an RTI field by activist Chandra Shekhar Gaur of Madhya Pradesh (Sengupta, 2021, June 2; Scroll, 2021, June 3).

Tendencies such as civic capitalism that focuses on philanthropy to a certain extent can be helpful in this context, but not the solution to the issues caused by inequality and structural violence. The primary reason being that they do not challenge the dynamics of power in the society. They rather urge businesses to do the work that governments should have done ideally *on their own* while the government serves as their regulator. It is more of a regulatory framework than an actually operating one, wherein the state assumes the role of a supreme regulator. In other words, there is a tendency towards the gradual demolition of the important role that the public sector plays in constructing effective economies, which works equally well for the marginalised sections of the population as it does for the affluent section. Civic capitalism does not challenge the austerity measures implemented by most neoliberal governments across the globe, because it does not attempt to negate the engagement of businesses in essential services *in toto*, but rather attempts to merely regulate them. The primary point which one has to understand surrounding any business – big or small – is that they are primarily meant to generate profits. A small businessman might not be reaping the same profits as Gautam Adani or Mukesh Ambani, but the small businessman is still running a business the survival of which is contingent upon the ways in which the business can extract the surplus labour of the workers who produce the commodities.

For example, in Mumbai's Dharavi, the small businesses suffered throughout the lockdown with limited support for the informal traders who could not even access bank loans or other aids and schemes coming from the government (Srivastava, 2020, July 7). The annual turnover of these small business, which create jobs for millions of people, ranges from US$ 650 million to US$ 1 billion (Gulankar, 2020, April 22). As Srivastava notes, the migrant exodus actually helped Dharavi because it reduced the workloads on health workers. The migrant workers' crises faced by the innumerable vulnerable workers in India again has proved that mere alteration of regimes would do nothing substantial for the working class and other marginalised sections of the population. Civic capitalism's idea that the market can be regulated for the benefit of the people is extremely short-sighted in nature. One of the reasons for this is that if under neoliberal capitalism one is talking about the regulation of the market by the state, then one simply has not understood the ways in which the state and the market are related to each other. The state today is a neoliberal state, and as such is inseparable from the market (Harvey, 2005). The ways in which the lockdown has affected the lives of migrant workers is a testimony to that.

Regardless of the scale of the businesses, at the end, commodities are produced in order to obtain profits and that the realisation of profit is the determining factor of the ways in which production is shaped under capitalism. The need for capital to valorise itself ultimately triumphs over all other dynamics involved in the socio-economic process that any business engages with. In this scenario, money acts as an agent that completely externalises the human labour embedded within these commodities to produce spiralling capitalist valorisation processes and methods of profit accumulation (Murray, 1993/2014, p. 43). Marx (1867/1976) describes commodities, as has already been stated, to be objects that are located outside of the human being and are characteristic of something that satisfies some form of human need as Marx had argued:

> Objects of utility become commodities, only because they are products of the labour of private individuals or groups of individuals who carry on their work independently on each other. The sum total of the labour of these private individuals forms the aggregate labour of society.
> (Marx, 1867/1976, p. 165)

Conclusion

Overoptimistic private funding has produced a globally connected world where capital has been allowed to be as free as possible, producing newer commodity-based economies because '[a]s economic growth transformed the lives of billions . . . there was no alternative to an order based on privatization, light-touch regulation, and the freedom of movement of capital and goods' (Tooze, 2021, 'Introduction'). This is exactly the kind of situation that led to COVID-19 becoming the crisis that it had become eventually. In India specifically, the introduction of neoliberalism resulted in newer forms of inequalities. Contemporary global capitalism makes it difficult for even intending governments to make changes in their ways of functioning because of external constraints that affect their economic functioning. Singh (2018), in his book on the problem of air pollution in India – a factor that is quite intimately related to COVID-19 because both of them affect the lungs in the human body – argues that industrial activity, even if it causes pollution and other issues, continues to decrease in many vulnerable lands because it would put most economic activities at risk. However, one of the major issues with Singh's narrative is that there is a seemingly disproportionate importance given to the power of the market. Singh writes:

> [A] market-based policy would need to be designed that provides incentives to improve energy efficiency in large industries. Under such a market-based policy, the targets would not be based on the whims of bureaucrats and planners but instead be arrives at scientifically, and then the market would be allowed to do its thing, rewarding those who can innovate and improve and punish those that don't.
> (Singh, 2018, p. 105)

Migrants feel attracted to the city because of the facilities that urban spaces provide, despite these spaces being prone to issues such as bad air quality, poor sanitation, migration, slum culture, and economic instability. They argue:

> Most third-world cities lack the infrastructure they need to serve their population. According to a recent report, India alone needs 4.5 trillion US dollars in infrastructure investment between 2016 and 2040, while Kenya needs 233 billion and Mexico 1.1 trillion. This means the relatively small parts of most cities with decent quality infrastructure are always hugely in demand and have astronomically high land prices. Some of the most expensive real estate in the world, for example, is in India. Starved of investment, the rest of the city develops in haphazard ways, with the poor [desperate for a place to live,] often squatting on whatever land happens to be unoccupied, whether or not it has sewer connections or water or water pipes.
> (Banerjee & Duflo, 2019, p. 34)

Nobody can prepare for a situation such as COVID-19. Van Bergeijk's (2021) analysis of the discourse surrounding pandemics proves that both market researchers and academic researchers have not paid much attention to the threat of a pandemic. That is primarily because:

> The downward distortions in the risk perceptions were in this case stimulated because the frequency of pandemics was historically low in the period after the Spanish Flu of 1918. . . . [Thus] the production of the facilities and services that are necessary during a pandemic is essentially intangible and invisible. . . . This is because the utility of preparation can only be demonstrated during an actual outbreak of sufficient scale. If the disease risk pool does not deliver new dangerous contagious diseases, then the preparations and investments in the health care sector may look like a waste of money *ex post*.
> (Van Bergeijk, 2021, p. 19)

The decisions that most societies take during pandemics are often based on instinctive responses (Aarts et al., 2021), vaccinations being one of them. The manner in which vaccines were accepted by the people or were rather made to accept by the respective governments speaks in terms of how secrecy around the manufacturing process and conceptualisation process of medicines and vaccines create the grounds for profit accumulation for those engaged in their production (Law, 2006). Also, the way in which those unwilling to take the vaccine were demonised in the public media, and vice versa, by bringing in discourses surrounding moral obligation, constructed the uncritical acceptance of governmental mandates as an act of public good (Giubilini, 2019) which is critically important to a disaster authoritarianism framework (Sampath & Ghosh, 2020, June 15).

The author here does not propose any anti-vaccination sentiments or arguments, but rather argues against the secrecy that has been generated around the vaccines, thereby creating grounds for multinational corporates to profit out of them. The pharmaceutical industry has been one of the most profitable industries in the world, and in 2004, the top ten pharma companies generated an income of more than US$ 205 billion (Law, 2006). However, a pandemic does not only stop by interventions made at a pharmaceutical level but rather requires a host of different sectors, which might not be directly related to the healthcare sector. India's response to the Acquired Immuno-Deficiency Disease (AIDS) can be taken as an example. Khorshed M. Pavri's (1992) book on the response and challenges of AIDS in India from a government-sponsored publishing house establishes the issues in dealing with major contagious diseases in India, which include poor public health infrastructure and practices.

Unlike AIDS, which had a propensity to infect more women than men[15] (Pavri, 1992), COVID-19 makes no such distinctions on the basis of class, caste, gender, or race. COVID-19, as such, does not make many distinctions between the rich and the poor, between men and women, or between Caucasians and Mongoloids. However, the ways in which people belonging to these social categories had been found to be at the most risk of contracting the disease and getting stigmatised deserves attention. Rob Wallace (2016) argues that, under conditions created by neoliberalism, it becomes easy for capitalism to divert the public health emergency caused by pandemics such as COVID-19 towards other issues that concern the origin place of the virus rather than its effects on the particular societies. The way in which the term 'Chinese Virus', first made popular by Donald Trump (Rogers et al., 2020, March 18), made its way to the popular lexicon of many Indians, including children (Acharjee & Arun, 2020, March 30), is a glaring testimony to the claims made by Wallace. Any disease possessing the implications which are as grave in nature as AIDS is related to broader structural issues surrounding public health problems (Pavri, 1992). Similar is the case with COVID-19. Neoliberal capitalism makes it possible for private corporate healthcare infrastructure to dominate over the publicly owned ones. As Prasad (2018) argues:

> Most hospitals in India were run either by government or private charities and Trusts till late 1970s. In the early 1980s, the state encouraged private nursing homes and small and medium hospitals to supplement government health care. In 1991 there was a drastic cut in the central government budgetary allocation for health care, which favoured the establishment of private hospitals in India.
>
> (Prasad, 2018, p. 52)

The policies regarding privatisation of the healthcare infrastructure were affirmatively promoted by the successive governments, finally culminating in allowing Foreign Direct Investment (FDI) in the healthcare sector in 2000. This, as Purendra Prasad has mentioned, has resulted in the establishment of the corporate hospitals in India, which then went on to benefit immensely during the pandemic. These are the conditions that allowed disaster capitalism to thrive in India during the pandemic. Under such conditions, the way in which the society responds to disasters such as COVID-19 has important implications for the society at large. However, at this point, it is also important to underscore two types of disaster capitalists. The first are the large monopolies, which Klein (2007, 2018) critiques in her numerous works on disaster capitalism. The second category, which is an exceptional case and relevant mostly to countries such as India, encompasses the petty production units and small businesses in India, who also increase their process when disasters strike the society in spite of procuring the commodities at normal market prices. This is not surprising, as human beings as a species have always acted out of individual interests exhibiting short-termism, whereby they have privileged the short-term benefits that they can receive over and above broader social questions of human suffering and community-hood (Aarts et al., 2021).

During disasters, corporate interests feed upon the tokenistic interests of the marginalised population, while maintaining a rhetoric of common good. More than the corporates, communities can resist the inequality in terms of accessibility that the privatisation of the healthcare sector in India has created more effectively than corporates or even statist bureaucracies. Functional communitarian education and awareness drives can make people aware of their rights and make them question the existing order of things. Jacky Law (2006) argues that when the masses become articulate as customers, the pharmaceutical companies cannot exploit them. Because they tend to articulate their positions on the variety of drugs available in the market through the ideological framework they have developed. In scenarios such as that, individuals treat good health not as a commodity but as something that they have a right to. Disaster capitalism does not intend to accelerate the pace of the journey towards that situation.

Disaster capitalism, during COVID-19, has enabled hoarding and black marketing of essential commodities. The ground for disaster capitalism to make profits out of the pandemic has not been created overnight, but rather it has been created through years of steady disinvestment within the public sector. The manner in which disaster capitalism has functioned during the pandemic in India has exhibited that tendencies to profit from disasters have now become 'everyday' in the societies that we inhabit reaching right into our bedrooms. From the medicines that one consumes, to the air that one breathes, almost everything has become commodities that capital can exploit. The situation is so dire that several states in India have been forced to consider an urban job guarantee scheme of 100 days' employment in light of how the pandemic has affected the workers in the informal sector of which around 70%, as per the research conducted by Bhalotia et al. (2020), have no guarantee of minimum wage. Further research by Dhingra and Kondirolli (2021) has argued that more than four-fifths of the individuals would actually like such a scheme, as against other forms of gestures such as cash transfers or the state providing incentives for employing people to the employers. However, mere reforms would never serve the purpose because they do not challenge the overarching social inequality.[16]

Neoliberalism has shaped the society in such a way that the state today has to always respond to the needs of the market (Byttebier, 2022). The constant privatisation of the healthcare services in the country has resulted in the creation of a precarious healthcare working class, which constitutes majority of the workforce in the sector today (Bismark et al., 2022), and India being no exception to that. The plight of the precarious and informal workers in the healthcare sector is such that the government, as of July 2022, has even denied having any knowledge of the number of deaths in the sector (The Quint, 2022, July 22). The government's emphasis on the use of digital modes also has to be questioned, considering that most of the internet providers in the country are essentially private bodies, and the government does not have many plans for reinvigorating the public sector in the near future. The COVID-19 pandemic exhibited that just as how disasters impact the everyday lives of the people in a unique fashion, so do the capitalists who profit from them. In situations such as these, the effective opposition to the rise of disaster capitalism has to involve both the individuals and the communities that these individuals form. For the post-COVID-19 world to move beyond the scars of COVID-19, it is essential to realise that all disasters are not merely events but rather processes that continue to affect human lives. And that involves talking about COVID-19 in a manner that speaks about the empowerment of the lowest strata of the marginalised population because the ones suffering the most – or at the risk of suffering the most – due to a disaster can provide the pathways towards understanding the nuanced nature of the disasters. This also necessitates a certain journey from macro politics to a kind of *hyper-micro* politics, whereby the individual is not only an objective unit of analysis but also a fully functional and dynamic subject having internal contradictions that shape and get shaped by the experiences of a disaster, be it natural or man-made.

In spite of her pro-ruling class approach, which to the current author makes a significant difference to how one analyses human tragedy, Gandhi-Mody (2022) did correctly highlight that when crises of an apocalyptic nature arise in the society, there arise self-survival instincts which might prove more harmful to civilisation than the disaster itself. When disasters strike a society, there are multiple issues that crop up, the most important of which is the allocation of essential resources. Erich Fromm argues:

> While it is true that man can adapt himself to almost any conditions, he is not a blank sheet of paper on which culture writes its text. Needs like the striving for happiness, harmony, love and freedom are inherent in his nature. They are also dynamic factors in the historical process which, if frustrated, tend to arouse psychic reactions, ultimately creating the very conditions of the society and the culture remain stable, the social character has a predominantly stabilising function. If the external conditions change in such a way that they do not fit any more with the traditional social character, a lag arises which often changes the function of character into an element of disintegration instead of stabilisation, into dynamite instead of a social mortar, as it were.
>
> (Fromm, 1955/2008, p. 79)

Lawrence Wilde (2004) asserts that the thoughts proposed by Fromm were:

> . . . on the basis of a dialectical view of modernity. On the one hand, scientific and technical developments point to the real possibility of abundance, a day when "the table will be set for all who want to eat," and when the human race will form a unified community with no need to live as separate entities. On the other hand, modernity discourages our natural sociality and restricts it to the public sphere.
>
> (Wilde, 2004, p. 3)

In the private sphere, individuals today are guided by feelings of egoism and selfishness rather than any overarching love for humanity. A social solution to the problems caused by disasters with regards to their effects on human psychology requires an ideological re-orientation of the members of the society, not only individually but also socially. Politicians advocating municipal socialism do not refer to overtly grand forms of ideological struggle against capitalism, but rather remain entrenched within a local reform-based politics that can be at odds distinctly with their politics at the national level (Leopold & McDonald, 2012, pp. 1841–1842). An example in this regard can be cited of the *Aam Aadmi Party* (AAP) in India, which is the ruling party in Delhi. As a party, AAP has been instrumental in ensuring community level developmental projects, especially in the sectors of education and healthcare.[17] However, at the national level, the party has been engaged in the dominant neo-fascist turn in Indian politics, vilifying Muslims and appeasing majoritarian ideals. In the national capital, where the AAP is the ruling government, it did an exemplary work in the healthcare sector through the Mohalla Clinics[18] it had established. However, the manner in which the Mohalla Clinics are structured also make them prone to catering only in cases of primary ailments, and not for situations presented by the pandemic (Banka, 2021, May 5). At the same time, because Mohalla Clinics are often extremely tiny structures with single entries and exits, any possible case of infection is likely to become highly widespread within the community that the clinic serves. This was the case in North-East Delhi in March 2020 when 800 people had to be quarantined because a doctor had tested positive at the clinic (Scroll, 2020, March 26). Additionally, there has been widespread discontent among the doctors and nurses at these clinics because of the lack of covid insurance for them from the Delhi government (Bedi & Sirur, 2020, December 6).

Mohalla Clinics have only recently started acting as COVID-19 vaccination centres (The Indian Express, 2022, June 27). It is worthwhile to mention that these clinics had suffered from widespread criticism for not being able to vaccinate people previously because of their limited capacity (Banka, 2021, May 5). Municipalities, district authorities, and other such ULBs are indispensable in the struggle against COVID-19. The 2020 Operational Guidelines regarding the vaccines for COVID-19 released by the Ministry of Health and Family Welfare (December 28, 2020) of the Government of India emphasised the role of the municipalities in the various health-related issues faced by people in different localities. The guidelines also instructed that anyone qualified enough to vaccinate must be employed and seen as a potential vaccinator along with directions for timely remuneration for these vaccinators and the other ASHA workers. Slums such as Dharavi where the care workers ensured that daily screening was performed and isolation protocols were followed. Srivastava (2020) writes that the enlisting of private clinics in Dharavi for testing was one of the major reasons for the slum being able to diagnose and treat many patients early on. The Brihanmumbai Municipal

Corporation (BMC), in general, has been a good model for municipalities across the nation because of the way it could mobilise material and human resources to perform the requisite tasks during the pandemic (Upadhyay, 2021, June 1). The strategy of the 4T's, specifically referring to the processes of tracing, tracking, testing, and treating, received widespread praise, even from the WHO (The Hindu, 2021, May 28).

It is true that Dharavi, which is home to around 8.5 lakh people with a population density of 3.54 lakh people per square kilometre, even exceeds the density of Mumbai itself, which is one of the world's most highly congested cities, showed good results in terms of the cases of COVID-19, however, the general awareness regarding the disease itself remained low (Yadavar & Agrawal, 2020, May 22). The BMC workers were able to earn the trust of the residents of Dharavi by employing women, around 6,000 of them – health workers and volunteers from Dharavi itself – who were equipped with instruments such as oximeters and thermometers to manage the pandemic in the area (Altstedter & Pandya, 2020, October 9). The way in which the BMC reacted to the pandemic, especially in the case of Dharavi, is exemplary and deserves praise. However, that being said, as Sagar Kumbhare writes in *The Wire*:

> The caste system continues to 'reserve' sewer and sanitation work for Dalits be it is Brihanmumbai Municipal Corporation or Nagar Parishad Delhi or the Private Sector. For instance, around 30,000 sanitation workers are employed by the Greater Mumbai Municipal Corporation and all 30,000 are Dalits. Estimates say that 40–60% of the six million households of Dalit sub-castes are engaged in sanitation work.
> (Kumbhare, 2020, May 7, Para 18)

These are some of the burning questions that remain unresolved within the economistic agenda, such as the ones which municipal socialists put forward. The municipal socialist alternative talks about reducing the rates of public services and to an extent, universalising them (Gehrke, 2016), many of which have been the stated goals of contemporary left-wing movements.

Although the word 'radical' might seem ill-fitting in the context considering that the philosophy does remains highly revisionist and reformist in nature, but their ventures in putting monopolies at the hands of the public representatives and socialising the profits of such businesses and services (Leopold & McDonald, 2012, pp. 1840–1841) can be utilised for forwarding more radical ventures. Through the utilisation of such 'stop-gap' arrangements, municipal socialism can resist the actualisation of capitalism's monopolistic desire of doing away with forms of public trading and services (Leopold & McDonald, 2012, p. 1842). Although such arrangements can only be temporary respites, their ability to mitigate impacts cannot be denied. However, mitigation does not mean resolution. Mitigation merely refers to a temporary removal of the immediate contradictions, while more often than not, leaving the fundamental contradictions for the future.

Within municipal socialist tendencies, contrary to Sidney Webb's arguments, the idea of the state as a centre of power is prevalent. Municipal socialism does not challenge authority, but rather seeks to achieve authority at a local level and argue that it can use that authority in a more egalitarian fashion. In certain ways, it is very similar to the way in which state capitalism posits itself as an alternative to free-market capitalism. Under state capitalism, the state becomes capitalist not only because it controls the industries and means of production but also because it holds the power to administer and regulate services essential to the sustenance of a society. Both municipal socialism and state capitalism are synonymous with vanguardism because there is still a difference between the leaders and the led – a crucial aspect of vanguardist state capitalism (Dunayevskaya, 1956a). Within municipalities, vanguardism can mean the dominance of the rich and elite within the neighbourhood. The Johnson-Forest tendency argued that Leninist vanguardism was a product of the times in which it was constructed, both ideologically and materially. According to James et al. (1986), vanguardism is an ideological ideology that advocates for the creation of a party of the elite who will eventually lead the revolutionary upsurge.

This is where Marx again becomes extremely relevant, especially Marx's and Marxist criticism of utopian socialists or Fabian socialists. Cornelius Castoriadis (1992/2010) argues that the very term 'utopia' revolves around a pessimistic idea of the workers' movement because 'the project of individual and collective autonomy (the two are inseparable) is not a utopia, but a social-historical project susceptible of being achieved, and which has never been shown to be impossible' (p. 3). Marx (1847/1976) further argued that an increase in wages would not necessarily liquidate all the gains made by the working class within the framework of class struggle because a rise in wages also creates the conditions for the growth of industrial capitalism which acts in favour of the growing class consciousness of the working class. Marx criticised the reductionistic, both from the economistic fetishists and the utopian socialists, critiques of the anti-capitalist movement and argued:

> The economists want the workers to remain in society as it is constituted and as it has been signed and sealed by them in their manuals. The socialists[19] want the workers to leave the old society alone, the better to be able to enter the new society which they have prepared for them with so much foresight.
>
> (Marx, 1847/1976, p. 210)

Marx was important in the socialist tradition because he never distanced himself from the actual struggles of the working class, unlike the other utopian socialists who preached only reorganisation and not a radical reconstruction of the foundations of the society (Dunayevskaya, 1956b). Lal (2020) argues that the ways in which, and the extent to which, the state had intervened in the COVID-19 crisis are unique such that the state *literally* advocated in favour of halting all forms of economic activities deemed 'non-essential'. According to Lal, this is the singularity that COVID-19 poses before the human society as a unique event.

The effects that COVID-19 would have on the future of mankind will be very diverse. For example, Allen (2020) points out the impact that COVID-19 might have on the overall demography of the world, because 'despite all the hype [about sex], all signs point to fewer babies being born as a result of Covid-19, not more' (Allen, 2020, p. 109). Allen points out the closure of many public spaces – especially those where young people used to meet – is having an adverse impact on the way in which people form relationships. Most people coming from the lower ends of the social hierarchy have to live through disasters almost on an everyday basis because neither the society nor the state takes their voices into cognisance for framing laws, policies, and regulations (Yee, 2018), and even the notions of civility as they exist. This also includes the methods through which newer processes of digitalisation and technological reliance are creeping into the human society, affecting our human instincts (Antomarini, 2021), and human and social instincts form the basis of everyday life.

A welfarist approach here can prove helpful, but it cannot be the solution to the multiple levels of crisis that COVID-19 has brought forward. Slavoj Žižek says, 'It is not simply that we don't know what's going on, we *know* that we *don't know*, and this not-knowing is itself a social fact; it is inscribed into how our institutions act' (2021, p. xii). The correct assessment of the situation, even if that is an utterly hopeless one, can in fact, help the society in moving towards better understanding of the future possibilities of human action and sustenance in the world (Žižek, 2021). As Pikoli (2020) argues, COVID-19 has made crisis into a global terminology often invoked by the common people. However, what many do not realise is that the crisis is an everyday affair for the lives of many coming from marginalised communities and sections because of the kind of work they do and the extent to which they become recipients of all forms of social stigma. COVID-19 changed little in most such lives. For them, the crisis is part of their everyday lives.

Notes

1 DiSalvo (2020, March 30) has narrated in detail about how the factories in the United States producing face masks are infested with brokers from all levels of the capitalist economy – from the state to the informal sellers – driven by large scale demand and the opportunity to profit from the same by exporting in large quantities without satisfying domestic demand. This in turn, leads to hoarding, black marketing, and profiteering, often at a local level. In China, as Julian Borger (2020, April 5) reported, the manufacturers were demanding payment in full before delivery of the products, asking for exorbitant prices while producing masks that often did not meet the requisite medical standards.

2 Medical device companies such as Morepan Labs have registered drastic increases in their profits throughout 2021 and 2022 (Financial Express, 2021, November 11; Express Pharma, 2022, May 5).

3 Katherine Eban (2019), an investigative journalist, studied the famed Indian Pharmaceutical company, Ranbaxy and narrates the issues with generic drugs and how these drugs have caused a stir in the global pharmaceutical market, which was once dominated by western companies. Eban narrates, 'For many years, few people wanted to take Indian medicine, let alone praise the companies making it. To the brand-name pharmaceutical companies that had spent decades and millions developing drugs, the Indian companies that copied their products were no better than thieves. They deserved to be sued rather than thanked. And to patients around the world, the MADE IN INDIA label connoted flea-market quality they'd prefer to avoid' (Eban, 2019, p. 77).
4 The ability to store and transport was one of the major reasons behind India's inaccessibility to the vaccine manufactured by Pfizer was transportation and the suggested storage mechanisms (Scroll, 2020, November 11).
5 However, the condition of the public sector pharmaceutical industries remains highly dilapidated. There are a total of five public sector undertakings in the pharmaceutical industry, the Indian Drugs and Pharmaceuticals Limited (IDPL), the Hindustan Antibiotics Limited (HAL), the Karnataka Antibiotics and Pharmaceuticals Limited (KAPL), the Bengal Chemicals and Pharmaceuticals Limited (BCPL), and the Rajasthan Drugs and Pharmaceuticals Limited (RDPL). The Annual Report of the Department of Pharmaceuticals suggested that 'IDPL and RDPL be closed and HAL and BCPL be put up for strategic sale' (Department of Pharmaceuticals 2021, p. 83). According to the official report, the only public sector undertaking that will remain unscathed for the time being is the KAPL, even though it is also set-up for disinvestment in the near future (Das, 2019, September 9).
6 The psychologist R.D. Laing coined the term, 'ontological security' to refer to the processes that allow individuals to experience the self as 'real, alive, whole, and in a temporal sense, a continuous person' (Laing, 1990, p. 39). Giddens (1990, 1991) spoke about the term corelating it to issues of self-identity and the altering environmental they find themselves in.
7 A migrant worker from Hyderabad informed the current author that in some markets, surgical masks had sold for as high a price as Rs 50 per piece during the days when masks were mandatory.
8 In the context of India, certain events stand out. For example, in Uttar Pradesh, seventy-two Anganwadi workers lost their lives while performing their duties, out of which only twelve families have received the promised compensation (Pandey, January 12, 2022).
9 António Guterres, the Secretary General of the United Nations, praised the kind of work that NGOs and community organisations such as Voluntary Action Network of India (VANI) and Child Rights and You (CRY) had done in India, as documented in the *Report on the Socio-Economic Impact of COVID-19* (India Blooms, 2021, March 1). He emphasised that NGOs played a crucial role in bringing economic and livelihood opportunities for the marginalised populace by working within the community. This also made it easy for them to focus on issues such as sanitation, awareness, and the like.
10 Often, migrants adopt professions based on their regions. For example, the juice sellers in the Indian city of Hyderabad come from a single district in Jharkhand and as such carry their kinship frameworks with them to their adopted cities (Kavita Krishnan, personal communication). As time progresses, it is only natural that these networks of relationships become a part of the space that these workers occupy.
11 All of them are districts in Madhya Pradesh and Maharashtra.
12 According to a data presented in 1999, 'the railways carry nearly 48% of the country's total freight traffic and about 21% of the passenger traffic' (Rao, 1975, p. 67).

150 *Pandemics of Capitalism and Everyday Disasters*

13 Finance capital, as Rudolf Hilferding (1915) describes, is a system where a tiny group of banks dominate over all other forms of capital, most notably industrial capital.
14 When the migrants were walking home, a lot of different institutions played a key role in either easing or toughening their journey, especially political formations, NGOs, trade unions, and community associations.
15 This is because women have more mucus area that gets exposed to the virus during penile penetration.
16 The example of Bismarck is crucial to be considered at this point. The first person to advocate for a health insurance for the workers was the Prussian chancellor, Otto van Bismarck, someone who was known to be dictatorial in nature. It was him who 'introduced "workers' accident insurance",' which was focused on providing minimum compensation to the worker in exchange for which the worker relinquished the right to make any legal allegations against the employers (Ramin, 2017, p. 14). As Ramin notes, this made Bismarck widely popular among both the employers and the employed, and that the idea subsequently became very popular both in Europe and North America. Engels (1880), however, was able to see through this and could fathom that such reforms merely advocate in favour of the continuation of labouring conditions and make no fundamental changes to the state of the worker.
17 See detailed reports at www.thehindu.com/news/cities/Delhi/aap-government-lists-top-10-achievements-of-five-years/article30392089.ece, www.livemint.com/education/news/focus-on-education-yields-rich-dividends-11581446664047.html and http://health.delhigovt.nic.in/wps/wcm/connect/doit_health/Health/Home/Directorate+General+of+Health+Services/Aam+Aadmi+Mohalla+Clinics [Accessed 03.12.2023]
18 Neighbourhood clinics are set up to serve local communities.
19 The Term 'Socialists' here refers to '*the socialists of that time: the Fourierists in France, the Owenites in England. F. E. [Note to the German edition, 1885.]*' (footnote on p. 209 in Marx and Engels Collected Works, Volume 6, Lawrence and Wishart, emphasis self).

References

Aarts, E., Fleuren, H., Sitskoorn, M., & Wilthagen, T. (2021). The dawn of a new common. In E. Aarts, H. Fleuren, M. Sitskoorn, & T. Wilthagen (Eds.), *The new common: How the Covid-19 pandemic is transforming society*. Springer.

Acharjee, S., & Arun, M. G. (2020, March 30). Life in the time of corona. *India Today*.

Adams-Prassl, A., Boneva, T., Golin, M., & Rauh, C. (2020). *Inequality in the impact of the coronavirus shock: New survey evidence for the UK*. Universities of Oxford. Retrieved December 3, 2023, from www.iza.org/publications/dp/13183/inequality-in-the-impact-of-the-coronavirus-shock-evidence-from-real-time-surveys

Ahmed, A. (2021, April 19). India to fund capacity boost at Serum Institute, Bharat Biotech as vaccines run short. *Reuters*. Retrieved December 3, 2023, from www.reuters.com/world/india/india-fund-capacity-boost-at-serum-institute-bharat-biotecg-as-vaccines-run-short-source-2021-04-19/

Aljazeera. (2021, May 5). "Sari is my mask": How the COVID pandemic has hit India's poorest. Retrieved December 3, 2023, from www.aljazeera.com/news/2021/5/5/sari-is-my-mask-how-the-pandemic-has-hit-indias-poorest

Allen, L. (2020). Covid-19 could see thousands of women miss out on having kids, creating a demographic disaster. In M. Glassey (Ed.), *2020: The year that changed us*. Thames and Hudson.

Alluri, A. (2021, May 1). India's covid vaccine shortage: The desperate wait gets longer. *BBC*. Retrieved December 3, 2023, from www.bbc.com/news/world-asia-india-56912977

Altstedter, A., & Pandya, D. (2020, October 9). How the world's biggest slum stopped the virus. *Bloomberg*. Retrieved December 3, 2023, from www.bloomberg.com/features/2020-mumbai-dharavi-covid-lockdown/

Antomarini, B. (2021). Contact in absentia: Towards a cybertouch. In K. Mahadevan, S. Kumar, M. Bhoot, & R. Kharat (Eds.), *The covid spectrum: Theoretical and experiential reflections from India and beyond*. Speaking Tiger.

Archer, A., & Wildman, N. (2021). Internet access as an essential social good. In E. Aarts, H. Fleuren, M. Sitskoorn, & T. Wilthagen (Eds.), *The new common: How the Covid-19 pandemic is transforming society*. Springer.

Arora, M., & Sidhu, S. (2020). *The ordeal of being corona warriors: An approach to medical and essential service providers*. National Book Trust.

Ashton, J., & Toland, S. (2021). *The new normal: A roadmap to resilience in the pandemic era*. William Morrow.

Bandyopadhyay, R., Bannerjee, P., & Samaddar, R. (2022). Introduction: The shiver of the pandemic. In R. Bandyopadhyay, P. Bannerjee, & R. Samaddar (Eds.), *India's migrant workers and the pandemic*. Routledge.

Banerjee, A. V., & Duflo, E. (2019). *Good economics for hard times*. Juggernaut.

Banerjee, S., & Mahale, A. (2020, May 8). 16 Migrant workers run over by goods train near Aurangabad in Maharashtra. *The Hindu*. Retrieved December 3, 2023, from www.thehindu.com/news/national/other-states/16-migrant-workers-run-over-by-goods-train-near-aurangabad-in-maharashtra/article31531352.ece

Banka, R. (2021, May 5). Mohalla clinics a waste if not used during pandemic: Delhi HC. *Hindustan Times*. Retrieved December 3, 2023, from www.hindustantimes.com/cities/delhi-news/mohalla-clinics-a-waste-if-nit-used-during-pandemic-delhi-hc-101620166912692.html

Barnagarwala, T. (2022, June 17). Covid-19: WTO agrees on partial patent waiver for vaccine production. *Scroll*. Retrieved December 3, 2023, from www.scroll.in/latest/1026391/covid-19-wto-agrees-on-partial-waiver-for-vaccine-production

Barnagarwala, T. (2022, July 19). Why India's efforts to boost its medical devices industry are falling short. *Scroll*. Retrieved December 3, 2023, from www.scroll.in/article/102853/why-indias-efforts-to-boost-its-medical-devices-industry-are-falling-short

Bauman, Z. (2000). *Liquid modernity*. Polity.

BBC. (2020, April 24). Coronavirus: State surveillance "a price worth paying". Retrieved December 3, 2023, from www.bbc.com/technology-52401763

Bedi, A., & Sirur, S. (2020, December 6). "We're no different from AIIMS, RML Doctors" – Delhi Mohalla clinic staff demand covid insurance. *The Print*. Retrieved December 3, 2023, from www.theprint.in/india/were-no-different-from-aiims-rml-doctors-delhi-mohalla-clinic-staff-demand-covid-insurance/561495/

Bell, B., Bloom, N., Blundell, J., & Pistaferri, L. (2020a). Prepare for large wage cuts if you are younger and work in a small firm. *VOX CEPR Policy Portal*. Retrieved December 3, 2023, from www.voxeu.org/article/prepare-large-wage-cuts-if-you-are-younger-and-work-small-firm

Bell, B., Codreanu, M., & Machin, S. (2020b). *What can previous recessions tell us about the Covid-19 downturn? A CEP Covid-19 analysis*. Centre for Economic Performance, London School of Economics and Political Science.

Berman, M. (1983). *All that is solid melts into air: The experience of modernity*. Verso.

Bhalotia, S., Dhingra, S., & Kondirolli, F. (2020). *City of dreams no more: The impact of Covid-19 on urban workers in India. Covid-19 analysis series*. Centre for Economic Performance, London School of Economics and Political Science.

Bhardwaj, D. (2021, May 10). From shortage last year, India now has surplus of PPE kits, N95 masks. *Hindustan Times*. Retrieved December 3, 2023, from www.hindustantimes.com/india-news/from-shortage-last-year-india-now-has-surplus-of-ppe-kits-n95-masks-101620620597446.html

Bhusan, R. (2021, April 29). Vaccination deals between Serum Institute, Bharat Biotech and States: What we know so far. *Money Control*. Retrieved December 3, 2023, from www.moneycontrol.com/news/trends/vaccination-deals-between-serum-institute-bharat-biotech-and-states-what-we-know-so-far-6829581.html

Bhutto, F. (2021, March 17). The world's richest countries are hoarding vaccines. This is morally indefensible. *The Guardian*. www.theguardian.com/commentisfree/2021/mar/17-rich-countries-are-hoarding-vaccines-us-eu-africa

Bismark, M., Willis, K., Lewis, S., & Smallwood, N. (2022). *Experiences of health workers in the Covid-19 pandemic: In their own words*. Routledge.

Blundell, J., & Machin, S. (2020). *Self-employment in the Covid-19 crisis. A CEP Covid-19 analysis*. Centre for Economic Performance, London School of Economics and Political Science.

Borger, J. (2020, April 5). Market for Chinese-made masks is a madhouse, says broker. *The Guardian*. Retrieved December 3, 2023, from www.theguardian.com/world/2020/apr/05/market-for-chinese-made-masks-madhouse-says-broker

Bourla, A. (2022). *Moonshot: Inside Pfizer's nine-month race to make the impossible possible*. Harper Collins Publishers.

Brown, G. (2021, November 26). A new covid variant is no surprise when rich countries are hoarding vaccines. *The Guardian*. Retrieved December 3, 2023, from www.theguardian.com/commentisfree/2021/nov/26/new-covid-variant-rich-countries-hoarding-vaccines

Business Standard. (2020, June 21). *India "pharmacy of the world" during Covid-19 crisis, says SCO Secy general*. Retrieved December 3, 2023, from www.business-standard.com/article/current-affaiars/india-pharmacy-of-the-world-during-covid-19-crisis-says-sco-secy-general-120062100435_1.html

Business Standard. (2021, June 3). *Active internet users in India likely to reach 900 MN by 2025: IAMAI*. Retrieved December 3, 2023, from www.business-standard.com/article/technology/active-internet-users-in-india-likely-to-reach-900-mn-by-2025-iamai-121060300710_1.html

Byttebier, K. (2022). *Covid-19 and capitalism: Success and failure of the legal methods for dealing with a pandemic*. Springer.

CANDID & Center for Disaster Philanthropy. (2022). *Philanthropy and Covid-19: Examining two years of giving*. CANDID & Center for Disaster Philanthropy.

Cao, S. (2021, April 28). Bill gates' comments on Covid-19 vaccine patent draws outrage. *Observer*. Retrieved December 3, 2023, from https://observer.com/2021/04/bill-gates-oppose-lifting-covid-vaccine-patent-interview/

Castoriadis, C. (1992/2010). The project of autonomy is not a utopia. In E. Escobar, M. Gondicas, & P. Vernay (Eds.), *A society adrift: Interviews and debates, 1974–1997, Cornelius Castoriadis*. Fordham University Press.

Chandra, B., Mukherjee, M., Mukherjee, A., Mahajan, S., & Pannikar, K. N. (2016). *India's struggle for independence*. Penguin India.

Chatterjee, A. K. (2019). *The great Indian railways: A cultural biography*. Bloomsbury.

Dadhich, A. (2020, April 22). The Covid-19 pandemic and the Indian pharmaceutical industry. *European Pharmaceutical Review*. Retrieved December 3, 2023, from www.europeanpharmaceuticalreview.com/article/117413/the-covid-19-pandemic-and-the-indian-pharmaceutical-industry/

Das, S. (2019, September 9). Pharma PSUs likely to sign MoU with LMA for sale of surplus land. *Business Standard*. Retrieved December 3, 2023, from www.business-standard.com/article/companies/pharma-psus-to-sign-mou-with-management-agency-for-sale-of-surplus-land-119090800954_1.html

Das, S. (2021, January 5). Bharat biotech chief takes on serum institute in Covid-19 vaccine war. *Business Standard*. Retrieved December 3, 2023, from www.business-standard.com/article/current-affairs/bharat-biotech-chief-takes-on-serum-institute-in-covid-19-vaccine-war-121010500047_1.html

Dasgupta, B. (2022). Corona pandemic, sudden visibility of migrant workers, and the Indian economy. In R. Bandyopadhyay, P. Bannerjee, & R. Samaddar (Eds.), *India's migrant workers and the pandemic*. Routledge.

Department of Pharmaceuticals. (2021). *Annual report 2020–21*. Ministry of Chemicals and Fertilisers, Department of Pharmaceuticals.

Department of Pharmaceuticals. (2022). *Annual report 2021–22*. Ministry of Chemicals and Fertilisers, Department of Pharmaceuticals.

Dhingra, S., & Kondirolli, F. (2021). *City of dreams no more, a year on: Worklessness and active labour market policies in urban India. Covid-19 analysis series*. Centre for Economic Performance, London School of Economics and Political Science.

Dighavkar, K. (2021). *The Dharavi model: How Asia's largest slum defeated Covid-19*. Notion Press.

DiSalvo, D. (2020, March 30). I spent a day in the coronavirus-driven feeding frenzy of N95 mask sellers and buyers and this is what I learned. *Forbes*. Retrieved December 3, 2023, from www.forbes.com/sites/daviddisalvo/2020/03/30/i-spent-a-day-in-the-coronavirus-driven-feeding-frenzy-of-n95-mask-sellers-and-buyers-and-this-is-what-i-learned

Dunayevskaya, R. (1949). Letter to Grace Lee, February 1. In *The Raya Dunayevskaya collection – Marxist-humanism: A half century of its world development*. Wayne State University Archives of Labor and Urban Affairs.

Dunayevskaya, R. (1956a). Ferdinand Lassalle: State socialist and the 1850s – years of reaction, and Proudhonism. In *The Raya Dunayevskaya collection – Marxist-humanism: A half century of its world development*. Wayne State University Archives of Labor and Urban Affairs.

Dunayevskaya, R. (1956b). Marx and the Utopian socialists. In *The Raya Dunayevskaya collection – Marxist-humanism: A half century of its world development*. Wayne State University Archives of Labor and Urban Affairs.

Dunayevskaya, R. (1958). *Marxism and freedom . . . from 1776 until today*. Bookman Associates.

Dutt, B. (2022). *To hell and back: Humans of Covid*. Juggernaut.

Eban, K. (2019). *Bottle of lies: Ranbaxy and the dark side of Indian pharma*. Juggernaut Books.

The Economic Times. (2020, March 5). *Coronavirus terror in India: Sanitisers, masks sold out, prices peak*. Retrieved December 3, 2023, from www.economictimes.com/industry/cons-prpducts/fmcg/coronavirus-terror-in-india-sanitisers-masks-sold-out-prices-peak/articleshow/74487298.cms

The Economic Times. (2020, March 19). *Coronavirus scare grips India: Price of N95 mask shoots up to Rs 500, sanitiser shortage in stores*. Retrieved December 3, 2023, from www.economictimes.com/magazines/panache/coronavirus-scare-grips-india-price-ofn95-maks-shoots-up-to-rs-500-sanitiser-shortage-in-stores/articleshow/74476650.cms

The Economic Times. (2020, June 7). *India surplus in face mask Production, allows exports to clear inventory: Industry*. Retrieved December 3, 2023, from www.economictimes.com/industry/healthcare/biotech/healthcare/india-surplus-in-face-mask-production-allow-exports-to-clear-inventory-industry/articleshow/76241893.cms

Engels, F. (1880). The socialism of Mr. Bismarck. In *Marx-Engels collected works* (Vol. 24). Lawrence and Wishart.

Express Pharma. (2022, May 5). *Morepan labs' annual FY22 revenue increases by 30 per cent*. Retrieved December 3, 2023, from www.expresspharma.in/morepan-labs-annual-fy22-revenue-increases-by-30-per-cent

Feldman, R., & Frondorf, E. (2017). *Drug wars: How big pharma raises prices and keeps generics off the market*. Cambridge University Press.

Financial Express. (2021, November 11). *Morepan records 70 percent increase in profit before tax in Q2 with consolidated revenue growth of 17%*. Retrieved December 3, 2023, from www.financialexpress.com/healthcare/pharma-healthcare/morepan-records-70-percent-increase-in-profit-before-tex-in-q2-with-consolidated-revenue-growth-of-17/2376167/

Fromm, E. (1955/2008). *The sane society*. Routledge.

Gandhi-Mody, P. (2022). *A nation to protect: Leading India through the covid crisis*. Rupa Publications.

Gans, J. (2020a). *Economics in the age of Covid-19*. The MIT Press.

Gans, J. (2020b). *The pandemic information gap: The brutal economics of Covid-19*. The MIT Press.

Gehrke, J. P. (2016). A radical Endeavor: Joseph chamberlain and the emergence of municipal socialism in Birmingham. *American Journal of Economics and Sociology*, 75(1), 23–57.

Giddens, A. (1990). *The consequences of modernity*. Polity.

Giddens, A. (1991). *Modernity and self-identity*. Polity.

Gilbert, S., & Green, C. (2021). *Vaxxers: The inside story of the Oxford AstraZeneca vaccine and the race against the virus*. Hodder and Stoughton.

Giubilini, A. (2019). *The ethics of vaccination*. Palgrave Macmillan.

The Global Times. (2022, January 17). *GT investigates: Rich countries hoarding vaccines in disregard of poorer regions breathes life into new variants, worsens economic disparity*. Retrieved December 3, 2023, from www.globaltimes.cn/page/202201/1246196.shtml

Greger, M. (2020). *How to survive a pandemic*. Bluebird.

Guerin, P. J., Singh-Phulgenda, S., & Strub-Wourgaft, N. (2020). The consequence of Covid-19 on the global supply of medical products: Why Indian generics matter for the world? *F1000Research*, 9(225). https://doi.org/10.12688/f1000research.23057.1

Gulankar, A. C. (2020, April 22). Social distancing not a choice in Dharavi, Asia's biggest slum. *The Federal*. Retrieved December 3, 2023, from www.thefederal.com/states/west/maharashtra/social-distancing-not-a-choice-in-dharavi-asias-biggest-slum

Harvey, D. (2005). *A brief history of neoliberalism*. Oxford University Press.

Harvey, D. (2006/2019). *Spaces of global capitalism*. Verso.

Harvey, D. (2014). *Seventeen contradictions and the end of capitalism*. OUP.

Hay, C., & Payne, A. (2015). *Civic capitalism*. Polity.

Hilferding, R. (1915). The work community of the classes? In M. E. Blum & W. T. Smaldone (Eds.), *Austro-Marxism: The ideology of unity* (Vol. II). Brill.

The Hindu. (2021, March 27). *Relatives of migrants crushed under train in Maharashtra's Karmad await death certificates*. Retrieved December 3, 2023, from www.thehindu.com/news/national/other-states/reatives-of-migrants-crushed-under-train-in-maharashtras-karmad-await-death-certificates/article34177503.ece

The Hindu. (2021, May 28). *Mumbai "Dharavi model" helps tame second Covid-19 wave in slum town*. Retrieved December 3, 2023, from www.thehindu.com/news/national/other-states/mumbais-dharavi-model-helps-tame-second-covid-19-wave-in-slum-town/article34664110.ece

The Hindu. (2021, May 30). *Plea calls for national security act against hoarding COVID-19 essentials*. Retrieved December 3, 2023, from www.thehindu.com/news/national/plea-calls-for-national-security-act-against-hoarding-covid-19-essentials/article34683948.ece

The Hindu. (2021, October 5). *COVID insurance scheme to cover Anganwadi workers*. Retrieved December 3, 2023, from www.thehindu.com/news/national/

anganwadi-workers-helpers-involved-in-covid-related-duties-to-get-rs-50-lakh-insurance-cover-official/article36840593.ece

India Blooms. (2021, March 1). *India celebrates role of NGOs in combating the Covid-19 pandemic*. Retrieved December 3, 2023, from www.indiablooms.com/life-details/L/5775/india-celebrates-role-of-ngos-in-combating-the-covid-19-pandemic.html

The Indian Express. (2021, April 26). *Hoarding of oxygen, medicines creates panic shortages: Experts*. Retrieved December 3, 2023, from www.indianexpress.com/article/india/hoarding-of-oxygen-medicines-creates-panic-shortage-experts-7289367/

The Indian Express. (2022, June 27). *Over 500 Mohalla clinics in Delhi will soon provide Covid-19 shots*. Retrieved December 3, 2023, from www.indianexpress.com/article/cities/delhi/over-500-mohalla-clinics-in-delhi-will-soon-provide-covid-19-shots-7994526/

James, C. L. R., Dunayevskaya, R., & Boggs, G. (1986). *State capitalism and world revolution*. Charles H. Kerr.

Jishnu, L. (2022, February 11). COVID-19: India trips on its patent waiver proposal. *Down to Earth*. Retrieved December 3, 2023, from www.downtoearth.org.in/blog/health/covid-19-india-trips-on-its-patent-waiver-proposal-81477

Jones, L. (2018). *Big one: How natural disasters have shaped us (and what we can do about them)*. Doubleday.

Jowett, F. W. (1907). *The socialist and the city*. George Allen.

Kakani, S., & DebRoy, S. (2022). *Mumbai fights back: A bureaucrat's account of how the maximum city took on Covid-19*. Notion Press.

Kalra, A., & Ghoshal, D. (2020, March 28). India needs at least 38 million masks to fight coronavirus: agency document. *Reuters*. https://news.yahoo.com/india-needs-least-38-million-122153834.html

Kapri, V. (2021). *1232 KM: The long journey back home*. Harper Collins Publishers India.

Kinnvall, C., & Mitzen, J. (2020). Anxiety, fear, and ontological security in world politics: Thinking with and beyond Giddens. *International Theory*, 12, 240–256.

Klein, N. (2007). *The shock doctrine: The rise of disaster capitalism*. Penguin.

Klein, N. (2018). *The battle for paradise: Puerto Rico takes on the disaster capitalists*. Haymarket Books.

Koshy, J. (2022, March 16). Patent rights on Covid-19 vaccines may be waived for five years. *The Hindu*. Retrieved December 3, 2023, from www.thehindu.com/sci-tech/health/patent-rights-on-covid-19-vaccines-may-be-waived-for-five-years/article65230047.ece

Krishnan, V. (2022). *Phantom plague: How tuberculosis shaped history*. Penguin Random House.

Kumbhare, S. (2020, May 7). Sanitation workers: At the bottom of the frontline against COVID-19? *The Wire*. Retrieved December 3, 2023, from www.thewire.in/article/urban/sanitation-workers-covid-19

Lahariya, C., Kang, G., & Guleria, R. (2020). *Till we win: India's fight against the Covid-19 pandemic*. Penguin.

Laing, R. D. (1990). *The divided self: An existential study in sanity and madness*. Penguin.

Lal, V. (2020). *The fury of Covid-19: The politics, histories, and unrequited love of the coronavirus*. Pan Macmillan.

Lalé, E., & Osotimehin, S. (2021). Technology and globalization in the post-COVID economy. In J. L. Denis, C. Régis, D. M. Weinstock, & C. Champagne (Eds.), *Pandemic societies*. McGill-Queen's University Press.

Law, J. (2006). *Big pharma: Exposing the global healthcare agenda*. Carroll and Graf Publishers.

Lebowitz, M. (2020). *Between capitalism and community*. Monthly Review Press.

Leopold, E., & McDonald, D. A. (2012). Municipal socialism then and now: Some lessons for the global south. *Third World Quarterly, 33*(10), 1837–1853.

Leys, C. (2008). *Total capitalism: Market politics, market state*. Three Essays Collective.

Lopez, I., & Bultman, M. (2022, June 21). Covid vaccine waiver deal threatens investment for future crises. *Bloomberg Law*. Retrieved December 3, 2023, from www.bloomberglaw.com/coronavirus/wto-approves-vaccine-patent-waiver-to-help-combat-covid-pandemic

Lowenstein, A. (2015). *Disaster capitalism: Making a killing out of a catastrophe*. Verso.

Malm, A. (2020). *Corona, climate, chronic emergency: War communism in the twenty-first century*. Verso.

Martin, R., Unsworth, S., Valero, A., & Verhoeven, D. (2020). *Innovation for a strong and sustainable recovery*. Centres for Economic Performance, London School of Economics and Political Science.

Marx, K. (1844/1975). Economic and philosophical manuscripts of 1844. In *Marx Engels collected works* (Vol. 3). Lawrence and Wishart. (Original work published 1844)

Marx, K. (1847/1976). Moralising criticism or critiquing morality. In *Marx Engels collected works* (Vol. 6). Lawrence and Wishart. (Original work published 1847)

Marx, K. (1867/1976). *Capital. Vol. 1: A critique of political economy*. Penguin. (Original work published 1867)

Means, R., & Smith, R. (1994). *Community care: Policy and practice*. Macmillan.

Ministry of Health and Family Welfare. (2020, December 28). *Covid-19 vaccines: Operational guidelines*. Government of India.

MN, P. (2020, May 13). Urban India didn't care about migrant workers till 26 March, only cares now because it's lost their services: P Sainath. *Firstpost*. Retrieved December 3, 2023, from www.firstpost.com/india/urban-india-didnt-care-about-migrant-workers-till-26-march-only-cares-now-because-its-lost-their-services-p-sainath-8361821.html

Monti Jr., D. J. (2013). *Engaging strangers: Civil rights, civic capitalism, and public order in Boston*. Fairleigh Dickinson University Press.

Morgan, D. R. (2013). Structural criminality within the "collective shadow": Disaster capitalism and the globalization of ruling power. *On the Horizon, 21*(3), 247–258.

Morris, M. D. (1991). The emergence of industrial labour force in India. In D. Gupta (Ed.), *Social stratification*. Oxford University Press.

Mukul, J. (2022). *The great shutdown: A story of two Indian summers*. Harper Collins Publishers India.

Murray, P. (2014). The secret of capital's self-valorisation "laid bare": How Hegel helped Marx to overturn Ricardo's theory of profit. In F. Moseley & T. Smith (Eds.), *Marx's capital and Hegel's logic: A reexamination*. Brill. (Original work published 1993)

Nath, D. (2020, September 14). Govt. has no data of migrant workers' death, loss of job. *The Hindu*. www.thehindu.com/news/national/govt-has-no-data-of-migrant-workers-death-loss-of-job/article32600637.ece

Nature Editorial. (2021, May 27). A patent waiver on COVID vaccines is right and fair. *Nature, 593*.

Nature Editorial. (2022, March 31). Time is running out for covid vaccine patent waivers. *Nature, 603*.

The New Indian Express. (2021, April 26). *Ramdesivir hoarding: 19 held across India for alleged black marketing of Covid-19 drug*. Retrieved December 3, 2023, from

www.newindianexpress.com/nation/2021/apr26/ramdesivir-hoarding-19-held-across-india-for-alleged-black-marketing-pf-covid-19-drug-2294783.html
Nichols, J. (2022). *Coronavirus criminals and pandemic profiteers: Accountability for those who caused the crisis*. Verso.
OECD. (2020, May 4). *The face mask global value chain in the COVID-19 outbreak: Evidence and policy lessons*. Retrieved December 3, 2023, from www.oecd.org/coronavirus/policy-responses/the-face-mask-global-value-chain-in-the-COVID-19-outbreak-evidence-and-policy-lessons-a4df866d/
OECD. (2022, April 4). *Global supply chains at work: A tale of three products to fight COVID-19*. Retrieved December 3, 2023, from www.oecd.org/coronavirus/policy-responses/global-supply-chains-at-work-a-tale-of-three-products-to-fight-covid-19–07647bc5/
Oriel, A., & Ghosh, K. (2022, May 31). India's poor forced to swallow the Bitter Pill as medical inflation nibbles at their life savings. *Outlook*. Retrieved December 3, 2023, from www.outlookindia.com/business/india-s-poor-forced-to-swallow-bitter-pill-as-medical-inflation-nibbles-at-their-life-savings-news-199526
Osho, Z., & Sareen, J. (2022). Strengthening healthcare delivery systems in low-income countries. In A. Thomas, K. S. Reddy, D. Alexander, & P. Prabhakaran (Eds.), *Climate change and the health sector*. Routledge.
Oxfam. (2021, November 16). *Pfizer, BioNTech and Moderna making $1,000 profit every second while world's poorest countries remain largely unvaccinated*. Retrieved December 3, 2023, from www.oxfam.org/en/press-releases/pfizer-biontech-and-moderna-making-1000-profit-every-second-while-worlds-poorest
Pandey, T. (2022, January 15). "Futile to die for duty": Most dead Anganwadis' kin haven't got Rs 50L relief UP govt promised. *The Print*. www.theprint.in/india/futile-to-die-for-duty-most-dead-anganwadis-kin-havent-got-rs=50l-relief-up-govt-promised/801977/
Pandey, V. (2021, May 5). Coronavirus: How India descended into Covid-19 chaos. *BBC*. Retrieved December 3, 2023, from www.bbc.com/news/world-asia-india-56977653
Parikh, S., Desai, M., & Parikh, R. (2020). *The coronavirus: What you need to know about the global pandemic*. Penguin.
Pavri, K. M. (2010). *Challenge of AIDS*. National Book Trust. (Original work published 1992)
Pikoli, P. (2020, October 26). What is a crisis? Online special: Living and thinking crisis. *Thesis Eleven*. Retrieved December 3, 2023, from www.thesiseleven.com/2020/10/26/what-is-a-crisis
Pithode, T. (2022). *The battle against covid: Diary of bureaucrat*. Bloomsbury.
Prabhakaran, P. (2022). Climate change and its impact on human health: An overview. In A. Thomas, K. S. Reddy, D. Alexander, & P. Prabhakaran (Eds.), *Climate change and the health sector*. Routledge.
Prasad, P. (2018). Health care reforms: Do they ensure social protection for the labouring poor? In P. Prasad & A. Jesani (Eds.), *Equity and access: Health care studies in India*. Oxford University Press.
The Quint. (2022, July 22). *"Govt. has no data on Anganwadi workers who died due to COVID-19": Smriti Irani*. Retrieved December 3, 2023, from www.thequint.com/news/politics/smriti-irani-tells-parliament-no-data-anganwadi-workers-died-covid-lockdown
Ramin, C. J. (2017). *Crooked: Outwitting the back pain industry and getting on the road to recovery*. Harper.
Ranald, P. (2022, February 23). Trade rules have thwarted global efforts to fight covid. The WTO must deliver on a vaccine IP waiver. *The Guardian*. Retrieved December 3, 2023, from www.theguardian.com/commentisfree/2022/feb/23/

trade-rules-have-thwarted-global-efforts-to-fight-covid-the-wto-must-deliver-on-a-vaccine-ip-waiver

Rao, M. A. (2015). *Indian railways*. National Book Trust. (Original work published 1975)

Reddy, K. S. (2019). *Make health in India: Reaching a billion plus*. Orient Blackswan.

Rogers, K., Jakes, L., & Swanson, A. (2020, March 18). Trump defends using "Chinese virus" label, ignoring growing criticism. *The New York Times*. Retrieved December 3, 2023, from www.nytimes.com/2020/03/18/us/politics/china-virus.html

Rushe, D., & Inman, P. (2022, May 3). Hopes rise for covid vaccine patent waiver after key countries agree on proposal. *The Guardian*. Retrieved December 3, 2023, from www.theguardian.com/world/2022/may/03/covid-vaccine-patent-waiver-hopes-rise-wto

Sampath, G., & Ghosh, J. (2020, June 15). The "shock doctrine" in India's response to Covid-19. *The Hindu*. Retrieved December 3, 2023, from www.thehindu.com/podcast/comment-the-shock-doctrine-in-indias-response-to-covid-19/article31831402.ece

Scroll. (2020, March 26). Covid-19: 800 people in quarantine after Delhi Mohalla clinic doctor, family test positive. *Scroll*. Retrieved December 3, 2023, from www.scroll.in/latest/957268/covid-19-delhi-mohalla-clinic-doctor-wife-and-family-test-positive-visitors-asked-to-quarantine

Scroll. (2020, November 11). *Pfizer vaccine's -70Degree Celsius storage requirement will be a challenge for India, says AIIMS director*. Retrieved December 3, 2023, from www.scroll.in/latest/978288/pfizer-vaccines-70deg-celsiusm-storage-requirement-will-be-a-challenge-for-india-says-aiims-director

Scroll. (2021, March 29). *Covid-19: At least 22 migrants die while trying to get home during lockdown*. Retrieved December 3, 2023, from www.scroll.in/latest/957570/covid-19-lockdown-man-collapses-dies-halfway-while-walking-home-300-km-away-from-delhi

Scroll. (2021, June 3). *Covid lockdown: Over 8,700 people, many of them migrant workers, died along railway tracks in 2020*. Retrieved December 3, 2023, from www.scroll.in/latest/996519/covid-lockdown-over-8700-people-many-of-them-migrant-workers-died-along-railway-tracks-in-2020

Selvaraj, S., Farooqui, H., & Mehta, A. (2019). Does price regulation affect atorvastatin sales in India? An impact assessment through time series analysis. *BMJ Open*, 9(1), e024200.

Sengupta, A. (1986/2021). Generic names versus brand names. In P. Purkayastha, I. Mukhopadhyay, & R. Chintan (Eds.), *Political journeys in health: Essays by and for Amit Sengupta*. Leftword. (Original work published 1986)

Sengupta, A. (2007). *Report on the conditions of work and promotion of livelihood in the unorganised sector*. National Commission for Enterprises in the Unorganised Sector.

Sengupta, A. (2018). Globalisation, intellectual property rights, and pharmaceuticals. In P. Prasad & A. Jesani (Eds.), *Equity and access: Health care studies in India*. Oxford University Press.

Sengupta, A. (2021, June 2). COVID lockdown: Over 8,700 died on railway tracks in 2020, many of them migrants. *Newsclick*. Retrieved December 3, 2023, from www.newsclick.in/COVID%20Lockdown-pver-8700-died-railway-tracks-202-many-migrants

Shalal, A., & Farge, E. (2022, March 17). U.S., EU, India, S. Africa reach compromise on COVID vaccine IP waiver text. *Reuters*. Retrieved December 3, 2023, from www.reuters.com/business/healthcare-pharmaceuticals/us-eu-india-s-africa-reach-tentative-pact-covid-vaccine-ip-waiver-sources2022-03-15/

Sharma, J. (2022). *Made in lockdown: India's MedTech growth powered by AMTZ*. Rupa.

Silver, A. (2022, June 20). European industry laments WTO waiver on covid vaccine patents. *Research Professional News*. Retrieved December 3, 2023, from www.researchprofessionalnews.com/rr-news-europe-regulation-2022-6-european-industry-laments-wto-waiver-on-covid-vaccine-patents/
Singh, S. (2018). *The great smog of India*. Penguin.
Sismondo, S. (2018). *Ghost-managed medicine: Big pharma's invisible hands*. Mattering Press.
Smith, M. C., Kolassa, E. M., & Pray, W. S. (2021). *Government, big pharma, and the people: A century of dis-ease*. Routledge.
Srivastava, R. (2020, July 7). Don't forget us in coronavirus battle, say businesses in India's Dharavi slum. *Reuters*. Retrieved December 3, 2023, from https:///www.reuters.com/article/us-heath-coronavirus-india-slum-trfn-idUSKBN248004
Stern, N., Unsworth, S., Valero, A., Zenghelis, D., Rydge, J., & Robins, N. (2020). *Strategy, investment and policy for a string and sustainable recovery*. Centre for Economic Performance, London School of Economics and Political Science.
Stern, N., & Valero, A. (2021). Innovation, growth and the transition to net-zero emissions. *Research Policy*, *50*(9), 104293. https://doi.org/10.1016/j.respol.2021.104293
Subramaniam, S. (2020, April 28). How the face mask became the world's most coveted commodity. *The Guardian*. Retrieved December 3, 2023, from www.theguardian.com/world/2020/apr/28/face-masks-coveted-commodity-coronavirus-pandemic
Tomes, N. (1998). *The gospel of germs: Men, women, and the microbe in American life*. Harvard University Press.
Tooze, A. (2021). *Shutdown: How covid shook the world's economy*. Viking.
Tumbe, C. (2018). *India moving: A history of migration*. Penguin.
Upadhyay, P. (2021, June 1). How BMC set a benchmark for other municipalities in covid management. *India Today*. Retrieved December 3, 2023, from www.indiatoday.in/coronavirus-outbreak/story/how-bmc-set-a-benchmark-for-other-municipalities-in-covid-management-1809689-2021-06-01
Valero, A., Riom, C., & Oliveira-Cunha, J. (2021). The business response to Covid-19 one year on: Findings from the second wave of the CEP-CBI survey on technology adoption. In *A CEP Covid-19 analysis*. Centre for Economic Performance: London School of Economics and Political Science.
Van Bergeijk, P. A. G. (2021). *Pandemic economics*. Edward Elgar.
Veeraraghavan, D. (2013). *The making of the madras working class*. Leftword Books.
Wallace, R. (2016). *Big farms make big flu: Dispatches on infectious diseases, agribusiness, and the nature of science*. Monthly Review Press.
Wilde, L. (2004). *Erich Fromm and the quest for solidarity*. Palgrave Macmillan.
The Wire. (2020, May 8). *Aurangabad: 16 migrant workers killed by goods train, 5 injured*. Retrieved December 3, 2023, from www.thewire.in/article/rights/aurangabad-migrant-workers-goods-train-killed
World Health Organization. (2020, March 3). *Shortage of personal protective equipment endangering health workers worldwide*. Retrieved December 3, 2023, from www.who.int/news/item/03-03-2020-shortage-of-personal-protective-equipment-endangering-health-workers-worldwide
World Health Organization. (2022, March 17). *Africa's COVID-19 Vaccine uptake increases by 15%*. Retrieved December 3, 2023, from www.afro.who.int/news/africas-covid-19-vaccine-uptake-increases-15
Yadav, S. S. (2022). *India's vaccine growth story: From cowpox to vaccine Maitri*. Sage.
Yadavar, S., & Agrawal, S. (2020, May 22). Dharavi is not just fighting coronavirus, but also dirty toilets and battered image. *The Print*. www.theprint.in/india/dharavi-is-not-just-fighting-coronavirus-but-also-dirty-toilets-and-battered-image/426523/

Yee, D. K. P. (2018). Violence and disaster capitalism in post-Haiyan Philippines. *Peace Review*, *30*(2), 160–197.

Zanoni, P., & Mir, R. (2022). COVID-19: Interrogating the capitalist organization of the economy and society through the pandemic. *Organization*, *29*(3), 369–378.

Žižek, S. (2021). Light at the end of the tunnel? Yes, but . . . . In K. Mahadevan, S. Kumar, M. Bhoot, & R. Kharat (Eds.), *The covid spectrum: Theoretical and experiential reflections from India and beyond*. Speaking Tiger.

Zuboff, S. (2019). *The age of surveillance capitalism*. Public Affairs.

Zuckerman, G. (2021). *A shot to save the world: The remarkable race and groundbreaking science behind the Covid-19 vaccines*. Penguin.

4 Benefits and Pitfalls of Local Governance during Apocalyptic Times

Introduction

COVID-19 has spread globally by banking upon globalised capitalist production and consumption relations. The onset of the COVID-19 pandemic has consolidated numerous aspects of past governmental systems, which many thought had served their course, such as the statist management of the society and welfarist public services. Different forms of technology-based surveillance mechanisms have emerged during the pandemic, mostly managed by the state, in the form of mobile applications, tracking mechanisms, and so on (Faizal & Rahman, 2020, May 14), which has effectively transformed those mechanisms into biopolitical assets possessed by the state for various functions as they deem fit. These mechanisms will not be easy to get rid of once the pandemic is over.

Michel Foucault (1979) argued that methods of surveillance is one of the key elements that governments employ during epidemics, and pandemics, as it help states to separate the sick from the well-off. At the same time, these are also methods through which seclusion is inflicted upon people, often making them dependent *completely* on the state. The ways in which surveillance techniques are being used globally suggests that the emerging global powers will be the ones who would possess 'a sophisticated network of totalitarian global power that is far more subtle and extensive than the world has ever known' (Morgan, 2013, p. 255).

Amidst the onslaught of COVID-19, the term 'apocalypse' has been rendered mainstream in the last few years. A major reason for that being the way in which climate change has been transforming the lives of human beings on the planet. Climate change has been resulting in a multitude of changes in the organisation of life on Earth by bringing into action extreme weather events, which are increasingly becoming frequent and more disastrous with every passing year (Foster & Clark, 2020). The disastrous changes in the climate, as many believe, such as Klein (2019), are results of the ways in which the elite section of the populace is restructuring the world and the lives of countless others in the world, which is pushing the world towards a perennial state of crisis and chaos.

DOI: 10.4324/9781003505167-5

Nations and societies fall into crisis quite often – more frequently than one would ideally want them to – and with these changes, it is expected that that frequency will increase over the years. More often than not, it is the elite who create the conditions under which these disasters seem imminent (Foster, 2020). Jared Diamond (2019) notes that when societies descend into states of crises, there are two kinds of responses: one social and the other individual. While both responses should ideally be in synchronisation with each other – negotiating between violent upheavals or peaceful transformations – it is true that individuals do not commit automatically to violent upheavals.

The ways in which the contemporary society is structured, it can be said with a certain level of certainty that the actual risk involved with public health is amplified within public perceptions (Kasperson et al., 2005). This is due to the manner in which various forms of media discourses and public opinions are propagated within the society often causing massive social reactions of an adverse nature. It is this fear of the coming apocalypse, which has been amplified during the pandemic. The fear has resulted in some people resorting to better practices with regards to their healthcare, sanitation, and safety, but it also means that people – who have access – make arrangements to sustain through the impending crisis. The shortage of toilet paper in many urban markets of the Global North during the days before the lockdowns in their regions is a proof of how human beings can behave in times of crisis.

With the coming of large-scale attacks on the environment, the fears of an impending apocalypse have been accentuated among the people, especially the vulnerable populace globally. Terms such as *Airpocalypse* have been used in recent times by scholars, such as Smedley (2019), to refer to the broader climatic changes that have been emerging globally. This is particularly relevant in the context of India, where the increasing pollution in cities such as Delhi has been causing massive healthcare crisis in the cities as well as the adjoining regions. Siddharth Singh (2018) writes that the fear of an apocalypse is disproportionately distributed among the population because the solutions that the state provides towards resolving the crises of any imminent disaster of an apocalyptic nature is suboptimal in character, which largely helps the elites and 'upper middle class – and increasingly even the middle class – [which] relies on private providers' for fulfilling their essential activities of sustenance (p. 9). The private sector's dominance in providing essential commodities has accentuated in recent years. Neoliberalism which had garnered widescale support for itself in the early 1990s, saying that it would make lives of the Indian population better, has utterly failed in providing nutritional security and dignified livelihood to the citizens.

The COVID-19 crisis has not emerged out of the present day government, but has instead been formed gradually over the last three decades with reductions in public expenditure and a constant valorisation of capital in the private sector. This reflected in the decline of 9% in the per capita real consumption expenditure in rural India – where often the most marginalised population lives – between 2011–12 and 2017–18 (Patnaik, 2021). Sinha and

Sinha (2018), on the other hand, write that one of the major achievements of the governments after neoliberalisation was the importance which was given to economic growth. However, as Dréze and Sen (2013) have already stated, mere economic growth rarely shows the complete picture of development in any country. Other factors such as nutrition and subjective poverty need to be considered because issues such as poverty, food security, and inequality have to go beyond numbers and have to include diverse factors – such as the distribution of food within the family, which might not always be directly related to family income but rather be informed by gender disparity, and the ways in which children and the elderly are treated within the family (Sen, 1970/2017).

This has been further accentuated by the *fact* that human societies today are characterised by constant fears of being under some form of risk. The idea that human beings are always under some form of risk is causing a distinct effect on the social fabric that human society has built over the course of many centuries. There have been many reports in recent times that have brought forward the concerns surrounding the numerous probable apocalyptic crises that India might be facing in the coming years. For example, there is a growing concern about the state of water in the largest of Indian cities caused by the combined effects of climate change and wastewater policies. With rapidly expanding urban spaces, cities such as Chennai and Bengaluru are facing a tremendous water crisis during the summer months (Padmanabhan & Srivastava, 2019, August 4). There has also been a considerable increase in the kind of urban settlements that can be considered to be slums. Slums in India are extremely common sights.

Slums do not arise out of vacuum, but are results of long-drawn processes of exclusion in the city spaces. It is not such that slums can only grow in colonial urban spaces (Sen, 1970/1990), but they can also grow up in certain planned spaces (D'Souza, 1970/1990), making these informal settlements one of the many issues that India's urban governance has had to face. Slums are usually places where aspects such as sanitation and healthcare are not much discussed. At the same time, slums are usually spaces where essential services such as electricity, water, and sewer pipes are disproportionately provided (Ramachandran, 1970/1990). The kind of urban planning that capitalism promotes makes it almost impossible for people to pay attention to factors such as sanitation when choosing where to reside. Bisen (2019) has argued that the failure of urban planning and the state actors has contributed to the growth of such informal settlements in urban spaces in India, which are now causing major hurdles to ensuring public health in these spaces. With the advent of industrialisation, it became natural for migrants to come to cities, but unlike other countries such as China and the United Kingdom where public housing is a major political agenda, India did not have any such policy in its agenda.

The migrant workers' crisis, which shook the nation in 2020, was a stark reminder of the fact that in spite of passing through more than 70 years as a free nation, India still does not possess municipal housing facilities. According to a news report in *The Wire* (June 20, 2022), around 1,13,998 migrants have left cities, showing that around 52% of the migrant labour from rural India have relocated back to their villages following the lockdown. Imaan (July 31, 2020) writes that the unavailability of shelter homes during the pandemic was a major cause of the crisis faced by the migrant workers, despite the directives of the Ministry of Housing Affair's *Deendayal Antyodaya Yojana-National Urban Livelihood Mission* that a shelter home should be capable of accommodating 100 people out of every 100,000 people in each city. For example, Delhi only has around 230 such homes, with a capacity to house only 17, 128 people – a meagre figure considering that India has around 1.7 million homeless people according to the 2011 Census.

When migrants enter the city, they come with their own sanitation practices, which are often at odds with how the urban spaces are designed in a compact and cosy manner (Bisen, 2019). At the same time, sanitation is also something that is intimately connected to the Hindu caste system, which makes it almost certain that mere changes at a policy level would not make much difference at the grassroots level (Coffey & Spears, 2017). Open defaecation was, and still is, a major issue concerning sanitation in India. The plans that the central government has towards implementing sanitation in the country are largely based on voluntary action by the citizens, aided by funding from the government, along with a particular emphasis on partnerships between various bodies and political leadership (Iyer, 2019). Reputed journalists and chroniclers, such as Singh (2019), of the twentieth-century India have given assent to the success that the Swachh Bharat Abhiyan has been in rural areas. However, the reality is far from that. Sanitation and other such healthcare policies cannot be seen in an isolationist framework and need to take positions regarding other forms of deprivation that run amok in India, especially in rural India (The Hindu Editorial, 2019, November 27).

Public policy amidst these vulnerabilities becomes a crucial area of analysis, as well as of struggle because 'public policy is the epiphenomenon of power. It defines the political goals of those who exercise power through the instrument of public policies' (Monti & Wacks, 2021, p. 16). Public policy is a site where powers are expressed. It often becomes simply about the effectiveness of the policy decision bypassing the moral predicaments (Joshi, 2021). Health emergencies present unique challenges to the public policy-making process because public policy then has to be formed taking into consideration a multitude of various factors, as well as make a constant effort to strike a balance between moral values and socio-political impediments. Thomas et al. (2022) argue that the health of a community is directly affected by the apocalyptic times that issues such as climate change and pandemics pose before the human society, and healthcare workers play a crucial role in that regard. However, during crises such as COVID-19, it is not only the healthcare workers but the entire gambit of the working class itself that forms the core of the social response towards COVID-19. Local administration, amidst such scenarios, plays a crucial role because it is the primary vehicle through which the social co-ordination is maintained, and the working class and other marginalised sections have to bear a disproportionate amount of that responsibility. This chapter takes these issues into cognisance and is divided into four subsections. While the first subsection discusses the state of community health, the second section analyses the dynamics between capitalism, neoliberalism, and local community-focused administration. The third subsection takes a more technical turn and discusses ULBs and municipalism and their relevance within COVID-19, and the fourth and final subsection analyses the state of the community under neoliberal capitalism.

Community Health, the Pandemic and Capital

The WHO (April 1, 2021) declares primary health to be one of the most fundamental aspects of the right to a good health that people ought to enjoy, regardless of their class, gender, race, or caste, as it is one of the most effective methods to ensure communitarian good health, both physically and mentally. And primary healthcare is often a domain that is left exclusively at the behest of the public sector. The growth of neoliberalisation has meant that public expenditure in healthcare is only limited to areas where the private sector is not interested in investing (Sundaraman et al., 2020). There has been a severe depletion of public and community health services in the country, which has placed a huge section of the urban poor in jeopardy (Mishra et al., 2021). The health that a community and the individuals therein enjoy is connected to a web of interconnected factors that include the air that one breathes, safe drinking water, food, and modes of accommodation (Thomas et al., 2022).

The community is an important aspect of urban life, and ULBs, in turn, are an indispensable part of the community. This chapter discusses about the ways in which the individual human being, the community, and the municipality are entangled within the urban societies. With the rise of venture and asset capital in the society under neoliberal globalisation, the municipalities are being strategically depleted of all the funds leaving them with no other option but to remain mute spectators in the cases of public emergencies such as COVID-19. India is a rapidly urbanising society. There are diverse views about the kind of urbanisation which has been happening in the country – some describe it as a positive change, while others see the process of urbanisation in India as an unplanned one eventually fated to collapse. Urbanisation in India is opening up new frontiers in terms of many important aspects of urban life such as housing, energy utilisation, healthcare, and the like.

The socio-economic growth that India will potentially register in the next decades to come will depend, to a certain extent, on the way in which India manages its urban areas. And two critical aspects in this transformation will be access to water and energy. It is futile for any nation to aim for economic superiority unless and until it can assure its citizens uninterrupted and secure access to clean air, water, and energy. These aspects of urban life have an impact not only on the health of the citizens but also on affect the very idea of multifaceted well-being in urban spaces,[1] which in turn is related to the idea of a sustainable urban renewal. Cities are important aspects of the much desired urban renewal in India, which often intersects with India's agreements with other major nation states on questions of sustainability, ecological equity, and climate justice (NITI Aayog, 2021). However, the effective and democratic management of any city involves institutionalisation and public accountability of the administrators, politicians, and others in positions of power. The idea of a localised welfare state was used as a foundation for the conceptual formation of the theory of municipal socialism by the liberal political figures of Manchester during the mid-nineteenth century (Bönker et al., 2016).

Local elections in this regard proved to be critical because they provide an opportunity to advocate for a greater control of municipal resources. The first formal local elections *as one knows it today* were held in 1889 for county councils in Britain, where the 'principle of representative local democracy' was highlighted by the contesting and voting population (Barron et al., 1991, p. 1). Since then, local governance has taken on a diverse path globally, with a highly fluctuating importance being given to it in various political and social cultures in a variety of different social socio-political systems. However, with globally increasing urbanisation, the local urban bodies have again found themselves to be at the centre of attention. Dense cities, such as Mumbai and Kolkata in India or Huanan in China, have found themselves to be at higher risks of COVID-19 than others. With poor sanitation facilities and high chances of contagion, these cities – despite possessing better healthcare facilities – have become particularly risky places to live in if one takes the pandemic into cognisance. City residents, however, are less at the risk of dying than non-urban residents during a health emergency (Kukla, 2021). In the case of India as well, during April 2021, when the second wave was rampaging through the country with more than 400,000 cases recorded on 30th of April 2021, more than 50% of the recorded deaths were from the rural areas (Sengupta, 2021, May 4).

The spirit of reconstructing itself from ruins has been often focused by municipal and administrative people tasked with looking after the urban spaces (Hein, 2005; Rozario, 2005). However, with growing complexities surrounding the ways in which cities have become populated – *and polluted* – in India over the last few decades, India still does not have adequate data on the impacts that the process of urbanisation has on the informal urban settlements. Increased seasonal and permanent migration in search of work has led to an increase in the informal settlements in the country. These informal settlements often develop into slums, which become highly challenging sites during a public health emergency such as COVID-19.

In slums, the population density far exceeds the population density in other neighbourhoods in the city. Priyali Sur and Esha Mitra's (2020, March 31) report for CNN has exposed the vulnerabilities that the slum dwellers of

India faced during the COVID-19 pandemic. They state that the slum dwellers in India face innumerable challenges with regards to accessibility to public resources and sanitation. Before the huge surge of cases in India, places such as Dharavi had around 1 toilet for almost every 1,440 people, which contributed to the massive destruction that the pandemic had brought forward in India Sur and Mitra (2020, March 31). One might agree or disagree about urbanisation, but the importance that urbanisation holds for the global population at this juncture cannot be overlooked. A report argues that by 2050, around 68%, which amounts to 6.7 billion, of the global population are expected to live in urban areas (Housing Research, 2021). According to Census 2011, the total urban population in India was around 377.1 million, which roughly constitutes around 31.2% of the total population (Ahmad, 2012). And by 2050, India is projected to add another 404 million people to its existing urban population (Department of Economic and Social Affairs, 2014).

Along with the increasing urbanisation, there have been rise in issues surrounding urban governance. The contemporary Indian urban society is a society that is almost perennially gripped by numerous imminent fears of crises. The huge proportion of vulnerable and marginalised people that make up a large portion of the total population of India live under constant fears of social, economic, and cultural onslaughts upon their autonomy by the ruling class. And with each crisis that the society faces, human beings have found themselves being confronted by newer challenges. Under contemporary capitalism driven by neoliberal economic reforms, free markets, and capitalism have resulted in increasing casual work and a tendential fall in wages globally (Panitch & Leys, 1997), and especially in India. The COVID-19 pandemic has exposed these blatant inequalities which have been brought forward by neoliberal economic reforms in India. However, to argue that neoliberalism has only had an effect on the lives of human beings economically would be a massive underestimation of the extent to which neoliberalism as a social system function.

Neoliberalism has become an entire *way of life* encompassing not only the economic aspects of contemporary human life but also its social and cultural modes and relations of production, distribution, and consumption. Tavleen Singh (2020), one of the well-known Indian journalists, points out that the socialist – or rather semi-socialist – era of India's economic policies, when the state yielded a disproportionate power over other entities, had yielded nothing except the rise of a bureaucracy and the only way to reform that was to introduce free market capitalism and liberalisation in India.[2] The neoliberal reforms in India have attempted to resolve the supposed problems associated with bureaucracy and the infamous *license raj* in India through rampant privatisation.

However, with the institutionalisation of neoliberalism, the proposed solution to this sluggishness was not a reorganisation or reform of the public sector, but rather, as Jalan (2019) highlights, it was a complete destruction of the monopoly of the public sector in certain aspects of India's economic structure. The neoliberal reforms in India were supposed to lead India from the days of 'dour socialist decades' (Singh, 2016, p. 135) towards a more prosperous future where industrialists could be less coy about the profits they made, and where private companies could dominate the society without many regulations being put on them. Any society which is based on free market capitalism celebrates the development of bourgeois individualism because that makes it extremely easy for capital to dominate individuals, especially the marginalised sections of the population. There is a corresponding weakening of the community as well as the communal ethos, which are being substituted by ethics propagated by the market. There is a collective weakening of the ethical commitments that one makes in one's everyday life, which leads to a complete devaluation of the ethical experience and ethical selfhood characterised by dissonance between approval and demand of the experiencing subject (Critchley, 2012). The importance of the community, in such a situation, has been felt multiple times when the society was struggling not only against the disease but also against the ways it was being managed by the government.

The importance of the community could not be avoided even by the state-sponsored research reports. Dixit and Chauhan (2020) have argued that because of the entrapment of individuals during the nationwide lockdown, the need for a community was felt more strongly by the people, especially children and adolescents. During the pandemic, the world came to realise that one cannot live as if one's immediate surroundings were on an isolated island, but rather that every human being in the world is connected to each other, if not physically then psychologically (Blackman, 2020). The pandemic has exposed the myth that had been constructed around the cultural and social benefits of bourgeois individuality. There are certain aspects of behavioural change that become mainstream with the domination of bourgeois individuality, namely capitalistic attitude towards the society, risk-taking mentality for securing profits, and the rise of the mainstream corporate-driven entrepreneurial attitude, all of which contribute to the growth of newer modes of capital production and circulation to emerge (Gantenbein et al., 2021).

Bourgeois individuality makes the exploitation of others a routine event in the lives of human beings. It works through the glorification of hedonistic tendencies and commodity culture – all of which contribute to the capitalist modes of value production. It keeps on generating newer social needs by working upon common human emotions, which under conditions of capitalist alienation, by reducing human existence to 'archaic' forms of possession of commodities as Fromm (1976, p. 22) would say – within a life that is never fulfilled, never complete. This is the kind of situation where new forms of capital, such as venture capital and asset capital, have come to play important roles in the economic structure of the society. Under neoliberal capitalism, venture capitalists have become the largest capital investors within the economy, holding much higher levels of economic and social power than other publicly accountable bodies. Disasters make this power visible. Klein

(2017a) argues that disasters often evade strict categorisation with reference to the effects that they create, and when disasters such as pandemic strike, there arise moments of extraordinary politics that are often used to push the agendas of privatisation and corporatisation, which benefits the lobbyists and staffers who advocate the interests of particular firms while being working either within or in close tandem with the establishment (Klein, 2017b, July 6).

Capitalism uses the human desire to possess and incorporate commodities, the basis of all consumption under capitalism (Marx, 1844; Fromm, 1976), to the service of capitalist accumulation. The contemporary social structure is such that it has allowed capitalism to restructure the world in its own image, highlighting solutions that urge individuals 'to become bourgeois themselves' (Marx & Engels, 1848, p. 488). The contemporary society is a society where commodities have become the dominant factor in determining the mode of life that one lives. Contemporary capitalism posits commodities – good health being one of them – as the only agents capable of bringing in happiness and aesthetic fulfilment, emphasising the idea that in the contemporary capitalist society, the commodity economy reigns supreme (Marx, 1976, p. 133). The domination of the commodity form is such that major public sector holdings are being disinvested today, as the government of India is increasingly moving towards asset monetisation through the strategic leasing of public assets to private bodies (Arun & Punj, 2021, September 27).

ULBs in this context have to suffer the most because the public services had often been under their administrative capacities, and a change in any of them often creates issues concerning accessibility for them and the people and communities that they serve. Local self-government, as Das (2002/2012) points out, faces challenges from three fronts: the centralised state, the administrative bureaucrats, and the feudal lords. The solution to this, however, as he proposes is privatisation of the resources thus allowing the market to dominate over polity. Municipal bodies have found themselves fighting an unequal fight with private companies, with major democracies across the globe accepting neoliberalisation as a socio-economic policy. Amidst these trajectories of municipal weakening, and with higher degrees of urbanisation, public health has also become an issue which has garnered widespread attention. The municipality is an important aspect of the public health policy executions. Because the municipality interacts directly with the community, it stands at an advantageous position with regards to working in conditions such as the ones presented by the COVID-19 pandemic. Municipalities and the PHCs under them become critical in contexts such as India, where as many as 44 out of 1,000 people become hospitalised in a year as per the National Sample Survey Office (NSSO) data in 2014 (Ghoshal, 2016, April 18). Such massive inequality has only grown, and it is expected that it will continue to grow. With the NITI Aayog approving the plan for going ahead with more vigorous private-public partnerships in the healthcare sector – with ample support from the World Bank – where the public sector healthcare centres are now required to share some of their services such as blood banks, electricity loads, in-patient payment services, and ambulances with the private ones (Sethi & Rao, 2017, July 19).

The NITI Aayog's plan also has some other points, such as the technicalities involved in referring a patient to another private hospital, which will be possible only after the approval of the district medical officer (Sethi & Rao, 2017, July 19). The public-private partnership (PPP) model in India's healthcare first came into the limelight when a report by McKinsey and Company highlighted the benefits that the private sector could bring to India. The report, which was endorsed by Ghulam Nabi Azad, the then Union Health Minister, spoke about the differences between the government being a provider or a payer for healthcare services for the citizens. The report, emphasising the importance of digitalisation, argued:

> Adopting the provider role would slow down social insurance growth and private provision in the absence of any government incentivisation. Adopting the payer role would slow down growth of public beds but that can be resolved by adopting PPP models because private provision is predicted to show strong growth.
> (Sharma, 2012, December 19, Para 3)

GE HealthCare was one of the first to enter the PPP complex with widely circulated prospects of bettering healthcare infrastructure in the country with the help of other larger conglomerates (The Economic Times, 2022, June 2, 2022, June 3). Foundations such as the *Adani Foundation* and Tata supported the initiation of PPP models in the healthcare sector, which has allowed them to invest huge sums of money into rural healthcare as part of its corporate social responsibility (CSR) initiatives (Akhter, 2020, June 22). This has also initiated a host of private corporations entering into various aspects concerning the healthcare sector of the country. For example, the TATA Trust and GE HealthCare Education Institute (GE HEI) had decided in 2016 to work together on bridging the gap with regard to the requisite skills and the existing technical or operating skills among the workers by training students passing the 12th standard exams through certification courses (The Economic Times, 2022, June 3). The decision came in the wake of the estimation that as of 2016, the required number of allied healthcare professionals was almost about 6.5 million with the supply being only about 30,000 (The Economic Times, 2022, June 3). With lessening public expenditure and a constantly increasing private sector influence in the sector, a decade later, one has begun to see the effects of the policy.

Along with the private sector, the NGOs, have played a critical role in the response shown by India towards COVID-19 by providing the government with important critical equipment and ground support (Anand, 2021, October 5). NGOs have been able to provide customised solutions to some of the issues that certain very specific communities face, especially during times such as pandemics initiated by COVID-19. Many experts suggest that private healthcare would have to play a special role if India were to move towards full immunisation (Gupta, 2020, October 24; Digital Medic, 2021, March 29). Reddy's (2019) analysis of the PPP model in healthcare suggests that it did not bring much significant reforms to the Indian healthcare sector. It ended up disproportionately serving the private corporations and as such needed more public supervision at a governmental level to ensure public accountability. The problems with contracts, service delivery, and accountability have ensured that the access to healthcare for poor people has not improved substantially even with the PPP model.

The move towards further privatisation of healthcare by the NITI Aayog has received varied responses. While private hospitals had seen this as progress in the right direction, the public sector saw the move as being detrimental to the cause of publicly funded healthcare services in the country. The plan emphasises the role that private hospitals can play in the treatment of ailments such as cancer, heart diseases, and respiratory diseases (Raghavan, 2017, July 24). The complete autonomy given to private hospitals in this regard will jeopardise, and has already been jeopardising, the existent public healthcare structure in the country. According to NSSO 2017–18, around 75% of all the treated ailments happened in private hospitals in urban areas, compared to 60% in rural areas (Nagpal & Dixit, 2020, November 20). The dip in rural areas might be due to the fact that private and corporate healthcare has not yet significantly penetrated these regions.

Urban health has historically been a topic that has not received much attention in India, at least in the realms of government analysis, funding, and reportage. Government emphasis has been much more on rural health than urban health, which has created a situation where only 5,190 operational Urban Primary Health Centres (UPHCs) are functional against a total target of 9,072 (Badgaiyan & Kumar, 2021, April 15) as of March 2019. In rural areas, there are a total of 24,855 PHCs (Mishra, 2021, April 29). And, in 2019–20, the Indian government spent around Rs 30,000 crore on rural healthcare, while only Rs 850 crore on urban areas (Badgaiyan & Kumar, 2021, April 15). According to Mishra (2021, April 15), one PHC is needed for every 30,000 people in general areas, and one for every 20,000 in difficult terrains. PHCs are critical components of the healthcare infrastructure of the nation, providing both preventive and curative treatment for 'everyday' diseases in country, especially in the rural areas.

The issue is not about the government spending on rural healthcare, but rather about it spending abysmally low on urban healthcare infrastructure. The lower expenditure on urban healthcare becomes extremely crucial in India because the differences, both in terms of quality of healthcare and the accessibility, between the public and private sector is on the ascent. People in cities – mostly the urban poor and the middle class – have to rely on private healthcare services instead of accessing the services provided by the municipal corporations and local representative bodies because of multiple issues – that range from factors pertaining to accessibility (Nagpal & Dixit, 2020, November 20), the quality of healthcare (Scroll, 2020, March 26), and their use for political gains (Express Healthcare, 2021, March 10).[3] The failure of municipal bodies or locally administered services to engage effectively with the crisis proves that utopian localism is not a viable solution, nor does blatant centralisation, either of capital or state bureaucracy.

Capital and Local Governance

Governing at a local level is a complex business in India. Local governance in India often finds itself at odds having to decide between political affiliations and social ones (Kundu, 2009). Local governance in India becomes extremely complicated in nature because India inherited a major part of its bureaucratic administration from the British. India inherited the bureaucratic model of administration that was characteristic of the colonial period, and even if the benefits of democratic administration were well-known, they did not emerge from the colonial state (Rai, 1965). Jawaharlal Nehru devised robust plans for implementing his version of socialism in India, which often meant the employment of centralised planning. Nikhil Menon (2022) in his recent book on the history of the now defunct Planning Commission writes that the body was formed as an initiative to invoke hope and spirit among the people of India. The Planning Commission in India focused on centralised economic planning, which was reflected in the ways in which the country advanced massive Five-Year Plans from 1947 until 2014, when the Planning Commission was scrapped and NITI Aayog was established. However, in doing so, Nehru implemented a centralised planning commission which very soon turned into a bureaucratic apparatus, and 'India's federal democracy . . . became more centralised than British India's unitary bureaucracy ever was' (Mukarji, 2012, p. 60).

This kind of paradoxical result of a historical process is a proof of the constant valorisation process of capital underway under neoliberal capitalism, which produces and keeps on reinforcing the exclusionary measures that capitalism puts into place both materialistically and psychologically. These exclusionary measures create diverse social realities, such that there is a distinct difference between how different people have experienced the pandemic with respect to their own social realities. Bhangay (2022) narrates how it was government-sponsored surveillance that enabled him to detect that he had been infected with COVID-19. He also narrates how the entire community had helped him to overcome the crisis he had faced during COVID-19 – both at the level of his own individual self and at the level of community. However, the kind of the pandemic that the Unnamed Migrant Worker (2022) from Bihar and Mohammed Shameem (2022) had experienced was grossly different than him. Migrant workers faced the worst aspects of the pandemic. They have been stigmatised beyond limits in urban India and have been forced to question their very existence in the society that neoliberal capitalism has created over the past few decades. An Unnamed Migrant Worker narrates, 'In our family, we were more concerned about making ends meet. That is the reality of daily wage earners. We didn't pay much thought on this new disease, and life went on as usual' (2022, p. 61).

Corporatisation of the world under neoliberal capitalism is one of the primary drivers of this form of exclusion that the workers have to face. The migrant workers in most urban spaces in India are scrapped off of their right to the city, which in concrete terms, 'means the right to live out the city as one's own, to live for the city, to be happy there' (Merrifield, 2017: 'Fifty Years On: The Right to the City'). It is the right to the city itself that can provide the inhabitants with the ontological security that they crave for, which can generate a sense of 'home' and 'belongingness'. The process of the formation of the community, integral to the generation of notions of 'home' and belongingness, which today goes through the institutional space of the university, can only be truly realised if the social totality retrenches itself from the dehumanising impacts of neoliberal capitalism which homogenises and routinises life. In other words, the autonomous model of community formation, the search for shared solutions to collective problems (Beck & Beck-Gernsheim, 2001; Bauman, 2001), and the realisation of collective outcomes of urban social processes (Suttles, 1973) will have to be reinstated. The obstacle to these realisations is the rendering invisible of the individual within the society as a subjective agent – whose autonomous agency needs to be re-established by processes of de-alienation. The urban way of life, as Monti (2000, p. 21) says is 'not something physical like a tall building or a bridge. Nor is it as familiar to us like our family, neighbourhood, or job. It is more like a set of public habits or customs'. It is the responsibility of the people residing in urban spaces and cities to interact with the established civic culture composed of urban rules, rites and norms, alter them if required, and ensure their intergenerational transmission (Monti, 2000, p. 22).

However, the rise of newer forms of capital have put a halt to these processes. Venture capital and private equity-funded start-ups have been emerging in almost every imaginable sector, creating major issues with local bodies already engaged in providing these services. As Chowkwanyun argues, 'All these new developments and new players [especially in the health sector – Big Banks, Big Tech, Big Medicine, and whatever else – make local struggles over medicine seem bygone, modest, quaint' (p. 228). These newer forms of capital have been emerging out of the capitalist developmental process. Under neoliberalism, venture capitalists have created these newer forms of capital, such as asset capital, which have come to dominate the society as has been validated by Mustafa (2020). The importance of assets such as housing and land, and the ability of venture capitalists[4] to turn that need into a successful business model with the help of *courageous* entrepreneurs has been noted in the autobiographical account by Chandra (2019).

With the neoliberal culture actively glorifying risk, the contemporary society has progressed from a stage of solid modernity that is from a society of producers towards being a society of consumers with a liquid modernity (Bauman, 2000). He believes that consumption is a concept, which is inherently related to the ideas of desire and possession. Bauman (2003, p. 9) writes that desire is the very root of consumption. It is the desire to completely consume a commodity or a metaphysical entity, such as a relationship. Bauman's major contribution to this debate remains his theorisation of 'Liquid Modernity', whereby the society is conceptualised as a society of consumers – a society that favours a certain non-orderliness in the society and its institutions, where no event is more likely to happen than another (Bauman, 2000). Such a society places consumption at the centre of its existence establishing, as Dunn (2008) says, a relationship between economy and culture such that:

> The essence of consumerism is the principle that consumption is an end-in-itself, its own justification. Deeply rooted in the profit motive, consumerism is now a widely shared ideology and worldview capable of creating strong attachments to consumption as a way of life. It is based on a belief in the enduring power of material possessions and commercial distractions to bring happiness and personal self-fulfilment.
> (Dunn, 2008, p. 8)

Consumer society is a society where consumer culture reigns supreme within the social structure. Consumerism is a result of the combined effects of commodity fetishism and capitalist alienation. A consumer society needs innumerable objects as a precondition to its formations – objects which can be destroyed and replenished at the will of capital. This proliferation of objects for consumption is propagated as a marker of democracy and growth (Baudrillard, 1970/1998, p. 51). Because growth today is often marked by the rise of consumerism, there is a constant influx of venture capital into the society, creating new goods in a highly privatised and exploitative mode of production.

This has been particularly bolstered by theories which have focused on venture capital being a key driver of economic growth for certain national economies. Venture capital, over the course of years, has developed a strong presence in the realm of innovative technology sector and the development of export markets (Klonowski, 2010). The continuous influx of venture capital into the Indian economy has resulted in a situation where middle-class youngsters have been given the opportunity to become successful entrepreneurs by taking risks. Rahul Chandra (2019), one of the early venture capitalists from India, argues that venture capitalists and the start-up ecosystem began to be built up in India since 1997 with the establishment of Silicon-Valley backed Draper International and Walden International setting up offices in India. These bodies were developed much later than the ULBs in India. However, the start-up ecosystem in India shares an intrinsic connection with the ULBs, one that has seldom been explored in academic literature. Start-ups in India often engage with the services that municipalities and other ULBs had been traditionally engaging with, such as the delivery of essential items, primary healthcare, and the like. Venture capital, because of its often localised character, plays a strong role in this regard.

Venture capital, though global, still retains a very strong local connection, which often makes it easy for local capitalists to seek venture capital to make inroads into the already existing local markets as well as to, at times, create newer markets for their products (Klonowski, 2022). It is, as Dijk et al. (2014) have written, 'becoming increasingly important as equity capital for start-up ventures; venture capital investments lead directly to the creation of new businesses and contribute to economic growth, employment, and innovation' (p. 1). Venture capitalism has grown in spite of classical and influential capitalist economists arguing against the risks associated with the continuous increase of assets in the society Rajan (2011). The prospects that venture capitalism provides for capitalist economic development have transformed it into an effective tool at the hands of capital to undermine local public sector-based planning by directly interfering with the process of fund raising by private firms, as Gompers and Lerner (2001) have emphasised. With the increasing amount of contractualisation, the incessant rise of start-ups has indeed become a force that is now being found to be directly competing with municipal services for space within the various urban communities. This has also been impacted by ideas coming from neoliberal scholars who have argued that contractualisation can indeed be beneficial both to the employee and the employer because it not only cheapens the price of the service but also provides more opportunity of personal growth for the worker (Mohan, 2015). In reality, privatisation and contractualisation of local municipal services is actually related to the growing fiscal conservatism that has gripped many local bodies across the world (Ascher, 1987).

With the rampant outsourcing of certain essential services such as sanitation and public distribution of essential goods, the administrative duties that an officer or a representative must perform have become extremely complicated in conditions created by neoliberal capitalism. Since the ancient times, India has had a system of administrative duties being performed by officers in cities as Aijaz (2007) highlights. In India, there are different kinds of ULBs that function at different levels, such as municipal corporations, municipal councils, and nagar panchayats, all catering to different quantitative samples.[5] Municipalities play an important role in the process of decentralisation and in bringing in more effective forms of local democracy (Burns et al., 1994). The primary debates about local democracy and its importance in the political system were taken up by Joseph Chamberlain, one of the major proponents of the *civic gospel* in Europe, who believed that the focus on local issues such as the democratic provisioning of gas, water, and housing, and their correct resolution is the fundamental element of all kinds of egalitarian politics (Gehrke, 2016). The focus on the local administrative unit and its functioning was one of the basic aspects of India's pandemic response.

The ULBs in India – the ones entrusted with local administration – had to perform some of the most important duties during the pandemic. However, in spite of that, their financial autonomy remains highly constrained. This constrained nature of the ULBs' financial fabric often results in them not being able to perform the duties that they are supposed to perform to the best of their capabilities. In the context of India, ULBs are not only important because they are the lowest, often called the third, tier of the government, but also because they are a part of the community they represent, much like the panchayats in rural India. Municipalities are one of the most important parts of the entire urban system of urban governance in the country. They are essential elements of the conceptualisation of the towns as how people like Thomas Attwood and Joseph Chamberlain of 'town councils as "real and legal political unions . . . which would give the people a better means of making their power felt' (Fraser, 1987, p. 34). The possibilities of local governance have even caused neoliberal thinkers, such as Gurcharan Das (2002/2012), to praise the promotion of local governance by states actively embracing neoliberalism.

Despite the grim reality of the pandemic, the demand for further state control of essential resources is increasing, and the public perception of the benefits of private ownership of life saving materials such as medicine and health instruments is plummeting, though not at an alarming rate. In this context, it is an interesting exercise to analyse the contemporary significance, if any, of a reformist strand of left-wing politics – municipal socialism. The term has been used to refer to all forms of local-level socialist planning initiatives, including along with 'municipal socialism', aspects of 'city socialism' (Rustin, 1986), progressive municipal enterprises (Cohn, 1910; Palmer, 1986), and so on. Municipal socialism emerged as a strand of the broad array of radical alternatives to civic capitalism, emphasising the advantages of municipal ownership and urban councils' borrowing powers (Gehrke, 2016, p. 26). It is a multifaceted praxis based socio-political theory constituting 'a set of roughly analogous historical movements that fought the private delivery of essential services and used local governments to advance "socialist" agendas', which encouraged increased sector employment, collective universal provisioning of utilities (Leopold & McDonald, 2012, pp. 1837–38, 1843–44), economic renewal, employment, socially necessary production (Rustin, 1986, pp. 75, 79), and so on.

Urban Local Bodies and the Pandemic

In a recent report, the NITI Aayog (2021) has stated that amidst the growing urbanisation in India, there is an increasing importance of the local administration. This manifests itself in the way different services and commodities are provided to the urban populace of the country, including services deemed essential for sustenance such as healthcare, community care, and sanitation. During the COVID-19 crisis, the municipalities were entrusted with the responsibility of effective distribution of vaccines in the urban areas (Ministry of Health and Family Welfare, 2020). The role given to the municipalities stems from the critical role that they play within the overall structure of healthcare provisioning in developing economies (Garcia-Subirats et al., 2014). The provisioning of public health measures is one of the most critical functions that ULBs perform in contemporary societies. If equipped properly with the adequate kind of financial resources, municipalities and local bodies can provide a much higher level of public health provisions than most private bodies (Barker, 1946; Ascher, 1987).

By doing so, ULBs not only enrich the communities but also create the conditions under which individuals belonging to these communities develop their own identities during a crisis such as COVID-19. Local bodies have an important role in situations such as COVID-19 because of their role as efficient bridges between the state and the communities, and between the communities and the individuals therein. This relationship can be further used to advocate for broader agreements between scientific advancements and policymaking – both of which are critical during a health emergency such as COVID-19. One of the major issues during a pandemic is to ensure that the '"ideal" solution can actually be delivered on the ground' (Woods, 2019, p. 27) – a task that is usually entrusted to the ULBs in urban India.

When ULBs respond efficiently to situations caused by disasters and emergencies, they often result in important improvements in the lives of common people, such as price control during a health emergency (Davies, 2021), which is often essential in these times of disaster capitalism being rendered mainstream in the society. Localised lockdowns constitute an important aspect of the non-pharmaceutical response to COVID-19. Policymakers have used localised lockdowns affecting mobility at a local level to control the pandemics rise in the society, and 'Even now that countries have started vaccinating their populations, large-scale nonpharmaceutical interventions continue to be important, particularly [in the LMICs], to avoid large increases in the number of cases' (Li et al., 2022, p. 812). However, under contemporary capitalism, it is extremely difficult for ULBs to engage in such activities, as most of the municipal bodies in India are in deep financial distress without much financial autonomy, with major streams of revenue such as land taxes, and other forms of property taxes, and the like decreasing or remaining stagnant for a long time (Raj, 2020, July 2). This becomes clear in the case of the Greater Hyderabad Municipal Corporation, which, in 2021, was not financially affluent enough to either provide salaries and pensions, or to carry the burden of the lockdowns (Ahmed, 2021, February 12).

Localised lockdowns have been widely used in the state of Telangana in scenarios where a returnee to a particular community or area has been found to be positive for the virus (Harsha, 2021, December 23), or when a resident is found positive for the virus (Rao, 2021, December 31). Both the reports cited in the last statement bring forward that when local bodies impose lockdowns, then the role of the local officers – both administrative and healthwise – increase manifold. Localised lockdowns are usually imposed in areas to suppress an outbreak, but they have not been used much before the

COVID-19 pandemic, except while maintaining law and order situations in certain very specific contexts (Li et al., 2022). They also note that localised lockdowns, drawing from their research conducted in Chile, are more effective in countering the spread of the virus than universal ones. This is because local lockdowns are often more efficient in controlling the mobility within a *local* neighbourhood, which in third world or developing economies is often densely populated. Local bodies such as municipalities play a pivotal role in this regard. It must be remembered that localised lockdowns do, in fact, slow down the recovery of the service sector (Magazine & Sasi, 2021, April 1).

Localised lockdowns perform better than global ones in terms of their ability to shut down the movement of people in specific regions, as they are better suited to respond to triggering events such as, when the administration has to close or reopen the area, when the number of positive cases reaches 1,000 for every 100,000 population (Karatayev et al., 2020). At the same time, local lockdowns also create conditions of crisis for certain people. It is essential to keep in mind that even within a community, there will be people who do not fit into the traditional conceptions of municipal well-being, often formed by ULBs based on the analysis of the urban middle class. Considering that vaccination rates will be unlikely to reach the desired levels in countries such as India, well calibrated localised lockdowns could indeed be a major move by the government in controlling the pandemic (The Hindu, 2021, May 26). Local lockdowns, however, have been strongly criticised by corporates who have outlined that all forms of lockdowns harm processes of economic recovery (Suneja, 2022, January 7). Bodies such as the Confederation of Indian Industry (CII), the Multiplex Association of India (MAI) and the Shopping Centres Association of India (SCAI) have vehemently protested against the localised lockdowns because they harm their revenue streams.[6] The SCAI stated, 'On an average during pre-Covid days, the industry was clocking Rs 15,000 crore [USD 1.5 Billion] per month and "had reached the same during mid of March 2021, but, with the local restrictions, almost 50 per cent revenue got slashed"' (Business Standard, 2021, April 18, Para 4).

Local lockdowns can often affect those that it is supposed to protect, but the causality of such suffering is different. Marginalised people suffer during local lockdowns because they not only suffer from the lack of welfare measures but also from the social stigma that often becomes a part of their selfhood. According to the Centre for Monitoring Indian Economy (CMIE), there had been a loss of around 122 million rural and urban jobs in April 2020 (The Wire, 2022, June 20). As the Stranded Workers' Action Network (SWAN) Report states:

> [The] localised restrictions combined with the lack of government response, have dealt a body blow to the majority of the country's workforce (90% of the informal sector), whose incomes have once again plummeted and whose livelihoods have come under increasing threat.
> (SWAN, 2021, p. 6)

When migrants and other such individuals are within the limits of municipalities, it often becomes the duty of the municipalities to provide them with adequate care and provisions. During COVID-19, the municipalities have failed to do so (Kapri, 2021; Dutt, 2022; Mukul, 2022). However, municipalities in India are often not equipped financially and structurally to perform these tasks (Bisen, 2019). At the same time, urban governance in India depends, to a large extent, on the ways in which the ULBs such as municipalities function. Urban Governance in India, however, functions in a very restricted sense because they are placed in a kind of political framework that is often characterised by a high anti-urban bias (Ahluwalia, 2019). This anti-urban bias means that the development of cities and the improvement of urban health have only remained a marginal issue in the Indian political milieu. This, in turn, is causing a major dip in the way human capital is being organised in India. And, as Pande (2020) argues, one of the most important problems that India faces in contemporary times is the problem of human capital:

> India has underinvested in its cities, its institutions and, most of all, its people. Unlike many of India's challenges, the failure to invest in human capital is not a product of the liberal-Hindutva ideological divide. It is the function of petty-political division, legacies of big government, lack of foresight, and the type of simple mismanagement that is common to developing countries.
>
> (Pande, 2020, p. 35)

The urban process in India has often relied heavily on the ULBs. ULBs in India perform six major functions: (i) Public Health and Sanitation: engaging mainly with the supply of water, vaccinations, waste disposal, sewerage, and so on; (ii) Medical Relief: works which deal with the establishment and maintenance of healthcare institutions and personnel; (iii) Public Works: engaging mainly with infrastructural development, regulatory powers, and so on; (iv) Education; (v) Development: engaging with the construction, development, and maintenance of markets, and so on; and (vi) Administrative Duties: which deal with annual reports, maintenance of municipal property, traffic regulation, and other administrative issues (Aijaz, 2007). In 1992, the 74th Constitutional Amendment to the 12th Schedule of the Indian Constitution redefined the power of the ULBs, giving them more powers with regard to public health, sanitation, solid waste management, and conservancy – factors that directly affect public health within a community or locality. The amendment also provided certain powers to the municipalities regarding economic and social planning, along with poverty alleviation, slum improvement, ecological regulation, and the like.

Despite the amendment, however, bottlenecks remain in the structural infrastructure of urban governance in India because municipalities are almost always under the patronage – both financially and socially – of higher bodies

(Ahluwalia, 2019). The amendment lacked precise judgements regarding the distribution of power between the municipalities and state governments resulting in municipalities frequently turning to state governments and their health departments for financial and institutional support. The urban population in India, which was only 18% in 1960, has grown up to 34% as of 2019. However, the ULBs have not been investing proportional amount of money into the urban municipal owned and managed healthcare system, which is starved of funds (Mishra et al., 2021). The same report from Newsclick says,

> Ministry of Health and Family Welfare data shows that there are serious shortfalls in the availability of Urban Primary Healthcare Centres (UPHCs) that come under ULBs, based on the government's own norms, with the national average at almost 40% (2020). The shortfalls ranged from 7% in Rajasthan to 100% in Lakshadweep.
> (Nagpal & Dixit, 2020, November 20, Para 5)

Thus, it is highly unsurprising that any responsibility which comes under the municipalities in India suffers from a problem of financial overburdening. And one of the major responsibilities of the municipalities is *Primary Healthcare* – the first line of defence against pandemics and epidemics. According to the *World Health Organisation* (April 1, 2021), Primary Health Care (PHC) is one of the most important aspects of the healthcare infrastructure in any country. The definition of PHC according to the WHO is:

> PHC is a whole-of-society approach to health that aims at ensuring the highest possible level of health and well-being and their equitable distribution by focusing on people's needs and as early as possible along the continuum from health promotion and disease prevention to treatment, rehabilitation, and palliative care, and as close as feasible to people's everyday environment.
> (WHO, 2021, April 1, Para 2)

In India, PHCs focus on four aspects: equitable distribution, participation of the community, cooperation of different sectors, and the use of appropriate technologies relevant to the healthcare requirements of the particular area. PHCs are critical to urban spaces because the private hospitals that populate the urban areas do not ideally engage with simple diseases such as malaria and fever but rather want to engage with more complicated diagnostic services and diseases (Jain, 2017, August 2). Under contemporary capitalism, the basic purpose of PHC, which according to the WHO is based on social justice, solidarity, and participation (WHO, 2021, April 1), becomes endangered. Patel and Pant argue:

> Cities arguably have a wider range of health and social infrastructure than rural areas. However, for countries in the global south, access to

these services for the urban poor may be restricted by their inability to pay . . ., inconvenient locations or times of operation, or poor quality of healthcare services. All of these can result in low utilisation of even the most basic preventive and curative health service. . . . With rapid urbanisation, the urban poor population is also increasing rapidly.
(Patel & Pant, 2020, p. 1)

The shift from publicly owned healthcare to a system dominated by private bodies has been particularly brutal to the poor, especially the urban poor whose numbers have been steeply rising (Mishra et al., 2021). During the pandemic, private bodies had all the opportunity to charge exorbitant amounts from the people. The kind of shock that the pandemic had created allowed these bodies to make some drastic changes in the way the society organises itself, such as the proliferation of digital platforms, online deliveries, and digital healthcare mechanisms. Municipal socialism, as a tendency, is drawn from and within the argumentative position put forward by the Fabian socialists, who argued that organic changes in the society have to be democratic, gradual, acceptable, constitutional, and peaceful (Webb, 1889/1948). The absence of municipal socialism as an argumentative position under these circumstances is indeed surprising, considering the opposition to neoliberal modes of capitalist accumulation (Leopold & McDonald, 2012, p. 1837) expressed by left-wing and CSOs in contemporary India. The arguments in favour of municipal socialism come at a time when the world has been led to a deathly crisis by the privatisation of services deemed essential for survival within a pandemic ravaged world.

Local governance has come to be one of the central concerns of India's pandemic response. At the same time, local governance has always been a contentious issue for socialist politics. Left-wing policies have mostly advocated for greater decentralisation of the process of governance in India, with further ability to control provisioning and distribution being vested upon local bodies. As Taylor-Gooby argues, 'Most left strategies include higher public spending and more equal social provisions, but public opinion rejects both tax rises and greater generosity to the poor of working age' (Taylor-Gooby, 2015, p. 126). The right-wing on the other hand, focuses more on 'private enterprise-led recovery, work ethic values and policies that exclude less deserving groups' (Taylor-Gooby, 2015, p. 126). The strategies that the left has adopted in most countries have been in accordance with these principles. The Socialist Left's advocacy for more public ownership of essential services has been one of the mainstays of left-wing economic arguments. Peter Taylor-Gooby's arguments point towards a trilemma, that the left faces when designing effective public policies, constructed by the need to respond to the economic crisis competitively at par with other forces, address popular public opinion questions, and the development of policies that are both generous and inclusive.

Reforms surrounding the institutionalisation of the local bodies capable of effecting change has always been a major focus of the parliamentary left.

It would be an undialectical method of analysis to directly categorise all parties who argue for the use of parliaments are abject revisionists in nature. Historically, important figures of the revolutionary left, such as Vladimir Lenin and James Connolly, have argued in favour of using the parliament without falling into any form of parliamentary cretinism. However, both Lenin and Connolly were resolute on the point that, even when using the parliament, the organisational form must be led by the workers and the anti-capitalist classes. However, this is not the case with political formations such as the Indian National Congress (INC) in India, the African National Congress in South Africa, or the Labour Party in Britain, which despite emphasising the role of elections and parliaments from a broadly left-wing position, remain unable to advocate effective policies for a total transformation of the capitalist system (Miliband, 1964).[7] Under institutions that have desired to manage rather than obliterate capitalism, there has been a gradual erosion of the socialist vision. This has been replaced by a pragmatic managerial attitude that has aided in the analysis of political issues through a managerial perspective (Panitch & Leys, 1997).

With the rise of finance capital, there has been an erosion of the powers that local institutions hold over the public provisioning of essential services. Finance capital has actively aided the construction of the *super elite* and *the new elites* in the society, who naturally, are putting an immense pressure on their respective communities for disproportionate access to services and products. Gerry Stoker argues:

> The higher status groups make disproportionate use of local services relative to their need. Contrary to the widespread belief that public expenditure benefits primarily the less well-off there is considerable evidence that many welfare services are distributed in a manner which favour higher social groups.
>
> (Stoker, 1991, p. 18)[8]

The rich and urban middle class in India had almost continuous access to groceries, medicines, and vaccines, facilitated by the utilisation of mobile applications and the internet. However, the marginalised populace of the country has been fighting an extremely unequal duel, not only against the pandemic but also against the onslaught of capitalist expropriation and accumulation. Capitalism has exhibited that it is extremely resilient in its struggle against other forms of social systems, in such a way that, as Bruno (2020) elaborates upon, it can be equated with the worst version of the utopia that human evolution could envisage for people entrapped at the bottom of the socio-economic hierarchy in a fashion that could make the fears of the *end of history* realistically feasible. Fears such as climate change and the long-lasting impacts that the COVID-19 pandemic might have on human society – not only with regards to health but also socially, economically, and culturally – have been major causes of anxiety, anger, and depression among people, including the elderly, young people, and women (Dixit & Chauhan, 2020; Nagpal & Dixit, 2020; Uppal & Sidhu, 2020).

Nagpal and Dixit's (2020) reports highlight that engagement with the community at a local level can be immensely helpful in the context of the lockdown imposed due to COVID-19. Therefore, it can be said that both the right and the left agree upon the idea that the community is at the base of the response towards the pandemic. At the core of the pandemic response strategy is the community and local governance. In countries such as New Zealand, who though with certain limitations, have done exceptionally well in terms of their responses to the pandemic have actively used the community to make individual citizens more receptive to the state's response towards the pandemic. Of course, New Zealand's pandemic response has its fair share of criticism, but it cannot be denied that in terms of the lives saved with reference to the ones who were (and are) in New Zealand during the pandemic, it fared much better than India and even the United States. Under capitalism, and especially under neoliberal Hindutva-aided capitalism, there is a constant depletion of this sense of community.

The Community at Work, but without *the Community*

Community formation processes are intimately related to trust and recognition. It often rests on the belief that familial and communitarian ties are manifestations of the networks of support and care that are essential to the formation of a society (Alexander et al., 2007, p. 793). Alleyne (2002) argued that the classical idea of a 'community' usually revolved around material factors like home and land. However, such classical ideas surrounding the community are difficult to be found within the social reality produced by advanced neoliberal capitalism. Lefebvre (2016, p. 39), while talking about communal societies, brought forward the element of interdependence and networks of presence and complementation in these societies. However, under contemporary capitalism, where transnational migration has become a norm (Castells, 2000), the premodern ideas of community have given way to the establishment of looser and more individualised networks of association directing the shift from *Gemeinschaft* to *Gesellschaft* (Tönnies, 1955/1989). This process takes place within the everyday lives of individuals, which is the site of humanisation (Lefebvre, 1991, p. 163). This process of humanisation is related to or rather takes place within a complex circuit of needs and desires, which supersedes the way in which Tönnies theorised the creation of a community based on a certain moral basis reflecting the family ties, land ownership, social norms, and so on (Giuffre, 2013, p. 20).

One of the basic characteristics of a community is the idea of trust among the members of the community. Trust is an important aspect of the overall paradigm of social interactions, where it affects social cooperation, individual confidence in the social mechanisms, and the way in which individuals perceive of others – both within and outside the immediate framework of the community (Kasperson et al., 2005). Trust also has a critical effect on the perception of risk that vulnerable communities possess. Social trust can be broadly argued to be revolving around four basic characteristics: commitment, competence, caring, and predictability (Kasperson et al., 2005). COVID-19 had endangered almost all of this. The community is also important because it will play an extremely critical role in the post-pandemic health management. Most of the adjustments that the human society would have to make in the post-covid scenario from a perspective of individual healthcare would be such as stress management fatigue and exercise aversion (Shivdasani, 2021).

Communities are intimately connected with ideas of safety and security. They are supposed to, ideally, provide the members with care and comfort pertaining to both the physical and psychological well-being of the members, which has been of paramount importance since the day COVID-19 became a permanent fixture in the world. Concurrent with the pandemic, there has also been a considerable increase in the costs of medicines, which is now set to adversely impact the poor and marginalised populace. It can be said beyond reasonable doubt that the poor will definitely get adversely impacted (Oriel & Ghosh, 2022, May 31). A strong and resolute community might not be able to reduce the price of the commodities, but it can result in better mitigation of the effects of such price rises by engaging with cooperatives and more participatory planning models. The community in India is extremely powerful, which often even engulfs the power of the state-form. There are numerous aspects such as caste, gender, and creed, that, even though the state has criminalised them, remain alive in these communities. However, it is not theoretically correct to argue that these have remained popular because the initial governments did not engage much with private provisioning of commodities. Public provisioning, even if it comes from a central level, does indeed have some benefits, because it tends to construct public accountability something that contemporary capitalism, as Nichols (2022) claims, does not encourage. As such, it has become one of the most pertinent causes of the spread of COVID-19 globally. However, public accountability does not emerge from a vacuum, but rather from the construction of the social capital that people possess, because the concept of accountability in a situation where people do not possess social capital to articulate and voice their concerns surrounding accountability remains a mere abstraction. Gurcharan Das (2002/2012) argues:

> [Nehruvian] Socialism tended to destroy social capital because it made us depend on the government for everything (a dependence that also suited our politicians). People forgot that they could rely on themselves. And the best work of some of the NGOs has been to remind people on the virtues of self-reliance.
>
> (Das, 2002/2012, p. 17)

Das, in this context, conflates Nehru's version of a welfare-state based socialism that functioned through the aegis of statist administration with actual revolutionary socialism that, unlike vulgar materialist socialism, works for the complete dissolution of authoritarian and disproportionately bodies such as the state. The question here is not whether socialism tends to destroy communities, but rather how Nehruvian socialism was implemented at the grassroots. There was a strong element of bureaucracy involved in how the entire process of social ownership was brought forward in postcolonial India, which transformed India into a state that gave more importance to the bureaucrats rather than the people whom the bureaucrats were supposed to serve. The major reason for such a disjunction can be said to have been the absence of the emphasis on the capacity of the state and then subsequently of the market to dominate the state. This can only be analysed if one sees the state in relation to the conditions of the marginalised people, especially the working class. Marx (1875) argued that to use the state as an organisational form does not address any of the questions that the marginalised population seeks to answer. The point here is to convert the state from an entity that is superimposed on the existing relations of production to one that is subordinate to the new ones that emerge out of a radical social change, such as the workers' revolution that Marx had been advocating for. He critiqued the fetish of the state form as a Lassallean distortion of the workers' movement (Marx, 1875; Hudis, 2020).

The major difference that Marx shared with the utopian socialists like Ferdinand Lassalle, or Robert Owen, was that he could accept the immense possibilities of actual movements of the workers and other marginalised communities that went beyond the moral doctrine (Dunayevskaya, 1956). The real problem lay with the conceptualisation of the relationship between the leaders and the led, as Dunayevskaya (1956) has pointed out in her critique of Lassalle, which has been mostly characterised by organisations favouring the insights provided by the leaders – often the intellectuals or professional politicians. Marx, on the other hand, believed that intellectuals and the activists needed to work hand in hand with each other within a relationship where there was no domination of one over the other because 'Revolutions require a passive element, a material element. . . . It is not enough for thought to strive for realisation, reality must also strive towards thought' (Marx, 1843, p. 183). This is where Nehruvian socialism found itself lacking. It employed a strong think tank, as Menon (2022) rightly puts forward, but did not focus much on altering the social reality that constituted both the administers and the administrated.

Marx here focuses on one of the key insights that one can garner from Hegelian dialectics namely 'that the object generates its own categories of knowledge. The Task of the theoretician is not to *impose* upon the object of investigation an arbitrary plan or schema, but rather capture and explicate its *self-movement*' (Hudis, 2020, p. 109). In India, this self-movement often does not emerge from individuals, but rather comes from communities within which the individual subjectivity gets subjugated. The community is an important aspect of the Indian society. Community in India is directly related to crucial urban aspects of housing, sanitation, and healthcare. And, in the Indian context, housing, sanitation, and healthcare are interrelated and as such are connected by threads of accessibility and discrimination.[9] The people living in such conditions, obviously, are more at risk of contracting the virus. The frontline workers working in these conditions are also more vulnerable than others. Sagar Kumbhare (2020) reported about a particular case where a sanitation worker assigned to Dharavi contracted the virus and then passed it on to his wife who eventually succumbed to the disease on the 12th of April 2020. Such instances again bring to the fore issues such as the constant denial of PPE kits to the poor sanitation workers, which makes them more vulnerable to the virus. The community can become an extremely crucial factor in these situations.

Under contemporary capitalism, venture capitalists have infiltrated this space. Chandra (2019) narrates in his book about how the shortage of affordable housing had prompted him to invest in finance companies engaged in housing loans. The crucial task for any form of municipal socialist tendency in India foundationally rests upon taking back the ground that has been ceded to venture and asset capital. There have been diverse approaches towards solving issues such as housing shortage in India. Vidya Mahambare (2015) argues that even when housing prices are on the rise, the advocacy should not focus on fully government-sponsored housing, but rather the emphasis should be on bringing down the real estate pricing policy to its fundamental values, which would off-set what she refers to as suboptimal measures, such as taxation of the super-rich, inheritance taxation, and the like. In states such as India, where structural modes of oppression and inequality are integrated directly into the society, municipal provisioning of public housing can prove to be more effective in achieving housing equality, which according to Ahmad (2012) is an urgent requirement for effecting changes in the living standards. This, in turn, will affect the standards of healthcare among the socially disadvantaged communities in India. Newton and Karran's (1985) analysis suggest that, with proper use of regulations and laws surrounding housing and other services, the municipality or the local body can indeed be a vehicle for massive socio-political change, with better quality of service being provided by the public sector with better level of protection for the citizens as consumers than what can be provided by the private sector. Barker (1946) had argued long back that local bodies managed publicly are the most effective bodies in putting up a resistance to the growing power of capital, especially in situations where healthcare becomes a priority.

During COVID-19, the community has found itself to be at the centre of attention. There are certain reports that have emphasised that the urban community has somehow managed to rejuvenate itself during the pandemic like Collins and Soulia (2021) in *The Front Steps Project*, where they focus on the prospects of pre-Covid isolated individuals coming together as a community during the lockdowns in the United States by increased participation in community ventures and collective sharing. At the same time, there are thinkers such as Kukla (2021) who have argued that 'COVID has shot down most third places [, places which are neither private nor public], or made those of us who are cautious afraid to use them' (p. 88). He argues that the kind of distancing mechanisms put in place by certain places may actually be hampering the very aesthetical sense of coming together as a community. This often depends on factors such as spontaneous interactions and unplanned gatherings, especially under conditions where the entire prospect of city-living itself has been put under question in terms of the lessened safety that it proposes during a health emergency. The state desired to use the communitarian nature of Indian society, especially with the lockdown, which has had tremendous psychological impacts on a great percentage of the population. The central government's usage of the community ranged from using community centres as promoters of their campaigns against the pandemic and for resource distribution.

Gandhi-Mody's (2022) pro-establishment narrative argues that 'Events' such as *Janta Curfew* or the lighting of *diyas*[10] in honour of the frontline workers, which were made part of the way India responded to the crisis caused by the pandemic, were actually events orchestrated to make the people aware of their responsibilities amidst the raging pandemic. The popular participation of these events reveals an important aspect of the Indian society as it exists today. With the use of hyper-nationalist propaganda, such events were portrayed to be tests of one's patriotism towards the nation. In addition to these measures, the way in which India responded to COVID-19 was reeked of bureaucracy and centralisation and depended immensely on the kind of fervour that had been generated by these activities. Priyam Gandhi-Mody's (2022) analysis of India's response to the pandemic is a testament to that mode of thinking, where the sensibilities of nationalism have triumphed over the rational logic provided by science – both natural and social. The continuous 'mounting' of positivity coming from the state, or the government, also constructs a kind of exploitation because it tends to make individuals unsusceptible to feelings of grief or mourning. This tends to render invisible the trauma that individuals and the society suffer through (Han, 2015, p. 28).

Irrational optimism has been an important aspect of the response that the far-right has exhibited towards managing the pandemic. The power of emotions and cultural nationalism, in the case of India's COVID-19 response, have transgressed scientific rationality. Historically, emotions, especially those associated with one's religious affiliations, have often played an indirect role in the spread of diseases. Because emotions play a major role in the way everyday life is structured, it is not unnatural that they have played a major role in the spread of contagious diseases. During the cholera pandemic of the early twentieth century, the pilgrimage sites that were often insanitary and dirty were one of the most widely spread sites of infections (Tumbe, 2020). This did not change much even during the COVID-19 pandemic.

One of the starkest examples in this regard is the 2021 *Kumbha Mela*. Some scholars consider the *Kumbha Mela* to be an example of India's tremendous human capital potential (Pande, 2020). However, the *Kumbha Mela*[11] has come under serious criticism during the pandemic. The Chief Minister of Uttarakhand, Mr. Tirath Singh Rawat, decided against cancelling the event despite numerous warnings. Instead, he decided to hold a short fair that would follow all the regular COVID-19 protocols mandated by the health ministry, including RT-PCR tests, regular sanitisation, and reduced times for the religious bathing ceremonies. However, as Gandhi-Mody narrates:

> [Despite the government's] best preparations, the waves of people arriving were too overwhelming for the government to ensure that COVID-19 protocol was followed. Within days, the city of Haridwar and neighbouring areas became COVID-19 hotspots with a surge of cases. Seven Hindu saints and 300 pilgrims tested COVID-19 positive within a week of the beginning of the festival.
> (Gandhi-Mody, 2022, pp. 188–189)

An effective municipality and its associated officers and workers become an important tool to resist such events and spread of harmful viruses and diseases. Caroline Keen's (2021) work on Sir Sidney Wadsworth, a British judge who served in the colonial Indian Civil Service (ICS), reveals the peculiar circumstances under which the civil administration system has developed in the country. Keen reveals that during the colonial rule, the Indian people had a peculiar allegiance to the colonial administrative officers: 'Time and time again Sidney was struck by "the readiness of the village people to accept an arbitrary decision from an impartial officer"' (Keen, 2021, p. 49). The book also narrates how the compilation of weekly epidemic reports and the local emphasis on sanitation and hygiene in a village called Gudur in Colonial India had helped in managing the smallpox and cholera epidemics in the village. The district officer in India is an important position and 'What [one] choose[s] to do on the chair is surprisingly substantial. In [some states], the District Officer is indeed the *mai-baap*.[12] He[/she] is accepted by all as the head of district administration and is the first port of call in times of crisis' (Mathew, 2020, p. 16). Urban governance today, however, does not only concern the district officer but also involves a multitude of different organisations, including developmental bodies, the public works department, and municipalities. Municipal socialism attempts to use all of these different bodies to advance the egalitarian vision. It was (and is) more of a practical advancement of the socialist idea than an ideological one. It was more than a mere electoral mode of advancement towards an envisioned socialist reality, but it hinged strongly on the reallocation of resources. Edgar J. Levey (1909) has defined municipal socialism as a method that lends voice to humanity's quest for collective living and to enable contemporary societies to perform the complicated functions that they are meant to perform. Levey argues:

> Viewed in its broadest aspect, it might mean merely the use which communities make of government in order to engage in cooperative effort.

But this would be almost equivalent to making it a synonym for government itself. What is commonly understood by the term municipal socialism is the use by municipalities of the powers of general taxation to obtain special advantages which do not ensure the benefit of those who chiefly defray the cost.

(Levey, 1909, p. 23)

Debates about whether local governance can play a major role in social transformation within Marxist and radical social theory run far and wide. Regardless of whether one is looking at an advanced industrial nation such as the United States of America or a developing nation such as India, the problem of the state, law, and its institutions has become a commonplace issue. Ernest Untermann describes the impact that a correct resolution of the municipal problems would have on the people in Urban spaces:

Municipal problems are now a part of the daily life of 47.1% of the American people. Of there, 33.1% live in cities with a population of more than 8,000 inhabitants, 4.2% in towards of more than 4,000 inhabitants, and 9.8% in towns of more than 1,000 inhabitants.

(Untermann, 1906/2002, p. 1)

Although, it is true that Untermann's work was written in the early twentieth century, the statistics still hold huge relevance today considering that more than 50% of the global population live in urban areas as of 2014 (Department of Economic and Social Affairs 2014), thus making them a part of some form of bodies concerned with urban governance. And the world today is increasingly becoming further urbanised, and by 2050, nearly 68% of the world's total population, which amounts to roughly 6.7 billion people, are expected to live in urban areas (Housing Research, 2021).

Municipalities can play an important role in the expansion of the network of amenities, such as piped gas and drinkable water, which are still hard to reach in Indian cities according to Singhal and Mathur (2021) and Aiyar (2020). The same goes for other essential services such as health and education. Without the help of the community, any municipality-based political establishment will find it extremely difficult to implement reforms that engage directly with the community. Municipal socialism is directly linked to the relationship that working-class politics shares with the communities (Towler, 1909). Local governance or the control over resources by municipalities is part of the long heritage of working class politics, which does not exclude even the Paris Commune. The extension of local self-governance is an issue that is intimately associated with the ways in which individuals function because local governance, mostly at the municipal level, is associated with the immediate community that the individuals are a part of. However, communities operating under capitalism are not free from the impact of capital's sustained logic. When more and more individuals from a certain community start getting upwardly mobile in large quantities, there also occurs a proportional growth of the community's own internally bred elite, which then carry the logic of capital with them back to the community.

Maya Bathija's (2014) work on the Sindhi business community shows that when certain individuals amass huge proportions of wealth, they inevitably end up as being the natural leaders of the community. These communities like the Sindhis and Baniyas in Europe and the United States, as Bathija (2014) and Inamdar (2014) note, gain tremendous economic and political capital, which makes them become the natural voice of the communities, thus further marginalising the poor in the community. One of the major demerits of municipal socialism is the way in which it decides to use the legal infrastructure in the society. Bernard Shaw (1930), however, was careful to argue that constitutional reforms are merely means and not the ends. However, Shaw's arguments in favour of municipal socialism often tend towards establishing municipal socialism as an end in itself. Bernard Shaw states:

> In the ability market, the municipalities have a decisive advantage in the superior attraction of public appointments for prudent and capable organisers and administrators. A municipality always get an official more cheaply than a company can. A municipality never becomes bankrupt, is never superseded by a new discovery, and never dismisses an official without giving his case prolonged consideration in committee, from which he has practically an appeal to the whole body.
>
> (Shaw, 1908, p. 10)

It is important at this point to state that Bernard Shaw was writing in a historical timeframe where neoliberalism was not even conceived. In most major democracies in the world today, municipalities do not have the ability to attract funds like the private corporations.

The community will be an extremely important aspect in the post-pandemic phase. The importance of the community is such that even neoliberal thinkers, such as Das (2002/2012), have been forced to praise the intense amount of communitarian bonds that characterise Indian society and the ways in which those bonds have helped the society in overcoming certain serious challenges. At the same time, Das (2002/2012) also praises the importance of the partnerships that the government and NGOs have developed to provide education and health using money from international sources such as the World Bank. However, during times of crisis, the problem is not only about the funding issues involved in such crucial sectors but also about the processes in which the service is rendered accessible to everyone. This gets reflected in the ways in which the pandemic could have been managed by the local bodies in an ideal situation. Various reports such as those brought forward by Bhalotia et al. (2020) and followed by Dhingra and Kondirolli (2021) on the urban workforce in India, point towards the complete collapse of the social system as one knows it. The private sector disdains the social ownership of the means of production, and as such creates conditions of extreme vulnerabilities for the marginalised populace.

Conclusion

Local bodies can play an important role in the resistance that societies show towards disasters. The role of district officer in India encompasses the role of disaster management as well, so that the district officer not only functions as an officer but also as a leading example for the community that one administers (Sinha, 2007). However, the kind of public and political accountability, or the lack thereof, that characterises Indian administrative or governance in the contemporary times does not allow local bodies and the people engaged in them to bring in effective policies. The constraining force of the market and the state, as a holistic power, acts upon these bodies, transforming them into mere agents of bourgeoisie law and order. The increase in the urban population of India has not been met with an adequate increase in urban health services (Sundaraman et al., 2020), which has severely affected the human capital that India possesses. To enrich the human capital, especially in a post-pandemic scenario, one needs to take into cognisance that there will be fundamental changes in the way the human capital itself is organised. However, in order to achieve that, one needs to move away from the idea that Das (2000) proposes, which sometimes seems to be in favour of completely doing away with the entirety of the public services. The vision should be based on intelligent scepticism, like the one proposed by Pande (2020), which takes into account both the benefits and the pitfalls of neoliberal economy policies. It recognises that though certain improvements have been made, the country still faces massive challenges in securing jobs for its large population, as well as overcoming the recent downturn in its economic growth.

In 1991, the Indian society faced a watershed moment with neoliberal policies becoming the primary instruments of economic growth. Intellectuals such as Das (2000) and Singh (2020) continue to laud the benefits of the neoliberal policies. Das (2002/2012) argued that the nineties were times when the individual Indian felt completely liberated. However, the nineties were also the times in which the public health infrastructure in India degraded greatly, creating the conditions under which COVID-19 became the catastrophe that has transformed itself into in the Indian context. In India, almost 60% of hospitalisation and 70% of the outpatient care are provided by the private sector (Sundaraman et al., 2020). The rise of private provisioning has severely impacted the community health centres (CHCs), which are pivotal elements of a responsible response to a disaster. When CHCs take certain decisions, they become examples for the entire community and the individuals therein. These decisions can make crucial differences to the way one manages one's role within the community (Thomas et al., 2022). However, it also raises concerns regarding the internal homogeneity and the existence of internal contradictions within a community. Municipal socialism accepts prima facie that a community is often homogeneous. It does not realise that it is often the community itself that becomes the cause for the continuation of anti-marginalised work profiles such as manual scavenging, since it is often the community and the individual within the community who give ascent to these modes of employment driven by a combination of heretical caste privileges and the inability of the state to provide adequate sanitary mechanisms (Wilson & Singh, 2016).

Despite its shortfalls, certain aspects of municipal socialism can be taken as tools to bring forward certain progressive reforms within the neoliberal state. Disasters like the present, especially in the context of the failure of the healthcare system in India, can be analysed as a failure of state's desire under neoliberal capitalism to externalise costs which might come into its way of accumulating profits (Matthewman, 2015, p. 98) in the healthcare sector. Municipal-based efforts often tread along the paths of getting into partnerships with private capitalists such as individual entrepreneurs or financial institutions, reproducing a hegemonic inequality within the society (Webb, 1891; Palmer, 1986, p. 21). In spite of the strides made by such arguments regarding greater power allocation to workers and progressive organisations and a gradual reduction of the influence of the market, strategies such as these can rarely operate in large scale economies with an active presence of large monopoly capitalists (Rustin, 1986, pp. 80–81, 83). Arguments of municipal socialism or city socialism are not always financially coherent and often do not focus on class struggle (Rustin, 1986, p. 79) or any partisan or non-partisan working-class consciousness (Robinson, 2015, pp. 615, 616). Along with its emphasis on the multiplication of bureaucratic professionals to handle public affairs (Cohn, 1910, p. 567), municipal progressiveness, often based on the idea of a certain municipal modernity (Robinson, 2015, p. 615), does not make a distinction between 'local authorities and local communities, or those who make decisions and those who must live them' (Randall, 1995, p. 43). This can also give rise to competition between different municipal centres, which can be detrimental during pandemics like the one brought forward by COVID-19 (Randall, 1995). When the support for the parliamentary left in a country with rich tradition of socialist and communist politics is dwindling, strands such as municipal socialism which emphasise 'city socialism' can prove helpful in bringing the support of the people back to the left (Rustin, 1986, p. 75). However, such support often comes at the cost of broader working-class solidarity across geographical boundaries.

Since April 2021, the insurgent rise of the COVID-19 pandemic has forced many state governments to openly invite tenders from foreign companies to supply vaccines,[13] while some have reduced their vaccination rates to as low as 500 per day per centre.[14] The Indian government's acts of exporting medical oxygen for profit during the pandemic[15] resulted in significant financial losses for the nation, with the average death rate exceeding of 3,000 per day during the months of April and May in 2021 (Dong et al., 2020).[16] Temporary 'stop-gap' measures cannot be taken as solutions to larger systemic inequalities created by neoliberal capitalism. The aftereffects of a disaster of any kind are that even if the disaster passes on, the victims of the disaster will remember it causing them trauma for the rest of their lives (Smedley, 2019).

No single explanation in terms of meta-narratives can provide one with the full scope of the ramifications of the crisis. It is always a combination of various theoretical endeavours that is required for understanding the effects of a disaster in totality. The resolution of the imbalances created by material inequalities require access to resources that go beyond the bare-minimum necessities to sustain life (Scheidel, 2018). If municipal socialism has to be effectively employed as a long-term strategy in devising solutions to problems caused by disaster capitalism, it has to address in further detail, as Palmer (1986) roughly highlighted in the case of the London Industrial Strategy, the questions concerning large-scale public ownership, decentralised planning, capitalist repercussions, and so on. Strategies which are 'in fact little other than a more democratic management of long-established systems of collective provision (or . . . collective consumption)' (Davies, 1988, p. 19), can only work when there is an overwhelmingly cooperative system in place that looks favourably upon such systems. In other words, without a change in the total system, such efforts would always be bottlenecked by existing larger processes.

The radical alternative to neoliberalism cannot be characterised as socialised or publicly owned neoliberalism, but rather as the destruction of neoliberal capitalism itself. Local governance can play a crucial role in that regard. Local administration can only be considered to be successful when certain factors have been enabled in the process such as the empowerment of marginalised individuals in the communities such that they are treated at par with others, producing the conditions for the transformation of formal equality into actually existing material equality. This enables people from marginalised individuals to self-uplift themselves, enabling them to work not only for their spatial communities but also for the entire 'community' to which they belong (Baviskar, 2009). Different epidemiological models have been employed globally in an attempt to identify different individuals, groups, and subgroups who might be carriers of virus in their respective communities (Carballosa et al., 2021).

Local administrative governance has proved to be quite effective in managing the pandemic, provided it is done with the right intentions. India has tried various methods to bring in effective local governance, engaging with both Nehruvian socialism and Gandhian socialism – one focused on change from the top through the usage of centralised planning, while the other focused on localised philanthropy. Both of these ideological formulations remained entrapped within a capitalist mode of development, and as such could only propose plans which benefitted the elites and the already existing socially stable groups, creating a highly segmented developmental society. Gandhian socialism was unable to develop a theoretically sound basis for morality, a central element of the discourses it generated. Nehruvian socialist models of development empowered the elites by making them the drivers of development in the country – both of them reinforcing caste Hindu traditions of morality and development (Desai, 1990). None of these traditions – and the plans and programmes which emanated from them – could empower to the fullest extent the marginalised of the country, who remained entrapped within a nexus of social evils, economic disparity, and discriminatory cultural ethos. All of these issues have come to haunt the country during the pandemic, converting COVID-19 into an everyday disaster. The solution to this is a fully decentralised and *horizontalist* community-based local governance, one where the human being is given precedence over the group morality and established societal norms.

Communities can be constructed similar to the cooperative societies. However, their limitations will have to be taken into cognisance. In his inaugural address to the IWMA, Karl Marx (1864/1985) had argued that, the working class has to engage in the cooperative movement through its various organisational forms, but the political action, and the necessity of the same, of the working class has to be affirmed. Similar is the case with communities, which constitute a majority of the non-capitalist players in the society. At the same time, it also has to be realised that capital today is globalised in character. Therefore, the model that communities propose should be internationalist in its character and approach towards the society, which can be an effective antithetical body in opposition to the global domination of capitalism. Marx said:

> One element of success they possess – numbers; but numbers weigh only in the balance, if united by combination and led by knowledge. Past experience has shown how disregard of that bond of brotherhood which ought to exist between the workmen of different countries and incite them to stand firmly by each other in all their struggles for emancipation, will be chastised by the common discomfiture of their incoherent efforts.
>
> (Marx, 1864, p. 12)

Local governance often makes it easy for the government to bring in measures of surveillance. During times such as pandemics, a strong state often tries to make decisions identifying individuals who *can be left to die* (Monti & Wacks, 2021). Local governance, as one knows, has to give away to much more democratic forms of governance. Under contemporary capitalism, public policy formation has increasingly become a domain where the states intervene in the lives of common people – that is the very definition of public policy though (Reddy, 2021) – to exert domination and control. Public policies are influenced by the socio-economic conditions, as well as the existent public perception and the ideological formulation of the contemporary government (Reddy, 2021). In situations such as this, the immediate community that an individual belongs to becomes the primary site of self-articulation, at least in the context of India, where group solidarities often dominate over individual consciousness. Communities can help in the protection of the human rights of the people, which often during emergencies such as Covid are endangered, and the policy makers – dominated by the society that constructed their mode of thinking (Marx & Engels, 1845–46) – are:

> tempted to state that, morally speaking, we must undoubtedly strive to save as many lives as possible, at any cost. Politically speaking, however, that may not be the case. Policy must be determined after weighing all of the options on the table, not just those moral consideration.
> (Maffettone, 2021, p. 65)

It becomes further complicated in India because compliance is often invoked in a manner that makes it equal to one's *Dharma* – a set of moral guidelines – which in the case of Indians, often translates into a method of coerced social control based on caste, gender, and social class (Monti & Wacks, 2021).

Social control becomes a weapon at the hands of the elite to dominate the discourses that generate during a crisis such as COVID-19. Apocalyptic tendencies are often not generated by those who suffer the most from them, but rather by those who possess enough resources to safeguard themselves, at least temporally. The increasing consumption of luxury products, the desire to obtain riches by extracting the earth's resources, and the constantly rising energy expenditure of all the major democracies in the world have been having a negative impact on the environment (Foster, 2020), which is increasingly pushing the world to the brink of extinction. Preparedness in such situations is a luxury that only a few can afford, as a reflexive reading of Bounds' (2021) work on New York city dwellers preparing for a disaster proves. Human rights in situations such as these can only be protected when communities emerge as an egalitarian and humanistic mode of organisation dialectically initiating the process of the transformation of the individuals in a manner that makes individuals come together as a coherent and united – yet diverse – body of thinking beings.

Notes

1 There are certain aspects out of all the different facilities that an urban space should provide to its citizens that are emphasised by various different scholarly think tanks. For example, Singhal and Mathur (2021) write, 'Access to energy is pivotal for any economic development and India's future development is heavily dependent on the sustainable growth of cities and access to clean and affordable energy' (p. 318).
2 According to some, the remnants of the *license raj* still persist within some sectors. For example, Sastri and Bandyopadhyay, while speaking about the development of technology in India, note '... sluggishness in bringing out timely, effective and easy-to-navigate frameworks to help develop and market science – and technology – based services or products has been the Achilles' heel of the Indian regulatory establishment' (Sastri and Bandyopadhyay, 2021, p. 42).

3 That is the problem that concerns most of the AAP or the All India Trinamool Congress (AITC) or even the Bharat Rashtra Samithi (BRS) government in Telangana. The relative success of Mohalla Clinics in Delhi can serve as an example of how public funding can help in ensuring healthcare for a broad mass of people. The AAP and its ministers have been continuously using the Mohalla Clinics to advance their version of egalitarian social restructuring. Recently, the Delhi government had also announced that they would be opening *Mahila Mohalla* Clinics to cater to the needs of women, along with the introduction of a health card and a digital platform called Health Information Management System (HIMS) (Express Healthcare March 10, 2021). Mohalla Clinics have been established by the AAP in Delhi to cater to the primary healthcare needs of the people of particular localities, especially the poor and marginalised sections. Mohalla Clinics have enabled greater control and flexibility for the government to control and restructure in the case of an outbreak within the clinics. For example, when a doctor tested positive in Northeast Delhi in March 2020, the Delhi government could immediately quarantine 800 people in the locality who had come in contact with the clinic (Scroll, March 26, 2020). However, it is important here to take into cognisance that Mohalla Clinics merely scratch the surface of the healthcare requirements of the society. Local residents in Delhi remain sceptical about them not only because of the ways in which they are managed by the state in terms of facilities but also because of the quality of healthcare. During the second wave of the pandemic, however, the Mohalla Clinics had been found to be at their wits end.
4 'Venture Capital is a high-risk investment with the potential for above-average returns and that's why it is often referred to as "Smart Money"'. 'Venture Capital firms not only invest money into companies, but also devote time to support and manage risks by leveraging their collective in-house and external expertise' (Mustafa, 2020, p. xiv).
5 In India, 'Municipalities are constituted by the State Government, which specifies the class to which a municipality shall belong in accordance with the provisions of the municipal Act. For this purpose, size of the urban population is the main criterion. However, in some States consideration is also given to other criteria, such as location of the urban area and the per capita income' (Aijaz, 2007, p. 10).
6 Farooqui's (April 05, 2021) report talks about how localised lockdowns in different parts of the country, and especially Maharashtra, have been adversely affecting businesses such as multiplexes and single screen cinemas. Despite the fact that, even if they reopen during these times, their operational expenses have remained constant, their footfall has singnificantly decreased. Localised lockdowns are indeed causing losses in power consumption, retail mobility, and GST collections as *Business Standard* (April 20, 2021) reports.
7 As Miliband notes, 'The achievements of the parliamentary party . . . were not such as to hide the limited nature of its impact and the ambiguity of its position. Whatever might be said for the inevitability of gradualness, [the parliamentary left-wing parties'] progress [bears] too close a resemblance to stagnation not to produce much frustration, recrimination, and criticism of the leadership' (Miliband, 1964, p. 25).
8 Stoker's arguments were made considering the provisioning of mostly health, education, housing, and transport, and can be witnessed in real life in the case of India.
9 In Dharavi, for example, there are only 225 public toilets that cater to a population of 8.5 lakh people according to Sah (2020), a volunteer with the SWAN. Ritika Sah further goes on to state, 'Crammed with makeshift tin and concrete shanties, Dharavi's houses are particularly vulnerable to the spread of a virus. It is common for more than a hundred people to use a single bathroom. It is quite likely that someone who has been infected with COVID-19 has used it that same day. In the 2.02 sq. km spread of Dharavi' (Sah, 2020, Para 5).

10 Traditional Indian lamps made of clay, usually lit during festivals such as Diwali.
11 The *Kumbha Mela*, a Hindu religious festival is celebrated to mark the completion of the revolution of Jupiter around the Sun after every 12 years. According to Hindu mythology, it coincides with the Hindu mythological event of the *samudra manthan* – a mythological event wherein the gods and demons in Hindu mythology churned the cosmological ocean in the hope of obtaining *amrit* (a nectar that supposedly provides immortality to the one who drinks it). This event is the largest gathering of people in the world and was held in Haridwar in Uttarakhand from 1st to the 17th of April in 2021.
12 Supreme authority.
13 See www.thequint.com/news/india/odisha-govt-floats-global-tender-to-procure-covid-vaccines. Also see www.hindustantimes.com/india-news/ten-states-gear-up-to-import-vaccines-bottlenecks-remain-101620757827529.html [Accessed 04.12.2023]
14 See www.bbc.com/news/world-asia-india-56345591 and www.livemint.com/news/india/mumbai-no-covid-vaccination-for-age-45-above-tomorrow-says-bmc-11619962486825.html [Accessed 04.12.2023]
15 See www.ndtv.com/india-news/india-oxygen-export-rose-over-700-in-january-2021-vs-2020-amid-pandemic-2418461 [Accessed 04.12.2023]
16 Data sourced from the *Center for Systems Science and Engineering* (CSSE) at John Hopkins University, Canada. Accessible at www.arcgis.com/apps/opsdashboard/index.html#/bda7594740fd40299423467b48e9ecf6 [Accessed 04.12.2023]

References

Ahluwalia, I. J. (2019). Urban governance in India. *Journal of Urban Affairs*, 41(1), 83–102.
Ahmad, S. (2012). Housing inequality in socially disadvantaged communities: Evidence from urban India, 2009. *Environment and Urbanization ASIA*, 3(1), 237–249.
Ahmed, M. H. (2021, February 12). Impact of coronavirus lockdown: GHMC in deep financial crisis. *The Siasat Daily*. Retrieved December 4, 2023, from www.siasat.com/impact-of-coronavirus-lockdown-ghmc-in-deep-financial-crisis
Aijaz, R. (2007). *Challenges for urban local governments in India*. Asia Research Centre Working Paper 19, London School of Economics and Political Science.
Aiyar, S. (2020). *The gated republic: India's public policy failures and private solutions*. Harper Collins Publishers India.
Akhter, S. (2020, June 22). PPP in healthcare can be successful with long-term commitment, patience, and sizeable investment: Vasant Gadhavi, Adani Foundation. *The Economic Times*. Retrieved December 4, 2023, from www.health.economictimes.indiatimes.com/news/hospitals/ppp-in-healthcare-can-be-successful-with-long-term-commitment-patience-and-sizeable-investment-vasant-gadhavi-adani-foundation/7649768
Alexander, C., Edwards, R., & Temple, B. (2007). Contesting cultural communities: Language, ethnicity and citizenship in Britain. *Journal of Ethnic and Migration Studies*, 33(5), 783–800.
Alleyne, B. (2002). An idea of community and its discontents. *Ethnic and Racial Studies*, 25(4), 607–627.
Anand, P. (2021, October 5). How NGOs have silently helped Indians combat the covid-19 pandemic. *The News Minute*. Retrieved December 4, 2023, from www.thenewsminute.com/article/how-ngos-have-silently-helped-indians-combat-covid-19-pandemic-156115
Arun, M. G., & Punj, S. (2021, September 27). Asset monetisation: The big push. *India Today*.

Ascher, K. (1987). *The politics of privatisation: Contracting out public services.* Macmillan.
Badgaiyan, N., & Kumar, A. (2021, April 15). The third tier of government can bolster urban health. *Mint.* Retrieved December 4, 2023, from www.livemint.com/opinion/online-views/the-third-tier-of-government-can-bolster-urban-health-11618417940856.html
Barker, B. (1946). *Labour in London: A study in municipal achievement.* Routledge.
Barron, J., Crawley, G., & Wood, T. (1991). *Councillors in crisis: The public and private worlds of local councillors.* Macmillan.
Bathija, M. (2014). *Paiso: How Sindhis do business.* Penguin Portfolio.
Baudrillard, J. (1970/1998). *The consumer society: Myths and structures.* Sage.
Bauman, Z. (2000). *Liquid modernity.* Polity.
Bauman, Z. (2001). *The individualized society.* Polity.
Bauman, Z. (2003). *Liquid love: On the frailty of human bonds.* Polity.
Baviskar, B. S. (2009). Including the excluded: Empowering the powerless through Panchayati Raj in Maharashtra. In B. S. Baviskar, & G. Mathew (Eds.), *Inclusion and exclusion in local governance: Field studies from rural India.* SAGE.
Beck, U., & Beck-Gernsheim, E. (2001). *Individualization.* Sage.
Bhalotia, S., Dhingra, S., & Kondirolli, F. (2020). *City of dreams no more: The impact of covid-19 on urban workers in India.* Covid-19 Analysis Series. Centre for Economic Performance, London School of Economics and Political Science.
Bhangay, K. (2022). It's all in your head until it happens. In D. Aggarwal & S. Sundaram (Eds.), *A world on hold: A living record of the global pandemic.* Om Books International.
Bisen, A. (2019). *Wasted: The messy story of sanitation in India: A manifesto for change.* Pan Macmillan.
Blackman, M. (2020). *A new normal. In what covid-19 revealed about us, and where we might go next.* Penguin.
Bönker, F., Libbe, J., & Wollmann, H. (2016). Remunicipalisation revisited: Long-term trends in the provision of local public services in Germany. In H. Wollmann, I. Koprić, & G. Marcou (Eds.), *Public and social services in Europe: From public and municipal to private sector provision.* Palgrave Macmillan.
Bounds, A. M. (2021). *Bracing for the apocalypse: An ethnographic study of New York's 'Prepper' subculture.* Routledge.
Bruno, P. (2020). *Lacan and Marx: The invention of the symptom.* Routledge.
Burns, D., Hambleton, R., & Hogget, P. (1994). *The politics of decentralisation: Revitalising local democracy.* Palgrave Macmillan.
Business Standard. (2021a, April 18). Localised lockdowns impacting business in organised retail, says SCAI. Retrieved December 4, 2023, from www.business-standard.com/article/current-affairs/localised-lockdowns-impacting-business-in-organised-retail-says-scai-121041800333_1.html
Business Standard. (2021b, April 20). Localised lockdowns already hitting economic activities: Report. Retrieved December 4, 2023, from www.business-standard.com/article/economy-policy/localised-lockdowns-already-hitting-economic-activities-report-121042000681_1.html
Carballosa, A., Balsa-Barreiro, J., Garea, A., Garcia-Selfa, D., Miramontes, A., & Muñuzuri, A. P. (2021). Risk Evaluation at municipality level at a COVID-19 outbreak incorporating relevant geographic data: The study case of Galicia. *Scientific Reports, 11*(21248). https://doi.org/10.1038/s41598-021-00342-2
Castells, M. (2000). *The rise of the network society.* Blackwell.
Chandra, R. (2019). *The moonshot Game: Adventures of an Indian venture capitalist.* Penguin.
Coffey, D., & Spears, D. (2017). *Where India goes: Abandoned toilets, stunted development and the costs of caste.* Noida: Harper Collins Publishers India.

Cohn, G. (1910). Municipal socialism. *The Economic Journal*, 20(80), 561–568.
Collins, K., & Soulia, C. (2021). *The front steps project: How communities found connection during the COVID-19 crisis*. West Margin Press.
Critchley, S. (2012). *Infinitely demanding: Ethics of commitment, politics of resistance*. Verso.
D'Souza, V. (1970/1990). Slums in a planned city: Chandigarh. In A. R. Desai & S. D. Pillai (Eds.), *Slums and urbanization*. Bombay: Popular Prakashan.
Das, G. (2000). *India unbound: From independence to the global information age*. Penguin.
Das, G. (2002/2012). *The elephant paradigm: India wrestles with change*. Gurugram: Penguin.
Davies, J. G. (1988). From municipal socialism to . . . municipal capitalism? *Local Government Studies*, 14(2), 19–22.
Davies, R. (2021). *Prices and inflation in a pandemic – a micro data approach*. Centre for Economic Performance, London School of Economics and Political Science.
Department of Economic and Social Affairs. (2014). *World urbanization prospects: The 2014 revision*. United Nations.
Desai, A. R. (1990). Caste violence in post-partition India. In A. R. Desai (Ed.), *Repression and resistance in India: Violence of democratic rights of the working class, rural poor, Adivasis and Dalits*. Popular Prakashan.
Dhingra, S., & Kondirolli, F. (2021). *City of dreams no more, a year on: Worklessness and active labour market policies in urban India*. Covid-19 Analysis Series. London: Centre for Economic Performance, London School of Economics and Political Science.
Diamond, J. (2019). *Upheaval: How nations cope with crisis and change*. Allen Lane.
Digital Medic. (2021, March 29). *The role of NGOs in covid-19 community-based education*. Retrieved December 4, 2023, from www.digitalmedic.stanford.edu/general/the-role-of-ngos-in-covid-19-community-based-education/
Dijk, E. Van., Schrevel, L., Stormbroek-Burgers, R. Van., & Blomme, R. J. (2014). How to create an effective venture capitalist-entrepreneurship relationship: An entrepreneur's perspective. *SAGE Open* [Online]. https://doi.org/10.1177/2158244014553602
Dixit, A., & Chauhan, R. (2020). *The future of social distancing: New cardinals for children, adolescent and youth*. National Book Trust.
Dong, E., Du, H., & Gardner, L. (2020). An interactive web-based dashboard to track COVID-19 in real time. *The Lancet Infectious Diseases*, 20(5), 533–534.
Dréze, J., & Sen, A. (2013). *An uncertain glory: India and its contradictions*. Penguin.
Dunayevskaya, R. (1956). Marx and the Utopian socialists. In *The Raya Dunayevskaya collection – Marxist-humanism: A half century of its world development*. Wayne State University Archives of Labor and Urban Affairs.
Dunn, R. G. (2008). *Identifying consumption: Subjects and objects in consumer society*. Temple University Press.
Dutt, B. (2022). *To hell and back: Humans of covid*. Juggernaut.
Express Healthcare. (2021, March 10). *Delhi budget free covid vaccine scheme at state-run hospitals special women Mohalla clinics*. Retrieved December 4, 2023, from www.expresshealthcare.in/news/delhi-budget-free-covid-vaccine-scheme-at-state-run-hospitals-special-women-mohalla-clinics/427739/
Faizal, M., & Rahman, A. (2020, May 14). COVID-19 and the acceleration of state surveillance. *The Interpreter*. Retrieved December 4, 2023, from www.lowyinsititute.org/the-interpreter/covid-19-and-the-accleration-of-state-surveillance
Farooqui, M. (2021, April 5). Malls, multiples owners upset over new restrictions, localised lockdowns. *Money Control*. Retrieved December 4, 2023, from www.moneycontrol.com/news/trends/entertainment/covid-19-spike-malls-multiplex-owners-upset-over-new-restrictions-localised-lockdowns-6731951.html

Foster, J. B. (2020). *The return of nature: Socialism and ecology*. Monthly Review Press.

Foster, J. B., & Clark, B. (2020). *The robbery of nature: Capitalism and the ecological rift*. Monthly Review Press.

Foucault, M. (1979). *Discipline and punish: The birth of the prison*. Vintage Books.

Fraser, D. (1987, April). Joseph Chamberlain and the municipal ideal. *History Today, 33*–39.

Fromm, E. (1976). *To have or to be?* Continuum.

Gandhi-Mody, P. (2022). *A nation to protect: Leading India through the covid crisis*. Rupa Publications.

Gantenbein, P., Kind, A., & Volonté, C. (2021). Individualism and venture capital: A cross-country study. *Management International Review, 59*, 741–777. https://doi.org/10.1007/s11575-019-00394-7

Garcia-Subirats, I., Vargas, I., Mogollón-Pérez, S., Paepe, P. De, de Silva, R. F., Unger, J. P., & Vásquez, M. L. (2014). Barriers in access to healthcare in countries with different health systems. *Social Science and Medicine, 106*, 204–213.

Gehrke, J. P. (2016). A radical Endeavor: Joseph Chamberlain and the emergence of municipal socialism in Birmingham. *American Journal of Economics and Sociology, 75*(1), 23–57.

Ghoshal, D. (2016, April 18). Charted: The astonishing cost of healthcare in India. *Quartz India*. Retrieved December 4, 2023, from www.qz.com/india/663718/charted-the-incredible-cost-of-healthcare-in-india

Giuffre, K. (2013). *Communities and networks: Using social network analysis to rethink urban and community studies*. Polity.

Gompers, P., & Lerner, J. (2001). The venture capital revolution. *Journal of Economic Perspectives, 15*(2), 145–168.

Gupta, K. (2020, October 24). India needs a public-private model for covid-19 immunisation. *ORF Online*. Retrieved December 4, 2023, from www.orfonline.org/expert-speak/india-needs-a-public-private-model-for-covid-19-immunisation/

Han, B.-C. (2015). *The burnout society*. Stanford University Press.

Harsha, P. N. S. (2021, December 23). Telangana village imposes self lockdown after Dubai returnee tests omicron positive. *The Siasat Daily*. Retrieved December 4, 2023, from www.siasat.com/telenagana-village-imposes-self-lockdown-after-dubai-returnee-tests-omicron-positive-2246428/

Hein, C. (2005). Resilient Tokyo: Disaster and transformation in the Japanese city. In L. J. Denis & T. J. Campanella (Eds.), *The resilient city: How modern cities recover from disaster*. Oxford University Press.

Housing Research. (2021). *State of Indian healthcare: Indian cities through the lens of healthcare 2021*. Housing Research. Retrieved December 4, 2023, from www.housing.com/research-reports

Hudis, P. (2020). Political organisation. In M. Musto (Ed.), *The Marx revival: Key concepts and new interpretations*. Cambridge University Press.

Imaan, A. (2020, July 31). India's migrant crisis pointed to another problem: Its lack of shelter homes. *Scroll*. Retrieved December 4, 2023, from www.scroll.in/article/968374/indias-migrant-crisis-pointed-to-another-problem-its-lack-of-shelter-homes

Inamdar, N. (2014). *Rokda: How baniyas do business*. Penguin Portfolio.

Iyer, P. (2019). Introduction. In P. Iyer (Ed.), *The Swachh Bharat revolution: Four pillars of India's behavioural transformation*. Harper Collins Publishers India.

Jain, M. (2017, August 2). Private sector profits in healthcare soar as Indian government investment stagnates. *Scroll*. Retrieved December 4, 2023, from www.scroll.in/pulse/845539/private-sectors-profits-in-healthcare-soar-as-indian-government-investment-stagnates

Jalan, B. (2019). *Resurgent India: Politics, economics and governance*. Noida: Harper Collins Publishers India.
Joshi, N. K. (2021). Ethics and public policy: How 'just' can public policy be? In R. Basu (Ed), *Democracy and public policy in the post-covid-19 world*. Routledge.
Kapri, V. (2021). *1232 KM: The long journey back home*. Harper Collins Publishers India.
Karatayev, V. A., Anand, M., & Bauch, C. T. (2020). Local lockdowns outperform global lockdown on the side of the covid-19 epidemic curve. *PNAS, 117*(39), 24575–24580.
Kasperson, R. E., Golding, D., & Tuler, S. (2005). Introduction. In J. X. Kasperson & R. E. Kasperson (Eds.), *The social contours of risk volume 1: Publics, risk communication and the social amplification of risk*. Earthscan.
Keen, C. (2021). *A judge in Madras: Sir Sidney Wadsworth and the Indian civil service, 1913–47*. Harper Collins Publishers India.
Klein, N. (2017a). *No is not enough: Resisting Trump's shock politics and winning the world we need*. Haymarket Books.
Klein, N. (2017b, July 6). How power profits from disaster. *The Guardian*. Retrieved December 4, 2023, from www.theguardian.com/us/us-news/2017/jul/06/naomi-klein-how-power-profits-from-disaster
Klein, N. (2019). *On fire: The burning case for a green new deal*. Knopf.
Klonowski, D. (2010). *The venture capital investment process*. Palgrave Macmillan.
Klonowski, D. (2022). *Venture capital redefined: The economic, political, and social impact of COVID on the VC ecosystem*. Palgrave Macmillan.
Kukla, Q. R. (2021). The COVID-19 pandemic and the loss of the urban. In J.-L. Denis, C. Régis, D. M. Weinstock, & C. Champagne (Eds.), *Pandemic societies*. McGill-Queen's University Press.
Kumbhare, S. (2020, May 7). Sanitation workers: At the bottom of the frontline against COVID-19? *The Wire*. Retrieved December 4, 2023, from www.thewire.in/article/urban/sanitation-workers-covid-19
Kundu, M. (2009). Panchayati raj or party raj? Understanding the nature of local government in West Bengal. In B. S. Baviskar & G. Mathew (Eds.), *Inclusion and exclusion in local governance: Field studies from rural India*. SAGE.
Lefebvre, H. (1991). *Critique of everyday life: Volume 1*. Verso.
Lefebvre, H. (2016). *Marxist thought and the city*. University of Minnesota Press.
Leopold, E., & McDonald, D. A. (2012). Municipal socialism then and now: Some lessons for the global south. *Third World Quarterly, 33*(10), 1837–1853.
Levey, E. J. (1909). *Municipal socialism and its economic limitations*. Ginn and Company.
Li, Y., Undurraga, E. A., & Zubizarreta, J. R. (2022). Effectiveness of localized lockdowns in the covid-19 pandemic. *American Journal of Epidemiology, 191*(5), 812–824.
Maffettone, S. (2021). Pandemic: Philosophy and public policy. In K. Mahadevan, S. Kumar, M. Bhoot, & R. Kharat (Eds.), *The covid spectrum: Theoretical and experiential reflections from India and beyond*. Speaking Tiger.
Magazine, A., & Sasi, A. (2021, April 1). Localised lockdowns in second wave set to hit services recovery. *The Indian Express*. Retrieved December 4, 2023, from www.indianexpress.com/article/india/coronavirus-localised-lockdowns-in-second-wave-set-to-hit-services-recovery-7253512/
Mahambare, V. (2015, February 9). Wealth inequality and housing reforms. *Mint*. Retrieved December 4, 2023, from www.livemint.com/Opinion/ZDkmQFSmM7hNM1ky3ZR
Marx, K. (1843/1975). Contribution to the critique of Hegel's philosophy of right: Introduction. In *Marx Engels collected works: Volume 3*. Lawrence and Wishart.

Marx, K. (1844/1975). Economic and philosophical manuscripts of 1844. In *Marx Engels collected works: Volume 3*. Lawrence and Wishart.
Marx, K. (1864/1982). Inaugural address of the IWMA. In *Marx Engels collected works: Volume 20*. Lawrence and Wishart.
Marx, K. (1867/1976). *Capital, volume 1: A critique of political economy*. Penguin.
Marx, K. (1875). Critique of the Gotha programme. In *Marx-Engels collected works: Volume 24*. Lawrence ad Wishart.
Marx, K., & Engels, F. (1845–1846/1976). The German ideology. In *Marx Engels collected works: Volume 5*. Lawrence and Wishart.
Marx, K., & Engels, F. (1848/1978). Manifesto of the communist party. In *Marx Engels collected works: Volume 6*. Lawrence and Wishart.
Mathew, C. K. (2020). *The historical evolution of the district officer: From early days to 1947*. Azim Premji University Press.
Matthewman, S. (2015). *Disasters, risks and revelation: Making sense of our times*. Palgrave.
Menon, N. (2022). *Planning democracy: Modern India's quest for development*. Cambridge University Press.
Merrifield, A. (2017). Fifty years on: The right to the city. In *The right to the city: A Verso report*. Verso.
Miliband, R. (1964). *Parliamentary socialism: A study in the politics of labour*. Monthly Review Press.
Ministry of Health and Family Welfare. (2020, December 28). *Covid-19 vaccines: Operational guidelines*. Government of India.
Mishra, A., Seshadri, S. R., Pradyumna, A., Pinto, E. P., Bhattacharya, A., Saligram, P., & Benny, G. (2021). *Health care equity in urban India*. Azim Premji University.
Mishra, S. (2021, April 26). Importance of upgrading India's network of PHCs and adopting telemedicine. *The Economic Times*. Retrieved December 4, 2023, from www.health.economictimes.indiatimes.com/news/health-it/importance-of-upgrading-indias-network-of-phcs-and-adopting-telemedicine/82309505
Mohan, T. T. R. (2015). *Rethinc: What's broke at today's corporations and how to fix it*. Random House.
Monti, A., & Wacks, R. (2021). *COVID-19 and Public Policy in the Digital Age*. Routledge.
Monti, D. J. (2000). Why cities still matter. *Society, 38*, 19–27.
Morgan, D. R. (2013). Structural criminality within the "Collective Shadow": Disaster capitalism and the globalization of ruling power. *On the Horizon, 21*(3), 247–258.
Mukarji, N. (2012). Decentralisation below the state level. In T. R. Raghunandan (Ed.), *Decentralisation and local governments: The Indian experience*. Orient Blackswan.
Mukul, J. (2022). *The great shutdown: A story of two Indian summers*. Harper Collins Publishers India.
Mustafa, M. (2020). *Demystifying venture capital: How it works and how to get it, insights from top VCs*. Simon and Schuster.
Nagpal, J., & Dixit, A. (2020, November 20). Municipal bodies failing to cater to health care needs of the urban poor, finds report. *NewsClick*. Retrieved December 4, 2023, from https:///www.newsclick.in/municipal-bodies-failing-cater-health-care-needs-urban-poor-report
Newton, K., & Karran, T. J. (1985). *The politics of local expenditure*. Macmillan.
Nichols, J. (2022). *Coronavirus criminals and pandemic profiteers: Accountability for those who caused the crisis*. Verso.
NITI Aayog. (2021). *Reforms in urban planning capacity in India: September 2021*. Government of India.

Oriel, A., & Ghosh, K. (2022, May 31). India's poor forced to swallow the bitter pill as medical inflation nibbles at their life savings. *Outlook*. Retrieved December 4, 2023, from www.outlookindia.com/business/india-s-poor-forced-to-swallow-the-bitter-pill-as-medical-inflation-nibbles-at-their-life-savings-news-199526

Padmanabhan, V., & Srivastava, P. (2019, August 4). Which Indian city will run out of water first? *Mint*. Retrieved December 4, 2023, from www.livemint.com/news/india/which-indian-city-will-run-out-of-water-first

Palmer, J. (1986). Municipal enterprise and popular planning. *New Left Review*, 1(159), 117–124.

Pande, A. (2020). *Making India great: The promise of a reluctant global power*. Harper Collins Publishers India.

Panitch, L., & Leys, C. (1997). *The end of parliamentary socialism: From new left to new labour*. Verso.

Patel, S., & Pant, P. (2020). Decentralisation and urban primary health services: A case study of Delhi's Mohalla clinics. *Commonwealth Journal of Local Governance*, 23. https://doi.org/10.5130/cjlg.vi23.6987.

Patnaik, P. (2021, September 24). Neoliberalism: An era of growth sans justice. *Frontline*. https://frontline.thehindu.com/cover-story/neoliberalism-economic-reforms-at-30-an-era-of-growth-sans-justice/article36295371.ece

Raghavan, P. (2017, July 24). NITI Aayog's healthcare PPP needs clarity: Hospitals. *The Economic Times*. Retrieved December 4, 2023, from www.theeconomictimes.com/industry/healthcare/biotech/healthcare/niti-aayogs-healthcare-ppp-needs-clarity-hospitals/articleshow/59728377.cms

Rai, H. (1965). The changing role of the district officer. *Indian Journal of Public Administration*, 11(3), 376–388.

Raj, C, A., & K., M. (2020, July 2). As covid-19 puts India's largest cities under strain, municipalities must rethink finance strategies. *Scroll*. Retrieved December 4, 2023, from www.scroll.in/article/966210/as-covid-19-puts-indias-largest-cities-under-strain-municipalities-must-rethink-finance-strategies

Rajan, R. (2011/2017). *Fault lines: How hidden fractures still threaten the world economy*. Harper Collins Publishers India.

Ramachandran, P. (1970/1990). The slum: A note on facts and solutions. In A. R. Desai & S. D. Pillai (Eds.), *Slums and urbanization*. Popular Prakashan.

Randall, S. (1995). City pride – from "municipal socialism" to "municipal capitalism"? *Critical Social Policy*, 15(43), 40–59.

Rao, C. S. (2021, December 31). Telangana: 4th omicron case in Sircilla, another village in lockdown. *The Times of India*. Retrieved December 4, 2023, from www.timesofindia.com/city/hyderabad/4th-omicron-case-in-sircilla-another-village-in-lockdown/articleshow/88602020.cms

Reddy, C. S. (2021). Theoretical framework and dynamics of public policy trajectory. In R. Basu (Ed.), *Democracy and public policy in the post-covid-19 world*. Routledge.

Reddy, K. S. (2019). *Make health in India: Reaching a billion plus*. Orient Blackswan.

Robinson, E. (2015). Defining progressive politics: Municipal socialism and anti-socialism in contestation, 1889–1939. *Journal of the History of Ideas*, 76(4), 609–631.

Rozario, K. (2005). Making progress: Disaster narratives and the art of optimism in modern America. In L. J. Vale & T. J. Campanella (Eds.), *The resilient city: How modern cities recover from disaster*. Oxford University Press.

Rustin, M. (1986). Lessons of the London industrial strategy. *New Left Review*, 1(155), 75–84.

Sah, R. (2020, June 4). The wages of covid-19 lockdown in Dharavi – A sense of panic, loss of self. *The Wire*. www.thewire.in/article/rights/dravai-covid-19-lockdown-workers

Sastri, S, & Bandyopadhyay, A. (2021). *The ventilator project: How the IIT Kanpur consortium built a world-class product during India's covid-19 lockdown.* Macmillan.

Scheidel, W. (2018). *The great leveler: Violence and the history of inequality from the stone age to the twenty-first century.* Princeton University Press.

Scroll. (2020, March 26). Covid-19: 800 people in quarantine after Delhi Mohalla clinic doctor, family test positive. *Scroll.* Retrieved December 4, 2023, from www.scroll.in/latest/957268/covid-19-delhi-mohalla-clinic-doctor-wife-and-family-test-positive-visitors-asked-to-quarantine

Sen, A. (1970/2017). *Collective choice and social welfare.* Penguin.

Sengupta, R. (2021, May 4). More than half of India's April COVID-19 deaths were in rural districts. *Down to Earth.* Retrieved December 4, 2023, from www.downtoearth.org.in/news/health/more-than-half-of-india-s-april-covid-19-deaths-were-in-rural-districts-76782

Sethi, N., & Rao, M. (2017, July 19). NITI Aayog and health ministry model contract for privatising urban health care. *Scroll.* Retrieved December 4, 2023, from www.scroll.in/article/844272/niti-aayog-and-health-ministry-prepare-model-contract-for-privatising-urban-health-care

Shameem, M. (2022). Digging deeper wounds. In D. Aggarwal & S. Sundaram (Eds.), *A world on hold: A living record of the global pandemic.* Om Books International.

Sharma, R. (2012, December 19). PPP is the way forward to improve healthcare in India: McKinsey. *Down to Earth.* Retrieved December 4, 2023, from www.downtoearth.org.in/news/ppp-is-the-way-forward-to-improve-healthcare-in-india-mckinsey-39883

Shaw, B. (1908). *The commonsense of municipal trading.* A. C. Fifield.

Shaw, B. (1930). Preface to the 1931 reprint. In B. Shaw, S. Webb, G. Wallas, The Lord Oliview, W. Clarke, A. Besant, & H. Bland (Eds.), *Fabian essays.* The Garden City Press.

Shivdasani, V. (2021). *Covid and post-covid recovery: Doctor Vee's 6-point plan.* Harper Collins Publishers India.

Singh, S. (2018). *The great smog of India.* Penguin.

Singh, T. (2016). *India's broken tryst.* Harper Collins Publishers India.

Singh, T. (2019). Chalo Champaran. In P. Iyer (Ed.), *The Swachh Bharat revolution: Four pillars of India's behavioural transformation.* Harper Collins Publishers India.

Singh, T. (2020). *Messiah Modi? A tale of great expectations.* Harper Collins.

Singhal, A, & Mathur, R. (2021). City gas distribution: Emerging potential. In V. S. Mehta (Ed.), *The next stop: Natural gas and India's journey to a clean energy future.* Harper Collins Publishers India.

Sinha, C. (2007). *Public sector reforms in India: New role of the district officer.* SAGE.

Sinha, Y., & Sinha, A. (2018). *India unmade: How the Modi government broke the economy.* Juggernaut Books.

Smedley, T. (2019). *Clearing the air: The beginning and end of air pollution.* Bloomsbury.

Stoker, G. (1991). *The politics of local government.* Macmillan.

Stranded Workers Action Network (SWAN). (2021). *No country for workers: The Covid-19 second wave, local lockdowns and migrant worker distress in India.* SWAN.

Sundaraman, T., Parmar, D., & Kriti, S. (2020). Public health and health services as global public goods. In *India exclusion report, 2019–20.* Three Essays Collective and Centre for Equity Studies.

Suneja, K. (2022, January 7). Avoid knee-jerk reactions, local lockdowns: CII president. *The Economic Times.* Retrieved December 4, 2023, from www.economictimes.com/news/economy/indicators-avoid-knee-jerk-reactions-local-lockdowns-cii-president

Sur, P., & Mitra, E. (2020, March 31). Social distancing is a privilege of the middle class. For India's slum dwellers, it will be impossible. *CNN World.* Retrieved

December 4, 2023, from www.edition.cnn.com/2020/03/30/india/india-coronavirus-social-distancing-intl-hnk/index.html
Suttles, G. D. (1973). *The social construction of communities*. The University of Chicago Press.
Taylor-Gooby, P. (2015). Public policy futures: A left trilemma? In J. Green, C. Hay, & P. Taylor-Gooby (Eds.), *The British growth crisis: The search for a new model*. Palgrave Macmillan.
The Economic Times. (2022a, June 2). PPP model in healthcare: Bettering healthcare in India. Retrieved December 4, 2023, from www.health.economictimes.indiatimes.com/microsite/gehealthierindia/news/detail/1023
The Economic Times. (2022b, June 3). GE Healthcare, Tata trusts join hands to train 10,000 youth in technical areas of healthcare. Retrieved December 4, 2023, from www.health.economictimes.indiatimes.com/microsite/gehealthierindia/news/detail/1023
The Hindu Editorial. (2019, November 27). Not so Swachh: On sanitation goals. Retrieved December 4, 2023, from www.thehindu.com/opinion/editorial/not-so-swachh/article30090214.ece
The Hindu Editorial. (2021, May 26). Calibrated closures: On localised lockdowns. Retrieved December 4, 2023, from www.thehindu.com/opinion/editorial/calibrated-closures-on-localised-lockdowns/article34644647.ece
The Wire. (2022, June 20). How many migrant workers left cities during the covid-19 lockdown? Retrieved December 4, 2023, from www.thewire.in/article/labour/how-many-migrant-workers-left-cities-during-the-covid-19-lockdown
Thomas, A., Alexander, D., & Gyani, G. (2022). Health sector leadership to combat climate change. In A. Thomas, K. S. Reddy, D. Alexander, & P. Prabhakaran (Eds.), *Climate change and the health sector*. Routledge.
Tönnies, F. (1955). *Community and association (Gemeinschaft und Gesellschaft)*. Routledge and Kegan Paul.
Towler, W. G. (1909). *Socialism in local government*. The Macmillan Company.
Tumbe, C. (2020). *The age of pandemics, 1817–1920: How they shaped india and the world*. Harper Collins.
Unnamed Migrant Worker. (2022). Whose country is it anyway? In D. Aggarwal & S. Sundaram (Eds.), *A world on hold: A living record of the global pandemic*. Om Books International.
Untermann, E. (1906/2002). *The municipality from capitalism to socialism*. Appeal to Reason.
Uppal, T., & Sidhu, S. (2020). *New frontiers at home: An approach to women, mothers and parents*. National Book Trust.
Webb, S. (1891). *The London programme*. Swan Sonnenschein & Co.
Webb, S. (1889/1948). Historic. In B. Shaw, S. Webb, G. Wallas, The Lord Oliview, W. Clarke, A. Besant, & H. Bland (Eds.), *Fabian essays*. The Garden City Press.
Wilson, B., & Singh, B. (2016). The long march to eliminate manual scavenging. In *India exclusion report, 2016*. Yoda Press and Three Essays Collective.
Woods, E. (2019). Science policy in a post-truth world. In S. Linden & R. E. Löfstedt (Eds.), *Risk and uncertainty in a post-truth society*. Routledge.
World Health Organisation. (2021, April 1). *Primary health care*. Retrieved December 4, 2023, from www.who.int/news-room/fact-sheets/detail/primary-heath-care

5 Radical Possibilities of the Apocalyptic Times

Introduction

The COVID-19 pandemic was unleashed onto the world in the midst of extreme economic instability, recession, climate change, bourgeoning racism, and extreme inequality (Alston, 2020). When COVID-19 became an everyday reality for a majority of the global populace, the idea that the world might be heading towards a globe-ending apocalypse loomed large, and to many it looked a highly probable outcome of the pandemic. Images and conceptualisations of the apocalypse have always occupied an important position in most human cultures. These ideas are often dominated by the religious beliefs that people hold, which have evolved over the centuries (Himmelfarb, 2010). In recent times, terms such as the *Sixth Extinction* have been used to refer to the probable apocalypse that human society is supposed to face as:

> Blessed with reason and insight, we move[d] toward the twenty-first century in a world of our own creation, am essentially artificial world in which (for some, at least) technology brings material comfort and leisure brings unprecedented artistic creation. So far, unfortunately, our reason and insight have not prevented us from collectively exploiting Erath's resources – biological and physical – in unprecedented ways.
> (Leakey & Lewin, 1995, p. 232)

Several versions of the post-apocalyptic society have come to influence human minds over the past few decades. Singularitarianism proposes a technological singularity between human beings and technological artefacts, with the possibility of creating a superhuman intelligence. Transhumanism or posthumanism believes that people and technology, and even non-human beings, will pose themselves as singular entities in the future (Wells, 2009). The proponents of these visions, however, argue in favour of a quick transformation to these ontologies. Pandemics and epidemics have been frequently evoked as being the markers and accelerators of such apocalyptic processes when they act in combination with other social and structural issues (De Bevoise, 1995).

However, the language that scientists speak often does not evoke the reactions that they should because the general populace, unlike those in positions of power, does not have the capacity to understand scientific language or their own existing vulnerability. This results in many not being able to comprehend the massive degradation of society that is being caused by capitalist developmental projects and its associated politics that dominate the everyday life under contemporary capitalism. This degradation often translates into giving preference to immediate visible threats while leaving out the long-term structural issues (Wells, 2019; Ramesh, 2018b). Naomi Klein (2014) writes that those in power usually deny the impending apocalyptic event because they believe that those with strong communitarian ideals moving towards egalitarian solutions are far more dangerous. This is because they can use the situation to steer the society towards a more egalitarian one as against the more individualistic one proposed by capitalism – which would in turn, significantly decrease the profits that large corporations and powerful people can extract out of the disaster.

Many people might have imagined the end of the world through a virus, but when one actually confronts one, then the reactions that one shows are usually not driven by rational actions, but rather by a fear of the unknown or of death. Fear is not only psychologically constructed but also socially constructed, generating 'reckless emotional reactions in the masses, which then find expression in racism and revolt' (Maffettone, 2021, p. 83). There is no way to provide a deterministic set of guidelines to predict human behaviour during times of crises, because the human brain is an unpredictable entity, and 'brains give rise to our ability to form relationships and make life meaningful [and s]ometimes, they break' (Kalanithi, 2016, 'In Perfect Health I Begin'). An apocalyptic scenario usually results in chaos, like the one that India, and especially the informal workforce, witnessed. It would be wrong to say that the general level of preparedness for an apocalyptic world-order ending event is uniformly prevalent across the globe. Certain societies are more prone to disasters and risks – such as Japan – and they devise and evolve their public policies accordingly. Such societies often internalise risk prevention because of the kind of geographical, social, and political conditions within which they are located (Alberg, 2017). However, that being said, it is expected that provided the kind of society that has been constructed through years of neoliberal and capitalist reforms, which have advocated in favour of a continuously diminishing state while leaving out more and more sectors open to international private finances to extract profit (Chandrashekhar & Ghosh, 2002), many of which work on the basic principle of cheap surplus labour exploitation that is available in the Global South.

The condition of the marginalised sections who form the source of cheap surplus labour has worsened with time, more so because the world today does not only face risks from the natural world but also often from man-made artefacts. Technology has made life easier for many, but it has also come with its own set of risks such as pollution, substandard living, conditions, and accidents (Roeser & Asveld, 2009). These have come to adversely affect the powerless populace. Clarke notes in this regard:

> The Immense destructiveness of technological weaponry, foreseen [by science fiction writers such as H. G. Wells], became apparent to all during the First World War. One of the many reactions to that conflict was the sudden shotgun wedding between the function of future-warfare and the tales of an end to civilization or to all life on earth.
> (Clarke, 2000, p. 21)

When COVID-19 emerged, the fear of such an end to civilisation turned into a concrete reality for many. In the pre-twentieth century world, the human society was confronted more by natural disasters such as earthquakes and floods. However, since the twentieth century, the human society has also been confronted by the possibilities of man-made disasters emerging out of rapid technological development (Daley, 2010). The nature of disasters and the theories based on them have also had to undergo significant changes, which have also caused a change in the way disasters impact societies and the responses that the society and the state show towards them. As Walter Scheidel argues:

> In premodern, agrarian societies, plagues levelled by changing the ratio of land to labor, lowering the value of the former . . . and raising that of the latter. . . . This served to make landowners and employers less rich, and workers better off, than before, lowering inequality in both income and wealth . . . demographic change interacted with institutions in determining actual shifts in prices and incomes.
> (Scheidel, 2018, p. 292)

Apocalyptic events are never equal in nature, but they rather tilt in favour of those who can articulate their self-identities in a manner which reduces their vulnerability, both financially and socially. There are not many who would have found hope in such a situation. However, there are a few who have found apocalyptic events such as nuclear wars and pandemics being the basis of a future egalitarian society. Juan Posadas, the Argentinian Trotskyist thinker, was one of them. Posadas argued that instead of thinking about the destruction that events such as an atomic war might bring, the anti-capitalist class should strive to use the war for its own benefits because 'as a class, the proletariat feels secure in history' (Posadas, 1972, p. 11).[1] Posadas (1979) believed in a 'world process of development' according to which there would be an accelerated collapse of the capitalist world order. Wars are some of the most important examples of disasters available to mankind – one that is not caused by natural issues but rather a result of the ways in which foreign policies and resources are managed and directed by the state. According to Posadas:

> War is a necessity of capitalism. It is part of capitalist competition and the accumulation of capital. It does not intervene directly

in commercialisation but in production and profit, because the arms industry constitutes more or less 20% of production in big capitalist countries.

(1978a, p. 1)

The processes through which Big Pharma benefits out of pandemics such as COVID-19 is by completely ignoring the natural world's limitations and continuing to exploit it (Wallace, 2016). COVID-19 has witnessed a dramatic rise in the prices of medicine globally, with newer treatments set to be priced higher than the existing ones, which largely depend on widespread vaccinations, along with an associated political pressure on those in power to intervene (Rowland, 2021, January 17; Lopez, 2022, March 24). It had already been reported in 2021 that once the pandemic's immediate threat is over, Pfizer was already eyeing to charge higher rates for its vaccines (D'Amelio, 2021, February 23). India has not been spared of this as well, with a price increase of 180% observed in the months of February and May in 2021 (Das, 2021, May 5). In the context of India, the Health Ministry had made it clear that the government cannot effectively control the price rise of essential drugs (News18, 2022, April 4). Before the pandemic became a reality, there were claims that the kind of controls that the Indian government had been putting up on the prices of essential medicines, along with the dilution of IPR regimes and the imposition of strict price caps, were hurting the healthcare industry because they tend to discourage innovation (Khan, 2019, October 29). Innovation, however, has a highly neoliberal nature under contemporary capitalism. The relationship that science and technology share with the market forces and their associated fluctuations, makes innovations cater to only those who can afford them. For example, the costs of production for all the major COVID-19 drugs were much lower than what was being charged (Hill et al., 2020) – this particularly affected the capability of the poor and marginalised people to access them.

The COVID-19 pandemic has been used by Big Pharma as a weapon for extracting massive profits, almost as one of mass destruction, which were primarily aimed as a kind of cushion for capitalism, whereby they could be used for regulating the economic crises that were almost always imminent under capitalism, akin to Posadas's (1977) conceptualisation of weapons of mass destruction.[2] Posadas argued that disasters bring out the most militant sections of the anti-capitalist classes into action by pushing them to action on a socialist basis. Posadas argued, 'The war is not going to be the disaster which the communist leaders imagine but will mean a rapid revolution. The revolution is not going to be delayed . . . as in the last war but will be very rapid' with the support of the Soviets (Posadas, 1979, p. 21). Gittlitz (2020) brings forward the aggressiveness with which Posadas was insistent on the idea that mass-scale disasters such as atomic wars and other such catastrophes would in fact play a positive role in the transformation of the society. Such theories, however, often focus on history as a one-dimensional process: 'Posadas believed that the senseless brutality with which General Augusto

Pinochet overthrew a democratically elected government would inspire a global revolution that would help bring the imaginary Communist International of Masses into being' (Gittlitz, 2020, p. 139).

However, arguing that such a transformation would be a simple matter is problematic because the contemporary industrialised society is characterised by widespread risks in the society, with different subjective human beings reacting to them in different ways (Cranor, 2009). Apocalyptic events represent the pinnacle of this situation, with widespread uncertainty about the manner in which particular individuals and groups react to such situations. Because it is customary for individuals to react in a way that protects their interests in the best possible way in the face of risks (Zandvoort, 2009). The kind of transformation that Posadas had been advocating would require everybody – even within the working class itself – to be equally impacted by an event such as a war or a pandemic. However, in the case of any such warfare, or disaster – or a pandemic – it would be unlikely that everyone would be equally impacted. For example, the death rate due to Covid was particularly high among migrants, around three times higher than those who had been born in Australia (Davey & Nicholas, 2022, February 17).

The OECD (2020, October 19) also noted that immigrants, minorities, and other such marginalised communities often are disproportionately affected by a health emergency such as COVID-19 because of their increased vulnerability. Migrants, usually outsiders within a particular community, have been frequently hounded for being potential carriers of the virus into a locality or a community. The ascription of the disease to the *Chinese People* by some of the most powerful people in power also did not make matters better, but rather contributed to the overall racialisation of a public health emergency, which is again connected to the larger structural faults of the capitalist system as a whole (Wallace, 2020). Most visions of the apocalypse or the journey towards the unknown are guided by human fear of the unknown and the 'other'. Lisboa (2011) takes the example of *King Kong*, the movie, to make this point, where she argues that:

> [The] story of King Kong is among other things an unedifying translation of the long-standing Western fear that nature's representatives of unbridled, elemental forces (apes, savages, black men) desire white flesh (a blonde woman) and, if allowed, will violate it to commit the ultimate desecration: forcible penetration of the white man's property, leading to miscegenation.
>
> (Lisboa, 2011, p. 2)

With COVID-19, the situation was no different. Rob Wallace (2016) argues that any epidemic or a pandemic worsens when the natural entities, such as viruses, are attributed to a particular race or a creed or a community. Such notions of biological inferiority are intimately connected with the ways in which the human society, especially the dominant section of the society, tries to demonise those who do not fit directly into the mainstream biological or social paradigm (Gould, 1981).

Left-wing tendencies such as apocalypse communism or disaster communism have existed for quite some time. Many of these tendencies advocate using disasters as a window to push the society towards more egalitarian systems of functioning. Such theoretical tendencies are distinct from others primarily because of the immense optimism that they possess regarding mass crises, which to them often create the conditions under which the present state of affairs can be completely done away with paving the path to replace it with an egalitarian vision of the future. Juan Posadas, one of the first proponents of apocalypse communism argued that mainstream thinkers – both on the left as well as on the right – provide a pessimistic idea of peace *as we know it*. Posadas had argued:

> Certain communist parties pose the problem of peace in a way that is not correct. One cannot simply say 'peace, peace'. It is essential to proceed from the fact that imperialism cannot make peace because that is against its interests. One cannot then create the illusion of peace. We want peace, but to make peace social transformations are necessary.
> (Posadas, 1980, p. 2)

The Posadist ideas about social transformation were based on the assumption that a socialist society would emerge from chaos. Posadas had often been ridiculed and laughed at by many on the left because of the kind of beliefs he possessed regarding 'conceptual' entities such as unidentified flying objects (UFOs), and aliens. Posadas, however, more than anything else, was a theorist of chaos and the methods through which chaos could lead the way towards a *socialist peace*. His optimistic ideas on the element of chaos becomes clear in the way in which he compares noise to music:

> Noise comes first. But in the human being, noise soon becomes sound, and sound soon becomes the musical note. The musical note is sound upgraded. The booms and rumbles of nature evoke strong feelings, and the human imagination retracts these musically.
> (Posadas, 1981, p. 3)

The writings of Posadas often focus on the optimistic possibilities of scientific development, wars, peace, and above all, the impending capitalist collapse, and the socialist response to it. Most of his theoretical explorations have revolved around the idea that the thought of lasting peace goes hand in hand with that of social transformation. In that way, he was very dialectical in his approach because he refused to analyse peace as a one-dimensional project, but rather saw it as a concurrent process where both workers' resistance and scientific development could go hand in hand. This gets reflected in the way in which Posadas (1978b) praised the Soviet space project, and the ways in which science could eliminate human suffering under socialism by engaging with 'a quest that transcends life on Earth' (p. 3). Posadas (1968) also had high expectations on the nuclear science project and, as such, argued that nuclear science advances could end hunger quicker than other structural reforms. Posadas had argued:

> Human intelligence stops at no boundary, not even that constituted by the human relations that gave birth to it. Intelligence sees through what stands before it. It has the ability to surmise, infer and foresee. It detects objects beyond those that are visible, and makes relations with them.
> (Posadas, 1981, pp. 2–3)

However, under contemporary capitalism the problem is that human intelligence itself has become a commodity. The growth of commodity culture in the society is a serious concern for social policy analysts to take into cognisance when devising their policies in times of crisis. David Harvey (2014) has argued, following Marx (1976), that it is the rapid rise of the psychology of appropriation that has led the human society to a state where commodities have become the personification of who one is. This has given rise to a host of different processes in the society, such as the domination of speculative capital over actually existing human beings, which is most prominently visible in the urban areas (Harvey, 2012).

Even though inequalities persist both in the urban and rural areas, when apocalypse strikes, it would be the urban spaces that would be under attack in the beginning. Cities in India have historically never been known for their sustainability of their economic efficiency, and as such require huge amounts of funding to be resistant to large-scale disasters. Over the past few decades, Indian cities have been desiring better infrastructure due to increasing urbanisation and the constant increase of population. The HPEC for Estimating the Investment Requirements for Urban Infrastructure Services (2011) argued:

> Cities and towns of India are visibly deficient in the quality of services they provide, even to the existing population. Considering that the Indian economy is now one of the fastest growing economies in the world, and standards are rising, current service levels are too low relative to the needs of the urban households. They are low relative to what will be required to sustain the economic productivity of cities and towns.
> (HPEC, 2011, p. xxiii)

The report also claimed that the number of metropolitan cities with more than 1 million population has increased from thirty-five to fifty during the period 2001–11 and is projected to increase further to eighty-seven by the year 2031. According to a subsequent report prepared by Ahluwalia et al. (2019), the situation has not improved sufficiently from 2011 to 2019 with municipalities still entrapped within acute financial and infrastructural crisis causing issues with proper service delivery in the urban areas. As per the 2019 report, the municipal revenues in India continue to account for merely 1% of the GDP in India, something which has not changed much since the report prepared by the HPEC (2011). They argue that 'If the urban local governments were to increase their expenditure to the much higher levels required, they will need to borrow from the capital market, given their declining revenues and also the dwindling basket of revenues' (Ahluwalia et al., 2019, p. 5).

The capital market under contemporary capitalism does not work in favour of providing more autonomy to these local bodies because they often create power struggles within the overall capitalist system. They, however, are usually the first to respond to crisis of any kind. Even if one has to propose a radicalisation of the apocalypse, these local bodies – often constituted by the members of the community themselves – will serve as important agents of transformation because of their participatory nature. Communities in this milieu can provide a much-needed impetus because they can be 'key actors in preparedness, mitigation, response, and recovery ... generating a sense of possibility and a sense of communal action in addressing emergencies and disasters since they are the ones immediately impacted' (Otieno, 2018, p. 207). The critical question remains how to empower such communities. The vision of Posadas remains terribly myopic here because he constantly emphasises the important role that the state would play in the transition, along with the armed forces:

> [T]he leaders who create *Revolutionary States* originate from the capitalist regime. They come from bourgeois organisations, bourgeois institutions, the army. The army often takes a leading role in the revolution because it is often the only constituted power. This is how the *Revolutionary State* comes about.
>
> (Posadas, 1969, p. 14)

This chapter analyses such arguments in light of the COVID-19 pandemic. The first section discusses the subsumed nature of the state under neoliberal capitalism, while the second section analyses the idea of trading by municipal bodies and their relationships with the state and society. The third section takes note of these discussions and analyses the nature of disruptions faced by the public services during the pandemic. The fourth and final section discusses the ideas behind the theories of apocalyptic communism.

Collectivisation, the Neoliberal State and Disaster Communism

Cities are crucial to the overall growth of societies globally. Despite being a major contributor to the GDP, urban spaces are spaces where massive inequalities persist. Not everybody in these spaces have, as Lefebvre (1996,

2003) and Harvey (2003b, 2008) would have put it, *the right to the city*. The increasing urban population, however, is also putting an abnormal stress on the environment, which is gradually creating the conditions for a major urban disaster. This has got manifested in the way in which the urban spaces have been subjected to immense pressures, both from the capitalist developmental process and its associated social and natural degradation.

Pande (2020) argues that since by 2030, it can be estimated that around 40% of the population of India will live in cities, it is important that the government and the state, along with the people and the communities that they form, realise the critical importance that cities harbour within themselves in the contemporary times. Pande (2020) writes:

> According to a study . . . in 2010, India's cities could generate 70 per cent of net new jobs created until 2030, in addition to producing around 70 per cent of Indian GDP and contributing to near fourfold increase in per capita incomes across the country. India's future, thus, lies in its cities.
>
> (Pande, 2020, p. 47)

It is evident from the way the pandemic has spread around the world, which has followed a similar – almost identical – pattern of the routes that global capital follows under contemporary capitalism (Liu, 2020). Under such circumstances, exclusion from accessing essential services and public resources has come as a major cause of concern. Exclusion from accessibility to public services and public goods is a major contributor to their exclusion. Mundane things such as public modes of transport are critical for the marginalised population to experience the urban space and its associated economic and financial benefits (Mohan, 2019). When cities were locked down in March 2020 along with the modes of transport, as Mukul (2022) states, the most vulnerable populace lost access to the most vital public good which was necessary for them to reach their homes, i.e. the means of mobility and transportation.

Urban spaces are the spaces that are likely to be impacted adversely by events such as the COVID-19 pandemic. The ways in which urban spaces are designed are such that they are intrinsically not meant to withstand large numbers of people within them. However, with increasing and unplanned urbanisation, these cities have far exceeded their carrying capacities. The largest cities in India were the worst affected by the pandemic. In terms of both infrastructure and economics, the largest cities in India, which include cities such as Delhi, Mumbai, Hyderabad, and Kolkata, have been at the focal point of the crisis that the pandemic has brought to India. These cities are not only spaces of political grandeur but also spaces where the local bodies had to perform some of the most daunting tasks imaginable amidst a pandemic.[3]

Local governance in India has been an important issue of national discussion and policymaking. It does not only engage with civic issues but also deals with economic development, as local governance is critically important to an efficient mode of using the locally available material and human resources (Isaac et al., 2000). Because of its focus on local dynamics, an efficient plan for local governance must be decentralised in both form and content. Isaac and Franke argue:

> Planning [is] a multi-level process. Land and water management, small-scale production – particularly agriculture and cottage industry – and locally specific services are best planned at the local level. By contrast, centralisation leads to narrow departmentalism, causing duplication and lack of complementarity among the programmes at the local level.
> (Isaac and Franke, 2000, pp. 14–15)

Municipal collectivisation is often invoked to be an important option to achieve these aims. The parliamentary left, including some of the trade unions in most countries, has been extremely vocal about the need of municipal collectivisation (Towler, 1909). Municipalisation, according to the revolutionary left, largely forms a part of the broader strategy of social transformation, and as such analyse municipalisation as a part and parcel of the development of capitalism. To most revolutionary socialists, municipal control over resources is the base upon which an international socialist tendency can be constructed. They advocate in favour of socialisation and nationalisation of all resources at a local municipal level, which potentially construct the ground for complete public ownership of all means of production. Public ownership, over time, can lead to increased participation of the marginalised populace in matters of governance rather than merely being supervised individuals. The focus on effective participation can be best transmitted through forms of egalitarian local administration functioning according to a democratically elected and accountable mode of governance (Debray, 1971).[4] The services delivered through the publicly funded resources:

> are superior to those delivered by the private sector because they ensure public accountability. Public input to the decision-making process and the fact that those making decisions are elected representatives who never answer to residents constitute the essence of public accountability. Such *accountability* is often offered as a justification for a municipality's involvement [in various essential sectors.]
> (Moses, 2022, p. 23)

Mere participation can never be a solution. As Isaac et al. (2000) note, the key point is the idea of accountability of the representatives to the people who elected them. Debray (1967) had argued that, if the Cuban revolutionaries under the leadership of Fidel Castro and Che Guevara had read about the Maoist revolution in China, it would have been highly probable that they would have been unable to perform the Cuban Revolution in 1953 – because the fetish with models is characteristic of all forms of revolutionary upheaval. The same goes for municipal egalitarian proposals in India. During the COVID-19 pandemic, Kerala heavily relied on the Cuban model, the success of which has only been partial. The existence of a left-wing municipal reform-based government within a democracy which largely ascribes to be the neoliberal model of authoritarian capitalism creates certain issues for the efficient functioning of a municipality moving towards socialistic governance at the local level. However, that being said, it is of course true that the control over services by municipalities often results in cheaper costs associated with the services and commodities (Darwin, 1903; Barker, 1946).

The models of *Local Administrative* Socialism, as W. G. Towler, the secretary of the London Municipal Society in 1909, iterated, 'has ceased to be an occasional topic for academic discussion in literary and debating societies, and the subject of loud-voiced oratory and turbulent imagery in our public' spaces (Towler, 1909, p. 1). The fact that the word 'socialism' still resounds, either positively or negatively, with a wide section of the people had been aptly exhibited during the lockdown imposed by the central and state governments in India – where a great proportion of the marginalised section of India's population suffered from hunger and deprivation at levels much higher than the one that they had experienced in their normal everyday lives before the COVID-19 pandemic.

The range of problems that urban governance faces in India is multifaceted, which span from financial incapability to administrative inefficiency. The per capita expenditure of municipalities in India, as of data from 2012 to 2013 Financial Year, is estimated at Rs 3,116. This also includes the per capita revenue expenditure and capital expenditure of Rs 1,986 and Rs 1,130, respectively (Mohanty, 2016). According to Bhavsar, Tiwari and Deshpande (2020), the uneven and often disproportionate allocation of resources across different municipalities in the country has resulted in municipalities being unequally equipped to engage in carrying out their supposed functions, something that has also been highlighted by Ahluwalia et al. (2019). The crucial issue of resource allocation and finances was taken up by the government of India in 2013 (Working Group of State Urban Development Secretaries, 2013).

The issue of public control over resources under these circumstances naturally became one of the most important and critical issues. One of the important aspects of municipal socialism is its relationship with municipal trading – a governing system under which local municipalities actively engage in commercial activities. There have been multiple debates on municipal trading with the Independent Labour Party (ILP), the Social Democratic Federation (SDF), and the Fabian Society led by people like Bernard Shaw and Sidney Webb, actively supporting municipal trading (Darwin, 1903). The question of municipal trading, something which occupies an important part of this chapter, is directly related to the finances that a municipality requires for effective functioning. In India, municipalities and ULBs have historically suffered from issues surrounding underfunding. According to Mohanty (2016), the:

> [The contemporary] revenue base [of municipalities] is narrow, inflexible, and non-buoyant. Ironically, the ratio of municipal taxes to combined central and state taxes has gone down from 2.11 percent to 1.79 percent between the two years. These trends are disturbing as urbanisation is increasing, so also is the contribution of cities to GDP.
> (Mohanty, 2016, p. 21)

The 74th Constitutional Amendment Act, or the *Nagarpalika* Act, which was introduced in 1992, regularised elections to urban municipalities, institutionalised certain affirmative actions pertaining to these bodies, and granted some financial and economic powers to the ULBs (Prasad & Pardhasaradhi, 2020). It provided a constitutional mandate for the decentralisation of governance in India by creating local self-governmental units at both urban and rural levels (TERI, 2010). Through this amendment, the ULBs were provided with crucial powers in the spheres of sanitation, public health, water provisioning, and so on. (Hamid, 2004). The constitutional amendment, though extremely important, faced problems concerning the differences which existed between the strengths of different municipal bodies across the country. The amendment was brought in to reform the ULBs' 'weak institutional framework, functional fragmentation, inadequate finances, absence of space for citizens' voice in governance, lack of professionalism, low public image, etc.' along with the lack of 'vibrancy and . . . inadequate devolution of powers, functions and finances', which often stemmed from the overarching powerful nature of the state (Prasad & Pardhasaradhi, 2020, p. 2).

The state should be, as Mander (2019) argues, formed on the basis of large-scale social solidarity where the state is supposed to care for every individual. Till the early 1990s, the national private sector still depended upon the government for support, but things changed drastically when the economy was opened up to the entire globe for investments. This created notions of achievements where individual efforts and the formation of an achievement-based society took precedence over the social structuring necessary for ensuring the transformation of efforts into achievements for the marginalised population (Mander, 2019). Correspondingly, while India has progressed economically, the most marginalised and vulnerable people of India did not get to experience the full ramifications of that progress. Privatisation usually puts this project of social solidarity in jeopardy. The term 'privatisation' typically refers to the processes in which 'the state sells its assets to a private company, along with all of the maintenance, planning and operational responsibilities that these assets entail' (McDonald & Ruiters, 2005, p. 14). After 1991, the rampant privatisation of the Indian economy and the public services has excluded many people from accessing the same and has created fertile grounds for disaster capitalism to emerge in times such as the COVID-19 pandemic. And the issue with disaster capitalism is that it creates a situation where the struggle for mere survival – a limiting case for human beings in the contemporary society – becomes the most important, and in many cases the only struggle that they have to necessarily engage in (Trimble, 2019). COVID-19 exhibited that this stands true even today.

One of the major debates following the crumbling of the healthcare infrastructure of the country is the usage of community monitoring. Under the National Rural Health Mission (NRHM) in India, community monitoring has been implemented at the pilot stage in nine states, out of which in seven states it still remains at the pilot stage except Tamil Nadu and Maharashtra where NGOs constructed mechanisms through which community monitoring could be taken forward (Priya, 2018). The benefits of community monitoring are diverse. They can help in the implementation of policies required for ensuring good health for the underprivileged and marginalised sections (Flores, 2016). If health emergencies such as the COVID-19 pandemic have to be effectively countered, then such communities need to be empowered. In doing so, it must be kept in mind that community monitoring should not be allowed to transform itself into community surveillance.

The propensity of monitoring mechanisms being converted into surveillance mechanisms has increased manifold during the COVID-19 outbreak, with state-sponsored and digital surveillance methods being rendered mainstream. Surveillance by the state was often portrayed to be a boon in the services of mankind, without going through the perils that it entails within itself in a post-pandemic scenario. Such kinds of surveillance enabled the use of digital connections to further the commercial profit: '*It revives Karl Marx's old image of capitalism as a vampire that feeds on human labour, but with an unexpected turn. Instead of labour, surveillance capitalism feeds on every aspect of every human's experience*' (Zuboff, 2019, 'Home or Exile in the Digital Future', emphasis self). Dismantling such surveillance models that have emerged and become normalised during the pandemic will not be a very easy task. While most civil rights activists have argued that the usage of these surveillance technologies should be timebound and relinquished once the threat is over, it is unlikely that the state will hear them because the technology-enabled state is beneficial to the state-form, which has in recent times been mounting increasing attacks on the privacy of the citizens (Faizal & Rahman, 2020, May 14).[5] In this day and age of big data, there can be innumerable uses of the data that these surveillance mechanisms can generate, which are often managed or developed by corporate actors or with the help of corporate firms.

For corporate businesses, the public sector and its associated services does not hold much promise. And, since the state today is inseparable from the market under neoliberalism, it becomes imperative for those interested in an egalitarian and more equitable future to understand the complex relationship between the state and the market under neoliberalism. David Harvey (2005) argues that the main focus of the neoliberal state remains in the process through which businesses can develop and investment can be boosted, with the neoliberal state trusting 'the integrity of the market and the solvency of financial institutions over the well-being of the population or environmental quality' (p. 71). When any form of socialism or communism talk about the desirability of a state-form or even a community-form, or for that matter, any higher administrative form emerging from within a disaster, it necessarily carries within itself the problems associated with vanguardism (Deb Roy, 2022a). Posadas (1969) analysed the establishment of the Revolutionary State as a stage of development that falls in between the Workers' State and Socialism.

Posadas argued that once the workers' state has been established, it could move towards becoming a revolutionary state with the expansion of science and technology. In addition to his undialectical approach towards science and technology, which the chapter will focus on, Posadas' vision was also myopic in terms of the roles that he assigned to the state. Posadas (1969) argued that the 'Revolutionary State' could steer the society towards an egalitarian future, even if their policies and governmental actions have nothing do with the working class. The Revolutionary State to Posadas:

> is not a new form of State. It is a manner of transition between the capitalist State and the Workers State. It is the form taken by world power dualities in specific countries. You could say that it is a form of dual power where proletarian power does not figure. The leaders come from capitalism, but they can be influenced.
>
> (Posadas, 1969, p. 11)

The uncritical analysis of leadership that Posadas exhibits was also one of the fundamental aspects of the problems associated with municipal socialism. Both of these tendencies do not question the fetish of the 'leadership' – which under apocalypse communism of the kind that Posadas argued in favour of posits the formation of a hyper-vanguard kind of an entity that is supposed to be superior to the general masses. The ways in which such tendencies rest upon the *so-called representatives of the people* have to be critically evaluated once the pandemic has ended. This is because the pandemic has exhibited the immense power of mutual aid and mutual collectivisation can provide during times of crisis, which works through voluntary participation, self-help, and building relationships between a wide range of movements based on the needs of the actors involved (Spade, 2020). Mutual aid, albeit with its own limitations, attempts to do away with the differences that are created between the leaders and the led, which are related to how one conceptualises the relationship between the base and superstructure within any social movement and in the society in general. Dissolving the distinction between base and superstructure in the society tends to be too negligent of the material conditions of human existence producing accounts which are 'counter . . . to the revolutionary materialism of Marx' (Dunayevskaya, 1973, p. 163).

A complete dissolution of the differences between the base and superstructure, as it had happened under Mao's leadership in China, tends to create alienated subjectivity that fails to consider the actual objective material conditions thus failing to evolve into a 'revolutionary humanist subjectivity' (Dunayevskaya, 1973; Anderson, 2021, p. 331). This humanist subjectivity has to be the base of the opposition towards all forms of 'extra human' abilities of a certain agent (Trimble, 2019, p. 24), which apocalyptic visions often present. COVID-19 also was no different. Mutual aid solutions to the problems caused by COVID-19 were proposed as potential solutions to the crisis brought in by the virus. Mutual aid solutions provided avenues where survival could be performed in conjunction with transformative changes in the society (Spade, 2020).

The supposedly supernatural ability of the virus makes it a potent killer, one that can feed upon the human fear of the unknown. As Kempner (2014) describes, the *hyperreal* overcomes and dominates over the real, only in this case, the hyperreal is indeed a real threat. The only way to counter this *real* threat is through a principle of collectivism, which proposes to build bridges between the individual and the collective. However, administrative modes of performing the same have to evolve beyond the narrow confines of administrative determinism of any kind. Ideas such as municipal collectivisation in the context of a disaster can only work when the conditions for the same have been created through years of non-capitalist policy reforms, which constitute the basis upon which an egalitarian collectivist model can be implemented. Such a model requires a dialectical approach towards everything existing, which most egalitarian tendencies after Marx lacked profusely. Juan Posadas (1978a) believed that automation and the improvement of technology would be important allies to the socialist vision of development on a global scale. Mitchell (2007), on the other hand, relates automation to the growing neoliberal apocalyptic tendencies that have become mainstream under contemporary neoliberalism. Bastani (2020) believes that the rapid rise in technological inventions and the corresponding political changes around them where labour itself will become redundant and automated luxury will be the primary driver of the society. However, Bastani focuses on a highly optimistic view of modern technology, one that is very difficult to be envisaged in the way that capitalism has been using technological development.

Technologies are not alien elements which are introduced into the society, but rather socially shaped having their own socio-political, economic, and cultural implications on individuals and communities (Mackenzie and Wajcman, 1999). The influence of technological innovations facilitates the integration of everyday life into a 'technological milieu', where objects previously seen as only appendages to social existence become essential artefacts influencing the rhythm or style of human existence (Lefebvre, 2002, pp. 74–75). Many such technological equipment often restrict the freedom of movement of the individuals and allow them to utilise their private spaces by making them completely segregated from the overall social space. Such technologies often act like individuals who provide not only physical comfort to their users but also provide mental security, akin to that of human beings (Latour, 1987) especially with some of these technologies becoming important actors in the fulfilment of everyday lives under capitalism (Greenfield, 2017).

Technology, as Dunayevskaya (1958) notes, was analysed and perceived differently by different individuals depending on the hierarchical structure to which they belonged (Dunayevskaya, 1958, p. 268). She brings out the worst aspects of the work that capitalism has put machines to, such as putting workers out of work and increasing their insecurities. Dunayevskaya (1958, p. 269) predicted the way in which technology and automation could divide the working class based on their knowledge of the machines, which were finding space in the capitalist production systems. The world that one inhabits today is a world where economics, and primarily mainstream economics, has established itself firmly as the only science and theory of the society, such that a nation or a society's progress has begun to be measured only through certain goals, measurements, and comparisons with others (Mitchell, 2007). The growth of the idea of quantifiability has been so rapid and extensive that even minor changes in the way certain sectors behave are measured in numbers and not in terms of the humanitarian quality that they propose. For example, the AAP has introduced a variety of schemes to cater to the basic healthcare needs of different communities in Delhi. Schemes such as *Delhi ke Farishtey* (Angels of Delhi), which effectively pays people a sum of Rs 2,000 to bring victims of road accidents to hospitals, have been very successful, and it is estimated to have saved the lives of around 16,000 people (Express Healthcare, 2021, March 10). It can be said beyond reasonable doubt that if the reward were not offered, then the scheme would not have met with the success that it has achieved.

Such events are located within the conflict between the 'I' and the 'We', and how the 'I' replaces the 'We' in the contemporary society, creating a psycho-social condition where power has been directly connected to space furthering the continuity of the *ego* (Han, 2019). This also creates innumerable hurdles for collectivist models of social cooperation. Such a replacement of the 'us' with 'me' affects the ways in which private solutions are posed as the only viable solutions towards issues, which then subsequently permeate across the society: 'Adoption of private solutions is now at both individual and institutional levels, at the top of the income pyramid, in the middle and even in the lower quintiles' (Aiyar, 2020, p. 36). There is no doubt that ideas such as municipal collectivisation can help in countering the effects of COVID-19. But at the same time, it is important to realise that municipalities themselves have been severely constrained in recent times, both financially and socially, as monopoly capital transformed the market into an omnipresent reality where everything has to be bought from the market – from the paracetamol that helps one to reduce body temperature to the oxygen that is required to save it.

The Question of Municipal Trading

The question of services has come to be a central one in the context of COVID-19. There is widespread scepticism among social scientists that the service sector will be uniquely impacted by the pandemic, which will require certain structural and functional changes (Lee & Han, 2021). In the context of India, the medium- and small-scale industries have been severely impacted by the pandemic, which has had an adverse impact on Dalits and people from other marginalised communities, especially the women who own and are employed by these small-scale industries (Singh et al., 2021). COVID-19 has particularly affected those industries who have been unable to digitise themselves. Large-scale digitalisation is already causing numerous issues with firms who do not have the infrastructure in place and as such are failing to respond adequately to the crisis (Xiang et al., 2021). Without any form of community assistance, most businesses, especially those that are small, are set-to be tremendously impacted by this massive digitalisation. The local bodies can be instrumental in providing the support that these businesses require in building up robust technological systems and ensure that the small businesses continue to function during and after the pandemic.

The relationship between the state and local governance is a complicated one in India. The Indian administrative structure is plagued by discontents between the state and the lower forms of administrative units, such as municipalities and panchayats. When disasters strike, it is usually the state that assumes a central role in the provisioning of services. The fundamental problem in this case is that the local bodies are starved off of the requisite funds that they ideally require to transform cities into the engines of growth that the capitalist world view proposes in the Indian context. Indian municipalities raise money through a variety of means. They are mainly property taxes, stamp duty, entertainment taxes, other local taxes, state and central grants, and the like (Raj, 2020, July 2). Municipalities are increasingly being maneuverer by the existent socio-economic situation to seek public-private partnership-based funding for some of the services that they ought to provide (HPEC, 2011). The report released in 2011 by the HPEC stated that urban areas contributed around 62–63% of the GDP in mid-2009–10, with industry and the service sectors contributing immensely to this. As a nation, the central government has been spending exorbitant amounts of money on urban development, albeit of a neoliberal nature. Shaguna Kanwar reports:

> The Ministry of Housing and Urban Affairs (MoHUA) got Rs 41,765 crore for the fiscal year 2018–19, a hike of 2.82% over 2017–18. The Smart Cities Mission, under which the ministry has announced 99 cities for central assistance, got the highest hike of 54.22% with Rs 6,169 Crore as against Rs 4,000 crore in Budget 2017–18.
>
> (Kanwar, 2018, July 30, Para 3)

Projects such as the *Mass Rapid Transit System* and *Metro Projects* are some of the areas which have received particular attention in recent times. However, only a negligible amount of this money goes towards the upliftment of the municipalities. Because of the way in which the urban administrative structure has been established, municipalities often find themselves at a disadvantaged position as far as the finances are concerned. The financial instability that the municipalities face in India has emerged out of the neoliberal mode of production and consumption, which has caused massive inequalities to emerge in India. This has already been stated in the previous chapters in detail. It must be taken into cognisance that the struggle against these inequalities takes place at an everyday level. Common people do not struggle against capitalism as an abstract concept, but rather against its concrete manifestations affecting their everyday lives (Mouffe, 2018, p. 39). And very often, people struggle through and against the local bodies, which gives capitalism all the more reason to keep these bodies under control by starving them off funds. There are numerous reports that talk about the disgraceful condition of the municipalities in India. The Working Group of State Urban Development Secretaries (2013) argues that even with constitutional reforms, the condition of municipal finances has not improved much in the post-1992 period. Financing of cities in India has not yet been developed to the extent as it has been developed in the Global North, such that:

> [The] responsibility for urban infrastructure still lies mainly with the states. Municipal bodies depend upon the states for the assignment of taxation powers, and fiscal transfers (including loans), and resort to market borrowing (albeit in a few cases), largely with state guarantee, for infrastructure responsibilities that are allocated to them. The tradition of levying user charges to cover even operating costs for infrastructure services has not yet developed in the country.
>
> (Garg, 2007, p. 108)

The HPEC (2011), a committee constituted by the government, argued that the ULBs in India are one of the weakest in the world both in terms of generating resources and financial autonomy. Under contemporary capitalism, the municipalities are undergoing changes with regard to their functioning and their position within the administrative structure (Teles, 2016). Municipalities globally are running into acute financial crises, which have made it difficult for them to function effectively as vehicles of public administration. Municipalities exist so that the residents of their respective localities can lead a 'good' life, especially in terms of their health and well-being (Jowett, 1907). According to Jowett, any socialist should hold the belief that:

> [The] public should own and manage every service which provides for the common good. He believes that all should co-operate to supply their common needs, rather than leave the work of providing those

needs to the chance operations of the conflicting interests of individuals, whose sole object is the making of profit.

(Jowett, 1907, p. 5)

However, any effective and sustainable 'socialist' project of any kind demands that the ones engaged within the movement have an ideological position, even if that is Stalinist in nature. Ideology is a major component of any socialist transformation. One of the major demerits of municipal socialism is that it does not propose any major ideological alterations within the anti-capitalist struggle, as such it does not advocate much in favour of the relationship between the reforms it proposes and the kind of implications that they might have or how they can be used with regards to the propagation of the revolutionary ideological consciousness among the workers and citizens of the municipalities. In countries where economic planning has taken a centre stage, such as Yugoslavia, there have been labour bureaucracies that have often displaced the actual workers involved in the process of production as the controllers of the process of production and regulation (Comisso, 1979).

When services are provided by the municipalities directly, there is a better chance of the common people being able to access those services. Especially in the domains of healthcare and essential services, municipalities can play an important role, as the COVID-19 pandemic has exhibited. However, to do that, municipalities, and other forms of ULBs require access to funds, *much more than what they have presently*. Budget allocation occupies a crucial part of determining how well a local body or community can resist public health emergencies such as COVID-19 (Hassan et al., 2022). The preventive measures taken by the governments across the globe such as the closure of certain public services, also put the communities, and in turn the ULBs, under greater pressure because along with the responsibilities entrusted to them regarding controlling the pandemic, they are also – to a certain extent – responsible for ensuring that the social and individual progress of the members of the community do not get affected by these strict measures. The extent to which municipalities can ensure that is getting further complicated with major corporations making tremendous inroads into the communities solving the issues pertaining to the communities.

Although the entry of corporations into local issues does not eradicate the relevance of municipalities in India because of their constitutional legalisation, it does reduce them to be mere spectators in the way in which the community is being managed. More often than not, in situations where the private bodies have gained prominence in the society, they attempt to bring in a certain standardisation of the services they provide, which they eventually use for more effective pricing of the services. Notwithstanding the standardisation exercise's eventual exploitative nature, this conforms to the dominant mode of social regulation under capitalism. Municipalities in India, on the contrary, according to the Working Group of State Urban Development Secretaries (2013), suffered from the absence of standardisation of services within the municipal bodies, which has not improved much even after the Nagarpalika Act's implementation.

Municipal trading, or in plain words the system through which municipalities and local bodies can engage in commercial ventures, seems to be a solution to this regard. Bernard Shaw (1908) advocates that municipal trading can offset the commercial enterprises which grow under industrial capitalism focused on extracting profit and interest on capital. Both Jowett and Shaw agree that, 'The importance of management as a factor in industrial success cannot easily be exaggerated; but management is nowadays as completely disassociated from ownership, and as easy to buy in the market, as machinery' (Shaw, 1908, p. 9). Shaw's argument about labour being merely a commodity in the market and as such becoming a tool at the hands of capital to exploit is in synchronisation with those of Marx (1976). Privatisation of public resources only worsens this situation. The current government in India is moving towards further privatisation of services by bringing in more vigorous private investments in the sectors of roadways management, railways, telecom, power transmission, aviation, natural gas, and the like. Since 1991, all the central governments have tended to bring in privatisation at various levels, but the speciality of the current government's move is the scale in which it is attempting to do so by using initial public offerings (IPOs) and divestment (Arun & Punj, 2021, September 27).

During the pandemic, such tendencies were blatantly visible in India. The public resources, which have been mostly financially deprived, have found themselves to be at the mercy of private bodies. For example, while the government has, in recent times, been finding it difficult to invest in healthcare, the profits reaped in by healthcare monopolies such as Apollo, Fortis, Narayana Hrudayalaya, Max India Limited, and Healthcare Global Enterprises Limited – whose total revenues in 2017 equalled 12,990 crore with a profit of Rs 1,890 crore growing by around 68.75% since 2012 – with an annual profit increase of 11.03% and revenue rise of 12.59% till 2017 (Jain, 2017, August 2). This becomes critical in countries such as India where nearly 6.3 crore people face poverty because of inaccessible healthcare according to the NHP Draft 2015. There have been increasing tendencies for private forms to partner with the state to make improvements in this area. The IT giant Accenture has the potential to enhance the infrastructure of the healthcare structure in the country by sponsoring around 5 million vaccine doses, donating around 1.5 lakh PPE kits, augmenting the capacities of around 22 hospitals and medical centres by supplying them with over 5,000 beds and 30 oxygen beds, along with other equipment (The Economic Times, 2021, August 25).

The same goes for other IT firms such as Cognizant and Infosys. Cognizant joined hands with the Maharashtra state government to provide 100 oxygen beds and other medical equipment such as defibrillators and patient monitors. They also donated Rs 60 crores and 92 lakhs for relief measures, which also contributed to the construction of a Covid Care facility in Mahalunge (The Indian Express, 2021, June 19), while also donating about US$ 2 million to

UNICEF India to aid in the acute oxygen shortage and medical service delivery issues, especially during the second wave of the pandemic (Mint, 2021, April 29) through its 'Operation C3' which translates into *Cognizant Combats COVID-19*. Infosys, along with other companies such as HCL and Tech Mahindra, has contributed to the relief measures during the COVID-19 crisis by collaborating with 172 hospitals in 34 cities emphasising the vaccination of the employees and the members of their families (Business Standard, 2021, May 25). Because the company did not suffer from major setbacks due to the pandemic, Infosys subsequently also increased its COVID-19 relief commitment to a staggering Rs 200 crore (Business Standard, 2021b, May 5) from the initially proposed Rs 100 crore (The Hindu, 2020, March 30).

Almost all of these major IT firms worked directly with the governments, both at the centre and in various states, during the pandemic building hospitals and providing critical medical support. While there is nothing wrong with private bodies helping those in need, the graver issue that remains unresolved is the complete apathy towards the empowerment of public services that the government's pandemic response showed. The government has been highly determined in divesting the public assets and using the money for infrastructural development (Arun & Punj, 2021, September 27). However, it is worth noting that public assets can be far more beneficial to inclusive infrastructural development if they are controlled by the local bodies because accountable local bodies can enable the widest outreach possible for the social and financial benefits that come from these assets. Administrative socialism, such as that advocated by Sidney Webb, Bernard Shaw, and other municipal (and Fabian) socialists, places a particular emphasis on municipal trading, especially within the sectors of health, education, and employment generation (Avebury, 1907; Towler, 1909).

Levey (1909) argues that the basic character of any form of municipal trading under municipal socialism does not prove to be threatening to established property because municipal socialism works competitively with the private monopolies in providing services and commodities at cheaper rates. Levey argues:

> Municipal socialism aims at the municipalisation of two kinds of human effort, the one economic, the other humanitarian, which though not wholly unrelated, are in the main distinct and to some extent even antagonistic to each other: (1) public ownership, operation or control of industrial functions, especially those which are monopolistic in character, such as water supply, lighting, street railways and telephone service; and (2) philanthropic improvement of social conditions.
> (Levey, 1909, p. 29)

Trading has come to be a central concern for fulfilling these objectives under contemporary capitalism. Some such as Lord P. C. Avebury (1907) have argued that municipal trading would, at the end, result in increasing municipal debts, as a result of which the cost of the services would increase. This would be detrimental to the interests of the workers themselves in the service of whom municipal socialism and municipal trading is aimed at. At the same time, this will make municipalities the direct employers of labour, leading them to be engaged in labour disputes like their private counterparts. Darwin (1903), on the other hand, states:

> Socialism and the desire for Municipal Trade are undoubtedly products of the same great political and social forces; the result, that is, of the increased power of the mass of the people, and of the great extension of the facilities for intercommunication of all kinds.
>
> (Darwin, 1903, p. 28)

To Darwin, the demand for socialism and that of municipal trade are intricately linked to each other within municipalities. However, Darwin acknowledges that socialists of the *advanced* kind and municipal trade advocates differ on the question of individual property holdings. Darwin, here, has classified individual and private property holding as one and the same. However, they are widely different in the sense that the point of critique of capitalism, by all tendencies of socialism, rests on the idea that private property benefits private expropriation, something that an individually held property may or may not do (Deb Roy, 2022). One example in this regard can be taken of the housing market in India. The aspects of housing and healthcare are related to each other. Housing enables one to reside within a fixed spatiality allowing one, in turn, to build up a community or be part of a community which can be critical in the construction of a healthy individual. Srinath Reddy argues:

> Health is often viewed as an individual attribute, to be enjoyed, tended to, and mended at a personal level. This perspective imposes the responsibility of ill health on the individual and also heaps the physical, financial, and emotional burdens of obtaining healthcare on that person. The role of a society's economic, social, and political systems in shaping the health of the population and impacting an individual's health is unsighted in such a blinkered view.
>
> (Reddy, 2019, p. 1)

The situation does not become easier with the rising inequality with regards to the condition of housing in India. As of 2012, India had an estimated shortage of 24.71 million houses, with around 49,000 slums and approximately 93.06 million people living in them (Ahmad, 2012). The vulnerability of the housing condition in India adds to the existing exploitation that marginalised groups, such as Muslims and Dalits face in their everyday lives in India. Proper housing has become absolutely essential during the pandemic, especially with the social distancing protocols. Sohail Ahmad (2015) has argued that the renters and slum dwellers have a poorer standard of living than those who own houses. However, as Ahmad (2015) correctly writes, the slum dwellers and renters more often than not get overlooked in housing policy frameworks. In 2012, the total wealth that Indian households possess was approximately Rs 350 trillion, with the richest 10% of urban households possessing around 50 times more wealth than those of the bottom 40%. The difference between the top 10% and the bottom 10% is skewed in favour of the former by almost 50,000 times (Mahambare, 2015, February 9). Municipal housing in conditions such as these can be extremely helpful. Schemes such as the *Pradhan Mantri Awas Yojana* (PMAY) received a massive amount of Rs 6,500 crore for the period 2018–19 (Kanwar, 2018, July 30), and its regional counterparts, such as the Dignity Housing scheme in Telangana, have failed to ensure proper housing to people. However, seven years after its initiation in 2015, the PMAY scheme as of 2022 can only boast of a completion rate of 60% in eleven of the thirty-five states (Gera, 2022, May 26), which though appreciable is not sufficient.

The PMAY, once an ambitious scheme to construct affordable houses for the economically weaker sections and the middle income group, was built on four options. These include *In-Situ Slum Development* (ISSR) referring to rehabilitation of slums through private participation, Affordable Housing in Partnership (AHP) with financial help of INR 1,50,000 from the central government, Beneficiary-led Individual House Construction/Enhancement (BLC) with a financial help of INR 1,50,000 from the central government to those who qualify to be in the EWS, and Credit-Linked Subsidy (CLS) which was designed to disburse loans from INR 6–12 lakhs for new housing or renovation (Kanwar, 2019, May 14). However, as Kanwar (2019, May 14,) has shown, the plan remains unsuccessful till date with a scheme utilisation of only 21%. Even within the successful percentage, a huge proportion has benefited only the middle and the relatively high income groups. As a report in *The Wire* published in 2019 states: 'Even with a focus on housing in the last few years, we have managed to construct only 18 lakh houses of the original 1.8 crore housing shortage. That is less than a mere 10% of the total urban housing needed' (Unni & Panwar, 2019, April 5, Para 5). According to research conducted by the Centre for Science and Environment (CSE) in Telangana, government-sponsored housing needs to be improved at multiple levels such as the layout, ventilation, heating mechanisms, and the like (CSE, 2021, December 26). And these aspects such as layout and ventilation had become central to accommodation requirements during the pandemic (World Health Organisation, 2021, December 23).

Housing and healthcare are related to each other, and it can be expected that the pandemic is only going to impact that relationship in a negative way. According to a report by Housing Research (2021), following the standards set by the WHO, the quality, location, and environmental context of housing plays a major role in determining the quality of healthcare of a community. The report further stated:

> Not only has the . . . global health crisis strongly reinforced the importance of access to healthcare, [but] the ensuing lockdowns also to

control the virus spread restricted people to stay at home, demonstrating the deep connection between health and housing. The lockdown, lack of access to quality living conditions and healthcare facilities, have further exacerbated the impact of the pandemic.

(Housing Research, 2021, pp. 1–2)

Because neoliberalism has converted the idea of good health into a commodity, it is only natural that health has become a driver of price fluctuations in the housing market. There is an increasing demand for detached or semi-detached housing because of the ways in which such housing has been related to better health, improved aesthetics such as gardens, and more space for working from home (Chesire et al., 2021) – issues which are central to the neoliberal professional middle class. Chesire et al. (2021) write that in London:

[A] post-pandemic stretching of the income distribution gave even more market power to the richest households. . . . They seem to have concentrated that power on escaping the effects of the worst impacts of the lockdown ad the pandemic and the increasing demand for home working most saliently by buying larger, more central houses.

(Chesire et al., 2021, p. 9)

One can notice similar processes happening in India as well. According to a report from JP Morgan (2023, December 7), housing prices in the United States are increasing at a pace which is the highest in over 40 years – a period which also included the 2008 global crisis. In New Zealand as well, the rising prices of housing has been a cause of concern for the Jacinda Ardern-led government (Hunt, 2021, March 29). The relationship between housing and public health is such that when one gets impacted, there is automatically a ripple effect on the other. Local governments, in addition to other aspects of community life such as public safety and urban planning, also play an important role in the maintenance of public health. Socialist municipalities ensure 'the health of the community by a code of minute regulations for the treatment of infectious diseases; and they . . . subsidise the local hospitals and dispensaries' (Crofts, 1885, p. 14). Public health, it can be argued, benefits immensely from local governance. Each neighbourhood in India is unique, and as such requires unique attention. The most important effect that municipal socialism *might* have in the Indian scenario is on the primary healthcare set-up. Priya (2018) argues:

A primary health care approach requires the design of health systems development (HSD) to incorporate, (i) centrality of primary-level care, (ii) use of appropriate technology at primary, secondary, and tertiary levels of care, and (iii) recognition of the determinants of health other than medical care.

(Priya, 2018, p. 25)

It is important here to emphasise that even though primary healthcare systems form the foundation of the healthcare infrastructure of the society, but that in no way remains the sufficient vehicle for ensuring proper health of all the citizens in the urban space, especially during a pandemic.

Municipal socialism is integrally related to the socialist usage of the laws and regulations established by capitalism. It aims at the complete obliteration of the middlemen and the private capitalist by extending municipal activities and power (Webb, 1889/1948). According to Webb, this can be performed by putting the municipality in charge of housing, infrastructure development, education, and public health. One of the methods through which the municipal socialists attempt to do this objective is by engaging in municipal trading. However, critics such as Avebury (1907) have argued that the municipality as such already has too many tasks to perform, and thus, it would be undesirable to put it in direct charge of any commercial venture. He also argued that municipal trading would eventually result in a loss-incurring venture which might also result in an increase of prices, thus adversely affecting the workers. This is partly because, as Barker (1946) explains, municipalities find it difficult to compete with private bodies, especially with the private bodies' ability to influence market prices. This can increase the costs associated with any project that the municipality undertakes. At the same time, there are certain tendencies within municipal socialism and its associated trading practices that could become the possible points of criticism, such as the issues associated with paying municipal employees more than those employed in the private enterprises – a point that has contributed significantly to the demonisation of the public sector in India.

Public Services and the Pandemic

Neoliberalism has caused an adverse impact on the public sector in India. India has historically been a nation that has often faced acute crises of basic essential elements such as food, water, and the like. Aiyar argues, 'The failures of public policy are at the intersection of need and entrepreneurship. Those who can solutions – where they find them and when they can pay for them – have already migrated to these private solutions' (2020, p. 27). Singh (2018) has stated that since the middle class, and specifically the urban upper middle class, dominates the flows of information in the society, it is often the issues which only affect them that get reported in the media. COVID-19 has brought in numerous analytical frameworks to the mainstream public discussion. It has not only enabled the problematisation of the peace that these discourses tend to create but also that of chaos itself. Questions such as *who benefits out of chaos* and *who loses out on peace* are one of the most prominent questions that the human society faces in contemporary times.

Capitalism that creates the conditions under which it becomes possible for private corporations to dominate in times of chaos (Klein, 2007). Large corporations play a global role in creating disastrous and potentially apocalyptic tendencies, both in India and beyond, leading to powerful nations dominating the discussion about climate change and other major disasters, usually asking, or coercing the smaller nations to adjust themselves (Narain, 2017). Corporations pay huge sums of money to keep themselves afloat in case a potential disaster were to strike. For a significant period, many researchers and activists spoke about disasters being the great equaliser. Disasters to many were:

> [The] one issue that affected everyone, rich or poor. It was supposed to bring us together. Yet all signs are that it is doing precisely the opposite, stratifying us further into a society of haves and have-notes, divided between those whose wealth offers them a not insignificant measure of protection from [disasters], at least for now, and those left to the mercy of increasingly dysfunctional states.
> (Klein, 2014, 'The Right Is Right')

This becomes evident in the way in which the housing crisis was managed by the state, where the government did not use the community halls and public spaces owned by businesses during the first lockdown but instead proceeded towards sending thousands of migrant workers back home with just four hours of time to pack their entire lives (MN, 2020, May 13). It would be a highly optimistic idea to assume that disasters create a level playing field for everybody.[6] As Steve Matthewman (2015) argues, disasters mean different things for different people, and there is no way that one can deny that. This is nothing new, especially in the context of India.

COVID-19 not only caused these older forms of exploitations to thrive and aggravate but also gave birth to newer forms of exploitations based on digital access to services. The major question to be raised in the context is whether it was COVID-19 that accentuated these differences, or the governmental response towards it. One of the new inequalities that COVID-19 birthed is in the realm of education and technology, and the relation between them. According to Chancel and Piketty (2017), the income inequality in India is the highest since the establishment of the Income Tax Act, 1922. The top 1% of the earning population of the country, whose earnings were less than 21% of the total income in the 1930s, 6% in the 1980s, now earn about 22% of the country's total income – the highest since 1922. With such widespread inequality, both economic and social, prevalent across the country, Dréze-Dréze and Sen (2013) firmly assert that mere economic growth cannot be the marker of progress of a nation such as India. Even though India's growth in GDP has been significant, raising from 3.7% in real GDP at market prices and 1.6% in real per capita GDP at market prices during 1951–81 to 7.7% and 6.4%, respectively, during 2003–18 (Panagariya, 2020), it is imperative to acknowledge that India is also among the most unequal countries in the world. The top 10% and 1% in the country possess around 57% and 22%, respectively, while the bottom 50% own only around 13% of the total national income (Chancel, et al., 2022). According to the *World Inequality Report* 2022, an average Indian earns around Rs 2,04,200 per year, while the bottom 50% earns Rs 53,610 and the top 10% earns Rs 11,66,520 – more than twenty times the income of the lowest 50%.

Amidst such a growing inequality, pandemics exhibit the power that public control of essential resources hold for the society. The complete collapse of the society during the COVID-19-initiated lockdown in the country demonstrated that the control of the resources by the public ensures equality in terms of distribution and usage by the common people. The community plays an active part in resisting this auto-exploitative tendencies which are inherent under neoliberal capitalism because the relationship between community and health is intimate. Municipalities can play a pivotal role here because by their very definition, municipalities and the members which constitute them at a representative level are a part of the community which the municipality serves. Crawford (1906) had argued, in the context of early 1900s Glasgow, that when services are controlled by public bodies, without being handed over to private corporations, they are maintained in a way that ensures a proper balance between the commercial viability of the services and still being as inclusive as possible without the interference of any direct interest of the people engaged in the delivery of the service.[7]

It is true that only 30% of the Indian population lives in urban areas, which is significantly lower than that of other countries such as China, Brazil, and South Korea. However, it is worth noting that 'India's urban population as presently defined will be close to 600 million by 2031, more than double that in 2001' (HPEC, 2011, p. xxii). This perceived, and possibly certain, explosion of urban population in the coming years has made public administration in India an important aspect of the broader national governance of the country as a whole. Public administration in India is divided into two components, one political and the other bureaucratic, with the former constituting of elected representatives and the latter mostly composed of permanent civil servants (Jalan, 2019). Effective forms of local governance are established through a proper maintenance of the different bodies engaged in governmental administration within the society (Teles, 2016). However, under newer models of capitalist domination, the inter-municipal cooperative models have begun to be threatened by competitive dominance of private bodies. There are also issues surrounding intergovernmental transfers occurring within the administrative structure, such as tax bases and tax yields of higher governmental bodies, and the sharing of these taxes with the local municipal bodies (Mohanty, 2016).

Neoliberalism capitalism often impinges on the efficacy that municipal bodies possess in the society in the sense that it often renders impossible the production of goods and services that lay adequate emphasis on the democratic formation of the enterprises, which ideally should form the core of municipalities (Cooke, 2008). The demand for furthering the power of the public sector, along with its associated nationalisation and ingrained egalitarianism is nothing new in India. The national liberation movement in India had paved the way for an egalitarian management of the national resources in the country. Ideologies such as secularism and public provisioning of food were often accorded important statuses. Chandra et al. stated, 'The basic pro-people or pro-poor orientation of the national movement and the notion that politics must be based on the people, who must be politicised, activised and brought into politics, also made it easier to give it a socialist orientation' (2016, p. 524). In independent India, public administration can play a tremendous role in this regard. Public administration, however, in a socialist sense, cannot only be about the law. Municipal socialism hinges on the belief that a smooth transition to socialism is not only possible but also imminent when the society is managed by municipal-directed public administration. It is almost as if 'progress consists in rescuing human affairs from the domain of chance and making them subservient to law' as Walter Vrooman (1895, p. 5) had once said. However, the deterministic opposition to municipal socialism does not gain much ground because human society has always been spontaneously creative in nature, such that the people themselves have given ascent to modes and methods of organising that have gone beyond the traditional norms set by the established order of the day. The Fabian Society in England was one of the many early socialist societies that advocated for more public control of avenues in Britain. Municipal socialism, as an ideology was widely popularised by the likes of Sidney Webb (1889/1948) and Bernard Shaw (1930) who referred municipalities as the fulcrum of change in society.[8]

In *The Manifesto of the Communist Party*, Marx and Engels (1848/1976) wrote about the importance of the political organisation of the workers, which far outweighed the logic provided by Fabian socialists such as Sidney Webb and Bernard Shaw. The uniqueness of the working-class revolution, as envisaged by Marx, lies in the fact that it was a social revolution led by the majority within the society, based on lines of class, in contrast to the bourgeoisie revolutions, which were basically composed of the minorities within the populace (Chattopadhyay, 2016). Regarding the highly debated concept of the relation between the party and the working class, the classical Marxist idea was very clear. For Marx and Engels (1848/1976), it was the *Communist Party* which represents the workers in the society, because forming a separate workers party would only negate their working-class roots. The role of the Communist Party, while working with the workers, was to raise the class consciousness of the workers. The true responsibility of such a Party was to strive towards the creation of a situation where the necessity of the Party itself dissolves.

The Communist Movement has to exist within the workers, not as a component, but as a totality in itself, for without the workers the movement would have no ontological basis in itself. The interventions of the movement in various societies can be decided based on the material conditions but, 'The immediate aim of the Communists is the same as that of all other proletarian parties: formation of the proletariat into a class, overthrow of the bourgeois supremacy, conquest of political power by the proletariat' (Marx & Engels, 1848/1976, p. 498). On the nature of political power, Marxism emphasised that political power was nothing but the sustained domination of one class over the other. During the course of the revolution, when the workers' movement would dissolve all existing class antagonisms, the political character would also be lost and a fraternal, non-oppressive, cooperative production-based society would be established. Marx argued that the working class should engage itself with the politics of cooperative production because it can potentially attack the very base of the bourgeois capitalist economic system (Marx, 1866/1985, p. 190). Marx also outlined the precautions that the workers' movement and the organisations therein should follow regarding the involvement of the working class within the cooperative movement, 'In order to prevent co-operative societies from degenerating into ordinary middle-class joint stock companies . . . all workmen employed, whether shareholders or not, ought to share alike' (Marx, 1866/1985, p. 190).

Forms of governance such as municipal socialism take root from some form of perceived radical realtering of the society. Shocks which have become the mainstream mode of governance (Klein, 2007) can be resisted by the effective use of local bodies formed out of a combination of egalitarian communitarian action and local administration centred on the well-being of the people. Contemporary arguments for municipal socialism are a result of the ways in which the left had responded to the crises caused by the Second World War, especially in Britain. Increasing trends of centralisation and policing had gripped the society after the Second World War (Stoker, 1991). For almost three decades after the Second World War, the importance of local governance has been highlighted both in economic and political spheres (Barron et al., 1991). And, when one talks about local governance, one also has to tread into the relationship between the society and the state. India, historically, has always had a weak state, but a strong social structure that made its effects felt quite prominently in the sphere of categorising individuals by their social attributes even though the state had deemed those social attributes to be obsolete (Das, 2002/2012).

Municipal socialism has been one of the many possibilities that exist in socialist theory and politics throughout the course of history to overcome the challenges of shaping post-war economies and societies. Under Margaret Thatcher, there was practically an 'enforced' characteristic of the state and the government, which culminated in the rise of a society that was highly policed in nature (Ewing & Gearty, 1990). When the state is administratively authoritarian, it is impossible for local governments to be completely free of authoritarian policies. Almost all major democracies in the world have had trysts with authoritarianism. India is having one at the present moment. Works by public intellectuals such as Arvind Narrain (2021) have exhibited that the contemporary situation in India is one where authoritarianism has almost made surveillance and policing look natural and completely justified to the eyes of a significant percentage of the population. Municipal socialism and its associated collectivism were constructed as a quest for the solidarity that human beings might show towards each other in times of needs and economic crises (Stoker, 1991).

Public expenditure, in countries such as India, has been a part of the post-independence plan for national development. Public expenditure was a key aspect of the freedom struggle and the vision of a post-independent progressive India.

> Starting with Dadabhai Naoroji and Ranade, the nationalists visualised a crucial role for the public sector in the building of an independent and modern economy. In the 1930s, Jawaharlal Nehru, Gandhiji, and the left-wing also argued for the public sector, especially in large scale and key industries as a means of preventing the concentration of wealth in a few hands.
> (Chandra et al., 2016, p. 523)

Rao's (2015) account of the history of the railways in India points one towards how the nationalisation process has worked in India. This process encompasses the formulation of the Indian Railway Board Act, 1905, which placed the railways under the jurisdiction of a union cabinet minister. During the period of 1924–44, the railways underwent a nationalisation process, and subsequently underwent a regrouping from 1948 to 1952, after independence, to bring the railways directly and totally under the administrative and financial control of the government.

However, Nehru was a pragmatic thinker. His mode of socialism was highly Fabian in nature, and as such did not confront capitalism directly. In a letter dated 15th of August 1949, Nehru argued that in Independent India, though the key industries would be a part of the state-funded public sector, private businesses would still be important for the nation to develop. As Nehru wrote:

> In our country, situated as it is, it is inevitable that the State should help in . . . planning on a large scale, even though a great part of our national economy be left to private sphere. But the State can only help people who help themselves and who bring a certain enthusiasm to the task. They must have a feeling that they are building something that is permanent, that, in fact, they are the builders of the new India.
> (Nehru, 1949/2015, p. 152)

Even though there was a certain progressiveness in the way Nehru articulated his vision for a scientifically oriented socialist India – in the propagation of which Nehru with all his limitations played a crucial role especially with his articulation of political freedom being related to economic emancipation – his ideas remained entrapped within a very bourgeois reformist framework

(Chandra et al., 2016). Both Jawaharlal Nehru and Mahatma Gandhi were not able to formulate a theoretical and practical plan to overturn the strong hegemonical influence that bourgeois ideology held over the Indian national movement. This becomes even clearer in Nehru's (1980/2017, p. 576) autobiography, where he argued that class 'war' and the confiscation of any private property without legitimate reasons were not in accordance with the ethos that the Congress practised and held dear.

There are certain marked differences which exist between public and private companies. Public sector holdings are usually more accountable to the general masses than their private counterparts, as can be seen in the cases of privately managed insurance firms and microfinancing companies which focus on the creation of revenue, as Chandra (2019) highlights. Contrastingly, companies such as the Life Insurance Corporation (LIC) of India were built upon the idea of ensuring social welfare and initiating inclusive infrastructural development in the country, especially in the sectors of power, sanitation, housing, transportation, and the like (Sahay, 2018). The demand for public ownership of such financial services and other essential services has always been somehow related to mass scale disasters wrecked by events such as industrial accidents, epidemics, and pandemics (Troesken, 2006, pp. 176–177).

Urban centres, which have been plundered by the capitalist desire to accumulate through rapid privatisation and a neoliberal drive of accumulation through dispossession (Harvey, 2003a), are in desperate need of communitarian interventions. Communitarian municipal interventions can help transform the ownership of essential services and goods from the hands of the few to the general public. This can in turn have an impact on the monetisation of such services for profits and could also play a role in rendering these services free of capitalist influence (Leopold & McDonald, 2012, p. 1840) for a post-pandemic future. Municipal socialism is not a revolutionary programme, and as a tendency, as Rustin (1986, p. 77) elaborates, it emphasises a socio-economic path that is focused on a 'left-wing supply side strategy' such as to ensure a general agreement upon the point that 'Unless the production of goods and services in key sectors is competitive, they cannot survive'. It does not oppose liberal restructuration, but rather argues for the benefits to be distributed favourably to the workers (Rustin, 1986), which gets adequately manifested in tendencies such as municipal trading and its supposed benefits.

Municipal trading cannot compete with the private sector under the conditions created by the neoliberalisation. The delivery of vaccines during the pandemic is an example of that. Bodies such as COVAX, a global collaboration of countries which propose vaccine delivery to deprived countries and communities, have been struggling to ensure their aims because it is almost for the public sector in most major democracies to ensure vaccines to the entire population without taking the help of the private sector (Gupta, 2020, October 24). The healthcare infrastructure of India has been characterised by a widescale privatisation since 1991. In 2017, there had also been discussion surrounding further privatisation of the sector in India (Sethi & Rao, 2017,

July 19). The elites have almost always supported the PP model, largely because it suits their own social and cultural agendas in the society. According to a report published in Business Line (2021, March 18), the PPP model can help bring in improvements in infrastructure, energy utilisation, education, urban development, tourism, and so on. In the sector of healthcare, PPP, as per the report by the President of GiveIndia, would help the government in ensuring healthcare to a large section of people by bringing in more expertise, finances, affordability, technology, and efficiency. The argument for PPP models in the healthcare sector get boosted by the fact that as of 2021, the ratio of doctors to every 1,000 people in India is 1:1444, while the WHO recommends a ratio of 1:1000. The PPP model in healthcare in the country has created a massive inequality in terms of accessibility and the quality of healthcare that people receive.

The current government in India, as of 2021, has been rapidly striving towards withdrawing itself from all forms of provisioning, including the essential ones such as healthcare and public provisioning of food. The current goverment:

> [relies] more on insurance-based health systems rather than universalisation and strengthening of public healthcare. As a result, what we are witnessing at the end of the day is minimum governance and complete abdication of its responsibilities.
> (Panwar & Ojha, 2021, May 25, Para 19)

During COVID-19, reports argued that, the PPP model worked very well in certain cities where the private sector accepted the bills provided by the government to the patients and helped the government in setting up oxygen banks, grievance redressal mechanisms, and so on (Times of India, 2021, October 11). However, in some major cities such as Delhi, the private sector was asking for bulk upfront payments from the patients to secure beds and services, in spite of which the beds available were often of substandard quality and were often not suited to the needs of the patients (Panwar & Ojha, 2021, May 25). The rampant privatisation of healthcare services in the country has ensured that a significant section of the populace has absolutely no access to healthcare services and is even ignorant of the ways in which they can access them.

Apocalypse Communism and the Public Services

The state and its role as an agent of development has been an important aspect of theories surrounding disaster or apocalypse communism. In the context of India, however, the state has often been equated with the public sector because of the overarching role of the public sector in pre-neoliberal India. The public sector in India is the culmination of Nehruvian socialism, which was the dominant ideology in the post-1947 period till 1991, which believed in the public provisioning of essential services and the government's continued role in ensuring the social ownership of the major means of production (Chandra et al., 2000). The contemporary society is a culmination of the ways in which previous historical revolutions, such as the Industrial Revolution, the American Revolution, the French Revolution, and the Russian Revolution, have affected the internal dynamics of the human society, raising questions about human freedom and its relationship with societal administration and modes of production (Dunayevskaya, 1958). The usage of bodies such as clubs, societies, and committees in generating newer tendencies within the old institutions during events such as the Paris Commune created conditions that enabled the marginalised sections to establish novel forms of self-administration, including bureaus of communication, coordination committees, and so on (Dunayevskaya, 1958).

Local governance, as Aslam (2007) notes, does not only refer to making laws and rules, but *'The objectives of local governance cannot be realised by passing legislations only. The related legislation is necessary, but it is not enough unless its spirit is translated into practice'* (Aslam, 2007, p. 51, emphasis self). Neoliberal capitalism makes it very difficult for municipalities to bring in effective policies for sustained self-government through a variety of measures. In sectors such as healthcare and education, the municipalities can play an important role. Because these are local bodies sharing organic connections with the communities, they can have greater impacts on the kinds of situation that disasters such as pandemic create within the communities. Many studies across the globe have proved that when essential services such as healthcare are managed by the publicly funded and controlled ULBs, they result in better inclusivity and accessibility for the general populace (Kuchibanda & Mayo, 2015; Søreide et al., 2019).

Lahariya et al. (2020) cite the example of Dharavi, the largest slum in Asia, to provide inputs towards establishing the benefits of the public healthcare system. The public health infrastructure in Dharavi, which is sprawling and congested, came under tremendous pressure because of the ways in which the pandemic progressed in cities like Mumbai. It is noteworthy to mention that, Dharavi has a population of 6.5 lakh, which roughly translates into a population density of 2,27,136 people per square kilometre within the region. Dharavi had been reporting up to ninety-nine cases per day on 8th of April 2021, which could come down to below five in May 2021. The Dharavi Model consisted of the 4Ts which referred to tracing, tracking, testing, and treating, a strategy – which received high praise from the WHO during the first wave of the pandemic in India (The Hindu, 2021, May 28). The report by the PTI, published in *The Hindu*, reproduces a statement made by Kiran Dighavkar, the assistant municipal commissioner of G-North ward, which Dharavi falls under in Mumbai: 'Door-to-door screening of people with symptoms, aggressive testing, regular screening and testing of Dharavi residents who work in different parts of Mumbai, including delivery personnel, industrial workers, helped to control the spread of the pandemic'

(Dighavkar, 2021, quoted from *The Hindu*, 2021, May 28). The steps taken by the Brihanmumbai Municipal Corporation (BMC) in Dharavi ensured that the number of cases could be reduced in that difficult terrain.

The response that Dharavi put forward towards COVID-19 made it possible for the area to have large gaps in terms of COVID-19 infections, such that it could be COVID-19 free from 17th of March 2022 to 5th of May 2022, which is exemplary considering the way in which Dharavi and other such slums are structured. The total number cases that Dharavi has encountered as of May 2022 stands at 8,653 with a death toll of around 419, according to the BMC (Business Standard, 2022a, May 5). However, the response that the BMC exhibited towards Dharavi might not even be out of the good of their hearts, but simply because Dharavi occupies an important position in the overall financial fabric of the city connecting major areas to each other (Yadavar & Agrawal, 2020). The response that most governments across the world demonstrated towards the pandemic comes in the backdrop of the importance that most governments lay on trade under the logic of capitalist globalisation.

Socialism within the municipalities is nothing but the use of the gradual degradation of the influence of finance capital during times of pandemics for the benefit of ushering in socialism at a local level with a prospect of expanding it to the wider society in general. However, under conditions created by neoliberal capitalism, municipal socialism of any variety is a difficult plan to be executed. Disasters such as COVID-19 are utilised by the forces of capitalism to ensure a steady sustenance and growth of capitalism in the post-COVID-19 era. The global supply chain of vaccines and the ways in which this supply chain aids capitalism in establishing, maintaining, and furthering social control at an international scale during disasters are examined. There is also a propensity to analyse such pandemics as being purely natural scientific in nature, while in reality:

> When serious infection disease outbreaks occur, many routine dimensions of everyday life can be thrown into disarray, an uncertainty, fear and anxiety are heightened, rapid changes are made, and restrictions are imposed in the attempt to thwart the spread of contagion.
> (Lupton, 2021, p. 14)

Neoliberal capitalism exploits this fear and anxiety and attempts to implement reforms that benefit private contractors who make sure that the common masses only see, hear, and sense what they want them to see, hear, and sense (Sexton, 2014). In bourgeois democracies, there exists a tendency that allows private contractors and entrepreneurs to greatly influence governmental elections and, in turn, the decisions that the elected governments take.[9] The quick coming-in of private enterprises to India post-1991 and the associated creation of an entirely multinational private financial structure became kind of a *shock* to the general populace, which increasingly saw itself becoming victim to the rising domination of financial power within the local administrative machinery. At the same time, it is quite natural that because of the ways in which the responsibilities of the municipalities have increased historically, which has resulted in the creation of newer departments and roles, there would also occur a creation of bureaucracy within these local bodies as had happened in the case of Europe in the early 1900s (The Times, 1902). Municipal socialism does not differentiate on the basis of the citizens' class, caste, race, or gender, but municipal elections in India do. Within municipalities, class and all of these factors plays a crucial role. Even if all the major public services are nationalised, class would continue to play an important role. Newton and Karran opine, 'the wealthier sections of society appear to make particularly heavy claims on local services such as roads, education, environmental control, and consumer protection, and may well do so for things such as parks, libraries and museums and art galleries' (1985, p. 65). Many conversations which the author has had with the informal workforce – both migrant and locale – in major Indian cities such as Delhi and Kolkata have confirmed that it is the wealthier sections of society, notably the new urban middle class, which benefits from most of the municipal reforms.

Municipal socialism as such has remained a highly revisionist paradigm. During India's pandemic response, municipalities faced the highest burden of the distributed responsibilities – orders regarding which came from the central and regional state governments. Analysing Tumbe's (2020) research into the relationship that pandemics share with human progress, one can get an idea of how the faults of the local governments usually result in increased chances of transmission of contagious diseases. This happens because when the central government makes a mistake, there is always an opportunity for local governments to rectify the mistakes. However, when the local governance makes mistakes and starts becoming discriminatory in nature, then there is usually no 'escape route' left for the marginalised population. Another reason associated with these is that because of the kind of people who contest in the municipal elections in India, who usually come from affluent families, they often carry with them sufficient financial and political clout to adjust state policies at local levels. For example, a proactive municipal council can make sufficient interventions to ensure that relief packages reach the people who need it the most.[10]

Municipal socialism was envisaged as something which was better than Statist Socialism (or State Capitalism as it transformed into in most of the scenarios). Sidney Webb declared:

> We threw ourselves with energy into the study and propaganda of 'Municipal Socialism,' the steady increase of which has resulted not merely in greatly widening the available experience of Collectivism, and in the placing, by 1919, of literally thousands of members of the Labour Party on Local Governing Bodies, but also in considerably filling out the vision of the organisation of the Socialist State.
> (Webb, 1919/1920, pp. xx–xxi)

It becomes evident at this point that both Sidney Webb and Bernard Shaw were unable to completely relinquish the fetish of the state form, and its supposed benefits. Cohn (1910, pp. 561–562) makes an important comment on the nature of municipal socialism, which is distinct from dominant state socialist utopian models. He states that the measures taken under such reformist models are actually part of the general ontology of the community. He also brings forward some instances from Europe where such socialistic tactics have been taken up by anti-socialist or non-socialist groups as part of their overall strategy towards community improvement uniting political factions over a common program (Cohn, 1910, p. 565). Klein (2018, 'A Solar Oasis') shows the benefits of such tangible modes of development in her case study of disaster capitalism in Puerto Rico, where such progressive initiatives could potentially generate a sense of communitarian solidarity amongst people hit by disasters, reinforcing a sense of belonging to their environment and society. The major difference, however, is that while state socialism usually remains an abstract notion to most citizens, municipal socialism is something that is very easy for them to witness, because it happens within their, as Lefebvre (1994) would say, lived spaces. In their everyday lives, common people do not struggle against capitalism, fascism, or neoliberalism, but they do so against the effects of these ideologies in practice. Sidney Webb, the noted Fabian socialist, argued that municipal socialism was the Fabian method of countering the demerits of state socialism. Local governance was something that the Fabians thought of:

> [As] organising production for the sake of the unemployed and as ultimately developing, side by side with capitalist enterprise, alternative factories and shops, which would, under the management of [Local] Councils, beat the profit-maker with his own weapons, at his own game.
> (Webb, 1919/1920, p. xx)

Organising the population through the municipalities is effectively a method which organises people based on their identities as consumers and not as producers. Every person within the municipality becomes a member of the same because of their identity as a consumer and not as a producer. In this regard, it is essential to emphasise here that everybody who is part of a society in most major democracies in the world is automatically part of a municipality as a consumer. Guild Socialism, on the other hand, focuses on the identity of the citizens as active producers. G. D. H. Cole's criticism of Fabian socialism – which can be almost equated with the views proposed by municipal socialism – was based on the idea that Fabian collectivism of any variety does not propose self-government of any social group, or the individuals therein. Instead, he advocates for a centralised welfare mechanism one that is not controlled by the workers and does not propose industrial democracy (Mukherjee, 1991), which was the core of the Guild Socialist tendency. The question of whether such professional guilds would have made affairs better during the pandemic is something that demands a larger engagement with Guild Socialism, which is beyond the scope of this particular work. The idea that was pertinent to advocates of municipal socialism was to put municipalities directly into their roles as organisers of the localities in which they were situated.

However, there are issues surrounding the extent to which ULBs and municipalities – even if they have all the good intentions of being more egalitarian in nature – can be distinguished from the dominant political and economic structure and ideology in the larger political society. To think that local representatives would be completely autonomous of all class interests would be a myopic argument. The response to the COVID-19 pandemic relied greatly on the public representatives at a local level. Even right-wing commentators such as Gandhi-Mody (2022) accepted that the presence of local representatives was critical to the overall success of the India's response. Even though Gandhi-Mody's narrative is almost exclusively based on the assumption that India's response was highly successful and scientific in nature, which people like Mander (2021) and Mukul (2022) have exhibited with facts that it was not. Her narrative is important because it speaks from the inner contours of the administrative set-up. She argues that the self-imposed curfew on the 22nd of March 2021 from 7 in the morning to 9 at night, was to enable the nation to prepare itself for the coming lockdown, which was supposed to be implemented in the coming days. However, the government did not consider that any public policy is only successful when there are sufficient resources at disposal to utilise. When there is an abundance of resources for the public to use, then the society moves in a particular manner, contrary to how it behaves when there is a resource crisis. The scope of this particular book does not allow an in-depth focus on resource utilisation. However, it can be said beyond reasonable doubt that the availability of resources has an indelible effect on the social characteristic that human beings possess. The social characters, in turn, that human beings possess are important aspects of the overall social fabric that they inhabit. Erich Fromm argues:

> [Social character is] the nucleus of the character structure which is shared by most members of the same culture in contradistinction to the individual character in which people belonging to the same culture differ from each other. The concept of social character is not a statistical concept in the sense that it is simply the sum total of character traits to be found in the majority of people in a given culture. It can be understood only in reference to the function of the social character.
> (Fromm, 1955/2008, pp. 76–77, emphasis original)

The idea of peace is an idea of immense contestation among the left. While revolutionary theorists such as Rosa Luxemburg and Sylvia Pankhurst emphasised the necessity of peace at all costs (Pankhurst, 1917; Wolfe, 1961), Lenin brought out the class nature of peace, one that was more dialectical in nature than either Luxemburg's or Pankhurst's. Lenin's (1915/1974) understanding of peace was based on an analysis of the class structure of the warring nation states. It is essential to mention here that though both Luxemburg and Pankhurst were excellent theorists and activists in their own light, their own ideas were not informed by a reading of Hegelian dialectics. Lenin's (1914–16/1975) reading of Hegel had transformed the ways in which Lenin theorised the issues of wars, nationalism, and the state. Similarly, disasters such as COVID-19 transform the ways human beings think and rationalise about their lives. Any vision of apocalyptic communism, or rather post-apocalyptic communism, can only work when one can analyse destruction as a dialectical process in itself, which embeds within itself not only the issues concerning the universal but also the particular, with a specific emphasis on the idea of belonging.

One of the major points to consider here is that when masses remain entrenched within conditions that make death a possible reality on a mass scale, such as those presented to the world during COVID-19, and especially the second wave of the pandemic in India, their daily routine often provides glimpses of the possible future course of action. It is true that conceptualising praxis as an essentialising factor creates the ground for fetishising the spontaneous action of the people in an undialectical fashion. However, as Raya Dunayevskaya (1980/2019) notes, movements from below harbour within themselves a unique sense of theory, such that they themselves construct newer forms of theory.

Conclusion

An apocalypse under neoliberalism would not be an event that proposes equality. Rather, it would propose the conditions under which human society would be left searching for the final remnants of humanity. Visions of apocalypses often entail within themselves ideas surrounding the complete extinction of humankind, and sometimes of the entire world itself. The risk of extinction as of 2009 was 3% per decade, and the estimate that civilisation as it currently exists will collapse at 10% per decade, or, put more simply, 1% every year, according to Wells (2009). And, the combination of capitalist development, technology, and pollution, and epidemics as well as pandemics, are all contributing to the acceleration of this process. The COVID-19 pandemic might be the warning that dinosaurs never received. As Wells argues, 'The collapse of civilization will be almost as deadly as extinction' (Wells, 2009, p. 5). Technology could not save the world from COVID-19, at least for a long time, and even when it did, it went along with the profits of capital and not with human lives.

Herbert Marcuse argued that technology under capitalism was no better than capitalism itself. Like capitalism, technology too:

> [As] a mode of production, as the totality of instruments, devices and contrivances which characterize the machine age is thus at the same time

a mode of organising and perpetuating (or changing) social relationships, a manifestation of prevalent thoughts and behaviour patterns, an instrument of control and domination.

(Marcuse, 1941/1998, p. 41)

Technology is an integral part of capitalism that has contributed to the production of what Marcuse referred to as being 'technological rationality' (Marcuse, 1941/1998, p. 44), which destroys individual rationality and makes human beings unable to critique the way machines dominate over the everyday lives of human beings. Under capitalism, technology is used by the forces of capital to create further alienation and oppression. One such example is the condition of healthcare in the country. Even when the private sector has been steadily progressing in the country, a large section of the populace has still succumbed to COVID-19 because of the lack of medical resources such as oxygen (Ghoshal, 2021, April 24).

All of these are happening in spite of the Bhore Committee Report – perhaps, the most important report in the history of Indian healthcare management – which states that 'No Individual should fail to secure adequate medical care because of an inability to pay for it' (Aiyar, 2020, p. 60). This committee, as Aiyar (2020) notes, focused on the crucial relationships between sanitation, availability of water, and the state of healthcare in the country, along with making an argument for increased healthcare expenditure in the budget so that every individual in India could have access to healthcare. However, as Kannabiran et al. (2021) show, the Indian state has failed to do so over the past 75 years but has instead, with neoliberal austerity reforms, ended up reinforcing further inequality and creating a highly privatised healthcare infrastructure which was easily dismantled when crisis came upon. The crisis has become further accelerated under the IPR regime, where capitalism depends on appropriation and building up models of ownership even within the healthcare sector. Das (2002/2012) argues that the neoliberal reforms enabled the people of India to think of themselves as active human beings who could function without the intervention of the state. He notes that the reforms were in synchronisation with the desire to:

decentralize decision-making, devolve power to the states, municipalities and panchayats and have people rely on themselves. This stood in contrast to Nehru's socialist vision that had prevailed during the past fifty years, with its emphasis on centralization, command and control bureaucracy and mammoth public sector monopolies. Socialism tended to destroy social capital because it made us depend on the government for anything. . . . People forgot that they could rely on themselves. And the best work of some of the NGOs has been to remind people on the virtues of self-reliance.

(Das, 2002/2012, p. 17)

However, the ways in which the individual has been constructed in India post the 1991 economic reforms demands a critical introspection. The individual has been created through a massive disinvestment in key sectors (Chandrashekhar & Ghosh, 2002), which also includes healthcare. The lack of funding for healthcare resources in India is such that:

> Over 9 lakh children die before they reach the age of five – that is over 100 per hour. The Global Burden of disease Report estimates that over 7.78 lakh people – adults and children – die of diarrheal diseases and 4.35 lakh of tuberculosis' which points towards poor health capacity and quality.
>
> (Aiyar, 2020, p. 57)

COVID-19 in India has transformed India into a country that has to face the stark reality that the reforms initiated in the country since 1991 have resulted in the creation of private healthcare infrastructure, weak community bodies, and a significant decrease in the incomes of a large section of the populace. Social co-operation would have played a key role in mitigating these impacts. Gurcharan Das argues that 'The rules of social cooperation are the rules of *dharma*' (Das, 2002/2012, p. 59). However, no social cooperation flows out of a vacuum, but is rather the construction of the society which the human beings, who are supposed to cooperate, inhabit (Dawson et al., 2018). It is true that during major disasters, people have been found to be cooperative, as Klein (2018) has also stated, but she also notes that things are worsening under neoliberal capitalism. At the same time, disasters, due to the nature of their impact under neoliberalism, also create a demand for more democratic and public control of essential services (Klein, 2018). During pandemics or a crisis which is based on a viral infection that is contagious in nature, the norms of social cooperation themselves get altered, significantly more so than in the event of an earthquake or flood. As Shah (2020) has elaborated, during a pandemic, when cooperation might itself become the cause of infection, such human conclusions might not hold much ground. Both disaster communism and municipal socialism do not address the contradictions, instead, they build upon them

However, both of them can be useful tools of analysis because, while both contain the perils of short-sightedness, they do not move towards the double negation. While municipal socialism emphasises the role of municipalities as governing bodies, disaster communism does that to the state-form, albeit in a modified way. However, such forms of non-capitalist or semi-capitalist structures are only the first negation of capitalist mechanisms. The method of absolute negativity as Dunayevskaya proposed, goes beyond this bare negation and calls for an absolute negation, which means doing away with 'not only . . . the old, but also [establish] the basis for a forward movement' (Hudis & Anderson, 2021, p. 27). Both these variants push human society towards a mode of non-autonomous dependency by putting forth newer structures of regulation or a belief in higher beings, as Posadas (1968) had argued to be the case referring to extra-terrestrial superior beings. Absolute negativity, as Hudis and Anderson state, not only means negating the external obstacles but also means negating the basis of all the internal obstacles to the path of human liberation – the very basis of value and commodity form – to move towards the negation 'for the positive is contained in the negative, which is the path to a new beginning' (p. 27). The narrow and limited logic of crude communism or other such forms of transcendence based on private property can only be overcome by a positive transcendence of private property. As Marx said:

> *Communism* as the *positive* transcendence of *private property human self-estrangement*, and therefore as the real *appropriation* of the *human* essence by and for man; communism therefore as the complete return of man to himself as a *social* (i.e., human) being – a return accomplished consciously and embracing the entire wealth of previous development. This communism, as fully developed naturalism, equals humanism, and as fully developed humanism equals naturalism; it is the *genuine* resolution of the conflict between man and nature and between man and man – the true resolution of the strife between existence and essence, between objectification and self-confirmation, between freedom and necessity, between the individual and the species. Communism is the riddle of history solved, and it knows itself to be this solution.
> (Marx, 1844/1975, pp. 296–297)

The abolition of private property in a humanist way does not merely mean doing away with private property, as the crude and vulgar forms of communism posed to do. That is only the *first negation*, the most important part of abolition is to move towards the *second negation* – the *negation of the negation* – ' "the permanent revolution" . . . integral to the creation of "new Humanism" "beginning from itself" ' (Dunayevskaya, 1973, p. 186). Human society under capitalism lacks the methods through which it can convert an apocalyptic event to an egalitarian one. Since the COVID-19 pandemic occurred at a juncture where neoliberalism has converted the state into a non-existent entity for the lives of many, it is almost obvious that most would embrace the state, as Matthewman (2020) argues, because it signifies for many a caring hand.

However, that caring hand often comes with the perils of state surveillance. Burke (2021) and Palaez (2020) both have written about the extraordinary response that Cuba has shown towards COVID-19 because of the ways in which it has empowered its local bodies and municipalities, which have played a critical role in the response towards the pandemic in Cuba. However, both of them have also noted about the production of governable subjects in Cuba through biopolitical control, which has also contributed to the process. It is customary to realise in the context of the current society that risks are often forcibly made acceptable to the society by political decision-making processes (Zandvoort, 2009), which mostly avoid dialogues with the marginalised sections. The process of emancipation starts when human society moves on its own, creating newer theories and newer *models* through its self-articulation of the situation, both philosophically and materially.

Notes

1. Posadas also argued, 'The present process is one of inevitable preparation for war by imperialism. This is going to require time, but war could break out any moment because it does not depend on the military preparedness of imperialism, but on the development of the world anti-capitalist social crisis. And this crisis will crush capitalism from every point of view. Capitalism is going to prepare and enter the war in the midst of revolution' (Posadas, 1979, p. 15).
2. As against the dominant left-wing perspectives, which more often than not advocate peace or rather a struggle between the classes situated within the warring geographies and social contexts, Posadas (1977) advocated in favour of the development of an anti-nuclear bomb, stating that: 'in front of any other weapon of mass destruction – an equally effective weapon will be found. We propose that the Soviet comrades study the means by which to reply to this militarily, and we propose that they prepare and mobilisations against such a bomb. No one can prevent it from being manufactured' (Posadas, 1977, p. 13).
3. Dighavkar (2021) argues in his book on the management of the pandemic in Dharavi that ULBs in places such as Dharavi in the financial capital of India face tremendous challenges in terms of finances and logistics, which adversely impact the public health scenario in these areas during times of distress such as the pandemic. He narrates how different actors, such as NGOs and civil society organisations, play an important role in safeguarding the people during a pandemic.
4. One can always take slums such as Dharavi as a reference point here. Dharavi had emerged as a COVID-19 hotspot in the heartland of Mumbai. In places such as Dharavi, where more than a million people live within 2.1 square kilometres of land – an area smaller than New York's Central Park – and with a population density of 3,33,333, measures such as social distancing and isolation are almost impossible to adhere to (Gulankar, 2022). In situations such as these, policies that are focused on participation rather than supervision often prove superior and more useful.
5. In terms of surveillance, there have been reports of, as Brar (2020, April 14) notes, the government using private sector tracing applications for tracking the individuals and then putting them into government-sponsored quarantine facilities. Aadil Brar (2020, April 14) argues that the rapid deployment of surveillance technologies is not a just an emergency protocol but also an indication of the ways in which technologies are being developed on an everyday scale by the state and corporates alike. The surveillance mechanisms deployed to track infections have already begun to be used for tracking and stigmatising sections of populations (Lyon, 2022).
6. Ambedkar, as Chinmay Tumbe, writes, wrote about how caste segregations make their mark amidst pandemics following an incident in 1943, 'It was reported from Nasik on 1st September that the Hindus of a village attacked an *Achchut* [untouchable] family; tied the hands and feet of an elderly woman, placed her on a pile of wood which was subsequently set on fire. All this because they thought she was the cause of the Cholera in the village' (quoted from Tumbe 2020, p. 41).

7 In India, as well, one example in this regard can be cited of the bank nationalisation policies of Indira Gandhi in 1969 (Ramesh, 2018a).
8 Shaw (1930) argued in favour of demanding an obliteration of the party system and replacing it with municipal governing bodies because he saw democracies managed by political parties as being unnecessarily chaotic – launching oppositions at policies merely for the sake of opposition – with party members voting for the positions of their parties regardless of the merit of the argument. Shaw believes that the replacement of the party system with municipal governance would ensure that 'the municipalities get through their work without excessive attendance . . . sitting all day and sometimes all night, . . . hopelessly unable to keep abreast of its business, and finds that it overworked ministers have no control of the departments they are nominally responsible for, and often no real knowledge of the work done by them, the effective Government being really the bureaucracy or permanent Civil service, which is unaffected by the Party system' (Shaw, 1930, pp. xiii–xiv). Shaw's argument makes sense only in the realm of theory because the realm of polity is where the actual social change happens.
9 Bimal Jalan (2005) argues that 'these coalitions of special interests ensured that the necessary change in the initial development strategy did not occur for as long as possible, and when it became unavoidable (due to external crises), it was slow and politically controversial' (p. 18).
10 Tarun Pithode (2022) writes about the process by which the response team worked at various district levels nationwide against the pandemic. Other such accounts of the bureaucratic management of the pandemic came from Kakani and DebRoy (2022) and Dighavkar (2021) regarding Mumbai and Dharavi, respectively. These narratives have provided some critical and much-needed insights into the way administrative bodies functioned during the pandemic, which focused on the coordination and exercise of local bureaucratic power in accordance with the directives passed on from the central government in Delhi.

References

Ahluwalia, I. J., Mohanty, P. K., Mathur, O., Roy, D., Khare, A., & Mangla, S. (2019). *State of municipal finances in India: A study prepared for the fifteenth finance commission.* Indian Council for Research on International Economic Relations.

Ahmad, S. (2012). *Housing inequality amongst disadvantaged communities in India.* United Nations University. https://unu.edu/publications/articles/housing-inequality-amongst-disadvantaged-communities-in-indian-cities.html

Ahmad, S. (2015). Housing poverty and inequality in urban India. In A. Heshmati, E. Maasoumi, & G. Wan (Eds.), *Poverty reduction policies and practices in developing Asia.* Springer.

Aiyar, S. (2020). *The gated republic: India's public policy failures and private solutions.* Harper Collins Publishers India.

Alberg, J. L. (2017). A light shall appear in the east: An introduction to this volume. In J. L. Alberg (Ed.), *Apocalypse deferred: Girard and Japan.* University of Notre Dame Press.

Alston, P. (2020). *The parlous state of poverty eradication: Report on the special rapporteur on extreme poverty and human rights.* Report No. S/HRC/44/40. www.chrgj.org/wp-content/uploads/2020/07/Alston-POverty-Report-FINAL.pdf

Anderson, K. B. (2021). *Dialectics of revolution.* Daraja Press.

Arun, M. G., & Punj, S. (2021, September 27). Asset monetisation: The big push. *India Today.*

Aslam, M. (2007). *Panchayati raj in India.* National Book Trust.

Avebury, P. C. (1907). *On municipal and national trading.* Macmillan and Co.

Barker, B. (1946). *Labour in London: A study in municipal achievement*. Routledge.
Barron, J., Crawley, G., & Wood, T. (1991). *Councillors in crisis: The public and private worlds of local councillors*. Macmillan.
Bastani, A. (2020). *Fully automated luxury communism: A manifesto*. Verso.
Bhavsar, D., Tiwari, P., & Deshpande, V. (2020). *Study of municipal governance assessment frameworks*. Center for Water and Sanitation, CEPT University.
Brar, A. (2020, April 14). COVID-19 boosts India's growing surveillance state. *The Diplomat*. www.thediplomat.com/2020/04/covid-19-boosts-indias-surveillance-state
Burke, N. J. (2021). Care in the time of covid-19: Surveillance, creativity and socialism in Cuba. In L. Manderson, N. J. Burke, & A. Wahlberg (Eds.), *Viral loads: Anthropologies of urgency in the time of covid-19*. UCL Press.
Business Line. (2021a, March 18). Why India needs private-public partnerships in healthcare. www.thehindubusinessline.com/opinion/why-india-needs-private-public-partnerships-in-healthcare/article/34099324.ece
Business Standard. (2021b, May 25). Infosys sees no major impact of Covid pandemic on client deliverables. www.business-standard.com/article/companies/infosys-sees-no-major-impact-of-covid-pandemic-on-client-deliverables-121052500852_1.html
Business Standard. (2022a, May 5). Infosys doubles its Covid-19 relief commitment to rs 200 crore. www.business-standard.com/article/current-affairs/infosys-doubles-its-covd-19-relief-commitment-to-rs-200-crore-121050501242_1.html
Business Standard. (2022b, May 5). Mumbai: Dharavi reports first covid-19 infection since March 17. www.business-standard.com/article/current-affairs/mumbai-dharavi-reports-first-covid-19-infection-since-march-17-12205041383_1.html
Centre for Science and Environment. (2021, December 26). Affordable housing – A lot more remains to be done, says CSE's pilot assessment in Telangana. www.cseindia.org/affordable-housing-alot-more-remains-to-be-done-says-cse-s-pilot-assessment-in-telangana-11106
Chancel, L., & Piketty, T. (2017). *Indian income inequality 1922–2014: From British raj to billionaire raj*. WID: World Working Paper Series N 2017/11.
Chancel, L., Piketty, T., Saez, E., & Zucman, G. (2022). *World inequality report 2022*. World Inequality Lab.
Chandra, B., Mukherjee, M., & Mukherjee, A. (2000). *India after independence: 1947–2000*. Penguin.
Chandra, B., Mukherjee, M., Mukherjee, A., Mahajan, S., & Pannikar, K. N. (2016). *India's struggle for independence*. Penguin India.
Chandra, R. (2019). *The moonshot game: Adventures of an Indian venture capitalist*. Penguin.
Chandrashekhar, C. P., & Ghosh, J. (2002). *The market that failed*. Leftword.
Chattopadhyay, P. (2016). *Marx's associated mode of production*. Praeger.
Chesire, P., Hilber, C., & Schöni, O. (2021). *The pandemic and the housing market: A British story*. Centre for Economic Performance, London School of Economics and Political Science.
Clarke, J. F. (2000). The tales of the last days, 1805–3794. In D. Seed (Ed.), *Imagining apocalypse: Studies in cultural crisis*. Macmillan.
Cohn, G. (1910). Municipal socialism. *The Economic Journal*, 20(80), 561–568.
Comisso, E. T. (1979). *Workers' control under plan and market: Implications of Yugoslav self-management*. Yale University Press.
Cooke, O. D. (2008). *Rethinking municipal privatization*. Routledge.
Cranor, C. (2009). A plea for a rich conception of risks. In L. Asveld & S. Roeser (Eds.), *The ethics of technological risk*. Earthscan.
Crawford, R. (1906). Glasgow's experience with municipal ownership and operation. *The Annals of American Academy*, 27, 1–19.
Crofts, W. C. (1885). *Municipal socialism*. Liberty and Property Defence League.

D'Amelio, F. (2021, February 23). Pfizer eyes higher prices for COVID-19 vaccine after the pandemic wanes: Exec, analyst. *Fierce Pharma*. www.fiercepharma.com/pharma/pfizer-eyes-higher-covid-19-vaccine-prices-after-pandmeic-exec-analyst

Daley, T. (2010). *Apocalypse never: Forging the path to a nuclear weapon-free world*. Macmillan.

Darwin, M. L. (1903). *Municipal trade: The advantages and disadvantages, resulting from the substitution of representative bodies for private proprietors in the management of industrial undertakings*. John Murray.

Das, G. (2002/2012). *The elephant paradigm: India wrestles with change*. Penguin.

Das, S. (2021, May 5). Key covid-19 drugs see 180% price increase over four months. *Business Standard*. www.business-standard.com/article/current-affairs/key-covid-19-drugs-see-180-price-increase-over-four-months-121050401326.html

Davey, M., & Nicholas, J. (2022, February 17). Covid death rate three times higher among migrants than those born in Australia. *The Guardian*. www.theguardian.com/australia-news/2022/feb17/covid-death-rate-three-times-higher-among-migrants-than-those-born-in-australia

Dawson, M. C., Rosin, C., & Wald, N. (2018). Resource scarcity between conflict and cooperation. In M. C. Dawson, C. Rosin, & N. Wald (Eds.), *Global resource scarcity: Catalyst for conflict or cooperation?* Earthscan.

De Bevoise, K. (1995). *Agents of apocalypse: Epidemic disease in the colonial philippines*. Princeton University Press.

Deb Roy, S. (2022). *Social media and capitalism: People, communities and commodities*. Daraja Press.

Deb Roy, S. (2022a). *Mass struggles and Leninism: Dialectics, contradictions and revolution*. Phoneme Books.

Debray, R. (1971). *Conversations with Allende: Socialism in Chile*. New Left Books.

Debray, R. (2016). *Revolution in a revolution*. Verso. (Original work published 1967)

Dighavkar, K. (2021). *The Dharavi model: How Asia's largest slum defeated covid-19*. Notion Press.

Dréze, J., & Sen, A. (2013). *An uncertain glory: India and its contradictions*. Penguin.

Dunayevskaya, R. (1958). *Marxism and freedom . . . From 1776 until today*. Bookman Associates.

Dunayevskaya, R. (1973). *Philosophy and revolution: From Hegel to Sartre, and from Marx to Mao*. Humanities Press.

Dunayevskaya, R. (1980/2019). Preface to the Iranian edition of Marx's humanist essays. In F. Dmitryev (Ed.), *Marx's philosophy of revolution in permanence for our day: Selected writings by Raya Dunayevskaya* (pp. 27–30). Brill.

Ewing, K. D., & Gearty, C. A. (1990). *Freedom under Thatcher: Civil liberties in modern Britain*. Clarendon Press.

Express Healthcare. (2021, March 10). *Delhi budget free covid vaccine scheme at state-run hospitals special women Mohalla clinics*. Retrieved December 4, 2023, from www.expresshealthcare.in/news/delhi-budget-free-covid-vaccine-scheme-at-state-run-hospitals-special-women-mohalla-clinics/427739/

Faizal, M., & Rahman, A. (2020, May 14). Covid-19 and the acceleration of state surveillance. *The Interpreter*. www.lowyinstitute.org/the-interpreter/covid-19-and-the-acceleration-of-state-surveillance

Flores, W. (2016). Public health for indigenous peoples in Guatemala: Monitoring from the bottom up. In D. A. McDonald (Ed.), *Making public in a privatised world: The struggle for essential services*. Zed Books.

Fromm, E. (1955/2008). *The sane society*. London: Routledge.

Gandhi-Mody, P. (2022). *A nation to protect: Leading India through the covid crisis*. Rupa Publications.

Garg, S. C. (2007). Overview of urban infrastructure finance in India. In G. E. Peterson & P. C. Annez (Eds.), *Financing cities: Fiscal responsibility and urban infrastructure in Brazil, China, India, Poland and South Africa*. SAGE Publications.

Gera, I. (2022, May 26). Home truths about urban housing scheme: 60% completion in 11 of 35 states. *Business Standard*. www.business-standard.com/article/economy-policy/home-truths-about-urban-housing-scheme-60-completion-in-11-of-35-states-122052600953_1.html

Ghoshal, D. (2021, April 24). Why India is facing an oxygen crisis as covid cases mount. *Reuters*. www.reuters.com/world/india/why-india-is-facing-an-oxygen-xcrisis-as-covid-cases-mount/

Gittlitz, A. M. (2020). *I want to believe: Posadism, UFOs and apocalypse communism*. Pluto Press.

Gould, S. J. (1981). *The mismeasure of man*. W. W. Norton and Company.

Greenfield, A. (2017). *Radical technologies: The design of everyday life*. Verso.

Gupta, K. (2020, October 24). India needs a public-private model for covid-19 immunisation. *ORF Online*. www.orfonline.org/expert-speak/india-needs-a-public-private-model-for-covid-19-immunisation/

Hamid, A. (2004). *74th constitutional amendment: An overview*. CCS Research Internship Paper. Centre for Civil Society.

Han, B. C. (2019). *What is power?* Polity.

Harvey, D. (2003a). *The new imperialism*. Oxford University Press.

Harvey, D. (2003b). The right to the city. *International Journal of Urban and Regional Research*, 27(4), 939–941.

Harvey, D. (2005). *A brief history of neoliberalism*. Oxford University Press.

Harvey, D. (2008). The right to the city. *New Left Review*, 1(53), 23–40.

Harvey, D. (2012). *Rebel cities: From the right to the city to the urban revolution*. Verso.

Harvey, D. (2014). *Seventeen contradictions and the end of capitalism*. Oxford University Press.

Hassan, S. A., Agarwal, P., Ganesh, T., & Mohamed, A. W. (2022). Optimum budget allocation for social projects to control the cOVID-19 pandemic: A multi-objective nonlinear integer mathematical model with a novel discrete integer gaining-sharing knowledge-based metaheuristic algorithm. In U. Rana & J. Govender (Eds.), *Exploring the consequences of the COVID-19 pandemic*. CRC Press and Apple Academic Press.

Hill, A., Wang, J., Levi, J., Health, K., & Fortunak, J. (2020). Minimum costs to manufacture new treatments for COVID-19. *Journal of Virus Eradication*, 6(2), 61–69.

Himmelfarb, M. (2010). *The apocalypse: A brief history*. Wiley Blackwell.

Housing Research. (2021). *State of Indian healthcare: Indian cities through the lens of healthcare 2021*. Housing Research. www.housing.com/research-reports

Hudis, P., & Anderson, K. B. (2021). Raya Dunayevskaya's concept of dialectic. In K. B. Anderson, K. Durkin, & H. A. Brown (Eds.), *Raya Dunayevskaya's intersectional Marxism: Race, class, gender, and the dialectics of liberation*. Palgrave Macmillan.

Hunt, E. (2021, March 29). New Zealand housing crisis: Jacinda Ardern says rent-increase warnings are 'speculative'. *The Guardian*. www.theguardian.com/2021/mar/29-new-zealand-housing-crisis-jacinda-ardern-says-rent-increase-warnings-are-speculative

Isaac, T. M. Thomas, & Franke, R. W. (2000). *Local democracy and development: People's campaign for decentralised planning in Kerala*. Leftword Books.

Jain, M. (2017, August 2). Private sector profits in healthcare soar as indian government investment stagnates. *Scroll*. www.scroll.in/pulse/845539/private-sectors-profits-in-healthcare-soar-as-indian-government-investment-stagnates

Jalan, B. (2005). *The future of India: Politics, economics and governance.* Penguin Viking.
Jalan, B. (2019). *Resurgent India: Politics, economics and governance.* Harper Collins Publishers India.
Jowett, F. W. (1907). *The socialist and the city.* George Allen.
Kakani, S., & DebRoy, S. (2022). *Mumbai fights back: A bureaucrat's account of how the maximum city took on covid-19.* Notion Press.
Kalanithi, P. (2016). *When breath becomes air.* Random House.
Kannabiran, K., Hans, A., Mohanty, M., & Pushpendra. (2021). Migration, work, and citizenship: COVID-19 and the faultlines of Indian democracy. In A. Hans, K. Kannabiran, M. Mohanty, & Pushpendra (Eds.), *Migration, workers and fundamental freedoms: Pandemic vulnerabilities and the states of exception in India.* Routledge.
Kanwar, S. (2018, July 30). Government schemes: Where are we on urban agenda? *The Wire.* www.thewire.in/article/urban/government-schemes-where-are-we-on-the-urban-agenda
Kanwar, S. (2019, May 14). How the PM's affordable housing scheme went from promising to dysfunctional. *The Wire.* www.thewire.in/article/urban/housing-urban-policy-scheme
Kempner, B. (2014). Feathering the truth. In N. Michalid & J. Watkins (Eds.), *Jurassic Park and philosophy: The truth if terrifying.* Open Court.
Khan, A. U. (2019, October 29). India's drug price fix is hurting healthcare. *Mint.* www.livemint.com/politics/policy/india-s-drug-price-fix-is-hurting-healthcare
Klein, N. (2007). *The shock doctrine: The rise of disaster capitalism.* Penguin.
Klein, N. (2014). *This changes everything: Capitalism vs. the climate.* Simon and Schuster.
Klein, N. (2018). *The battle for paradise.* Haymarket Books.
Kuchibanda, K., & Mayo, A. W. (2015). Public health risks from mismanagement of healthcare wastes in Shinyanga municipality health services, Tanzania. *The Scientific World Journal* [Online]. https://doi.org/10.1155/2015/981756
Lahariya, C., Kang, G., & Guleria, R. (2020). *Till we win: India's fight against the covid-19 pandemic.* Penguin.
Latour, B. (1987). *Science in action: How to follow scientists and engineers through society.* Harvard University Press.
Leakey, R., & Lewin, R. (1995). *The sixth extinction: Patterns of life and the future of humankind.* Anchor Books.
Lee, J., & Han, S. H. (2021). Preparing for accelerated third order impacts of digital technology in post pandemic service industry: Steep transformation and metamorphosis. In J. Lee & S. H. Han (Eds.), *The future of service post-COVID-19 pandemic, volume 1.* Springer Nature.
Lefebvre, H. (1994). *The production of space.* Blackwell.
Lefebvre, H. (1996). *Writings on cities.* Blackwell.
Lefebvre, H. (2002). *Critique of everyday life: Volume 2.* Verso.
Lefebvre, H. (2003). *The urban revolution.* University of Minnesota Press.
Lenin, V. I. (1915/1974). On the slogan for a United States of Europe. In *Lenin collected works: Volume 21.* Progress Publishers.
Lenin, V. I. (1914–16/1975). Philosophical notebooks. In *Lenin collected works: Volume 38.* Progress Publishers.
Leopold, E., & McDonald, D. A. (2012). Municipal socialism then and now: Some lessons for the global south. *Third World Quarterly, 33*(10), 1837–1853.
Levey, E. J. (1909). *Municipal socialism and its economic limitations.* Ginn and Company.
Lisboa, M. M. (2011). *The end of the world: Apocalypse and its aftermath in western culture.* Open Book Publishers.

Liu, A. (2020). "Chinese Virus," world market: The best safeguard against the novel coronavirus is the ability to voluntarily withdraw oneself from capitalism. In J. Kindig, M. Krotov, & M. Roth (Eds.), *There is no outside: Covid-19 dispatches*. Verso.

Lopez, I. (2022, March 24). Pfizer covid pill targeted in bid for Biden to spur drug access. *Bloomberg Law*. www.news.bloomsberglaw.com/health-law-and-business/pfizer-covid-pill-targeted-for-biden-to-spur-drug-access

Lupton, D. (2021). Contextualising covid-19: Sociocultural perspectives on contagion. In D. Lupton & K. Willis (Eds.), *The covid-19 crisis: Social perspectives*. Routledge.

Lyon, D. (2022). *Pandemic surveillance*. Polity.

Mackenzie, D., & Wajcman, J. (1999). *The social shaping of technology*. Open University Press.

Maffettone, S. (2021). Pandemic: Philosophy and public policy. In K. Mahadevan, S. Kumar, M. Bhoot, & R. Kharat (Eds.), *The covid spectrum: Theoretical and experiential reflections from India and beyond*. Speaking Tiger.

Mahambare, V. (2015, February 9). Wealth inequality and housing reforms. *Mint*. www.livemint.com/Opinion/ZDkmQFSmM7hNM1ky3ZR

Mander, H. (2019). Reimaging the good state in India. In *India exclusion report, 2018–19*. Three Essays Collective and Centre for Equity Studies.

Mander, H. (2021). *Locking down the poor: The pandemic and India's moral centre*. Speaking Tiger.

Marcuse, M. (1941/1998). Some social implications of modern technology. In D. Kellner (Ed.), *Collected Papers of Herbert Marcuse volume 1: Technology, war and fascism*. Routledge.

Marx, K. (1844/1975). Economic and philosophical manuscripts of 1844. In *Marx Engels collected works: Volume 3*. Lawrence and Wishart.

Marx, K. (1866/1985). Instructions for the delegates of the provisional general council: The different questions. In *Marx Engels Collected Works: Volume 20*. Lawrence and Wishart.

Marx, K. (1976). *Capital: Volume 1*. Penguin.

Marx, K., & Engels, F. (1848/1976). Manifesto of the communist party. In *Marx-Engels collected works: Volume 6*. Lawrence and Wishart.

Matthewman, S. (2015). *Disasters, risks and revelation: Making sense of our times*. Palgrave.

Matthewman, S. (2020, July 15). Disaster communism. *Thesis Eleven*. www.thesiseleven/2020/07/15/disaster-communism/

McDonald, D., & Ruiters, G. (2005). Theorizing water privatization in southern Africa. In D. A. McDonald & G. Ruiters (Eds.), *The age of commodity: Water privatization in southern Africa*. Earthscan.

Mint. (2021, April 29). *Cognizant to contribute about ₹10 cr towards fight against COVID-19 in India*. www.livemint.com/companies/news/cognizant-to-contribute-about-rs-10-cr-towards-fight-against-covid-19-in-india-11619715954467.html

Mitchell, T. (2007). *Evil paradises: Dreamworlds of neoliberalism* (M. Davis & D. B. Monk, Eds.). The New Press.

MN, P. (2020, May 13). Urban India didn't care about migrant workers till 26 March, only cares now because it's lost their services: P Sainath. *Firstpost*. www.firstpost.com/india/urban-india-didnt-care-about-migrant-workers-till-26-march-only-cares-now-because-its-lost-their-services-p-sainath-8361821.html

Mohan, D. (2019). Exclusion from mobility and access: Denial of public good. In *India exclusion report, 2018–19*. Three Essays Collective and Centre for Equity Studies.

Mohanty, P. K. (2016). *Financing cities in India: Municipal reforms, fiscal accountability and urban infrastructure*. SAGE.

Morgan, J. P. (2023, December 7). *The American homeowners' dream vs. recent reality.* www.jpmorgan.com/insights/real-estate/housing-market/the-american-homeowners-dream-vs-recent-reality

Moses, M. (2022). *The municipal financial crisis: A framework for understanding and fixing government budgeting.* Palgrave Macmillan.

Mouffe, C. (2018). *For a left populism.* Verso.

Mukherjee, S. (1991). G. D. H. Cole's critique of Fabianism. In M. M. Sankhdher & S. Mukherjee (Eds.), *Essays on Fabian socialism.* Deep and Deep Publications.

Mukul, J. (2022). *The great shutdown: A story of two Indian summers.* Simon and Schuster.

Narain, S. (2017). *Conflicts of interest: My journey through India's green movement.* Penguin.

Narrain, A. (2021). *India's undeclared emergency: Constitutionalism and the politics of resistance.* Context.

Nehru, J. (1980/2017). *An autobiography.* Penguin.

Nehru, J. (2015). From a letter dated 15 August 1949. In M. Khosla (Ed.), *Letters for a nation: From Jawaharlal Nehru to his chief ministers, 1947–1963.* Penguin India.

News18. (2022, April 4). Govt doesn't control medicine prices, says health minister amid medicine price hike. www.news18.com/news/business/govt-doesnt-control-medicine-prices/

Newton, K., & Karran, T. J. (1985). *The politics of local expenditure.* Macmillan.

OECD. (2020, October 19). What is the impact of the COVID-19 pandemic on immigrants and their children? *OECD Policy Responses to Coronavirus.* www.oecd.org/coronavirus/policy-responses/waht-is-the-impact-of-covid-19-pandemic-on-immigrants-and-their-children/

Otieno, A. (2018). Promoting human rights to resist disaster capitalism. *Peace Review: A Journal of Social Justice, 30,* 206–214.

Palaez, J. C. (2020, November 13). Cuba: Autocratic governance and pandemic juncture. *Thesis Eleven.* www.thesiseleven.com/2020/11/13/cuba-autocratic-governance-and-pandemic-juncture/

Panagariya, A. (2020). *India unlimited: Reclaiming the lost glory.* Harper Collins Publishers India.

Pande, A. (2020). *Making India great: The promise of a reluctant global power.* Harper Collins Publishers India.

Pankhurst, S. (1917, March 24). Whose Russian revolution? *Woman's Dreadnought.*

Panwar, T., & Ojha, A. (2021, May 25). How 'privatisation' and 'PPP Models' have left Indians to die. *Citizen Matters.* www.citizenmatters.in/privatisation-ppp-governance-failure-impact-on-healthcare-and-lives-25222

Pithode, T. (2022). *The battle against covid: Diary of bureaucrat.* Bloomsbury.

Posadas, J. (1968). Flying saucers, the process of matter and energy, science and socialism. In *Socialism and human relationships with nature and the cosmos.* Scientific, Cultural and Political Editions.

Posadas, J. (1969). *The revolutionary state, its transitory role and the construction of socialism.* Scientific, Cultural and Political Editions.

Posadas, J. (1972). War is not the end of the world: It is an atomic 'Charco'. In *Posadas "On War".* Posadists Today.

Posadas, J. (1977). The neutron bomb: A social counter-revolutionary weapon. In *Nuclear energy, war and socialism.* Scientific, Cultural and Political Editions.

Posadas, J. (1978a). The crisis of capitalism, war and socialism. In *War, peace, and the function of the socialist countries.* Scientific, Cultural and Political Editions.

Posadas, J. (1978b). Childbearing in space, the confidence of humanity, and socialism. *Quatrieme Internationale Posadiste.* www.quatrieme-internationale-posadiste.org/pdf-texte/EN/JP-Childbearing-in-space-JP-final.pdf

Posadas, J. (1979). The war and the elimination of the capitalist system on a world scale. In *Nuclear energy, war and socialism*. Scientific, Cultural and Political Editions.
Posadas, J. (1980). The conception of the communist parties on the problem of peace. In *Nuclear energy, war and socialism*. Scientific, Cultural and Political Editions.
Posadas, J. (1981). On the socialist future of humanity. *Quatrieme Internationale Posadiste*. www.quatrieme-internationale-posadiste.org/pdf-texte/EN/FutureOfHumanity.pdf
Prasad, R., & Pardhasaradhi, Y. (2020). Twenty-five years of the constitution seventy-fourth amendment act (74th CAA), 1992: Promise and performance. *Indian Journal of Public Administration* [Online]. https://doi.org/10.1177/0019556120923900
Priya, R. (2018). State, community, and primary health care: Empowering or disempowering discourses. In P. Prasad & A. Jesani (Eds.), *Equity and access: Health care studies in India*. Oxford University Press.
Raj, C. A., & K., M. (2020, July 2). As covid-19 puts India's largest cities under strain, municipalities must rethink finance strategies. *Scroll*. www.scroll.in/article/966210/as-covid-19-puts-indias-largest-cities-under-strain-municipalities-must-rethink-finance-strategies
Ramesh, J. (2018a). *Intertwined lives: P. N. Haksar and Indira Gandhi*. Simon and Schuster.
Ramesh, M. (2018b). *The climate solution: India's climate-change crisis and what we can do about it*. Hachette India.
Rao, M. A. (2015). *Indian railways*. National Book Trust.
Reddy, K. S. (2019). *Make health in India: Reaching a billion plus*. Orient Blackswan.
Roeser, S., & Asveld, L. (2009). The ethics of technological risk: Introduction and overview. In L. Asveld & S. Roeser (Eds.), *The ethics of technological risk*. Earthscan.
Rowland, D. (2021, January 17). With America's attention on Covid-19, drugmakers are quietly raising US prescription prices. *USA Today*. www.usatoday.com/story/news/health/2021/01/17/drug-companies-are-quietly-raising-prices-ambien-covid-pandemic/
Rustin, M. (1986). Lessons of the London industrial strategy. *New Left Review*, 1(155), 75–84.
Sahay, K. (2018). *The LIC story: Making of India's best-known brand*. Macmillan.
Scheidel, W. (2018). *The great leveler: Violence and the history of inequality from the stone age to the twenty-first century*. Princeton University Press.
Sethi, N., & Rao, M. (2017, July 19). NITI Aayog and Health Ministry prepare model contract for privatizing urban health. *Scroll*. www.scroll.in/article/844272/niti-aayog-and-health-ministry-prepare-model-contract-for-privatising-urban-health-care
Sexton, T. (2014). Flea market capitalism. In N. Michalid & J. Watkins (Eds.), *Jurassic Park and philosophy: The truth if terrifying*. Open Court.
Shah, S. (2020). *Pandemic: With a new preface*. Penguin.
Shaw, B. (1908). *The commonsense of municipal trading*. A. C. Fifield.
Shaw, B. (1930). Preface to the 1931 Reprint. In B. Shaw, S. Webb, G. Wallas, The Lord Olivier, W. Clarke, A. Besant, & H. Bland (Eds.), *Fabian essays*. The Garden City Press.
Singh, A. S., Venkataramani, B., & Ambarkhane, D. (2021). Post-pandemic penury of the financially marginalized in India: Coping with the new normal. In J. Lee & S. H. Han (Eds.), *The future of service post-COVID-19 pandemic, Volume 1*. Springer Nature.
Singh, S. (2018). *The great smog of India*. Penguin.
Søreide, H., Kyrjebø, D., & Råholm, M. (2019). Challenges in municipality health-care services – the nurse leaders' perspective. *Nursing Open* [Online]. https://doi.org/10.1002/nop2.270.

Spade, D. (2020). *Mutual aid: Building solidarity during this crisis (and the next)*. Verso.
Stoker, G. (1991). *The politics of local government*. Macmillan.
Teles, F. (2016). *Local governance and inter-municipal cooperation*. Palgrave Macmillan.
TERI. (2010). *Enhancing public participation through effective functioning of ward committees*. Project Report No. 2009UD04.
The Economic Times. (2021, August 25). Accenture working with 15 NGOs as part of covid-19 pandemic relief in India. www.economictimes.com/tech/information-tech/accenture-working-with-15-ngos-as-part-of-covid-19-pandemic-relief-in-india/articleshow/85620844.cms
The High Powered Expert Committee (HPEC) for Estimating the Investment Requirements for Urban Infrastructure Services. (2011). *Report on Indian urban infrastructure and services*. ICIER.
The Hindu. (2020, March 30). Infosys foundation commits Rs 100 crore. www.thehindu.com/news/national/karnataka/covid-19-infosys-foundation-commits-100-crore/article31212252.ece
The Hindu. (2021, May 28). Mumbai's 'Dharavi model' helps tame second covid-19 wave in Slum Town. www.thehindu.com/national/other-states/mumbais-dharavi-model-helps-tame-second-covid-19-wave-in-slum-town/article34664110.ece
The Indian Express. (2021, June 19). Maharashtra joins hands with Cognizant Foundation to set up 100-bed Covid care facility in Pune. www.indianexpress.com/article/cities/pune/state-govt-joins-hands-with-cognizant-foundation-to-dedicate-100-bed-covid-care-facility-in-pune-7364588/
The Times. (1902). *Municipal socialism: A series of articles*. George Edward Wright.
Times of India. (2021, October 11). PPP Model worked well during pandemic. www.timesofindia.com/city/ahmedanad/ppp-model-worked-well-during-pandemic
Towler, W. G. (1909). *Socialism in local government*. The Macmillan Company.
Trimble, S. (2019). *Undead ends: Stories of apocalypse*. Rutgers University Press.
Troesken, W. (2006). *The great lead water pipe disaster*. MIT Press.
Tumbe, C. (2020). *The age of pandemics, 1817–1920: How they shaped India and the world*. Harper Collins.
Unni, A., & Panwar, T. (2019, April 5). What the last five years of urban policies reveal about our cities. *The Wire*. www.thewire.in/article/urban/urban-planning-india-elections
Vrooman, W. (1895). *Government ownership in production and distribution*. Patriotic Literature Publishing Co.
Wallace, R. (2016). *Big firms make big flu: Dispatches on infectious disease, agribusiness, and the nature of science*. Monthly Review Press.
Wallace, R. (2020). *Dead epidemiologists: On the origins of COVID-19*. Monthly Review Press.
Webb, S. (1889/1948). Historic. In B. Shaw, S. Webb, G. Wallas, The Lord Olivier, W. Clarke, A. Besant, & H. Bland (Eds.), *Fabian essays*. The Garden City Press.
Webb, S. (1919/1920). Introduction. In G. B. Shaw (ed.), *Fabian Essays in Socialism*. The Fabian Society.
Wells, D. W. (2019). *The uninhabitable earth: Life after warning*. Tim Duggan Books.
Wells, W. (2009). *Apocalypse when? Calculating how long the human race will survive?* Springer and Praxis Publishing.
Wolfe, B. D. (1961). Introduction. In R. Luxemburg (Ed.), *The Russian revolution, and Leninism or Marxism*. Ann Arbor Press.
Working Group of State Urban Development Secretaries. (2013). *Approach to the finances of municipalities: A report to the 14th finance commission*. Ministry of Urban Development and National Institute of Urban Affairs.

World Health Organization. (2021, December 23). *Coronavirus disease (COVID-19): Ventilation and air conditioning.* www.who.int/news-room/questions-and-answers/item/coronavirus-disease-covid-19-ventilation-and-air-conditioning

Xiang, S., Rasool, S., Hang, Y., Javid, K., Javed, T., & Artene, A. E. (2021). The effect of COVID-19 pandemic on service sector sustainability and growth. *Frontiers in Psychology* [Online]. https://doi.org/10.3389/fpsyg.2021.633597

Yadavar, S., & Agrawal, S. (2020, May 22). Dharavi is not just fighting coronavirus, but also dirty toilets and battered image. *The Print.* www.theprint.in/india/dharavi-is-not-just-fighting-coronavirus-but-also-dirty-toilets-and-battered-image/426523/

Zandvoort, H. (2009). Requirements for the social acceptability of risk-generating technological activities. In L. Asveld & S. Roeser (Eds.), *The ethics of technological risk*. Earthscan.

Zuboff, S. (2019). *The age of surveillance capitalism: The fight for a human future at the new frontier of power*. Public Affairs.

6 Morbidities of Disaster Civility

Introduction

Notions of civility are intimately related to broader social processes and social cohesion. The civility that has come to influence the material world has been closely connected to the ways in which capitalist economic and cultural processes have come to influence society at large. Events such as earthquakes and pandemics often bring forward the contradictions that surround the questions of civility in relation to one's social existence in society. Within the realm of social life, civic order is often enforced violently – physical or structural – on certain individuals (Monti & Wacks, 2021).

A normalised civic order is often the result of a major event which has had an important effect on the society as a whole. For example, Angela Saini (2019), in a recent book, notes about the influence that certain culinary practices gained during colonisation continue to have on Indian eating habits. The alterations within the general sensibilities, everyday practices, and social customs are a crucial part and parcel of the ways in which capitalist globalisation attempts to restructure global markets and societies (Leys, 2008). There is a widespread consensus among people that COVID-19 has resulted in a loss of this civility among people. The impact of COVID-19, as Keane (2020) argues, was unevenly distributed, with the virus exposing the worst vulnerabilities which exist within the healthcare infrastructure of almost every country on the globe.

The 'seminal event', as Davis (2020) terms COVID-19 to be, has caused numerous important events and processes to unfold globally, altering the worldly experience of many. One of the major aspects that has been impacted by this *seminal* event is the civility that human society had grown accustomed to. With the lockdowns put in place by numerous governments globally, there has been a strong decline in the civic relations that some of the vulnerable sections of the population requires to sustain in the society, such as the elderly and the disadvantaged (Chauhan & Harsheeta, 2020; Nagpal & Dixit, 2020). Bonotti and Zech (2021) have argued that civility is an important aspect of the pandemic because the society almost always expects that people will behave in a certain way, which maintains the accepted norms of the society. This becomes further complicated because there have always been contested definitions of civility within academic and scholarly literature. Bonotti and Zech argue:

> Existing work provides different and often contrasting definitions of the concept. . . . On the one hand, civility is often associated with . . . norms of etiquette and politeness: to be civil, in this first sense, implies to speak and act in ways that comply with . . . norms. On the other hand, it is linked with the idea of public-mindedness: to be civil, in this second sense, means to display a commitment to the public good, not just to one's personal or sectarian interest, and to treating others as free and equal.
>
> (Bonotti & Zech, 2021, p. 59)

COVID-19 has endangered certain important methods of generating civility and civic relations among the people, such as the extracurricular activities taken up in schools, which generally contribute a lot towards generating civic engagement among the children (Putnam, 2000). Community activities outside the space of the school also play a critical role in this regard (Longo, 2007). With the lockdown in place, these activities have been halted.

The lockdown that was imposed in India in March 2020 turned into a human tragedy, as the local bodies struggled to arrange transportation, shelter, and food for the migrant workers returning home – who, at times, had to travel thousands of kilometres to reach their homes due to the harsh roads and drivers, and often on foot with their families and children (Biswas, 2020, March 30; Pande, 2020, May 20; Mukul, 2022). The migrant exodus was a proof that governments across the globe can potentially use a crisis such as the pandemic to infringe upon basic human rights of the people (ICNL, 2022). In India, the magnitude of the crisis was so huge that the prime minister had to seek forgiveness from the migrant workers for the way in which the lockdown had been imposed and subsequently announced a bailout of US$ 22 billion for the country's poorest population (BBC, 2020, March 29). However, the way in which the government reacted to the crisis in the realm of business was very different. The government has decided to focus its attention towards sectors such as aviation, tourism, and hospitality, which have been severely impacted by COVID-19-induced localised lockdowns, with a stimulus package of INR 6.28 lakh crore with an emphasis on loan guarantees and concessional credit to businesses (Business Today, 2021, May 25; Singh, 2021, May 25; The Hindu, 2021, June 28). Naomi Klein argues that such subsidies by the government to large corporates are an integral part of the ways in which capitalism tends to work through the shocks that the natural world presents. Klein argues that 'They're not doing this because they think it's the most effective way to alleviate suffering during a pandemic – they have these ideas lying around that they see now an opportunity to implement' (Solis, 2020, March 13, Para 6). The proof of this can be seen in the ways in which vaccines were put out in the marketplace for people to make profits, even though both the manufacturers and the government knew very well that vaccines during a pandemic are essential for survival.

The governments have allowed Big Pharma to make profits out of the calamity by providing licenses and authorisation to many of the Big Pharma conglomerates the flexibility to fix prices and dominate the supply of the vaccines along with exemption from batch inspection and a complete removal of all forms of public control (Sridhar, 2021). As Ramachandran (2021) has pointed out, the ways in which the government has completely toed the argumentative lines put forward by the global pharmaceutical conglomerates has resulted in a situation where the general population has been forced to accept the outcomes of trials and data from contexts very different from their own. At the same time, the complete absence of important and critical data from the public domain contributes to the rising secrecy, which in turn strengthens the supremacy of the Big Pharma by making them akin to a Hobbesian Leviathan – an entity to which one has completely surrendered their independent critical self. This is not an ideal situation and considering that:

> [the] world will not be the same after COVID-19 [, humanity] will have to find newer ways of dealing with public health emergencies, considering the developed countries of the West are the worst affected despite their state-of-the-art health infrastructures. The United States, in particular, must have realised that its excessive expenditure on the war against terror was flawed and misdirected.
> (Mustafa, 2020, April 17, Para 1)

Tendencies such as civic capitalism – the primary focus of this chapter – become popular, in circumstances such as this, because they tend to theorise the mechanisms through which capitalism can be made to work for the people, and the role that states and businesses play in keeping the society functional. With COVID-19, it is beyond reasonable doubt that segregations in the society will become more acute than ever before because of the effects that the pandemic has had on people's ways of living and means of employment. COVID-19 has brought into the limelight the acute inequalities that plague the human society under the dominance of the market within free market capitalism and neoliberalism. Since 2020, COVID-19 and the response towards it by various states and regions has played a key role in the way civic relations are formed globally. Be it within the realm of social ethics or collective responsibility, the way in which COVID-19 has escalated the need for mutual cooperation has made it significantly safe to assume that it will continue to affect the private and public lives of individuals and social groups for a long time to come. In addition to the virus, there will also remain the vestiges of the inhuman nature with which the market treated the workers, women, and other marginalised sections of the population during the pandemic, especially the migrant workers.

The ways in which different governments responded to the crises caused by the widespread spread of COVID-19 had one aspect in common, which was that almost all major democracies kept the interests of the market at the forefront of their pandemic response policies. Neoliberal market policies as they exist today are all encompassing in nature, with little or almost no regard for the human suffering they bring forward in their drive towards development and progress. Since the 1980s, under the intellectual legitimacy provided by the Chicago School of Law and Economics, there has been a conscious construction of a global market, which has strategically destroyed the bases of the old systems in place. The most important aspect of society that this global market has destroyed is the security that the working class enjoyed, as Guy Standing (2006) mentions, under both left- and right-wing governments.

The nature of collective bargaining under non-neoliberal forms of governance was such that the nominal wage and the social security, which is always needed for the development of the modes of consumption and the maintenance of workers as consumers, were in place (Aglietta, 1979). In doing so, most governments globally have ensured that the consumer identity of their workers remains intact, while their identity as actual self-asserting human beings remains subordinated. Under contemporary regimes that advocate for rampant economic growth with little or almost no regard for the human costs of development, there has been a conscious effort by many social thinkers to manage capitalism, rather than completely do away with it (Panitch & Leys, 1997). Civic capitalism as a political-economic argument stems from the manner in which Colin Hay (2013) described the Anglo-Liberal model of the growth of capitalism, which was constructed upon market liberalism, neoliberal ideology, hegemonical growth models, bureaucratic elitism in policymaking, cheap supply of raw materials, risk and debt accumulation, extreme dependency on consumption of commodities and a rampant deregulation of the market, among other factors.

COVID-19 has caused dual shocks to emerge, one health centric and the other economic; and the lockdowns and the impending recessions which have been witnessed by the human society during COVID-19 are likely to continue affecting human society for years to come (Hupkao et al., 2020; Davies, 2021). Hupkau et al. (2020) have argued that the shocks caused by COVID-19 are likely to have an intergenerational effect, specifically on the children of those who have been affected by either the virus or the response to the pandemic by various governments. When pandemics emerge, their effects do not only remain constrained within the healthcare sector, but also have overlapping effects on other domains of human survival. Nancy Tomes' (1998) *The Gospel of Germs* provides one with a descriptive analysis of how germs and their spread through the society initiates newer social habits, customs, and rituals, especially those that involve direct contact, such as shielding sneezes and coughs, handshakes, kissing, and the like. Ashton and Toland (2021) and Renner (2020, April 15) have also talked about how the COVID-19 pandemic has caused changes in the way people eat, sleep, and even dream, often stemmed by the withdrawal from the usual environment that they have been habituated to. It is in this context, theories such as civic capitalism, have come into question. The basic idea behind civic capitalism remains the reinvention or rather, the rearticulation of capitalism in a way that benefits the common people. However, during a pandemic, things become a lot more complicated than they usually are.

There are multiple issues which crop up during a pandemic as serious as COVID-19. These issues largely pertain to issues concerning healthcare, mortality, lifestyle, breach of privacy, and the like. Mundane aspects of everyday life, such as sleeping, have become immensely important during the pandemic, and the world has seen rampant variations within these crucial aspects of everyday life (Ashton & Toland, 2021). Health workers have found themselves to be at the centre of crisis. Curtis and Johnson (2022) have stated that the covid crisis has resulted in a massive mental health crisis among people, especially healthcare workers. The community healthcare workers have faced an extremely difficult time during the pandemic with additional responsibilities being thrust on them such as containment, contact tracing, community surveillance, and the propagation of information regarding safety and hygiene (Saha et al., 2021, September 29). This chapter analyses such issues, informed by a perspective of civic capitalism, in relation to the various perspectives discussed in the previous chapters. The first section discusses the various theoretical trajectories that have contributed to the idea of civic capitalism, while the second section discusses how businesses – the core of civic capitalist theories – have failed to fulfill their social responsibilities. The third and final section discusses the neoliberal nature of the pandemic and analyses the complete subsumption of the state by neoliberal business models.

Civic Capitalism's Trajectories

The construction of the market and the desire for socio-economic supremacy has been an important part of the human civilisation since centuries. In ancient India, the mainstream business modelwas based on kingship-based state control, accompanied by a primacy of private enterprise, which corresponded to the functioning of the state (Trautmann, 2012). The contemporary capitalist society has two aspects entrenched within itself through which various proponents of the theory of civic capitalism attempt to talk about the same. These two aspects are the market – which includes the businesspeople engaged in these markets – and the state – including the politicians and bureaucrats who constitute the political fabric in almost all major democracies in the world. Under neoliberalism, both the state and the market function as a holistic united entity. Notions of civility here are often negligent of the alternate civilities practiced by marginalised groups and sections of the society (Rucht, 2011).

Monti (1999) and Monti et al. (2007) argue that businesspeople and women contribute significantly to society's total requisite labour and as such deserve the attention of the people. The way in which Monti et al. (2007) define civic capitalism emphasises the kind of work that businesspeople and entrepreneurs perform for the community by keeping it together and by giving back to the communities from which they come from. Monti (1999) argues that businesspeople, and especially women, act as community boosters by engaging in more civic-oriented activities than others, such as the construction of libraries, large-scale donations, and the like. During COVID-19, one has seen a plethora of such activities from the businesspeople. Giant business corporations such as the IT giant Infosys can be taken as examples in this regard. Infosys has also been engaged in some affirmative actions during the pandemic, such as providing insurance covers and financial assistance to the kins of those who died from COVID-19 among its employees, which include employment opportunities for spouses and educational assistance for kids of the victims (Bhattacharyya, 2021, May 13). In addition to the Rs 200 crore that Infosys had committed to relief efforts during COVID-19, it has also contributed to the construction of a 350-bed cardiac care unit within the Jayadeva Hospital in Bengaluru, which according to reports had cost them around Rs 103 crores (Business Line, 2021, November 18).

Almost all forms of philanthropic endeavours by these corporations come at a price. When major capitalist philanthropists make donations or interfere with certain processes, they mostly do so to make inroads into profitable markets (Moloo, 2018). Wars, perhaps, remain the most important example in this regard amidst all other kinds of disasters. According to Rosenthal (2015), capitalism invented wars so that major corporations and billionaires could make humanitarian interventions. Another example can be cited of the ways in which major multinational bodies operate. Because most of the money that these bodies – such as the WHO – receive is obtained from private foundations, there are very few decisions that they can make, *even if they wanted to*, which goes against the private bodies or advocates for their reduced capacities in the society (McGoey, 2015). Faas (2018) argues that entrepreneurial solutions to the crisis presented by emergencies such as COVID-19 do not produce any argument that re-theorises or rearticulates policies and the existing economic state of affairs, but instead remain focused on increasing local productivity, which could potentially benefit them in the form of gaining more state subsidies in the future by *cashing-in on* the activities during a disaster.

Philanthropical activities and gestures have recently come under serious state surveillance, which has created issues with how philanthropy has functioned during COVID-19 (Sidel, 2022, May 11). At the same time, issues surrounding tax exemptions have also caused major issues in heightening the philanthropic and charitable drive of common people and corporations in India (Sanjay & Indiaspend, 2021, September 27). Philanthropic interventions have attempted to solve the systemic crisis within the existing systems through the influx of 'private' money into the system in order to improve the possibility of people receiving timely and good care during the crisis by improving the healthcare capacity and meeting other socio-economic needs of the vulnerable populace (Venkatachalam et al., 2020, July 16).

NGOs have played a key role in this regard, who have collaborated with donors, other CSOs, and the government to improve the conditions of healthcare capacity and delivery in the country during the pandemic (Mehta, 2021, August 5). The Indian Philanthropy Alliance (IPA) (2022) also has argued that philanthropy has played a key role in India's COVID-19 strategy, with organisations and trusts such as Sehgal Foundation, Indiaspora, The Antara Foundation, and the like making significant contributions towards ensuring educational continuity, healthcare delivery, knowledge propagation, and so on during the pandemic, using technology and community connections. Philanthropy in India has, however, also faced issues concerning the continuous influx of money into NGOs and organisations that have better industrial standing than others (Vaid & Shetty, 2021, September 7). This becomes particularly important in the context of COVID-19, when a large proportion of Indian people have begun to believe that the government and businesses should contribute more towards charities that could potentially contribute more towards the betterment of the infrastructure (Sanjay & IndiaSpend.com, 2021, September 27) in the country which has found itself wanting in the face of the challenge posed by COVID-19.

Monti's ideas about civic capitalism are slightly different from the recent ideological construction of civic capitalism as has been put forward by Hay and Payne (2015). Monti (2013) argues that both the state and the market are almost equal in their statures, under contemporary capitalism. However, he does not focus much on the relationship that they have come to share under neoliberal regimes, where the latter has come to abjectly dominate the former. Monti et al. (2007) argue:

> People that own and run businesses often practice a kind of civic-minded capitalism in which doing well does not preclude the possibility of doing good but actually encourages it. Successful businesspeople are not required to give back to the community and some embrace the idea and practice more readily than others.
>
> (Monti et al., 2007, p. 354)

Civic-minded capitalism grows most profusely within liberal democracies because liberal democracies provide the ideal grounds for:

> [A large] majority control of government via free and fair elections, genuine party competition, a vivid interest group process, and diverse other forms of political participation; the maintenance and development of human rights and civil liberties for all citizens, ensuring equal treatment even for unpopular minorities or causes; the conscious

development and pursuit of greater political and social equality; and widespread political legitimacy for the state, in part based on the existence of multiple (plural) centres of power, information and influence within society.

(Dunleavy, 2018, p. 17)

If one goes through each of the four characteristics that Dunleavy puts forward, one can realise the importance that liberal democracies hold in any potential construction of civic capitalism, the definitions of which have varied over the years. Hay and Payne (2015) define civic capitalism in a slightly different way. According to them, people engaged in different businesses that adhere to the market as a dominant force in the society cannot ensure social justice because 'The market can never be a guarantor of equity or justice. . . . [If] we are to have social and economic justice, it has to be imposed upon the market by the state in [the citizens'] name' (p. 13). They argue that it is not businesspeople who can bring in equity and justice within the society, but rather the state which can do that. This is distinct from the kind of definitions that Monti and his co-scholars put forward, which focuses more on businesses and the market to ensure civility within the society. Regardless of the definition that one follows, civic capitalism is distinct from other modes of capitalism because it encourages:

> [The] emergence of a more consciously held, open-ended and dynamic ideology that puts markets at the service of the public as citizens; a more interventionist role for the state . . . ; the coordinated re-regulation of markets and risk management, both as a collective public good and an antidote to unstable growth; the need for sustainability . . . ; the promotion of sustainable development . . . ; the development of an alternative currency of economic success . . . ; the integration into this alternative model of development of a genuine social dimension that opens up different and more civic social policies and partnerships; a shared commitment to reducing prevailing levels of inequality . . . ; and the creation of more intensive and sophisticated, flexible and deliberative, mechanisms of global governance capable of serving, and in part also reflecting, the guiding intelligence of the global economy.
>
> (Hay & Payne, 2015, pp. 7–8)

Liberal democracies provide the most ideal ground for the generation of civic capitalism because concepts such as sustainable development, alternative models of market mechanisms, and the like can only become prominent under liberal democracies. Also because liberal democracies provide two important tools to capitalism of all kinds: a free market and burgeoning economic well-being of a particular class of the society. According to Colin Hay and Anthony Payne (2015), civic capitalism is based on the market being made to work for the people by the active regulatory mechanisms put in place by the state, which considers the regulation of markets as its civic duty. Moreover, civic capitalism will supposedly put more emphasis on the generation of sustainable modes of production and consumption based on investment, rather than debt accumulation and consumption aided by debt. The mode of capitalism that Hay and Payne (2015) advocate for is supposed to be both productive and sustainable at the same time. It is similar to the ways in which Al Gore argued about the gradual alteration in the way capitalism will function such that 'The interests of the shareholders, both public and private, over time, will be best served by companies that maximise their financial performance by strategically managing their economic, social, environmental and ethical performance' (Gore, 2007, p. xxiv). One can find similar emphasis in Unsworth et al.'s (2020) strategy for building UK better from the crisis caused by the coronavirus through 'investment in a strong, sustainable, inclusive and resilient recovery' (p. 3). However, one of the major hindrances towards companies and corporations actually doing this is the way they are structured into the global financial ecosystem, which leaves them no choice but to disregard the ethical aspects of their accumulation of profits that influences the dominant perceptions and modes of civility in the society upon which all varieties of civic capitalism depend upon.

Civility in the society is often the result of a long-drawn ideological and material struggle within the elites. Marx and Engels (1845–46/1976) had famously argued that the class which controls the means of production in the society also controls the general intellect, which is rendered mainstream in the society. Civic capitalism is *almost* an accurate example of that kind of a dominance. Monti's theory of civic capitalism rests upon the power that the philanthropists possess over the society. Monti's theory remains short-sighted because it completely disregards the history of capitalist philanthropy, which has always operated through a nexus of capitalist charity and development (Moloo, 2018). Capitalist philanthropists are the ones who proposed *race science* arguing that medical statistics should be collected on the basis of race, reinstating the racial segregations that exist in the world. This allows racist capitalist systems to inflict biological oppression on the racial minorities, often through methods such as race science which have begun to be reused in the contemporary times (Rosenthal, 2015, Saini, 2019).

Civic capitalism emphasises the role of mainstream policymaking, which focuses on the continuation of the notions of civility – and its many contradictions – as they exist under contemporary capitalism. It argues that mainstream policies if implemented properly, can bring in more equity within the society provided most businesses and the state behave in a civic-oriented manner. Most left-wing policies must focus on a host of different dimensions, including a competent response to economic crisis such that both electoral – the pragmatic aspects of policy making – and ideological progressive checkboxes are ticked (Taylor-Gooby, 2015).

Civic capitalism attempts to mediate through this trilemma by posing the state as a regulator of services deemed essential. The Austro-Marxist, Rudolf

Hilferding argued that when large areas of the economy are put under state control, it automatically translates into the conscious suppression of the autonomous regulations that pre-existed the control of the state (Bottomore, 1981). Civic capitalism, of the variety that Hay and Payne (2015) theorise, does not provide any viable solutions to this issue. Instead, civic capitalism tends to believe that the state exists in an ideal condition, whereby the state has the best interests of the citizens in its mind. In contrast, the concept of civic capitalism that Monti (2013) highlights, hinges on the belief that businesses do a majority portion of the socially necessary labour required to keep society adrift. The regulation of the market society is an extremely perilous task in a situation where profits are being produced at a rapid pace and getting concentrated at the hands of a tiny minority without much resistance. With the era of welfare capitalism long past, monopolistic capitalism has been an active participant in the marginalisation of labour. Mainstream economics act as justifiers for this marginalisation and exploitation by arguing that the growth of the labour force is a proof of the idea that the competition for low wages among corporates reflects the construction of a world where economic differences between different societies are set to disappear (Foster & McChesney, 2012).

The contemporary society is a space where business interests and the interests of the state have fused together, as Leys (2008) has highlighted. Major international financial bodies have begun to have drastic impacts on the local politics of a region under neoliberal capitalism because of the rising globalisation of capital in the twenty-first century (Leys, 2008). This trend, however, is nothing new in the case of India. The East India Company – the primary agents of colonisation of India – was constituted by a mixture of politicians, merchants, mariners, and businesspeople from Britain (Roy, 2012). The contemporary situation of the Indian healthcare infrastructure is a proof of this. Right from the colonial times to the present, the condition of healthcare in India has always been insufficient for the kind of population that India has – both quantitatively and qualitatively, as many such as Aiyar (2020) and Rao (2017) have highlighted.

The Failure of the Business Regime

Local bodies are critical to the response that any society exhibits towards disasters and apocalyptic events, and are therefore crucial for ensuring the effective delivery of essential services. Free market capitalism desires disasters because it allows it to push forward its own set of agendas, which often tends to dilute the influence that these local bodies have. Gurcharan Das (2012) argues that free markets depend on a strong rule of law to bring in an equality of opportunities to the citizens. However, as the lockdowns and the migrant exodus have shown, free market capitalism rarely provides citizens with equal opportunities, but rather creates newer forms of inequalities where certain segments of the population *are often left to die* during emergencies by both the market and the state (Ananta, 2020). This is co-existent with the global vaccine nationalism exhibited by the majority of nations in the Global North, which has left many of the Global South *begging* for resources. The scarcity of resources to fight the pandemic, combined with the rise of neoliberal authoritarianism, has been creating a situation where human rights violation, according to McCann and Ó hAdhmaill (2021), have become normalised and widespread in many countries of the Global South.

Lockdowns and the inability to contribute physically have led to an increase in online donations, with some online portals such as GiveIndia's *India Covid Response Fund* registering almost 3,50,000 donating users every day for 2021 since its launch, raising almost Rs 220 crore in the year comprising donations from Rs 50 to Rs 5 crore. Similarly, Razorpay reported that there had been a 180% increase in online donations between the 24th of March and the 23rd of April, the period of the first lockdown (Sanjay & Indiaspend, 2021, September 27). Venkatachalam et al. (2020, May 18, 2020, July 16) identify certain key aspects that need to be realised if such philanthropic interventions have to be made more impactful in the context of the crisis that COVID-19 presents before the social order. These include a focus on issues concerning equity and justice, flexible funding structures, address critical, humanitarian, yet unconventional needs of the people, and increased collaborative efforts between governments, CSOs, philanthropists, communities, and businesses. With COVID-19, more and more Indians have been seeing philanthropy as something that is beneficial to the society in the long run, as (Shashidhar, 2022, June 7; Irani, 2021, June 11) prove. Since the pandemic, there has been a constant rise in the amount of money that family philanthropy has raised, but that has been seriously constrained by the ways in which the government has been bringing in newer and more stringent laws concerning funding of civil society and non-profit organisations along with funds such as PM CARES. This has contributed to more funds being diverted to governments operating at a central level rather than grassroots organisations (Dayal, 2022, July 20).

In India, variants of philanthropy are deeply rooted within the culture itself, with a significant proportion of the population donating large sums of money to religious and other community institutions every year. This constitutes a tremendous amount of informal donations in the form of individual charity (Sanjay & Indiaspend, 2021, September 27). In 2021, the World Giving Index reported that India ranked the 14th most charitable country in the world (Mehta, 2021, August 5). The World Giving Index Report 2019 by the Charities Aid Foundation (2019) puts India at 82nd position, with countries such as the United States and New Zealand being ranked higher in terms of giving than India. The Doing Good Index (DGI) 2022 reports that India's position within the world of philanthropy has worsened because of the tax laws in place, and it has been 'Doing Okay' since 2018 (Doing Good, 2018, 2020, 2022). The DGI 2022 also reports that corporate funding now accounts for almost 16% of the funding that Social Delivery Organizations

(SDOs) – that they studied – receive in India. About 50% of the SDOs receive corporate funding, which is almost similar to the 51% reported to be in the DGI 2020. While in 2020, 37% of the SDOs received government grants, the percentage increased to 42% in 2022. The percentage of government grants contributing to the SDOs budget has increased from 9% in 2020 to 15% in 2022. However, if one considers the source of funding, there is a decline of 5% in government funding in 2022 as compared to 2020, and both domestic and foreign funding sources have increased by 2%. At the same time, while in 2020, 15% of the SDOs reported having connections to the business and political elites, which is a significant decline from the 34% in 2018. Almost all the reports emphasised that one of the major reasons for low levels of charity in India is that Indians prefer to donate more to religious institutions.

David Harvey (2005) argues that under neoliberal capitalism, human well-being is directly related to the liberation of individual entrepreneurial skills, something which does not challenge the established framework of private property, free trade, and commodity production. The rise of corporate culture, on the other hand, in India has resulted in relief work evolving into brand building exercises that encompass celebrities in the field of sports, entertainment, and politics (Bamzai, 2020, March 28). Disasters for the corporates is an opportunity not only for profit maximisation but also for their philanthropic interests to be given vent to. During COVID-19, philanthropical resources were put to use quite voraciously by the large monopolies. In the United States, there was involvement from 323 independent, community, and corporate foundations amounting a total of 1.462 million US$ in the 2021 Fiscal Year-End (FYE) which is around 19% and 31% lesser than FYE 2020 (Candid & Center for Disaster Philosophy, 2022). The number of community and independent foundations – 212 and 93 in 2021, respectively, and 265 and 102 in 2020, respectively – was significantly higher than that of corporate foundations, which was only at 31 in 2020 and 18 in 2021. In India, as the report by Candid and the CDP states, *GiveIndia* has raised almost US$ 70.5 million from around 1.6 million donors, Dasra has raised US$ 10.2 million from 474 funders and has already put in use US$ 6.5 million to around 140 non-profits, and Give2Asia has donated a sum of US$ 7.7 million to India. In 2021, the human services organisation received the highest amount of donations, while public safety along with community and economic development-based organisations received the lowest (Candid & Center for Disaster Philanthropy, 2021).

Vidya Shah, the Executive Chairperson of EdelGive Foundation, pointed towards the herd mentality that often exists amongst donors, which sometimes makes donations happen in bulk only after a credible donor has begun the process of donation (Vaid & Shetty, 2021, September 7). Vidya Shah mentions that this herd mentality actually is harmful in the long run because when money is not available from many different sources, the existent money almost always finds its way to certain fixed sectors and organisations which might or might not be beneficial to the target receivers.[1] According to an interview given by the GiveIndia CEO, the culture of 'giving' increases during disasters, but the focus needs to be on rehabilitation of people, which is a long-term process (Irani, 2021, June 11). There were also certain structural problems associated with the concentration of wealth that had been unearthed during the pandemic, such as that most wealthy families are based in metropolitan cities, specifically Mumbai, Delhi, and Bengaluru, which collectively account for 77% of the total ultra-high-net-worth individuals (Sheth et al., 2021).

Businesses operating under monopoly capitalism have failed to provide security to their employees, especially the informal and outsourced workforce they employ. Most retail workers that the author has had conversations with during and after the pandemic have stated that they have been provided with little to almost no employment benefits. Of course, a large proportion of them losing access to these basic amenities is because of the way informal employment functions in India, which mostly relies on lower wages being offered to vulnerable workers with almost no documentation of the kind of work they are supposed to do and the kind of work they end up doing. The informal migrant workforce was one of the worst affected by the COVID-19 pandemic, more so by the response that the state put forward. The point that must be highlighted in this context is that a lot of these migrants would, over time, return to the same city from which they had travelled back. In parts of Delhi, Bengaluru, Gurgaon, and Hyderabad, this process has already begun. Women living in *jhuggis*[2] in and around Delhi are already contemplating the immense loss of jobs that might be coming their way once all the residents around their *jhuggis* begin to leave for their offices on an everyday basis. One of the women stated:

> Earlier, the people used to employ us for their convenience. If I could not go to work, I could send my daughter or somebody else to do my job and I could split the wages with them. But after Covid, they have suddenly become so much conscious that they refuse to accept anyone else. Also, it becomes further difficult because they have employed me back after a lot of requests, and I do not want to endanger that in any way. If I do not have this job, then I will have to go back to my village.

Such traumatic events alter the perception that many of the individuals hold towards a particular social institution, especially if the concerned person comes from a vulnerable social or cultural group. When disasters create conditions in which people have to leave the places they had been living in, they leave behind a sense of belonging (Diaz-Quiñones, 2019). As the first chapter has already stated, disaster capitalism does not pay heed to such issues of belongingness, but instead focuses more on the profits that it can extract from the situation. That being said, the responses to disasters can be structured in such a way that even if migrant workers and other such vulnerable sections of the population have to leave their place of occupation, they do not have to sacrifice their dignity and livelihood in the process. Sainath correctly mentions that it was entirely possible for the state to take over the various public spaces, such as marriage halls, business centres, and community halls, and use them as centres for letting the migrant workers stay. Sainath says:

> When we arrange trains for the migrants, we charge them full fare. Then we put in AC trains and Rajdhani class fares of Rs 4,500. To make it worse, you say the tickets can be booked online, assuming they all have smartphones. Some of them buy those tickets. But in Karnataka, they cancel them because the chief minister meets the builders, who say the slaves are escaping. What you are witnessing is the quelling of an anticipated slave rebellion.
>
> (MN, 2020, Para 5)

Arguments of civic capitalism do not address this issue in an adequate manner. Daniel Monti (2013) argues that all human beings within a particular social context take advantage of the peaceful conditions created by civic capitalism while continuously posturing themselves as being better than the ones already existing. Social groups, under such modes of thinking, treat people in a way that they themselves would ideally want to be treated. However, when one notices the kind of hatred, negligence, and stigmatisation that these migrant workers encounter on an everyday basis in urban India, one is tempted to believe that any kind of hypothesis based on a civic order has to understand that the civic order in place is a capital-driven one. In the context of India, the civic order is largely influenced by feudal values, wherein social attributes such as caste and gender play an integral part.

Things such as civic order and civic charity are the domains of the privileged under capitalism because they control the way value systems are structured in the society, which results in the production of ideas (Marx & Engels, 1845–46/1976). And, established virtue and value systems in any society play an important role in the way in which philanthropy and civic charity are structured in the society (Holland, 2007). Monti et al. (2007) opine that, activities such as giving back to the community:

> were once the special province of conspicuously wealthy persons or the highest born and regarded people in a community. That changed with the rise of small businessmen in medieval towns and cities and the claims they made to rights and duties once reserved for the community's most prominent men and women. Tradesmen – the people we call entrepreneurs today – became bigger and more important not just by managing exchanges of goods and services or by 'spreading the wealth' by hiring local people . . . [but] also tilted to earn public regard.
>
> (Monti et al., 2007, p. 354)

Monti further argues:

> Someone from an unaccredited group could do a good deed without any public benefit falling back onto the good-deed doer's group. People from better-established groups might acknowledge the good deed, but the recognition would stop there. At the same time, a misdeed by someone from an unaccredited or discredited group could be used to justify attacks upon other people in the miscreant's group.
>
> (Monti, 2013, p. 10)

The first prime minister of India, Jawaharlal Nehru, was quite critical of how Monti's 'unaccredited groups' would function in India. First of all, it is essential to clarify the concept of unaccredited group in India, which would basically almost always refer to Dalits, Muslims, and women who have faced discrimination in accessing the vaccine (VP, 2021, November 23). There are also issues such as digital inequality, which has made access to vaccines and other essential services difficult for a significant part of the population. The vaccine distribution in India for the 18–44 age-group exhibits this tendency quite blatantly. With the central government directing the people to register on the internet for receiving the vaccine (Bhanj, 2021, March 2; Koshy, 2021, April 28) without taking into consideration issues such as internet penetration and digital literacy, the vaccine rollout is destined to further highlight the fault lines within the Indian society in terms of class, caste, and gender along with the uneven development that bolsters the urban-rural divide (Avadhani & Reddy, 2021, May 7). This will also have implications for the pace of vaccination in the country, which is already reeling at a pace slower than most countries of its size and dimension (Walsh, 2021, April 10).

Borer and Monti (2006) have pointed out that even though certain businesspeople and women tend to contribute a lot more to the civic causes, their contribution often gets overlooked. It is true that, in spite of the important contribution that women make to society, they have faced an increasingly difficult time during the lockdowns with increasing cases of violence against women being registered. As Uppal and Sonie write in their government funded report:

> The National Commission for Women . . . has been receiving complaints mostly via emails. In the first week of March (2–8), the Commission had received 116 complaints of crimes against women from across the country. During the Lockdown period from 23–31 March, the number of complaints increased to 257. According to the NCW data, during the Lockdown period, there have been 69 cases of domestic violence, 77 cases under Right to Live with Dignity, 15 cases of harassment of married women in the home, two dowry deaths, and 13 cases of rape or attempt to rape. The number of domestic violence cases in the week

prior to the Lockdown was 30, harassment of married women 13, Right to Live with Dignity 35.

(Uppal & Sidhu, 2020, p. 25[3])

The reasons for this might be multifarious in nature, including issues surrounding the sense of being captive[4] and the obliteration of one's private space during the lockdown.[5] The erosion of the private space of individuals is a construction of the neoliberal order. Patriarchy is 'a system of social structures and practices in which men dominate, oppress and exploit women' (Walby, 1990, p. 20). Domestic violence is a part of the patriarchal social order and as such has been a part of the social order for decades, where men have been provided with both the social and familial power along with additional privileges to exploit and oppress women (Tonsing & Tonsing, 2017). Ronnie and Shannon (2013) have argued that the way in which the private sphere 'idealized by the notions of hearth and home – denigrated and endangered women in part by isolating them and rendering them subject to male control' (p. 39). This has come to be escalated during the lockdown because it has created the conditions under which the idea of male control and its associated manifestations of violence can be easily exercised.

Muslims in India have also been facing a similar sort of situation in the public sphere. The public sentiment regarding the Muslims in India has already been suffering greatly in recent times, and the incidents surrounding the Tablighi Jamaat are a glaring example of this. The Tablighi Jamaat had held a four-day conclave in Malaysia in February 2020. The problems began when more than 620 people connected with the event tested positive for COVID-19, with most of the then 73 cases in Brunei and 10 cases in neighbouring Thailand being connected to the event, which made Malaysia seal its borders (Radhakrishnan, 2020). The *New York Times* reported on March 3 that the Tablighi Jamaat meeting has been the largest vector of the virus in Southeast Asia (Philip, 2020b, March 31). It was the same organisation, which then held a gathering at Delhi's Nizamuddin Markaz (centre), where the organisation organised an annual conference on the 3rd of March in 2020, with an attendance of 250 people from abroad who then for various reasons stayed in India, and:

> one of its members . . . told BBC Hindi that hundreds of delegates left before the lockdown came into effect on 24 March, but that more than 1,000 followers. Including many foreigners, got stranded, as all modes of transport and international flights were cancelled.
>
> (BBC, 2020, April 2, Para 9)

Newspaper reports of the attendees trying to flee the country added to the media frenzy which was created by this particular event (Dwarkanath, 2020, April 5), aptly aided by the political situation prevalent in the nation. The kind of response, both from the privately owned media and the government-sponsored media houses, proved that the repercussions of any event cannot be separated from the existing socio-political situation in the society. The jingoistic outburst around the Tablighi Jamaat did not stop even after recovering from COVID-19, the infected attendees of the conference had donated plasma for furthering the treatment against COVID-19. However, that did not deter discourses such as 'Corona Jihad' from being circulated within the mainstream and right-wing media (Sharma & Gupta, 2020, April 27). Some of the reporters even went to the extent of accusing the organisation and its members of committing crimes against humanity, such as Bismee Taskin's (2020, April 1) report for *The Print*. The central government, instead of countering the rampant communal narrative, opted to utilise certain alternative and independent media outlets to justify itself, while omitting the errant news channels untouched (Shantha, 2020, November 18).[6] Gandhi-Mody (2022) also talks about the Tablighi Jamaat in her book. She writes about how the gathering went ahead despite repeated warnings from the Delhi state government and the central government, and how this affected the public perception of the organisation: 'Due to the panic and fear of the unknown disease and a perception being built up in the media, folks began to blame the Tablighi Jamaat as the group responsible for spreading the virus in the country' (Gandhi-Mody, 2022, p. 75).

The problem with Gandhi-Mody's narrative is that most of the sources she cites remain from the popularly perceived establishment-backed media houses. Her arguments remain laden with the arguments that the establishment provided for the complete vilification of the entire Muslim community, which followed after the Jamaat was publicly proclaimed to be the *only* carrier of the virus in India, including the strongarming of Muslim voices in the country during the pandemic. The demonisation of the minorities in India had escalated greatly during the lockdown period. Although, as Komireddi (2019) has argued that the problems did not begin with the BJP, but rather escalated with the BJP coming to power.[7] The BJP's insistence on portraying the Muslims as the *other* has created a highly vulnerable state of being for them. In its drive to evoke feelings of 'genuine nationalism', it has constantly demonised and impoverished the Muslim populace. The implications of this have been felt across the pandemic response, which did not take the deprived state of the Muslims into account. Jawaharlal Nehru (1950/2015) argued that it is virtually impossible for any form of loyalty to germinate under pressure and that labelling and hate-mongering does not help the cause of integration of the nation. Nehru stated:

> [The] only real long-term policy we can have is to consolidate India by making all the minorities in the country feel completely at home in the State, and indeed by removing all sense of difference from the political point of view between the so-called majorities and minorities.
> (Nehru, 1950/2015, p. 47)

Under neoliberalism, these sentiments that Nehru had been talking about have drastically increased manifold. It is indeed neoliberal capitalism, that produces the conditions – social, cultural, and economical – within which such tendencies become violent in nature or possess the highest probability of becoming mainstream political ideological constructions.

Anand Teltumbde (2018) argues that the continuous demonisation and exclusion of certain communities or groups from the mainstream scheme of things has been aggravated under the regime of the right-wing BJP government, which has increased the internal contradictions existing in the Indian society, especially between the workers in general and the other *non-working class* in the traditional sense, but non-capitalist classes. There have been certain factors which have contributed to this. For example, while talking about the Tablighi Jamaat, Faizan Mustafa (2020, April 17) reports that things have further worsened with fake news and the suppression of governmental data becoming institutionalised under the contemporary regime in India. Mustafa argues that, holding the conference because of the existing laws in the country which did not prohibit religious gatherings from taking place, was not illegal in any way contrary to how it was reported in mainstream media. This became further problematic for the minorities in India because of the relative lack of representation of the minorities within the country's political system. According to Aakar Patel (2020), one of the major causes of concern at this juncture is the absence of Muslim and representations from other marginalised communities in the parliament. In the case of Muslims, it is at its lowest historically. Because of such systemic inequalities existing within the system, the pandemic has also affected the Muslim population differently, especially the poorer Muslims.[8]

Lockdowns initiated as a response to the Covid crisis have shown that businesses cannot sustain the multitude of ways in which individual human subjectivities engage with situations of crisis. The attention, in those situations, immediately turn to the governmental public administration. Public administration in India is a tumultuous task, even for the highly experienced public administrators. Padma Ramachandran (1995) has laid out the difficulties that public administrators in India face on an everyday basis in implementing their duties.[9] That being said, the current author does not desire to indicate that public administrators are indispensable. It is also correct that public administrators and bureaucrats in India often engage in acts of violence against the poor in India. The situations constructed by the response to the COVID-19 pandemic were also not that different. There were reports of public administrators using police personnel to beat street vendors, delivery executives, and hawkers (The Telegraph, 2020, March 24; Scroll, 2021, May 11; Siddiqui, 2021, May 22; Pandey, 2021, May 23). However, the situations within which COVID-19 has pushed human society into, the role and importance of public administration, were felt deeply. Public administration, like public policymaking, in India is a difficult task with multiple issues, which include not only coordination among various levels of bureaucracy but also within the administrative body itself.

Ramachandran (1995) argues that public administration is a discipline that touches almost every aspect of civic life, and therefore requires further infrastructure development in the country. Ramachandran has pointed out that the lack of public expenditure in the education of students as public administrators, like what goes in into educating the doctors, the engineers or even the army, has created a lack of effective public administrators in India. In many countries, such as India and Pakistan, times of crisis usually involve the implementation of the army on a massive scale to manage the society during those times. The question that arises at this point is that public administrators in India, in spite of all the shortcomings that Ramachandran has brought forward, it cannot be denied that the task of civil servants and administrators had increased manifold during the pandemic. Their separation from their families and the constant ordeal of being responsible for the many lives that exist within their managed territories often lead these civil administrators – otherwise highly competent and efficient personnel who have been selected through one of the toughest examinations of the world (AECC Global, 2022, April 27) – to become akin to automated responders to standard solutions in extraordinary times. Businesses benefit from the erosion of *original thinking*, feelings, and emotions which according to Erich Fromm have become commonplace under capitalism:

> From the very start of education original thinking is discouraged and ready-made thoughts are put into people' heads. How this is done with young children is easy enough to see. They are filled with curiosity about the world, they want to grasp it physically as well as intellectually. They want to know the truth, since that is the safest way to orient themselves in a strange and powerful world. Instead, they are not taken seriously, and it does not matter whether this attitude takes the form of open disrespect or of the subtle condescension which is usual towards all who have no power.
>
> (Fromm, 1942/2001, p. 213)

Neoliberalism actively embraces the complete obliteration of the sense of sympathetic feelings among the citizens. The exodus faced by the migrant workers is a striking example of this. The SWAN, an organisation which was working throughout the lockdown in India, especially with migrant workers, stated that out of the 6,319 workers that it spoke to till June 2020, 52% had rations which could last only for a day or less. In Dharavi, as Sah (2020, June 4) states, 60% of the 338 workers that SWAN spoke to, had rations only for a day. It is worthwhile to mention that in June 2020, Dharavi recorded a total of 1,849 cases of COVID-19 (Mumbai Mirror, 2020, June 3), greater than the then total number of cases in Assam and Kerala (Sah, 2020, June 4). Places such as Dharavi in India were not only suffering from the way in which the policies were being made – which did not take them into account much – but also by the misinformation that was spread among them (Lahariya et al., 2021). Even the Department of Economic and Social Affairs (2020, June 11) considers the dissemination of accurate and reliable information regarding the pandemic as a critical service during the pandemic. Businesses remain inept to make inroads into this sphere because they often engage with the society at a macro level but do not do so at a micro level, especially in places such as Dharavi.

The commodities that businesses produce are not products of the *businesses* themselves, but rather of the labour power that they employ, and often pay cheaply. The reality is even starker in countries such as India, where the working class is reeling under pressure from the globalised neoliberal production models. Inequalities exist not only among countries of the Global North and Global South but there are inequalities even within the countries of the Global North and Global South, which have to be acknowledged. John S. Saul, an important contemporary Marxist thinker, has argued that the countries of the Global South are far more heterogeneous economically than those of the Global North (Saul, 2006). This is easily visible in the manner urban neighbourhoods are constructed in India, or, for that matter, anywhere in today's globalised society. The ways in which certain neighbourhoods are constructed in certain areas bear resemblance, based on the class they represent, to neighbourhoods in other countries more than they do with other areas of their own society (Farrall et al., 2020). Various factors play crucial roles in this regard, from gentrification (Stein, 2019) to authoritarian and neoliberal economic reforms (Harvey, 2019). The manner in which politics operates in the contemporary society converts the businesspeople from being mere voters, and as such equal stakeholders in the political outcomes of elections in liberal democracies. Many aspects of this transformation have to do with the conversion of all forms of capitalism into crony capitalism, which has been further bolstered through the continuous and fascistic use of the power of mainstream media. The utilisation of media has been one of the cornerstones of the ways in which the current prime minister of India, Narendra Modi, has conducted his entire election campaigns in both 2014 and 2019. While analysing the rise of Jeremy Corbyn, Jeremy Gilbert (2016) brought forward the importance that political media had occupied in the current political ecosystem. Gilbert noted that under contemporary capitalism, the media plays a vital role in the manner in which leadership positions and personnel are perceived by the common people.

The BJP government has mastered the manner in which the interests of large businesses can be made to look entwined with those of the common populace in the country.[10] The ways in which the present regime have been endorsed by the business community of the country has proved that in terms of the ways in which businesses and workers look at events have remained drastically at odds even after more than 70 years of independence. The confluence of the state and the market, as people like Harvey (2005) and Leys

(2008) had been speaking about, becomes abjectly clear in the case of media, especially under the contemporary ruling class in India. The state and market under neoliberalism are meshed with each other. Inamdar (2014), Chandra (2019), and Eban's (2019) studies have pointed out the interdependence that they share with each other. Neoliberal developmental projects' insistence on turning cities into business hubs has prompted tenders being floated for the construction of housing colonies and ensuring transportation for the urban middle class inhabiting those places, as well as enabling the growth of microfinance private companies for disbursing loans to the people. Civic capitalism is infested with symptoms of morbidity, not only because it merely advocates in favour of showing ideological gratitude to businesses for following the mandates put up by the state, and the state for working for the citizens, but also because it tends to neglect the contribution that labour has to play in the sustenance of the society by focusing more on the concept of citizenship than of class and labour. Forms of civic capitalism that have been brought out by theorists such as Daniel Monti and Colin Hay do not talk much about the actual workers, who constitute the society as it exists for everyone to enjoy, but rather talk more about the ways in which a more representative system of democratic governance can be implemented. One of the major issues with civic capitalism is that their theories may have implications for small businesses and petty production units.[11] These tactics employed by monopoly capital reflects the ubiquity of capital in maintaining its overwhelming presence in the society.

These mechanisms, which have been accelerated as part of the massive digitalisation, have resulted in a complete subversion of the local merchants and businesspeople. Small local businesses are important for capitalism because they ensure that a part of it is always present in the market, bringing into effect the metamorphosis of productive and industrial capital to commodity capital and further into commercial capital. In doing so, capital ensures that it is reproduced at a social level. However, capital also has a tendency of gobbling up these small businesspeople with the help of monopoly capital. Most of the services that small businesses use are often informal in nature, performed mostly in cash and by migrant workers in India's urban spaces, as Srivastava (2020) noted in her report for Reuters on Dharavi in Mumbai.[12] During disasters, the activities at the local or municipal level are far more equipped to help those in need than those at city or state levels. But, with the rise of monopoly capital, it has become extremely difficult for these businesses to survive. COVID-19 and its associated lockdowns have made it almost mandatory for the businesses to innovate, in spite of suffering from decline in turnovers both in the domains of products and processes with some companies 'continuing to employ such process innovations [which] will increase the productivity of employees in their current tasks or allow employees to be allocated to more productive ideals' (Riom & Valero, 2020, p. 9).

Large businesses are more likely to adopt technological innovations faster than smaller ones, be it in the United Kingdom or India. Although the rate of such innovations made during the pandemic is unlikely to persist (Roper & Turner, 2020, August 5), COVID-19 has initiated a leap in the way one understands technology. Technological innovations, previously treated as scared have now become profane. They have become an element of everyday use by a majority of the people in the world. Amidst this, COVID-19 has initiated one of the greatest and the most rapid race for technological innovation among the capitalists in the technology sector. With platforms such as Google Meet and Zoom becoming indispensable in sectors such as pandemic management and education, it is essential to establish a relationship between these technological innovations and the various different social contexts in which they find themselves in. The digitalisation of society is a reality in the contemporary India, and there is no escape from this harsh reality. It will also be a lack of common understanding to assume that the drive towards digitalisation which has been initiated by COVID-19 will dissipate once the pandemic is over. With the coming of COVID-19 as a global pandemic along with its associated lockdowns and other public health measures in place, most essential services that do not strictly require physical presence, such as education and public training, have been forced to move towards a partial or fully online model. This has been actualised through the use of Information and Communication Technologies (ICTs). Amidst these massive digitalisations, the citizens' perspective is rarely invoked, which often gets lost within the quality assurance surveys conducted within the bureaucratic digital models of assessment. Digitalisation has both social and psychological aspects, having a significant impact on the articulation of the social reality as one knows it. Examples of social changes include the creation of atomised individuals who are completely alienated from the social reality (Lefebvre, 1991b), the creation of abstract spaces referring to spaces where exchange relations dominate (Lefebvre, 1991a), and the evolution of highly controlled spaces through the use of surveillance and repressive diktats.

In the sphere of education, the psychological implications can include the intense amount of stress and anxiety that cause hindrances to the overall learning of the students by creating hurdles in their internalisation of the processes of digital or online education (Cao et al., 2020; Chakraborty et al., 2020; Essadek & Rabeyron, 2020). Digitalisation and their application are not simple processes, but rather encompass broader aspects such as social class, accessibility, and socio-economic marginalisation processes. While it is true that digitalisation has enabled the continuation of certain important aspects of contemporary social life such as education and public interaction during the pandemic, it has also come at the cost of anxiety and stress causing emotional, learning, and behavioural problems among children and adolescents (Dixit & Chauhan, 2020), and with massive psychosocial impacts such as increased loneliness and desperation among the elderly (Nagpal & Dixit, 2020). For example, in the realm of education, while the necessary requirement to continue the process of education has been realised, this massive and sudden need to digitalise education has created certain problems – for students, teachers, and the educational institutes in general. An in-depth analysis of the situation remains beyond the scope of this particular book, but considering that in India, a large proportion of children and young adults do not have access to education in general (Ramachandran & Ramkumar, 2005), it can be estimated that a further proportion of these individuals will be marginalised with the onslaught of digitalisation – especially when digital education is promoted as the sole means of imparting education. The ways in which newer forms of technology have been introduced into the everyday life of citizens during COVID-19 has massively impacted the individuals and the communities of which they are parts of, including their ways of organising their communities. Han (2013) argues that these newer technologies, which are facilitating the creation of virtual communities (Deb Roy, 2022), have 'made [the] community – the *we* – deteriorate markedly. It is destroying the public sphere and heightening human isolation' creating egoistic individuals (Han, 2013, p. 44).

Even with widespread digitalisation, a wide plethora of services still remain outside the affordable limits of the poor and the working class. Another case in point are the people with disabilities. With COVID-19, it is medically possible that people with pre-existing conditions might experience a harsher stint with the virus (Lewin, 2020), and they were often left at the mercy of the situation. The way in which disability services are maintained in India has raised numerous questions over the past few decades. During COVID-19, the disabled people found themselves to be further marginalised within the health framework of the country. According to Chauhan and Harsheeta (2020), apart from the demand for fixing the costs associated with essential medical and transportation services, disabled people were also worried about whether they would be treated equally and if their special health services could be maintained during the lockdown phase.

Capitalism, as Russell and Malhotra (2019) have opined, creates the notion of 'disability' as an anomie to promote its own interests whereby the labour power of a section of the population is rendered useless, which makes 'Disabled workers face inherent economic discrimination within the capitalism system, stemming from employers' expectations of encountering additional production costs when hiring or retaining' them (Russell & Malhotra, 2019, 'Introduction'). There are other important issues that disabled people face in their everyday lives, which become critical issues within a pandemic ravaged world, such as insurance and social security (Russell, 2005/2019), expensive corporate driven in-home services (Russell & Malhotra, 2002/2019), and the like. All of these issues contribute to the conversion of human beings into objects of exploitation by commodifying the disabled body. Russell and Malhotra (2002) argue that under corporate-driven capitalist systems, disability is portrayed as a social problem that can be only dealt with by keeping the disabled population out of the mainstream society. This, in turn, creates numerous employment issues for the disabled people, who often face economic hardships due to employers' expectations and social exclusion (Russell & Malhotra, 2002) – the resolution of which fall outside the domain of conventional policies (Russell, 2001/2019).

Murthy et al. (2020) state in their empirical report published by the Indian Institute of Public Health (IIPH) that 81.6% of the disabled people have faced moderate to high levels of stress during the pandemic. Some of this stress can be attributed to the additional stigmatisation, discrimination, and isolation that disabled people face in their everyday lives, which was aggravated during the lockdown. Around 42.5% of the disabled people reported that it had become extremely difficult for them to get treatment during the lockdown, out of which 12.7% had pre-existing medical conditions and around 58% expressed their difficulties in getting routine treatment during the lockdown. The numbers for accessibility to emergency services are lower – 16.6% needed emergency services and only 45% could access them (Murthy et al., 2020). Services for disabled people benefit greatly when community organisations, or the communities directly engage with disabled individuals as their own. However, as Naomi Klein (2007) argues, under neoliberal capitalism there occurs a depletion of the community as one knows it. Previously, disasters may have been occasions when people united in solidarity, forgetting their internal differences and contradictions, but they are often not so anymore. Naomi Klein argues:

> Not so long ago, disasters were periods of social levelling, rare moments when atomised communities put divisions aside and pulled together. Increasingly, however, disasters are the opposite: they provide windows into a cruel and ruthlessly divided future in which money and race buy survival.
>
> (Klein, 2007, p. 413)

Neoliberalism, which desires to weaken all forms of social solidarity (Harvey, 2006/2019, 'Neo-liberalism'), has played a critical role in this. Neoliberal capitalism attempts to render mainstream which coexists and completely becomes one with the extremely powerful capitalist state and deregulation of the economy (Harvey, 2014, p. 42). This makes it further difficult to actualise or even conceive of the emergence of a social cooperation among citizens to help each other during times of disaster. Under neoliberalism, where everybody has been forced into a bubble of self-preservation, the social order 'encourages . . . individuals to treat public issues as personal troubles' forcing the search for alternatives to tread along pre-defined market mechanisms (Matthewman, 2015, p. 99), thus evading the larger structural and ideological questions about capitalism. The community structure in India, however, has survived through the worst prospects of the pandemic. In fact, the community has, as some believe, emerged stronger after the pandemic with increased sensibilities of solidarity. The way community associations and self-help groups (SHGs) have functioned during the second wave of the pandemic in India has been exemplary.[13]

The Neoliberal Apocalypse

Neoliberalism has produced a situation under which the apocalypse not only appears possible but also imminent – both in form and content. The methods in which capitalism behaves under neoliberal policies are extremely harsh on both the human society and the natural world. The change in climate and the subsequent scarcity of resources is one of them. The continuous degradation of the quality of air and water in India has contributed to the worsening of the spread of COVID-19 in the country (Spears, 2019; Ramesh, 2021). Just as how *Big Firms* need *Big Flus* to survive as Rob Wallace states, capitalism also needs wars and its associated arms production to survive (Posadas, 1981b; Lowenstein, 2015). The primary agents behind such policies of capitalist states and societies remain the bourgeois intellectuals and the financial sectors, who leave no stone unturned to create inequality and insecurity in the world on a global scale, which leaves no option but for anti-capitalist forces to retaliate through the same methods, including violent actions (Posadas, 1981d).

Visions of apocalypse communism as highlighted by Posadas (1981c) often remain highly prideful of the functions of the army in the society when the army becomes political in nature. However, the problem with optimistic visions about army, under contemporary capitalism, relates to the ways in which policing is being promoted by almost all the major capitalist democracies in the world. The insecurity that characterises most capitalist regimes globally makes them take drastic steps such as wars to preserve their supremacy (Posadas, 1980). Neoliberal capitalism has conveniently created a situation where most aspects of human life today are under the influence of capitalist profit extraction. COVID-19 pandemic has exhibited that, provided science is used for the benefit of the people at large, it can indeed be a vehicle of change in the society. The quick turnaround of the vaccines for COVID-19 has exhibited that science and technology do possess the ability to restructure human lives amidst chaos (Miller, 2021). Furthermore, the way in which the results of innovations, such as vaccines, have been monetised for profit, points towards the limitation of science and technology under capitalism. Juan Posadas argued:

> Science is not independent. It is not comparable to the activity of growing a plant, because when we do, we can still decide what we will reap in spite of being subject to nature. Things are different when it comes to science because it is subject to those who pay.
>
> (Posadas, 1968, p. 1)

Such conceptualisation of technology is nothing new. Previously the Dutch Council Communist Anton Pannekoek and Herbert Marcuse had also written in detail about the relationship between technology and capitalism. Technology was a crucial part of the formulation of the socialism in the twenty-first century perspective, which took shape in Latin America. Harnecker (2007) in her work has engaged in considerable detail with the changes which have been ushered into the capitalist relations of production by the growing scientific knowledge and technological advancements. However, as the Dutch Socialist and reputed astronomer Pannekoek would argue, these developments have taken place within a context where capitalism has used science and technology for its own benefits rather than using technology for the greater social good, converting science to nothing but *bourgeois science* (Steen, 2019).

When apocalyptic tendencies emerge in the society or even in the body of an individual human being, it is very easy for certain things to become commodities – for example, as Kalanithi (2016) says, breath becomes air in case of a health crisis when an individual is on medicated oxygen. During the second wave, a significant number of people have already gone through the process. Healthcare needs and food are often two of the initial entities that become scarce during apocalyptic times. Between them, food is often the first entity to become scarce during such times. As GRAIN (2016), a small international non-profit organisation, has laid out in a report in 2016, the relationship between climate change and food security. They argue that industrial food production has seriously endangered the food security of the marginalised sections of the population in countries in the Global South. They also report that the effects of the industrial food production are most highly felt among the small and marginal farmers. With COVID-19 as well, there was the upsurge of a massive amount of food insecurity among the marginalised populace, especially in the Global South due to numerous factors, including trade restrictions (Glauber et al., 2020; Hansda, 2022).

One of the major causes of food insecurity in India, in addition to the inflation, is the complete destruction of the PDS, which has failed to function well in most states in the country. For example, it has already been stated that the PDS system was fairly well developed in Kerala in the early 1990s (Swaminathan, 2000). The Kerala Model of Democratic Communism paints a different picture than other states in the country. The state with the lowest poverty rate is Kerala with 0.71% MDPI (Hindustan Times, 2021, November 27). Also, the percentage of people owning houses is highest in Kerala, at 82%, which leads the state placed second, that is Punjab, by around 5% (Mahambare, 2015, February 9). The relative success of Kerala – to be analysed more critically in the conclusion – in managing the pandemic paves the path towards conceptualising the relationship between different factors in the context of a health emergency. One of the major reasons for this is that Kerala has been able to focus on the continued provisioning of public goods, even under neoliberal regimes.

Public goods are usually defined as 'a good, service or capability that is necessary for a life with dignity' (Sinha et al., 2019, p. 133). Food, the most important of all public goods, is necessary for sustaining life of any form, and scarcity of food has been a characteristic feature of the COVID-19 pandemic in India for the marginalised. Human beings might not live only for food, but they do need food to survive (Dunayevskaya, 1984). For example, in Bihar, an 8-year-old child died because of starvation – accompanied by fever and diarrhoea – caused by the lack of food because there was no work available during the lockdown and the shopkeepers had stopped issuing credits – a common practice in India – in March 2020 (Ray, 2020, March 30). The migrant and contractual workers like the boy and his family found themselves to be left at the mercy of the state, which often provided remunerations but those were highly inadequate (Yadav, 2020, March 24). And, in light of a poor PDS, the crises caused by the shortfall of food and supplies became further elevated. The death of the boy, who could not even afford the medicine, in a timely fashion, that the doctor at his local government hospital had prescribed. Such deaths point towards the larger structural defects in the healthcare system in India, which cause malnutrition that increases the chances of such deaths. Malnutrition is highest among the poorest population of India, especially the women and children (Sinha et al., 2019). According to UNICEF (2022), over 25% of the women in India who are of reproductive age are undernourished, which also makes any large scale post-birth nutritional programmes for children redundant because they are born undernourished, despite the large-scale economic progress of the nation (Abraham, 2019, July 10). Deaths such as these make one think about the fact that there have been reports of the government not taking warnings of health officials and experts – employed by the government itself – seriously regarding the deadly B.1.617 variant, which with the other variants caused the massive second wave of COVID-19 in India and continued to allow election rallies, religious gatherings, and similar activities (Ghoshal & Das, 2021, May 1; Ghoshal & Siddiqui, 2021, June 15).

In normal times, there is a scarcity of the resources, which has been used by disaster capitalists to increase prices and increase their probability of profit accumulation. Resource scarcity is one of the major problems that human society has been confronting in the last few decades. In fact, the problem has always been there, it is merely that human society has come to realise it in the recent few decades, when climate change has become a concrete threat. As Andreas Malm (2016) has argued, climate and the natural world has increasingly found itself to be the centre of attention, while newer theories are being proposed regarding the causality of historical events. This has also been bolstered by the fact that the constantly depleting natural resources available has been a major cause for concern for environmental thinkers globally. With COVID-19, the conflicts around scarce resources such as water which have characterised India and its relations with its neighbours will eventually escalate as nations struggle to hold on to the limited resources in light of the economic downturn which has characterised COVID-19. Natural resources have, under capitalism, become a major marker of geopolitical influence (Ramesh, 2018). At a micro level, the inability to share a common natural resource has resulted in numerous conflicts, and such conflicts, as Mridula Ramesh narrates, are only set to increase in the coming years. The scarcity of resources – both natural and man-made – will also have an impact on the social relations among people. It must be realised that 'social relations are strongly influenced by competition and any form of scarcity will exacerbate existing tensions between countries or among class, cultural or ethnic divisions within countries' (Dawson et al., 2018, p. 16). Amidst this situation, it is almost always the vulnerable and the most marginalised who often get left out of the provisioning means available in any society. COVID-19 was not the only crisis of an apocalyptic nature that India was facing back in 2020. India under contemporary times is also facing a major environmental crisis (Narain, 2017; Ramesh, 2021). Though it is difficult to establish a direct connection between climate change and COVID-19 as Malm (2020) highlights. It is true that one can be saved from COVID-19, although it is unlikely that climate change will occur. However, if one takes out the specific characteristics of both of them, then there are some similarities at a macro level. For example, both COVID-19 and Climate Change, as Malm (2020) highlights, have brought forward the vulnerabilities that the marginalised sections face under capitalism.

Naomi Klein (2007) argues that when large-scale disasters become a reality, such as a hurricane or even the contemporary pandemic, human beings do not ideally want to begin their lives afresh with a black slate but rather desire to harvest their new lives out of the remnants of their old lives. It is well known that Posadas was so enthusiastic about nuclear warfare, but he did not consider that nuclear warfare would potentially result in a blank slate for a significant amount of the population, both in the Global South and in the Global North. The problem with most of the approaches towards understanding the post-apocalyptic views of Posadas is his approach towards the ways in which disasters transform human society. To Posadas (1979), the changes that occur within a revolutionary society happen very fast. However, as history has exhibited and Lenin (1905) has rightly said in his *Revolutionary Days*, while it is true that during times of revolutionary upheavals, social change occurs in an accelerated fashion, but at the same time, it is also essential to realise that for social change to occur at a rapid pace, the social context for that change takes place slowly. Resetting social structures mechanically will often lead one to argue that society works one-dimensionally, which conveniently neglects the fact that disasters have different meanings for different people (Matthewman, 2015). Human beings in situation where *they have to rebuild from scratch* often have to face uncomfortable decisions over the cost that they have to pay regarding their act of regeneration. Trimble (2019) shows this through the concepts of the *Last Man* and the *Economic Man*, and argues that, 'Visions of apocalypse that closely align their Last Man with the worldview, practices, and values of economic Man expose the colonial dimensions of the apocalyptic imaginary: its investment in blank slates, a logic of closeness', along with the regeneration of the world through violence (Slotkin, 1973; Trimble, 2019, p. 143).

The elites often find it easy to regenerate their lives from a blank slate, while for most of those on the margins, it is a process laden with difficult decisions. Both disaster communism and municipal socialism has the potential to work best in scenarios that already present some sort of equity, and at least, a sense of equality among the people. When large-scale disasters hit human societies, it is often the most vulnerable who get affected the most. COVID-19 has proved that, beyond doubt. The extent to which a local body might be successful in addressing the concerns of the marginalised populace in a post-pandemic situation depends on the structure of the body before the pandemic. India is, however, a country where even in 2020, a significant population of the vulnerable and poor children die because of premature birth, under-nutrition, pneumonia, and diarrhoea as Aiyar (2020) notes. Aiyar further continues:

> A Study led by the John Hopkins Bloomberg School of Public Health revealed that India topped the list for pneumonia and diarrhoea deaths – claiming 2,96,279 lives, that's thirty-three per hour, in 2015, and 2,60,990 or twenty-nine deaths per hour in 2016. Yes, immunization helps, but the average score flatters to deceive. The 2019 John Hopkins study shows that even in states where immunization coverage is 70 per cent, 'less than half of the children in a poor, urban area within that state fully immunized'.
> (Aiyar, 2020, pp. 56–57)

India thus is not one of those equitable scenarios. India is marked by numerous inequalities, not only economic but also social. Dréze and Sen (2013) have argued that private bodies can only help in inclusive growth and development when the state acts as an influential coordinator. Municipalism to most revolutionary socialists are merely an extension of the capitalist scheme of things. The Social Democratic Federation declared that municipalisation:

> like the Trusts, is only a development of Capitalism, and is run in the interest of the capitalist class. But it is capitalism in its most advanced stage. It is a form of collectivism; it demonstrates the practicability of public ownership, and supplies . . . the embryo of the industrial organisation of Socialist Society. . . . [T]he S.D.F. stands for the municipalisation and nationalisation of all monopolies as a step further towards the complete socialisation of all industries, and of all the means and instruments of production.
> ('The Social Democratic Federation, Its Objects, Its Principles, and Its Work', quoted from Towler, 1909, p. 3)

The success of any variant of disaster communism or municipal socialism depends to a large extent on the ways in which policies of nationalisation are taken up by the state. In the successive paragraphs, the chapter will critically evaluate the ways in which the lack of nationalisation, and administrative centralisation have played their roles in India's pandemic response. In doing so the chapter, and the book as it proceeds, talk about two methods of nationalisation keeping in mind the ways in which nationalisation policies often work in most societies. The first one being Plain and Simple Nationalisation and Socialisation referring to policies of nationalisation that only focus on nationalisation without focusing much about the broader social struggles that such policies inevitably become a part of. The second, and the preferred one, being Nationalisation and Socialisation for Holistic Social Progress, which refers to the ways in which nationalisation can be used as a tool for broader social progress and radical reforms. The history of nationalisation goes a long way in the context of India. Once India had gained her independence from the British in 1947, Jawaharlal Nehru, the first prime minister of India, and the Karachi Session of the INC, laid emphasis on the nationalisation of key industries, but at the same time, they also did not completely eradicate the necessity of private corporations.

The debate between Civic capitalism, of both varieties, and apocalypse communism is related to this struggle between private corporations and public bodies. Pande (2020) has elaborated on the two divergent views that gripped the Indian state in 1947 – the one proposed by Nehru which had a paternalistic attitude towards the market and emphasised protectionism to ensure social justice and socio-economic well-being; and the other proposed by Gandhi, which, even though it was anti-capitalist, like Nehru's, was focused on the creation of small republics of self-sufficient villages distinct from the plans of urbanisation that had been taken by the capitalist and the socialist countries. One of the major questions that tendencies such as disaster communism, municipal socialism, and civic capitalism have to face in the context of India is the perennial debate between Gandhian socialism and Nehruvian socialism, which has been a major feature of Indian democracy since 1947. Nehruvian socialism was focused on a strong and central state. Similarly, Posadas too focused his attention on the creation of a revolutionary state as a transitional model from capitalism to socialism. Both of them focused on the centrality of planning to advance egalitarian thought and structure in their respective contexts. However, there were certain differences between them. Posadas's state was based on the idea of a revolutionary dictatorship, while Nehru's was more democratic in nature. Most importantly, Posadas never gave away the class dimension of the struggle, however, flawed his application of the same might have been, but Nehru's socialism was more evolutionary than that of Bernstein and Kautsky. Nehru focused on the elimination of land lordship and other such evils that one usually associates with rural India (Singh & Hussain, 2021). Nehru was someone who, like Posadas, was mired with controversies. As Palat (2022, February 12) wrote in a recent article, Nehru was considered to be a bureaucracy friendly prime minister by the right, while the left found him too inadequate to bring in any structural change in the society.[14]

While Nehru's focus lay on planning, which in turn, led the way to his ideas surrounding the relationship between urbanisation and modernity. For

Gandhi, rural India should have been the focus of the national development project (Gandhi, 1979), while for Nehru, the rural communitarian society did not really become central to his project of development even though he did accept its centrality in the Indian society (Nehru, 1946/2016). Nehru insisted that within the community that rural India celebrated, the individual was often placed in an inferior position, which did not fit in well with the modern industrial society-based vision of India that he possessed, as Gopal (1986) has highlighted. Nehru, as Crocker (2009) notes, might have been *just* too modern and liberal for India to bring in a structural change within the society. However, that being said, Nehru was extremely crucial to bring in certain planning reforms in India, which have continued to serve India even in the contemporary times (Chandra et al., 2000). Nehru was highly materialistic in his outlook in the sense that he attempted to bring in social reforms through the state. Mahatma Gandhi tried to do the same through his insistence on trusteeship, which in plain words means, the dominance of philanthropy over means of social ownership and restructuring of the economy. Raghavan Iyer notes:

> Gandhi sensed that all our resources and possessions, at any level are not merely fragments of the Divine but are also inherently mortal and mutable. The Divine in its active aspect is ceaselessly creative and ever fluid in form. By analogy, human needs and material circumstances alter even while cultural patterns and social customs purport to maintain temporal continuity through established traditions.
>
> (Iyer, 1985, p. 4)

Nehru, above all, was a democratic socialist who believed that it is only a combination of socialism and democracy that can save India from capitalism and dictatorship. His tryst with Marx and Gandhi, and with both nationalism and socialism simultaneously, had left him with a confused state of affairs, which gets reflected in the way in which his progressive ideals still remained within the confines of the bourgeois model of development (Chandra et al., 2000). M. K. Gandhi believed that the act of renunciation that rich people ought to show would lead them towards regeneration of their human selves (Iyer, 1985). Civic capitalism of the kind that Daniel Monti talks about tends to transform this tryst with trusteeship into a fetish, where entrepreneurs become the drivers of the society.

The mutual aid movements conducted during COVID-19 have shown that the world can survive without the philanthropists. Samantha Klein (2020, June 1) argues that even though disaster capitalism is on the rise during the pandemic, there are certain terrific examples of human solidarities that focus on mutual aid and the culture of giving. It is this 'culture of giving' that has now been taken over by the corporates. The COVID-19 crisis has exhibited that philanthropic gestures can never account for the complete sphere of work that public sectors and community organisations perform during a health emergency. Community participation will be a key to furthering accountability within the sphere of urban governance and administration (HPEC, 2011). Disaster capitalism attempts to weaken the communitarian feeling among the people by acting upon the fears that people possess with regards to their own self-preservation during a pandemic. This often results in municipalities not being forced to be accountable to the public, but rather being converted into agencies benefitting the elite in the society who can articulate their self-preservation better, both financially and socially. Public accountability, under such circumstances, can only increase when the focus shifts back to the autonomy of the community.

Jewett et al. (2021) have argued that community resilience shown towards health emergencies such as pandemics have an intrinsic relationship with the social capital that members of the community possess. The chances that a municipality will be able to do that depend, to a large extent, on the financial autonomy that a municipality possesses. Tendencies such as municipal socialism, even though based on sound theoretical endeavours, will have a chance of survival in a world that is rapidly moving towards more rampant and exploitative neoliberal policies and governance, only if the municipalities have a certain autonomy. And, if municipalities have to be autonomous in nature, then they need to move towards more radical forms of financial autonomy (Moses, 2022). In India, certain urban reforms such as JNNURM have indeed improved the financial situation in many municipalities, but the municipalities still lack the human resources and institutional capacity to utilise them (Bhavsar et al., 2020). However, a reformed mode of democratic privatisation or independent enterprise-based reforms might not be the best solution in this context because one would still have to deal with inequality in the domains of social capital and community participation. Patel and Pant (2020) in their work on the *Mohalla Clinics* of Delhi run by the AAP have argued that community participation cannot emerge in particular sectors unless there is a general consensus and constitutional legality regarding the same in the very structure of the ULBs and governance.

ULBs in India have historically been – or at least till the 74th CAA – dominated by the influence of the larger and more powerful governing bodies of the state (Sivaramakrishnan, 2000), which at times, also resulted in irregular elections of local bodies. However, as Sivaramakrishnan (2013) has noted, there is an increasing need to revisit the impacts the amendment has had on urban governance because the process of urbanisation in India has been further complicated with the passing years after the neoliberal reforms. Mishra et al. (2021) have also argued that public policy making needs to be able to tackle the problems caused by the possible existence of corruption within the municipalities themselves. The powers vested to the municipalities with regards to controlling epidemics have to be seen in synchronisation with the existent political and social framework in place in the broader perspective. An egalitarian model of local governance has huge potential to achieve this. However, whether local governance would do this or not depends on the context within which those municipalities are located. Gurcharan Das (2012) has argued that India's problem is that it has always had a weak state and a strong social order, such that the state is not the problem, but the social order dominated by Brahmins and other caste Hindus is the primary contradiction in Indian society. He uses this analogy to justify the proliferation of the neoliberal reforms in India.

The *Dharma of Capitalism* to Das (2012) is one where the productive forces, which includes the market as a leading force, are given free rein to bring about progress and prosperity in the society taking India out of the Fabian socialism of Nehru. He does however acknowledge that capitalism in India is still not completely institutional in nature and suffers from the remnants of the old family-based industrialists' domination over the market. However, that being said, the growth of Indian capitalism over the past few decades has indeed relied on these familial ventures (Raianu, 2021). However, corporate rivalries have grown up even within these ventures as Gupta's (2019) analysis of the Tata versus Mistry conflict highlights. This is because of the transformation that these ventures have undergone under global capitalism. This goes on to prove that capitalism in India has evolved greatly since the days of the ancient merchants and the East India Company because of the structural adjustments in the Indian economic system, and as such the creation of capital and profits today is not the exclusive domain of any community, caste, or religion (Damodaran, 2008). In India, the research on how business is done, as well as the history of business in India has mainly focused on certain communities as Harish Damodaran (2008) has rightly pointed out. Works from Mukund (2012), Inamdar (2014), Timberg (2014), Levi (2015), Subramaniam (2016), and Goswami (2016) have continued to follow this tradition. These works have focused on the various caste and communitarian aspects of the ways in which Indian capitalism has developed over the past century, which has often treated individual capitalists being capitalists because they were part of a certain community, caste, or religion. However, it can be assumed – and safely so – that the growth of capitalism today does not depend merely on certain communities but has rather been transformed into an all-encompassing social process itself. Under neoliberalism, however, this process has totally engulfed the state itself, leaving as such little difference between the market and the state. The conditions created by COVID-19 in India leaves capitalism in India, as Posadas (1981a) had argued to be in the case of global capitalism, with little options because it cannot 'use the world as it likes' (Posadas, 1981a, p. 44).

Conclusion

A major part of civic capitalism theories is based on how capitalism can be made to work for the people, or rather how capitalism can be reengineered in a way in which it becomes beneficial to the people. However, in order to be beneficial to the people in general, capitalism has to be made to work for the most vulnerable sections of the populace, which during the pandemic were the informal frontline workers and the migrant workers. The failure of the various charities and philanthropists[15] to counter the structural injustice meted out to these people reflects the kind of deprivation that these people have been made to experience, which has put an unjust burden of civic attachment on them – towards a society that lacks any attachment towards them. Monti et al. (2003) have argued, and correctly, that the role and types of civic attachments have varied greatly over the past decades and centuries. The civic attachments of the twenty-first century are different than those of the past. Under capitalism, there has been a constant degeneration of the human psyche itself, which makes models based on egalitarian charity seem unlikely to succeed under neoliberalism. Even neoliberalism could not effectively do away with some of the intrinsic features of the Indian community based social set-up, which focus on mutual aid and human sensibilities of togetherness and empathy towards other fellow human beings. However, neoliberalism has surely degraded these feelings, an idea to which almost every social activist that the author has had conversations with agrees.

There is a depleting sense of the community in India, even in the hinterlands, caused by the rampant migration that Indian people have to engage in to satisfy their needs of sustenance. Sinha and Sinha (2018), in their work, have argued in favour of the Gandhian Trusteeship Model, and critiqued the socialist leanings of Nehruvian governance, which to them had too much of centralisation embedded within it – something that Nehru borrowed from the erstwhile Soviet Union under Stalin. This subsequently resulted in the gross violation of individual freedom and also created numerous hurdles for entrepreneurial ventures and getting personal work done by institutionalising the corruption that germinates within the bureaucracy when it is bestowed upon with too much power as Gurcharan Das (2000) writes.

Most of the criticisms that Das (2000) and Jalan (2005) have pointed out regarding the bureaucracy as it existed – and continues to exist – in India are to a certain extent justified. However, the kind of demonisation of the public sector that these authors resort to is grossly overstated. Jalan argued, 'The public sector does not really work for the public at large. The value added by the enterprises has been low, and instead of adding to public savings, they are now a major drain on the fiscal resources available to the government' (2005, p. 153). Jalan argues that the government should only play a political role within the provisioning of essential services such as education, health, roads, and water, but that this role has to be ably aided by the private sector such that free market competition can be brought in more effectively within the country. Because to Jalan, that would ensure the reduction of state's economic role while disabling monopolistic tendencies. Nehru's policies regarding the social ownership of the means of production – even though he largely spoke about the social ownership of the key industries – to them, was an admixture of 'Keynesian macroeconomics, Stalinist public investment policy, and Gandhian rural development' (Das, 2000, p. 90). Nehruvian socialism to Das

(2000) was extremely short-sighted because it did not pay much attention to exports and remained focused on social ownership of the key industries.

The Gandhian Trusteeship Model lands a strong criticism of this. According to the model proposed by Gandhi, it was trusteeship and not social ownership that could be the vehicle of change in the society. Trusteeship or such models of philanthropy, however, have failed to overcome the global crisis that COVID-19 has brought in. The United Nations was quick to recognise the important role that public service can play in the struggle against the pandemic. The Department of Economic and Social Affairs (2020, June 11) stated that due to the sudden onset of the pandemic, the public servants – which include teachers, sanitation workers, social welfare workers and officers, and the like – globally have found themselves engaged in an unequal battle against the virus in an attempt to restore continuity within the public sector. The Policy Response from the United Nations states:

> In the ongoing COVID-19 Pandemic, however, public servants are working under life-threatening circumstances. In all COVID-19 pandemic affected countries they are both expected to deliver services despite the pandemic while at the same time suffering its impact, either by being directly infected or having family members who are.
> (Department of Economic and Social Affairs, 2020, June 11, Para 5)

A lot of the charity and relief-centric works that most corporations have been engaging with during the pandemic are considered to be a part of their CSRs, which is a part of the overall global capitalist infrastructure (Balakrishnan et al., 2017). Sheth et al. (2022) in their latest report on Indian philanthropy have confirmed that CSR financing has grown at almost 15% annually over the last 7 years contributing to around 23% of total donations and charity drawn amounts in Financial Year 2021–22 – a rapid rise from the 15% in Financial Year 2015. They further state that the projections for the increase of CSR are that it would occupy around 32% of the total private giving by 2026–27 Financial Year, growing at almost 19% every year from 2021. The GTM can be a useful tool here, but the idea behind GTM was based on the voluntary renunciation of wealth (Kesavalu, 2004). Mainstream theoretical schools have often highlighted the role that accepted norms and practices play in the internal integration that characterise most modern societies – both nationally and globally (Rucht, 2011). These accepted norms and practices constitute the established practices of civility in the society, which the market and the state-form both exploit. Most of the criticisms which have emerged against the dominant mode of capitalist production systems in the recent past have not attacked the point of production under capitalism, and civic capitalism is no different.

Raya Dunayevskaya (1965) argued that the basic contradiction within all modes of capitalism – industrial, finance, neoliberal, digital, and so on or a combination of all of these – is the point of production under capitalism.

The inability of major theoretical paradigms to address the concerns related to this basic and fundamental contradiction under capitalism is also evident in civic capitalism. The basic tenet of Hay and Payne's (2015) civic capitalism model is the argument in favour of an increasing control of the state over businesses in such a way that the market can be made to work for the majority of the citizens. Hay and Payne (2015) also argue that civic capitalism, because of the involvement of the state as a regulator, will result in 'the development of a genuine social dimension that opens up different and more civic social policies and partnerships' (p. 8).

At the same time, Monti's (2013) definition of civic capitalism focuses on the idea that the world as it exists should be preserved and that the society should move towards more civic formations such that social inequality should not be demonised but rather be taken as an axis around which notions of civility can be developed so as to ensure utilitarian notions of happiness. The issues engaged with by civic capitalism are intimately associated with the struggles between people desiring to become 'new saviours' and the 'old saviours' of the society. Daniel Monti (2013) argues that the solution to the struggle between 'new' and 'old' elites is that the new elites should build a new structure instead of struggling to occupy the old one. Of course, the context in which Monti was writing from was Boston in the United States, and the context of this particular book is from India, but certain similarities with regards to urban centres being hubs of immigrants and local-immigrant conflicts remain similar in both contexts. Undoubtedly, factors such as migration and informalisation of the labour force, which have become important aspects of the pandemic in India, will continue to play a major role even in the post-pandemic phase. Colin Hay (2013) argues, through a much wider scale of analysis, that when trading mechanisms and businesses get interconnected, the first set-up that experiences a crisis caused by an economic downturn is the source of *all* businesses. In the case of the 2008 financial crisis, as both Hay (2013) and Harvey (2014) have elaborated, it was the United States of America – and the same has been repeated in the context of the COVID-19 – the global supply chain. As Hay further notes:

> As growth turns negative, unemployment is bound to rise, albeit once again and with some time-lag effect. The result, inevitably, is that, without any change in the eligibility criteria, the number of legitimate welfare claimants and total welfare expenditure both rise – with increased numbers of citizens claiming unemployment and associated benefits, a variety of means-tested payments and subsidies, access to a range of public services to which they were not previously entitled.
> (Hay, 2013, p. 19)

When economies enter recession, it naturally means that certain economic adjustments have to be made, keeping in mind the unemployed citizens and the manner in which resources and expenditures can be effectively managed

(Taylor-Gooby, 2015). In the context of India, this situation is a bit more complicated because the contradictions do not centre only around class, but rather encompass aspects of caste, gender, and race in a far more complicated manner than anywhere in the Global North or even in the rest of the Global South.

To better understand civic capitalism and its morbidities, the crisis caused by the mass exodus of migrant workers in India during the first lockdown, which has proved to be one of the greatest failures of state policy in recent times in India, can be taken as an example. It not only points towards the failure of neoliberal regime-oriented policy changes in India, it also urges one to delve deeper into the ways in which the pandemic has exposed the vulnerabilities of the business regime in India. In spite of his insistence on the benefits that businesspeople bring to the community, Monti et al. (2007) also agree with that. They argue:

> The possibility that more businesspeople today make an explicit connection between their economic and social interests might have been anticipated with the emergence of 'social entrepreneurs'. These are men and women that add a for-profit component to their non-profit organization in order to accomplish their larger social mission. . . . If they do not make a profit, they cannot write a grant proposal or wait for a donor to step up and fund their social program; they disappear.
> (Monti et al., 2007, p. 354)

This provides the ideal ground for tendencies such as trusteeship to emerge, which contracept the struggle emerging from the non-capitalist classes against the domination of capital. Dharmadhikari writes in this regard:

> Capitalism means an order of things in which the basis of distribution is purchase or barter. Unless you have the purchasing power, you are unable to get anything that you need, even food for hungry. It is an irony of fate that things can only be bought, forcibly snatched, or acquired, but nobody can get it because they are just 'needed'. This is why, in the preset day social order, needy persons are deprived of the primary amenities of life. Therefore, everything has got exchange value, that is price. It is a price-based economy and not a need based or value-based economy. It is a diabolical social order.
> (Dharmadhikari, 2007, Para 3)

Charity tries to dislodge this domination of the price by providing money to people whom they deem fit. However, as Marx (1867/1976) had predicted, the crisis of capitalism cannot be solved by mere restructuring of prices because prices themselves, as a concept, are an exploitative framework designed to extract surplus value and profit. Under capitalism, both the rich and the poor depend on the market for their own renewal (Warnecke-Berger, 2020) and as a result, the market becomes the soul and substance of the violence that characterises all matured and burgeoning capitalist societies. Civic order, in reality, is enforced by the law and order in place in these societies, which often overlooks the nuanced reality of the oppressed sections of the society. Often, the quest for civic order might even take violent forms, where the dominant group attempts to *discipline* the others by force of violence. All democracies entail within themselves a possibility of majoritarian violence (Waghmore & Gorringe, 2019), as exhibited during the pandemic by constant news of violent incidents against the Muslim population of India (Salam, 2021).

Civic order under capitalism of all forms, works on the principle of the ruling classes directing the working class and other non-capitalist classes. Civic capitalism of the kind that Hay and Payne (2015) argue for depends to a large extent on the state acting as a regulator of the market. However, under neoliberalism, the state itself becomes subordinate to the market (Harvey, 2005; Leys, 2008). The contemporary Indian state *as it exists* is an ideological and material construction of the neoliberal reforms that had been introduced in India in 1991. One of the major advantages that theories such as municipal socialism provide in the case of disasters such as the present one is that they provide an ontological basis for socialist epistemology. For example, one of the major crises that emerged during the first wave of the COVID-19 pandemic in India was the one faced by migrant workers in the country, where scores of migrant workers had to walk to their homes, sometimes over thousands of kilometres[16] because of the lockdown initiated by the central government. The proliferation of the migrant workforce in Indian cities can be considered to be one of the impacts of the large-scale neoliberalisation of civic life, which has been in place since the economic restructuration of the Indian state in 1991 (Patnaik, 2020, p. 44).

A municipal socialist position would have been able to mitigate the impact of the crisis on the migrant workers by furthering municipal control over housing arrangements, providing subsidies to the informal workforce, and so on enabling them to survive the lockdown, the timing and implementation of which itself were grossly hurried and immature in nature.[17] Civic capitalism, as Hay and Payne (2015) have argued, is basically about making the market work for the people rather than the reverse way around which is the usual under free market capitalism. However, while the prospect of increasing control by the state might seem fascinating to most proponents of plain and simple nationalisation, as scholars such as Karl Korsch (1975) and Raya Dunayevskaya (1985) have exhibited, plain and simple nationalisation of resources does not contribute much to the emancipation of the marginalised sections. Both Korsch and Dunayevskaya have argued in favour of nationalisation of the resources. However, both of them had also pointed out that mere nationalisation would serve no purpose. Karl Korsch (1975) argued:

> [The] mere socialising of the *means of production* is in no way connected with the elimination of private self-interest from the motivations

of production; instead, through socialising the means of production in [the] first phase of communal economy, private self-interest can be of even greater service as motivation for the most profitable and prolific possible production on a still greater scale of production.

(p. 78)

Apart from Korsch, Raya Dunayevskaya was one of the most articulate philosophers who stood opposed to this determinist belief that mere nationalisation could result in any form of socialism. In an interview with the *Chicago Literary Review*, she had said:

To my utter shock and disbelief, I realised that with the outbreak of the war, Trotsky, who had been fighting the Stalinist bureaucracy for over a decade, would now turn to the workers and ask them to defend Russia, because it was a 'workers' state though degenerate' . . . I was not only opposing the Hitler-Stalin pact, but I was also opposing Trotsky's conception that nationalised economy equalled workers' state.

(Dunayevskaya, 1985, p. 10228)

Nationalisation also has a larger politics behind it, but when such demands are entrapped within an economistic understanding, they become unable to articulate a political vision around those demands. Civic capitalism, as Hay and Payne (2015) argue, on the other hand, proposes something unique in the sense that it does not advocate nationalisation per se, but rather advocates for a regulation regime at the head of which lies the state. However, once the state is at the helm of affairs, the conditions become ripe for the state to self-transform into the *capitalist machinery* on its own, operating independently of the people. James et al.'s (1986) analysis of state capitalism has proved that mere replacement of the capitalist infrastructure by the state would never result in the complete emancipation of labour in the society because labour would still be subservient to larger powers. COVID-19 is supposedly set to cause numerous long-term health concerns for those infected with the virus, including pulmonary damages, widespread post-viral fatigues and the possibility of certain chronic cardiac complications (Lewin, 2020).

Because of the kind of healthcare infrastructure that India has, which is highly privatised in nature and has been taking a toll on the marginalised population, as Rao (2017) has argued, it is unlikely that charities will be able to provide the necessary solutions – simply because of the scale of the problem. Charities by major corporations cannot guarantee a radical community-based restructuring in the society because it is the constant devaluation of the community itself that has allowed these philanthropic ventures to be successful in the society. The activities of various trusts and organisations that Venkatachalam, Yeh, and Memon (2020, May 18; 2020, July 16) take into their framework are mostly dominated by the *super elites*. And, if any of the desired egalitarian characteristics that Venkatachalam, Yeh, and

Memon point out have to be reached in the context of India, these will have to include the communities in their frame of action, something that they have been doing for quite some time now. The problem, however, is that they are including them in a manner which promotes an alienated sense of community and not the radical community that might be helpful in a post-pandemic situation. Civic capitalism of any kind – whether it be the one focused on the state as a regulator or the businesspeople as regulators – cannot effectively resolve the situation of crisis that the pandemic has forced upon the marginalised populace. As Andreas Malm (2016, 2020) rightly argues, capitalism cannot be expected to solve the crisis that it itself has produced, and philanthropy is a part of the overall capitalist framework.

Venture capital is mostly constructed of the *risk capital*, constituted out of the money, provided by different foundations – something which Buffet (2013) identified as the basis of a new system in itself. The management of the elites' wealth by trusts that can be then used for greater good holds promise to many of the world's leading economists (The Times of India, 2020, February 5). However, under contemporary capitalism, trusts themselves have become vehicles of exchange between the market and the state, and their potential to act as social levellers has significantly decreased. Both trusteeship models and philanthropic charity indicate the inequality that exist within the society. Corporate philanthropy today, as McGoey (2015) points out, is largely a method to get exempt from taxation. Many charities have done some commendable work in the domain of public health – there is no way one can deny that. However, the donations rarely reflect or make structural changes to the vulnerabilities that the extremely marginalised face (McGoey, 2015).

The contemporary world is a world where the population looks towards the billionaires to solve the crisis that they themselves have produced over the years (Klein, 2017). Philanthropy, in such a situation, merely exists as a ploy to manage the dissent that might arise out of the massive inequality that capitalist exploitation produces on an everyday basis (Barker, 2020). Philanthropy tends to dislodge the arguments which are put forward for more equality in the society, by pushing the society towards accepting their hegemonic influence, both materially and psychologically. Civic capitalism, as it exists in both of the variants discussed here, fails to address the effects that neoliberalism has produced by critically evaluating the changes that have come within the very nature of the state and the market. The market today is not composed mainly of do-gooders, but rather comprises of a complicated network of profit-seeking corporations and individuals who exert their hegemony on the marginalised sections, by not only oppressing them economically as *homo economicus* but also socially as *social beings* themselves. In this milieu, the state-form merely acts as an agent of legalisation of oppression, not only because the state itself is today made up of the market but also because it has few other options in its arsenal than to follow the market if it has to avoid extinction. The civility that arises out of such conditions is nothing but 'disaster civility' whose civic nature is constructed out of the complete dehumanisation of human beings in the society, especially the marginalised sections.

Notes

1. Shah further states, '. . . there were also gaps in how philanthropists responded to the pandemic, particularly to the second wave. The first wave of the pandemic showed us, especially with the migrant crisis, how a shortage of food and shelter, and no livelihood security, devastated families. Despite knowing this, during the second wave, all donour attention went to hospital beds, oxygen concentrators, and medical supplies' (quoted from Vaid and Shetty, 2021, September 7, Para 3).
2. Tiny informal housing colonies, usually found in North India, especially in Delhi.
3. This has been written based on a statement given by Rekha Sharma, Chairperson of the NCW, dated 2nd of April, 2020.
4. Statement by Vani Subramaniam from Saheli Trust, as referred to in Uppal and Sidhu, 2020, p. 26.
5. According to Jaya Velankar, Director of Jagori, as referred to in Uppal and Sidhu, 2020, p. 26.
6. There were also reports that around 1,000 people being stranded after the event with no clear idea of what would happen to them (BBC, 2020, April 2), with certain reports stating that more than 2,000 foreigners had entered India since the beginning of 2020. A significant percentage of them being untraceable as of March 2020 (Philip, 2020a, March 31). The plight of the attendees of the event has been such that even after a year or so, they are still awaiting trial or are struggling to go back to their homes (Shantha & Chauhan, 2021, May 9).
7. The Indian state policy towards religious minorities has been a confused one, according to noted sociologist T. K. Oommen (2016), with the state merely determining minorities on the basis of numbers. Muslims in India have historically been at the receiving end of both structural and physical violence, as Oommen (2016) highlights with frequent stigma by the ascription of labels such as 'pro-Pakistan', 'anti-national', and the like. The National Commission for Minorities Act, 1992 of the Indian government established the National Commission for Minorities (NMC) to examine issues pertaining to violations of minorities' rights with a specific focus on the investigation of complaints. The NMC received 350 complaints during 1993–95, when Chandra Shekhar was the prime minister, from the Samajwadi Janata Party (Rashtriya) that is the Socialist People's Party (National). Around 2,625 complaints were received every year during the period 2001–03 when the central government was being run by the National Democratic Alliance (NDA) led by the BJP – increasing the number of complaints almost by 7.5%, proving that the 'value orientation of the party in power influences the quantum of violence against minority communities. The content of complaints is indicative of the nature of tension: non-recognition by the government of minority managed institutions, unlawful interference in the management of these institutions, refusal to provide infrastructural facilities in areas inhabited mainly by minorities, and the like' (Oommen, 2016, pp. 129–130).
8. Harsh Mander (2021) writes that gatherings such as the Tablighi Jamaat's have occurred in other places as well, which relate to the Hindu religion, but that did not garner the kind of attention that the Jamaat did even though the gathering held by the Jamaat was held at a time when the government itself had not been taking the pandemic seriously.
9. Accounts such as Pithode's (2022) lay out the immense complexities within which public administration had to, and is still continuing to, pass through during the

10 times of COVID-19 – shifting of offices, reduction of staff personnel, separation of the personnel from their families, and the like – in addition to other administrative issues, such as city-mapping for efficient drug delivery, and lockdown implementation on places such as shopping malls.
10. Harsh Mander argues in this regard: 'Given Modi's public position on the 2002 massacre, the obliteration of his role in it was even harder to accomplish than the reinvention of the two earlier prime ministerial candidates fielded by the BJP. But the leaders of industry, as much as large segments of the middle classes impatient to see his installation as the one man who could accelerate economic growth rejected the idea that his ambitions to attain the highest post in national politics were disqualified by his alleged role in one of the most brutal communal massacres after Independence' (Mander, 2015, p. 171).
11. Small businesses under contemporary forms of capitalism have begun to get integrated within larger monopolies such as Amazon and Flipkart in India by registering themselves as sellers, opening storefronts, etc. Small businesses are generally impacted positively by this step because they usually have a flagship brand value associated with niche commodities or have used such platforms to become more sophisticated in nature to the customer by using their automated and digital systems in place (Deb Roy, 2022).
12. In Delhi's Mayapuri, a small industrial hub, the lockdown had almost rendered the small industries bankrupt. Conversations with an owner of a small manufacturing unit in Mayapuri, who also doubles up as a worker in his own factory during the day, revealed that during the lockdown, his own condition was so miserable that it had became impossible for him to sustain the workers that he employs. In times of disaster, local businesses have the utmost capacity to help people in need. However, it is doubtful whether these businesses and their owners will continue to behave similarly under the control and regulations of the state, especially under neoliberalism, where large monopoly business owners have effectively merged with the state.
13. Pithode (2022) narrates the case of one such SHG with which he had worked in Madhya Pradesh in securing enough masks for people. According to him, along with the Directorate of Medical Educationin Madhya Pradesh: 'The district administration had to ensure supplies of masks and sanitisers, which were going out of stock. The women self-help groups came forward with the proposal of ensuring supplies at reasonable rates. As soon as this was approved, women self-help groups started manufacturing masks and sanitisers in large quantities, which not only helped in ensuring supplies for hospitals but also reduced the cost of these products in the market, helping people at large' (Pithode, 2022, p. 37).
14. Nehru, as Palat highlights, was opposed to class warfare because he thought that class struggle resulted in innumerable atrocities. At the same time, he was also opposed to the rampant development of capitalism in the country because he was also influenced by Marx and the Fabian Society to give in to the ideals of capitalist development completely.
15. The benefits of donating to charities were a part of the Indian freedom struggle itself in the form of the Gandhian Trusteeship Model. The Gandhian Trusteeship Model (GTM) was based on M. K. Gandhi's campaign against social evils such as poverty, exploitation, and injustice by utilising the role that rights and responsibilities play in the creation of economic value in the country (Kesavalu, 2004) – these ideas formed the core principles of the ideology of Gandhian Socialism. The relationship between Gandhian Socialism and Civic Capitalism is a complicated one. However, it is an important one in the context of India.
16. See Retrieved December 6, 2023, from www.bbc.com/news/world-asia-india-52086274
17. See Retrieved December 6, 2023, from https://thewire.in/government/india-covid-19-lockdown-failure

References

Abraham, T. (2019, July 10). The malaise of malnutrition. *The Hindu*. Retrieved December 6, 2023, from www.thehindu.com/opinion/op-ed/the-malaise-of-malnutrition/article28335228.ece

AECC Global. (2022, April 27). Which is the toughest exam in the world? Retrieved December 6, 2023, from www.aeccglobal.in/blog/which-is-the-toughest-exam-in-the-world

Aglietta, M. (2015). *A theory of capitalist regulation: The US experience* (D. Fernbach, Trans.). Verso. (Original work published 1979)

Aiyar, S. (2020). *The gated republic: India's public policy failures and private solutions*. Harper Collins Publishers India.

Ananta, J. (Ed.). (2020). *When the people are not "we, the people"*. SAHMAT.

Ashton, J., & Toland, S. (2021). *The new normal: A roadmap to resilience in the pandemic era*. William Morrow.

Avadhani, R., & Reddy, R. (2021, May 7). *Digital divide curbs vaccine access in rural Telangana*. Retrieved December 6, 2023, from www.thehindu.com/news/national/telangana/digital-divide-curbs-vaccine-access-in-rural-telangana/article34508753.ece

Balakrishnan, J., Malhotra, A., & Loren, F. (2017). Multilevel corporate responsibility: A comparison of Gandhi's trusteeship with stakeholder and stewardship frameworks. *Journal of Business Ethics*, 141.

Bamzai, K. (2020, March 28). Why India's wealthy happily donate to god and govt but loathe helping needy and poor. *The Print*. Retrieved December 6, 2023, from www.theprint.in/opinion/india-wealthy-happily-donate-to-god-govt-loathe-helping-needy-poor/390206/

Barker, M. (2020). *Under the mask of philanthropy*. CreateSpace Independent Publishing.

BBC. (2020, March 29). *India's PM seeks "forgiveness" over lockdown*. Retrieved December 6, 2023, from www.bbc.com/news/world-asia-india-52081396

BBC. (2020, April 2). *Tablighi Jamaat: The group blamed for new Covid-19 outbreak in India*. Retrieved December 6, 2023, from www.bbc.com/news/world-asia-india-52131338

Bhanj, J. D. (2021, March 2). *Vaccine portal faces glitches*. Retrieved December 6, 2023, from www.thehindu.com/news/cities/Delhi/vaccine-portal-faces-glitches/article33966738.ece

Bhattacharyya, R. (2021). Employers lend support to covid victims' kin; offer insurance cover, financial assistance among other relief measures. *The Economic Times*, May 13, 2021. Retrieved December 6, 2023, from www.theeconomictimes.com/news/company/corporate-trends/employers-lend-support-to-covid-victims-kin/articleshow/82592282.cms

Bhavsar, D., Tiwari, P., & Deshpande, V. (2020). *Study of municipal governance assessment frameworks*. Center for Water and Sanitation, CEPT University.

Biswas, S. (2020, March 30). Coronavirus: India's pandemic lockdown turns into a human tragedy. *BBC*. Retrieved December 6, 2023, from www.bbc.com/news/world-asia-india-52086274

Bonotti, M., & Zech, S. T. (2021). *The human, economic, social and political costs of COVID-19*. Palgrave Macmillan.

Borer, M., & Monti, D. (2006). Community, commerce and consumption: Businesses as civic associations. In M. Borer (Ed.), *Varieties of urban experience*. University Press of America.

Bottomore, T. (1981). Introduction to the translation. In *Finance capital: A study of the latest phase of capitalist development* (M. Watnick & S. Gordon, Trans.). Routledge & Kegan Paul.

Buffett, P. (2013). The charitable-industrial complex. *New York Times*, July 26. Retrieved December 6, 2023, from www.mkgandhi.org/articles/the-charitable-industrial-complex.html

Business Line. (2021, November 18). *Infosys foundation builds a 350-bed cardiac care unit at Karnataka government-run hospital*. Retrieved December 6, 2023, from www.thehindubusinessline.com/news/infosys-foundation-builds-a-350-bed-cardiac-care-unit-at-karnataka-government-run-hospital/article37552897.ece

Business Today. (2021, May 25). *Modi govt plans stimulus package for sectors impacted by second Covid-19 wave*. Retrieved December 6, 2023, from www.businesstoday.in/latest/economy-politics/story/modi-govt-plans-stimulus-pacakage-for-sectors-impacted-by-second-covid-19-wave-296972-2021-05-25

Candid & Center for Disaster Philanthropy. (2021). *Philanthropy and Covid-19: Measuring one year of giving*. Retrieved February 2, 2023, from https://disasterphilanthropy.org/resources/philanthropy-and-covid-19/#:~:text=In%20the%20report%20titled%20"Philanthropy,19%2Drelated%20efforts%20during%202020.

Candid & Center for Disaster Philanthropy. (2022). *Philanthropy and Covid-19: Examining two years of giving*. Retrieved February 2, 2023, from https://disasterphilanthropy.org/resources/philanthropy-and-covid-19-examining-two-years-of-giving/

Cao, W., Fang, Z., Hou, G., Han, M., Xu, X., Dong, J., & Zheng, J. (2020). The psychological impact of the COVID-19 epidemic on college students in China. *Psychiatry Research*, *284*. https://doi.org/10.1016/j.psychres.2020.112934

Chakraborty, P., Mittal, P., Gupta, M. S., Yadav, S., & Arora, A. (2020). Opinion of students on online education during the Covid-19 pandemic. *Human Behavior and Emerging Technology*. https://doi.org/10.1002/hbe2.240

Chandra, B., Mukherjee, M., & Mukherjee, A. (2000). *India after independence: 1947–2000*. Penguin.

Chandra, R. (2019). *The moonshot game: Adventures of an Indian venture capitalist*. Penguin.

Charities Aid Foundation. (2019). *World giving index: Ten years of giving trends*. Charities Aid Foundation.

Chauhan, R., & Harsheeta. (2020). *Making sense of it all: Understanding the concerns of persons with disabilities*. National Book Trust.

Crocker, W. (2009). *Nehru: A contemporary's estimate*. Random House India.

Curtis, L., & Johnson, S. (2022). *A nurse's story: My life in A&E during the covid crisis*. PAN Books.

Damodaran, H. (2008). *India's new capitalists: Caste, business, and industry in a modern nation*. Permanent Black.

Das, G. (2000). *India unbound: From independence to the global information age*. Penguin.

Das, G. (2013). *India grows at night: A liberal case for a strong state*. Penguin. (Original work published 2012)

Davies, R. (2021). *Prices and inflation in a pandemic – a micro data approach*. Centre for Economic Performance, London School of Economics and Political Science.

Davis, W. (2020, August 6). The unravelling of America. *Rolling stone*. Retrieved December 6, 2023, from www.rollingstone.com/politics/political-commentary/covid-19-end-of-american-era-wade-davis-1038206/

Dawson, M. C., Rosin, C., & Wald, N. (2018). Resource scarcity between conflict and cooperation. In M. C. Dawson, C. Rosin, & N. Wald (Eds.), *Global resource scarcity: Catalyst for conflict or cooperation?* Earthscan.

Dayal, S. (2022, July 20). Philanthropy during Covid-19 in India. *Candid*. Retrieved December 6, 2023, from www.blog.candid.org/post/philanthropy-during-covid-19-in-india/

Deb Roy, S. (2022). *Social media and capitalism: People, communities and commodities*. Daraja Press.

Department of Economic and Social Affairs. (2020, June 11). *The role of public service and public servants during the COVID-19 pandemic*. United Nations Policy Brief #79. Retrieved December 6, 2023, from www.un.org/development/desa/dpad/publication/un-desa-policy-brief-79-the-role-of-public-service-and-public-servants-during-the-covid-19-pandemic/

Dharmadhikari, C. S. (2007). Trusteeship: A technique of social change. *Gandhi Today, 4*. Retrieved December 6, 2023, from www.mkgandhi.org/articles/trusteeship1.htm

Diaz-Quiñones, A. (2019). Foreword. In Y. Bonilla & M. LeBrón (Eds.), *Aftershocks of disaster: Puerto Rico before and after the storm*. Haymarket Books.

Dixit, A., & Chauhan, R. (2020). *The future of social distancing: New cardinals for children, adolescent and youth*. National Book Trust.

Doing Good. (2018). *Doing good index 2018*. Centre for Asian Philanthropy and Society.

Doing Good. (2020). *Doing good index 2020*. Centre for Asian Philanthropy and Society.

Doing Good. (2022). *Doing good index 2022*. Centre for Asian Philanthropy and Society.

Dréze, J., & Sen, A. (2013). *An uncertain glory: India and its contradictions*. Penguin.

Dunayevskaya, R. (1965). Marx's humanism today. In E. Fromm (Ed.), *Socialist humanism*. Doubleday.

Dunayevskaya, R. (1984). *Nationalism, communism, Marxist humanism and the Afro-Asian revolutions*. News and Letters.

Dunayevskaya, R. (1985). Interview with Chicago literary review (March 15, 1985). In *The Raya Dunayevskaya collection – Marxist-humanism: A half century of its world development*. Wayne State University Archives of Labor and Urban Affairs.

Dunleavy, P. (2018). Auditing the UK's changing democracy. In P. Dunleavy, A. Park, & R. Taylor (Eds.), *The UK's changing democracy: The 2018 democratic audit*. LSE Press.

Dwarkanath, N. (2020, April 5). 8 Caught at Delhi airport trying to flee to Malaysia, may have attended Tablighi Jamaat event. *India Today*. Retrieved December 6, 2023, from www.indiatoday.in/india/story.tablighi-jamaat-8-malaysians-try-to-escape-through-delhi-airport-1663528-2020-04-05

Eban, K. (2019). *Bottle of lies: Ranbaxy and the dark side of Indian pharma*. Juggernaut Books.

Essadek, A., & Rabeyron, T. (2020). Mental health of French students during the COVID-19 pandemic. *Journal of Affective Disorders, 277*, 392–393.

Faas, A. J. (2018). Petit capitalisms in disaster, or the limits of neoliberal imagination: Displacement, recovery, and opportunism in highland Ecuador. *Economic Anthropology, 5*, 32–44.

Farrall, S., Hay, C., & Gray, E. (2020). *Exploring political legacies*. Palgrave Macmillan.

Foster, J. B., & McChesney, R. W. (2012). *The endless crisis: How monopoly-finance capital produces stagnation and upheaval from USA to China*. Monthly Review Press.

Fromm, E. (1942/2001). *The fear of freedom*. Routledge. (Original work published 1942)

Gandhi, M. K. (1979). Letter to Nehru dated August 23, 1944. In *The collected works of Mahatma Gandhi* (Vol. LXXVII). Government of India.

Gandhi-Mody, P. (2022). *A nation to protect: Leading India through the covid crisis*. Rupa Publications.

Ghoshal, D., & Das, K. N. (2021, May 1). Scientists say India government ignored warnings amid coronavirus surge. *Reuters*. www.reuters.com/world/asia-pacific/exclusive/scientists-say-india-government-ignored-warnings-amid-coronavirus-surge-2021-05-01/

Ghoshal, D., & Siddiqui, Z. (2021, June 15). Health experts say India missed early alarm, let deadly coronavirus variant spread. *Reuters*. www.reuters.com/business/healthcare-pharmaceuticals/health-experts-say-india-missed-early-alarm-let-deadly-coronavirus-variant-2021-06-15/

Gilbert, J. (2016). The question of leadership. In *Corbyn and the future of labour: A verso report*. Verso.

Glauber, J., Laborde, D., Martin, W., & Vos, R. (2020). Trade restrictions are worst possible response to safeguard food security. In J. Swinnen & J. McDermott (Eds.), *COVID-19 and global food security*. International Food Policy Research Institute.

Gopal, S. (1986). *Selected works of Jawaharlal Nehru. Vol. 4: New series*. Oxford University Press.

Gore, A. (2007). *Earth in the balance: Forging a new common purpose*. Earthscan.

Goswami, C. (2016). *Globalization before its time: The Gujarati merchants from Kachchh*. Portfolio.

GRAIN. (2016). *The great climate robbery: How the food system drives climate change and what we can do about it*. New Internationalist Publications.

Gupta, D. (2019). *Tata vs Mistry: The battle for India's greatest business empire*. Juggernaut Books.

Han, B. C. (2013). *In the swarm: Digital prospects*. (E. Butler, Trans.). The MIT Press.

Hansda, R. (2022). COVID-19, India, small-scale farmers, and indigenous Adivasi communities – the answer to the future lies in going back to the basics. In P. Castellanos, C. E. Sachs, & A. R. Tickamyer (Eds.), *Gender, food and COVID-19*. Routledge.

Harnecker, M. (2007). *Rebuilding the left*. Zed Books.

Harvey, D. (2005). *A brief history of neoliberalism*. Oxford University Press.

Harvey, D. (2014). *Seventeen contradictions and the end of capitalism*. OUP.

Harvey, D. (2019). *Spaces of global capitalism*. Verso. (Original work published 2006)

Hay, C. (2013). *The failure of Anglo-liberal capitalism*. Palgrave Macmillan.

Hay, C., & Payne, A. (2015). *Civic capitalism*. Polity.

The High Powered Expert Committee (HPEC) for Estimating the Investment Requirements for Urban Infrastructure Services. (2011). *Report on Indian urban infrastructure and services*. ICIER.

The Hindu. (2021, June 28). *Govt. unveils Rs. 6.28 lakh crore stimulus post second covid wave*. Retrieved December 6, 2023, from www.thehindu.com/business/Economy/nirmala-sitharaman-unveils-new-covid-recovery-pacakage-expands-credit-relief/article35020572.ece

Hindustan Times. (2021, November 27). *Which states and UTs are among India's poorest? List here*. Retrieved December 6, 2023, from www.hindustantimes.com/india-news/which-states-and-uts-are-among-india-s-poorest-list-here

Holland, M. S. (2007). *Bonds of affection: Civic charity and the making of America – Winthrop, Jefferson, and Lincoln*. Georgetown University Press.

Hupkau, C., Isphording, I., Machin, S., & Ruiz-Valenzuela, J. (2020). *Labour market shocks during the Covid-19 pandemic: Inequalities and child outcomes*. Centre for Economic Performance, London School of Economics and Political Science.

Inamdar, N. (2014). *Rokda: How baniyas do business*. Penguin Portfolio.

Indian Philanthropy Alliance. (2022). *Indian philanthropy members respond to Covid-19*. Indian Philanthropy Alliance. Retrieved December 6, 2023, from www.indianphilanthropyalliance.org/new-addressing-covid-19

International Center for Not-For-Profit Law (ICNL). (2022). *Coronavirus and civic space*. Retrieved December 6, 2023, from www.icnl.org/coronavirus-response

Irani, D. (2021, June 11). Philanthropy had changed in the times of Covid-19. *Forbes India*. Retrieved December 6, 2023, from www.forbesindia.com/blog/storyboard18/philanthrophy-has-changed-in-the-times-of-covid-19

Iyer, R. (1985). *Gandhian trusteeship in theory and practice*. Crest Associates.

Jalan, B. (2005). *The future of India: Politics, economics and governance*. Penguin Viking.
James, C. L. R., Dunayevskaya, R., & Boggs, G. (1986). *State capitalism and world revolution*. Charles H. Kerr.
Jewett, R. L., Mah, S. M., Howell, N., & Larsen, M. M. (2021). Social cohesion and community resilience during COVID-19 and pandemics: A rapid scoping review to inform the United Nations research roadmap for COVID-19 recovery. *International Journal of Health Services*. https://doi.org/10.1177/0020731421997092
Kalanithi, P. (2016). *When breath becomes air*. Random House.
Keane, J. (2020, April 17). Democracy and the great pestilence. *Eurozine*. Retrieved December 6, 2023, from www.eurozine.com/democracy-and-the-great-pestilence
Kesavalu, Y. (2004). Gandhi Marg, 25(4). Retrieved December 6, 2023, from www.mkgandhi.org/articles/trusteeship.htm
Klein, N. (2007). *The shock doctrine: The rise of disaster capitalism*. Penguin.
Klein, N. (2017). *No is not enough: Defeating the new shock politics*. Penguin.
Klein, S. (2020, June 1). Disaster capitalism in the wake of coronavirus. *Currents: A Student Blog*. Retrieved December 6, 2023, from www.smea.uw.edu/currents/disaster-capitalism-in-the-wake-of-coronavirus/
Komireddi, K. S. (2019). *Malevolent republic: A short history of the new India*. Context.
Korsch, K. (1975). What is socialisation? A program of practical socialism. *New German Critique*, 6, 60–81.
Koshy, J. (2021, April 28). *Vaccine registrations begin for those above 18, amid glitches*. Retrieved December 6, 2023, from www.thehindu.com/news/national/covid-19-vaccine-registration-for-those-above-18-begins-amid-glitches/article34428071.ece
Lahariya, C., Kang, G., & Guleria, R. (2021). *Till we win: India's fight against the Covid-19 pandemic*. Penguin.
Lefebvre, H. (1991a). *The production of space*. Basil Blackwell.
Lefebvre, H. (1991b). *Critique of everyday life* (Vol. 1). Verso.
Lenin, V. I. (1905). Revolutionary days. In *Lenin collected works* (Vol. 8). Progress Publishers.
Levi, S. C. (2015). *Caravans: Punjabi Khatri merchants on the silk road*. Allen Lane.
Lewin, E. (2020, June 24). What are the long-term health risks following COVID-19? *NewsGP*. Retrieved December 6, 2023, from www.racgp.org.au/newsgp/clinical/what-are-the-long-term-health-risks-post-covid-19
Leys, C. (2008). *Total capitalism: Market politics, market state*. Three Essays Collective.
Longo, N. V. (2007). *Why community matters: Connecting education with civic life*. State University of New York Press.
Lowenstein, A. (2015). *Disaster capitalism: Making a killing out of a catastrophe*. Verso.
Mahambare, V. (2015, February 9). Wealth inequality and housing reforms. *Mint*. Retrieved December 6, 2023, from www.livemint.com/Opinion/ZDkmQFSmM7hNM1ky3ZR
Malm, A. (2016). *Fossil capital: The rise of steam power and the roots of global warming*. Verso.
Malm, A. (2020). *Corona, climate, chronic emergency: War communism in the twenty-first century*. Verso.
Mander, H. (2015). *Looking away: Inequality, prejudice and indifference in new India*. Speaking Tiger Books.
Mander, H. (2021). *Locking down the poor: The pandemic and India's moral centre*. Speaking Tiger.

Marx, K. (1867/1976). *Capital* (Vol. 1). Penguin.
Marx, K., & Engels, F. (1845–46/1976). The German ideology. In *Marx Engels collected works: Volume 5*. Lawrence and Wishart.
Matthewman, S. (2015). *Disasters, risks and revelation: Making sense of our times*. Palgrave.
McCann, G., & Ó hAdhmaill, F. (2021). International human rights and global welfare in the midst of the COVID-19 pandemic. In G. McCann, N. Mishra, & P. Carmody (Eds.), *COVID-19, the global South and the pandemic's developmental impact*. Bristol University Press.
McGoey, L. (2015, November 10). The philanthropy hustle. *Jacobin*. Retrieved December 6, 2023, from www.jacobin.com/2015/11/philanthropy-charity-bangacarnegie-gates-foundation-development
Mehta, S. (2021, August 5). How a global Covid-19 pandemic made us rethink philanthropy. *Financial Express*. Retrieved December 6, 2023, from www.financialexpress.com/lifestyle/health/how-a-global-covid-19-pandemic-made-us-rethink-philanthropy/2304887/
Miller, J. (2021). *The vaccine: Inside the race to conquer the COVID-19 pandemic*. St. Martin's Press.
Mishra, A., Seshadri, S. R., Pradyumna, A., Pinto, E. P., Bhattacharya, A., Saligram, P., & Benny, G. (2021). *Health care equity in urban India*. Azim Premji University.
MN, P. (2020, May 13). Urban India didn't care about migrant workers till 26 March, only cares now because it's lost their services: P Sainath. *Firstpost*. Retrieved December 6, 2023, from www.firstpost.com/india/urban-india-didnt-care-about-migrant-workers-till-26-march-only-cares-now-because-its-lost-their-services-p-sainath-8361821.html
Moloo, Z. (2018, February 6). The problem with capitalist philanthropy. *Jacobin*. Retrieved December 6, 2023, from www.jacobin.com/2018/02/charity-philanthropy-howard-buffet-congo
Monti, A., & Wacks, R. (2021). *COVID-19 and public policy in the digital age*. Routledge.
Monti, D. (1999). *The American city*. Blackwell.
Monti, D., Butler, C., Tilney, K., & Weiner, M. F. (2003). Private lives and public worlds: Changes in Americans' social ties and civic attachments in the late-20th century. *City and Community*, 2(2), 143–163.
Monti, D., Ryan, A. D., Brush, C., & Gannon, A. (2007). Civic capitalism: Entrepreneurs, their ventures and communities. *Journal of Developmental Entrepreneurship*, 12(3), 353–375.
Monti, D. J., Jr. (2013). *Engaging strangers: Civil rites, civic capitalism, and public order in Boston*. Fairleigh Dickinson University Press.
Moses, M. (2022). *The municipal financial crisis: A framework for understanding and fixing government budgeting*. Palgrave Macmillan.
Mukul, J. (2022). *The great shutdown: A story of two Indian summers*. Simon and Schuster.
Mukund, K. (2012). *The world of the Tamil merchant: Pioneers of international trade*. Allen Lane.
Mumbai Mirror. (2020, June 3). *Dharavi reports 19 Covid-19 cases on Wednesday; Total cases climb to 1,849*. Retrieved December 6, 2023, from www.mumbaimirror.indiatimes.com/coronavirus/news/dharavi-reports-19-covid-19-cases-on-wednesday-total-cases-climb-to-1849/articleshow/76179743.cms
Murthy, G. V. S., Kamalakannan, S., Lewis, M. G., Sadanand, S., & Tetali, S. (2020). *A strategic analysis of impact of Covid-19 on persons with disabilities in India*. Indian Institute of Public Health.

Mustafa, F. (2020, April 17). The coronavirus spread and the criminal liability of the Tablighi Jamaat. *The Wire*. Retrieved December 6, 2023, from www.thewire.in/article/communalism/coronavirus-criminal-liability-of-tablighi-jamaat

Nagpal, J., & Dixit, A. (2020). *Vulnerable in autumn: Understanding the elderly*. National Book Trust.

Narain, S. (2017). *Conflicts of interest: My journey through India's green movement*. Penguin.

Nehru, J. (1946/2016). *The discovery of India*. Penguin.

Nehru, J. (2015). From a letter dated 1 March 1950. In M. Khosla (Ed.), *Letters for a nation: From Jawaharlal Nehru to his chief ministers, 1947–1963*. Penguin.

Oommen, T. K. (2016). State formation, minoritization, and violence in postcolonial India. In K. Kannabiran (Ed.), *Violence studies*. Oxford University Press.

Palat, M. K. (2022, February 12). Nehru's socialism was evolutionary, inclusive and not based on class. *The Hindu*. Retrieved December 6, 2023, from www.thehindu.com/society/nehrus-socialism-was-evolutionary-inclusive-and-not-based-on-class/

Pande, A. (2020). *Making India great: The promise of a reluctant global power*. Harper Collins Publishers India.

Pandey, A. (2021, May 23). As Telangana tightens covid lockdown norms, e-commerce delivery boys face Police wrath. *India Today*. Retrieved December 6, 2023, from www.indiatoday.in/coronavirus-outbreak/story/as-telangana-tightens-covid-lockdown-norms-e-commerce-delivery-boys-face-police-wrath

Panitch, L., & Leys, C. (1997). *The end of parliamentary socialism: From new left to new labour*. Verso.

Patel, A. (2020). *Our Hindu Rashtra: What it is. How we got here*. Westland Books.

Patel, S., & Pant, P. (2020). Decentralisation and urban primary health services: A case study of Delhi's Mohalla clinics. *Commonwealth Journal of Local Governance, 23*. https://doi.org/10.5130/cjlg.vi23.6987

Patnaik, P. (2020). Neoliberalism and fascism. *Agrarian South: Journal of Political Economy, 9*(1), 33–49.

Philip, S. A. (2020a, March 31). How Tablighi Jamaat emerged as the "largest known" Covid-19 source in South Asia. *The Print*. Retrieved December 6, 2023, from www.theprint.in/india/how-tablighi-jamaat-unknowingly-emerges-as-largest-known-covid-19-source-in-south-asia/391918/

Philip, S. A. (2020b, March 31). More than 2,100 foreigners linked to Tablighi Jamaat entered India since 1 January. *The Print*. Retrieved December 6, 2023, from www.theprint.in/india/more-than-2100-foreigners-linked-to-tablighi-jamaat-entered-india-since-1-january/392228/

Pithode, T. (2022). *The battle against covid: Diary of a bureaucrat*. Bloomsbury.

Posadas, J. (1968). Flying saucers, the process of matter and energy, science and socialism. In *Socialism and human relationships with nature and the cosmos*. Scientific, Cultural and Political Editions.

Posadas, J. (1979). The war and the elimination of the capitalist system on a world scale. In *Nuclear energy, war and socialism*. Scientific, Cultural and Political Editions.

Posadas, J. (1980). On the war preparations of capitalism and its historic insecurity. In *War, peace, and the function of the socialist countries*. Scientific, Cultural and Political Editions.

Posadas, J. (1981a). The war preparations in the midst of the capitalist crisis. In *War, peace, and the function of the socialist countries* (Vol. 1). Scientific, Cultural and Political Editions.

Posadas, J. (1981b). War preparations and the function of the socialist countries. In *War, peace, and the function of the socialist countries* (Vol. 1). Scientific, Cultural and Political Editions.

Posadas, J. (1981c). The significance of the discussion in the Polish army. In *Poland: The advance of socialist democracy and of socialist influence in the world* (Vol. 1). Scientific, Cultural and Political Editions.
Posadas, J. (1981d). Reagan's threats and the war preparations of imperialism. In *War, peace, and the function of the socialist countries* (Vol. 1). Scientific, Cultural and Political Editions.
Putnam, R. D. (2000). *Bowling alone: The collapse and revival of American community*. Simon and Schuster.
Radhakrishnan, S. (2020, April 1). Tablighi Jamaat and Covid-19: The story so far. *The Hindu*. Retrieved December 6, 2023, from www.thehindu.com/news/national/tablighi-jammat-and-covid-19-the-story-so-far/article61955229.ece
Raianu, M. (2021). *TATA: The global corporation that built Indian capitalism*. Harvard University Press.
Ramachandran, P. (1995). *Public administration in India*. National Book Trust.
Ramachandran, P., & Ramkumar, V. (2005). *Education in India*. National Book Trust.
Ramachandran, R. (2021, January 29). Vaccine politics. *Frontline*.
Ramesh, M. (2018). *The climate solution: India's climate-change crisis and what we can do about it*. Hachette India.
Ramesh, M. (2021). *Watershed: How we destroyed India's water and how we can save it*. Hachette India.
Rao, K. S. (2017). *Do we care? India's health system*. Oxford University Press.
Ray, U. K. (2020, March 30). COVID-19 lockdown: 8 year old dies of hunger as family struggles to make ends meet. *The Wire*. Retrieved December 6, 2023, from www.thewire.in/article/rights/bihar-starvation-deaths-lockdown
Renner, R. (2020, April 15). The pandemic is giving people vivid, unusual dreams. Here's why. *National Geographic*. Retrieved December 6, 2023, from www.nationalgeographic.com/science/article/coronavirus-pandemic-is-giving-people-vivid-unusual-dreams-here-is-why
Riom, C., & Valero, A. (2020). *The business response to Covid-19: The CEP-CBI survey on technology adoption*. Centres for Economic Performance, London School of Economics and Political Science.
Ronnie, C., & Shannon, O. (2013). "Can you hear me now . . . good!" Feminism(s), the public/private divide and citizens United v. FEC. *UCLA Women's Law Journal*, 20(1), 39–70.
Roper, S., & Turner, J. (2020, August 5). What will coronavirus mean for innovation by firms? *Economics Observatory*. Retrieved December 6, 2023, from www.coronavirusandtheeconomy.com/question/what-will-coronavirus-mean-innovation-firms
Rosenthal, S. (2015, April 28). Philanthropy: The capitalist art of deception. *Socialist Worker*, 402.
Roy, T. (2012). *The east India company: The world's most powerful corporation*. Allen Lane.
Rucht, D. (2011). Civil society and civility in twentieth-century theorizing. *European Review of History*, 18(3), 387–407.
Russell, M. (2019). Between dependence and independence: Rethinking a policy wasteland. In K. Rosenthall (Ed.), *Capitalism and disability: Selected writings by Marta Russell*. Haymarket Books. (Original work published 2001)
Russell, M. (2019). Targeting disability. In K. Rosenthall (Ed.), *Capitalism and disability: Selected writings by Marta Russell*. Haymarket Books. (Original work published 2005)
Russell, M., & Malhotra, R. (2019). Capitalism and the disability rights movement. In K. Rosenthall (Ed.), *Capitalism and disability: Selected writings by Marta Russell*. Haymarket Books. (Original work published 2002)

Sah, R. (2020, June 4). The wages of Covid-19 lockdown in Dharavi – a sense of panic, loss of self. *The Wire.* Retrieved December 6, 2023, from www.thewire.in/article/rights/dravai-covid-19-lockdown-workers

Saha, D., Pal, S., & Bhatia, S. (2021, September 29). With COVID duty continuing, community health workers deserve better working conditions. *The Wire.* Retrieved December 6, 2023, from www.thewire.in/article/health/covid-19-duty-continuing-community-heath-workers-deserve-better-working-conditions

Saini, A. (2019). *Superior: The return of race science.* Beacon Press.

Salam, Z. U. (2021, July 2). The virus of hate. *Frontline.*

Sanjay, S., & IndiaSpend.com. (2021, September 27). Indians say they donated a lot more to charity in the first year of the pandemic. *Scroll.* Retrieved December 6, 2023, from www.scroll.in/article/1006257/indians-say-they-donated-a-lot-more-to-charity-in-the-first-year-of-the-pandemic

Saul, J. S. (2006). *Development after globalisation: Theory and practice for the embattled south in a new imperial age.* Three Essays Collective.

Scroll. (2021, May 11). *Watch: Policemen beat up street vendors for allegedly violating lockdown rules in Karnataka.* Retrieved December 6, 2023, from www.scroll.in/video/994636/watch-policemen-beat-up-street-vendors-for-allegedly-violating-lockdown-rules-in-karnataka

Shantha, S. (2020, November 18). COVID, communal reporting and centre's attempt to use independent media as Alibi for inaction. *The Wire.* Retrieved December 6, 2023, from www.thewire.in/article/communalism/tablighi-jammat-communal-reporting-ib-ministry-coronavirus

Shantha, S., & Chauhan, M. S. (2021, May 9). Tablighi Jamaat: A year on, some attendees still await trial, others struggle to return home. *The Wire.* Retrieved December 6, 2023, from www.thewire.in/article/rights/tablighi-jamaat-one-year-trial-struggle-return-home-covid-19-legal-action

Sharma, A., & Gupta, C. (2020, April 27). Audit of bigotry: How Indian media vilified Tablighi Jamaat over coronavirus outbreak. *Newslaundry.* Retrieved December 6, 2023, from www.newslaundry.com/2020/04/27/audit-of-bigotry-how-indian-media-velified-tablighi-jamaat-over-coronavirus-outbreak

Shashidhar, A. (2022, June 7). COVID-19 made Indians more open to charity. *Fortune India.* Retrieved December 6, 2023, from www.fortuneindia.com/enterprise/covid-19-made-indians-more-open-to-charity/108484

Sheth, A., Ayilavarapu, D., Pandit, R., & Sinha, M. M. (2021). *India philanthropy report 2021.* Dasra and Bain and Company. Retrieved December 6, 2023, from www.bain.com/insights/india-philanthropy-report-2021/

Sheth, A., Ayilavarapu, D., Pandit, R., & Sinha, M. M. (2022). *India philanthropy report 2022.* Dasra and Bain and Company. Retrieved December 6, 2023, from www.bain.com/insights/india-philanthropy-report-2022/

Siddiqui, F. R. (2021, May 22). Vegetable vendor dies after being beaten by two cops in Unnao. *Times of India.* Retrieved December 6, 2023, from www.timesofindia.com/city/kanpur/vegetable-vendor-dies-after-being-beaten-by-two-cops

Sidel, M. (2022, May 11). *Civil society and the state in Asia in the covid era: A comparative look at key themes across the region.* Centre for social impact and philanthropy blog. Ashoka University. Retrieved December 6, 2023, from www.csip.ashoka.edu.in/civil-society-and-the-state-in-asia-in-the-covid-era-a-comparative-look-at-key-themes-across-the-region/

Singh, S. (2021, May 25). India plans stimulus package for sectors worst affected by second wave. *The Economic Times.* Retrieved December 6, 2023, from www.economictimes.com/news/economy/finance/india-plans-stumulus-pacakage-for-sectors-worst-affected-by-pandemic/

Singh, T., & Hussain, A. (2021). *Nehru: The debates that defined India.* Fourth Estate.

Sinha, D., Mander, H., & Shrimali, P. (2019). Food, nutrition and exclusion. In *India exclusion report, 2018–19*. Three Essays Collective and Centre for Equity Studies.
Sinha, Y., & Sinha, A. (2018). *India unmade: How the Modi government broke the economy*. Juggernaut.
Sivaramakrishnan, K. C. (2000). *Power to the people? The politics and progress of decentralisation*. Konark Publishers.
Sivaramakrishnan, K. C. (2013, March 30). Revisiting the 74th constitutional amendment for better metropolitan governance. *Economic and Political Weekly, 43*(3).
Slotkin, R. (1973). *Regeneration through violence: The mythology of the American frontier, 1600–1860*. Wesleyan University Press.
Solis, M. (2020, March 13). Coronavirus is the perfect disaster for "disaster capitalism". *VICE*. Retrieved December 6, 2023, from www.vice.com/en/article/5dmqyk/naomi-klein-interview-on-coronavirus-and-disaster-capitalism-shock-doctrine
Spears, D. (2019). *AIR: Pollution, climate change and India's choice between policy and pretence*. Harper Collins India.
Sridhar, V. (2021, July 2). A blank cheque to vaccine majors? *Frontline*.
Srivastava, R. (2020, July 7). Don't forget us in coronavirus battle, say businesses in India's Dharavi slum. *Reuters*. Retrieved December 6, 2023, from https:///www.reuters.com/article/us-heath-coronavirus-india-slum-trfn-idUSKBN248004
Standing, G. (2006). *The corruption of capitalism: Why rentiers thrive and work does not pay*. Biteback Publishing.
Steen, B. (2019). "A new scientific conception of human world": Anton Pannekoek's understanding of scientific socialism. In C. Tai, B. van der Steen, & J. van Dougen (Eds.), *Anton Pannekoek: Ways of viewing science and society*. Amsterdam University Press.
Stein, S. (2019). *Capital city: Gentrification and the real estate state*. Verso.
Subramaniam, L. (2016). *Three merchants of Bombay: Business pioneers of the nineteenth century*. Portfolio.
Swaminathan, M. (2000). *Weakening welfare: The public distribution of food in India*. Leftword Books.
Taskin, B. (2020, April 1). Dear Muslims, Tablighi Jamaat committed a crime against humanity: Don't defend them. *The Print*. Retrieved December 6, 2023, from www.theprint.in/opinion/pov/dear-muslims-tablighi-jamaat-commtted-a-crime-against-humanity-dont-defend-them/392698/
Taylor-Gooby, P. (2015). Public policy futures: A left trilemma? In J. Green, C. Hay., & P. Taylor-Gooby (Eds.), *The British growth crisis: The search for a new model*. Palgrave Macmillan.
The Telegraph. (2020, March 24). *Cops beat up people out to buy*, sell food. Retrieved December 6, 2023, from www.telegraphindia.com/india-cops-beat-up-people-out-to-buy-sell-food
Teltumbde, A. (2018). *Republic of caste: Thinking equality in the time of neoliberal Hindutva*. Navayana.
Timberg, T. A. (2014). *The Marwaris: From Jagat Seth to the Birlas*. Allen Lane.
The Times of India. (2020, February 5). *Mahatma Gandhi's model of trusteeship is relevant even today, says Nobel Laureate*. Retrieved December 6, 2023, from www.timesofindia.indiatimes.com/city/ahmedabad/mahatmas-mode-of-trusteeship-is-relevant-even-today/
Tomes, N. (1998). *The Gospel of germs: Men, women, and the microbe in American life*. Harvard University Press.
Tonsing, J. C., & Tonsing, K. N. (2017). Understanding the role of patriarchal ideology in intimate partner violence among South Asian women in Hong Kong. *International Social Work, 62*(1), 161–171.
Towler, W. G. (1909). *Socialism in local government*. The Macmillan Company.

Trautmann, T. R. (2012). *Arthashastra: The science of wealth*. Allen Lane.
Trimble, S. (2019). *Undead ends: Stories of apocalypse*. Rutgers University Press.
UNICEF. (2022). *Women's nutrition: The diets of women in India are often too poor to meet their nutritional needs*. Retrieved December 6, 2023, from www.unicef.org/india/what-we-do/womens-nutrition
Unsworth, S., Andres, P., Cecchinato, G., Mealy, P., Taylor, C., & Valero, A. (2020). *Jobs for a strong and sustainable recovery from Covid-19*. Centres for Economic Performance, London School of Economics and Political Science.
Uppal, T., & Sidhu, S. (2020). *New frontiers at home: An approach to women, mothers and parents*. National Book Trust.
Vaid, D., & Shetty, S. (2021, September 7). Reflections: Philanthropy in India during Covid-19. *India Development Review*. Retrieved December 6, 2023, from www.idronline.org/article/philanthrophy-csr/reflections-philanthrophy-in-india-during-covid-19/
Venkatachalam, P., Yeh, D., & Memon, N. (2020, May 18). *Philanthropy and the Covid-19 response in India*. The Bridgespan Group.
Venkatachalam, P., Yeh, D., & Memon, N. (2020, July 16). Philanthropy's distinct role in India's COVID-19 response. *Devex*. Retrieved December 6, 2023, from www.devex.com/news/opinion-philanthropy-s-distinct-role-in-india-s-covid-19-response-97702
VP, A. (2021, November 23). Patients' rights and inequality in vaccine survey. *OXFAM*. Retrieved December 6, 2023, from www.oxfam.org/press-release/patients-rights-and-inequality-vaccine-survey
Waghmore, S., & Gorringe, H. (2019). Towards civility? Citizenship, publicness and the politics of inclusive democracy in India. *South Asia: Journal of South Asian Studies*. https://doi.org/10.1080/00856401.2019.1573714
Walby, S. (1990). *Theorizing patriarchy*. Blackwell.
Walsh, J. (2021, April 10). India's covid outbreak is now the world's worst as it lags in vaccinations. *Forbes*. Retrieved December 6, 2023, from www.forbes.com/sites/joewalsh/2021/04/10/indias-covid-outbreak-is-now-the-worlds-worst-as-it-lags-in-vaccinations/?sh=483d23d64d2a
Warnecke-Berger, H. (2020). Capitalism, rents and the transformation of violence. *International Studies*. https://doi.org/10.1177/0020881720912898
Yadav, A. (2020, March 24). "Hard to plan survival": Migrants, contract workers on looming uncertainty amidst lockdown. *The Wire*. Retrieved December 6, 2023, from www.thewire.in/article/labour/migrant-contract-workers-looming-uncertainty

Conclusion

COVID-19 has altered the course of human history, creating innumerable ripple effects across the various spehes of social life. Historically, as Roy (2020) states, pandemics have been vehicles through which people could envisage a break with the past. The pandemic might wane off with time, and the effects of the dreaded *long Covid* might not be as disastrous physically as they are today, but the kind of changes that COVID-19 has brought in within the social fabric will stay with the human society for a long time to come. The policy changes during COVID-19, as many have pointed out, are expected to remain in force even after the pandemic. These can include the effects that the vaccine to COVID-19 has on the women's menstrual cycles (Sheikh, 2022) or the recent surge in the popularity and the perceived viability of virtual healthcare, which had been growing even before the pandemic (Kompalli, 2019) and has been bolstered by the pandemic. COVID-19 has had a massive impact on not only the physical fabric of the society but also on the mental fabric, causing issues of mental health across a wide array of individuals in the society, globally (Barnagarwala, 2022).

The effects of COVID-19 on the human society cannot be seen in isolation, but rather has to be analysed in light of the constantly degrading relationship that human beings share with the natural world. This has been constantly pushing the human society towards a socio-ecological collapse. The ways in which capitalism has developed in the contemporary world have created a situation where it has become a part of the everyday reality, modifying it in the most profound ways possible. Activities such as panic buying and hoarding have been rendered mainstream causing a strain on the *moral fabric* of the society itself (Scroll, 2021), while human factors such as empathy and compassion have been turned into mere policy catchwords without much emphasis on the social nature of these qualities. The impact that COVID-19 had on India has to be analysed in the context of a few very important and relevant questions, in addition to the inequality that characterises the healthcare sector in India (Sundaraman et al., 2020), such as 'How do 35 crore people in India survive on Rs 32 per person per day in urban areas and Rs 26 per person per day in rural areas?' (Prasad, 2018, p. 50). The problems that

India has been facing because of such extreme inequalities have now assumed global proportions, as Brunnermeier states:

> As a result of the COVID-19 crisis, the world must address a critical question: How can societies be reshaped so that we can face inevitable, severe shocks with resilience? To answer that question, this book proposes a shift in our mindset and our social interactions. Rather than lethargically avoiding risks, we should proactively develop societies that are resilient to adverse shocks.
>
> (Brunnermeier, 2021, p. 1)

While the argument is appreciable and is true to a certain extent. The question is that whether such a risk-free society is feasible under capitalism, or even under the theoretically decentralised and practically centralised state-form as it exists in most major democracies. Capitalism has increasingly come to depend upon the global chains of production and supply to sustain itself, something which was halted by the COVID-19 pandemic, leaving the capitalist order searching for newer methods of economic and social sustenance (Lin, 2022). Some companies in India have suggested that the localised lockdowns during the second wave have drastically affected them negatively because of the changing regulations in different places where different stages of their entire process of stocking and retailing take place, even though there was no significant demand (Law, 2021). The world, it can be safely assumed, was simply not prepared for a pandemic to emerge, and so when it had to confront the pandemic, it reacted to the same with the only option it could think of, which consisted of massive chaos and an overt desire for control. Mandates on masks, PPE Kits, tracking applications, and the like have become one of the most prudent examples of how governmentality and surveillance mechanisms have fused together because of the pandemic. All of these factors have contributed to the response to the COVID-19 pandemic becoming more of a political and spiritual project (Hadas, 2022).

Cities, the spaces where these changes in the society are most visible, in this context become important because states such as India consider cities to be the vehicles of growth (NITI Aayog and Asian Development Bank, 2022). However, they continue to remain relatively silent on the autonomy of local governance. Cities, as Pelling (2003) shows, remain uniquely vulnerable to catastrophic disasters. It is undoubtable that states still dominate the ULBs in spite the implementation of the 74th Constitutional Amendment in 1992, which sought to provide the ULBs in India with more autonomy (Jha, 2020). COVID-19 has showed that, while cities are crucial to growth and stability, they can also be the sites of extreme vulnerability during a healthcare crisis such as the COVID-19 pandemic. According to an Asian Development Bank (2020) report, around 95% of all COVID-19 cases had come from urban areas.

This makes cities an important part of any analysis of the COVID-19 pandemic. It is important to mention here that cities have been analysed in a multitude of different ways. While Sassen (1991) has analysed cities as being representatives of contradictions of capitalism, Pinnock (1989) saw cities as being representatives of garrisons. Florida (2002) and Scott (2006), in recent times, have talked about cities being spaces where 'the creative class' thrives. Neil Smith (1996) had argued that cities under neoliberal governments are designed in ways that are revanchist in nature and, as such, desire to negatively affect minorities, women, and other dissenters who might speak up against the mainstream social order. During the pandemic, the relationship between all these different views were exposed to the common people. With the migrant exodus in India, it was clear that while capitalist globalisation had been successful in creating a diverse range of employment opportunities in the cities, it has at the same time failed to provide women, workers, and other marginalised sections of the populace with much socio-economic or cultural security.

In a recent article published in *Deccan Chronicle*, Datta Ray (2022) writes, 'The quality of Indian life is exposed not by a tycoon or two strutting on the world stage but by India's fall from 131st to [the] 132nd among 191 countries in the UN Development programmes latest Human Development Index' (Para 1). The constant dehumanisation of the marginalised sections, which becomes a norm under capitalism as Marx (1844) had argued, makes it look normal to overlook the facts that India ranks 101st among 116 countries as per the Global Hunger Index 2021 report (Grebmer et al., 2021), with a per capita food consumption lower than Bangladesh and Nepal as per the International Food Policy Research Institute (IFPRI) (2022). The combination of these factors contributed to the catastrophe, which, in the words of Daniyal (2021), jotted down the trajectory of the Indian state from being an emerging superpower to a failed one during the COVID-19 crisis. He also wrote about the probability of an impending viral apocalypse in India being widely circulated in international media such as *The Australian* (Sherwell, 2021). In spite of early warnings, the Indian government did not react proactively to the rising chances of infection that a viral outbreak poses in a globally interconnected world – where around 3,301 people flew out of Wuhan's airports every day, the epicentre of the pandemic (Pulla, 2020). It would be wrong to say that the non-responsiveness of the government at the initial stages was merely a coincidence, but rather the non-responsiveness has to be analysed in light of the changes which have occurred in the world under neoliberal regimes. This have a propensity to favour profit over the lives of people, more so than ever in recent human history.

The world is undergoing a significant change in terms of how it is organised by and for the people, with governments across the globe responding to the crisis in a way that has provided a new lease of life for newer capitalistic tendencies to emerge in the society. Tendencies such as disaster capitalism and civic capitalism have begun to feature in major global debates. The apocalyptic tendencies which characterise the world today are a result of the different combinations of economics, cultural modifications, and social reconstructions that have been used under capitalism (Magnuson, 2018). The capitalist society is a society where financialisation is the order of the society such that even with regular crises becoming normalised in the society, capitalism does not want to move away from the rampant financialisation and monetisation which characterise the contemporary society. The logic of capital itself revolves around the idea that investors need to get returns from the investment that they make in the process of capitalist expansion process. The non-capitalist class has been found to be at the worst receiving end of the pandemic, with many of them finding it – even after two and a half years – increasingly difficult to sustain themselves because of the kind of effects that the pandemic has had on their lives, economically, culturally, and socially.

Crises such as the COVID-19 pandemic have revealed that inequality and socio-economic and cultural shocks – such as the pandemic – share a dialectical relationship with each other, which is informed by the ways in which both of them affect and aid in the generation of each other (Scheidel, 2018). This becomes further complicated because pandemics such as COVID-19 exhibit the ways in which different actors in the society are affected and affect the existent social dynamics in the society. The marginalised sections of the society become the worst victims of a healthcare crisis such as COVID-19 because they face a double oppression – one caused by years' of malnourishment and undernourishment, which leaves them with weaker immune systems, and the other caused by the unequal access to healthcare that characterise most liberal democracies under capitalism. The contemporary state creates a situation where the migrant workers are often seen as nothing better than disposable beings in the society, whose existence has been carefully engineered by the dominant force to be something which causes physical and mental problems for the locales (Ghosh & Chaudhury, 2020).

Disasters have historically been used as drivers for enriching a small section of the elites, but that in no way means that this has to be a general rule. Klein (2017) argues that shocks can also provide gateways towards a more critical understanding of the society, which can lead to a more equitable and decent solution to the crisis. According to Naomi Klein and many others, COVID-19 has exhibited blatantly that human lives are interconnected – in a much more profound manner than capitalism would have us believe (Klein, 2017, September 29; Solis, 2020). The method of dialectics will be an important one in the construction of a humanist vision of the world after the COVID-19 pandemic because of this interconnectedness. Dialectical analysis analyses the relationship between the subject and the object in such a way that it analyses 'the conception of reality as totality; the unity of inner and the outer; the relationship between the whole and the parts which constitutes the passage from existence to reality' (Dunayevskaya, 1958b/2002, p. 95). If the post-COVID-19 society is not analysed dialectically, then one will again be prone to making crude analysis of the social structure under capitalism, which often falls into the trap of economism. Reductionist political economy tends to focus on this particular aspect of contemporary capitalism (Lefebvre, 1991b, p. 58), or in other words, in spite of their Marxist claims, they fail to realise that:

> The whole point, however, is that Marx . . . did not confine himself to 'economic theory' in the ordinary sense of the term, that, while explaining the structure and the development of the given formation of the society exclusively through production relations . . . (he) clothed the skeleton in flesh and blood.
> (Lefebvre, 1991b, p. 3)

A dialectically critical look at the relationship between philosophy and the social reality, not only allows one to look at the overall totality of existent reality but also enables one to delve into the multiplicity of issues that co-exist within any society, most precisely within any moment with revolutionary possibilities, such as COVID-19. Dunayevskaya's (1987/2002) philosophical vantage point on dialectics as a philosophy of revolution remains a highly relevant tool in any contemporary revolutionary analysis because it helps in analysing the ways in which the relationship between dead and living labour is fundamental to the articulation of human society under capitalism. Preston and Firth write, 'In the current COVID-19 crisis the whole economic system appears to be "contaminated" from banknotes to packaging and supply chains. Labour itself becomes a possible source of viral contamination' creating what they refer to as the *Viracene* (Preston & Firth, 2020, p. 13). Pandemics, they argue, make one realise the sociality of commodity production regimes under capitalism, thus again bringing one back to the most fundamental contradiction under capitalism – the contradiction between labour and capital. The greatness of Marx's theory was that it could point towards the final dismantling of the capitalist system as a whole (Dunayevskaya, 1981) as such that 'The law of motion of capitalistic society is . . . the law of its collapse' (Dunayevskaya, 1958a, p. 124).

The central point regarding understanding Marx's notion of accumulation is to emphasise the law of motion within capitalist societies. Marx considered that the contradiction between capital and labour was the central question under all capitalist societies. It is the power over the purchasing of capital that gives the power to the capitalists to control the society, but at the final stage (or rather the stage of the complete development of capitalism) when the power of capital grows extravagantly, it supersedes the power of the individual capitalist as Marx (1844, p. 247) predicts. In general terms, any form of socialism, as Fiamingo (1898) notes while talking about municipal socialism in Europe, refers to a system where production is held in common, or in other words, where the means of production is socialised. However, with COVID-19, it has become clear that mere social ownership would not be of much help, but rather it is necessary to completely eliminate the idea of ownership itself.

316 *Conclusion*

COVID-19 has affected the society at multiple levels. One of them is the ways in which it has exposed the relationship that local governance shares with centralised planning. Dialectics helps one in understanding the cause and effects of the horrors caused by the complete disjunction between local governance and centralised statist governance during the COVID-19 pandemic, or the issues with the complete overwhelming of the former by the latter without making one dominate over the other. The issue of local governance often converges with that of civic pride in an urban context, something that has at times been conceived of being directly and essentially related to the existent architecture of a city (Groten, 2021). This relationship has been further complicated by the onslaught of the COVID-19 pandemic, which has exposed that modern urban architecture itself might be a reason behind the spread of COVID-19 in major metropolitan cities in the world.

The current urban architecture that is prevalent in most cities is built around the constant devaluation of the lives and liberty marginalised sections of society under neoliberal capitalism, as many such as Harvey (2012) and Stein (2019) have argued. The neoliberal reforms, which were initiated in the early 1990s in India, have sparked an array of structural and ideological changes in the Indian society that have further rendered mainstream exclusionary practices along economic and socio-cultural practices. Desai (1984) had argued that in order to make sense of the complicated times that the Indian society presents before academics and social analysts, one has to move beyond the boundaries of traditional disciplines and focus on the ways in which the dehumanisation of human beings can be countered within the aegis of social analysis. In these scenarios, tendencies such as municipal socialism and civic capitalism must evolve from their reliance on centuries-old theoretical paradigms, the problems of which have been analysed by Goldfrank and Schrank (2009) in the context of Latin America. They argue, taking municipal socialism as an example, that such responses to crisis are particularly common in urban spaces which have a high union density, a significant proportion of middle class in the population and popular movements. In the context of India, perhaps, one could take the example of Delhi to a certain extent, which satisfies these criteria. Reforms at the local level also have to deal with the complexities that arise with lockdowns and how they affect businesses (Bagus et al., 2021). It is essential to realise that a reform at the local level might not be the solution to all the problems which have emerged or escalated during the pandemic.

Local solutions would almost always require some form of assistance from the universal bodies to implement the necessary policy reforms (Chowkwanyun, 2022). It is crucial to realise that many of these issues have been a part of the society for a very long time. There have been multiple explorations into the different issues that experiments with socialism have thrown up at a local level. Boddy and Fudge (1984) argue that local politics' revival, on the progressive side, requires a strong alliance between the traditional support bases and the new urban populace, at least as far as electoral politics is concerned. They argue, in the context of England, that

> An important influence on the emerging practice and analysis of the new urban left [in the 1980s] has been the intellectual input of work which has started to make sense of local politics and local government in relation to capital, the capitalist state and notions of class and power.
> (Boddy & Fudge, 1984, p. 8)

Their discussion followed from other discussions such as Cockburn's (1977) article *The Local State*, which has been one of the major explorations from the left on the question of local governance. This article focused on the overarching presence of the state in everyday life in the society, which complicate and reduce the capacity of local bodies to act autonomously (Dunleavy, 1984). Administrative changes at the local level often fail to invoke the confidence of prominent individuals who are otherwise quite progressive and moral (Robinson, 2015). Both Boddy (1984), Mohanty (2016), and Moses (2022), along with several reports from the Government of India, which have been cited in the present book, have highlighted that local bodies across the democratic world have also been facing a financial shortfall for decades, one that has grown in proportion to neoliberalism. In this situation, any regional administration which has historically invested in projects designed to increase their cash flow have found themselves in at an advantageous position during the pandemic as Adikesavan's (2020) piece on the 'Kerala Model' exhibits. The requirement in this context is a radical reimagination of local politics itself, one that goes beyond the deterministically futurist ideas.

Žižek (2021) argues that any estimation of the future is contingent upon factors – many of which remain to be unknown – which cannot possibly be taken into cognisance while devising a futurist notion. Bello (2022) notes that in the wave of changes that the pandemic has brought forward, the far-right remains at an advantageous position in making use of those changes for political benefits. Even in India, the advantageous positioning of the far-right is because of the ways in which the capitalist developmental process has been ushered in in the context of India, which has resulted in the creation of what Kaur (2020) has recently referred to as an economy of hope countering the erstwhile socialist experiments under Nehru's semi-Fabian socialism. Global and contemporary National Capitalism in India has left no stone unturned to disregard the 4% growth that India showed until 1964, which economist Jean Dréze aptly mentions as a breakthrough (NP, 2013). It is true that India is not the same as it was before 1991, and there are numerous changes that have occurred both in the social culture and in the socio-economic structure of the country. In times such as these, it is tempting to argue that the era of any kind of socialist experiment is long over as the Business Line (2018) opinion column noted in 2018. However, as the pandemic has shown, India still needs a public sector and a political structure that believe in the same to counter the effects of crises such as COVID-19 (Newsclick, 2022).

The loss of public funding has resulted in a significant section of the population losing the capacity to react to the effects of catastrophes such as COVID-19 (Dean & Heron, 2020). Private providers, either directly of healthcare or of insurance, are not efficient enough to counter the crisis because they are not conditioned to incentivise public welfare over and above profit accumulation (Chang, 2020; Barnagarwala, 2020, March 24). At the same time, the crisis is just too huge for charities to come in and handle the same. The glorification of charity itself speaks of how the social structure under capitalism, which is bereft of much welfare mechanisms, is conditioned to benefit the elite (Davis, 2020), who attempt to justify their huge wealth through their self-glorification of their activities within an achievement-based society where such acts garner widespread public applause from the bourgeois press and are part of the overall construction of capitalism in a humane manner (Vanheuverswyn, 2006; Kilby, 2015). In such social situations, the market plays the role of the most important mediator of social relations, constituting a social conditioning where *to have* becomes more important than *to be* as Fromm (1976) had noted long back. The pandemic has seen market-based clashes over critically important entities such as vaccines (Ghoshal & Ravikumar, 2021). The ways in which Big Pharma and Big Tech struggled with each other in a rapid competition to accumulate profits during the pandemic again prove that the market is not positioned in a manner that it can give precedence to human life over monetary gains. It is only the non-commercialised alternatives such as the ones based on community and alternative care frameworks which can do that, as Sengupta's (2013) detailed article shows. Even if they do not overhaul the complete privatised system, they can still be more efficient tools in achieving the objectives of the Alma Ata Declaration of the WHO (1978), which argued that health is a state of complete mental, physical, and social well-being rather than being only related to one's physical condition. This was one of the precursors to the Universal Health Coverage concept, which spoke about the importance of accessing healthcare without financial hardships (Sengupta, 2018). The pandemic showed that the world is still trailing behind a lot of these objectives even with all the technological development in the sector of healthcare.

Capitalist development usually takes place under the guise of the potential existence of a more prosperous life (Mies & Shiva, 2014), while in reality it leads to the complete opposite (Foster & Clark, 2020). This encapsulates the constructed necessity of a commodity economy and a capitalistic way of life, divorced from all forms of human relationships. In situation such as these, if the progressive agenda has to make a mark in the post-pandemic world, it has to focus on the dialectical relationship that is shared between the whole and the parts, or in other words, the relationship that exists between the problems faced by individuals in their concrete everyday lives and the issues faced by them because of the abstract universal nature of the state. The hope that the marginalised sections of the society rest on the state needs to be critically analysed, keeping in mind that the state-form is essentially a form maintained by the forces of global capital. It cannot be denied that in states such as China, the reaction to COVID-19 has indeed benefited the authoritarian regimes in gaining legitimacy and *some kind of* public approval, even from multinational bodies, with many nations following suit in establishing censorship regimes, including India (Schwartz, 2020; Simon & Mahoney, 2022).

The diversity that India possesses makes it a unique case among other nation states. It is a country where, according to Pew Research Center, 36% Hindus do not prefer to have a Muslim neighbour, while still 53% adults say that that the religious diversity benefits the country. It is a country where 20% of Muslims in Northern India said that they have faced discrimination due to their faith at some point in their lives, while around 65% of the total population believes that religious hate and violence are a major problem (Biswas, 2021). In dire situations such as these, as Baiocchi (2020), 'simply stating the opposite . . . is a slogan, but not an alternative' (Para 3). While the tactics employed by the likes of China, which focused on strict authoritarian disciplining as highlighted by Hessler (2020), might seem enticing in the wake of a global pandemic, it must also be mentioned that all forms of authoritarian control, even if that is for a short period of time, come with the risk of altering the social fabric of the society. These authoritarian forms of disciplinary biopower, as Foucault (1977) had highlighted, arise from a detailed and historical conditioning of the society through various disciplining bodies and institutions – which as Foucault (1978) had elaborated upon, span both the individual and the population levels. This has helped in the elevation of mandated duties such as the affirmative desire to take the vaccine to a kind of civic duty, a notion that has been advocated by scholars such as Gleisler (2021).

Randolph (2021), on the other hand, analyses the government's role in the entire pandemic as being one that is laden with ideas surrounding the methods of governmentality that make it mandatory for people to live, rendering mainstream surveillance methods by constantly referencing the rhetoric of public health mechanisms. Trantidis (2020) argues that the measures taken during the pandemic could very well become permanent parts of human lives after the pandemic. These can create the conditions, both social and psychological, which as Fromm (1942) had argued, where human beings, because of the immense amount of uncertainty they face, submit their entire selves to authoritarian control. This becomes especially prominent in contemporary post-truth societies, where objective facts often become secondary factors (Boyd, 2019). This, in turn, leads one back to argue, like Wagner (2020), that more than the virus, the lockdowns are the entities that deserve more attention. Not taking recourse to either Fromm or Foucault, Mann and Wainwright (2018) have stated that contemporary changes characterised by extended conflicts and grave problems, require interventions within the realm of political sovereignty of a planetary nature. This assertion is pertinent due to the planetary nature of the crisis (Therborn, 2020) and the methodology employed to analyse sovereignty. Mann and Wainwright assert that the emergence of figures such as Trump, Bolsonaro, or Modi is a part of a larger crisis that the human society is facing, which is ecological, political, and economic – all at the same time (Wainwright, 2019).

The critical question to ponder at this point for natural scientific, technological, and social thinkers is whether one is living through times where such tendencies are going to aggravate, or whether there is a potential solution to the crisis. James Hansen, one of the world's most respected climate scientists, has argued that the threat of climate change that looms over the human society is perhaps, now, past the limits from where it could be reverse engineered (Angus, 2011). There are others, such as Al Gore, who have worked their way through the climate change debate in a more pro-capitalist manner. In his Foreword written for *Capitalism at the Crossroads*, Gore (2007) argued that sustainability is a key element in the way businesses handle themselves under contemporary capitalism. Though Gore had written in the future tense back in 2007, that in 2022 one can safely assume that the future he was talking about is now knocking at the doorsteps of contemporary societies. However, one of the major problems facing businesses and states in turning towards sustainability is the way in which most businesses are structured under global capitalism, along with the deep connections which these businesses form with the state. A recent report by Nahm et al. (2022) has stated that India had spent only about 2% of its COVID-19 relief package on sustainable projects such as electrifying vehicles, and improving energy efficiency, while spending around 10% in projects which would, in all probabilities, go on to increase the greenhouse gas emissions.

With COVID-19, many new questions have cropped up, which have been exhibiting that the manner in which businesses have prepared their strategies in the decades leading up to the pandemic are unsustainable and are pushing the human society towards a catastrophe. The reactions to such catastrophes differ in terms of their political and ideological origins. Davis (2012) argues that the social conditions that remain fertile to propagate the chances of a catastrophe are often beneficial to the right wing because the right can effectively designate the causes of a catastrophe to any gains made by the left. This then allows the right to analyse the situation on its own terms creating fault lines of race, class, gender, and the like, as was easily visible during the pandemic. One can notice similar trajectories in the ways in which Islamophobia and the fear of contracting COVID-19 went hand in hand, under the governance of the BJP in India attempting to turn the healthcare emergency into a political one – in a divisive manner (Menon, 2020).

The lockdown, as Nivedita Menon, writes represented the political moment where democratic and human rights could be suspended, the effects of which have been disastrous for Muslims, Dalits, and other marginalised sections of the population. A crisis that evolves from such a situation gives a new lease of life to right-wing populism, which, as Brubaker (2020) argues, thrives on generating the idea of a crisis. These forces get further bolstered by what Fromm (1994) referred to as the loss of human control over the circumstances, which becomes a significant concern in times of rapid technological progress, such as the twenty-first century. The rapid technological progress is having an enormous impact on the acceleration of global climate change, which is already being reflected in the widespread acceleration of the frequency of catastrophic natural disasters such as the recent floods in Pakistan (Hanif, 2022). The pandemic has exposed the vulnerabilities that human society faces even with the widespread advancement in the field of technology and digital infrastructure. COVID-19 has exposed the relationship that exists between the digital and the biological, one which gets reinforced by the way in which scientific decisions are vulnerable to political decisions and sometimes vice versa (Žižek, 2021). Scientific Development, as Shiva (2008) argues, while always tries to portray itself as being neutral, frequently serves the interests of those in power. Science and technology, as such, are parts of the society and get shaped by them (Mackenzie & Wajcman, 1999). They also shape the social processes themselves. Anton Pannekoek, a member of the Council Communist, had argued that science under capitalism was merely bourgeois science that serves the interests of the elite (Steen, 2019). Disasters such as COVID-19 disrupt the organic process of the formation of politics. In fact, capital abhors the organic development of political tendencies within the society, because organic development creates the conditions under which the self-development of the people becomes a reality.

Disasters such as COVID-19 give voice to authoritarian socialist tendencies that posit the state as a superior figure. Such arguments, like the one that figures like Posadas advocated for, justify the formation of a hyper-vanguard. During disasters, the dominant forces in the society often discuss the benefits of supporting authoritarian forces, such as the market or the state. Within this milieu, the kind of response to the pandemic from major economies and states is nothing but the regularised capitalist response to crises of any kind. The definition of a successful nation, to most advocates of neoliberal policies, rest along the lines of evaluating growth rates in isolation from other factors such as political freedom, equitable opportunities, and socially peaceful and inclusive environment that are equally important to the development of a country (Das, 2002/2012). Democratic or compassionate capitalism, a term that neoliberal apologists often use, is akin to all other forms of capitalism because they do not attack the central power structure and commodity-form functioning under capitalism. These arguments often do not pay much attention to the importance that mass struggles have in the politico-ideological construction of a social structure.

The movement towards absolute liberation starts with the masses themselves. As Naomi Klein argues, shocks such as COVID-19 prevent the formation of organic moments that could facilitate the creation of a progressive mode of political activism among the people (Solis, 2020). These kinds of circumstances make one look towards the community for solutions. And, with the community – under contemporary capitalism – comes the question of local governance. The bodies that had been tasked with the difficult job of managing the pandemic at a community level and maintaining the restrictions imposed by the states. The COVID-19 pandemic provides an insight into the combined effects of biopolitics, surveillance, and disciplining in the society that Foucault (1978) had highlighted (Hannah et al., 2020) – many of which had been accelerated in the society through the utilisation of local bodies. The focus on the importance of local politics renewed debates about the tendencies of local ownership and municipal development during the pandemic. Saunders (1984) argues that two different political tendencies are not wholly incompatible in the administration of a particular society under contemporary capitalism. Saunders' *dual state* theory, which argues that the broader state remains much more focused on profit-seeking ventures, has been discussed extensively by Dunleavy (1984), who argues that the role of local bodies has been significantly curtailed because of the kind of domination that states themselves have come to self-posit in the realms of economy and administration, leaving local bodies with little autonomy in certain sectors such as education and community planning.

The conditions under which municipalities and other forms of local bodies function today are not much different from how *The Times* (1902) had described them to be in a collection of a series of articles which argued that the municipalities had found themselves to be at a disadvantageous position while competing with other private traders as well as remained conflicted with other issues such as fair wages, and their perspective on the employment of direct labour. Events such as the COVID-19 pandemic require decentralised policymaking processes that take the local contradictions and issues into account (Williams & Law, 2020), but almost all the major nation states in the world took recourse to centralised policymaking citing that as a better alternative. The desire for more centralised planning during conditions created by the COVID-19 pandemic and the relative inadequacy of the structures of local governance in resisting them, speaks of the ways in which decentralised planning structures need to be provided with more autonomy – both financially and socially. However, in countries such as India, where internal contradictions reign supreme at multiple levels, even decentralisation is not easy to achieve because local bodies, as Saunders (1984) explain, remain more open to succumbing to popular pressures because of their differing priorities.

Decentralised planning structures can be an antidote to the rampant commercialisation of the society, which becomes a norm under capitalist modes of production. A proper decentralised planning structure entails within itself not only autonomy but also all the facets of a proper grassroots with local democratic control, and the resolution of issues surrounding bureaucratic accountability and the like (Fudge, 1984). This would mean that local bodies remain proficient enough to counter the so-called new *society of enrichment*, which uses the existing social value systems and portray certain social aspects as enriching experiences to further its own goals of accumulation (Boltanski & Esquerre, 2020). Such alterations within the relationship between the people and the objects around them create a new ruling class along with the existing one, which then creates a new 'value (a "greatness") that will convey their hold on the world' (Boltanski & Chiapello, 2005b, p. 173). This stems from the deep capitalist desire to transform everything, including the immaterial forms of cultural expressions, into commodities meant for consumption.

Boltanski and Chiapello argue that, today, because of the ways in which capitalism has engulfed even the modes of critique, something which they label as the *New Spirit of Capitalism* (Boltanski & Chiapello, 2005b, 2005a), it is important to talk about newer forms of critique. Economic analysts have been trying to understand for decades, perhaps centuries, the causality behind the apparent dynamism within capitalism and its stability within the social consciousness in spite of its economic instability. This should be the focus of an artistic critique of capitalism, using a term emphasised by Boltanski and Chiapello (2005b), focused on the forces of the market working towards creating standardised and homogenously pervasive societies, which leaves almost everybody *located anywhere in the world* vulnerable to pandemics such as COVID-19. Diverse tendencies have attempted to provide a way out of the crisis. Frameworks such as *total liberation* (Pellow, 2014) have argued that the liberation from the apocalyptic tendencies of capitalism can only be effectively devised by taking into account both the inequalities and the enabling mechanisms pertaining to those inequalities.

COVID-19 has invigorated the widespread debates around the structural inequalities of capitalism. Neoliberal privatisation has created an immense inequality in the area of healthcare accessibility in South Asia (Sengupta et al., 2017/2020). The pandemic has revealed that inaccessibility to healthcare is one of the most critical inequalities of the contemporary world. When health crises such as COVID-19 emerge in the society, it becomes necessary to consider the disproportionate amounts of consciousness that people possess regarding their own social existence under capitalism. Naomi Klein (2017) argues that the resistance to shocks such as COVID-19 always requires a plan, a decent one that the people can understand and become a part of. When conditions such as the COVID-19 pandemic emerge in the society, it becomes essential to formulate a plan – one that is more inclusive both locally and globally, rather than exclusive.

The state and bourgeois life have an intrinsic connection with each other and continuously reinforce each other (Marx & Engels, 1845) because the political class has indeed become a social class (Marx, 1843). Under contemporary capitalism, this nexus between the state and the market, signifying the political class and the social class respectively, constitutes the ground through which, according to the Global Health Security Index, 2019 report, India scores a meagre 52.4 and has dropped further to 42.8 in the 2021 report (Cameron et al., 2019; Bell et al., 2021). The globe itself, according to the 2021 report, remains massively unprepared for any future pandemics.

Times such as these require global co-operation and combined efforts at multiple levels to counter future pandemics, as some experts have pointed out (Auto, 2022). This is not the first time that experts have argued for, as Boseley (2015) had advocated, in favour of mobilising global research funds to counter the growing inefficacy of antibiotics against the rapidly modifying microbial infections. She argued that in order to counter the global challenge posed by microbial infections, one needs to move towards more collective forms of action that transcend statist and corporate interests, benefiting both the elite and the poor. Slavoj Žižek argues:

> Our great advantage is that we *know* how much we don't know, and this knowing about out not-knowing opens up the space of freedom. We act when we don't know the whole situation, but this is not simply our limitation: what gives us freedom is that the situation – in our social sphere, at least – is in itself open, not fully (pre)determined. And our situation in the pandemic is certainly open.
>
> (Žižek, 2021, p. 114)

It is crucial that, in such open situations, the direction of the critique be towards devising effective strategies which take into cognisance the fact that in spite of the repeated claims made by the elite that they do not have sufficient funds to counter the effects of other catastrophic processes, such as climate change and global warming, funds surprisingly were available in abundance during COVID-19 (Stevano et al., 2021). Certain voices have sung praises about the rapid philanthropic efforts that have been ushered in by a section of the business and industrial community during the pandemic. It is true that the philanthropic interventions made by many of the industrialists and businesspeople have indeed been a major factor in the way different states have reacted to the crisis, *and they have often been instrumental in saving lives*. However, the manner in which different philanthropists have reacted to the crisis is symbolic of the inner contradictions of the capitalist mode of production itself, one that provides certain individuals with the power to donate while creating others who have no option but to be at the mercy of those donations. The power that philanthropists have over the society must be analysed in relation to the disproportionate share of their wealth that they possess. Glennie (2011) argues that charity and philanthropy are indeed beneficial because they emphasise co-operation rather than conflict, where human suffering is considered to be something which can be mitigated by philanthropic efforts.

Co-operation is a vital concept in the context of COVID-19, but it is important to realise that it is only a particular kind of co-operation that can offset the effects of the pandemic. Enforced co-operation from above does not help the society in mitigating the effects of the crisis, but rather, the requirement is of a massive rearticulation of mutual aid (Spade, 2020). The state, during the crisis, increasingly came to depend on local bodies (Firth, 2020), as many accounts such as Dighavkar's (2021) and Pithodes' (2022) have come to elaborate. The radical mutual aid is much better suited to counter the disastrous effects of COVID-19 than the philanthropic gestures, because mutual aid concerns the activities engaged in by marginalised human beings *for marginalised human beings* and does not succumb to the glorification of corporate donations and charities. The critique of philanthropy that has emerged during COVID-19 rests on the fact that it serves no other purpose than the institutionalisation of the private sector in essential sectors. For the post-Covid world, philanthropy will emerge as a major hurdle towards the effecting of major structural and radical social changes in the society. Philanthropical gestures result in the management of dissent by the complete institutionalisation of the marginalised voices into the state (Barker, 2020). This becomes crucial because COVID-19 has exposed that the key workers employed in certain sectors are critical to the well-being of the populace (Williams & Law, 2020). And these key workers often come from the most marginalised sections of the Indian social structure.

Policy-based changes made by governments have wide implications. However, under capitalism, they do not cause many changes to occur in the lives of the marginalised populace in an affirmative manner. For example, such gestures do not bring many changes to the lives of the women farmers who have been facing uncertainty and vulnerability for decades because of the ways in which the twin frameworks of capitalism and patriarchy operate within the Indian society. IndiaSpend (2020) reports that 45% of the farmers did not get any work during the lockdown period, and even those who did were forced to work for wages lower than INR 3,000 per month. Most of the women farmers – about 74% of the total respondents in the IndiaSpend survey – said that they had to sell their produce at reduced rates from that fixed by the government to private players. Additionally, there was a wide-scale disparity in the agricultural labour employment percentage. Many of these problems can be quite effectively countered by a strong and efficient local governance. As the book has shown, many tendencies have spoken quite eloquently about local governance, including municipal socialism and Fabian socialism. Webb (1919), in fact, had even argued that the Fabian socialists were more concerned about local governance than the trade unions and the cooperatives. While one may argue that Webb was correct about trade unionism, although that can be widely debated, it is difficult for one to agree with him wholeheartedly on the relationship that he draws between cooperatives and municipal socialism. The problem with many like Webb and Shaw was that they saw local governance, trade unionism, and the cooperative movement as distinct bodies pursuing different aims. However, all these different bodies, act together in the process of the construction of the society that marginalised people live through every day.

Henri Lefebvre (1991a) argued that the ways in which people experienced their everyday life, especially in urban spaces, is directly related to the ways in which 'Spatial Practices' (the Perceived Space), 'Representations of Space' (the Conceived Space), and 'Representational Space' (the Lived Space) interact with each other (Lefebvre, 1991a, p. 33) – these are widely known as *Lefebvre's Triad*. A spatial practice 'embraces production and reproduction, and the particular locations and spatial sets characteristic of each social formation. Spatial practice ensures continuity and some degree of cohesion'. Social spaces, including urban spaces, have an effect on the social practices that are prevalent within those spaces. These spaces are also a creation of the society within which they are located (Lefebvre, 1991a, p. 27). Finally, 'Representational Spaces' which embody the 'complex symbolisms, sometimes coded, sometimes not, linked to the clandestine or underground side of social life' (Lefebvre, 1991a, p. 38). This is the 'lived space' that the inhabitants experience on an everyday basis, where the individuals seek to physically interpret, alter, and appropriate the social space (Lefebvre, 1991a, p. 39) by manoeuvring through the forces which colonise or deprive them of their own consciousness (Merrifield, 2006, p. 12). Representational spaces are the spaces of the inhabitants and the users (Lefebvre, 1991a). Communities and their internal dynamics take an active part in the formation of these spaces. Within the representational spaces, the individuality of the inhabitants develops through their interactions with the existing social diversity and everyday patterns of life (Watkins, 2005).

When one's everyday life is affected – as is the case with COVID-19 – the individual's self is also affected. Self-identity, in the words of Giddens (1991, p. 52), 'is not something that is just given, as a result of the continuities of the individual's action-system, but something that has to be routinely created and sustained in the reflexive activities of the individual'. The identity of an individual, according to Giddens (1991, p. 54), is constructed not in the responsive reactions or behaviour of others 'but in the capacity *to keep a particular narrative going*' (emphasis original). Under the state's governmentality, the common citizens had no option but to resort to doing this on behalf of the state. The neoliberal governmentality, which as Foucault (2008) had showed, that spans the social reality under capitalism has been weaponised by capitalism to create subservient subjects in a much more violent manner during the pandemic. The extent to which one could follow or comply with the rules set by the authorities determines the extent of one's internalisation. The desire to get internalised frequently makes one change their preferences, even if that is enforced. This desire initiates the modifications of the lived space of these individuals, the *representational space of everyday life*, which is often heavily at odds with their native lifestyles within their private and public spaces. The use of private space draws from these differences which are essential components of the capitalist urban imagination. When a poor person uses an oximeter or some other medical device, it is not always out of a necessity but also out of a desire to become a part of the community. They become essential parts of the relations of production in a pandemic-ridden society.

Human societies today, definitely need to move towards more participatory models of governance. Tripathi (2020) has argued that the exclusion of certain sections of the populace, such as the migrant workers, can be addressed through bringing in reforms that consider them a part of the community. This approach would bring them under the aegis of the various policies and reforms from which they often remain deprived of resulting in poorer health and access to well-being mechanisms that are readily available to others. Sainath (2020), on the other hand, had argued that the government – if it wants to mitigate the effects of COVID-19 – needs to move towards bringing in more structural changes that cater to the poor and have the ability to counter the debt crisis that the marginalised population face in their everyday lives. This will also negatively affect their access to healthcare and immunity levels. The tryst with local governance, which would go on to play an important role if any of these suggestions are implemented, under contemporary capitalism cannot be analysed without taking the state into account. The state as it exists under capitalism is a result of the ways in which social divisions are gradually institutionalised through years of capitalist and neoliberal reforms in the society (Ramírez, 2021). Local governance and community organisations have the potential to perform crucial functions in the ways in which COVID-19 has shaped the society which human beings have come to inhabit. The importance of governance and responding to emergency-like situations at a local level has gained prominence in the models propounded at a global level to address COVID-19. Models such as the one that has been highly successful in Kerala – though relatively – have to be revisited in light of the structural changes that COVID-19 has brought in within the society. The analysis of these models has to consider both the benefits and problems associated with the institutionalisation of the local government in the lives of the people. Widely known as the *Kerala Model*, the left-wing government in Kerala has been successful in handling the COVID-19 crisis relatively better than most other states in India. It has even managed to garner the praise of the *New York Times* which praised the timely, systematic, and proactive manner of the state government (Bhagat, 2021), with *The Guardian* referring to K. K. Shailaja, the then Health Minister of Kerala as 'the Coronavirus Slayer' (Spinney, 2020).

The success of the Kerala Model has been accounted to many factors. Thomas (2021) and Bajpai and Wadhwa (2020) have highlighted the broad reforms regarding healthcare and education, which have taken place in Kerala, and those that have increased the general awareness about the disease. The prompt actions of the Health Ministry of the Kerala state government under the Communist Party of India (Marxist)-led Left Democratic Front (LDF) have ensured that the state could relatively avert the havoc that the disease had caused in other states such as Uttar Pradesh and Delhi. Jacob (2021) writes that despite the high number of cases, the model still remains successful according to experts, because it has been able to, through various means developed over years of infrastructural investment, detect more cases with increased testing and isolation mechanisms in place than others. Kerala has performed well during the pandemic, there is no denying it. However, the model that Kerala proposes has not been able to garner unanimous support. It has been referred to by many as not being a sustainable one because it fails to consider certain issues such as employment, which are making a significant population of Kerala move abroad to places like Dubai as cheap labour, along with other issues such as its response towards climate change, as some such as Balakrishnan (2019) have pointed out. While others such as Dennis (2021) have argued that Kerala has been a unique success story that could show economic progress while still retaining its socialist ethos. Apart from the Kerala Model, the Red Volunteers movement in West Bengal – a state where the left has a significant social presence after having governed the state for 34 years till 2009 – also gained a significant amount of media attention (Sengupta, 2021). This is due to the ways in which it substituted the state itself in certain aspects in the state of West Bengal, as Dhar (2021) argues, by working through communities and strategies of mutual aid. The ways in which the Red Volunteers reacted to the pandemic exhibited that states which have some presence of the left in the political sphere are better suited to react to healthcare crisis, even if they are not governing the region directly.

Marx (1870) had argued that social gains are usually usurped by the elite because they remain in a better position to do that, both economically and culturally, stemming from their domination over the society physically and psychologically. Models such as the one in Kerala and the Red Volunteers' movement can potentially disrupt these tendencies. But to do that, they will need to reinvent the dialectical framework of analysis emphasising the contradiction between living labour and dead labour. These models often resort to temporary *stop-gap* solutions, which are too restricted in their overall viability of becoming major factors in effecting structural changes in the society. They are, however, the glimpses of the working-class organisational forms that can, as Stall (2016) had argued, alter the capitalist structure of the world moving beyond the reliance that societies have come to gain on private charities during times of crisis. These private charities, as Lenin (1915/1974) had argued, only focus on peace because it is beneficial to them in the process of accumulation, and more so because they remain afraid of the idea of a revolutionary overhaul of their hegemonical domination. It is clear that capitalism does not promote peace, but neither does undialectical versions of egalitarian thought. Ideas such as those coming from Juan Posadas, at least in the context of COVID-19, do not help much because Posadas (1979) had argued that if a revolution were to break out in such times, the conditions would be very different from what mainstream socialists and communists perceive them to be. While, in reality, the conditions that COVID-19 presented were exactly what many socialist thinkers had predicted them to be. COVID-19 failed to improve the lives of the working class and the marginalised sections. Instead, as Basole et al. (2021) state, the pandemic has further increased informality and poverty. It has also pushed a significant section of even the middle class towards poverty (Singh & Kumar, 2021). At the same time, the pandemic has also resulted in increased violence against women (Raj, 2020), which has been a generalised trend under neoliberalism (Collier, 2008).

A conceptualisation of freedom in these circumstances requires not only a reorganisation of material production mechanisms but also of the ways in which people think ideologically. A plain and simple 'reset' often becomes akin to plain and simple wage struggles, which, even though revolutionary, cannot overcome the contradictory nature of capitalism in its entirety because they never move beyond the realm of the primary negation. COVID-19 creates the ideal conditions for survival of the capitalist leviathan, whereby processes of profit extraction become almost mainstream. The government can provide thousands of dollars to the elites and the capitalists to bring them out of the crisis caused by COVID-19, while the necessary funds required to help the poor effectively still remain out of reach (Duflo & Bannerjee, 2020; The Hindu, 2021). In his *Elements of Law, Natural and Politic*, Hobbes argues that human passions and desires are intimately related to the notion of power, which is central to the dynamics of human behaviour (Tuck & Silverthorne, 1998). The pandemic has increased the propensity of citizens to, what Hobbes mentions as, be obligated to obey. Tendencies such as Posadism harbours within itself a major element of fatalism, which rests on the fatalistic belief that a higher being than a human actually exists, and that they might be able to help the human society in overcoming the crisis (Posadas, 1968, 1968a). They do not consider that, much like the state, which encompasses all the characters of transforming itself into a coercive institution, as Bloch (2000) had written, any superpowered being also possesses the same qualities of becoming a 'global tyrant' (Paik, 2010, p. 12). The major problem with such ideas is that they do not emphasise sufficiently the capacity that human beings themselves possess. Instead, they always factor in a higher body to intervene. Erich Fromm's (1942/2001) humanist psychoanalysis points one towards the idea that under conditions of capitalist expansion, the market becomes the overarching force that dominates the society, creating atomised individuals, so that the idea of freedom itself becomes an emotional burden to many.

The loss of the desire to be free becomes critical in situations such as the COVID-19 pandemic because of the changes in the most intimate processes of life that COVID-19 has affected, which include one's own idea of selfhood and the processes of coming of age (Golechha, 2020; Bristow & Gilland, 2021). Diseases such as HIV-AIDS, which has significantly affected human history, are known to have a distressing effect on the elderly and those in perpetual need of some form of care (Wagner, 2020). However, the world that has come up in the contemporary times is one where there is a crisis of care caused by widespread financialisation and commercialisation of the society under neoliberalism (Dowling, 2021). While the idea of care has suffered through decades of capitalist exploitation and globalisation, during the pandemic the crisis of care gained a new momentum (The Care Collective, 2020). The loss of the ethical and caring framework is a result of the neoliberal domination of the society (Filip, 2020), which accelerates all kinds of tendencies that emphasise the loss of feelings such as empathy and compassion, leading the entire society towards becoming a dehumanised market, just as how Marx (1844, 1976) had predicted it to be. Capitalism today, as Flusser argues sees human beings as nothing more than '"digital computations" of whirring dots in possible combinations' (Han, 2013, p. 42), who can be used at will for accumulating profits. Human beings, in a post-COVID-19 society, will continue to be seen as nothing more than economic entities, unless a radical break occurs with capitalism – a simple thing theoretically. Brecht had argued in his play *The Mother* that the simple things are often the hardest to perform. Taking cue from that, Slavoj Žižek writes:

> There are many obstacles that make it so hard to do, above all the global capitalist order and its ideological hegemony. Do we then need a new Communism? Yes, but what I am tempted to call a *moderately conservative Communism*: all the steps that are necessary, from global mobilization against viral and other threats to establishing procedures which will constrain market mechanisms and socialize economy, but done in a way which is conservative (in the sense of an effort to conserve the conditions of human life – and the paradox is that we will have to change things precisely to maintain these conditions) and moderate (in the sense of carefully taking into count unpredictable side-effects of our measures.
>
> (Žižek, 2021, p. 116)

The radical proposal that many like Žižek are putting forth today would require the establishment of a certain 'narrative justice', which renders visible the invisible exploited masses whose identities are shaped by labour, sociability, and cultural expressions (Barca, 2020). They all face the consequence of capitalist oppression, which have to be analysed in light of capitalism not being a mere economic system but a dominant mode of social ontology.

In conditions like the present, which Moore (2015) describes to be a world where capitalism has become a part and parcel of *the web of life*, social theories have to be structured, especially in a post-COVID-19 world, in such a way that they favour the most vulnerable populations as Sengupta and Jha (2021) show. Amidst such situations, there have been reports of how effective local governance models are in distributing aid and relief to the marginalised (Sahin & Abbas, 2020). The pandemic has highlighted that the human society, in spite of the claims of *we are all in this together*, does not face catastrophic events as one unified body. This is due to the fact that different sections of the society are exposed to different vulnerabilities on social, economic, and cultural terms (Cubukcu, 2020), and as such COVID-19 is unlikely to create a 'sense of *us*' as Gessen (2020, Para 9) argues. Shukla (1969) argued about the relevance of the Gandhian alternative of trusteeship management as an alternative to class conflict, whereby he advocated a top-down approach towards social reform in India. Gandhi (1929/1969) believed that because of the unique conditions that India presented with its tradition of cooperation, the interests of the employer and the employed could be fused with each other if the employer could be infused with the feeling of spiritual oneness with the world populated by the employed. However, as Ghosh (1989) had argued, the application of the model remained extremely limited in independent India. The Gandhian idea of trusteeship was more or less devised on religious and spiritual terms – the same broad corpus of philosophy that has been used by individuals and institutions in analysing the numerous catastrophic events of the twenty-first century (Keller, 2021). Most of them, however in the context of COVID-19, belong to the right-wing because of the fact that COVID-19 was not a catastrophe born out of man-made intervention but rather perceived as a heavenly judgement by many, similar to meteor strikes or an extra-terrestrial invasion. Different catastrophes evoke a different set of reactions, but 'the End can only be evaded by a change of character and culture that is difficult to conceive' (Clark, 2000, p. 35).

Social movements, in a post-COVID-19 world, cannot be only about plain and simple redistribution, but rather they have to be about the abolition of the commodity-form and the value production mechanism that accompanies the same. The state-form, as it exists today, needs to be analysed more critically in light of the outright domination that it proposes to have in the lives of the citizens. Raya Dunayevskaya (2018) had argued that it would be wrong to analyse capitalism only as a result of the free market, but rather one has to also understand that the state – when it tries to replace the rule of capital – also runs the risk of becoming capitalist itself because the conditions of commodity production and the contradiction of labour and capital do not change much. The conditions created by COVID-19 are diverse. The pandemic has had a significant impact on the mental well-being of the people, with a notable effect on women among the people, which in countries such as India frequently suffers under normal conditions because of social taboos and bureaucratic mismanagement (Agarwal, 2020). In order to create a socially equitable post-COVID-19 world, the world needs to move towards generating plans that do not merely focus on new developments, but instead focus on the fulfilment of needs. This will be further diversified with the kind of impact that the pandemic has had on the mental health of the people. For example, Shaguna Kanwar (2019) notes that the current urban planning mechanisms in India, including the famed smart cities projects would fulfil very few urban needs in reality. Similar is the case with the plans and reforms that will be implemented subsequent to COVID-19. Unless and until the needs of the marginalised are considered *very specifically*, they will continue to be used in a way that does not benefit those who need them the most.

Universal basic services, according to Frankel (2022), need an interventionist state in order to connect them to an employment guarantee program, which would enable the individuals to engage with the society in a more dignified and productive manner. Stevano et al. (2021) also argue that, in the context of COVID-19, employment would have to be one of the fundamental areas of importance in a post-COVID-19 world, because 'depending on job type, the pandemic has differentiated effects on workers' earnings, the likelihood of becoming unemployed, ability to work from home and exposure to the disease, with those in informal, precarious and front-line work most severely affected' (2021, p. 4). However, the conditions created by capitalist employment measures almost always put the health of the workers at risk, as has been enumerated by Das's (2022) study of Marx's (1976) *Capital* from a perspective of the health of the workers, by creating living and work conditions that increase the risk of contracting diseases such as COVID-19. It is essential to realise that healthcare and capital have an intrinsic relationship with each other. The health of the workers is directly proportional to the productivity of capital, however, as Das (2022) argues, capitalism makes sure that the health of the workers remains under the strict control of the forces of capital. The manner in which the workers' health was treated by the states and the markets was akin to treating them as animals (Zaretsky, 2020). In the Indian city of Mumbai, where 42% of the population lives in overcrowded informal settlements such as Dharavi, the Anganwadi workers found it extremely difficult to even deliver the basic care that many lactating and pregnant women need (Mishra & Gaurav, 2022). Additionally, their work was made more difficult because they did not have access to proper protective equipment in certain cases. This made their work more dangerous than usual. This was explained in Tripathi's (2021) article on Matilda Kullu, an Anganwadi worker in rural Odisha. Migrant workers, as has been stated numerous times in the current book, have been one of the other most affected sections of the marginalised populace of the country. The pandemic has added to the precarity that they already face in their everyday lives, creating a situation where being panic-struck turned into a new normal for them, as Jesline et al. (2021) have exhibited in detail in their review article.

With the possibility of the *long Covid* becoming increasingly probable day by day, these vulnerable people will be put at further risk unless a radical structural change occurs. Zhang (2022) informs that the novel Coronavirus might have more possible mutations than the number of atoms in the universe, and as such it is expected to return periodically – either in the form of an outbreak or a pandemic, if not managed properly. And the kind of vaccines that are being developed need to be more robust and require an immense amount of funding that goes beyond political interests (Ghosh, 2021; Zhang, 2022). COVID-19 will be one of the most 'persistent' events for decades to come, because:

> [It] has served as a salutary reminder of the potential fragility of our relationship with nature. It has forced us as individuals to accept unprecedented constraints on our ability to go about our everyday business, including not least our ability to travel long distances by car or on a plane, while governments have found themselves intervening in the economy in a fashion not seen since wartime.
>
> (Curtice, 2020, p. 205)

The effects of the pandemic are a culmination of the constant devaluation of human lives that has become the norm under capitalism. COVID-19 has exposed that the healthcare systems globally remain underfunded, and as such remain incapable of protecting the marginalised populace from the effects of a global healthcare crisis caused by viral diseases such as COVID-19. The constant privatisation of healthcare services has resulted in a constant accessibility crisis for the poor and the marginalised, one that is unlikely to disappear even when COVID-19 has waned away. It has to be taken into cognisance that the contemporary world is a world that is best described as being a post-truth-based world, and as such the perceptions of risk among the people have become highly complicated to analyse in terms of the reliability that numbers and statistics pose (Humpherson, 2019; Spiegelhater, 2019). The only solution in sight which would potentially be in a favourable position to counter the effects of disasters such as COVID-19 is a future where people themselves are *in charge*, both formally and materially. That would enable a more egalitarian management of the community-bodies which have come to be seminally important during the COVID-19 pandemic. The organisations and bonds of solidarity which have organically developed among the people need to be nurtured in a post-COVID-19 world, but it should be done in such a way that neither the market nor the state-form becomes the dominant factor in the lives of the people.

COVID-19 has affected the very idea of the self in individuals, especially within those coming from marginalised backgrounds, and as such demands a solution. As Sainath (2020a) writes, a solution is required which involves a rapid nationalisation and formalisation of work for the informal sector – much like the Kerala Model (Jose, 2021a, 2021b). Tendencies such as Posadism lay hopes on higher bodies because, to them, as Gittlitz (2018) argues, any form of higher beings would have solved the contradictions that common human beings face and as such would be able to help human societies in resolving the contradictions surrounding nation states and capitalism. However, as the COVID-19 pandemic exposes, neither a higher body nor pure nationalisation would solve any of these completely. These solutions contradict the fundamental idea that 'man makes his own history; he is his own creator' (Fromm, 1961, p. 12).

Hope, in these circumstances, can be a critical weapon to possess. Ernst Bloch (1995a, 1995b, 1996) and Erich Fromm (1968) in their works have highlighted the immense power that hope possesses in a crisis-ridden world. Bloch (1995a, 2000) argued that hope and utopian vision can be a powerful weapon in the hands of the marginalised as it was something that could effectively venture beyond the limits posed by the present. Hope, however, in contemporary times, has often been stripped off of its role in shaping actions, and as such has stopped being social in nature to many (Petersen, 2015). Erich Fromm (1968), on the other hand, saw the idea of hope as being at the risk of getting engulfed by capitalist consumption-driven social structure. Social change in a post-COVID-19 world has to recover this hope from the clutches of capitalism consumerism and generalised commodity production, and as such, has to flow from the people themselves. Capitalism, over the years in India, has produced an immense inequality of wealth, which has been blatantly exposed during the pandemic. However, it cannot be argued that these inequalities and the sparks of rebellion that have erupted because of them during the pandemic will automatically lead to a social overhaul without the conscious effort of the marginalised sections. Bloch's *militant optimism* can be an important element in this context because it attempts to tread a middle path between naive optimism and abject pessimism struggling against the hopelessness that has gripped the contemporary society (Menozzi, 2020).

The COVID-19 pandemic exposes the vulnerability that capitalism faces in its everyday existence and, as such, also lays bare the utopian possibilities of transcendence of the society as one knows it (Buzgalin, 2020; Smith, 2020). The subjectivity of hope, as Aidnik (2021) writes following Ernst Bloch, will probably be a critical part of that process. This would require the conscious effort of both the intellectuals and the marginalised masses, only the dialectical unity of which could lead the society towards a more egalitarian future in a post-COVID-19 world. Social movements, which take place, stemming from this dialectical unity, can understand the true value of freedom – a life without toil and alienation (Dunayevskaya, 1958a) – and as such can move towards it while negating both the market and the state. These movements could potentially negate the conditions that arise from the contradictions presented by contemporary capitalism and move towards analysing freedom through the progress of history – a central concept within Marxian thought (Dunayevskaya, 1965). This implies taking into consideration the dual probabilities of a crisis leading to a positive social transformation, as well as the probability of a catastrophic crisis being a mere vehicle of social change that is best suited for right-wing populism in the contemporary times (Lilley, 2012; Walby, 2015).

Freedom not only refers to a social existence free of oppression but also means a life without alienation. It refers to a life where life becomes, as Dunayevskaya (1958a, p. 10) says, 'the play of human faculties'. This freedom can only be attained if human beings understand and realise, consciously, the dialectical progress of history, whereby they realise their own potential as actually living actors capable of effecting change as 'Man's true history does not begin until he is free, can develop all his innate talents, which class society, especially value-producing capitalism, throttles' (Dunayevskaya, 1973, p. 74). Following Marx's (1875) argumentative framework, one can say that these movements need to move towards a negation of all forms of higher bodies, including the neoliberal mode of statism, religious bigotry, and market chauvinism, and reinvent the subjective basis of the objective world – where the individual is in a dialectical relationship with the society at large.

The fundamental question under any form of capitalism – one mediated by the state, the market, or a combination of both as is usually the case – is the social character of labour. It is this peculiar character of labour, coupled with market and property relations, which gives rise to the excess wealth that has come to characterise the global elite, who have become the shroud beneath which the bodies of the countless victims of COVID-19 from the working class and other marginalised sections remain buried and hidden, *at least for now*.

References

Agarwal, P. (2020, May 16). We must intervene now to check the Covid-19 induced mental health pandemic. *The Wire*. Retrieved February 2, 2023, from www.science.thewire.in/health/we-must-intervene-now-to-check-the-covid-19-induced-mental-health-pandemic

Aidnik, M. (2021, July 8). From the depths of the pandemic towards an ecosocialist Utopia. *ROAR*. Retrieved February 2, 2023, from www.roarag.org/pandemic-ecosocialism-utopia

Angus, I. (2011). *Too many people? Population, immigration, and the environmental crisis*. Monthly Review Press.

Asian Development Bank. (2020). Creating investable cities in a post-COVID-19 Asia and the Pacific—Enhancing competitiveness and resilience through quality infrastructure. Retrieved February 2, 2023, from www.adb.org/sites/default/files/project-documents/54036/54036-001-tar-en.pdf

Auto, H. (2022, August 2). Rise above blame games to common challenge, urges top zoonotic diseases expert Wang Linfa. *The Straits Times*. Retrieved February 2, 2023, from www.straitstimes.com/world/united-states/rise-above-blame-games-to-common-challenge-urges-top-zoonotic-diseases-expert

Bagus, P., Peňa-Ramos, J., & Sánchez-Bayón, A. (2021). Capitalism, COVID-19, and lockdowns. *Business Ethics, the Environment and Responsibility* [Online First]. https://doi.org/10.1111/beer.12431

Baiocchi, G. (2020, August 14). The Utopian counterfactual. *Thesis Eleven*. Retrieved February 2, 2023, from www.thesiseleven.com/2020/05/14/the-utopian-counterfactual/

Bajpai, N., & Wadhwa, M. (2020). *Covid-19 in India: Issues, challenges and lessons*. ICT Working Paper # 34. Center for Sustainable Development.

Balakrishnan, P. (2019, August 22). The 'Kerala model' is unsustainable. *The Hindu*. Retrieved February 2, 2023, from www.thehindu.com/opinion/op-ed/the-kerala-model-is-unsustainable/

Barca, S. (2020). *Forces of reproduction*. Cambridge University Press.

Barker, M. (2020). *Under the mask of philanthropy*. CreateSpace Independent Publishing.

Barnagarwala, T. (2020, March 24). The pandemic's hidden cist: Much-hyped health insurance scheme failed to cover hospital bills. *Scroll*. Retrieved February 2, 2023, from www.scroll.in/article/1020201/the-pandemics-hidden-cost-much-hyped-health-insurance-scheme-failed-to-cover-insurance-costs

Barnagarwala, T. (2022, March 22). The pandemic's hidden cost: Suicides among Indians who lost jobs and income. *Scroll*. Retrieved February 2, 2023, from www.scroll.in/article/1019925/the-pandemics-hidden-cost-suicides-among-indians-who-lost-jobs-and-income

Basole, A., Abraham, R., Lahoti, R., Kesar, S., Jha, M., Nath, P., Kapoor, R., Mandela, S. N., Shrivastava, A., Dasgupta, Z., Gupta, G., & Narayanan, R. (2021). *State of working India 2021: One year of Covid-19*. Azim Premji University.

Bell, J., Nuzzo, J. B., Bristol, N., Essix, G., Isaac, C., Kobokovich, A., Meyer, D., Mullen, L., & Rose, S. (2021). *Global health security index 2021*. John Hopkins University, Nuclear Threat Initiative and The Economist.

Bello, W. (2022). The race to replace a dying neoliberalism. In S. Alexander, S. Chandrashekeran, & B. Gleeson (Eds.), *Post-capitalist futures: Paradigms, politics, and prospects*. Palgrave Macmillan.

Bhagat, S. V. (2021, May 23). As India stumbles, one state charts its own Covid course. *The New York Times*. Retrieved February 2, 2023, from www.nyti.ms/3hRRXov

Biswas, S. (2021, July 8). Pew survey: India is neither a melting pot nor a salad bowl. *BBC*. Retrieved February 2, 2023, from www.bbc.com/news/world-asia-india-57723926

Bloch, E. (1995a). *The principle of hope* (Vol. 1). MIT Press.

Bloch, E. (1995b). *The principle of hope* (Vol. 2). MIT Press.

Bloch, E. (1996). *The principle of hope* (Vol. 3). MIT Press.

Bloch, E. (2000). *The spirit of Utopia*. Stanford University Press.

Boddy, M. (1984). Local councils and the financial squeeze. In M. Boddy & C. Fudge (Eds.), *Local socialism: Labour councils and new left alternatives*. Macmillan.

Boddy, M., & Fudge, C. (1984). Labour councils and new left alternatives. In M. Boddy & C. Fudge (Eds.), *Local socialism: Labour councils and new left alternatives*. Macmillan.

Boltanski, L., & Chiapello, E. (2005a). *The new spirit of capitalism*. Verso.

Boltanski, L., & Chiapello, E. (2005b). The new spirit of capitalism. *International Journal of Politics, Culture and Society, 18*(Annual), 161–188.

Boltanski, L., & Esquerre, A. (2020). *Enrichment: A critique of commodities*. Polity.

Boseley, S. (2015, May 11). Experts call for global research fund for antibiotics, Ebola and other neglected diseases. *The Guardian*. Retrieved February 2, 2023, from www.theguardian.com/society/sarah-boseley-global-research-fund-for-antibiotics-ebola-and-other-neglected-diseases

Boyd, I. L. (2019). Risk and uncertainty in the context of government decision-making. In S. Linden & R. E. Löfstedt (Eds.), *Risk and uncertainty in a post-truth society*. Routledge.

Bristow, J., & Gilland, E. (2021). *The Corona generation: Coming of age in a crisis*. ZERO Books.

Brubaker, R. (2020, July 13). Paradoxes of populism during the pandemic. *Thesis Eleven*. Retrieved February 2, 2023, from www.thesiseleven.com/2020/07/13/paradoxes-of-populism

Brunnermeier, M. K. (2021). *The resilient society*. Endeavor Literary Press.

Business Line. (2018, March 9). A new paradigm: Time to bid adieu to Nehruvian socialism. *Business Line*. Retrieved February 2, 2023, from www.thehindubusinessline.com/opinion/a-new-paradigm/

Buzgalin, A. (2020, April 17). The Coronavirus is stirring the impulse to communism. *Rosa Luxemburg Stiftung*. Retrieved February 2, 2023, from www.rosalux.de/en/news/id/42001/the-coronavirus-is-stirring-the-impulse-to-communism

Cameron, E. E., Nuzzo, J. B., Bell, J. A., Nalabandian, M., O'Brien, J., League, A., Ravi, S., Mayer, D., Snyder, M., Mullen, L., & Warmbrod, L. (2019). *Global health security index 2019*. John Hopkins University, Nuclear Threat Initiative and The Economist.

The Care Collective. (2020). *The care manifesto: The politics of interdependence*. Verso.

Chang, C. (2020, March 4). There are no private solutions to a public health crisis. *Vice*. Retrieved February 2, 2023, from www.vice.com/article/qjdeq5/there-are-no-private-solutions-to-a-public-health-crisis

Chowkwanyun, M. (2022). *All health politics is local: Community battles for medical care and environmental health*. University of North Carolina Press.

Clark, S. R. L. (2000). The end of the ages. In D. Seed (Ed.), *Imagining Apocalypse: Studies in cultural crisis*. Macmillan.

Cockburn, C. (1977). The local state: Management of cities and people. *Race and Class, 18*(4). https://doi.org/10.1177/030639687701800403

Collier, C. N. (2008). Neoliberalism and violence against women: Can retrenchment convergence explain the path pf provincial anti-violence policy, 1985–2005? *Canadian Journal of Political Science*, 41(1), 19–42.

Cubukcu, A. (2020, May 30). Another end of the world is possible. *Thesis Eleven*. Retrieved February 2, 2023, from www.thesiseleven.com/2020/07/30/another-end-of-the-world-is-possible

Curtice, J. (2020). Ready to deal with another crisis? *IPPR Progressive Review* [Online]. https://doi.org/10.1111/newe.12209.

Daniyal, S. (2021, June 6). 'Emerging superpower' to 'failed state': How perceptions of india changed drastically under Modi. *Scroll*. Retrieved February 2, 2023, from www.scroll.in/article/996356/emerging-superpower-to-failed-state-how-percepions-of-India-changed-drastixally-under-Modi

Das, G. (2002/2012). *The elephant paradigm: India wrestles with change*. Penguin.

Das, R. J. (2022). Capital, capitalism and health. *Critical Sociology* [Online First]. https://doi.org/10.1177/08969205221083503

Datta Ray, S. K. (2022, September 28). The other side of life in the 5th largest economy. *Deccan Chronicle*.

Davis, G. (2020, July 31). Charity in time of plague. *Thesis Eleven*. Retrieved February 2, 2023, from www.thesiseleven.com/2020/07/31/charity-in-time-of-plague

Davis, J. (2012). At war with the future: Catastrophism and the right. In S. Lilley (Ed.), *Catastrophism: The Apocalyptic politics of collapse and rebirth*. PM Press.

Dean, J., & Heron, K. (2020, June). Revolution or ruin. *E-flux Journal*. Retrieved February 2, 2023, from www.e-flux.com/journal/110/335242/revolution-or-ruin/

Dennis, S. (2021, April 4). The Kerala model at the crossroads. *The Hindu*. Retrieved February 2, 2023, from www.thehindu.com/opinion/lead/the-kerala-model-at-the-crossroads/

Desai, A. R. (1984). *India's path of development: A Marxist approach*. Popular Prakashan.

Dhar, D. (2021, October 26). In India, communists are leading the fight Against COVID-19. *Jacobin*. Retrieved February 2, 2023, from www.jacobin.com/2021/10/indian-left-red-volunteers-west-bengal-mutual-aid-and-covid-relief

Dighavkar, K. (2021). *The Dharavi model: How Asia's largest slum defeated Covid-19*. Notion Press.

Dowling, E. (2021). *The care crisis: What caused it and how can we end it?* Verso.

Duflo, E., & Bannerjee, A. (2020, March 29). A prescription for action: Nine steps after the next 21 days. *Indian Express*. Retrieved February 2, 2023, from www.indianexpress.com/article/opinion/columns/india-lockown-coronavirus-infection-abhijit-bannerjee-esther-duflo-6336624/

Dunayevskaya, R. (1958a). *Marxism and freedom... from 1776 until today*. Bookman Associates.

Dunayevskaya, R. (1958b/2002). Letter to Herbert Marcuse July 15, 1958. In P. Hudis & K. B. Anderson (Eds.), *The power of negativity: Selected writings on the dialectic in Hegel and Marx by Raya Dunayevskaya*. Lexington Books. (Original work published 1958b)

Dunayevskaya, R. (1965). Marx's humanism today. In E. Fromm (Ed.), *Socialist humanism*. Doubleday.

Dunayevskaya, R. (1973). *Philosophy and revolution: From Hegel to Sartre, and from Marx to Mao*. Humanities Press. (Original work published 1973)

Dunayevskaya, R. (1981/1982). *Rosa Luxemburg, women's liberation and Marx's philosophy of revolution*. Humanities Press. (Original work published 1981)

Dunayevskaya, R. (1987/2002). Presentation on the dialectics of organisation and philosophy. In P. Hudis & K. B. Anderson (Eds.), *The power of negativity: Selected writings on the dialectic in Hegel and Marx by Raya Dunayevskaya*. Lexington Books. (Original work published 1987)

Dunayevskaya, R. (2018). The theory of state capitalism: The Soviet Union as capitalist society. In J. Asimakopoulos & R. Gilman-Opalsky (Eds.), *Against capital in the twenty-first century*. Temple University Press.

Dunleavy, P. (1984). The limits to local government. In M. Boddy & C. Fudge (Ed.), *Local socialism: Labour councils and new left alternatives*. Macmillan.

Fiamingo, G. (1898). Municipal socialism in Europe. *Journal of Political Economy*, 396–401.

Filip, B. (2020). *The rise of neo-liberalism and the decline of freedom*. Palgrave Macmillan.

Firth, R. (2020). Mutual aid, anarchist preparedness and COVID-19. In J. Preston & R. Firth (Eds.), *Coronavirus, class and mutual aid in the United Kingdom*. Palgrave Macmillan.

Florida, R. (2002). *The rise of the creative class*. Basic Books.

Foster, J. B., & Clark, B. (2020). *The robbery of nature: Capitalism and the ecological rift*. Monthly Review Press.

Foucault, M. (1977). *Discipline and punish: The birth of the prison*. Penguin.

Foucault, M. (1978). *The history of sexuality* (Vol. 1). Random House.

Foucault, M. (2008). *The birth of biopolitics: Lectures at the College de France, 1978–1979*. Palgrave Macmillan.

Frankel, B. (2022). From technological Utopianism to universal basic services. In S. Alexander, S. Chandrashekeran, & B. Gleeson (Eds.), *Post-capitalist futures: Paradigms, politics, and prospects*. Palgrave Macmillan.

Fromm, E. (2001). *The fear of freedom*. Routledge. (Original work published 1942)

Fromm, E. (1961). *Marx's concept of man*. Continuum.

Fromm, E. (1968). *The revolution of hope: Toward a humanized technology*. Harper and Row.

Fromm, E. (1976). *To have or to be?* Continuum.

Fromm, E. (1994). *On being human*. Open Road.

Fudge, C. (1984). Decentralisation: Socialism goes local? In M. Boddy & C. Fudge (Eds.), *Local socialism: Labour councils and new left alternatives*. Macmillan.

Gandhi, M. K. (1969). Capital and labour. In *Gandhiji on trusteeship management*. Indian Centre for Encouraging Excellence. (Original work published 1929)

Gessen, M. (2020, May 26). Life, liberty, and the pursuit of spitting on other people. *The New Yorker*. Retrieved February 2, 2023, from www.newyorker.com/news/our-columnists/life-liberty-and-the-pursuit-of-spitting-pver-other-people

Ghosh, A. K. (2021). *Billions under lockdown: The inside story of India's fight against COVID-19*. Bloomsbury.

Ghosh, A. K., & Chaudhury, A. B. R. (2020). Migrant workers and the ethics of care during a pandemic. In R. Samaddar (Ed.), *Borders of an epidemic: Covid-19 and migrant workers*. Calcutta Research Group.

Ghosh, S. (1989). Trusteeship in industry: Gandhiji's dream and contemporary reality. *Indian Journal of Industrial Relations*, 25(1), 35–44.

Ghoshal, D., & Ravikumar, S. (2021, January 5). Indian vaccine makers end spat, pledge 'smooth rollout' of Covid-19 shots. *WTVBAM*. Retrieved February 2, 2023, from www.wtvbam.com/2021/01/05/indian-vaccine-makers-end-spat-pledge-smooth-rollout-of-covid-19-shots/

Giddens, A. (1991). *Modernity and self-identity*. Polity.

Gittlitz, A. M. (2018, July 14). The secret history of Marxist Alien hunters. *The Outline*. Retrieved February 2, 2023, from www.theoutline.com/post/5384/the-secret-history-of-marxist-alien-hunters

Gleisler, M. (2021, April 7). COVID vaccine: Where does freedom end and civic duty begin? *BIG THINK*. Retrieved February 2, 2023, from www.bigthink.com/13-8/freedom-end-civic-duty-begin

Glennie, J. (2011, April 22). Slavoj Žižek's animated ideas about charity are simplistic and soulless. *The Guardian*. Retrieved February 2, 2023, from www.theguardian.com/global-development/poverty-matters/2011/apr/22/slavoj-Žižek-animated-ideas-about-charity

Goldfrank, B., & Schrank, A. (2009). Municipal neoliberalism and municipal socialism: Urban political economy in Latin America. *Urban Worlds*, *33*(2), 443–462.

Golechha, M. (2020). COVID-19, India, lockdown and psychosocial challenges: What next? *International Journal of Social Psychiatry*, *66*(8), 830–832.

Gore, A. (2007). Foreword. In S. L. Hart (Ed.), *Capitalism at the crossroads*. Wharton School Publishing.

Grebmer, K., Bernstein, J., Wiemers, M., Schiffer, T., Hanano, A., Towey, O., Cheilleachair, R. N., Foley, C., Gitter, S., Ekstrom, K., & Fritschel, H. (2021). *Global hunger index report 2021: Hunger and food systems in conflict settings*. SIPRI.

Groten, M. (2021). Glasgow's new town hall: Imperialism, nationalism and civic pride, 1877–1889. *Urban History*, *48*, 644–662.

Hadas, D. (2022, August 5). After Covid: Pandemic restrictions stumble on like zombies. *City Journal*. Retrieved February 2, 2023, from www.city-journal.org/after-covid

Han, B. C. (2013). *In the swarm: Digital prospects* (E. Butler, Trans., 2017). The MIT Press.

Hanif, M. (2022, September 26). Pakistan's biblical floods and the case for climate reparations. *The New Yorker*. Retrieved February 2, 2023, from www.newyorker.com/news/pakistans-biblical-floods-and-the-case-for-climate-reparations

Hannah, M. G., Hutta, J. S., & Schemann, C. (2020, May 5). Thinking through Covid-19 responses with Foucault – an initial overview. *Antipode Online*. Retrieved February 2, 2023, from www.antipodeonline.org/2020/05/05/thinking-through-covid-19-responses-wthpfoucault-an-initial-overview

Harvey, D. (2012). *Rebel cities: From the right to the city to the urban revolution*. Verso.

Hessler, P. (2020, August 10). How China controlled the Coronavirus: Teaching and learning in Sichuan during the pandemic. *The New Yorker*. Retrieved February 2, 2023, from www.newyorker.com/magazine/2020/08/17/how-china-controlled-the-coronavirus

The Hindu. (2021, June 28). Govt. unveils Rs. 6.28 lakh cr. stimulus post second covid wave. *The Hindu*. Retrieved January 2, 2023, from www.thehindu.com/business/Economy/nirmala-satharaman-unveils-new-covid-recovery-pacakage-expands-credit-rellief

Humpherson, E. (2019). Trustworthiness, quality, and value: The regulation of official statistics in a post-truth world. In S. Linden & R. E. Löfstedt (Eds.), *Risk and uncertainty in a post-truth society*. Routledge.

IFPRI. (2022). *Climate change and food systems: Global food policy report 2022*. IFPRI.

IndiaSpend. (2020, June 29). Women farmers face uncertain future as lockdown affects income. *IndiaSpend*. Retrieved February 2, 2023, from www.indiaspend.com/women-farmers-face-uncertain-future-as-lockdown-affects-income/

Jacob, S. (2021, December 13). Despite higher Covid cases, Kerala model still a success: Experts. *Business Standard*. Retrieved February 2, 2023, from www.business-standard.com.article/current-affairs/despite-higher-cases-kerala-model-still-a-success

Jesline, J., Romate, J., Rajkumar, E., & George, A. J. (2021). The plight of circular migrants during Covid-19 and the impact of circular migration in India: A systematic review. *Humanities and Social Sciences Communications* [Online]. https://doi.org/10.1057/s41599-021-00915-6

Jha, R. (2020). *The unfinished business of decentralised urban governance in India*. ORF Issue Brief No. 340. Observer Research Foundation.

Jose, S. (2021a, June 14). The story behind the 'Kerala model' of Covid control: Part 1. *Counter Currents*. https://countercurrents.org/2021/06/the-story-behind-the-kerala-model-of-covid-control-part-one/

Jose, S. (2021b, June 15). The story behind the 'Kerala model' of Covid control: Part 2. *Counter Currents*. https://countercurrents.org/2021/06/the-story-behind-the-kerala-model-of-covid-control-part-two/

Kanwar, S. (2019, May 16). Without an overhaul, smart cities won't fulfil urban needs. *The Wire*. Retrieved February 2, 2023, from www.thewire.in/article/urban/smart-cities-mission-reality

Kaur, R. (2020). *Brand new nation: Capitalist dreams and nationalist design in twenty-first century India*. Stanford University Press.

Keller, C. (2021). *Facing Apocalypse: Climate, democracy, and other last chances*. Orbis Books.

Kilby, J. (2015, December 17). The season of giving: Philanthropy or exploitation. *Socialist Appeal*. www.socialist.net/the-season-of-giving-philanthropy-or-exploitation

Klein, N. (2017). *No is not enough: Resisting Trump's shock politics and winning the world we need*. Haymarket Books.

Klein, N. (2017, September 29). A new shock doctrine: In a world of crisis, morality can still win. *The Guardian*. Retrieved February 2, 2023, from www.theguardian.com/news/2017/sep/29/a-new-shock-doctrine-in-a-world-of-crisis-morality-can-still-win

Kompalli, P. (2019). The coming of age of virtual hospitals. *Asian Healthcare and Management, 43*.

Law, A. (2021, May 20). Localised lockdowns have affected sales in second covid Wave, says Jyothy labs. *The Hindu Business Line*. Retrieved February 2, 2023, from www.thehindubusinessline.com/companies/second-covid-wave-has-not-hit-demand-but-localised-lockdowns-have-hit-sales-jyothy-labs/article34605280

Lefebvre, H. (1991a). *The production of space*. Basil Blackwell.

Lefebvre, H. (1991b). *Critique of everyday life* (Vol. 1). Verso.

Lenin, V. I. (1974). Bourgeois philanthropists and revolutionary social-democracy. In *Lenin collected works* (Vol. 21). Progress Publishers. (Original work published 1915)

Lilley, S. (2012). The Apocalyptic politics of collapse and rebirth. In S. Lilley (Ed.), *Catastrophism: The Apocalyptic politics of collapse and rebirth*. PM Press.

Lin, W. (2022). Automated infrastructure: COVID-19 and the shifting geographies of supply chain capitalism. *Progress in Human Geography, 46*(2), 463–483.

Mackenzie, D., & Wajcman, J. (1999). *The social shaping of technology*. Open University Press.

Magnuson, J. (2018). *Financing the Apocalypse: Drivers for economic and political instability*. Palgrave Macmillan.

Mann, G., & Wainwright, H. (2018). *Climate Leviathan: Our new planetary future*. Verso.

Marx, K. (1870). The civil war in France: Address to the general council of the international working men's association. In *Marx-Engels collected works* (Vol. 22). Lawrence and Wishart.

Marx, K. (1875). Critique of the Gotha programme. In *Marx-Engels collected works* (Vol. 24). Lawrence and Wishart.

Marx, K. (1975). Contribution to the critique of Hegel's philosophy of law. In *Marx Engels collected works* (Vol. 3). Lawrence and Wishart. (Original work published 1843)

Marx, K. (1975). Economic and philosophical manuscripts of 1844. In *Marx Engels collected works* (vol. 3). Lawrence and Wishart. (Original work published 1844)

Marx, K. (1976). *Capital* (Vol. 1). Penguin. (Original work published 1867)

Marx, K., & Engels, F. (1975). The holy family. In *Marx-Engels collected works* (Vol. 4). Lawrence and Wishart. (Original work published 1845)

Marx, K., & Engels, F. (1975). The German ideology. In *Marx Engels collected works* (Vol. 5). Lawrence and Wishart. (Original work published 1845–46)

Menon, N. (2020, August 3). Coronacapitalism and Hindu Rashtra in India. *Thesis Eleven*. Retrieved February 2, 2023, from www.thesiseleven.com/2020/08/03/coronacapitalism-and-hindu-rashtra-in-india

Menozzi, F. (2020, July 20). Militant optimism: A state of mind that can help us find hope in dark times. *The Conversation*. Retrieved February 2, 2023, from www.theconversation.com/militant-optimism-a-state-of-mind-that-can-help-us-find-hope-in-dark-times

Merrifield, A. (2006). *Henri Lefebvre: A critical introduction*. Routledge.

Mies, M., & Shiva, V. (2014). *Ecofeminism*. Zed Books.

Mishra, D. K., & Gaurav, N. (2022). Challenges faced by Anganwadi Centres in delivering nutritional meals to pregnant women, lactating mothers and children in Mumbai during COVID-19. *Advances in Public Health, Community and Tropical Medicine* [Online First]. https://doi.org/10.37722/APHCTM.2022.301

Mohanty, P. K. (2016). *Financing cities in India: Municipal reforms, fiscal accountability and urban infrastructure*. Sage.

Moore, J. W. (2015). *Capitalism in the web of life: Ecology and the accumulation of capital*. Verso.

Moses, M. (2022). *The municipal financial crisis: A framework for understanding and fixing government budgeting*. Palgrave Macmillan.

Nahm, J. M., Miller, S. M., & Urpelainen, J. (2022, March 3). G20's US$14-trillion economic stimulus reneges on emissions pledges. *Nature*, 603, 28–31.

Newsclick. (2022, February 19). Only Nehruvian 'socialism' 2.0 can solve India's problems. *Newsclick*. Retrieved February 2, 2023, from www.newsclick.in/only-nehruvian-socialism-20-can-solve-indias-problems

NITI Aayog. (2022). *Cities as engines of growth: Strengthening the states for broad based urban development*. NITI Aayog and Asian Development Bank.

NP, U. (2013, July 21). 'Nehruvian socialism' a derogatory term, 4% growth till 1964 was a breakthrough: Jean Dréze. *The Economic Times*. Retrieved February 2, 2023, from www.theeconomictimes.com/opinion/interviews/nehruvian-socialism-a-derogatory-term-4-growth-till-1964-a-breakthrough

Paik, P. Y. (2010). *From Utopia to Apocalypse: Science fiction and the politics of Catastrophe*. University of Minnesota Press.

Pelling, M. (2003). *The vulnerability of cities: Natural disasters and social resilience*. Earthscan.

Pellow, D. (2014). *Total liberation: The power and promise of animal rights and the radical earth movement*. University of Minnesota Press.

Petersen, A. (2015). *Hope in health: The socio-politics of optimism*. Palgrave.

Pinnock, D. (1989). Ideology and urban plain: Blueprints of a garrison city. In W. James & M. Simon (Eds.), *The angry divide: Social and economic history of the Western Cape* (pp. 150–168). David Philip.

Pithode, T. (2022). *The battle against Covid: Diary of a bureaucrat*. Bloomsbury.

Posadas, J. (1968). Flying saucers, the process of matter and energy, science and socialism. In *Socialism and human relationships with nature and the cosmos*. Scientific, Cultural and Political Editions.

Posadas, J. (2008). The intellectuals and the technicians, the development of the socialist revolution, and the IV international. In *What is a soviet*. Scientific, Cultural and Political Editions. (Original work published 1968a)

Posadas, J. (1979). The war and the elimination of the capitalist system on a world scale. In *Nuclear energy, war and socialism*. Scientific, Cultural and Political Editions.

Prasad, P. (2018). Health care reforms: Do they ensure social protection for the labouring poor? In P. Prasad & A. Jesani (Eds.), *Equity and access: Health care studies in India*. Oxford University Press.

Preston, J., & Firth, R. (2020). The *viracene* and capitalism. In J. Preston & R. Firth (Eds.), *Coronavirus, class and mutual aid in the United Kingdom*. Palgrave Macmillan.

Pulla, P. (2020, January 30). Why India should worry about the new Coronavirus. *The Wire*. Retrieved February 2, 2023, from www.thewire.in/article/health/wuhan-coronavirus-sars-mers-flu-pandemic-quanrantine-bats-wet-markets

Raj, V. (2020). Stay home stay unsafe: The violent fallout of a gender-blind COVID-19 response. In S. E. Thomas, I. Jaising, A. Agarwal, M. Arya, P. Dhawan, & V. Sharma (Eds.), *The gendered contagion: Perspectives on domestic violence during Covid-19*. Centre for Women and the Law.

Ramírez, C. M. S. (2021). *Knowledge capitalism and state theory: A "space-time" approach explaining development outcomes in the global economy*. Palgrave Macmillan.

Randolph, N. (2021). Making live and letting die in Covid-19: The biopolitics of race, space and freedom. *Spectra*, 8(2), 7–18.

Robinson, E. (2015). Defining progressive politics: Municipal socialism and anti-socialism in contestation, 1889–1939. *Journal of the History of Ideas*, 76(4), 609–631.

Roy, A. (2020). *AZADI: Freedom. Fascism. Fiction*. Haymarket.

S, A. (2020, April 10). A new 'Kerala' model for infra growth. *Business Line*. Retrieved February 2, 2023, from www.thehindubusinessline.com/opinion/a-new-kerala-model-for-infra-growth

Sahin, E., & Abbas, K. (2020). Communal lifeboat: Direct democracy in Rojava (NE Syria). In M. Sitrin & C. Sembrar (Eds.), *Pandemic solidarity: Mutual aid during the Covid-19 crisis*. Pluto Press.

Sainath, P. (2020a, April 8). Suggestions on what India should do about Coronavirus crisis. *The Quint*. Retrieved February 2, 2023, from www.thequint.com/coronavirus/p-sainath-suggestions-on-what-india-should-do-about-coronavirus-crisis

Sainath, P. (2020b, March 27). In India, neither tokenism nor panic can help counter this unique crisis. *The Wire*. Retrieved February 2, 2023, from www.thewire.in/article/government/india-coronavirus-migrants-agriculture

Sassen, S. (1991). *The global city: New York, London, and Tokyo*. Princeton University Press.

Saunders, P. (1984). Rethinking local politics. In M. Boddy & C. Fudge (Ed.), *Local socialism: Labour councils and new left alternatives*. Macmillan.

Scheidel, W. (2018). *The great leveler: Violence and the history of inequality from stone age to the twenty-first century*. Princeton University Press.

Schwartz, J. (2020, February 8). Coronavirus and China's 'authoritarian advantage'. *The Diplomat*. Retrieved February 2, 2023, from www.thediplomat.com/2020/02/coronavirus-and-chinas-authoritarian-advantage/

Scott, A. (2006). Creative cities: Conceptual issues and policy questions. *Journal of Urban Affairs*, 28(1), 1–17.

Scroll. (2021, May 6). COVID-19: 'Our moral fabric has been dismembered', says Delhi HC on hoarding, black-marketing. *Scroll*. Retrieved February 2, 2023, from www.scroll.in/latest/994236/covid-19-our-moral-fabric-has-been-disembered/

Sengupta, A. (2013). Creating, reclaiming, defending non-commercialised alternatives in the health sector in Asia. In D. A. McDonald & G. Ruiters (Eds.), *Alternatives to privatisation: Public options for essential services in the global South*. Leftword.

Sengupta, A. (2020). Forty years of Alma-Ata declaration. In P. Purkayastha, I. Mukhopadhyay, & R. Chintan (Eds.), *Political journeys in health: Essays by and for Amit Sengupta*. Leftword. (Original work published 2018)

Sengupta, A. (2021, August 15). 'Red volunteers' make a mark amid COVID crisis in West Bengal. *The Federal*. Retrieved February 2, 2023, from www.thefederal.com/states/west-bengal/red-volunteers-make-a-mark-amid-covid-crisis-in-west-bengal/

Sengupta, A., Mukhopadhyay, I., Weerasinghe, M., & Karki, A. (2020). The rise of private medicine in South Asia. In P. Purkayastha, I. Mukhopadhyay, & R. Chintan (Eds.), *Political journeys in health: Essays by and for Amit Sengupta*. Leftword. (Original work published 2017)

Sengupta, S., & Jha, M. K. (2021). Social policy, Covid-19, and impoverished migrants: Challenges and prospects in locked down India. In M. Pawar (Ed.), *Covid-19 pandemic: Impact on and implications for community and social development*. Sage.

Sheikh, K. (2022, September 27). New study shows Covid vaccines can temporarily alter menstrual cycle. *The New York Times*. Retrieved February 2, 2023, from www.nyti.ms/3CeUx1w

Sherwell, P. (2021, April 25). Modi leads India into a viral apocalypse. *The Australian*.

Shiva, V. (2008). Decolonising the North. In M. John (Ed.), *Women's studies in India: A reader*. Penguin.

Shukla, C. M. (1969). Introduction. In *Gandhiji on trusteeship management*. Indian Centre for Encouraging Excellence.

Simon, J., & Mahoney, R. (2022, April 25). How China's response to COVID-19 set the stage for a worldwide wave of censorship. *The New Yorker*. Retrieved February 2, 2023, from www.newyorker.com/news-desk/how-chinas-response-to-covid-19-set-the-stage-for-a-wave-of-censorship

Singh, K. D., & Kumar, H. (2021, April 16). COVID-19 pushes India's middle class toward poverty. *The New York Times*. Retrieved February 2, 2023, from www.nyti.ms/3snnXT2

Smith, J. (2020, March 31). Why Coronavirus could spark a capitalist supernova. *Open Democracy*. Retrieved January 2, 2023, from www.opendemocracy.net/em/oureconomy.why-coronavirus-could-spark-a-capitalist-supernova

Smith, N. (1996). *The new urban frontier: Gentrification the Revanchist city*. Routledge.

Solis, M. (2020, March 13). Coronavirus is the perfect disaster for 'disaster capitalism'. *VICE*. Retrieved January 2, 2023, from www.vice.com/en/article/5dmqyk/naomi-klein-interview-on-coronavirus-and-disaster-capitalism-shock-doctrine

Spade, D. (2020). *Mutual aid: Building solidarity during this crisis (and the next)*. Verso.

Spiegelhater, D. J. (2019). Trust in numbers. In S. Linden & R. E. Löfstedt (Eds.), *Risk and uncertainty in a post-truth society*. Routledge.

Spinney, L. (2020, May 14). The Coronavirus slayer! How Kerala's rock star health minister helped save it from Covid-19. *The Guardian*. Retrieved January 2, 2023, from www.theguardian.com/world/2020/may/14/the-coronavirus-slayer-how-keralas-rock-star-health0minister-helped-save-it-from-covid-19

Stall, P. (2016, December 21). Seize the charities. *Jacobin*. Retrieved January 2, 2023, from www.jaco9bin.com/2016/12/[rivate-charity-holidays-philanthropy-poverty-inequality/

Steen, B. (2019). 'A new scientific conception of human world': Anton Pannekoek's understanding of scientific socialism. In C. Tai, B. van der Steen, & J. van Dougen (Eds.), *Anton Pannekoek: Ways of viewing science and society*. Amsterdam University Press.

Stein, S. (2019). *Capital city: Gentrification and the real estate state*. Verso.

Stevano, S., Franz, T., Dafermos, Y., & Waeyenberge, E. V. (2021). COVID-19 and crises of capitalism: Intensifying inequalities and global responses. *Canadian Journal of Development Studies*, 42(1–2). https://doi.org/10.1080/02255189.2021.1892606

Sundaraman, T., Parmar, D., & Kriti, S. (2020). Public health and health services as global public goods. In *India exclusion report, 2019–20*. Three Essays Collective and Centre for Equity Studies.

Therborn, G. (2020, July 6). Opus Magnum: How the pandemic is changing the world. *Thesis Eleven*. Retrieved January 2, 2023, from www.thesiseleven.com/2020/07/06/opus-magnum-how-the-pandemic-is-changing-the-world

Thomas, J. J. (2021, June 27). The achievements and challenges of the Kerala 'model'. *The India Forum*. Retrieved January 2, 2023, from www.theindiaforum.in/article/achievements-challenges-kerala-model

The Times. (1902). *Municipal socialism: A series of articles*. George Edward Wright.

Trantidis, A. (2020, May 4). Liberty in the wake of Coronavirus. *Econlib Articles*. Retrieved January 2, 2023, from www.econlib.org/library/Columns/y2020/Transtinidiscoronavirus.html

Tripathi, B. (2020, May 3). Migrants build cities but face exclusion during crisis: Here's how this can change. *IndiaSpend*. Retrieved January 2, 2023, from www.indiaspend.com/migrants-build-cities-but-face-exclusion-heres-how-this-can-change/

Tripathi, N. (2021, November 24). Matilda Kullu: The purpose of saving lives. *Forbes India*. Retrieved January 2, 2023, from www.forbesindia.com/article/wpower-2021/matilda-kullu-the-purpose-of-saving-lives

Tuck, R., & Silverthorne, M. (1998). Introduction. In *Thomas Hobbes, on the citizen*. Cambridge University Press.

Vanheuverswyn, M. (2006, July 7). The philanthropy of Warren Buffet: Capitalism with a human face? *In Defence of Marxism*. Retrieved January 2, 2023, from www.bolshevik.info/philanthropy-charity-warren-buffet-capitaism-with-a-human-face

Wagner, P. (2020, July 24). COVID-19, HIV/AIDS, and the "Spanish flue": Historical moments and social transformations. *Thesis Eleven*. Retrieved January 2, 2023, from www.thesiseleven.com/2020/07/24/covid-19-hiv-aids-and-the-spanish-flu-historical-moments-and-social-transformations/

Wainwright, J. (2019). We need planetary sovereignty to address the climate crisis. *Wattsup with that*. Retrieved January 2, 2023, from https://wattsupwiththat.com/2019/01/16/claim-we-need-planetary-sovereignty-to-address-the-climate-crisis/

Walby, S. (2015). *Crisis*. Polity.

Watkins, C. (2005). Representations of space: Spatial practices and spaces of representation: An application of Lefebvre's spatial triad. *Culture and Organization, 11*(3), 209–220.

Webb, S. (1948). Introduction to the 1920 reprint. In B. Shaw, S. Webb, G. Wallas, The Lord Oliview, W. Clarke, A. Besant, & H. Bland (Eds.), *Fabian essays*. The Garden City Press. (Original work published 1919)

Williams, K., & Law, J. (2020). The conditions of system failure. *IPPR Progressive Review* [Online]. https://doi.org/10.1111/newe.12220

World Health Organization. (1978). *Declaration of Alma-Ata*. Retrieved January 2, 2023, from www.who.int/publications/almaata_declaration_en.pdf

Zaretsky, E. (2020, May 14). Culling the heard: A modest proposal. *London Review of Books*. Retrieved January 2, 2023, from www.lrb.co.uk./blog/2020/may/culling-the-herd-a-modest-proposal

Zhang, S. (2022, July 28). How long can the Coronavirus keep reinfecting us? *The Atlantic*. Retrieved January 2, 2023, from www.theatlantic/health/archive/2022/07/coronavirus-will-never-run-out-ways-reinfect-us/670976/

Žižek, S. (2021). The 'great reset'? Yes, please – but a real one! In K. Mahadevan, S. Kumar, M. Bhoot, & R. Kharat (Eds.), *The Covid spectrum: Theoretical and experiential reflections from India and beyond*. Speaking Tiger.

Index

Aam Aadmi Party (AAP) 145, 196n3
AAP *see* Aam Aadmi Party (AAP)
Abhishek, S. 5
Abstract Negativity 54
Accredited Social Health Activist (ASHA) schemes 39, 91, 126, 145
Acquired Immuno-Deficiency Disease (AIDS) 29, 141
ActionAid 57n19
Action COVID-19 Team 90
active pharmaceutical ingredients (APIs) 50
Adani, G. 139
Adani Foundation 170
Affordable Housing in Partnership (AHP) 228
Agarwal, A. 89
agrarian sector 79
agruculture 78
Ahluwalia, I. J. 212–213, 216
Ahmad, S. 186, 227–228
AHP *see* Affordable Housing in Partnership (AHP)
Aidnik, M. 334
AIDS *see* Acquired Immuno-Deficiency Disease (AIDS)
Aijaz, R. 175
AIMED *see* Association of Indian Medical Device Industry (AIMED)
Airpocalypse 162
AITC *see* All India Trinamool Congress (AITC)
Aiyar, S. 230, 244, 245, 286
AKCDA *see* All Kerala Chemists and Druggist Association (AKCDA)
Allen, L. 148
Alleyne, B. 183
All India Trinamool Congress (AITC) 196n3

All Kerala Chemists and Druggist Association (AKCDA) 50
Alma Ata Declaration 318
Amazon 104n11
Ambani, M. 139
American India Foundation 57n19
AMTZ *see* Andhra Pradesh MedTech Zone (AMTZ)
Anand, G. 51–52
Anderson, K. B. 246
Andhra Pradesh MedTech Zone (AMTZ) 86, 95
Anganwadi workers 39, 126, 332
Annual Report of the Department of Pharmaceuticals 149n5
The Antara Foundation 264
APIs *see* active pharmaceutical ingredients (APIs)
apocalypse communism 10, 211, 219, 237–243, 282, 287
Apollo 225
Arabian Peninsula: MERS 3
Ardern, J. 229
Arendt, H. 55n5
Arogya Setu App 122
ASHA *see* Accredited Social Health Activist (ASHA) schemes
Ashton, J. 261
Asian flu (influenza) virus 3
Aslam, M. 238
Assam 133, 137, 276
asset capital 168
Association of Indian Medical Device Industry (AIMED) 126–128
AstraZeneca 95, 102, 130
Atma Nirbhar relief package 15
Australia 46, 210; zoonotic virus 3
authoritarianism: contemporary 101; populist 101

autonomy 10, 167; financial 177
Avebury, P. C. 226–227, 230
avian flu/bird flu 4
avis, M. 73, p 102
Azad, G. N. 170

Baiocchi, G. 319
Bajpai, N. 327
Balakrishnan, P. 328
Bandyopadhyay, A. 95, 195n2
Bangalore 137
Bangladesh 313; zoonotic virus 3
Barker, B. 186, 230
Barman, A. 15
Basole, A. 328
Bastani, A. 220
Bathija, M. 190
Bauman, Z. 174
BBIL see Bharat Biotech International Limited (BBIL)
BCPL see Bengal Chemicals and Pharmaceuticals Limited (BCPL)
Beck, U. 27
Bell, D. 89
Bello, W. 317
Bengal Chemicals and Pharmaceuticals Limited (BCPL) 149n5
Bengaluru 163
Berman, M. 122–123
Bhalotia, S. 143, 190
Bhangay, K. 172
Bharat Biotech International Limited (BBIL) 16, 130–132
Bharatiya Janata Party (BJP) 19, 33, 52, 277, 298n7, 320
Bharat Rashtra Samithi (BRS) 196n3
Bhavsar, D. 216
Bhopal 126
Bhore, J. W. 56n15
Bhore Committee 41, 56n15; Bhore Committee Report 244
Bhutto, F. 120
Big Pharma 6, 44, 86–92, 116, 118–121, 132, 209, 260, 318
Big Tech 6, 318
Bihar 133
biopolitics 7, 9, 42, 47, 125, 161, 246, 322
Bisen, A. 51–52, 74
Bismarc, O. van 150n16
Bismark, M. 126
Biswas, S. 2
BJP see Bharatiya Janata Party (BJP)

Black Death of 1346 1, 3
Blakeley, G. 9
Bloch, E. 20, 329, 333, 334
Blundell, J. 129
BMC see Brihanmumbai Municipal Corporation (BMC)
Boddy, M. 316–317
Boltanski, L.: *New Spirit of Capitalism* 323
Bonilla, Y. 93
Bonotti, M. 258–259
Borer, M. 272
Borger, J. 148n1
Bourla, A. 132
Boseley, S. 324
Bounds, A. M. 195
bourgeois individualism 168
Bourla, A. 132
Brar, A. 247n5
Brazil: Zika virus 4
Brecht: *The Mother* 330
Brihanmumbai Municipal Corporation (BMC) 82, 145–146, 239
Broder, D. 19
Brown, G. 120
Brown, M. 12
BRS see Bharat Rashtra Samithi (BRS)
Brubaker, R. 320–321
Brunnermeier, M. K. 312
Bruno, P. 182
Buckshee, D. 15
Burke, N. J. 246
business regime, failure of 267–281

Cadila Pharmaceuticals 50
Candid 120
capital 9, 46, 95, 165–172; asset 168; economic 15; finance 182; global 6, 33, 53; and local governance 172–176; monopoly 13, 47, 192, 221, 270, 278; risk 297; social 15, 50; venture 168, 173–175, 196n4
capitalism 4, 7, 9–10, 13, 53, 208–209, 220, 312; civic 10, 136–139, 261–267, 288, 295, 297, 314; contemporary 20–21, 33, 54, 129, 169, 207; corporate 72; disaster *see* disaster capitalism; free-market 147, 267; global 15, 29, 97, 115, 116, 140; monstrosity of disasters under 67–104; and nature, relation between 49; neoliberal 8, 32, 52, 87, 128, 135, 137–139, 172–173, 183, 232; pandemics

of 115–150; state-capitalism 101; welfare 267
capitalist accumulation 42, 169, 181
capitalist development 4, 48, 135, 173, 207, 214, 243, 299n14, 317, 318
capitalist mode of production 21, 32, 69, 72, 91, 324
capitalist neoliberal economies 6
capitalist oppression 67, 330
Caritas 57n19
caste-based violence 56n10
Castoriadis, C. 147
Castro, F. 215
CDP *see* Center for Disaster Philanthropy (CDP)
Center for Disaster Philanthropy (CDP) 120
Centre for Monitoring Indian Economy (CMIE) 56n16, 178
Centre for Science and Environment (CSE) 228
Chamberlain, J. 175, 176
Chancel, L. 231
Chandra, R. 173, 174, 186, 233, 236, 278
Charities Aid Foundation 268
Chatterjee, A. K. 135
Chauhan, R. 168, 280
CHCs *see* community health centres (CHCs)
Chennai 163
Chesire, P. 229
Chhattisgarh 133
Chiapello, E.: *New Spirit of Capitalism* 323
Child Rights and You (CRY) 149n9
Chile 178
China 99, 100, 319; COVID-19 pandemic 29; Maoist revolution 215; public housing 163; vaccine expenditure 121
Chowkwanyun, M. 173
CII *see* Confederation of Indian Industry (CII)
circular migrants 8
city socialism 192
civic capitalism 10, 136–139, 261, 288, 295, 297, 314; trajectories of 262–267
civic order 295
civil society organisations (CSOs) 43, 181, 264
Clarke, J. F. 208

class exploitation 35
climate change 11, 17, 32, 71, 72, 98, 100, 116, 161, 163, 164, 182, 206, 231, 283–285, 320, 321, 324, 328
climate justice 166
CLS *see* Credit-Linked Subsidy (CLS)
CMIE *see* Centre for Monitoring Indian Economy (CMIE)
Cockburn, C.: *The Local State* 317
Cognizant 225
Cohn, G. 241
Cole, G. D. H. 241
collectivisation 213–221
Collins, K.: *The Front Steps Project* 186
commodity fetishism 91, 117, 174
communal violence 56n10
Communist Movement 233–234
community accountability 51
community at work 183–191
community health 165–172
community health centres (CHCs) 191
Concrete Universality 54
Confederation of Indian Industry (CII) 178
Connolly, J. 182
consumerism 174
consumer society 174
contractualisation 175
co-operation 324
Corbyn, J. 277
corporate capitalism 72
corporate social responsibility (CSR) 170
corporatisation 169, 173
COVAX 236
Covaxin 37, 130
COVID-19 pandemic 1–9, 11, 17–18; neoliberalism, implications of 43–48; second wave 5, 7; socio-political causality of 29–36; unequal 27–57; vaccines 2, 14–15; *see also individual entries*
Covishield 37
CoWin 122
Crawford, R. 232
Credit-Linked Subsidy (CLS) 228
Crocker, W. 288
CRY *see* Child Rights and You (CRY)
CSE *see* Centre for Science and Environment (CSE)
CSOs *see* civil society organisations (CSOs)

348 *Index*

CSR *see* corporate social responsibility (CSR)
Cuba 99, 100; Cuban Revolution 215–216
Curtis, L. 262

Dadhich, A. 121
Damodaran, H. 290
Daniyal, S. 8
Darwin, M. L. 227
Das, G. 36, 48, 52, 69, 169, 176, 184, 190, 191, 244, 245, 291, 332; *Dharma of Capitalism* 290
Das, P. K. 20
Davis, J. 320
Davis, W. 258
DC *see* District Collectorate (DC)
Dean, J. 98
DebRoy, S. 126, 248n10.
decentralised planning structures 322
Defoe, D.: *Journal of the Plague Year'*, *A* 3
Delhi 137, 164, 214, 237, 274, 316, 327
Delhi ke Farishtey (Angels of Delhi) 221
Dennett, P. 12
Dennis, S. 328
Department of Economic and Social Affairs 277, 292
Department of Pharmaceutical: Report for 2020–21 118
Desai, A. R. 1–2, 12–13, 30–31, 99, 316
Deshpande, V. 216
DGI *see* Doing Good Index (DGI) 2022
Dhar, D. 328
Dharavi 14, 104n13, 126, 139, 146, 167, 186, 196n9, 238, 247n4, 332
Dharmadhikari, C. S. 294
Dhingra, S. 49–50, 143, 190
Dhole, M. 4
Diamond, J. 162
Dighavkar, K. 126, 238, 247n3, 248n10, 325
digital apartheid 122–128
Dignity Housing scheme, Telangana 228
Dijk, E. Van. 175
DiSalvo, D. 148n1
disaster capitalism 6, 10, 35, 44, 46–47, 68, 72, 76–77, 91, 92, 94, 96, 98, 129, 144, 241, 289, 313
disaster civility, morbidities of 263–299
disaster communism 10, 211, 213–221, 245, 286, 287

discrimination 5, 34, 84; gender 35
District Collectorate (DC) 31
District Medical Office (DMO) 31
Dixit, A. 168, 183
DMO *see* District Medical Office (DMO)
Doing Good Index (DGI) 2022 268
domestic violence 57n17, 273
Dréze, J. 163, 231, 286
Drugs and Cosmetics Act, 1940 38
Drugs (Price Control) Order, 2013 7
dual state theory 322
Dunayevskaya, R. 14, 54, 129, 185, 221, 243, 245, 292, 295, 296, 315, 331
Dunleavy, P. 322
Dunn, R. G. 174
Dutt, B. 35, 39, 49, 82

East India Company 267, 290
Eban, K. 119, 149n3, 278
Ebola 3, 4
ecological equity 166
economic capital 15
economic liberalisation 34
Economic Man 285
economic reforms of 1991 116
education 80; continuity of 45–46; school 47
Einstein, A. 32
Eleventh Five-Year plan 36
Empowered Committee 43
Engels, F. 233–234, 266; *The Manifesto of the Communist Party* 233
Epidemic Diseases Act, 1897 38
Essential Commodity Act, 1955 38, 40
essential equipment crisis 122–128
Europe: Black Death of 1346 1, 3
event, definition of 55n5
everyday dehumanisation 117

Fabian socialism 241, 325
Fabian Society 216
Facebook 6
Fang, F. 100
FAO *see* Food and Agriculture Organization (FAO)
Farooqui, M. 196n6
FDI *see* Foreign Direct Investment (FDI)
Federal Emergency Management Agency (FEMA) 74
Feldman, R. 119, 125

FEMA *see* Federal Emergency Management Agency (FEMA)
Fiamingo, G. 315
Fifth Five-Year plan 56n12
finance capital 182
First Five-Year plan 56n12
Firth, R. 315
'flattening of the curve' 73
Florida, R. 313
Food and Agriculture Organization (FAO) 78
food scarcity 12, 79–80
food security 47, 77, 78, 283
Foreign Direct Investment (FDI) 142
Fortis 225
Foucault, M. 161, 319, 322, 326
Fourth Five-Year plan 56n12
4T's (tracing, tracking, testing, and treating) 146
France: public healthcare expenditure 72
Franke, R. W. 215
Frankel, B. 331
free-market capitalism 147, 267
Fromm, E. 20–21, 54, 101, 144, 168, 242, 318, 319, 321, 329, 333
Frondorf, E. 119, 125
Fudge, C. 316–317

Gandhi, I. 248n7
Gandhi, M. K. 236, 287, 288, 330–331
Gandhian socialism 10, 193–194
Gandhian Trusteeship Model (GTM) 292, 299n15, 331
Gandhi-Mody, P. 187, 242, 274
Gaur, C. S. 138
GDP *see* gross domestic product (GDP)
GE HealthCare Education Institute (GE HEI) 170
GE HEI *see* GE HealthCare Education Institute (GE HEI)
gender discrimination 35
generic medicines 119
genuine nationalism 274
Ghosh, J. 52, 122
Ghosh, S. 331
Giddens, A. 123, 326
Gilbert, J. 277
Gilbert, S. 2
Gittlitz, A. M. 209–210, 333
GiveIndia 89, 90, 269–270; India Covid Response Fund 268
Glasgow Water Company 13
Gleisler, M. 319

Glennie, J. 324
Global Health Security Index, 2019 report 323
Global Hunger Index Data 2021 79, 313
Global North 99–101, 118, 120, 162, 223, 268, 277, 285, 294
Global South 2, 9, 18, 49, 53, 54, 76, 89, 99, 100, 118, 120, 207, 268, 277, 283, 285, 294
Gokhale, M. 35
Goldberg, S. 94
Goldfrank, B. 316
Gompers 175
Goodman, P. S. 102
Google 6
Google Meet 104n11, 279
Gopal, S. 288
Gore, A. 266; *Capitalism at the Crossroads* 320
Goswami, C. 290
Goswami, O. 52
GRAIN 283
Greater Hyderabad Municipal Corporation 177
Green, C. 2
Greger, M. 115–116
gross domestic product (GDP) 37, 78, 90–92, 227, 231
GTM *see* Gandhian Trusteeship Model (GTM)
Guerin, P. J. 121
Guild Socialism 241
Guinea: Swine flu 3
Gupta, S. 20
Guru, G. 84
Guterres, A. 149n9

HAL *see* Hindustan Antibiotics Limited (HAL)
Han, B. C. 280
Hansen, J. 320
Hardikar, J. 68
Harnecker, M. 283
Harsheeta 280
Harvey, D. 135, 214, 218–219, 269, 277, 293, 316
Hay, C. 264–267, 278, 293, 295, 296
healthcare corruption 87
Healthcare Global Enterprises Limited 225
Health Information Management System (HIMS) 196n3

350 *Index*

Heron, K. 98
Hessler, P. 319
Hilferding, R. 135, 150n13, 266–267
HIMS *see* Health Information Management System (HIMS)
Hindustan Antibiotics Limited (HAL) 149n5
Hobbes, T. 11, 100–101; *Elements of Law, Natural and Politic* 329
Honigsbaum, M. 16–18, 35
Horton, R. 28
Housing Research 228–229
HPEC for Estimating the Investment Requirements for Urban Infrastructure Services 212, 213, 222, 223
HPEC Report of 2011 79
Hudis, P. 246
Hupkau, C. 14, 41
hurricane Katrina 74
Hyderabad 149n10, 214
hyper-micro politics 144

ICAR *see* Indian Council for Agricultural Research (ICAR)
ICDS *see* Integrated Child Development Services (ICDS)
IDPL *see* Indian Drugs and Pharmaceuticals Limited (IDPL)
IFPRI *see* International Food Policy Research Institute (IFPRI)
IIPH *see* Indian Institute of Public Health (IIPH)
ILP *see* Independent Labour Party (ILP)
Imaan, A. 164
Inamdar, N. 190, 278, 290
INC *see* Indian National Congress (INC)
Independent Labour Party (ILP) 216
India Exclusion Report 2016 34, 51
Indian Constitution: 12th Schedule 179
Indian Council for Agricultural Research (ICAR) 78
Indian Drugs and Pharmaceuticals Limited (IDPL) 149n5
Indian Institute of Public Health (IIPH) 281
Indian National Congress (INC) 182
Indian Patents Act of 1970 87, 121
Indian Philanthropy Alliance (IPA) 264
Indian Railway Board Act, 1905 235
IndiaSpend 325
Indiaspora 264

inequality 7, 15, 16, 85, 101, 117, 244, 316; bourgeoning 70; vaccine 116
Infosys 225, 226, 263
initial public offerings (IPOs) 225
Innovative Emergency Management 74
In-Situ Slum Development (ISSR) 228
Institute of Medicine 17
Institut Montaigne 51
Integrated Child Development Services (ICDS) 80, 126
Intellectual Property (IP) 130
Intellectual Property Rights (IPRs) 16, 89, 119, 131
International Dalit Solidarity Network 104n10
International Food Policy Research Institute (IFPRI) 313
Invest India 125
IP *see* Intellectual Property (IP)
IPA *see* Indian Philanthropy Alliance (IPA)
IPOs *see* initial public offerings (IPOs)
IPRs *see* Intellectual Property Rights (IPRs)
Isaac, T. M. Thomas 215
ISSR *see* In-Situ Slum Development (ISSR)
Iyer, K. 67, 68
Iyer, R. 288

Jacob, S. 327, 328
Jaishankar, S. 57n24
Jalan, B. 36, 52, 167–168, 248n9, 291
Jallianwala Bagh massacre 104n14
James, C. L. R. 147, 296
Japan 207
Jayadeva Hospital, Bangaluru 263
J. B. Chemicals 50
Jenner, E. 33
Jesline, J. 332
Jewett, R. L. 289
Jha, M. K. 53, 330
Jharkhand 133
Johnson, S. 262
Jowett, F. W. 223–225
JP Morgan 229

Kakani, S. 126, 248n10
Kalanithi, P. 283
Kamath, A. 45
Kannabiran, K. 244
Kant, A. 43
Kanwar, S. 20, 228, 331

KAPL *see* Karnataka Antibiotics and
    Pharmaceuticals Limited (KAPL)
Kapri, T. 35, 39
Kapri, V. 82
Karnataka Antibiotics and
    Pharmaceuticals Limited
    (KAPL) 149n5
Karran, T. J. 186, 240
Kaur, P. 20
Kaur, R. 317
Keane, J. 258
Keen, C. 188
Kelman, E. 73, 93
Kempner, B. 220
Kerala 216, 276, 327–328
Kerala Model of Democratic
    Communism 283, 317, 327,
    328, 333
Klein, N. 1, 6, 18, 72, 88, 92, 94–97,
    102, 124, 142, 161, 168–169, 207,
    259, 281, 314, 321, 323; *Shock
    Doctrine, The* 74
Klein, S. 288
Koley, T. K. 4
Kolkata 137, 166, 214
Kondirolli, F. 49–50, 143
Korsch, K. 295–296
Koshy, J. 131
Krishnan, M. 74
Krishnan, V. 43–44, 56n11, 57n21, 125
Kukla, Q. R. 186–187
Kumar, A. 20
Kumar, V. 45
Kumbha Mela 187–188, 197n11
Kumbhare, S. 146, 186

labour codes 18, 19
Lahariya, C. 126, 238
Laing, R. D. 149n6
Lal, V. 32, 52–53, 99, 147–148
Lassalle, F. 185
Last Man 285
Latin America 283
Law, J. 143
Law, S. 95, 138
LDF *see* Left Democratic Front (LDF)
Lebowitz, M. 123
LeBrón, M. 93
Lefebvre, H. 183, 213, 241, 325–326
Lefebvre's Triad 326
Left Democratic Front (LDF) 327
Lenin, V. 182, 242–243, 328;
    Revolutionary Days 285

Lerner, J. 175
Levey, E. J. 188–189, 226
Levi, S. C. 290
Leviathan 11, 100–101
Leys, C. 267, 277–278
Liberia: Swine flu 3
life expectancy, politics of 81–86
liquid modernity 174
Lisboa, M. M. 210
Local Administrative Socialism 216
lockdown 2, 7, 8, 12, 15, 20, 32, 34,
    39–43, 46, 48, 49, 53, 55n3, 56n10,
    57n17, 57n22, 68, 73, 75, 77, 80,
    82, 84, 86, 89, 93, 99, 101, 118,
    122, 127, 128, 133–136, 138, 139,
    162, 164, 183, 186, 216, 228–229,
    231, 232, 242, 258, 261, 267, 268,
    272–276, 278, 279–281, 284,
    294, 295, 299n9, 299n12, 316,
    319, 320, 325; global 42; localised
    42, 177–178, 196n6, 259, 312;
    nationwide 17, 31, 42, 168
Lupton, D. 9
Luxemburg, R. 242

Machin, S. 129
Madhiwalla, N. 88
Madhya Pradesh 134
Mahambare, V. 186
Mahapatra, A. 4
Maharashtra 218
Maharashtra Industrial Development
    Corporation (MICD) 134
MAI *see* Multiplex Association of
    India (MAI)
Malaria 19, 55n3
Malaysia: zoonotic virus 3
Malhotra, R. 280–281
Malm, A. 284, 285, 297
Mander, H. 242, 258, 298n7, 299n10
man-made disasters 73
Mann, G. 101, 319, 320; *Climate
    Leviathan* 11
manual scavenging 83–85
Mao Zedong 220
Marcuse, H. 243–244, 282
marginalisation 30, 118
Marx, K. 13, 54, 70, 97, 139, 147, 188,
    194, 212, 219, 225, 233–234, 246,
    266, 294, 313, 315, 328, 330, 334;
    Capital 332; *The Manifesto of the
    Communist Party* 233
Marxism 234

Mass Rapid Transit System 223
material vulnerability 5
Mathur, R. 189, 195n1
Matthew, R. 104n12
Matthewman, S. 74, 95–96, 231
Max India Limited 225
Mbembe, A. 7
McCann, G. 268
McGoey, L. 297
McKinsey and Company 170
media 33–34, 55n7, 55n8
medical device industry 118
Memon, N. 297
Menon, N. 172, 185, 320
MERS *see* Middle East respiratory syndrome (MERS)
Metro Projects 223
MICD *see* Maharashtra Industrial Development Corporation (MICD)
Mid-Day meals 80
Middle East respiratory syndrome (MERS) 3, 4
migrant workers 14, 15, 19, 39, 40, 42, 53, 67–68, 72, 82, 83, 90, 101, 133–139, 172, 173, 231, 259, 260, 270, 271, 276, 278, 291, 295, 314, 327, 332; crisis 7–8, 104n8, 163–164
Migrant Workers Solidarity Network (MWSN) 8
migration 133–139
Miliband, R. 196n7
militant optimism 20, 334
Minimum Retail Pricing (MRP) 40
Ministry of Health and Family Welfare 145
Ministry of Housing Affair: *Deendayal Antyodaya Yojana-National Urban Livelihood Mission* 164
Ministry of Housing and Urban Affairs (MoHUA) 222
Mir, R. 97
Mishra, A. 9
Mission *Sanjeevani* 43
Mitchell, T. 220
Mitra, E. 166–167
MNCs *see* multinational corporations (MNCs)
Moderna 102, 119, 120
Modi, N. 19, 100
Mohalla Clinics 145, 196n3, 289
Mohanty, P. K. 217, 317

MoHUA *see* Ministry of Housing and Urban Affairs (MoHUA)
Monkey Pox 18–19
Monti, D. J. 136–137, 173, 263–267, 271–272, 278, 288, 291, 293, 294
Moore, J. W. 330
Morepan Labs 148n2
mortality rates 85
Moses, M. 317
Mosley, M. 54
MPI *see* Multidimensional Poverty Index (MPI)
MRP *see* Minimum Retail Pricing (MRP)
Mukherjee, U. 35
Mukul, J. 214, 241, 242
Mukund, K. 290
Multidimensional Poverty Index (MPI) 77
multinational corporations (MNCs) 87, 137
Multiplex Association of India (MAI) 178
Mumbai 126, 136, 137, 139, 166, 214, 238, 332
municipal socialism 10, 123–124, 176, 181, 191–193, 230, 233, 234, 236, 240, 241, 325
municipal trading 222–230
Mustafa, F. 275
Mustafa, M. 173
mutual aid solutions 220
MWSN *see* Migrant Workers Solidarity Network (MWSN)

N95 masks 127
NABARD: Department of Economic Analysis and Research 78
Nagarpalika Act 217, 225
Nagpal, J. 14, 183
Nahm, J. M. 320
Nail, T. 75
Nambiar, D. 51, 81
Narayana Hrudayalaya 225
Narrain, A. 234
National Capitalism 317
National Commission for Women (NCW) 57n17
National Containment Plan 31
National Containment Plan 31
National Family Health Survey (NFHS-5) 79–80
nationalism/nationalisation 134, 137

National Pharmaceutical Pricing
  Authority (NPPA) 40, 50
National Rural Health Mission
  (NRHM) 218
National Sample Survey Office (NSSO)
  169, 171
National Security Act (NSA) 119
natural disasters 2, 73, 129, 208, 321
NCW *see* National Commission for
  Women (NCW)
necro-politics 7
Nehru, J. 78, 172, 187–188, 235–236,
  274–275, 287–288, 290, 299n14
Nehruvian socialism 10, 36, 185, 193,
  237, 287, 291–292
neo-fascism 13
neoliberal apocalypse 282–290
neoliberal capitalism 8, 32, 52, 87, 128,
  135, 137–139, 172–173, 183, 232
neoliberal economic reforms 7, 30, 70
neoliberal healthcare ecosystem 71
neoliberal healthcare infrastructure 69
neoliberalism 10, 36–43, 55, 76,
  84, 92, 138, 140, 142, 162, 229,
  230, 245, 276, 281; development
  of 67; implications of 43–48;
  institutionalisation of 167–168
neoliberal market: policies 261;
  structures 39
neoliberal market policies 261
neoliberal privatisation 81
neoliberal state 213–221
Nepal 313
New Health Policy (NHP) of 2017 91
Newton, K. 186, 240
New Zealand 46, 99–100, 183, 229
NFHS-5 *see* National Family Health
  Survey (NFHS-5)
NGOs *see* non-governmental
  organisations (NGOs)
NHP Draft 2015 225
NHP *see* New Health Policy (NHP)
  of 2017
Nichols, J. 184
Nigeria: Swine flu 3
Nipah virus 3
NITI Aayog 43, 56n12, 69, 77, 169,
  170, 171, 176
Nocca Robotics 86, 89, 95
non-governmental organisations
  (NGOs) 18, 42, 43, 89, 119, 128,
  150n14, 170, 190, 218, 264
North Korea 99

NPPA *see* National Pharmaceutical
  Pricing Authority (NPPA)
NRHM *see* National Rural Health
  Mission (NRHM)
NSA *see* National Security Act (NSA)
NSSO *see* National Sample Survey
  Office (NSSO)

OECD *see* Organisation for Economic
  Co-operation and Development
  (OECD)
Ó hAdhmaill, F. 268
Ola 14
ontological security 123, 173
Oommen, T. K. 298n7
OOP *see* out-of-pocket (OOP)
  expenditure
Operational Guidelines 2020 145
Organisation for Economic
  Co-operation and Development
  (OECD) 49, 117, 126–127
Osho, Z. 118
out-of-pocket (OOP) expenditure 40,
  71, 90
outsourcing 103n5
Owen, R. 185
Oxfam India 5, 57n19
Oxford-AstraZeneca vaccine 2
Oximeters 40

Pakistan 276
Palaez, J. C. 247
Palat, M. K. 287, 299n14
Pande, A. 36, 179, 191, 214
Pankaj, A. K. 53
Pankhurst, S. 242
Pannekoek, A. 282, 283, 321
Pant, P. 289
Parikh, S. 116
Paris Commune 189, 238
Participatory Research in Asia
  (PRIA) 83
Patel, A. 275
Patel, S. 289
Pavri, K. M. 141
Payne, A. 264–267, 293, 295, 296
PDS *see* Public Distribution
  System (PDS)
Pelling, M. 3123
Perrow, C. 46
personal protection equipment (PPE) 40,
  85, 126, 127, 186, 225, 312
Petrongolo, B. 14

Pew Research Center 319
Pfizer 95, 102, 130, 132, 149n4
Pfizer-BioNTech vaccine 2, 119, 120
pharmaceutical industry 87
PHC *see* primary health centre (PHC)
Philippines: zoonotic virus 3
Piketty, T. 231
Pikoli, P. 148
Pinnock, D. 313
Pithode, T. 39, 126, 248n10, 298–299n9, 299n13, 325
Planning Commission 172
PMAY *see* Pradhan Mantri Awas Yojana (PMAY)
PM CARES 268
PMGKY *see Pradhan Mantri Garib Kalyan Yojana* (PMGKY)
PM SVANidhi scheme 55n2
political opportunism 18
Posadas, J. 11, 32, 98, 208–213, 219, 220, 246, 247n1, 247n2, 285, 287, 290, 328
Posadism 329
PPE *see* personal protection equipment (PPE)
PPP *see* private-public partnerships (PPP)
Prabhakaran, P. 116
Pradhan Mantri Awas Yojana (PMAY) 228
Pradhan Mantri Garib Kalyan Yojana (PMGKY) 15
Prasad, P. 90–91, 142
Preston, J. 315
Preston Model 12
The Prevention of Black Marketing and Maintenance of Supplies of Essential Commodities Act, 1980 38
PRIA *see* Participatory Research in Asia (PRIA)
primary health centre (PHC) 37, 89, 126, 169, 171, 180–181
primitive communism 57n23
private equity-funded start-ups 173
private-public partnerships (PPP) 169–171, 237
privatisation 36, 37, 169, 175, 236; healthcare 86–92, 142; neoliberal 81
Priya, R. 47, 229
profit accumulation 20, 33, 73, 94, 98, 103, 121, 139, 141, 284, 318
psychological vulnerability 5

public accountability 39, 51, 166, 171, 184, 215, 289
Public Distribution System (PDS) 15, 80–81
public expenditure 8, 17, 235
public goods, definition of 283
public healthcare, and disasters 70–77
Public Health Management Cadres 91
public services: apocalypse communism and 237–243; disruption of 77–81; pandemic and 230–237
Puerto Rico: disaster capitalism 241

Quammen, D. 16, 18

Rajan, R. 175
Rajasthan Drugs and Pharmaceuticals Limited (RDPL) 149n5
Ramachandran, P. 260, 275, 276
Ramesh, M. 284
Ramin, C. J. 94, 150n16
Rao, M. A. 235, 296
Rapid Community Response to COVID-19 89–90
Rawat, T. S. 188
Ray, D. 313
RDPL *see* Rajasthan Drugs and Pharmaceuticals Limited (RDPL)
Reddy, K. S. 171
Reddy, S. 37
reductionist political economy 315
Red Volunteers' movement 328
regionalism 134
Remdesivir 119
Renner, R. 261
revolutionary socialism 185
Revolutionary State 98
risk capital 297
Robbins, R. 102
robotization 20
Ronnie, C. 273
Rosenthal, S. 263
Rowlatt Act 104n14
Roy, A. 19
Ruparel, P. 86
rural distress 68
Russell, M. 280–281
Rustin, M. 236
Ryan, F. 1

Sainath, P. 6, 7, 15, 79, 133, 134, 271, 327, 333
Saini, A. 258

sanitation 8, 14, 28, 29, 45, 51, 52, 57n22, 71, 74–77, 82–85, 104n9, 104n13, 120, 140, 146, 162, 164, 166, 167, 175, 176, 179, 186, 188, 217, 236, 244
Santosh, S. 9
Sardesai, R. 55n8
Sareen, J. 118
SARS *see* severe acute respiratory syndrome (SARS)
Sassen, S. 313
Sastri, S. 95, 195n2
Saul, J. S. 277
Saunders, P. 322
Save-LIFE Foundation 57n19
Save the Children 57n19
SCAI *see* Shopping Centres Association of India (SCAI)
Scheidel, W. 96, 208
Schrank, A. 316
Scott, A. 313
SDF *see* Social Democratic Federation (SDF)
SDOs *see* Social Delivery Organizations (SDOs)
Second Five-Year plan 56n12
Sehgal Foundation 264
self-help groups (SHGs) 281
self-preservation 7, 10, 281, 289
Sen, A. 163, 231, 286
Seneral: Swine flu 3
Sengupta, A. 18, 88–89, 132–133, 318
Sengupta, S. 330
Serum Institute of India (SII) 16, 37, 51, 129, 131, 132
Seventhy Five-Year plan 56n12
74th Constitutional Amendment Act 217, 289
severe acute respiratory syndrome (SARS) 3, 4, 15, 17
Shah, S. 55n3, 81
Shah, V. 269–270
Shailaja, K. K. 327
Shameem, M. 172
Shannon, O. 273
Shantz, J. 11
Sharma, J. 86, 95, 116–117
Shaw, B. 190, 216, 225, 226, 233, 248n8, 325
Sheth, A. 292
SHGs *see* self-help groups (SHGs)
Shiva, V. 321

Shopping Centres Association of India (SCAI) 178
Shraya, V. 46
Shruti, I. 82–83
Shukla, C. M. 330
Sidhu, S. 272–273
Sierra Leone: Swine flu 3
SII *see* Serum Institute of India (SII)
Silchar 124
Singh, A. K. 56n13
Singh, B. 83–84
Singh, S. 44–45, 82, 140, 162, 191
Singh, T. 164, 166
Singhal, A, 189, 195n1
Sinha, A. 163, 291
Sinha, Y. 162–163, 291
Sismondo, A. 88
Sismondo, S. 48, 88
Sivaramakrishnan, K. C. 289
Sixth Extinction 206
Sixth Five-Year plan 56n12
slums 14, 30, 163, 166–167
Smedley, T. 162
Smith, M. C. 38, 125
Smith, N. 313
social capital 15, 50
Social Delivery Organizations (SDOs) 268–269
Social Democratic Federation (SDF) 216, 286
social distancing 14, 20, 34, 101, 227, 247n4
socialism 11; city 192; Fabian 241, 325; Gandhian 10, 193–194; Guild Socialism 241; municipal 10, 123–124, 176, 181, 191–193, 230, 233, 234, 236, 240, 241, 325; Nehruvian 10, 36, 185, 193, 194, 237, 287, 291–292; revolutionary 185
social segregation 35
social solidarity 7, 217, 281
socio-economic growth 165–166
solidarity: human 13; social 7, 217, 281
Soulia, C.: *The Front Steps Project* 186
South Africa 119, 130, 132
South Korea: bird flu 4
Spanish flu 104n7, 104n14
spitting, ban on 57n21
Sridhar, V. 21
Srivastava, H. N. 76, 278
Srivastava, R. 145
Stalinism 11

Stall, P 328
Standing, G. 261
state-capitalism 101
statism 55, 101
Statist Socialism 240
Stein, S. 316
Stevano, S. 331–332
stigmatisation 84
Stoker, G. 182, 196n8
Stranded Workers Action Network (SWAN) 7, 8, 178, 276
Subramaniam, V. 290
Sur, P. 166–167
surgical masks 127
surplus labour 139
surveillance 161, 218
surveillance capitalistic model 2
sustainability 166, 212, 320
Swabhiman Society 89
Swachh Bharat Mission (Clean India) 14, 56n9
Swaminathan, M. 80
SWAN *see* Stranded Workers Action Network (SWAN)
SWASA face masks 126
Swine flu 3

Tablighi Jamaat 273, 275
Tamil Nadu 218
Taskin, B. 274
TATA Trust 170
Taylor-Gooby, P. 181
TB *see* Tuberculosis (TB)
telemedicine 122
Teltumbde, A. 275
Tenth Five-Year plan 36
Third Five-Year plan 56n12
Thomas 327
Thomas, A. 164
Timberg, T. A. 290
TINA 97
Tiwari, P. 216
Toland, S. 261
Tomes, N. 125; *The Gospel of Germs* 261
Torrent Pharmaceuticals 50
Towler, W. G. 216
Trade-Related Intellectual Property Rights (TRIPS) 89
transhumanism 206
Trantidis, A. 319
travel restrictions 46
Trimble, S. 285

Tripathi, B. 326–327, 332
TRIPS *see* Trade-Related Intellectual Property Rights (TRIPS)
Trivedi, D. 33
Tronti, M. 103
Trotskyism 11
Trump, D. 100, 142
Tuberculosis (TB) 56n11, 57n21
Tumbe, C. 42, 136, 240, 247n6

Uber 14
UFOs *see* unidentified flying objects (UFOs)
Uganda: Zika virus 4
ULBs *see* urban local bodies (ULBs)
UNAIDS *see* United Nations AIDS charity (UNAIDS)
unemployment 56–57n16
UNESCO *see* United Nations Educational, Scientific and Cultural Organization (UNESCO)
UNICEF India 226
UNICEF *see* United Nations Children's Fund (UNICEF)
unidentified flying objects (UFOs) 211
Union of Soviet Socialist Republics (USSR) 16
United Kingdom (UK) 17, 278; civic capitalism 266; economy 5; pharmaceutical sector 88; public healthcare expenditure 72; public housing 163; young and lowest-paid workers 41
United Nations 32, 292
United Nations AIDS charity (UNAIDS) 130
United Nations Children's Fund (UNICEF) 68, 284
United Nations Educational, Scientific and Cultural Organization (UNESCO) 77
United States of America (USA) 16, 17; 2008 recession 69; Afghanistan War 55n6; COVID-19 pandemic 69; pharmaceutical sector 88; public healthcare expenditure 72; vaccine expenditure 121
Universal Health Coverage 318
Unninathan, S. 5
Unsworth, S. 266
Untermann, E. 189
UPHCs *see* Urban Primary Health Centres (UPHCs)

Uppal, T. 14, 272–273
Upreti, B. R. 104n12
urban health 171
urban healthcare infrastructure 171
urbanisation 10, 28, 74, 167; capitalist 19
urban local bodies (ULBs) 39, 43, 138, 165, 169, 174–183, 216, 217, 223, 224, 238, 242, 289, 312
Urban Poor 30
urban population 79
urban poverty 30
Urban Primary Health Centres (UPHCs) 171
USA *see* United States of America (USA)
USSR *see* Union of Soviet Socialist Republics (USSR)
Uttar Pradesh 133, 327

vaccines 2, 5, 33, 119–121; inequality 116; inequity 14–15; shortages of 128–133
Van Bergeijk, P. A. G. 141
VANI *see* Voluntary Action Network of India (VANI)
Veeraraghavan, D. 136
Venkatachalam, P. 296–297
venture capital 168, 173–175, 196n4
Vietnam 99
violence: caste-based 56n10; communal 56n10; domestic 57n17, 273
Vishwaguru 27
Voluntary Action Network of India (VANI) 149n9
Vrooman, W. 233
vulnerability 44, 84, 116, 164; material 5; psychological 5; social 68
Vyas, S. 84

Wadhwa, M. 327
Wadsworth, Sir S. 188
Wagner, P. 319
Wainwright, H. 101, 319, 320
Wainwright, J.: *Climate Leviathan* 11
Wallace, D. 81, 102n4
Wallace, R. 81, 102n4, 128, 142
Wallace, R. G. 16
Waterman, P. 53
WCD *see* Women and Child Development (WCD) Ministry

weapons of mass destruction 209
Webb, S. 147, 216, 226, 230, 233, 240, 241, 325
welfare capitalism 267
welfare state 12–13, 166, 184
Wells, H. G. 208, 243
West Bengal 133, 328
Western Africa: Swine flu 3
WHO *see* World Health Organization (WHO)
Wholesale Price Index (WPI) 50, 125
Wilde, L. 144
Wilson, B. 83–84
Women and Child Development (WCD) Ministry 80
workers' accident insurance 150n16
Working Group of State Urban Development Secretaries 223, 224
World Bank 52, 169
World Giving Index Report 2019 268
World Health Organization (WHO) 121, 128; Alma Ata Declaration 318; on costs of surgical masks 125; on COVID-19 pandemic 2, 9, 27–28, 30; health financing profile 71; on PHC 180; on primary health 165; on private-public partnerships 237; on SARS 3
World Inequality Report 2022 101
World Inequality Report 2022 232
World Trade Organization (WTO) 131
World Vision 57n19
WPI *see* Wholesale Price Index (WPI)
WTO *see* World Trade Organization (WTO)
Wuhan 17, 29, 31

Yang, G. 100
Yee, D. K. P. 98
Yeh, D. 296–297
Yugoslavia 224

Zanoni, P. 97
Zech, S. T. 258–259
Zhang, S. 332
Zika virus 3–4
Žižek, S. 2, 9, 54, 148, 317, 324, 330
Zoom 104n11, 279
zoonotic viruses 3
Zydus Cadila 50

For Product Safety Concerns and Information please contact our EU
representative GPSR@taylorandfrancis.com
Taylor & Francis Verlag GmbH, Kaufingerstraße 24, 80331 München, Germany

www.ingramcontent.com/pod-product-compliance
Lightning Source LLC
Chambersburg PA
CBHW061343300426
44116CB00011B/1969